Information Technology
in a
Global Society

for the IB Diploma

Stuart Gray

Information Technology in a Global Society

Image copyright and credits are cited on page 368.

This textbook has been developed independently of the International Baccalaureate®.

Information Technology in a Global Society

for the IB Diploma

Stuart Gray

Using this textbook

Information Technology in a Global Society is the first textbook written specifically for the new IB Information Technology in a Global Society syllabus, covering technical systems, social impacts and ethical issues, and each area of application. The book has a number of features to enhance teaching and understanding and ensure students get the best experience possible from the ITGS course.

Chapter Contents

Each chapter starts with a set of **clear objectives** tied directly to the ITGS syllabus, so you can be sure that all aspects of the course are being covered.

The course content is covered through **up to date examples**, supported by varied exercises, with a mix of **ethical discussion** points, **classroom activities**, guided and unguided **practical activities**, and **exam style questions** to cover the syllabus content from a variety of assessment angles. **Theory of Knowledge** (TOK) links are provided where appropriate, enabling integration with the IB core. The **fully cited examples** in each chapter mean students can extend their learning with wider reading—an essential part of IB courses.

Each chapter is illustrated with clear photographs and original diagrams to highlight and clarify key points and concepts. **Common mistakes**, based on the author's experience with ITGS students and examination grading, are highlighted and corrected so that they will not be repeated in the future!

Key Language and Glossary

Each chapter has a comprehensive review section which includes all key language used in that chapter. At the back of the book you will find a complete glossary of all key language found in the text, with precise definitions and links to relevant chapters.

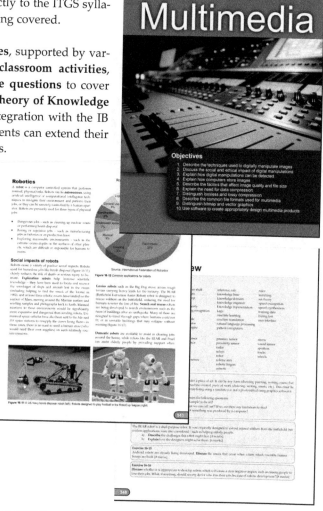

Chapter 6

Online Support and Resources

This textbook's website, www.itgstextbook.com, provides additional resources to support the use of the book. Students can find useful links to examples and case studies related to the topics covered in the text, while teachers can find additional activities, exercises and exam questions, and rubrics for the main exercises.

Contents

Contents

Contents

Chapter 1
Introduction

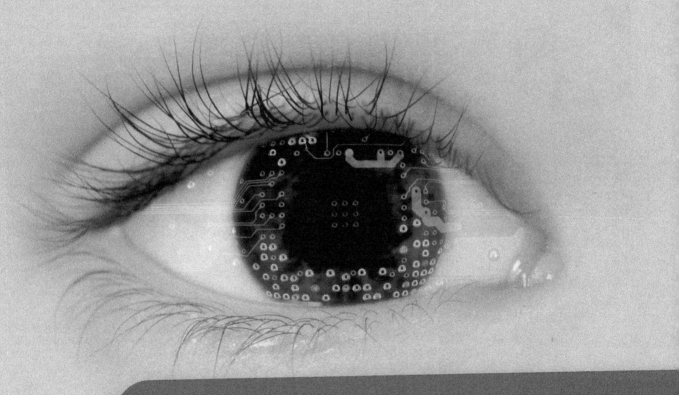

Objectives

1. Explain the key components of the ITGS triangle
2. Identify examples of information technology
3. Analyse a scenario using the ITGS triangle:
    a. Identify the stakeholders involved
    b. Identify the relevant information technology
    c. Explain the social impacts
    d. Explain the ethical issues

What is ITGS?

Information Technology in a Global Society is the study of how developments in Information Technology affect people and society. These **social impacts** can be positive or negative—in many cases, benefits for some people come at the expense of drawbacks for other people. In ITGS you will study situations from across the world – from the local community to an international level—and in different areas including education, business, healthcare, and the military. **Ethics**, the study of what is right and what is wrong, is an important part of ITGS. There are many uses of IT which are completely legal but which raise social and ethical concerns, and may be objectionable to some people.

A key part of ITGS is making decisions about the use of technology by weighing up its positive and negative impacts. You should be able to arrive at well argued conclusions about how, where, when, or even if, different technologies should be used. Below are some examples of ITGS topics and the social impacts and ethical issues they raise:

Workplace surveillance – Many organisations monitor their employees' activities, including the email they send and the web pages they view. Employers do this to improve productivity and reduce time wasted by workers, but some workers may feel their privacy is being invaded. Do the benefits of increased productivity outweigh the uncomfortable feeling of being monitored? To what extent should monitoring be allowed – are there any activities that should not be monitored? Should employees expect any privacy while using work computers? Should employers be legally required to inform employees if they are being monitored?

Graphics editing – Computer graphics techniques have advanced to the point where images can be altered in ways which are virtually impossible to detect. One common use of graphics software is to change the appearance of models featured on the covers of magazines. Who might be affected by changing images in this way? What might be the effects, and how serious are they? Should it be legal to manipulate images but display them as though they are real? Are some edits acceptable, but others unacceptable? If so, who is responsible for enforcing these rules: photographers, editors, the government?

E-waste – The average life time of a computer is relatively short, meaning thousands of new computer purchases are made each year. Many discarded devices are exported to developing countries where they are recycled in hazardous conditions, polluting the environment and causing serious health impacts for the recyclers. Who is responsible for helping solve these problems? Should users be responsible for the safe disposal of equipment, or should manufacturers, who created the equipment in the first place, be required to take it back for recycling?

Violence in computer games – Increasingly powerful home computers and games consoles have enabled increased realism in computer games, many of which depict very violent actions. While films and other media often depict violence too, in computer games the player is more intimately involved, often as the perpetrator. Some people believe violent games have a negative effect on young players. What should be done to keep violent games away from people who might be affected by them? Is there a limit to what it is acceptable to include in computer games? Are computer games different to other forms of entertainment media?

Internet censorship – Many countries filter Internet access, blocking pages deemed inappropriate. Some countries do very little filtering, removing only extreme content which may be harmful to society, while others filter a much higher percentage of material. This raises many ethical issues about the right to Internet access and whether people need protecting from potentially harmful content. Who should be responsible for deciding what is inappropriate material? Should anything be allowed on the Internet? Is one solution suitable for everyone? How do we even know if our Internet connections are being filtered?

The ITGS Triangle

There are four core aspects of ITGS. These aspects – social and ethical significance, IT systems, application to specific scenarios, and stakeholders, are shown in figure 1-1. These aspects are interrelated, and cannot exist without the others. Every topic studied in ITGS must cover each of these core elements.

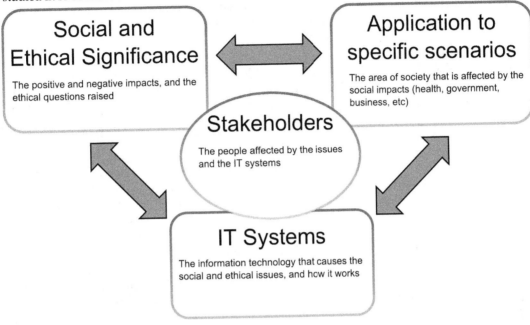

Figure 1-1 The ITGS Triangle
Text adapted from *Information technology in a global society guide*, Copyright © International Baccalaureate Organisation 2010. Used with permission.

Setting up an RSS reader

RSS stands for Really Simple Syndication – which doesn't give much indication of what it actually does. RSS is a 'push-technology' which allows users to view updates to web sites without having to repeatedly visit the site. By configuring an **RSS news reader** with **RSS feeds**, changes to monitored sites are automatically displayed in the reader.

RSS technology is often used on sites where information changes frequently—such as on blogs, news pages, or price alert sites. Many web browsers such as Firefox have built in RSS capabilities, and standalone RSS readers are available. There are also online news readers, allowing you to access your news feeds from any Internet connected computer. Popular standalone readers include RSSOwl, while online options include Google Reader and Bloglines.

To set up an RSS reader

1. Download and install the required software, or create an account if using an online reader
2. Web sites that support RSS will display an orange RSS icon somewhere in their page or near the web browser's address bar. Clicking on the RSS icon causes the address of the feed to be displayed in the address bar—you can tell this has happened because the address will end in .rss or .xml.
3. You need to copy this URL and paste it into your news reader, using the 'new feed' or similar option.
4. The feed should appear and automatically display the most recent updates to that web site. Every time you open the RSS reader, the updates since your last visit will be displayed.
5. Most news readers let you configure how often they check for updates.

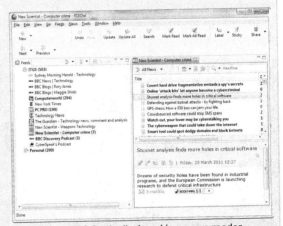

Figure 1-2 RSS feeds displayed in a news reader

Strand 1: Social and ethical significance

Issues of social and ethical significance can arise whenever information technology is used. These issues have **social impacts** – either positive or negative – on **stakeholders**. Impacts affect stakeholders in a variety of ways including economically, legally, and psychologically. Issues of social and ethical significance also raise ethical questions about systems, such as *'who is responsible if the system fails?'* or *'is this an ethical way to use technology?'*. Often, a single IT system causes several social impacts and raises several ethical questions. The ITGS issues of social and ethical significance are:

Reliability and Integrity

Reliability refers to how well a computer system works: if it functions as intended, or fails and crashes. IT failure can cause loss of data, time, or money. In the worst cases, failure can even cause injury or death. **Integrity** refers to the correctness of data. Data can lack integrity if it is incomplete, out of date, or has been deliberately or accidentally changed. Problems may also arise if two copies of the same data are stored and only one copy is updated, causing inconsistency.

Security

Security is concerned with protecting IT systems from **unauthorised users**. Security measures such as passwords, firewalls, and locks are used to restrict access to machines and networks. Security is closely related to issues such as privacy and integrity, because a security breach in an IT system can cause loss of control over the data stored in it.

Privacy and anonymity

Privacy is the ability to control how data about us is used. This includes deciding who we give our data to, who they share our data with, how long data is stored, and how the data is used. IT makes covert data collection relatively easy and large databases of information can reveal a great deal about people's lives, even if their names are not directly recorded. If a person has total privacy, hiding their identity, they become **anonymous**. This can be positive (for example, in witness protection) or negative (such as a user committing cyber bullying anonymously). Excessive privacy also helps hide criminals and terrorists from law enforcement. Finding the right balance of privacy is a big challenge in IT.

Intellectual Property

Intellectual property refers to 'creations of the mind', including photographs, films, essays, and art works. **Copyright law** is designed to protect intellectual property from unauthorised reproduction. Modern IT systems make it easy to break copyright laws by providing ways to quickly and easily distribute copies of work, with little fear of being caught.

Authenticity

Authenticity involves a user proving their identity to gain access to a computer system. The most common examples of authentication are the usernames and passwords used to login to many computer systems. Biometric authentication using fingerprints or retinal scans is also becoming more common. For transactions across the Internet, digital signatures can be used to prove users' identities.

The Digital Divide and Equality of Access

IT has not developed at the same rate for everybody in all parts of the world. Even within individual countries there are often groups or individuals who lack access to technology or services such as the Internet. Often this is for economic

Figure 1-3 Information technology is used in many areas of life including transportation, education, exploration...

reasons – IT and its related services are often expensive to buy and maintain. However, lack of literacy or language skills (particularly English), a lack of training, or a lack of basic resources such as electricity may also cause problems and create a **digital divide** between the 'IT-rich' and the 'IT-poor'.

Surveillance
Surveillance involves using IT to monitor people – either with or without their knowledge or permission. Surveillance can be performed by governments and law enforcement, or by private groups such as employers. Surveillance is an increasing issue as world governments search for ways to fight global terrorism and crime. Surveillance is often closely tied to the issue of privacy, especially when it is performed without the subjects' prior knowledge or consent.

Globalisation and Cultural Diversity:
IT has helped to reduce global boundaries and speed up the global spread of news and culture. This is especially true in recent years with the rapid spread of the Internet to even very remote areas of the world. This spread has benefits, but may also cause problems such as the erosion, or even complete loss, of traditional cultures, values, and languages.

Policies
Policies are rules designed to control the way people use IT. Policies may be designed by individuals or organisations such as schools or businesses, or they may take the form of laws created by governments. The fast pace of IT development means policies often lag behind reality, as developments allow new ways to use – and abuse – information technology, before they can be regulated.

Standards and Protocols
Standards and **protocols** are technical rules that designers of hardware and software should follow. They are needed to ensure different systems are compatible with each other. For example, the JPEG image standard ensures images created by any camera can be opened by any JPEG-compatible graphics program. Similarly, the http protocol ensures web browsers and web servers can communicate and exchange information, and the USB standard ensures any USB device will work with any USB port on any computer. Without standards, compatibility and interoperability would be difficult.

People and Machines
People and Machines concerns the way that humans interact with IT, including physical interaction through user interfaces, and our psychological response to IT. For example, many people trust computers intrinsically, and this has consequences when they fail. At the extreme, people may become so reliant on IT as to become addicted. In some cases decisions may be left to technology even though they would be better made by a human.

Digital Citizenship
Digital citizenship involves being a good citizen in a digital world. This means using information technology ethically, in a way which does not harm other users or their hardware and software. It also means using IT in a way that respects the law (for example, with reference to copyright), and in a way that does not expose yourself to danger (for example, young children posting personal information on the Internet and being unaware of the possible consequences).

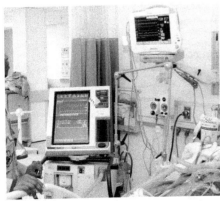  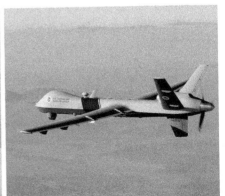

...as well as in medicine, home entertainment, and the military.

Analysing ITGS Situations

When analysing ITGS scenarios, it is important to remember that any IT system can cause several **issues of social and ethical significance**. In turn, each of these issues may cause several **social impacts** (actual effects on people), and raise several **ethical questions**. Figure 1-4 shows guidelines for analysing the issues of social and ethical significance, impacts, and ethical questions.

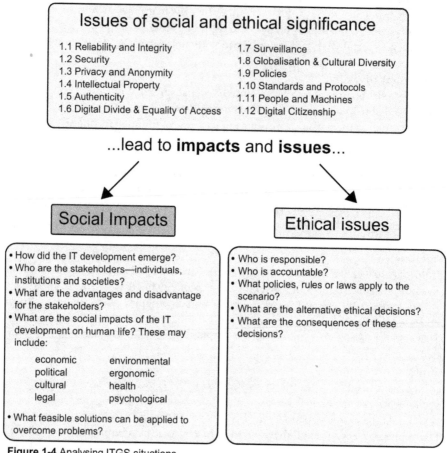

Issues of social and ethical significance

1.1 Reliability and Integrity
1.2 Security
1.3 Privacy and Anonymity
1.4 Intellectual Property
1.5 Authenticity
1.6 Digital Divide & Equality of Access

1.7 Surveillance
1.8 Globalisation & Cultural Diversity
1.9 Policies
1.10 Standards and Protocols
1.11 People and Machines
1.12 Digital Citizenship

...lead to **impacts** and **issues**...

Social Impacts

- How did the IT development emerge?
- Who are the stakeholders—individuals, institutions and societies?
- What are the advantages and disadvantage for the stakeholders?
- What are the social impacts of the IT development on human life? These may include:

economic	environmental
political	ergonomic
cultural	health
legal	psychological

- What feasible solutions can be applied to overcome problems?

Ethical issues

- Who is responsible?
- Who is accountable?
- What policies, rules or laws apply to the scenario?
- What are the alternative ethical decisions?
- What are the consequences of these decisions?

Figure 1-4 Analysing ITGS situations.

Diagram text adapted from *Information technology in a global society guide*, Copyright © International Baccalaureate Organisation 2010. Used with permission.

Evaluating Impacts

A large part of the ITGS course focuses on analysing and evaluating the impacts of IT systems and coming to conclusions about its use—it is not enough to merely describe the impacts of a system. The questions below can help you evaluate a situation and come to a conclusion. Not every question will apply to every situation.

- Are the impacts serious? Are they life or death, or merely an inconvenience?
- Is the impact a long term of short term impact?
- Is there an easy solution to the problem?
- Are all stakeholders affected or just a few?
- Are the affected stakeholders a large group or a small group?
- Is the impact a local issue or a global issue?
- Is it the impact likely to lead to further problems?

By considering the answers to several of these questions, the importance of the social impacts can be evaluated.

Analysing the One Laptop Per Child Project

Analysing

The One Laptop Per Child (OLPC) project provides cheap laptops to children in developing countries. This clearly raises the issue of the **Digital Divide**. Reducing the digital divide causes several impacts. First, it may produce a **positive economic impact**, if it can improve education and stimulate the economy of the country. It may also cause a **positive cultural impact**, as Internet access will provide access to a much wider range of educational material. However, this cultural impact may also be negative, as exposure to foreign cultures may erode local ones.

The issue of the Digital Divide also raises ethical questions. **Responsibility** is a key concern—who will be responsible if the laptops are stolen, or if they break down? Who will be responsible for training teachers and students to use the laptops effectively?

Alternative decisions must also be considered—perhaps most importantly, whether it is appropriate to spend so much money on computer technology in areas that may lack clean water, schools, and healthcare.

Other issues are also raised: **Security** and **Digital Citizenship** are concerns, and could have negative impacts unless students are trained to correctly use the laptops.

The OLPC project demonstrates how one example of IT has social and ethical significance, positive and negative impacts, and raises ethical questions. A range of stakeholders are affected, including children, governments, and the families and teachers of the children, and implicitly the manufacturers of the laptop.

Figure 1-5 The OLPC project provides laptops to governments of developing countries

Evaluating

The guiding questions on page 6 can be used to evaluate the impacts of the OLPC project.

The positive educational impact of the OLPC is likely to be a long term impact, and will affect a large number of students, plus their families because the children take the laptops home. Improved education is also a very important as it underlies several other issues facing developing countries. These factors make this a significant impact.

The issue of responsibility in the event of theft is important, however, there are clear solutions to this problem. The OLPC has anti-theft systems built in, which can disable the laptop remotely. This should reduce the impact of theft, reducing it to a short term problem —until people realise there is no point stealing the computer.

The cultural impact is debatable, since it may be either positive or negative. The potential erosion of culture may affect a very large group of stakeholders, and is likely to be a long term effect. However, this may be outweighed by the educational benefits that access to the computers and the Internet bring.

The ethical question of appropriateness is also tricky—the potential alternative uses of the money (clean water, hospitals, and schools) could help a very large number of people, and in quite significant ways, since lack of clean water and limited healthcare cause large numbers of deaths in developing countries. However, it is also possible that the OLPC could help address these issues, both by improving educational standards—known to have a knock-on effect on health—and by raising the countries' profiles internationally, which could attract funding and support for these other projects.

As with many issues in ITGS, there is no one correct answer when considering the effects of the OLPC project. Answers are likely to vary from person to person, and from place to place. The most important skill in ITGS is the ability to **understand** the impacts an IT system has, and then **evaluate** them to come to a well argued conclusion.

Strand 2: Application to specific areas

IT is ubiquitous – it exists all around us. Laptop computers, smart phones, and games consoles are obvious examples of IT in our everyday lives. But IT also exists in many other places: in our cars, controlling the engine and braking systems; in factories, manufacturing products; in aircraft control systems; and in the banking sector, enabling the global financial markets to operate. IT also controls many of our essential services, including water and power distribution. ITGS examines the effects of information technology in six specific areas:

Business and employment—Many businesses make heavy use of IT to develop, advertise, and sell their products and services. E-commerce has opened markets for even the smallest businesses, allowing them to compete on a global scale. Many services such as ticket booking, banking, and shopping can now all be done online from the comfort of our homes. Many workers can now engage in teleworking, enabling people to work from home or while on the move. But IT can also cause problems in businesses, with security breaches and employee time-wasting being common concerns.

Education and training—The availability of vast amounts of information for free on the Internet has opened up new educational possibilities for many people. Sites like Wikipedia allow information, once only available in expensive paper encyclopaedias, to be read online, for nothing, in dozens of different languages. Formal education organisations have also taken advantage of the Internet to allow distance-learning, while in traditional classrooms many schools are now furnishing teachers and students with laptops and Internet access as standard. Initiatives like the Flat Classroom project[1] have even been successful in fostering collaboration from classrooms across the world.

Environment—Robotic vehicles are rapidly taking over the job of exploring Earth's extreme environments: the deep ocean, the polar icecaps, and dangerous volcanic craters. Improvements in satellite technology have allowed high resolution mapping of the earth from space, while advanced computer models are used to try to predict the future climate of our planet. Yet technology also has a cost for our environment: IT equipment contains many hazardous chemicals, and vast, heavily polluted dumping grounds in developing countries are a forlorn testament to the speed at which technology changes.

Health—IT has helped advance healthcare in daily tasks such as patient record keeping, as well as more unusual tasks such as robot assisted surgery. IT also raises several health issues, especially among the young, with concerns over addiction, injury from excessive use, and the psychological consequences of being in constant contact, thanks to social networking, email, and mobile phones.

Home and Leisure—Our leisure time has been significantly changed by developments which let us watch high quality films, listen to CD-quality music almost anywhere, and stay in touch with family and friends globally. The increased use of the Internet has led to widespread illegal downloading of copyrighted films, software, and music: and the entertainment industry seems unable to stop this trend. IT has also changed how we receive news and stay in contact with friends: 8 times as many people read The New York Times online compared to the printed edition, while social network Facebook has 500 million users, each with an average of 130 friends[2].

Politics and government—IT is used throughout the political process: Barack Obama's 2008 election campaign is famous for extensively using technology for advertising, gathering support, and fund raising. Many of these technologies had not even existed at the previous election. Many countries, including the US, now use e-voting machines and some are considering allowing citizens to vote via the Internet. Once in power, governments are starting to use IT to increase efficiency and transparency, and allow citizens access to services and information. IT has not been embraced by all governments however, and a number of regimes across the world routinely restrict citizens' access to technology or services such as the Internet. The use of IT in Politics and Government includes use by military and police forces, and advancements in military robotics often raise ethical questions.

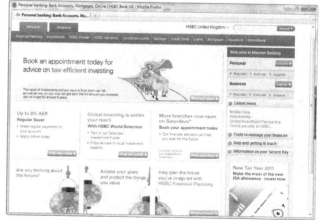

Figure 1-6 The business topic covers everything from the transportation industry to online banking

Strand 3: IT Systems

Although ITGS focuses on the social and ethical significance of information technology, students need to study the underlying technology as well. The IT Systems part of the course examines how these underlying systems work in order to better understand how the systems differ from previous systems, and how they affect society.

All IT systems take data as **input** and **process** it according to programmed instructions into **output**. All IT systems have these three essential components: input, processing, and output. Normally a system will also store the data it processes on some form of permanent **storage device** (see chapter 2), and increasingly data will also be communicated to other systems via **networks** (chapter 4). It is also important to remember that an IT system is not just the hardware and software, but also the people who use the system and the data which is processed. All information systems consists of:

1. **hardware** to input, process, and output data (figure 1-7)
2. **software** to control the hardware
3. **people** to use the system
4. **data** on which the system performs work

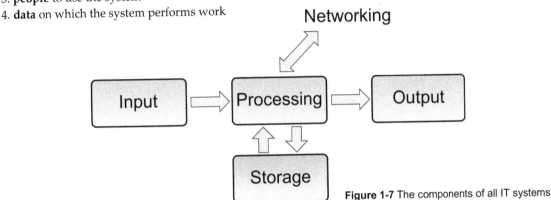

Figure 1-7 The components of all IT systems

Technology versus Information Technology

Students sometimes have difficulty distinguishing between **technology** and **information technology**. Figure 1-7 shows the key elements that all information technology systems have. For a topic to be relevant to ITGS, it has to have information technology at its core. Issues such as DNA cloning, which clearly involve IT but are not a direct result of IT developments, are not relevant to ITGS. The table below shows examples of ITGS topics and examples of common misunderstandings.

Topic	ITGS?	Explanation
Increase in online copyright infringement (music and films)	Yes	The IT systems involved are personal computers and peer-to-peer networks. Without these technologies, the problem would not exist to the same extent. The social issue here is intellectual property, causing an economic and legal impact.
CCTV cameras and privacy	No	Although CCTV cameras have input (the images) and record it, the computer merely records the image. It is the human who performs the 'processing'.
Smart CCTV	Yes	Smart CCTV involves the computer using Artificial Intelligence (AI) to automatically analyse the video images and look for suspicious behaviour. In this case the system processes the images in order to make decisions about them. This raises several issues including reliability and privacy.
DNA cloning	No	Although IT is used by scientists, it is not central to the issue of DNA cloning. IT did not cause DNA cloning – scientific knowledge did. DNA cloning also raises ethical issues – but again, the issues are not caused by the IT system.
Internet addiction	Yes	The Internet is a key information system, allowing widespread spread of ideas and communication. Internet addiction is an example of the issue People and Machines (how people and computers interact) and is a serious social issue in some places. Without the Internet, the issue would not exist.

Chapter Review

Key Language

ITGS Core Terms

application areas	information technology	stakeholders
ethical issues	social and ethical significance	
ethics	social impacts	

Strand 1—Social and Ethical Significance

anonymity	ergonomic impact	protocols
authenticity	globalisation	psychological impact
compatibility	health impact	reliability
cultural diversity	integrity	security
cultural impact	intellectual property	standards
digital citizenship	legal impact	surveillance
economic impact	policies	the digital divide
environmental impact	political impact	unauthorised access
equality of access	privacy	

Strand 2—Application to specific scenarios

Business and employment	Environment	Home and leisure
Education and training	Health	Politics and Government

Strand 3—IT Systems

input	processing	storage
networking	RSS feed	
output	RSS reader	

Exercise 1-1
Match the terms on the left with the descriptions on the right.

1) Privacy   A) Refers to creations of the mind which are protected by copyright law

2) Globalisation   B) Regulations governing the way IT can be used

3) Equality of Access   C) Concerns whether hardware and software work as intended

4) Reliability   D) The use of IT to monitor people causes concerns about this

5) Policies   E) These help ensure that files created in one application can open in another

6) Surveillance   F) The difference between those who have access to IT and those who do not

7) Intellectual Property   G) Relates to who data is shared with and how it is used

8) Standards   H) This involves proving our identity

9) Authenticity   I) Protecting computers, networks, and data from hackers

10) Security   J) IT and quicker communication facilitate this

Exercise 1-2
Read 5 or 6 news articles from the technology sections of newspapers (see page 11 for suggested reading). Determine whether the articles deal with technology or information technology and briefly **explain** your reasoning. [4 marks]

Exercise 1-3

Staying up to date with the latest IT news is essential to success in ITGS. Set up an RSS reader (see page 3) on your computer to automatically fetch the technology headlines from a variety of web sites (a list is given under Further Reading in this chapter review). Remember that ITGS covers local as well as global issues, so your local newspapers – online or on paper—are also important sources. Find a list of RSS readers on the book support website.

Exercise 1-4

Find two ITGS related news articles. Analyse them and describe: the key stakeholders, the IT systems involved, and the area of application (Business, Health, Politics, Home & Leisure, Education, Environment). **Explain** the social impacts and ethical issues caused by the technology – aim for a mix of positive and negative social impacts. [6 marks]

Exercise 1-5

Use the Internet to research how information technology has changed our society in the last few years. Look for key facts and statistics, and link them with ITGS social and ethical considerations on pages 4 to 5. Create a digital presentation that demonstrates these facts and the ITGS key terms for social impacts. Use any IT tools you want: perhaps a digital video camera, an online animation creator, or a presentation package. [10 marks]

Exercise 1-6

Look at the following examples and decide whether they are suitable ITGS topics based on the criteria on page 9.

  a) The use of computer games by the military to train soldiers
  b) The use of web sites or virtual worlds to provide virtual 'field trips' to school children
  c) The increased incidence of violence on television
  d) The increased incidence of apparent Internet addiction in some countries
  e) The rise of online crime
  f) The release of a new portable music player

Exercise 1-7

Consider the following ITGS situations. Briefly discuss the potential positive and negative impacts for each. Try to use the key language on page 6.

  a) The use of software controlled medical devices
  b) The creation of digital copies of famous works of art
  c) The increased use of mobile phones by young people, especially school children
  d) The use of the Internet to cast votes in national elections

Exercise 1-8

TOK Link

Search engines like Google and Yahoo are our 'window' into the Internet, providing us access to the top ranked sites for different topics. What factors might affect a site's search ranking? How do these relate to the ITGS issues of social and ethical significance? How might search engines affect our knowledge and understanding of the world around us?

Further Reading

The following sites provide useful articles related to ITGS and contain useful background reading which will help widen your understanding of the topics involved:

  BBC News – Technology (http://www.bbc.co.uk/news/technology)
  Sydney Morning Herald (http://www.smh.com.au/technology)
  The Telegraph – Technology (http://www.telegraph.co.uk/technology)
  The New York Times technology section (http://www.nytimes.com/pages/technology/index.html)
  Wired (http://www.wired.com)
  Science Daily—Computers and Maths News (http://www.sciencedaily.com/news/computers_math)
  The Atlantic—Technology (http://www.theatlantic.com/technology)

References

1 Davis, V. (2011). Flat Classroom Project. Available: www.flatclassroomproject.org. Last accessed Nov 2011.

2 Facebook. (2011). Facebook Statistics. Available: www.facebook.com/press/info.php?statistics. Last accessed Nov 2011.

Chapter 2
Hardware

Objectives

1. Describe the available types of computer
2. Describe common input, output, and storage devices
3. Describe the role of the main computer components
4. Use the correct units to describe the specification of a computer
5. Explain how a computer's specification affects its performance and use
6. Select a suitably specified computer based on a user's needs
7. Explain how data is stored inside a computer

Hardware

This chapter covers computer **hardware** – the tangible, physical parts of the computer which work together to input, process, store, and output data. Computer hardware comes in many different shapes, sizes, and specifications, from low power systems in basic mobile phones to state-of-the-art supercomputers that run simulations of the Earth's environment. Computer hardware cannot function without software, which is covered in chapter 3.

Although ITGS is not a Computer Science course, knowledge of hardware is still fundamental to the course. Hardware affects both the performance and the way in which IT systems are used. In the most extreme examples, some systems may be unusable by some disabled users unless they have specialist hardware or software (which is clearly an **Equality of Access** issue).

Even if you have experience of hardware from previous IT courses, you should review the concepts in this chapter because hardware is – literally – behind everything you will learn in ITGS.

Types of Computer

Supercomputers

Supercomputers represent the cutting edge of computing technology. They are the largest, fastest, most powerful, and most expensive computers available. Supercomputers achieve incredibly high processing speeds through **multiprocessing**, with hundreds or even thousands of separate **processors** working together. Most supercomputers will have thousands of **gigabytes** of **primary storage** and many **terabytes** of **secondary storage** space. Supercomputers are easily big enough to fill large rooms, requiring significant amounts of power to operate and cool them. In some cases even liquid cooling is used to keep them operating at the correct temperature.

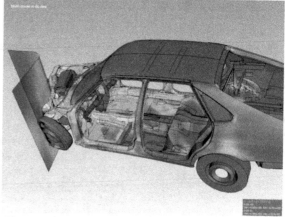

Figure 2-2 Supercomputers can be used to run computer models of car crashes, simulating physical forces and damage.

Their power means supercomputers are only affordable for government facilities or scientific research laboratories, where they are used for tasks involving extremely complex and intensive mathematical calculations, such as running earth climate models, analysing the effects of nuclear explosions, and advanced scientific research. Figure 2-3 details some of the top supercomputers.

Mainframes

Mainframes are also very powerful computers which share many features with supercomputers. However, while supercomputers are optimised for very high speed calculations, mainframes are optimised for high **data throughput**. This means they are able to read extremely large amounts of data from storage, process it, and store the results very quickly. The calculations mainframes perform are not necessarily highly complex, but their sheer volume means a lot of computing power is needed. Tasks requiring these capabilities include payroll processing, airline reservation management, and banking. Banks, for example, process tens or even hundreds of thousands of transactions every second, from a variety of networked offices, including credit card checks, pay-

Figure 2-1 Computer models used to predict climate change require the type of computing power only available in supercomputers.

The World's Fastest Supercomputers

Rank	Name	Owner	Processor	Number of cores	Operating system	Use
1	Tianhe-1A	National Supercomputing Center in Tianjin	Intel Xeon 2930 MHz	186,368	Linux	Research
2	Cray XT Jaguar	Oak Ridge National Laboratory	AMD Opteron 6-core 2600 MHz	224,162	Linux	Research
3	Nebulare	National Supercomputing Centre, Shenzhen	Intel Xeon 2660 MHz	120,640	Linux	Research
4	NEC / HP TSUBAME 2	Tokyo Institute of Technology	Intel Xeon 2930 MHz	73,278	Linux	Research
5	Cray XE Hopper	National Energy Research Scientific Computing Center	AMD Opteron 12-core 2100 MHz	153,408	Linux	Research

Figure 2-3 Supercomputers feature thousands of processor cores to enable extremely fast processing. Source: Top500 Project[1]

ments, cash withdrawals, and money transfers. Because **uptime** is critical in mainframes, they usually feature redundant **failover systems** (see page 38).

Desktop computers

Desktop computers have fallen significantly in price in the last decade, while the amount of available computing power has significantly increased. Desktop computers are common in homes, offices, and schools because they are relatively cheap compared to **laptop computers** with equivalent hardware specifications. Desktop computers are also more comfortable to use for long periods of time because they have adjustable monitors and separate keyboards and mice. This can help avoid health issues related to poor **ergonomics** (see page 266). Another advantage is that desktop computers use generic parts with standard interfaces: this makes upgrading and repairing them easier than with some laptop computers which have custom, manufacturer specific, components. This is important because discarded computer components, known as e-waste, are becoming a serious environmental concern (see page 244).

Home Theatre PCs (HTPC) are desktop computers designed specifically for multimedia entertainment in the home, including accessing the Internet, viewing films, and listening to music.

Laptop computers

The term **laptop** covers a wide range of portable computers from those designed for simple Internet access and word processing, to those powerful enough to replace an average desktop computer. Laptops generally feature a standard keyboard (although some omit the numeric keypad), an LCD screen of between 14 and 17 inches, and a Wi-Fi card to allow wireless access to the Internet.

When designing laptop computers, heat generated by the internal components – especially the processor – is always a concern. Thin laptop cases provide less room for ventilation than desktop cases, and using a laptop on a soft surface such as a cushion or a bed can easily lead to the case vents becoming blocked and the laptop overheating. Excess heat also requires additional cooling, which consumes more power and decreases battery life.

Figure 2-4 The NASA Columbia supercomputer, used for advanced computer modelling and simulation. Columbia has 10240 processor nodes, 20 TB of primary storage, 440 TB of secondary storage, and can perform over 51 trillion operations per second. Columbia runs Linux and custom software to perform advanced mathematical modelling and simulation of space for future NASA missions[4].

Figure 2-5 An IBM System Z (left) is one of the latest models of mainframe computers, with up to 96 processor cores and 3 terabytes (TB) of RAM. The XO Laptop (right) was created by the One Laptop Per Child (OLPC) project. It is a low specification laptop with a 400 MHz processor 512MB RAM, and 4 GB of secondary storage, and is designed especially for children in developing countries.

Another concern for laptops is the relative ease with which they can be stolen or accidentally left behind by their owners (on public transport, for example). This could have serious **security** and **privacy** consequences if the data on the laptop is not protected against **unauthorised access**. For this reason it is a good idea to use security measures such as **passwords** and **disk encryption** (see page 109) on all portable devices. Some laptops feature mounting points for cable locks (called **Kensington Locks**) so the computer can be secured to a desk while unattended.

Netbooks

Netbooks are laptop computers with lower specifications than normal, designed for maximum portability. They are not designed to be a primary machine for office work, but instead to provide access to the Internet and email in a convenient and portable way. Netbooks typically have a very slow processor, a small amount of RAM, and a small, low resolution screen. The benefit of this reduced

Staying in Sync

Mobile phones, PDAs, and other portable computers often come with software to allow **data synchronisation** with a 'main' desktop or laptop computer. The connection can take place using a **USB** cable, **infra-red** (IrDA) or **Bluetooth** connection, and usually allows emails, contact details, photos and other files to be synchronised between the devices.

specification is lower weight and greatly increased battery life – sometimes as much as 9 hours. The **hard disk** may also be replaced with a **solid state flash drive** in order to further reduce weight and power consumption, and increase reliability.

Personal Digital Assistants

Personal Digital Assistants, or PDAs, are somewhere between mobile phones and netbooks in terms of their size and functionality. Also called **palmtop computers**, PDAs usually have a larger screen than mobile phones. As many PDAs do not have a keyboard, the screen is used either for **touch input** using a **soft keyboard**, or **handwriting recognition**. In both cases a special pen called a **stylus** is used. Although many PDAs have Internet access, they are best suited to quick viewing or input of information rather than long sessions of continuous use. Some hospitals are now equipping their doctors and nurses with PDAs to allow rapid retrieval and updating of patient records, and well as rapid communication between staff members (see page 256).

Smart Phones

Smart phones have more features than merely making voice calls and sending text messages. Smart phones usually include built in digital cameras with the ability to record video, sound, and images. Many can also run applications (or **apps**) which are downloaded from online stores, sometimes for free. These applications usually

Lost Laptops

In 2008 a British Royal Navy officer faced a court martial after his work laptop, which had been left in his car overnight, was stolen. The stolen laptop contained the banking, passport, address, and national insurance details for 600,000 people[2]. The implications were frightening: in addition to providing everything a criminal needed to commit **identity theft**, the laptop contained home addresses of serving members of the armed forces, as well as those in the recruiting process – information which could be extremely valuable to terrorist groups.

The loss was not the UK government's first – others include a flash drive detailing 84,000 criminals, including high risk offenders (August 2008)[5]; details of up to 900,000 Royal Air Force personnel on three flash drives (September 2008)[6], details of 1,700,000 armed forces recruits from a lost hard drive (October 2008)[7], and many other cases[8]. The biggest loss was in 2007 when the Revenue and Customs (HMRC) service lost two unencrypted CDs containing the personal data of 25 million citizens[9].

Such cases highlight the value of personal data and the risks of storing it – especially in portable devices which are easily lost or stolen. Worryingly, these organisations often had strict rules regarding data security, yet failed to enforce them. These failures indicate a need for education – for **data subjects**, who must be careful which data they disclose and to whom – and for **data users**, who must be trained in proper security procedures. There is also a need for greater control of data at higher levels of organisations – for example, in the HMRC case, a single employee could download the entire database of 25 million records onto a CD – an inappropriately large amount of power for one individual. By tightening security controls throughout an organisation, serious data losses like this could be prevented.

offer more advanced functions than the contact mangers, calendars, and reminder features found on most mobile phones. Some perform the same function as a GPS, providing maps and directions, allow editing of images and video taken with the phone's camera, or provide entertainment such as games. Some applications even allow the creation of office documents, such as spreadsheets or word processed documents. To facilitate this, smart phones either have full (although small) keyboards, or use soft keyboards (see page 19).

Internet access is standard on smart phones, allowing access to the world wide web and email. If the phone uses higher speed 3G or 4G technology for Internet access, it may also be possible watch streaming video (for example TV programs).

Figure 2-6 Computers come in all shapes and sizes, including PDAs (left), smart phones (centre), and netbook computers (right).

Exercise 2-1
Read the description of smart phones on these pages. **Describe** three technical developments that have contributed to the development of phones with these capabilities. [6 marks]

Figure 2-7 PDA computers are well suited to maintaining calendars, appointments, email, and contacts on the move.

Figure 2-8 GPS and satellite navigation systems contain embedded computers

Embedded systems

An **embedded system** is a specialised computer which is 'hidden' inside another device. Embedded systems are found in cars, where they control the anti-lock braking and engine management systems; in traffic lights, where they synchronise the lights; and in washing machines, where they control the wash cycles and manage water efficiency. Smaller portable devices like digital watches, digital cameras, and GPS systems also contain embedded systems. Even smart cards (see page 22) contain very simple embedded microprocessors and data storage devices. Unlike other computer types, embedded computers are typically special purpose, programmed to perform only one type of specific task. An important aspect for many embedded systems is reliability since they are often required to run for very long periods without restarting. Many embedded systems are also real-time systems, meaning that they have to provide immediate output.

Exercise 2-2

Use the Internet, manufacturers' web sites, and advertisements to find examples of different computer types: desktop, laptop, PDA, handheld, smart phones, and supercomputers.

Create a table that compares the major specifications of each type. Include at least: the number of processors, processor speed, RAM, hard disk capacity, and cost, using the correct units for each.

Exercise 2-3

Convergence is the idea that computers today can perform tasks that were once performed by many separate devices. One simple example is modern games consoles that can now play games, play DVD or Blu-ray films, and allow access to the Internet: each of these tasks used to require a separate piece of equipment.

Take your mobile phone as an example. Is it an example of convergence? What tasks can you perform using it? How did you perform these tasks before mobile phones had these capabilities? **Explain** your answer. [4 marks]

Exercise 2-4

The IT industry is known for its rapid pace of development, with new products continually being released, each claiming to be better than its predecessor. New computers have faster processors, higher capacity hard disks, and more RAM. New phones have additional features and faster network connections. Yet this rapid development comes at a price: each year thousands of tonnes of old electronics are unsafely discarded, threatening the health of people and the environment. Heavy metals in dumped equipment leach into soil and ground water, and workers dismantle equipment in dangerous conditions in developing countries.

What can be done about this problem? Safely recycling electronic waste is expensive – who should be responsible for paying this price – the manufacturers, the customers, or somebody else? **Discuss** possible solutions. [8 marks]

Input Devices

Input devices are items of hardware that allow entry of information into the computer. This information may be text, images, sound, or even movements. Typically input devices are specialised to enter one type of information. Some are designed especially to help users with disabilities use the computer, helping to create **equality of access** for these users (see page 29).

Keyboards

Most computer users are familiar with the standard QWERTY keyboard that is present on virtually all laptop and desktop computers. Despite dating back to typewriters in the 1870s, the keyboard layout has changed very little over the years.

Some alternatives to QWERTY keyboards have been created: **Dvorak keyboards** use a completely different layout which is claimed to increase typing speed by rearranging commonly paired letters. There are also variations of QWERTY that swap a small number of the keys, especially in Eastern Europe and in Asia.

Multimedia keyboards are standard QWERTY keyboards with additional 'hotkeys' for opening common applications like web browsers or media players. A very common enhancement to a standard QWERTY keyboard is the inclusion of a 'Windows key' on most PCs – this quickly brings up the Start Menu in Microsoft Windows and can also be used to perform specific shortcuts such as locking the computer or showing the desktop.

Laptop computers often feature a special function key (often labelled 'Fn') which is used in conjunction with other keys to control features like the sound volume, screen brightness, or use of an external monitor or projector.

Concept Keyboards

On a **concept keyboard** (see figure 2-11) each key is programmed to perform a custom function. Typically there are no pre-set keys such as numbers or letters – instead, each key performs one compound task. Concept keyboards are useful in situations where the user needs to make a quick selection of choices from pre-set options, but does not need to regularly enter text or numeric data manually. They are often used in restaurants to enter the items a customer has purchased. In this case, each key can be programmed to represent a different item – one key for a hamburger, one key for fries, one key for a soda, and so on. This allows the operator to make rapid input from a variety of pre-set choices.

Figure 2-9 Multimedia buttons allow quick access to additional functions

Soft keyboards

A **soft keyboard** (also called a **software keyboard**, **on-screen keyboard**, or **virtual keyboard**) is a keyboard that is represented by a series of buttons drawn on a monitor or screen. The user select options using a pointing device like a mouse, or a touch screen. A soft keyboard uses a combination of hardware (the monitor or touch screen) and software (the program that displays the options).

Soft keyboards are useful because they can be more accessible than regular keyboards – for example, the size of the keys can easily be increased for users who have difficulties with small keys, and the language of the keyboard can be changed much more easily than with a hardware keyboard. They are also useful for small devices such as PDAs and smart phones, where it is not possible to include full sized keyboards – or even any keyboard at all.

Even on desktop and laptop computers, soft keyboards can be useful in security conscious environments. Some banks use soft keyboards on the login pages of their online banking web sites to reduce the risk of key logging attacks (see page 94).

Mice

A mouse is the standard pointing device on most desktop computers. A typical computer mouse has two buttons and many also have a scroll wheel in the centre to perform tasks like scrolling through documents or web pages. Some have additional buttons in the middle or around the side, which can be programmed to perform customizable commands (such as a sequence of key presses in a game).

Figure 2-10 A virtual keyboard used by an online banking site. The positions of the keys are randomized to prevent spyware from capturing passwords.

Figure 2-11 A concept keyboard that might be used in a restaurant to speed up the entry of orders

Trackballs

A **trackball** consists of a relatively large ball which is fixed in place so that the user can spin it around, controlling a pointer on the screen. One of the advantages of trackballs over mice is that they do not move across the desk, which makes them ideal for use in areas where space is tight. For this reason, some early laptops had trackballs, and some recent models of mobile phone also include them. A trackball can also be built-in to a computer system easily, making it hard to detach or steal (unlike a mouse). This has made them popular in some computer kiosks which are used in public areas.

A trackball can be much more usable than a mouse for people with movement difficulties in their arms or hands. Since using a trackball requires only movement of the thumb or fingers, they can make computers accessible to people who are unable to move a mouse across a desk.

Touch pads

Touch pads are common input devices on laptops, where there is usually not enough space for a mouse. As well as moving the pointer by tracing their finger across the touch pad, users can also use bars at the side to scroll text on the screen. **Multi-touch** touch pads allow more complex actions to be performed using several fingers – for example, moving two fingers away from each other to zoom in.

Touch screens

Touch screens allow users to interact with computers using their hand or a specially designed pen called a **stylus**. Touch screens are often used in airports for passengers to complete self-check-in procedures, or in self-service photo kiosks. Automatic Teller Machines (ATMs) in banks also frequently use them.

Figure 2-12 Two common input methods—a trackball (left) and touch screen with stylus (right)

Figure 2-13 Touch screens often use a stylus pen for input, and are common on mobile devices where there is no space for a regular sized keyboard.

Touch screens are also useful on small portable devices such as mobile phones. Many mobile phone operating systems now include support for **multi-touch**—being able to control the device using a single finger or making complex gestures using multiple fingers.

Microphones

A **microphone** allows sound data to be input into the computer. Many laptops have microphones built in to them, and external microphones can also be used. Microphones are often used with video-conferencing and **Voice over IP** (VoIP) software. This lets users talk – often with video too – between two computers over the Internet – usually for much less than the cost of a telephone call.

Once sound has been recorded, it is merely a collection of digital data – the computer does not 'understand' the meaning of the sounds. To recognise the words being spoken, **voice recognition software** is required. This allows a person to dictate words into a word processor to write a document, rather than typing. The software breaks down the recorded sound into parts, tries to match them with the sounds of letters and words, and then produces the corresponding character on the screen.

Voice-control software is similar except the user speaks commands to the computer operating system (e.g. *open word processor* or *delete file*). Voice recognition and voice command software are not always useful in busy, noisy work environments, but they can be useful for users who are unable to type, perhaps due to injury or disability (see page 29).

Figure 2-14 Self-service check in machine at London's Heathrow airport. Using a touch screen and a software keyboard, machines like this can easily switch between several different languages and provide accessibility options.

Game controllers

Joysticks and **game pads** are two common input devices used by games players. There are many different configurations available that include a variety of buttons and features. More exotic input devices include steering wheels and pedals for driving games, musical instruments, and dance mats on which the user stands and controls the game by moving their feet.

One of the more unusual game controllers in recent years is the controller used by Nintendo's Wii games console. This controller is held in the hand in mid-air, and internal **motion sensors** interpret the user's movement into actions in the game. If the user holds the controller and moves their arm in a golf-style swing, the character on screen will mimic their movements. These types of controllers are used in a variety of games including golf, bowling, and boxing – where the user punches the air in front of them to make their virtual character fight on screen.

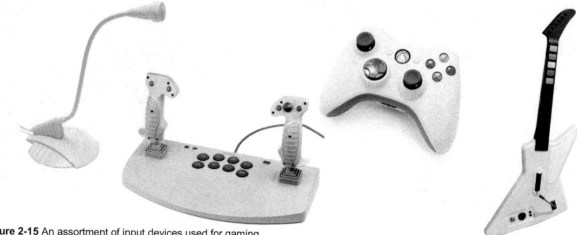

Figure 2-15 An assortment of input devices used for gaming.

Barcode scanners

A **barcode scanner** uses a laser to shine light onto a barcode label. The thickness of the lines and the spacing between the lines on the barcode determine the amount of reflected light. This is then interpreted as a number by the barcode scanner. Barcodes are most commonly used on items in supermarkets but they also have other applications such as identifying packages that are sent by courier firms. **UPC (Universal Product Code)** is one standard which defines how a barcode stores its information. Page 23 explains how barcodes work in more detail.

Magnetic Stripe Readers

Bank cards, credit cards, hotel key cards and some frequent traveller cards feature a **magnetic stripe** on the reverse side, and in many places tickets for public transport now use the same technology to process passengers through automated gates, and to reduce fare dodging. These magnetic stripes store a small amount of data which is read using a **magnetic stripe reader**.

Although magnetic stripes are often considered relatively secure, it is possible to purchase stripe writers to alter the data on such cards. This can be done to create a clone of an existing bank card which might be indistinguishable (to a computer) from a genuine card. The clone card could still be spotted by a person because it would lack the colours, logo, security holograms and signature of a genuine card.

Smart cards

Smart cards are plastic credit card style cards that differ from normal 'dumb' magnetic stripe cards by having a higher storage capacity and an **embedded processor**. The processor is powered on when the card is inserted into a **smart card reader**; the processor then controls access to the data stored on the card. This allows the data to be encrypted for increased security.

Smart cards are frequently used in bank and credit cards, and related electronic cash systems such as public transport or loyalty card systems. Some governments

Figure 2-16 Cards for public transport systems, like this London Oyster card, often use embedded RFID chips.

Exercise 2-5: Healthy Computer Gaming?
Some people have claimed the new generation of motion input devices and games consoles can help young people improve their fitness. Some schools have even bought games consoles for their PE departments. Research the use of these devices. **Analyse** the benefits and problems. Do you think the benefit is significant? [8 marks]

How Barcodes Work

Barcodes are used in supermarkets to identify different types of products. This speeds up many processes in the supermarket, from customer purchases to managing stock levels.

Each product of the same type (for example, every 1 litre bottle of water from the same manufacturer) is given the same barcode. The barcode contains a unique identification number to identify that type of product—it does not contain any other data about the product, such as a description or the price. The barcode number is used to retrieve data information from the supermarket's database, as explained below.

5 901234 123457 >

Step 1—Scan the barcode
A barcode reader scans the barcode using a laser. The amount of light reflected back is interpreted as different numbers by the computer.

Step 2—Verify the barcode
The last digit of the barcode number is a **check digit**. This helps the computer determine if the barcode has been scanned correctly. Page 157 explains how check digits work.

Step 3—Find the product's data
The barcode only contains a unique product identification number—it does not contain the price of the product or any other information. To retrieve this data, the barcode number is used to search the product database.

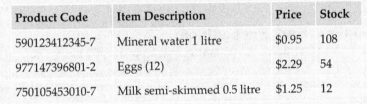

Product Code	Item Description	Price	Stock
590123412345-7	Mineral water 1 litre	$0.95	108
977147396801-2	Eggs (12)	$2.29	54
750105453010-7	Milk semi-skimmed 0.5 litre	$1.25	12

590123412345-7   Mineral water 1 litre $0.95

Step 5—Return the product's data
Once the product's record is found, the number of items in stock is decreased and the product's description and price is returned to the Point of Sale (POS).

Advantages
Using barcodes and a database like this has several advantages:
- Prices can easily be changed simply by changing a single database field. No barcodes need to be changed. This saves time and reduces the chances of mistakes.
- Supermarkets can easily keep track of stock—each time an item is scanned, the 'quantity' field in the database can be reduced by one.
- Automatic stock ordering can be performed if the quantity of an item drops below a predetermined level. This reduces the chance of the supermarket running out of stock. Advanced systems can even order more items depending on variables such as the weather or time of year—for example, ordering more ice cream during a heat wave, or more drinks during the holiday period.

Figure 2-17 MICR is frequently used on cheques because it can be read by both people and machines.

issue smart cards as identity cards, which can also be used for authentication when claiming services such as health care, or when voting. Although smart cards are more expensive than regular plastic cards, they reduce costs for many operators by reducing fraudulent transactions.

Normally a smart card contains a unique identification number which can then be used to access a database for further details related to the card. For example, swiping a smart card at a subway station will access a central transport database, and record the card's number and the time and location of the journey. Depending on the system the amount of money remaining for future travel might be stored on the smart card or the central database, or both.

Optical Mark Recognition

Optical Mark Recognition (OMR) is an input method for speedily reading and counting multiple choice style answer papers. If you have ever taken a multiple choice test like the US SAT, or filled in lottery tickets, your work has probably been checked by an **Optical Mark Reader**. An OMR system uses reflected light to determine whether or not a mark exists in a box on a piece of paper, and then tallies the results.

Magnetic Ink Character Recognition

Magnetic Ink Character Recognition (MICR) is a specialised technology that uses ink containing iron particles, making it magnetic. MICR text is written in a special font, making it human-readable, while the varying amounts of iron in each letter allow the computer to differentiate them. Probably the most common use of MICR is on the bottom of cheques.

Scanners

A **scanner** is a device for **digitizing** a piece of paper. A digital image of the paper being scanned is stored as a standard image file (JPEG, TIF, PNG). This happens even if the page being scanned contains text. The **resolution** of the scanner, measured in **DPI (Dots Per Inch)**, determines the quality of the image produced—this is particularly important when scanning photographs for digital archiving. Modern photo scanners might have maximum resolutions around 4800 dpi. Page 127 describes DPI and PPI in more detail. Many scanners come with **OCR (Optical Character Recognition)** software to convert a scanned image containing text back into 'normal' text which can be edited in a word processing program. Typically OCR software will not work well, if at all, with hand written text.

Figure 2-18 Scanning technologies: Optical Mark Recognition recognises pen and pencil marks as they are placed in the boxes—the numbers are there for the human to read—the computer determines the answer by the position of the box on the page.

Sensors and Probes

Sensors are used for measuring some aspect of the physical world, such as humidity, temperature, light, or pH. Such data is typically **analog data** (continuous data), so it needs to be converted to **digital data** before it can be processed or stored by a computer. An **Analog-to-Digital Converter** (ADC) does this task. Sensors are useful for collecting data at regular intervals without human intervention: for example, measuring the temperature every ten minutes for many hours. They are also useful in situations that are too dangerous for humans, such as monitoring the activity of an active volcano. The Spirit and Opportunity robots designed by NASA used a variety of sensors for recording data about the surface of Mars, and sending it back to Earth. Page 238 contains more details about **Data Logging**.

Digital cameras

Digital cameras and **digital video cameras** have gradually replaced film models over the last decade. Although many digital cameras could be considered computers in their own right, they are also a useful way of inputting image, video, and sound straight into a computer. This can be done using a **USB** or **FireWire** connection, or by putting the camera's **memory card** into a card reader in the computer. Page 34 describes the types of memory card available.

Web cams

A **web cam** is a relatively low resolution video camera. Many modern laptops have web cams built into their screens, and external models can also be bought. Web cams are normally used to record the computer user, often for the purposes of **video conferencing**. Some vendors also sell software that allows web cams to be used as cheap security cameras, with the computer being used to record and monitor activity.

Radio tags

Radio tags are used for locating or tracking objects. They emit Very High Frequency (VHF) radio signals which can be picked up and located by a receiver. Radio tags are frequently used to track wildlife, especially endangered species, by attaching the tag as a collar or a leg ring. The advantage of using radio tags to track animals is that the technology has a relatively long range and allows animals to be monitored without disturbing them. Radio tags can also be used in combination with the **Global Positioning System** (GPS) to generate alerts if tagged animals enter certain areas – for example, farm land. This can allow wildlife managers to deal with the animal before it causes a problem.

Figure 2-19 A wolf in Yellowstone National Park is tracked using a radio tag collar (top). Radio tags can also be used to track animals in the ocean (bottom).

Radio Frequency Identification

Radio Frequency Identification (RFID) is a technology which some people believe will replace barcodes in the near future. An RFID system consists of two components: an **RFID tag** which is attached to the surface of an item (or sometimes even inside it), and an **RFID reader** to query the tag and retrieve its information. RFID tags have a greater storage capacity than barcodes and are contactless – that is, the reader does not have to be very close to the tag and it does not require line of sight to the tag.

A major application of RFID tags is in supermarkets. Individual pallets of goods are tagged as they leave the manufacturer, allowing them to be tracked to the warehouse,

Figure 2-20 Uses of RFID tags. Top to bottom: in a passport; in groceries; embedded in animals to aid identification; in a car flap which opens only for a specific animal, using a tag in its collar.

and ultimately to the shelf. This has great benefits for efficiency and loss reduction. Tagging of individual items, such as clothes, also has benefits, such as allowing workers to stock shelves more effectively and ensure goods are always available. For example, an employee scanning a shelf visually might notice that only half the stock of jeans has been sold—but an employee using an RFID scanner can quickly determine which size and colour jeans are missing, ensuring a variety of products is always on the shelf.

Other applications of RFID include implanting the chips into the skin of pets to enable their identification: the RFID tag can contain the name, address, and contact details of the owner, unlike a barcode which can contain very little information (and would be easily lost if attached to an animal!). Additionally, the RFID tag can store the details of the animal's vaccinations – essential information when trying to import animals into other countries. An embedded RFID tag has the advantage that, unlike paperwork, it cannot be lost or easily forged.

RFID is also being used in new passports issued by many countries, including the US and the UK. The RFID chip is designed to speed up the passport control by allowing the passport to be read from a greater distance, and improve security by allowing biometric data to be stored. Page 293 discusses the use of such passports.

Concerns about RFID

RFID has also raised some concerns. The ability to make extremely small tags—similar in size to a grain of rice—raises worries about privacy, surveillance, and the possible surreptitious tagging of items. The ability the embed tags within objects, rather than on their surface, and the relatively large reading distance of RFID readers, increases these concerns.

Because each individual RFID tag is unique, it also allows tracking of individual items—or the people buying those items. For example, a tag embedded in a product could be read by RFID readers in the shop's shelves. The shop owners could then view the path the customer takes through the shop – including the other products they stop at, pick up, or buy. Over time a complex record of customer activity can be built up, enabling the shop to develop much more advanced product placement or targeted advertisements. A tag in a long lasting item such as a pair of shoes could even allow tracking over multiple visits. However, there is no evidence that any of these techniques have been used yet.

Input devices of the future?

The decreasing size of mobile devices often makes it difficult to input data using a conventional device like a mouse, keyboard, or even a touch screen.

One solution, designed by researchers at Microsoft and Carnegie Mellon University, is the idea of Skin Input, or Skinput. This system uses a small projector to project images of menus and options directly onto the hand or arm surface. The user taps the appropriate option and the Skinput system detects the choice by measuring the inaudible sound waves that travel through the skin and bone when the arm is tapped. With training, the research team claimed over 90% accuracy in detecting correct taps to the skin[10].

The team believe the technology will be useful for a variety of small devices including MP3 players.

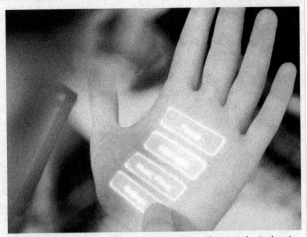

Figure 2-21 A user selects from menu options projected onto their hand using the Skin Input system. (Image courtesy of Microsoft Research and Carnegie Mellon University)

Output Devices

Output devices are any items of hardware that the computer uses to present data to the user. Like input devices, output devices can output text, images, video, sound or other types of data. Even movements can be output using robotic arms.

Screens

Screens are one output device found in almost all computer systems. **CRT (Cathode Ray Tube)** displays are the big, deep, monitors that used to be used on almost all desktop computers. They have now been almost completely replaced by **LCDs (Liquid Crystal Displays)**.

LCD displays are generally cheaper, thinner, lighter, and produce higher quality images than CRT displays. Their small size is useful when displays need to be wall mounted, used in confined spaces such as in instrument panels, or in portable devices such as music players.

LCD screens have a **native resolution**, which refers to the fixed number of dots that make up the screen. Although an LCD can display an image in different resolutions, the image will be scaled to match the LCD's native resolution. For this reason, the best image quality is obtained when using an LCD at its native resolution.

If data needs to be shown at a much greater size than CRT or LCD will allow, a **projector** can be used. These are often used when data needs to be presented to a large audience, such as in a classroom or a business conference. Some classrooms make use of **interactive whiteboards**— a combination of projector and touch screen (see page 227).

Speakers

Speakers come in many forms, from simple ear phones to complex multi-speaker arrangements. As well as entertainment purposes, speakers have essential functions in other areas. In busy environments where a person must absorb a lot of information at once (such as an aircraft cockpit), some feedback can be given as audio output, either as beeps or as a human voice. This is especially useful in emergency situations where sound is more likely to be noticed than flashing lights or displays.

Figure 2-22 Sound output is often used in aircraft cockpits.

Printers

Printers produce **hard copies** of documents and files. Printers vary in how they produce an image, which has a direct effect on the quality of the printout and the cost of the printer. The speed of a printer, expressed in **pages per minute (PPM)** may also be an important factor when considering a purchase.

Years ago dot matrix printers were very common. They created an image by hitting the paper through an ink-ribbon with a series of pins to form a shape, similar to a typewriter. As a result they were incredibly noisy and quite slow. Dot matrix printers are generally obsolete now.

Much more common are **inkjet printers**, which work by squirting ink onto a page through a series of nozzles. The quality of the printer can be measured by the number of **dots per inch (DPI)** that the printer is able to produce. Some printers, often sold as photo printers, have a higher DPI and are capable of very high quality printouts when using the correct ink and special paper. Page 127 discusses DPI in more detail.

Laser printers produce higher quality printouts than inkjet printers but are also more expensive, especially colour versions. They often print at up to 40 ppm.

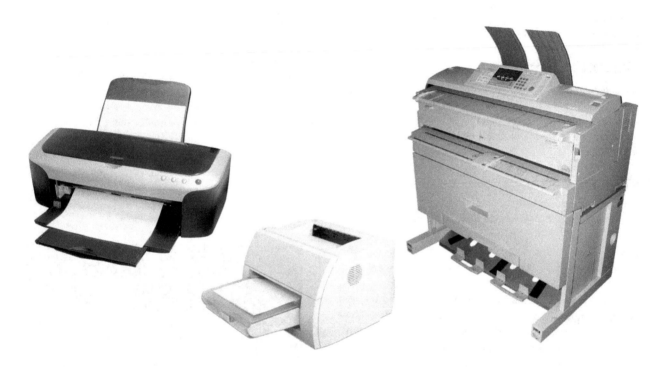

Figure 2-23 Printers come in many forms: inkjet printers (left) are often used with desktop computers as they offer good value for money; laser printers (middle) offer faster print speed and higher quality; specialised art printers (right) are used for larger print sizes and professional quality.

Ethics: running costs and environmental costs

Running costs should also be considered when purchasing a new printer. Some modern inkjet printers are so cheap that it can be less expensive to replace the printer than buy a new set of ink cartridges for it! This is especially true if the printer requires you to replace all inks at once rather than allowing you to replace individual colours as they run out. The use and replacement of ink also brings environmental concerns: of the 700 million ink cartridges used in the US each year, 95% are discarded in landfill sites. This clearly has a huge impact on both disposal sites and in terms of the resources needed to manufacture new cartridges (each cartridge requires 2 ½ ounces of oil to manufacture)[3].

Figure 2-24 Millions of empty ink cartridges are thrown away each year.

Computer Access for Disabled users

Computer systems which can be used by users with disabilities are said to be **accessible**. User disabilities can include hearing problems, mobility problems, and vision problems.

Vision impaired users

Vision impaired users have a variety of options, depending on the severity of their disability. Users with partial sight might find the **screen magnification**, **large pointer**, and **high contrast** options helpful. If users have difficulty seeing the components of the screen (such as the mouse pointer), using a microphone and **speech control software** might assist with input problems. Similarly, **text-to-speech** software can be used to read out loud the contents of the screen. Windows and MacOS both feature basic text-to-speech utilities.

A blind user might also use a **Braille keyboard** to input text. Rather than simply placing Braille dots on a standard keyboard, a Braille keyboard uses a small number of keys that can be pressed in different combinations to produce the letters of the alphabet. **Braille printers** are also available, which produce documents using the Braille system of writing by impacting the paper to raise small bumps.

Mobility Problems

Users with mobility problems in their arms may find a trackball more useful than a mouse because it requires less arm dexterity to use. Software utilities such as **sticky keys** can also help because they allow keys (for example the shift key) to be 'stuck down' after pressing, rather than requiring the user to hold down multiple keys at once.

Head control systems use a web cam and special software to track the movement of the user's head and convert this into pointer movement. Some hardware and software developers are taking this system a step further and attempting to implement **eye tracking software** to follow the movement of a user's eyes around the screen, with the cursor following their gaze. **Input switches** are pads that can be pressed with the user's hands, feet, or even head in order to input data. In many cases they are relatively large and padded, as they are designed for users with limited control over their movements.

If a user has severe mobility difficulties and speech problems, there are still input options. A **head wand** can be worn and used to touch keys or switches. **Sip and puff** input devices allow the user to control a computer literally by blowing or sucking on a small plastic tube. The change in air pressure is then read by the computer and interpreted as a command. This can be extended to measure the strength of sips and puffs, for example strong and weak.

Figure 2-25 Screen magnification tools enlarge the area of the screen around the pointer (top); inverted colour schemes are easier to read for some users (middle); a disabled computer user casts a vote using a head wand (bottom).

Processor Technology
Microprocessors

At the centre of all computers is a **processor** (also called a **Central Processing Unit (CPU)** or a **microprocessor**). The processor is responsible for performing all instructions and tasks that the computer does. Instructions (**software**) are loaded from **secondary storage** into **RAM** and then the processor executes each of these instructions one by one. The speed of the processor determines how quickly tasks can be completed.

One of the main concerns computer manufacturers have about the processor is keeping it cool. Processors generate a large amount of heat and without cooling they can quickly overheat and even melt. Most desktop and laptop computers use a metal heat sink to dissipate heat, with a fan on top to draw air over the metal and improve cooling. Higher end computers such as supercomputers may even use liquid cooling to maintain low operating temperatures.

Clock Speed

The speed at which a processor executes instructions is called the **clock speed** and is measured in **Megahertz (MHz)** or **Gigahertz (GHz)** (and perhaps in the future, **Terahertz (THz)**). The higher the clock speed, the more instructions a processor can perform in a given period of time.

However, comparing the clock speeds of processors from different companies is not always useful since on some processors some instructions may a different number of clock cycles to complete. Thus, a processor with a lower clock speed can sometimes be faster than a processor with a higher clock speed.

Increasing the clock speed of a processor also increases the amount of heat it produces. This can be a problem even for desktop computers, but is a particular issue for smaller devices such as laptops and mobile devices.

Some manufacturers design their processors with variable clock speeds, which reduce when the processor is under less load and increase when the processor is being heavily utilised. This **speed throttling** saves power and reduces heat output when the computer is idle.

> **Common Mistake**
> A common mistake is to refer to the computer box that sits under your desk as the 'CPU'. In fact the best term for this is the 'system unit'. CPU refers **only** to be processor inside a computer.

Figure 2-26 The underside of a microprocessor (top). The gold pins are used to provide a connection with the motherboard. The top side of the processor with a heat sink attached (bottom). The heat sink's fins increase the surface area to aid cooling.

MIPS

MIPS (**Millions of Instructions Per Second**) is another measure of processor performance. Like clock speed, MIPS figures should be used with caution because it is possible to quote misleading figures based on instructions which execute the quickest, rather than those that represent real life computing tasks.

A modern desktop computer might have a processor running at between 2 and 3 GHz and capable of performing about 50,000 Million Instructions per Second.

Multicore processors

Increased processor performance can also be achieved by adding additional processor **cores**. Each core is capable of running an individual program thread at once, boosting performance. While computers with only one core give the appearance of performing more than one task at once using **multi-tasking** (switching rapidly between running programs), **multicore** computers can truly run more than one task at the same time. Multiple cores can also work together on the same task to get the job performed in less time. Multicore processors offer huge performance benefits, especially when software is designed to take advantage of this approach. **Dual core**, **quad core**, and even eight core processors are becoming more common.

Motherboards

The processor connects directly to the computer's **motherboard**, which in turn provides ports and connections for all other parts of the system. The motherboard also has slots for the RAM, connectors for hard disks, slots for attaching expansion cards like video cards or sound cards, and connectors for the mouse and keyboard. Many modern motherboards also have built-in video and sound capabilities, so they feature connectors for monitors and speakers as well.

Figure 2-28 Modern processors allow you to reduce their clock speed to lower power consumption when they are idle and increase laptop battery life.

Figure 2-27 A typical computer motherboard

Common Mistake: Multitasking

A processor cannot perform more than one instruction at a time. When you are using a word processor, listening to music, and running a web browser, your computer's processor is switching between each of these tasks very quickly – far quicker than you could notice. This type of system is known as **multi-tasking**. To truly perform multiple tasks at once, a **multicore** system can be used.

Quad-core: 4 times quicker?

It is not true that a dual-core processor will double a computer's performance, a quad-core processor will quadruple it, and so on. Although multicore systems offer large performance gains, the relative gain drops as more cores are added. There are two main reasons for this:

Sequence: many tasks cannot be completed in parallel – there are some parts which must be completed before other parts can be attempted. This may leave some cores idle, waiting until a separate part of the task is finished.

Organisational overhead: many consumer-level multicore systems have one area of RAM, shared by all cores. This causes an overhead as each core must wait in turn to access the RAM and other devices like secondary storage. High end systems like supercomputers alleviate this bottleneck by having dedicated memory areas for each processor.

Consider this example: if you had to write a 1000 word English essay about Shakespeare, you might be able to complete it in 2 hours. If you had a friend to help, you could probably write it together in 1 hour. But if you had three friends to help you, would it be possible to write the essay in 30 minutes? What if there were 120 people? Could the essay be written in one minute? Certainly not – for two reasons. Firstly, the work would need to be divided between each person, deciding who writes which section, and then recombined later (this is organisational overhead). Secondly, not everyone would be able to write the essay independently – each paragraph depends to an extent on the one before it; similarly with each sentence; and certainly if we want to write something which makes sense, each word depends on the preceding word. So writing an essay is a task which does not lend itself to parallelism — it is sequential.

Storage devices

Storage devices are used to store both the data that a computer system processes and the software programs that tell it how to process that data. Storage devices differ according to their storage capacity, their physical size, the speed at which data can be accessed, and whether they store data temporarily (**volatile storage**) or permanently (**non-volatile storage**).

Primary Storage

Primary storage refers to the high speed, electronic memory found inside a computer. Primary storage is the only storage that the processor can access directly because it is connected directly to the bus on the motherboard. This makes primary storage much faster than **secondary storage**. (Although hard disks are inside the computer system unit, they are still considered secondary storage because they are not directly connected to the processor).

Random Access Memory

Random Access Memory (RAM) is a temporary (volatile) storage area for programs and data that are being used in a given moment. When a program or piece of data is first needed, it is loaded from secondary storage into RAM. The processor then fetches the instructions and data from RAM, executes them, and saves the results back to RAM. Because RAM loses its contents when the power is removed (i.e. it is volatile), you must save your data to secondary storage before turning off your computer.

RAM exists in relatively small amounts compared to secondary storage (a few gigabytes compared to hundreds of gigabytes). This is because RAM only has to store the program and data being used at any given moment, while the secondary storage holds all programs and data, even if they are not currently being used.

Figure 2-29 RAM chip from a typical desktop computer

Read Only Memory

Read Only Memory (ROM) is a type of primary storage whose contents cannot be changed. Because of this, the contents of ROM are programmed at the time of manufacture. The ROM in a typical computer contains the BIOS (Basic Input and Output System) software, which tells the computer how to boot up, perform a self-check, and locate secondary storage devices. Then the operating system will be loaded from secondary storage into RAM, and started.

Secondary Storage

Secondary storage devices are used to store all of the data and programs installed on a computer system – even if they are not currently being used. Any program that is run or data that is used will be copied from secondary storage to primary storage before being used. Secondary storage is slower, but also cheaper, than primary storage.

Magnetic Tapes

Magnetic tapes have been used in computing for many years. In the 1980s many home computers by companies like Amstrad and Sinclair used magnetic audio tapes to store all their software and data.

These days, much higher capacity magnetic tapes are used by organisations that must handle large amounts of data. It is slow to access data on tapes because they are sequential, so the tape must be spun through to find the right place. Because of this, they are used mainly for backing up and archiving data. Their reliability and their low price make them ideal for this type of data, since it will not need to be accessed very often.

	Primary Storage	Secondary Storage
Speed	Electronic – very fast to access data	Mechanical – slower to access data
Storage capacity	1 GB – 4 GB	100 GB - 2TB
Storage type	Volatile (RAM) Non-volatile, read-only (ROM)	Non-volatile
Cost	Expensive	Cheaper

Figure 2-30 Primary versus Secondary storage

Magnetic Disks

Magnetic **hard disks** are by far the most common type of secondary storage found in computers today. They consist of a series of disk platters spinning at up to 10,000 rpm inside a solid case. A read/write head moves backwards and forwards over the disk and magnetically charges areas of it to store data.

The high capacity, high speed, and relatively low price of hard disks makes them ideal for most personal computers. Their main disadvantage is that they are relatively fragile: a knock or a bump while the computer is switched on can easily be enough to make the read/write head hit the disk surface, damaging or destroying it. For this reason, some portable devices like MP3 players, some netbooks, and the One Laptop Per Child laptop use solid state storage instead of magnetic hard disks. Hard disks are also susceptible to damage from magnets.

External hard disks are portable disks often used for backups or transferring large files. Inside the case, external hard disks are the same as internal hard disks. The case simply allows the disk to connect via a USB, FireWire, or eSATA connector, and may also provide a connection for an external power supply.

Optical Storage

Optical disks like **CDs**, **DVDs**, and **Blu-ray** disks read and store data using lasers. Small 'lands' and 'pits' in the disk surface reflect laser light in different ways: the difference between these is interpreted as either a binary 1 or a 0 by the computer. Early versions of these technologies – CD-ROM, DVD-ROM, BD-ROM allowed only reading of data from pre-recorded disks. Over time, recordable versions (CD-R, DVD-R, BD-R) were developed that allowed a user with the appropriate recorder to save or 'burn' data to disks once. Later on, rewritable versions of the disks became available, allowing data to be saved and erased many times (CD-RW, DVD-RW, BD-RW).

Compact Disks store between 650 MB and 700 MB of data; DVDs allow 4.7 GB, while dual-layer (DL) DVDs allow up to 8.5 GB. The latest Blu-ray disks can store between 25 GB and 50 GB.

Optical disks are sometimes used for creating backups of files on personal computers, although the increasing capacity of hard disks is making them less useful for this. However, CDs and DVDs are still the most popular medium for the distribution of software in stores, and Blu-ray disks are the standard format for storing High Definition (HD) films.

Figure 2-31 Hard disks: two external models (left and right), and an internal hard disk with the case removed (centre)

Optical disks are relatively delicate: even small scratches on the disk surface can cause problems for the laser which reads them. Also, the cost of the writeable disks themselves can be quite high, especially in the case of newly released technologies such as Blu-ray.

Flash memory

Flash memory is a technology that stores data using electronic logic dates. Flash storage devices have no moving parts, giving them three main benefits over hard disks:

1. They are less susceptible to damage from drops and knocks when in use, making them ideal for portable computers, especially those intended for harsh environments (e.g. for use by young children).
2. They use significantly less power than hard disks (because there is no moving disk to power), which is useful for extending battery life on portable computers. This is especially important when a charger cannot be used (such as on many trains or on aircraft) or for devices that need to stay on for long periods of time (such as music players or mobile phones)
3. They offer much faster access than hard disks, which is useful for 'instant-on' devices which need to quickly load an operating system and user interface.

The main downside is that flash memory devices are still expensive, and only available in relatively low capacities. Currently flash memory is used heavily in memory cards for digital cameras and also in some netbook computers in place of a hard disk. USB based flash memory sticks are also commonly used as portable storage devices. Memory cards like **CompactFlash cards**, **SD cards** or **MMC cards** are generally available in sizes up to about 32 GB. USB **flash drives**, and flash based storage to replace hard disks are found in slightly bigger sizes, up to about 128 GB.

Camera memory cards need to be inserted into a card reader to be used on a computer. Laptop computers often have built in readers which are capable of reading multiple card formats.

Figure 2-33 Various solid state memory: CompactFlash (top), SD (middle), and a USB flash drive (bottom).

Common Mistake

It is common for people to use the term 'USB' to refer to flash drives. However, USB strictly refers to the connection on the computer – a USB port can be used to connect flash drives, printers, mice, keyboards, digital cameras, and many other peripherals. Therefore it is better to refer to **flash drives**, **USB memory sticks**, or **USB drives**.

Storage Type	Speed	Capacity	Price
Magnetic disks	Fast	Up to 2 TB	Cheap
Magnetic tapes	Slow (serial access)	Up to 5 TB	Very cheap
Optical disks	Medium	Up to 50 GB	Cheap
Flash memory	Very fast	Up to 500 GB	Very expensive

Figure 2-32 Comparing secondary storage devices

Hard disk security and privacy

As more and more details about our lives are stored on computers, the security of our data becomes increasingly important, especially when computers are lost or stolen, or old hardware is thrown away. In 2003, two MIT students conducted a study on 158 second-hand hard disks purchased from the online auction site eBay. The students used freely available software to attempt to recover previously stored data from the disks[11]. They found that:

- 117 drives (74%) contained data that they could recover and read
- 12 drives (9%) had been correctly erased
- 29 drives failed to work

Among the data recovered, the students found pornography, credit card numbers, financial data, and medical records – all extremely sensitive information. Some of the data could easily be used by criminals to commit fraud or identity theft. Other material might leave the previous owners open to blackmail. Material remaining on a hard disk from a previous owner could also cause problems for the hard disks' new owner if the material were illegal. This case highlights the need for education and training about the risks of discarding old equipment and the necessity of ensuring data is correctly and securely erased.

Where does data go when it is deleted?

Typically, the answer to this question is 'nowhere'. The MIT students above were able to recover data from hard disks because deleting a file on a computer does not normally remove the file's actual data. Instead, deleting the file removes the pointer to the data from the hard disk's File Allocation Table (FAT), which acts like an index to each file on the disk. Thus the computer's operating system cannot 'see' the file by reading the FAT, but the data itself remains on the disk until it is overwritten by new files – which may take months. Consider the analogy of an index in a book: if the index is removed it is much harder to find the material you want, but the information is still there – you just have to search page by page until you find it. This is effectively what disk recovery software does, searching the disk sector by sector to find previously deleted data.

Deleting a file, emptying the recycle bin or trash can, and even formatting a disk do not remove any files from the disk—the File Allocation Table is merely altered to give the impression that there are no files present.

Solutions

There are only two ways to ensure data is fully removed from your hard disk: by either physically destroying the hard disk, or by using special disk wiping software. Good methods for destroying hard disks include shattering the disk platters into pieces, drilling holes into the disk, or using a disk shredding machine. A strong magnet can also be used to wipe the data, although it is difficult to see whether this has worked or not.

If the intention is to reuse the disk, a less exciting solution is to use specialist **disk wiping** or **secure deletion** software (sometimes called **shredding software**). This overwrites all data on the hard disk with random data, making the old data inaccessible. Usually it repeats this process several times. Disk wiping software takes a long time to finish the job – especially on larger capacity hard disks—because it must overwrite every single sector on the disk. However, disk overwriting gives a good guarantee of privacy. Secure wiping software can be purchased and there are also free programs to perform the task.

Storing Data: Bits and Bytes

Whether you are viewing a web page, watching a video, running a game, editing an image, or reading an e-book, your computer is representing all of its data internally as binary digits—ones and zeroes. These ones and zeroes are known as **bits**. On their own, bits are not very useful because they only represent one of two states: on or off, yes or no, one or zero.

Eight bits are grouped together into more meaningful units called **bytes**. Bytes themselves are grouped into increasingly larger units called **kilobytes**, **megabytes**, **gigabytes**, and **terabytes**. Figure 2-34 shows common units used to describe computer storage capacity.

One byte can store a value between 0 and 255 (2^8 values). These values are interpreted by the computer in different ways: a byte might represent a letter in a document, or it might represent the colour of a pixel on the screen. Regardless of what you do with computers, underlying everything are bits and bytes. Computers communicate data by using predefined **standards** that govern the meaning of each bit and byte. Two common standards for storing text are ASCII and Unicode.

ASCII

ASCII (American Standard Code for Information Interchange) is a standard coding scheme for representing text using the English alphabet. Using ASCII, each byte of data represents a single character. When the computer comes across a given byte in a text file which uses ASCII encoding, it displays the corresponding character on the screen. Similarly, when a character is typed using a text editor, the ASCII code for that character is recorded as a binary number. Table 2-35 shows a subset of the ASCII coding scheme.

Because ASCII uses one byte per character, the maximum number of characters ASCII can represent is 128 (2^7). (There are 8 bits in a byte, but the eighth bit is used for error-checking). 128 characters might sound like a lot, but remember that different ASCII codes are needed for uppercase and lowercase letters, symbols, and numbers. As such, ASCII fails to include characters from many languages which include accents or completely different characters (such as Cantonese or Arabic).

Some companies developed 8-bit versions of ASCII, allowing 256 characters – but the companies didn't agree on which characters each code represented, causing compatibility problems when displaying documents on different computers. Today ASCII is being superseded by Unicode.

Unit	Size	Example
Bit	One binary digit (0 or 1)	
Byte (B)	8 bits	A single character of text consumes between 1 byte and 4 bytes of space (see ASCII and Unicode)
Kilobyte (KB)	1024 bytes	
Megabyte (MB)	1024 KB	
Gigabyte (GB)	1024 MB	In 2011 most home and laptop computers have between 2 GB and 8 GB of RAM
Terabyte (TB)	1024 GB	In 2011 the largest common hard disks are between 1 TB – 2 TB
Petabyte (PB)	1024 TB	
Exabyte (EB)	1024 PB	
Zettabyte (ZB)	1024 EB	
Yottabyte (YB)	1024 ZB	

Figure 2-34 Computer storage units

ASCII Code	Character		ASCII Code	Character
32	Space bar		65	A
33	!		66	B
34	"		67	C
35	#		68	D
36	$		69	E
37	%		70	F
38	&			
39	'		97	a
40	(		98	b
41	)		99	c
42	*		100	d
43	+		101	e
44	,		102	f
45	-		103	g

Figure 2-35 A sample of ASCII codes and their corresponding characters

Unicode

Unicode is a more modern coding scheme which aims to solve some of the problems of ASCII. Unicode uses up to 4 bytes to represent each character, allowing many thousands of characters to be represented (there are 32 bits in 4 bytes, so 2^{31} characters can be represented). These characters include non-English alphabets, and right-to-left (RTL) languages like Hebrew and Arabic. (In Ancient Greece, boustrophedon writing was often used, in which the characters in alternating lines of text were flipped and read in opposite directions. Although there weren't many computers in the 8th century BC, if there had been, the Greeks would have been pleased to know that Unicode has support for such bi-directional writing).

Modern operating systems such as Windows Vista, Windows 7, Mac OS X, and Linux distributions use Unicode as their character representation standard.

Plain Text

ASCII and Unicode are both examples of **plain text** standards. They specify the characters that make up a text but they do not include ways to specify other formatting attributes such as the font type, the font size, features like bold or underline, or coloured text. Plain text files are usually saved by programs known as text editors. Although many word processors have options to export documents as plain text, doing so will cause any formatting options to be lost.

To use more advanced formatting features, a word processor must be used. Word processors still use the ASCII or Unicode standards to represent text, but save documents in their own file formats which allow the inclusion of text formatting data plus more advanced features like image placement, columns, and tables. Some formats, like Rich Text Format (RTF) and OpenDocument (.odt), have openly published specifications, allowing them to be relatively compatible across different word processors. Other formats such as Microsoft Word's .doc format are proprietary. Page 137 details the most common file formats used for exchanging text data.

Graphics Standards

Computer graphics are represented as bits and bytes just like all other computer data. Different file formats such as BMP, JPEG, and PNG store the image data in different ways, but in general all true colour images use a similar scheme. Typically each pixel in an image uses three bytes of storage space—one byte to represent the amount of red in that pixel, one byte for the amount of green, and one byte for the amount of blue. Page 122 gives more details of exactly how computers store image and video data using schemes like this.

Failover systems

A **failover system** or **standby system** is one designed to keep a system running if the primary system fails—perhaps due to hardware or power failure. Failover systems are usually **redundant systems**—they provide the same functionality as the primary system, but do nothing unless the primary system fails, at which point they can be switched to automatically.

In situations where high reliability is needed, distributed redundant servers or redundant networks may be used to provide a failover system in case the primary server or network fails. Housing these at different geographical locations provides greater protection again serious disasters such as a fire, flood, or earthquake at the original location.

Figure 2-36 An array of hard disks in a server, arranged to provide data redundancy.

A **RAID (Redundant Array of Independent Disks)** array is a failover system for hard disks. RAID uses multiple hard disks connected together to create a fault-tolerant system. A common approach is called mirroring – one hard disk contains a complete, exact copy of another hard disk in the RAID array. Every time data is written to one disk, it is also copied (mirrored) to the other. Thus, if one of the hard disks fails, the computer can switch over to the other disk and continue operation with interruption (although possibly with some performance loss). In a hot-swap system, the failed hard disk can even be removed and replaced without switching off the computer. This is very useful in server environments where users expect a continuous service and downtime needs to be avoided.

Although RAID is very useful if a hard disk fails, it is not a replacement for data backups. Because all data is mirrored to both disks, if data is corrupted by a computer virus, all copies of the data will be damaged identically. Similarly, a flood or fire is likely to damage both disks since they are in the same physical location.

An **Uninterruptible Power Supply** (UPS) provides a redundant power source in case of a mains electricity failure. On detecting a power failure a battery in the UPS will provide enough power for a short period of time, which should be sufficient for the mains power to be restored or for an alternative power source such as a generator to be switched on. It also provides time to save any data and shut down the attached computer correctly. Many UPS systems also include hardware to condition the power line—ensuring that the voltage remains stable, avoiding dips or spikes, and removing noise and interference.

Uninterruptible Power Supplies designed for desktop computers are relatively small and inexpensive, and typically provide power for around 30 minutes. For larger scale uses, such as server rooms or data centres, large cabinets or rooms of batteries might be needed in order to provide sufficient power.

Figure 2-37 Desktop UPS system

Ports & Connectors

Various ports and connectors are used to connect input, output, storage, and networking devices. Using standard ports allows hardware devices to be compatible with many different systems, saving on costs for both users and manufacturers. Below are some of the most common ports and connectors used in modern computer systems.

	VGA	Used for connecting a standard monitor, either CRT or LCD, to a computer or games console. Projectors and interactive whiteboards also use VGA connections.
	DVI	Digital Video Interface (DVI) and the newer High Definition Multimedia Interface (HDMI) are used to connector digital displays to digital video sources. These connectors are especially designed to handle the requirements of High Definition (HD) signals.
	SATA and eSATA	A high speed standard for connecting hard disks, DVD and Blu-ray players. eSATA is a version of SATA used for connecting external devices (e.g. backup drives).
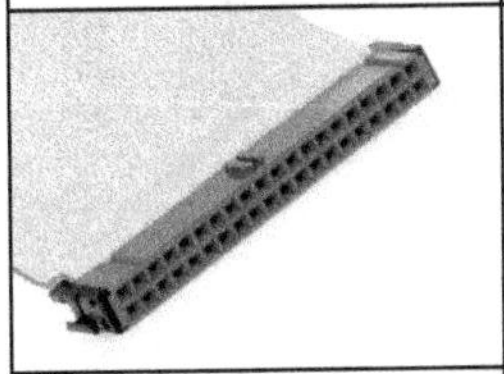	IDE	An older standard for connecting hard disks. Although slower, IDE is still widely used for devices like CD and DVD drives.
	USB	Universal Serial Bus: A modern standard used for connecting a wide variety of peripherals including mice, keyboards, external hard disks, digital cameras, printers, scanners, and flash drives. There are several versions of the standard – the most recent being USB 3.0.
	FireWire (IEEE 1394)	A high-speed interface used for different peripherals including digital video cameras and external hard disks. FireWire is less common than USB connections, but offers a much higher transfer rate
	Ethernet	A standard for wired Internet access, available on virtually all computers.
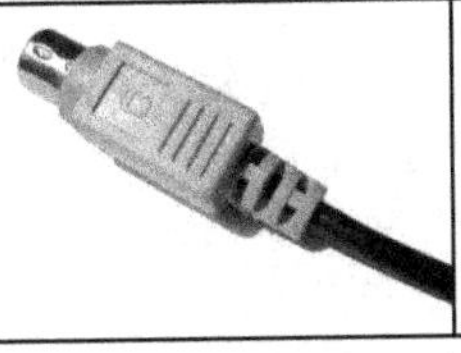	PS2	An older standard for connecting mice and keyboards. Generally superseded by USB.

Figure 2-38 Common ports and connectors

Chapter Review

Key Language

Types of computer

desktop computer	laptop	netbook	smartphones
embedded systems	mainframe	personal digital assistant	supercomputers
home theatre PC			

Input

barcode scanners	keyboard	scanner	Universal Product Code
concept keyboard	MICR	sensors	voice control
digital cameras	magnetic stripe readers	smart card readers	voice recognition
digital video cameras	microphones	soft keyboard	webcam
digitise	multi-touch	stylus	
Dvorak keyboards	multimedia keyboard	touch pad	
game controllers	OCR	touch screen	
joystick	optical mark recognition	trackball	

Output

CRT monitor	interactive whiteboard	native resolution	printers
hard copy	laser printer	output	projectors
inkjet printer	LCD screen	pages per minute	speakers

Storage

bit	FireWire	mouse	secure deletion
Blu-ray	flash memory	non-volatile storage	solid state storage
byte	gigabyte (GB)	optical storage	terabyte (TB)
CD-ROM	hard disk	petabyte (PB)	USB
CompactFlash	IDE	primary storage	volatile storage
data synchronisation	input	RAID	yottabyte (YB)
DVD	kilobyte (KB)	Random Access Memory	zettabyte (ZB)
eSATA	magnetic storage	Read Only Memory	
exabyte (EB)	megabyte (MB)	SATA	
external hard disk	MMC	secondary storage	

Processing Technologies

clock speed	hardware	motherboard	processor
CPU	megahertz (MHz)	multi-core	software
dual-core	microprocessor	multiprocessing	speed throttling
gigahertz (GHz)	MIPS	multitasking	terahertz (THz)

General terms

ASCII	Kensington lock	radio tag	Unicode
convergence	plain text	RFID reader	UPS
failover system	radio frequency identifica-	RFID tag	uptime
Global Positioning System	tion (RFID)	Rich Text Format (RTF)	VoIP

Computer Accessibility

braille keyboard	head control systems	input switches	sticky keys
braille printer	head wand	screen magnification	text-to-speech
eye tracking software	high contrast mode	sip and puff	

Exercise 2-6

Consider the following examples of information technology. **Identify** all of the input, output, and storage technologies used by each:

a) An ATM (Automatic Teller Machine)
b) An airport self check-in machine
c) A mobile phone (cell phone)
d) An in-car GPS navigation system
e) An aircraft cockpit
f) A cleaning robot

Exercise 2-7

Find and **describe** a suitable computer for the user in each situation below, using adverts from the Internet, magazines, or newspapers. The computer must have appropriate hardware specifications for the situation. In some cases additional input and output devices may be needed too. Try to find a solution that offers good value for money. [12 marks]

a) **Scenario:** A family wanting a computer for general use (browsing, typing up homework, playing simple games)
b) **Scenario:** An amateur film maker who wants to record her own films (she already has a digital camera for this) and then edit them on her computer.
c) **Scenario:** A businesswoman who wants a computer to use during her daily train commute. The typical journey lasts 2- 2.5 hours so she has plenty of time to work on company reports and spreadsheets. She also needs the ability to catch up with her email, and access files stored on her company's network.

Exercise 2-8

Research the One Laptop Per Child (OLPC) computer (this computer is also variously known as the $100 laptop and the XO PC). Try to find detailed specifications of the computer. The designers have made some interesting choices compared to the average laptop computer. **Justify** the individual specifications of the OLPC with reference to its target market (hint: there are many reasons other than pure cost). [8 marks]

Exercise 2-9

(a) State the units typically used to measure: [2 marks]
    (i) Processor speed
    (ii) Hard disk capacity

(b) State **two** ways of connecting an external hard disk to a computer.   [2 marks]

(c) Distinguish the terms *primary storage* and *secondary storage*.   [4 marks]

(d) A digital camera produces files that are 1,500 KB each. Calculate how many photographs can be   [2 marks]
stored on a standard CD-R.

Exercise 2-10

(a) Define the term *embedded computer*.   [2 marks]

(b) Identify **two** input mechanisms often used by disabled computer users.   [2 marks]

(c) Distinguish the terms *supercomputer* and *mainframe*.   [2 marks]

(d) Identify common applications for the following input and output devices: [4 marks]
    i.   Touch screen
    ii.   OMR
    iii. Barcode readers
    iv. Track ball

References

1 TOP 500 Project. (2010). *TOP 500 Supercomputer Sites.* Available: www.top500.org/. Accessed April 2011.

2 BBC. (2008). *Police probe theft of MoD laptop* . Available: http://news.bbc.co.uk/2/hi/7197045.stm. Last accessed Nov 2011.

3 Earth Solutions. (2010). *GO Green.* Available: www.earthtonesolutions.com/. Accessed April 2011.

4 NASA. (2007). *High End Computing Capability.* Available: http://www.nas.nasa.gov/hecc/resources/columbia.html. Last accessed Nov 2011.

5 Robinson, J. (2008). PA Consulting data loss sacking 'is a lesson to all suppliers'. Available: http://www.information-age.com/home/information-age-today/643396/pa-consulting-data-loss-sacking-is-a-lesson-to-all-suppliers.thtml. Last accessed Nov 2011.

6 BBC. (2008). Personnel records stolen from MoDBB. Available: http://news.bbc.co.uk/2/hi/uk_news/england/gloucestershire/7639006.stm. Last accessed Nov 2011.

7 BBC. (2008). Up to 1.7m people's data missing. Available: http://news.bbc.co.uk/2/hi/uk_news/politics/7667507.stm. Last accessed Nov 2011.

8 BBC. (2009). *Previous cases of missing data.* Available: news.bbc.co.uk/2/hi/uk_news/7449927.stm. Accessed April 2011.

9 BBC. (2007). Discs 'worth £1.5bn' to criminals . Available: http://news.bbc.co.uk/2/hi/uk_news/politics/7117291.stm. Last accessed Nov 2011.

10 Harrison, C. (2010). *Skinput: Appropriating the Body as an Input Surface.* Available: http://www.chrisharrison.net/index.php/Research/Skinput. Last accessed Nov 2011.

11 Roberts, P. (2003). *MIT: Discarded hard drives yield private info.* Available: http://www.computerworld.com/s/article/77623/MIT_Discarded_hard_drives_yield_private_info. Last accessed Nov 2011.

Chapter 3
Software

Objectives

1. Distinguish operating system software and application software
2. Justify the choice of a suitable operating system
3. Describe the categories of application software
4. Describe the types of user interface
5. Describe the types of software licence
6. Explain how software features can help disabled users
7. Explain the possible impacts of software failure

Software

Computer software or programs are the sets of instructions which hardware follows in order to perform tasks. Software processes input data and transforms it into useful output. From the most powerful supercomputers to the simplest mobile phones, all information technology requires software to operate. Software is often said to run 'on top' of hardware, providing the interface between it and the user.

Operating Systems

Operating System (OS) software, also called **system software**, is responsible for managing and controlling all of the computer's hardware. When you first switch on a computer, the operating system software is loaded into the computer's memory (RAM) and started before you can perform any other tasks. The operating system runs the entire time you are using the computer and provides the **user interface** to let you manage programs and data. On its own, the operating system software does not enable you to produce work (for example, documents, photographs, or emails): instead, it provides a **platform** on which application software can run. The operating system's tasks include:

Task and memory management – Many users run multiple pieces of software at once, for example a word processor, a web browser, and a music player. Even if it is not obvious, most computers are running many programs in the background, such as anti-virus software or networking software. It is the job of the operating system to manage these programs, assign them the resources they need, and protect or isolate programs from each other so that one program cannot corrupt another program's data. If one program crashes, the operating system should be able to shut down or kill the process without affecting other programs. Similarly, if programs need to use devices like the hard disk or the printer, it is the job of the operating system to assign these resources to programs in a controlled manner.

Security management – the operating system provides security for multiple users by requiring each user to authenticate themselves with a username and password. The OS also manages users' home directories, keeping their contents safe from other users. Shared folders, files, and peripheral devices are handled in a similar way, with the operating system maintaining a list of permissions that control users' access (see file permissions, page 92).

If the computer is attached to a network, the operating system might include **firewall software** to restrict incoming and outgoing traffic and prevented unauthorised access (see page 73).

Providing a user interface – the operating system provides an interface to allow the user to interact with and operate the computer. Typically this will be either a **Command Line Interface** (CLI), where the user types a series of commands using the keyboard, or a **Graphical User Interface** (GUI), operated with a mouse or similar pointing device. The interface allows the user to start and stop programs, switch between programs, and create, copy, and delete files (see page 60).

Platforms

The term 'platform' is often used to describe a particular combination of hardware and operating system. 'Windows running on x86 ('PC') hardware' and 'Linux on running x86 hardware' are two examples of platforms. 'MacOS X on Apple hardware' is another example.

Some operating systems run on multiple types of hardware—for example, Linux distributions are available that run on many different hardware configurations from mobile phones to supercomputers and everything in between. This allows, in theory, application **software compatibility** across different hardware platforms.

Similarly, some applications software is **cross-platform** or **multi-platform**, meaning that it works on several different platforms. For example, Microsoft Office is available for both Windows and Mac OS X, while LibreOffice has versions for Windows, MacOS, and Linux. Using the same application software on different operating systems helps maintain **file compatibility** between the systems.

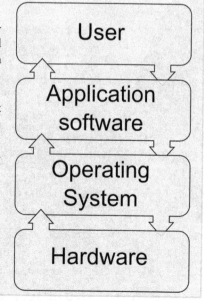

Communicating with hardware – the operating system controls all hardware devices such as disk drives, printers, and screens that are attached to the computer. It does this transparently to the user. For example, when a file is saved in a word processing program, the user enters the file's name. The user does not need to know (or care) in which physical platter or in which sector of the hard disk the file will be saved. It is the job of the operating system to control the disk, telling the hard disk which data to save, and in which sector to save it.

Operating systems use software called **device drivers** to understand how to communicate with the various hardware devices attached to the computer. This means a piece of hardware can work even if it was released long after the operating system was shipped: the device manufacturer simply writes a device driver to tell the operating system how to communicate with the hardware. This is why many devices require an installation CD when first used – the CD contains the device drivers that must be installed before the device will work.

Common Operating Systems

Microsoft Windows—the most common operating system for personal desktop and laptop systems. The latest version, Windows 7, offers an improved user interface, a redesigned task bar, performance improvements, improved security features, and the latest version of Microsoft's web browser, Internet Explorer.

MacOS 10—Apple's OS for its Mac computers is based on Unix, a system designed around security. Apple have added a user-friendly graphical interface on top of this. MacOS only runs on Apple hardware.

Unix—originally developed in the 1970s, Unix and Unix-like operating systems are known for security, stability, and scalability – the ability to take advantage of many types of hardware configurations, such as multiple processors. These traits make Unix a popular choice on high end hardware like supercomputers and mainframes. Embedded devices (see page 18) which must run for long periods of time without restarting often use Unix based systems. For example, the popular TiVo Digital Video Recorder uses a modified Linux OS.

Linux—a 'Unix-like' OS which is free software (see page 55). There are many different versions of Linux, called distributions, aimed at different markets. Two common distributions targeted at desktop users are Fedora and Ubuntu. Both provide a modern graphical user interface and feature a wide range of free software.

SymbianOS—a popular OS for mobile phones, managed by Nokia. Some sources suggest that Symbian has up to a 36% share of the mobile phone market.

Android—based on Linux and developed by Google, this is one of the newest phone operating systems. Android runs on handsets from a variety of manufacturers (Google do not manufacture phones) and has quickly gained market share.

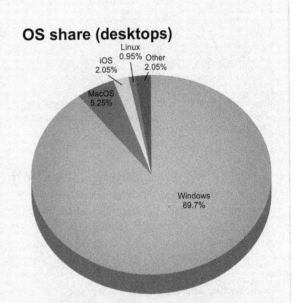

OS share (desktops)

Linux 0.95%
iOS 2.05%
Other 2.05%
MacOS 5.25%
Windows 89.7%

Figure 3-1 Source: NetMarketShare

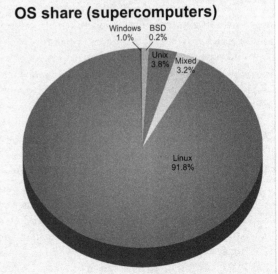

OS share (supercomputers)

Windows 1.0%
BSD 0.2%
Unix 3.8%
Mixed 3.2%
Linux 91.8%

Figure 3-2 Source: Top500 Project

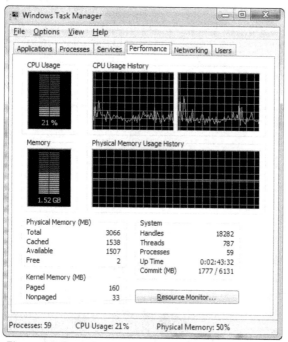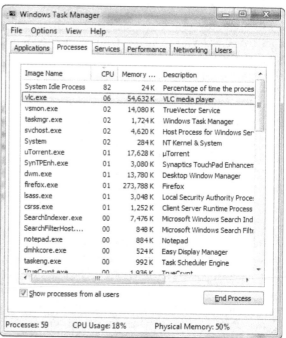

Figure 3-3 Operating systems control the many background tasks running on a computer, allocate resources to them, and monitor computer performance.

Selecting and Installing an Operating System

Most computers come with an operating system pre-installed by the manufacturer. This can be replaced with an alternative operating system, or upgraded to a new version of the existing operating system if one has been released. It is also possible to install more than one operating system at once and choose which to use when the computer starts up — this is known as dual booting. A dual-boot system presents a list of available operating systems to the user when it is switched on. To switch between the operating systems, the computer must be rebooted.

When selecting and installing an operating system, there are several steps to follow:

1. Check hardware compatibility – ensure the operating system has device drivers for the hardware you want to use. These may be part of the operating system or may be available on the hardware manufacturer's web page.
2. Check software compatibility – ensure that any application software you need to run will work on the new OS (including the specific version you are installing).
3. Check hardware requirements – operating systems have minimum requirements in terms of hard disk space, RAM, and processor speed.
4. Obtain the operating system media and any licences required.
5. Back up any existing data you wish to keep and test the backup to ensure it works (see page 49).
6. Partition and format the hard disk – operating systems should be installed in their own partitions – separate areas of the hard disk that appear as though they are separate disks.
7. Run the installation program and configure the operating system – including the language, keyboard layout, time zone, and bundled software you wish to install. You will also need to create at least one user account at this time.
8. Activate or register the operating system – some operating systems, such as Microsoft Windows, require online or telephone activation before they can be fully used. Other operating systems offer you the chance to register the software, perhaps in order to receive free updates or information.
9. Update the operating system – many operating systems have regular updates to boost performance and security. These can usually be downloaded with an included utility program. It is good security practice to keep the operating system up to date (see page 95).
10. Install any required application software.
11. Restore any data from backup copies.

Utility software

Utility software is the basic software included with operating systems to performing common 'housekeeping' tasks, helping to maintain and manage the computer. Examples of tasks performed by utility software include:

Disk defragmentation Optimises hard disk performance by arranging files into contiguous sectors (see page 48)

Backup programs Used to compress and back up important files (see page 49)

Encryption Secure files, folders, and disks in the event of theft or loss of the computer (see page 106)

System monitoring Monitors system resources such as processor and memory usage and optimises them to improve performance (see figure 3-3)

Disk clean up Detects and deletes unneeded files, such as temporary files created by some applications, that have built up over time. This helps reclaim valuable disk space.

Accessibility options Sets options for disabled users, such as increased font size or screen contrast (see page 29).

Anti-virus software Used to detect and remove malicious software such as viruses, Trojan horses, and spyware (see page 96).

System updates Updates the operating system with the latest security and performance 'patches' released by the software's creators (see page 95).

Compression software Used to compress files to save disk space or network bandwidth, and decompress them again (see page 124).

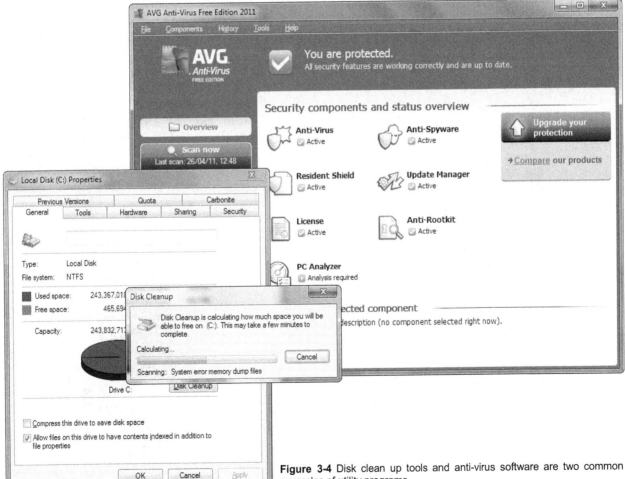

Figure 3-4 Disk clean up tools and anti-virus software are two common examples of utility programs.

Disk Fragmentation

Storage media like hard disks are divided into logical areas called **sectors**. When files are stored, one or more sectors are used to store their data. Each sector can only contain the data for one file. In some operating systems, files are always stored in the first available free sector. If a file needs more than one sector (which most do), the next available free sectors are found, even if they do not occur in a continuous block. This causes **disk fragmentation**: a file is stored in several sectors which are scattered across different parts of the disk. This can reduce disk performance because it is slower to read or write sectors from many separate places than from continuous sectors.

Fragmentation in action

Step 1

In the first diagram below, five files have been saved to the disk (ITGS.doc, English.rtf, TOK.ppt, Science.doc, and Geography.doc). Each file is saved in a separate sector. Two of the files consume more than one sector (ITGS.doc and TOK.ppt). In both cases, the two sectors that make up these files are in a contiguous block (i.e. they are next to each other). This is the ideal situation because they can be read very quickly. The final sector of the disk is free.

Step 2

In the second diagram, two files (English.rtf and Science.doc) have been deleted, leaving the third and sixth sectors free.

Step 3

In the third diagram, a new file (Art.tif) has been saved. Following the rules of the file system, the new file's data goes straight into the first available free space – straight after ITGS.doc. But this new file needs three sectors, and the gap is only one sector, so two more free sectors need to be found elsewhere on the disk. The next free sector is after TOK.ppt, but that is only one sector, so even more space is required. Another free sector is at the end of the disk, and this is where the final sector of Art.tif is stored. The problem now is that Art.tif is split into three **fragments**, in non-contiguous blocks. This makes reading Art.tif from disk slower, because the disk read head must move to multiple locations to access the file.

With a large number of files, disk fragmentation can cause serious performance problems. The diagram below is only an illustration: in reality, disk sectors are usually 4 KB, so there will be thousands of sectors on a high capacity disk. Likewise, most files will use many more sectors than illustrated here. On a frequently used hard disk, where data is often saved, deleted, and amended, files can be divided into dozens or even hundreds of fragments, drastically reducing disk performance.

ITGS.doc	ITGS.doc	ITGS.doc
ITGS.doc	ITGS.doc	ITGS.doc
English.rtf	FREE	Art.tif
TOK.ppt	TOK.ppt	TOK.ppt
TOK.ppt	TOK.ppt	TOK.ppt
Science.doc	FREE	Art.tif
Geography.doc	Geography.doc	Geography.doc
FREE	FREE	Art.tif
Step 1	Step 2	Step 3

Defragmentation

Most operating systems include a defragmentation utility. These programs try to rearrange file allocations so files are stored in contiguous sectors, and all files within the same directory are also stored together. This speeds up both individual file access and directory access. Some defragmentation programs, such as the one bundled with Microsoft Windows, can give priority to files which are accessed frequently, such as those needed during the boot process.

Some file systems suffer less from fragmentation than others: the reiser4 and ext4 Linux file systems, and the MacOS X file system are all designed to reduce fragmentation problems.

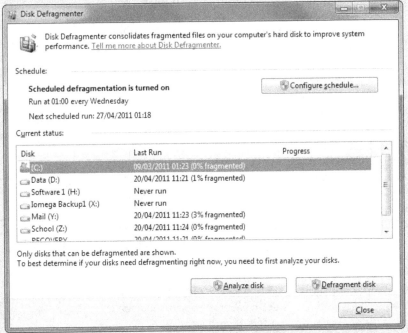

Figure 3-5 Disk defragmentation software optimises disk performance

Backups

Regularly creating and testing backup copies of data is an essential computing task. Businesses rely on their customer, product, and sales data to operate, while more and more of our personal photos, music, documents, and communications are stored only on computers. Data can be deleted or corrupted due to hardware failure, software errors, user error, or malicious software. Portable devices containing important data – especially small devices like USB flash drives – can easily be misplaced or stolen. Natural disasters like fires or floods can also destroy data.

Data can be backed up to a variety of devices including internal or external hard disks, writeable optical disks such as CD-Rs or DVD-RWs, or specialist backup devices such as tape drives. There are also an increasing number of online backup options available, where data is stored on a remote Internet server.

A **full backup** is, as its name suggests, a complete backup of all data on a computer system. An **incremental backup** is used to backup only the files that have changed since the last backup (either full or incremental). An incremental backup is quicker than a full backup because relatively few files will have changed and need copying.

A backup of important data is no use if it is left next to the computer and the building suffers from a flood, fire, or theft. For this reason, backup copies should be kept off-site in a secure location away from the main copy of the data. Businesses will often invest in fire-proof safes in which to store their backups. Remote 'cloud' based Internet backup options are also helpful here.

Security of backups is also important. If data is valuable enough to be backed up, it could also be valuable to a potential thief. Although a computer system may have usernames and passwords to prevent unauthorised access, many people forget to apply the same security rules to backup copies of data. Backup copies should always be stored in an encrypted form and in a physically secure location to prevent unauthorised access.

Many companies don't try to **restore** the data from their backup copies until they have suffered some form of data loss. In these situations, over 70% find that their backup copies contain errors and not all data is retrievable[1]. An important part of the backup procedure is to try to restore the files from the backup on a regular basis – perhaps to a spare hard drive. This will draw attention to any problems in the backup process so that they can be fixed before a real disaster strikes.

Application software

In contrast to operating system software, **application software** allows the user to perform tasks to solve problems, such as creating documents, managing finances, or editing images. For this reason it is sometimes called **productivity software**.

There are many types of application software, each specialising in a different task. **Word processing software** allows the creation of typed documents such as letters, memos, and business proposals. A word processor has features optimised for text creation, including formatting, spelling check, and language tools. Most word processors also include numbered lists, index creation, and referencing or footnote features. Another common tool is **mail merge**, which allows a single template document to be customised for individual people—for example, creating a thousand copies of a document each with a different name in the greeting line (see page 192).

Desktop Publishing (DTP) software (also called **page layout software**) allows the creation of documents such as leaflets, brochures, posters, newsletters, and maga-zines. DTP software is often confused with word processing software, but DTP software allows much greater control over the page layout than a word processor, and can prepare documents for output on professional commercial printers. These extra features may come at the expense of some text-creation tools. Many authors create their text in a word processor first and then import it into DTP software for layout. See page 136 for more details on using DTP software.

Presentation software focuses on the creation of slides for giving verbal presentations, as is frequently done by business workers, speakers at conferences, and teachers. Presentation software typically revolves around a series of text bullet-points and one or more images. Slides are formatted to the size of a computer screen rather than a printed page, and presentation software is almost always used in conjunction with some form of overhead projector. Page 138 describes good presentation techniques.

Spreadsheet software is used to perform tasks involving lots of calculations, such as managing finances or student grades. Spreadsheets divide a worksheet into a grid of cells labelled with letters and numbers. Individual cell

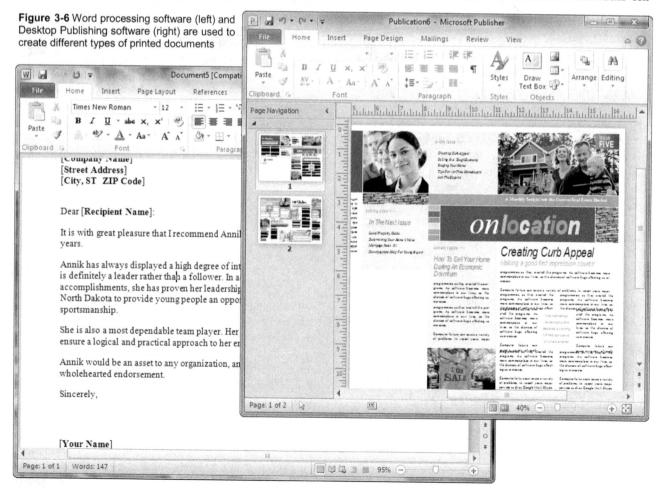

Figure 3-6 Word processing software (left) and Desktop Publishing software (right) are used to create different types of printed documents

references (for example 'A1') are used in formulae to calculate values in other cells. Spreadsheets support **automatic recalculation** so that if the value in one cell changes, any other cells referring to that cell will update to reflect the change. For example, if a student's grade in one assignment is changed, the cell containing the total score from all assignments will automatically change as well. See page 194 for more details.

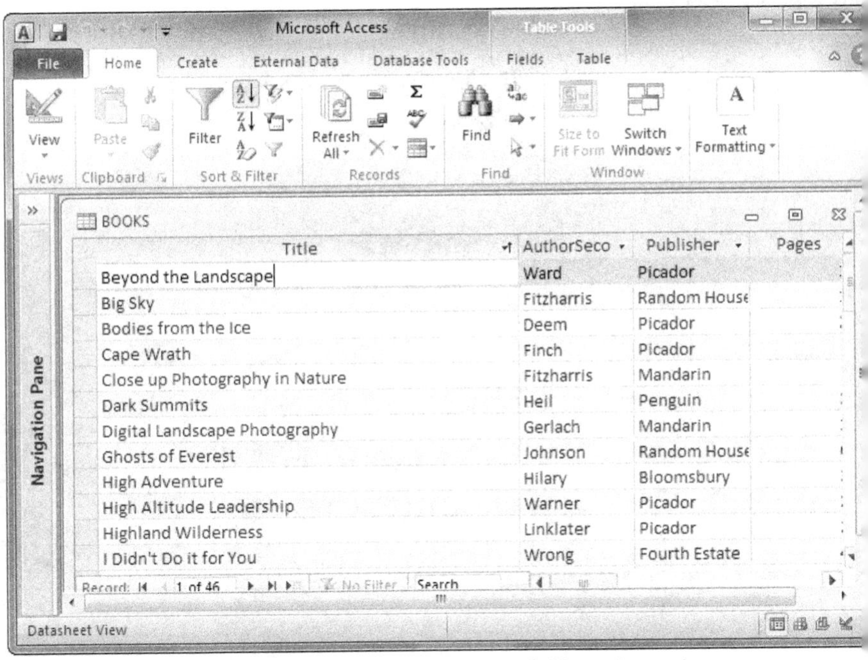

Database software is used to create, store, structure, and sort a collection of data about a set of items, search for certain data using queries, and produce printed reports. A database may be relatively simple (like a collection of DVDs) or more complex, like a shop's database of customers, suppliers, products, and sales. In extreme cases, web sites like Amazon and Facebook use extremely complex **Relational Database Management Systems** (RDBMS) to manage data about millions of items. See page 143 for more details about databases.

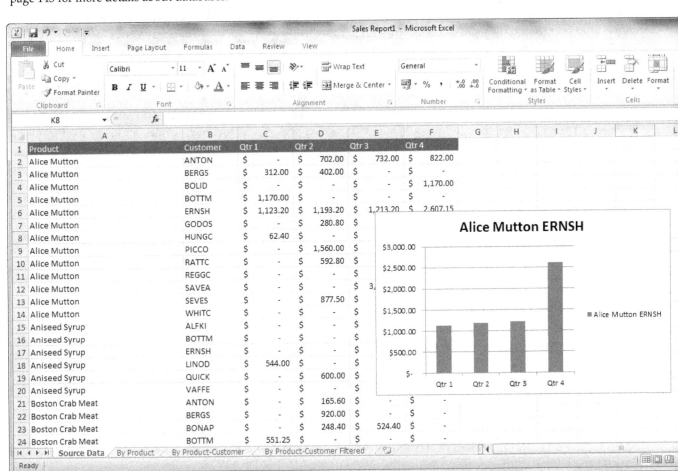

Figure 3-7 Database software structures data in tables, fields, and records

Figure 3-8 Spreadsheet software is used for calculations and data analysis

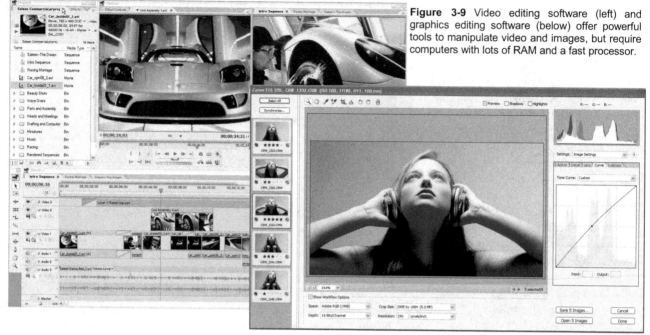

Figure 3-9 Video editing software (left) and graphics editing software (below) offer powerful tools to manipulate video and images, but require computers with lots of RAM and a fast processor.

Web browsers are an essential tool for many users, especially with the increased use of web based email, social networking, and the development of cloud computing. Modern web browsers have a variety of built in tools to protect users' security and privacy while online, and some include extensions to allow additional features to be added to the browser.

To design and create web sites, **web development software** is used. This typically includes a code editor which allows users to enter HTML, CSS, and JavaScript code. More advanced programs also include a graphical editor, allowing pages to be created without knowledge of HTML. Web development software also lets users check their web sites for compatibility with different web browsers and with web standards. Page 198 explains how web sites are developed.

Graphics software is used to create or edit digital images. Basic graphics software allows the creation of images by drawing individual pixels and shapes. More advanced software provides powerful effects to manipulate images, including adding blurs, changing brightness, contrast, and colour levels, cropping and rotating images, and adding special effects. Some graphics software even provides tools to mimic those used by an artist, such as pencil, watercolours, or charcoal. **Vector graphics** software focuses on the creation of images using mathematical shapes. **3D rendering** software allows the creation of 3D objects which can be given colour, texture, and lighting, and rendered to produce a final image. Expert users can create 3D images which are hard to distinguish from real photographs, and such images are often used in television and film special effects. **Computer Aided Design** (CAD) software focuses more on product design, using 3D graphics to represent components and allowing designers to create prototypes within the computer. Page 115 contains more information about the types of graphics software available.

Audio software is used to record, edit, and mix digital audio. Multiple tracks of sound can be recorded and com-

Creating this textbook

A range of software was used to create this textbook, each program specialising in one part of the process:

- A word processor was used to create and edit the text, and spell check it. At this stage, no formatting of the text was done.
- A vector graphics editor was used to create the diagrams and charts. The diagrams were saved as SVG files in case future editing was needed, and exported as PNG files.
- Graphics software was used to crop, resize, and alter the colour balance of the images. The DPI of the images was also changed and the images were exported as TIF files.
- A DTP package was used for page layout and formatting. From there the pages were output as a PDF file ready for professional printing.

bined, and various effects and fades can be applied, as well as basic changes such as altering the volume. Audio software is heavily used in the music, film, and television industries, as well as by users who want to record podcasts or enhance their home videos.

Video editing software allows images, sound, and video to be combined. Basic video packages allow cuts to be made and simple titles to be added. More advanced software can combine and overlay video and images from multiple sources, synchronise audio to video, and add special effects.

Multimedia software like Adobe Flash is used to create interactive graphical presentations, as might be found on some web sites, in simple games, or in some computer aided training packages.

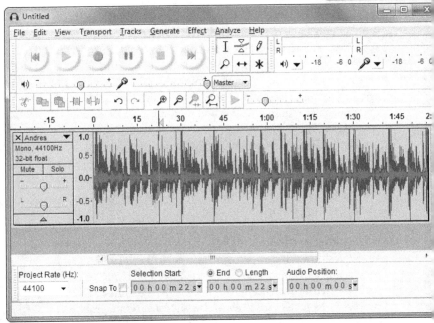

Figure 3-10 Audio editing software can record and edit digital audio (above) and perform a wide variety of enhancements, alterations, and effects (below).

Custom or Off-the-Shelf Software?

If off-the-shelf-software purchased from a store does not meet an organisation's requirements, they can hire a software development company to produce custom (also called bespoke) software tailored to their specific needs. This is useful if an organisation's needs are very specific and not catered for by mainstream software developers, but can also be more expensive. Another alternative is for an organisation to develop its own software—the feasibility of this option will depend on the IT expertise the organisation has. Page 310 covers custom software in more detail.

Accounting software helps manage finances, from small personal finances to large businesses with hundreds of employees, suppliers, and accounts being processed. Accounting software is more specialised than spreadsheet software and includes the necessary features to manage accounts payable, accounts received, payrolls, sales, and billing, while maintaining the information legally required for tax and auditing purposes. Double entry book keeping is required by many users, while large companies may need the ability to operate using multiple currencies or with multiple sets of rules and processes depending on the country of operation. Because many of these functions are so specialised, accounting software is often customisable to suit each individual user's needs.

Note taking software is designed for users who frequently attend lectures, classes, or conferences. It differs from word processing software because the text entered is free-form — it is not restricted by the structure of lines on a page, unlike a word processor. Note taking software also allows easy integration of diagrams, images, audio and video recordings into documents. Often touch input devices are used to enter handwriting into note taking software, which may or may not be converted into editable text using OCR techniques.

Often separate application programs which perform related tasks are sold together in **application suites**. For example, an office suite might contain a word processor, spreadsheet, presentation program, and other tools commonly used by businesses. A web design suite might include web development software applications and graphics design software. An advantage of application suites is that their price is often lower than buying each program separately and, because the programs are all from the same company, they are likely to integrate with each other much more effectively.

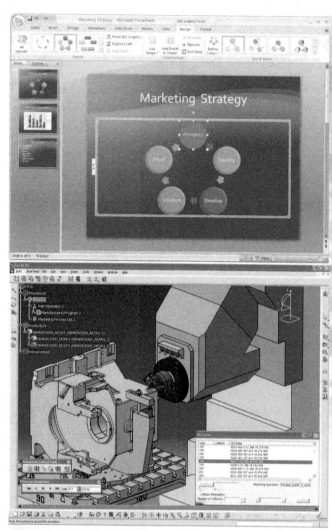

Figure 3-11 Presentation software (top) is widely used by teachers and conference speakers. CAD software (above) facilitates product design. Accounting software (below) keeps track of finances.

Common Mistake

Database software (figure 3-7) and spreadsheet software (3-8) are often confused. Databases are designed for the storage and retrieval of large amounts of organised data. Spreadsheets are designed to perform calculations on primarily numeric data. They are often used for accounting and similar tasks. Spreadsheets are not suitable for storing data such as lists of contacts or product information. See page 143 for more information about databases and page 194 for spreadsheets.

Software Licences

Computer software is a form of **intellectual property** and is therefore protected by **copyright laws**. Different types of software have different restrictions on how the software can be used, including the circumstances under which it can be sold or copied for other users, whether the **source code** is available, and whether you are allowed to modify the software.

Commercial software is software which is licensed or sold for profit by the companies that create it. When you buy commercial software you are in fact buying a licence to use the software. Commercial software has very strict licences preventing you from making copies of the software for other users, from having access to the source code, and from changing the software. Microsoft, Adobe, Apple, and IBM are very large companies that create a lot of commercial software.

Shareware is software which is distributed for no cost and is free to use for a limited period of time. After that period of time (usually 30 days), the user is expected to pay for the software if they continue to use it, or delete it. Some shareware may stop functioning after the time period expires, or the software's author may rely on the honesty of users to pay if they find the software useful.

Freeware can be distributed for no cost, but the software's copyright is still maintained by the author. This means that although you are allowed to copy the software you are typically not allowed to modify it or sell it. Freeware should not be confused with open source software, which grants more rights.

Public domain software is software for which the creator has relinquished all rights. This means that anyone can do anything with the software including selling it, changing it, and giving it away. Software typically becomes available as public domain if its copyright has expired or if the creator has specifically waived their rights under copyright law.

The central idea of **Free and Open Source Software** (also called open source, FOSS, or software libre) is that users have the freedom to use the software as they please. The source code of FOSS is always available for anyone who wants it. This makes it possible for users with program-

Figure 3-12 The office suite LibreOffice (a branch of OpenOffice) and the web browser Firefox are two very well known examples of FOSS.

Why use commercial software?

There are several reasons that companies and people still pay for commercial software, even though similar FOSS programs are available. Some of the advantages of commercial software include better **technical support,** which is usually available from the manufacturer, including telephone support, user manuals, and web site forums. Sometimes support for FOSS can be more difficult to find. Commercial software is often designed to be **integrated** with other products from the same software company (for example Microsoft's Internet, Office, and database products integrate very well). For a company this can help improve work flow and helps provide a consistent user interface. It also means that if a problem occurs, there is no need to contact multiple companies to establish where the fault lies.

Finally, because commercial software is much more common than FOSS in many industries, staff with relevant **experience and training** may be more readily available (and therefore cheaper) than those with the relevant FOSS skills. This is particularly true for desktop applications.

Licence	Price	Redistribution allowed	Re-selling allowed	Modifications allowed
Commercial	Not free	✗	✗	✗
Freeware	Free	✓	✗	✗
Shareware	Free initially	✓	✗	✗
Public domain	Free	✓	✗	✓
Free and Open Source	Free or sold	✓	✓	✓

Figure 3-13 Each type of software licence presents different freedoms and restrictions

ming experience to alter the software, adding features, fixing bugs, and customising the software to suit themselves. Users who make changes to open source software must publish their changes under the same licence: this is done to allow everyone to benefit from the improvements.

Unlike commercial software, users of open source software are encouraged to distribute the software freely to other users, and make changes they find desirable. Confusingly, it is even permitted to sell open source software, provided that you still follow the rules of making the source code available to users for free. Companies often create customised versions of FOSS and make money by selling boxed versions complete with user support and documentation, which would not be available in the free versions.

Perhaps the most famous examples of open source software are the Linux operating system, the LibreOffice office suite, the Firefox web browser, and the MySQL database programs, all of which are used by thousands of users worldwide.

Free and Open Source Software should not be confused with freeware. While freeware is free (no cost), Free and Open Source Software is 'free as in freedom' - it gives you the freedom to use it as you wish.

> **Common Mistake**
>
> A common mistake is to think that because the source code is available, anyone can maliciously edit FOSS and damage your computer. Of course, this is not correct— even if a malicious user does alter the source code, they still have to install the new, altered, software on your computer. If a malicious user has access to install software on your computer, it is irrelevant whether the software is open source or not—you have a large security problem regardless!

Open source versus Closed Source

Commercial software companies consider the source code of their software to be hugely valuable business assets. Programmers of free and open source software on the other hand openly encourage users to download, view, and change the source code. Why is there such a difference in viewpoints, and why is source code such a big concern?

Source Code

A program's source code is the instructions that make up the program. Computer programmers write source code in a programming language such as C, Java, or Basic, which are much more readable for human beings than the binary that computers understand. Source code has to be converted into binary (executable) code by a translator program before it can be run by the computer. This is a one-way process: source code can be translated into executable code, but executable programs cannot be converted back into the original source code. This is important because it means that if the programmer wants to make further changes to the program, the source code is needed.

Free as in Freedom

Programmers of free and open source software (FOSS) make their source code available to anyone because they want to encourage sharing and innovation. A common philosophy is that a person should be able to make changes to their software to suit their needs. Because FOSS also requires users to publish the source code for any changes they make, everyone can benefit when somebody improves the software. Thus if somebody creates, for example, an improved grammar checker for the popular LibreOffice software, they must make that code available so that everybody can benefit from the new features.

For the same reason, commercial software companies keep their source code tightly guarded—because they make a great deal of money not just by selling initial copies of the software, but also by selling upgrades and new versions. By being the only company to make these new versions available, they can harness the market.

Is Open Source more secure?

Security is a big topic in IT, and especially in open source software. Proponents of open source software often use the argument that because many people have examined the source code (because it is freely available), there is a higher chance of security problems being spotted – and therefore a higher chance that somebody will fix them. They also argue that because security problems can be spotted, users are aware of their security situation and can make informed decisions about what products to use and which to avoid. They argue that security bugs in commercial software may only be known to the developers, leaving users to make uninformed decisions.

On the other hand, some argue that open source software is less secure, precisely because the source code is available. They argue that malicious users can use the source code to spot security problems and, instead of reporting or fixing them, exploit them.

Transparency

One big advantage of open source software is transparency: because the software it available for all to see, the way the software works can be verified. In some situations this can be vitally important—for example, in an electronic voting machine (see page 295), the source code could be used to prove that the software counts votes correctly and does not accidentally or deliberately manipulate the results. With commercial software, this would not be possible.

```java
462
463     private void calcBallAngle(Bat bat, Ball ball) {
464         final int centre = bat.getY() + (bat.getHeight() / 2);
465         final int diff = ball.getY() - centre;
466
467         final float change = (diff * Ball.RANDOM_ANGLE_FUDGE_FACTOR) + Util.nextInt(-Ball.RANDOM_ANGLE, Ball.RANDOM_AN
468
469         ball.adjustAngle(change);
470     }
471
472
473     private void checkCollisions() {
474         for (int i = 0; i < balls.size(); i++) {
475             final Ball b = balls.get(i);
476
477             // Only check collisions if ball is on this level and has been launched.
478             if (b.getLevel() == levelNum && b.isLaunched()) {
479                 level.checkBoundaryCollisions(b, dangerMode);  /* Balls versus level bounaries */
480                 checkBatCollisions(b);
481
482                 /* Balls versus blocks */
483                 final Block blk = level.checkBlockCollisions(b);
484                 if (blk!=null) {
485                     if (blk.getPower()==0) {
486                         soundManager.playBrick();
487                         score += blk.getScore();
488                         if (level.getRemainingBlockCount() == 0) level.restartTimers();
489
490                         if (blk.isBonus()) {
491                             processBonus(blk.getBonusType(), b);
492                         } else {
```

Figure 3-14 Part of the source code for a program written in Java

Commercial Licences

Users of commercial software need an appropriate licence to use it in order to comply with copyright laws. There are several types of licence – though not all software companies sell every type. The terms and conditions of the software licence usually forbid certain practices such as modifying the software, and are covered in the **End User Licence Agreement (EULA)** which you approve when you install the software.

Single user licence – allows only one user to use the software. It may allow installation on several computers (for example, a laptop and a desktop) but only one copy should be used at once.

Multi-user licence or **concurrent licence** – Allows a fixed number of users to install and use the software. The number of users is specified when the licence is bought. Often companies sell multi-user licences for three or four users, aimed at families who want to install the software on each computer in a household. The number of concurrent users can be checked by having the software 'phone home' every time it is run, or by using a network server on a LAN to manage and keep track of licences.

Site licence – Allows the software to be installed on as many computers as desired, and used by as many users as needed, provided that they exist in the same organisation or on the same physical site. Site licences are useful for large organisations who might have fluctuating numbers of computers and do not want the difficulty of keeping track of individual licences. Because of their flexibility, site licences are expensive. They often come with discounts for upgrading to new versions of the software.

Copy protection mechanisms

Software companies have tried many methods to protect their software from illegal copying and distribution (sometimes called **piracy**). Some software embeds the name of the authorised user into it, allowing the source of any illegal copies to be identified. A more common approach is the use of **serial numbers**, found in the software's packaging and entered during the installation process, to uniquely identify copies. The software may register the serial number online during installation to prevent the same number being used multiple times. **Product activation** is another common method in which the software contacts the software company's servers and sends identifying information such as its serial number, user, location, and even machine specification. Software which detects it has been installed on unauthorised computers (for example, by checking the machine specifica-

Paying for FOSS

Free and Open Source Software does not always cost nothing. FOSS gives you the right to sell it, and some companies make money by selling the software along with hardware, installation, documentation, and technical support services. Business users in particular are often willing to pay extra for value added features such as technical support, especially businesses who may lack their own IT staff. For example, Red Hat (www.redhat.com) sells Red Hat Enterprise Linux, aimed at enterprise and mainframe users, from its web site, together with paid subscriptions which offer technical support and software updates. Although the source code of Red Hat Enterprise Linux is also freely available under a FOSS licence, it does not come with any of this support.

tion and comparing it to the specification of the machine on which it last ran) may stop functioning or enter a reduced functionality mode.

Many games CDs and DVDs use copy protection methods including **Digital Rights Management** (DRM) to stop duplicates of the disks being made. This reduces the number of illegal copies by making copying difficult and by programming the software to require the original disk to be present in order to work.

Software organisations such as the **Business Software Alliance** (BSA) and the **Federation Against Software Theft** (FAST) represent software companies and work to reduce illegal copying. Their campaigns include lobbying governments for stricter copyright enforcement, and educating users about copyright. The BSA also offers rewards in some circumstances for people who report cases of copyright infringement to them. A 2010 report by the BSA estimated the global piracy rate to be 43%, with the total value of pirated software being $51.4 billion worldwide[8].

Cloud Computing

Cloud computing is a relatively new phenomenon in computing which takes a different approach to the storage and availability of software and data. Instead of being stored on a local computer or network server, cloud computing applications are web-based, stored on a remote server on the Internet ('in the cloud'). To use cloud computing applications, the user starts their computer as usual (so an operating system is still required) and then uses their web browser to access the cloud computing system. After account authentication, the application software runs inside the web browser. When the user saves their data, that too is saved 'in the cloud' – on the remote Internet server. No data is stored on the user's computer.

Several large companies now offer cloud computing services. Google Apps is one such system which offers word processing, spreadsheet, and presentation software to users with a Gmail account. Google also provides enhanced services for education and business users. Microsoft's Office Web Apps offers cloud computing versions of their popular Office software for free, but with only basic features enabled. Zoho Office Suite also provides many cloud based applications for users.

Advantages	Disadvantages
Software and data are available from any location that has Internet access, regardless of the computer being used.	Reliability: A fast and reliable Internet connection is required. Unreliable connections may result in inability to work for long periods of time. If lots of users are using the cloud computing system, a lot of bandwidth is needed.
There is no need to manage, maintain, and upgrade a network of computers with lots of application software installed. Upgrades to the cloud software are automatically available on all computers immediately.	Security: You are reliant on the cloud computing provider having adequate security measures to prevent your data falling into the hands of unauthorised users both during transit and when stored on the remote server.
Reliability & Integrity: there is less need to maintain backup and test procedures for data stored on the cloud.	Reliability & Integrity: You are relying on the cloud computing provider to have adequate backup procedures to prevent loss of data if their systems fail.
Some cloud computing applications let multiple users work simultaneously on the same document (collaborative working).	Globalisation and Cultural Diversity: There are concerns about the legal status of data stored on cloud computing servers in different parts of the world. Varying international laws may mean that data is subject to government inspection or may be considered illegal, even though it would not be in the user's home country.

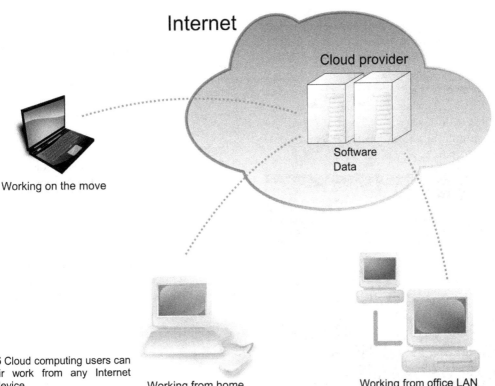

Figure 3-15 Cloud computing users can access their work from any Internet connected device.

User Interfaces
Graphical User Interfaces (GUI)

A **graphical user interface** (GUI) uses visual buttons, menus, icons, and windows to represent different parts of the computer, including the hardware, software, and data. A GUI is usually controlled by a pointing device like a mouse, although a variety of hardware can be used including touch sensitive devices and even voice command software (see page 21).

GUIs are often considered easier for users, particularly those with limited computing skills or experience. They remove most of the need to remember the complex commands that are needed for Command Line Interfaces. Most modern operating systems have a GUI.

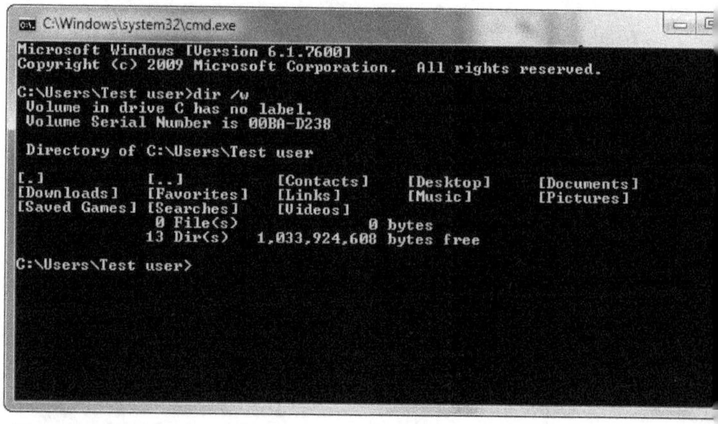

Figure 3-17 Command Line Interfaces are powerful tools for those who know the necessary commands and options

Command Line Interface (CLI)

In a **Command Line Interface** (CLI), the user interacts with the computer solely by typing commands. Depending on the command, the user may also specify additional parameters such as the files to operate on, or options to control exactly how the command works. Command line interfaces were some of the earliest computer interfaces, and most modern operating systems have a command prompt (also called a **terminal**) built in. In Windows, the command prompt can be accessed by clicking Start, Run, and typing 'cmd' and pressing enter. In Mac OS X, the 'Terminal' tool is available in Applications, Utilities.

Since many modern operating systems use graphical user interfaces which are easy and fast to use, it can be hard to see why anybody would choose to use a command line interface. However, for some tasks, especially those that need to be performed on multiple files or objects, command lines make work quicker and easier. For example, listing all files in a folder is easy in a GUI—but saving the list to disk, or printing it out, is much harder. A command line makes such tasks very easy.

Similarly, copying every file ending in .doc, or every file modified since a certain date (regardless of which folder they are in) to another disk would takes hours using a GUI and would be error prone. But a single typed command can be used to perform that task.

Command line interfaces often employ wildcards to increase their flexibility. A wildcard is a character that stands in for other characters. For example, in the Windows command line, the ? and * characters are wildcards. The former represents 'any one character' while the latter represents 'zero of more characters'. So the command `dir important.*` will list any file or folder called 'important', regardless of its file extension.

Menu Driven Interface

Menu-Driven Interfaces (MDI) let the user make selections from a series of predetermined options. Options may be spread across multiple screens or menus. Automatic bank tellers (ATMs) are a common example of menu driven interfaces: the user chooses from some initial selections ('Cash', 'Transfer', 'Balance'), and then further menus appear depending on the option selected ('Cash' usually leads to different options for different amounts of cash, or the option to specify your own amount).

MDIs may also be used in restaurants where the cashier must select from a fixed but quite large range of products. Initial menu options might include the food type (starter, main course, dessert), with sub options for each specific item (salad, soup, etc.).

Figure 3-16 A graphical user interface controlled by touch

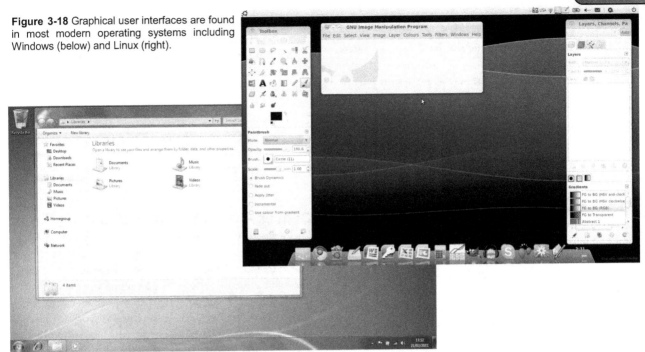

Figure 3-18 Graphical user interfaces are found in most modern operating systems including Windows (below) and Linux (right).

Getting Help

Commercial software applications sometimes include a printed user manual with installation instructions, descriptions of the software's features, and tutorials to complete common tasks.

Read me files are often included with software programs and detail last minute changes or known problems which may not have been included in the printed documentation. Read me files are often included with updates to explain what has been added in the new versions.

Increasing, the web is used to provide user support. Both commercial and FOSS applications often have dedicated web sites with documentation, **FAQs (Frequently Asked Questions)** and **tutorials**. If users cannot find an answer, online forums run by the software company or members of the software community can provide an invaluable source of help.

Programs can also include online help. Context sensitive help provides assistance for the specific feature being used when the user requests help. **Wizards** (called **Assistants** in MacOS) can guide users through a complex task by breaking it into steps and asking a series of questions – they are often used for software installation and configuration.

Third party documentation, in the form of tutorials or printed books, are also a common source of help. Most book shops carry a range of books for different applications and levels of ability.

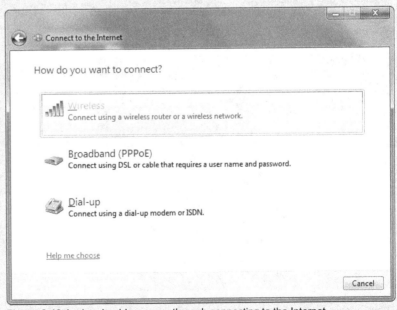

Figure 3-19 A wizard guides a user through connecting to the Internet

Software Reliability

All IT systems are a combination of **hardware**, **software**, **people**, and **data**. Problems with any of these parts, or a combination of them, can cause an IT system to fail. All software contains **bugs** – errors and mistakes made by the programmers as they create programs. As software complexity increases, so does the number of bugs, and as software becomes more commonplace in our lives, so the chances of these bugs affecting us also increases.

In recent years major email, social networking, and VoIP services have all suffered large scale 'blackouts' of their services. While these may lead primarily to inconvenience, other failures can have much more serious impacts. Failure of banking networks or credit card authorisation networks can cause serious problems for businesses that rely on these services, especially online transactions, costing business and possibly future customers. In the worst cases, computer failure can cause physical harm to people. Systems where failure could cause injury or death are known as **safety critical systems**, and special measures must to taken to keep the number of failures as low as possible, as well as to fail safely when a problem does occur. Some (in)famous software bugs are described here.

Year 2000 problem or 'Millennium bug'

Although not technically a software bug, the Year 2000 problem reveals a lot about the assumptions humans make when using computers. Computer software created before the 1990s often stored dates using two digits instead of four. This was to save money: memory was expensive and every digit saved helped. As the year 2000 approached, a problem became apparent: these systems represented the year 2000 as '00' – a figure which is smaller than the preceding year ('99'), and indistinguishable

Figure 3-20 An artist's impression of the doomed Mars Climate Orbiter probe

from the years 1900, 1800, and so on (all also '00'). This caused problems with some date calculations: in 1999, a person born in 1980 would have their age correctly calculated (99-80 = 19 years). But a year later, that same calculation would produce invalid results (00 - 80 = -20 years)!

The millennium bug received enough publicity before the year 2000 that most problems were fixed. However, there were some instances of credit cards being refused because their expiry date was considered to be in the past, and similar errors.

Denver Airport Baggage System

This system was designed to automatically transfer passengers' bags from the check-in desk to the aircraft. It was due to open in October 1993 but was delayed until February 1995, at a cost of over US $1 million per day (in addition to the $234 million initial costs). This system highlighted how hard it is for computers to work in the real world: the problems faced included bags falling out of baggage carts, getting stuck on carts or in conveyor belts, and labels getting dirty, preventing the computer from reading them. The system was abandoned in 2005, partly because it was costing $1 million per month to maintain[2].

National Cancer Institute, Panama City

In 2000, in a series of accidents at least 28 patients received overdoses and 18 later died after a computerised treatment system miscalculated radiation doses. A method used by doctors to get around a limitation in the software sometimes resulted in miscalculated doses.

The doctors were required by law to manually confirm the radiation dose calculations before treatment, but did not do so. As a result, two of them were subsequently sentenced to four years in prison[3].

Mars Climate Orbiter

The Mars Climate Orbiter was designed to land on Mars and study the Martian surface, but it was destroyed as it attempted to land because, NASA believe, it entered the atmosphere at a higher speed than intended. The official accident report discovered that some of the software developers for the project had used metric units (Newtons) for their calculations, while other developers had used Imperial units (pounds). This simple miscommunication over which units were being used caused the incorrect speed which led to the loss of the $327 million probe[4].

Case Study: Therac-25

Therac-25 was a computer controlled machine for administering radiation treatment to cancer patients, manufactured by Atomic Energy Canada Limited (AECL). Therac-25 had two modes: a lower energy electron mode designed to focus on a specific part of the body, and a high energy x-ray mode designed to distribute energy over a wider area of the body. A tungsten shield moved into place during the x-ray mode to protect the patient from harm. The shield was not needed during the lower energy electron mode. Therac-25 was first used in 1982 and reused software from Therac-6 and Therac-20. Because there had been no problems with those previous machines, the Therac-25 designers removed hardware safety locks which physically prevented certain erroneous conditions. This was to be a critical mistake.

Accident 1, June 1985. This accident caused a large overdose to be given to a breast cancer patient. A nurse noticed the patient was 'warm' after treatment but the hospital denied any mistake. Indeed, the patient was sent for future treatments. However, she had been severely injured, lost the use of one of her arms, and had to have both breasts removed.

Accident 2, July 1985. A Therac-25 machine gave an error message during treatment. The machine displayed the message 'No Dose', prompting the hospital technician to start the machine again. The technician did this five times, not realising that each time, the patient *had* in fact been given a radiation dose. Overall, the patient received 13,000 – 17,000 rads (200 rads is a typical dose and 1000 rads can be fatal). After this accident, an AECL engineer investigated the Therac-25 machine but was unable to determine the cause of the fault.

Accident 3, December 1985. Accident three was similar to accident 1. The patient eventually recovered from his injuries. After this accident, hospital staff contacted AECL about problems with the Therac-25 machine. A month later AECL replied, stating *'After careful consideration, we are of the opinion that this damage could not have been produced by any malfunction of the Therac-25 or by any operator error'* and *'[there have] been no other instances of similar damage to other patients.'*

Accident 4, March 1986. This accident was one of the most severe: a Therac-25 machine paused with a 'Malfunction 54' error during the treatment. As in accident 2, the technician was prompted to restart the machine, and did so. Unfortunately she had stumbled onto two faults in Therac-25 at the same time: one which gave a (single) overdose to a patient, and the 'No Dose' error. The patient received two large overdoses and died five months later. A contributing factor was broken audio/visual equipment, stopping the nurse seeing that the patient was hurt and trying to escape the room.

Accident 5, April 1986. In the same hospital as accident 4, with the same technician, the same 'Malfunction 54' error occurred. This time the technician stopped treatment immediately, but it was too late: the patient received an overdose, suffered severe neurological damage, and died three weeks later. After this accident the operator remembered the sequence of input she had made to cause the 'Malfunction 54' error message. Working with the hospital's physicist, she was able to eventually reproduce the error message at will. The speed at which the data was entered was critical in causing the error to occur. If data was entered and then quickly altered, the error would occur. The next day they reported this to an AECL engineer and two days later AECL acknowledged the error. Further testing revealed the dosage during the error to be up to 25 times higher than the amount required to kill a person.

Accident 6, January 1987. Despite the cause of the fatal overdoses being known, a Therac-25 machine at the same hospital as accident 3 was still in use. A technician received an error message during treatment of a patient and an overdose was administered. The patient died three months later.

By the time Therac-25 was removed from service, three people had been killed and three more seriously injured. The system had two main faults. The first, 'Malfunction 54', gave an overdose to the patient because the software did not move the tungsten shield into place during the high powered x-ray mode. The second error, 'No dose', caused a false message to be displayed, even though a radiation dose *had* been delivered. This fooled the operators into giving a second (normal) dose, thus causing an overdose. Accident 4 was particularly unfortunate because both errors occurred, giving the patient multiple overdoses. The tragedy of Therac-25 is that the programming errors were very simple errors, and existed in all previous versions of Therac but had been prevented by the hardware safety locks — the same safety features the Therac-25 designers removed because of the unbroken safety record of Therac-6 and Therac-20[5,6,7].

Chapter Review

Key Language

accounting software
application software
application suite
assistant
audio software
automatic recalculation
backup
browser
Business Software Alliance
closed source
cloud computing
command line interface
commercial software
compatibility
concurrent licence
copyright
cross-platform

database software
defragmentation
desktop publishing software
device drivers
DTP
End User Licence Agreement
Federation Against Software Theft
firewall
fragmentation
free and open source software
freeware
frequently asked questions
full backup
graphical user interface

graphics software
GUI
incremental backup
mail merge
menu-driven interface
multi-user licence
multimedia software
network licence
open source
operating systems
platform
presentation software
product activation
productivity software
public domain
read me file
restore (a backup)

safety critical system
serial number
shareware
single-user licence
site licence
source code
spreadsheet software
TCO
tutorials
user interface
utility software
video editing software
voice controlled interface
web development software
web-based software
wizard
word processing software

Exercise 3-1

Choose one scenario and produce a short persuasive presentation **justifying** either switching to FOSS or continuing to use commercial software. Your argument should take into account the specifics of the scenario. [10 marks]

Scenario 1 A large business has offices all over the country in many towns and cities. Each location has between 10 and 100 computers on their own network, with a server. Each office is connected to the main office in the capital city. The company has a 4 year hardware life-cycle. They run Microsoft Windows, Office, and Exchange. They have an upgrade agreement so they get big discounts on the latest Microsoft versions.

Scenario 2 A medium sized photographic and printing business has 50 desktop computers and 2 servers. The computers are about 5 years old. They mostly run Windows XP, with some still using Windows 2000. The desktops all use commercial software such as Photoshop, Internet Explorer, and Outlook. Staff frequently exchanges emails and files with clients who mostly use Windows.

Scenario 3 A large secondary school with 800 students has two computer laboratories with 50 Windows PC in total, and one learning resource centre with 20 Apple Macs. The school also has laptop carts with Windows netbooks that can be moved from classroom to classroom. A significant number of students also bring their own laptops to school. The school wants to increase the number of laptops available in the carts, increase the use of e-learning by teachers, and decrease total cost of operations – but they are unsure of the direction to take their IT strategy.

You will need to research both types of software—a good persuasive argument is balanced and covers all angles. You should refer to specific examples of software and apply them to the scenarios.

Exercise 3-2

Perform additional research on the Therac-25 case (sources for further reading are given). Split into pairs, with each pair representing a major stakeholder: AECL, the Therac-25 programmers, the hospital managers, and the patients.

Consider whether the responsibility is the same for each accident. What might have been done instead? Prepare a debate to discuss the question 'Who is responsible for the injuries and deaths caused by Therac-25?'. [10 marks]

Exercise 3-3

Match the terms on the left with the definitions on the right.

1)	CLI	A)	The instructions which make up a software program
2)	Public domain	B)	Software which is sometimes needed to make a new piece of hardware work
3)	Application software	C)	One method used to reduce illegal copying of software
4)	Freeware	D)	When software and data are saved on remote Internet servers
5)	Device drivers	E)	Software which helps users perform work, such as creating documents
6)	Source code	F)	A system that lets users control the computer by typing commands
7)	Serial number	G)	A reduction in disk performance when files are repeatedly changed over time
8)	Full backup	H)	Software which can be freely distributed but not usually changed
9)	Cloud computing	I)	Software over which the author has given up all rights
10)	Operating system	J)	A single document which is automatically customised for many individuals
11)	Fragmentation	K)	A complete copy of all data on a system
12)	Mail merge	L)	Software which manages the computer hardware and provides a user interface

Exercise 3-4

Research three famous computer failures. **Describe** the events, including the cost (in money or materials) of the failure. Try to determine whether the failures were caused by errors with hardware, software, people, or data. [12 marks]

Exercise 3-5

Every computer system has bugs—it is impossible to build a computer system that is 100% reliable. This means we need to build computer systems that are 'safe enough'. How could we determine an acceptable failure rate? What would be an acceptable rate for software controlling an aircraft or a medical device? **Explain** your answer. [4 marks]

Exercise 3-6

An online advert for a computer shows the following specifications:

Intel Pentium 4 2.0 GHz single core
1 Gigabyte (GB) DDR RAM Memory
40 GB Hard Drive
CD Drive (Plays Music & Data CD's)
10/100 Networking (Cable-DSL Internet Ready)
8 x 2.0 USB Ports
Microsoft Windows XP,
Office suite CDs included (Open Office is Microsoft Office compatible), anti-spyware and Anti-virus software
Also Includes: Power cables, Keyboard, Mouse, New Speakers

(a) State the amount of: [2 marks]
    i.   Primary storage
    ii. Secondary storage
(b) Define the term *operating system*. [2 marks]
(c) Discuss whether this computer would be a suitable purchase for an student starting IB year 1. [6 marks]

References

1 Boston Computing Network. (2010). *Data Loss Statistics.* Available: http://www.bostoncomputing.net/consultation/ databackup/statistics/. Accessed January 2011.

2 Calleam Consulting Ltd. (2008). *Denver Airport Baggage System Case Study.* Available: http://calleam.com/WTPF/? page_id=2086. Accessed Nov 2011.

3 Borrás, C. (2006). *Overexposure of radiation therapy patients in Panama: problem recognition and follow-up measures.* Available: http://journal.paho.org/uploads/1162234952.pdf. Accessed Nov 2011.

4 NASA. (1999). *Mars Climate Orbiter.* Available: http://mars.jpl.nasa.gov/msp98/orbiter/. Accessed Nov 2011.

5 Leveson, N. & Turner, C.. (1993). *An Investigation of the Therac-25 Accidents -- Part II.* Available: courses.cs.vt.edu/ cs3604/lib/Therac_25/Therac_2.html. Accessed April 2011

6 Leveson, N. (1995). *Therac-25 Accidents: An Updated Version of the Original Accident Investigation Paper.* Available: sunnyday.mit.edu/therac-25.html. Accessed April 2011.

7 Huff et al. (2002). *Therac-25 Case Materials* . Computing Cases. Available: computingcases.org/general_tools/ teaching_with_cases/teaching_w_cases_intro.html. Accessed May 2011.

8 Business Software Alliance. (2010). *09 Piracy Study.* Available: http://portal.bsa.org/globalpiracy2009/index.html. Last accessed Nov 2011.

Chapter 4
Networks

Objectives

1. Describe the roles performed by computers on a network
2. Distinguish PAN, LAN, MAN, and WAN networks
3. Describe the types of LAN networks which exist
4. Explain the ways computers can connect to a network
5. Explain how computers communicate on a network
6. Explain how network performance can be monitored
7. Explain the impacts of network failure

Networks

Networks are increasingly important as more devices like laptops, PDAs, and smart phones feature wireless networking options. The Internet has grown from 361,000,000 users in 2000 to 1,971,000,000 users just ten years later. Networks allow global collaboration and sharing of information and ideas like never before. In this chapter you will discover how networks operate and how it is possible to locate and access information on computers across the world from the comfort of your home.

Network Components

Clients and Servers

Computer networks exist in many places, from small home networks with just a few family computers, to huge corporate networks with thousands of devices attached. All but the smallest of networks tend to be **client-server networks**—the computers attached to the network act in one of two roles—as servers (of which there tends to be fewer) or as clients (of which there tends to be more).

Servers are computers that are assigned responsibility for certain tasks for the whole network, and provide services to other computers (the clients). **File servers** store users' files and data, and control access to them. **Application servers** perform a similar function for software applications, which can be delivered to any client computer on the network. They may also manage software licences (see page 55). **Print servers** manage any printers attached to the network, controlling access to them and maintaining a queue of documents waiting to be printed.

Many organisations have large databases of information, either for internal use by staff or external use by customers. A **database server** hosts this information and manages access to it.

Several security functions are also performed by servers. An **authentication server**, sometimes called a **domain controller**, is responsible for processing login requests and determining whether a user should be allowed access to the network and its resources. If a network is connected to the Internet, a server will often be dedicated as a **firewall**, managing security of information coming in and out of the network (see page 73). If an organisation hosts its own web site, rather than using an external hosting company, it will need a **web server** to store the web pages and serve them to users who connect. Similarly, an **email server** handles email for a network if an external service is not used.

In smaller networks one server may perform several or even all of these tasks, while on large networks each task may have an individual server, or even a group of servers, dedicated to it. Server computers normally have a higher specification than regular desktop computers because they must deal with many clients requests at once. They often feature multiple processors and extra RAM. If the server is responsible for storing a lot of data such as user files, a web site, or a shared database, it will probably have multiple hard disks offering several terabytes of storage, often arranged as a RAID array for maximum reliability and fault tolerance (see page 38).

Client computers are regular desktop, laptop, or mobile computers that connect to a network to use its services. Small home networks may feature only two or three client computers while a large business may have hundreds of client computers in one location or spread across the country or the globe. When connecting to a network, clients normally have to **authenticate** themselves using a username and password.

Shared devices

Sharing devices such as printers over a network provides many benefits. Most obviously, if an item such as a printer is attached to one computer and shared, there is no need to buy a separate printer for every user, thus saving large amounts of money. Most printers are not used constantly, so even a large number of users can share just one device without having to wait in line. Sharing devices also means users have a choice of devices—for example choosing between a low quality black and white inkjet printer and a high quality colour laser.

Figure 4-1 Many modern servers are blade servers, making it easy to connect many of them into a server enclosure (above).

Figure 4-2 Network hub

Shared devices may connect directly to a **network hub** or **switch** using an **Ethernet** or USB connection, or they may be attached to a server or client computer. In the latter case they will only be accessible if the connected computer is switched on and if they have been explicitly shared by the owner.

Hubs, routers, and switches

Hubs, **routers** and **switches** all perform a similar basic task, but the way in which they operate is different and has implications for network performance and cost. Hubs, routers, and switches all include a number of Ethernet ports, allowing multiple computers to be connected to them. The number of ports depends on the model: 8, 16, 32 and 64 ports are common configurations. If a network administrator needs more ports it is easy to link two or more devices together. Many devices also have **Wi-Fi** capabilities to allow clients to connect wirelessly. Most feature a series of status lights to indicate whether a cable is connected at both ends (this is useful when trying to fix a network connection where the cable is many metres long), and whether data is being sent over the connection. The difference between hubs, switches, and routers is how they broadcast data.

Hubs are the most basic and cheapest of these devices: when a hub receives data, it simply re-broadcasts it to every connected device— including the one that sent it! Computers simply ignore data if it is not intended for them. This method of operation has implications for network performance because a lot of **bandwidth** is wasted sending unnecessary data over the network.

Switches are like smarter versions of hubs. They inspect the data they receive to determine the intended destination, and then forward it to only the intended recipient. This saves a bandwidth compared to a hub.

Hubs and switches are both used to connect multiple computers on the same **Local Area Network** (LAN). **Routers** have a slightly different task: they connect two or more separate networks. For example, a switch will connect all the computers on a school network, while a router will connect the school network with another network, such as the Internet. The router acts as a **gateway** through which all data entering and leaving the network passes. This enables a router to perform a number of additional tasks, including filtering information that passes through it (perhaps only allowing access to certain computers).

Broadband routers are often supplied by **Internet Service Providers** (ISPs) when installing Internet access at a home or small business. Broadband routers effectively combine the functions of a router (connecting your home network to the Internet), with the features of a switch (allowing you to connect multiple computers to form a home network).

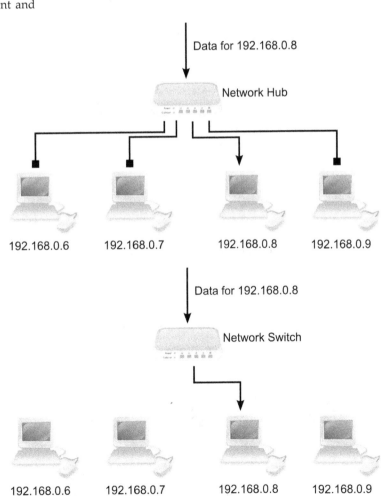

Figure 4-3 Hubs broadcast data to all connected computers (top), while switches send it only to the intended recipient (bottom)

Network Architecture

Network architecture refers to the way computers are logically organised on a network, and the role each takes. In a **client / server network**, one of the most common architectures, one or more computers act as servers that provide services to the rest of the network (the clients). This is a very common arrangement because having a central server provides many advantages. Files located on a server can be accessed by their owners from any client, meaning users are not tied down to one particular computer. This reduces the impact on work if a client computer needs repair, and also makes it easier to backup files regularly as they are stored in a central location. Se-

curity can also be improved because the server will authenticate users and control access to shared resources, which is easier and less error-prone than managing security on separate clients.

In a **thin client network**, the client computers rely heavily on a server not only to store files and applications, but to run software on the client's behalf. The thin client merely acts as a terminal for accepting input and displaying output. In extreme examples, the server will even run the operating system on behalf of the thin client: the client contains only enough software to initialise the hardware and network connection, and connect to the server. The heavy reliance on servers for the bulk of their work

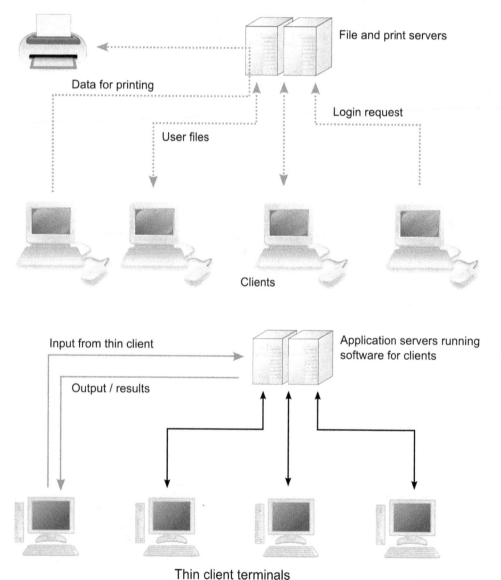

File and print servers

Data for printing

Login request

User files

Clients

Input from thin client

Application servers running software for clients

Output / results

Thin client terminals

Figure 4-4 In client / server networks (top), servers centrally manage access control and provide a single location for file storage. In thin client networks (bottom), servers provide even more functionality, even running applications on behalf of the clients, which merely provide the input and output.

Monitoring networks

Network monitoring systems are used by **network administrators** to continually monitor a network and its users. The administrator can be automatically notified by email or pager if any networked devices fail or if the network starts to exhibit performance problems. Two protocols which are commonly used to monitor networks are Simple Network Monitoring Protocol (SNMP) and Windows Management Instrumentation (WMI). Network monitoring systems perform checks including:

- Checking if pages on a organisation's web site are accessible
- Checking that response time from a web site is within an acceptable range
- Checking email servers are receiving email and able to send outgoing email
- Checking that network traffic is being routed correctly, for load balancing.
- Monitoring of server resources (CPU utilisation, disk space, memory) - for load balancing purposes
- Checking if bandwidth is being used efficiently
- Performing traffic shaping — giving more bandwidth to higher priority applications or users
- Looking for unusual traffic patterns which could indicate an intrusion or infection by a worm or virus

Network monitoring software records data into a **log file** which can be checked later by the network administrator.

If a network administrator is alerted to a problem but is away from the network, **remote access** can be used to investigate the problem. Remote access tools allow a user to login to a system as though they were actually physically present, including seeing a copy of the computer's screen and user interface and interacting with it. Because a network administrator's account is a desirable target for unauthorised users, remote access is usually restricted to particular computers and communication sent over a virtual private network (VPN).

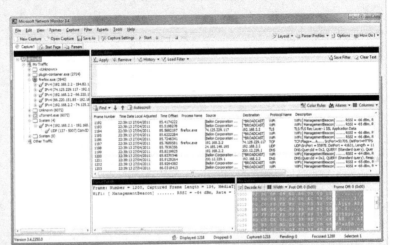

Figure 4-5 Microsoft Network Monitor showing network traffic.

Audit Trails

Individual users can also be monitored, including their login and logoff times, files and web sites accessed, emails sent and received, and even key strokes made. This information is usually recorded in a system record called an **audit trail**, which provides a chronological list of all actions taken. Audit trails are useful tools for ensuring network policies are being followed by users, and for investigating problems or potential security breaches. In fields where information security and privacy are critical, audit trails are an essential tool in ensuring network policies and local laws are being followed. Page 188 covers monitoring employees actions in more detail.

Load Balancing

Load balancing is an optimisation technique to make sure that bandwidth and network facilities such as servers are efficiently used. Larger web sites have multiple web servers servicing the needs of site visitors. Load balancing ensures that visitors are equitably distributed among the different servers, helping prevent individual servers from being swamped by traffic, and improving the response time for everyone. Load balancing can be achieved through configuration of networks switches. Load balancing can take place dynamically, so if one machine is performing a CPU-intensive task, less work can be assigned to it until the task is finished. Similarly, the load balancer can automatically stop delegating tasks to a server if it stops responding for any reason. In this situation, the load balancer helps implement a failover system (see page 38).

means thin clients can have very low specifications compared to so-called **fat clients** found on other networks. In particular, thin clients often have no secondary storage devices, a relatively slow processor, and only a small amount of RAM.

Peer-to-peer Networks

On a **peer-to-peer network** every client (peer) has equal status and there is no central authority or server. Peer-to-peer networks are common in homes and small businesses where a dedicated server is not needed or is too expensive. On a peer-to-peer network each computer shares the files from its own hard disk and other machines are able to access them (assuming they are shared with the correct permissions). As there is no central server, user accounts have to be made on each machine for each user who wants access. Peer-to-peer networks are limited in their usefulness once more than a few users are connected, as the lack of a central server to provide file storage and security features quickly becomes a problem.

Peer to peer networks should not be confused with peer to peer file sharing tools. Peer to peer file sharing tools are a way of sharing files over the Internet without a central server. Every user both downloads the data they need and uploads the data they have. This allows quicker downloading than from a single server.

Peer to peer file sharing have acquired a reputation as a means to illegally spread copyrighted material, though they have many legitimate uses. They are covered in more detail on page 275.

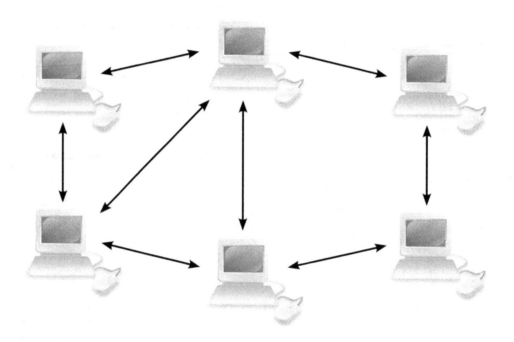

Figure 4-6 Peer to peer networks have no central authority or control

---

Exercise 4-1

Investigate the local area network at your school. Which services are provided by servers, and which are undertaken by clients? Would you classify it as a client/server, thin client, or peer-to-peer network? **Explain** your answer.

Exercise 4-2

Construct a diagram that shows a local area network which you know, such as the one at your school or your home. On the diagram be sure to include the key elements of networks: clients, servers, shared devices, hubs and switches, and routers. Where possible indicate the type of connection that is used between the devices (see page 76).

Exercise 4-3

In what types of situations would a thin client network be useful? **Explain** the advantages compared to a traditional 'fat client' network. [6 marks]

Firewalls

A **firewall** is hardware or software that determines which data is allowed to enter and leave a network. Hardware firewalls can be dedicated computers or can be built into network routers. Software firewalls are programs that can be installed to do the same job. If a software firewall is installed on a desktop computer (rather than a server), it is sometimes referred to as a **personal firewall**.

Firewalls help secure a computer by preventing network access from external unauthorised users, and also control which users and programs are allowed to connect to an external network such as the Internet. Firewalls can be configured to allow or block traffic using a number of methods:

IP addresses – IP addresses of specific computers can be allowed or denied access. For example, if a **Denial of Service** (DoS) attacked is being committed, the IP addresses of the attacking machines can be blocked.

Domain names – access to particular web sites, such as a social networks, can be blocked by specifying their name.

Protocols & Ports – different protocols such as HTTP (web browsing), SMTP and POP3 (mail), and FTP (file transfer) can be blocked or allowed as needed. These protocols usually use a standard port – for example, port 80 for HTTP. Either protocol or port can be blocked.

Application program—individual programs can be granted or denied network access. This can be useful for programs that connect to the Internet without consent – such as programs that try to automatically update themselves or report usage statistics.

Firewalls also raise some ethical issues. While they allow home users and organisations to control access to their networks, ISPs and governments can use similar technology to deny access to some services. Page 290 examines the ethical issues related to government control of information on the Internet.

Proxy Servers

Proxy servers act as a middle step between two computers—usually between a computer on a LAN and a web server on the Internet. All communication between the two passes through the proxy, allowing it to perform a number of tasks, including caching, filtering, and logging data. Because of this, proxy servers are a common way to implement firewall functionality and record logs of users' web activity.

Caching is a process used to speed up activities such as web browsing. Proxy servers keep a copy of commonly requested material, such as a web page, in a storage area called a **cache**. When a user requests the web page, the proxy server provides it from the local cache rather than retrieving it from the Internet, speeding up the process and reducing bandwidth use.

Figure 4-7 Firewall rules in the Microsoft Windows firewall

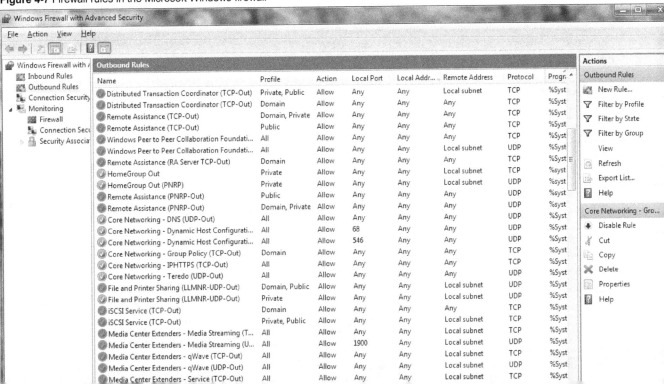

Types of network

Local Area Networks (LAN)

Networks are often classified according to their geographical size. A network is considered a **Local Area Network** (LAN) if it is confined to one geographical area such as a home, an office building, or a school campus. Even though the area may be quite large (as on a school campus) all of the computers belong to the same organisation. LANs are common because they provide many advantages, allowing users to log in from anywhere in the organisation, offering easy sharing of peripherals, files and applications, and helping the organisation manage its systems centrally. Users can also quickly communicate using email, and work together using collaborative tools.

Wireless LANs (WLAN)

A **Wireless LAN** (WLAN) is a local network in which some or all devices connect wirelessly. In businesses and schools it is common for some computers to have wired access using Ethernet cables while other devices like laptops and PDAs connect using Wi-Fi connections. In other places, such as freely provided networks in some cities, only wireless access may be offered. Wireless networks need special security precautions, explained on page 110.

Personal Area Networks (PAN)

A **Personal Area Network** (PAN) is created when devices such as mobile phones or PDAs are connected to a computer. A PAN is normally no bigger than a few metres – the space of a desk or a small room. A PAN is normally used to transfer data or synchronise devices (for example, updating contact details from a phone to a laptop or downloading photos). Bluetooth, USB cables, and IrDA (infrared) are common ways of creating PANs.

MANs and WANs

Metropolitan Area Networks (MAN) cover relatively large areas like very large university campuses or even cities. Usually a MAN is a series of local area networks connected together. For example, different government departments in the same city might connect their LANs to form a MAN, enabling more effective sharing of information.

Even larger networks, covering multiple cities or countries, are known as **Wide Area Networks** (WAN). The best example of a WAN is the Internet – a WAN formed by connecting many computers and LANs together to form a network of networks. Other examples of WANs include businesses that have offices in multiple cities: connecting the networks at each office location with each other forms a WAN. In order to ensure security of business data travelling over the network, VPNs are often used too.

Storage Area Networks (SAN)

A **storage area network** is a specialised network dedicated to storing data. SANs contain multiple hard disks which are attached to a LAN using high speed optical fibre connections. The SAN storage appears to client computers as local storage (i.e. as though it is a hard disk inside the client computer) and can be used in the same way. It is even possible to use servers without local hard disks and configure them to boot from a SAN. The advantage of a SAN is that all storage is maintained in a single location – making backup tasks much easier. It is also easier to add storage and distribute it across network clients.

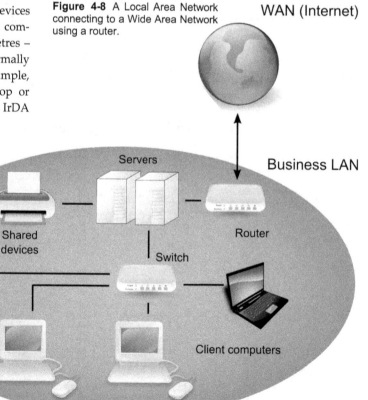

Figure 4-8 A Local Area Network connecting to a Wide Area Network using a router.

WAN (Internet)

Business LAN

Servers

Router

Shared devices

Switch

Client computers

Client computers

Virtual Private Networks (VPN)

Wide area networks like the Internet are inherently insecure because of the way data travels across them (see page 80). There are ways around this, such as encrypting email, but it is cumbersome and error prone to do this manually for every communication. A **Virtual Private Network** (VPN) uses encryption to create an **encrypted tunnel** from one computer to a local network in another location, over a public network. For example, a travelling businessman in a London hotel can use a VPN to connect to his company's LAN in the main New York office, allowing him to access the LAN's resources (such as shared files and printers) as though he were actually in the New York office. The VPN software automatically encrypts all data sent backwards and forwards through the tunnel, meaning transactions are secure from eavesdroppers.

VPNs are particularly useful when an organisation has a lot of users who travel a lot and must connect from remote locations which may not be secure (such as cafes, hotels, or airports). Commercial software vendors as well as open source projects offer various VPN software.

Virtual LAN (VLAN)

A **Virtual LAN** connects geographically separated computers or LANs into one virtual network. The concept is similar to a VPN except entire networks connect with each other, rather than just individual computers. VLANs are becoming more common as businesses increasing have geographically separated offices, but need to share more and more business information between them.

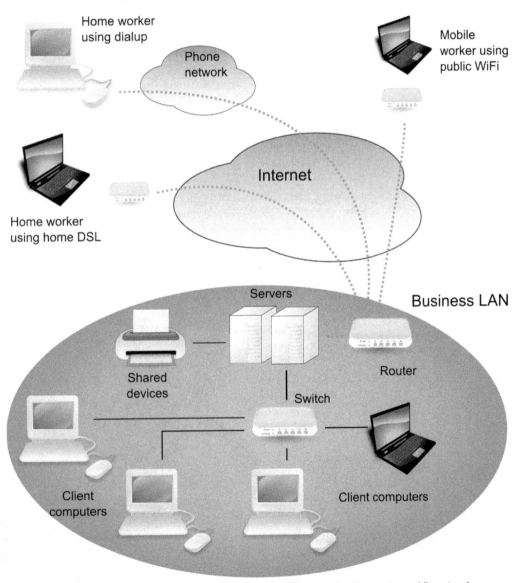

Figure 4-9 Virtual Private Networks are often used for security when sending data over a public network.

Network Connections
Wired Connections

A wide variety of methods are used to connect computers to one another. The option used will depend upon the distance between the computers, the bandwidth required, the cost of the connection, and whether a wireless or wired connection is desired.

Fibre optic cables transfer data by sending light down an extremely thin glass tube. Fibre optic connections are extremely fast, able to transfer data at well over 40 **Gbps** (Gigabits per second), and each cable is able to contain multiple independent optical fibres. Fibre optics also suffer less signal loss than other cables when travelling long distances. However, they are also extremely expensive – around $70 per metre. This has meant uptake by home and even business users has been relatively slow. At the moment fibre optics are mainly used for high speed **backbone** connections which deal with huge volumes of traffic.

Cable Internet access is one of the most common forms of broadband Internet access in homes. Cable uses the existing cable television network to transfer data, removing the need to install an additional cabling just for Internet access. In the same way, **DSL** (Digital Subscriber Line) connections use existing telephone networks. A **cable MODEM** is used to convert the data for use over the network.

The main advantage of these methods is that relatively high speed connections can be achieved without the need to lay additional networks dedicated to computer data. This also helps reduce the cost. One problem with cable networks is that users in the same area (for example, the same street or block) will normally share the same network, reducing bandwidth if there are many concurrent users.

Dialup is a relatively old technology that connects computers to a network using a standard telephone line. Because computers are digital but telephone lines are analogue, the computer must be connected to a **MODEM** (Modulator-Demodulator) to use the telephone network in this way. Dialup connections were common before broadband Internet access became widely available. The main problems with dialup are the relatively slow speed (up to 56 **Kbps**) and the fact that the telephone line cannot be used for anything else while connected. Another problem is that dialup connections, like telephone connections, must be paid for by the minute —which can quickly become very expensive.

The term **Ethernet** can be used in a number of ways, but in this context refers to the Ethernet cables that are the standard cables used for many Local Area Networks (LANs). Ethernet cables can transfer data at high speed over relatively short distances (usually less than 100 metres). Different versions of Ethernet exist, including fast Ethernet (100 Mbps) and 10 Gbit Ethernet (10 Gbps). Even faster connections can be attained by using multiple cables – 100 Gbit Ethernet uses this technique. Computers on Ethernet networks must have a network card that supports the network speed being used.

Figure 4-10 Modems (left) are used to connect a computer to a telephone line, while Bluetooth is used to connect devices over a short range (middle, right).

Wireless Connections

WiMax (Worldwide Interoperability for Microwave Access) is a wireless technology designed to transfer data over distances up to 50 kilometres. Bandwidth is relatively high – over 50 **Mbps** – but reduces with distance. WiMax is well suited to providing Internet access to homes in areas where laying cables would be difficult, or providing hotspot access to a large areas, such as cities.

Wi-Fi (Wireless Fidelity) is a standard for wirelessly connecting devices in a relatively small area, such as an office. Wi-Fi devices connect to a wireless router, and from there to the Internet. Wireless networks have become common as the number of laptop computers and mobile devices increases. Many hotels, cafes, and shops now offer **wireless hotspots** to their customers, allowing Internet access while on the move (page 110 covers the security precautions related to public wireless hotspots). Wi-Fi networks are based on the IEEE 802.11 series of standards, which includes 802.11b, 802.11g, and 802.11n. The primary difference between these standards is their bandwidth, with 802.11n offering up to 108 Mbps.

Bluetooth is a wireless technology used only for short distance or **personal area networks** (PANs). Bluetooth is often used to connect computers to mobile phones, cameras, game controllers, and other peripheral devices. It is also used to connect wireless headsets to music players or mobile phones.

3G and **4G** (3rd Generation and 4th Generation) are standards for wireless communication that operate using the mobile phone network. Smart phones and the MODEMS in some laptop computers use these standards. Because they use the mobile phone network, 3G and 4G

Measuring Network speed

The amount of data a network can transfer at once is referred to as its **bandwidth**. Older, dialup network connections are referred to as **narrowband** because of their low speed. More modern cable connections are referred to as **broadband** connections. Higher bandwidth networks are needed for tasks that involve large amounts of data transfer, including video conferencing, Voice over IP (VoIP) calls, and quickly downloading large files.

Bandwidth is measured in **bits per second** (bps), **kilobits per second** (Kbps), **megabits per second** (Mbps), and **gigabits per second** (Gbps).

connections do not require the user to be near a Wi-Fi hotspot, making them good solutions for mobile Internet access.

While the 3G standard offers at least 200 kbps, 4G offers speeds of at least several mbps. However, speed varies greatly depending on signal quality, and some phone companies limit data usage to a few gigabytes and charge heavily for additional data.

> **Common Mistake**
> Network speeds are measured in **bits per second** (bps), not bytes per second. This is a common source of confusion. If your Internet connection is 1 Mbps, the speed is not 1 megabyte per second, but 128 kilobytes per second (since there are 8 bits in a byte).

Technology	Used for	Typical Speeds
Wi-Fi	LAN	Up to 108 Mbps
Ethernet	LAN	100 Mbps—10 Gbps
Fibre optic	WAN	Over 40 Gbps
WiMax	WAN	Up to 70 Mbps
Cable / DSL	WAN	10 Mbps—100 Mbps (home connections are usually bandwidth capped)
Dialup	WAN	56 Kbps
3G	WAN	200 Kbps
4G	WAN	5—20 mbps in use
Bluetooth	PAN	Up to 2 Mbps

Figure 4-11 Speeds of typical network connections

Communicating on a network

In order to send and receive data on a computer network, there needs to be a way of identifying both the sender and the receiver.

MAC Addresses

A **MAC (Media Access Control) address** is a unique number built into virtually every network device. Unlike IP addresses which can be shared in some cases, each MAC address is unique. Typically MAC addresses are stored in a device's ROM, since they are not designed to be changed. For this reason a MAC address is sometimes called a **hardware address**. MAC address filtering is sometimes used on wireless networks to prevent access by unauthorised devices. However, although designed to be unique and permanent, it is relatively easy for a competent user to change, or spoof, their MAC address.

Protocols

A **protocol** is a set of rules about how to do something. Communication on a network could not occur without networking protocols. Different protocols are used for different types of communication.

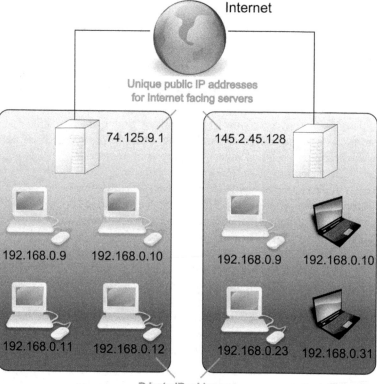

Figure 4-12 Private IP addresses are used on a LAN

IP

The **Internet Protocol** (IP) governs how devices on a network are identified and how information is routed between them. Despite its name, the Internet Protocol is used on many networks, not just on the Internet.

On an IP network each machine is assigned an **IP address** which uniquely identifies it on that network. An IP address contains of four groups of digits separated by dots (such as **192.168.2.5**). IP addresses can be configured manually on each computer on the network, but in order to avoid address conflicts (where two or more devices have the same IP address), addresses are normally assigned to computers by a **DHCP (Dynamic Host Control Protocol) server**, which keeps track of the addresses it has assigned.

With millions and millions of computers in the world, each one cannot have a unique IP address. Therefore the IP protocol features **private addresses** which are only used by computers on private networks such as LANs. The computers communicate within the LAN using these private addresses. Because they are only used with individual networks, the same private address can be used by other computers on other networks. For example, in figure 4-12, the private IP address 192.168.0.10 is used by two computers—but there is no conflict because they are on separate networks.

When a private network is connected to the Internet, the network gateway (typically the router) is assigned one **public IP address** which represents the entire network on the Internet (see figure 4-12). Public IP addresses must be unique.

TCP

The **Transmission Control Protocol** (TCP) is the 'other half' of one of the most common network protocols, **TCP/IP**. While the IP protocol deals with the addressing of individual devices and routing data between them, TCP deals with ensuring that data is sent and received correctly. If a packet of data is lost on the network due to an error, TCP is in charge of making a request for the data to

How are IP addresses assigned?

When your router connects you to the Internet, it is assigned an IP address by your ISP. This may change each time you connect (dynamic IP) or it may remain the same (static IP). But how does your ISP know which IP address to assign you to avoid conflicts with the millions of other Internet users? All IP addresses are managed by IANA, the Internet Assigned Numbers Authority. IANA assigns blocks of IP addresses to different Regional Internet Registries (RIR), who manage IP addresses in different geographical regions. For example, LACNIC (Latin America and Caribbean Network Information Centre) manages all territory south of Mexico. In turn, these regional authorities assign addresses to Internet Service Providers. Finally, when you connect to your ISP, it assigns you one of the IP addresses from its allocation. A side effect of this assignment is that a user's location can be deduced from their IP address, since a record exists of which IP addresses are assigned to each geographical region and ISP. This **geolocation** has implications for privacy, and is one of the main reasons why it is virtually impossible to maintain anonymity on the Internet.

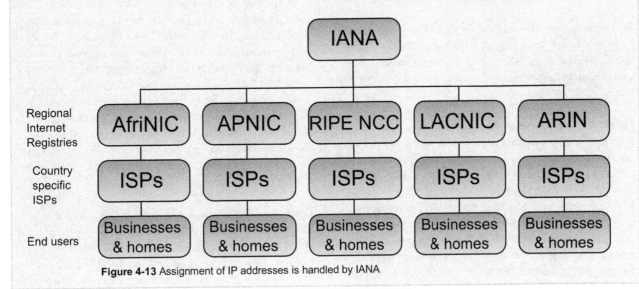

Figure 4-13 Assignment of IP addresses is handled by IANA

be re-sent. For ITGS, it is sufficient to understand that TCP/IP is a group of rules that government how data is sent over a network, and that an IP address is used to identify machines on that network. TCP/IP is used on the Internet as well as many LANs.

Ports

Ports identify the services available on networked computers. For example, when connecting to a web server to retrieve a web page, your computer will connect to port 80 because that is the standard port used by the **HTTP protocol**. Similarly, when web server software is run on a computer, it will 'listen' to port 80, waiting for connection attempts. Ports are used so that one computer can offer many different services in a standard way. Some common ports are given below:

Port	Service	Port	Service
25	SMTP (email)	53	DNS (see page 80)
80	HTTP (web)	443	HTTPS (web secure)
110	POP (email)		

The future of IP Addresses

The current IP addressing system (technically called IPv4) uses 32 bit addresses, meaning there are a total of around 4.3 billion possible IP addresses (2^{32}). According to the Internet Assigned Numbers Authority (IANA), there were 150 million unassigned addresses remaining in September 2010[1]. This might seem like a lot, but new addresses are being assigned at a rate of 243 million a year. In other words, very soon there will be no IP addresses left for new users! The solution to this is the adoption of a new standard, IPv6. IPv6 uses 128 bit addresses, given a total of 2^{128} (4.3×10^{38}) addresses – easily enough for the foreseeable future.

Try It Online
Visit www.itgstextbook.com for examples of online tools related to networking and IP addresses.

The Internet

The Internet Backbone

The Internet is a network of networks. All over the globe, networks from schools, businesses, organisations, universities and homes are joined together to create one much larger network. Local networks such as home or business users are connected via **Internet Service Providers** (ISP). In turn ISPs are connected to national Network Service Providers (NSP). NSPs are large companies that sell access to the Internet **backbone**—the series of high speed links which connect major geographical areas.

Backbone cables often run under oceans and are usually high speed fibre optic cables. Backbones need to be high speed because huge amounts of Internet traffic – everything from 'below' them on the network - travels through them.

Figure 4-14 shows a section of the undersea backbone in Africa. There are major backbones running off the East and West coasts of Africa, making land at key points. For example, the relatively new Seacom backbone runs through the Indian Ocean and makes land in Mombasa, Kenya. From Mombasa, this connectivity 'filters down' to the rest of Kenya—to Kenyan Internet Service Providers and then down to individual Kenyan homes and businesses. The Seacom backbone provides an essential link to East Africa because there is virtually no land based backbone infrastructure. This means almost all Internet traffic from Kenyan users will travel through the Seacom backbone to its destination.

Data Routing

The infrastructure of the Internet is important when considering how data is communicated between computers.
It should be clear that when you send an email or access a web page, your data does not go directly to recipient's computer. For that to be possible, you would need a direct cable between your computer and every person or web site you were ever going to communicate with –

clearly not possible. Instead data must travel through many other systems before it reaches its destination. This happens extremely quickly so you are unlikely to notice it except for routes that require many 'hops'.

For example, consider a computer which sends an email from a Mombasa, Kenya to Vigo, Spain. When the user in Mombasa clicks send, the data travels from his computer (via the LAN if he is using one) to his Internet Service Provider. His ISP sends the data to a National Service Provider, which is connected directly to the Internet backbone (in this case, probably the EASSy or Seacom cables shown in figure 4-14). The data travels through the backbone, utilising the cables up the east and north coasts of Africa, and through the Mediterranean, possibly moving between backbone connections (the precise route may vary). An Internet backbone hits land near Vigo, Spain. At this point the reverse happens—the email travels from a Spanish NSP, down to the recipient's ISP, then to the recipient's computer. If the recipient was not near a undersea backbone connection, the process is similar, except additional land-based backbone may be used before reaching the destination ISP.

Data travelling across the Internet is this manner enables fast global communication, and is relatively tolerant of faults because data can be re-routed to alternative paths if needed. However, there are also implications for privacy and security. Any of the systems through which data passes en route to its destination can potentially view or alter that data. This means it is a bad idea to send sensitive information such as personal details or credit card numbers through email. Online shopping and banking systems also face this problem, which is why data to such sites is always protected with SSL or TLS encryption to guard against electronic eavesdroppers (see page 108).

Internet Failure?

In early 2008 tens of millions of people in the Middle East and Asia lost their Internet connections. The cause: a primary backbone cable, running under the sea from Italy to Egypt, had been accidentally cut by a ship performing work on the sea bed. Because there were few alternative connections to Egypt, up to 60% of the available bandwidth was lost, with tens of millions of users affected[2].

Failures like this highlight our growing dependence on the Internet for many of our daily activities. India, reported to have lost 50% of its Internet capacity, has a booming hi-tech industry which is extremely reliant on fast, available Internet access, while users in Pakistan and Saudi Arabia were also affected.

Internet Backbone

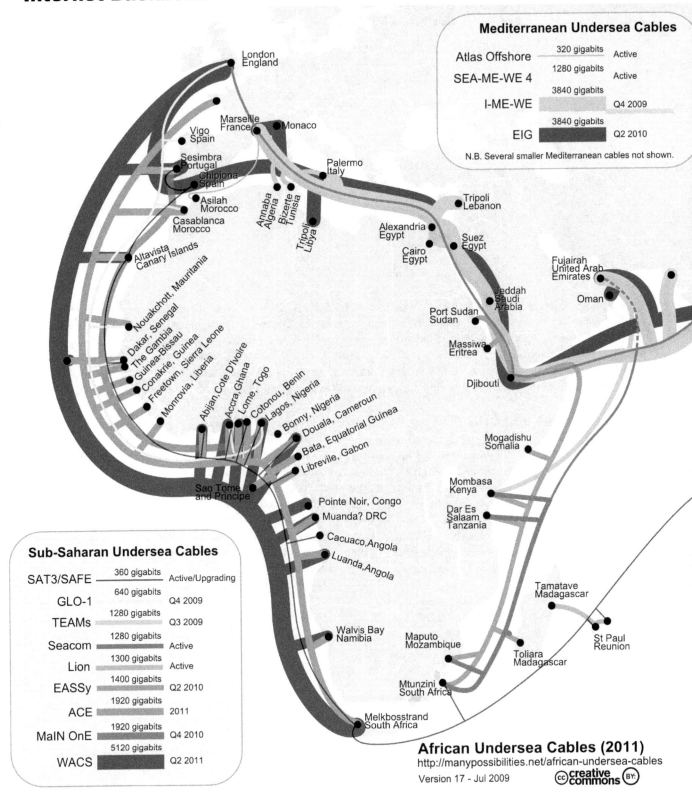

Mediterranean Undersea Cables

Atlas Offshore	320 gigabits	Active
SEA-ME-WE 4	1280 gigabits	Active
I-ME-WE	3840 gigabits	Q4 2009
EIG	3840 gigabits	Q2 2010

N.B. Several smaller Mediterranean cables not shown.

Sub-Saharan Undersea Cables

SAT3/SAFE	360 gigabits	Active/Upgrading
GLO-1	640 gigabits	Q4 2009
TEAMs	1280 gigabits	Q3 2009
Seacom	1280 gigabits	Active
Lion	1300 gigabits	Active
EASSy	1400 gigabits	Q2 2010
ACE	1920 gigabits	2011
MaIN OnE	1920 gigabits	Q4 2010
WACS	5120 gigabits	Q2 2011

African Undersea Cables (2011)
http://manypossibilities.net/african-undersea-cables
Version 17 - Jul 2009   © creative commons (BY)

Figure 4-14 Undersea cables form the majority of the African Internet backbone. Connectivity is carried into the African interior through land based backbones which connect with the undersea cables.

Trace Route

To view the precise route data takes as it travels to a destination, you can use the Tracert command. To do this you need to open a command prompt (the Terminal on MacOS). Enter the tracert command and a destination, for example:

```
tracert www.google.com
```

After a short pause, the 'hops' in the route start appearing:

```
Tracing route to www.l.google.com [74.125.229.210]
over a maximum of 30 hops:
 0 192.168.2.2  [Originating computer]
 1 190.53.3.1   [Amnet ISP, El Salvador]
 2 205.211.227.2 [Amnet ISP, El Salvador]
 3 200.12.229.65 [Amnet ISP, El Salvador]
 4 84.16.9.13   [Telefonica ISP, Spain]
 5 94.142.126.30 [Telefonica ISP, Spain]
 6 213.140.43.141 [Telefonica ISP, Spain]
 7 84.16.6.118  [Telefonica ISP, Spain]
 8 209.85.253.118 [Google, Atlanta]
 9 216.239.46.94 [Google, New York]
10 74.125.229.210 [Google, California]
```

The output indicates the IP address of each 'hop'. Hop zero (192. 168.2.2), is a private IP address—the machine from which the trace was started. Hop 1 (190.53.3.1) belongs to Amnet, an ISP in El Salvador. Hops 2 and 3 are also located in El Salvador. Hop 4 (84.16.9.13) belongs to Telefonica, a Spanish ISP with ties to Central America. The IP addresses in hops 5, 6, and 7 also belong to Telefonica. The IP addresses in steps 8, 9, and 10 all belong to Google, Inc. Hop 8 is apparently located in Atlanta, Georgia, hop 9 in New York, and hop 10 in Mountain View, California, where Google is based. So in this example data has travelled through nine different computer systems to reach its final destination.

Domain Names and DNS

Although IP addresses help computers identify each other on a network, they are not very useful for humans because they are hard to remember and they give no indication of the purpose of a computer. Instead, **URLs** (Universal Resource Locators) are used, such as `www.itgstextbook.com/index.html`. These are generally short enough to remember but provide enough details about the owner or content of the web site (if the name is chosen wisely). A URL has several parts:

> `itgstextbook.com` – The domain name
> `.com` – The Top Level Domain (TLD)
> `www.itgstextbook.com`—The hostname
> `index.html`—The file name

There are a variety of top level domains including:
> Org—Mainly used by charities and non-profits
> Mil—Military sites
> Edu—Educational sites
> Gov—Government sites
> Country specific TLDs such as uk, us, sv, and ke.

A system called the **Domain Name System** (DNS) is responsible for translating domain names that people type into their web browser address bars into IP addresses that computers can use to locate each other. DNS consists of servers connected to the Internet whose purpose is simply to map these domain names to IP addresses. Domain names and numeric addresses are interchangeable—for example, entering 74.125.229.51 in a web browser address bar will take you to the same place as typing www.google.com—to the computer it makes no difference (but the latter is easier for us to remember). An attempt to falsify DNS data to commit crimes is called **DNS poisoning** (see page 105).

Internet Protocols

HyperText Transfer Protocol (HTTP) is the protocol that governs communication between web servers and web browsers (which is why every web address starts with the letters http). Every time you visit a web site, your browser is using http to communicate with the web serv-

> **Did You Know?**
> Some top level domains have been removed over the years. Czechoslovakia (cs), Yugoslavia (yu), East Germany (dd), Zaire (zr) and Nato (nato) have all fallen into disuse since the creation of the domain name system.

er which houses the site. **HyperText Transfer Protocol Secure** (https) is a version of the http protocol designed to encrypt data to provide communication secure from eavesdroppers. This is essential for sensitive transactions such as sending passwords or bank account details. Https uses **Transport Layer Security** (TLS) or **Secure Socket Layer** (SSL) encryption to achieve this security. A secure web connection is indicated by a **https** at the start of the web site address and there is often a padlock icon somewhere in the browser window too.

Synchronous or Asynchronous Transfer

Data transfer between computers can occur either synchronously or asynchronously. In **asynchronous transfer**, the sender and receiver are not synchronised in terms of time. This means the recipient does not know when to expect data to arrive. The sender must therefore attach information to each to piece of data transferred, telling the receiver where the data starts and stops. Asynchronous transfer is fine for simple, irregular communication, but the need to add start and stop indicators wastes bandwidth and reduces overall communication speed.

In **synchronous transfer**, the sender and receiver synchronise times and agree on a transfer rate before the start of the transfer. They then transfer data at fixed, regular intervals. This allows faster data transfer.

Protocols in Action: How HTTP works

When you enter a web site address in your browser, the IP address of the site is found using DNS. Your browser makes an initial request for the main page of the web site (usually called index.htm or index.html) with the http GET command:

```
GET index.html HTTP/1.0
```

In turn the web server will send a response, such as the one below:

```
HTTP/1.0 200 OK
```

The number 200 is the HTTP code for success, followed by the message 'OK'. After this will come the contents of the requested file, which the browser will parse and display.

If a web page has graphics in it, your browser will make individual GET requests to retrieve those files too. The web browser doesn't return the graphics along with the initial file because you might not want the images – you might be using a text-only web browser or have switched images off in your browser. A request for an image might look something like this:

```
GET imgs/logo.jpg HTTP/1.0
```

Similarly, if you click a link on a web page, the browser sends a HTTP request for that resource:

```
GET exam_timetable.html HTTP/1.0
```

Each time the destination web server will return a response and the required data. If you have ever seen an error message like '404 – File not found' in your browser, then you have seen the HTTP protocol in action. 404 is the error that the web server returns instead of '200' when you have requested a file that cannot be found:

```
HTTP/1.0 404 Not found
```

Receiving this response from the web server prompts your browser to display an error message page. Using the HTTP protocol web servers and web browsers are able to communicate and send information in both directions. All of this 'conversation' happens invisibly, and so quickly that you wouldn't even notice it. Yet without the HTTP protocol web browsing would not be possible, because there would be no standard way for your web browser to request resources from a web server, and there would be no way for it to return the data you wanted.

The Internet or the Web?

Many people use the terms *Internet* and *World Wide Web* interchangeably, but technically they are distinct. The Internet is the physical network of computers across the globe, using the TCP/IP protocol to operate.

The World Wide Web is just one of the services that runs over the Internet, providing access to interlinked web pages containing text and images. As described on page 82, the World Wide Web uses the HTTP protocol.

There are many other services that also run over the Internet, each using their own protocols. Email, instant messaging (IM), peer-to-peer file sharing networks (not to be confused with peer to peer networks described on page 72) , Voice over IP (VoIP), and FTP are all services that use their own protocols running on top of the Internet's TCP/IP protocol. For example, email uses the SMTP (Simple Mail Transfer Protocol) and POP3 (Post Office Protocol), while FTP uses the File Transfer Protocol, and many peer-to-peer systems use the BitTorrent protocol.

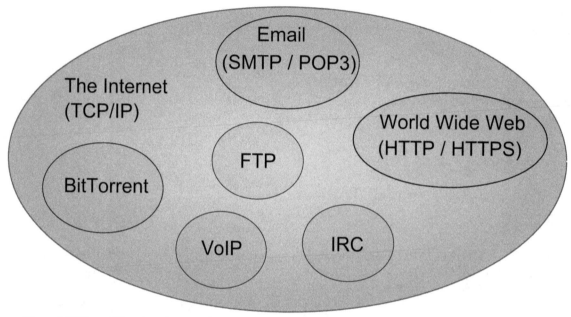

Figure 4-15 Many different services run through the Internet

Egypt 'switches off the Internet'

On 28 January 2011, headlines flew across international news networks: 'Egypt switches off Internet', 'Egypt severs Internet connection', and 'Egypt Disconnected'. What had occurred turned out to be the biggest shut down of Internet access in history, ironically motivated in part by the Internet and its ability to unite people. The previous days had seen growing unrest in Egypt with many anti-government protesters taking to the streets. Seemingly unable to prevent the protests, and with news that protesters were using services like social networks and instant messaging to organise themselves, the Egyptian government literally switched off the Internet for almost the entire country. Even mobile devices and smartphones were affected. No difficult technical tricks were used—instead, the nation's ISPs were simply instructed to stop their services. In moments, a nation of nearly 83,000,000 was disconnected.

However, despite the block a small number of users were able to get Internet access using dialup modems[3]. In the rest of the world, both mainstream and social media buzzed with up-to-the-minute news and images of the protests. Despite their attempts to control the Internet, the government faced increasing numbers of protesters, with up to 250,000 in Cairo alone by January 31, and protests carrying on through much of 2011.

What is web 2.0?

Web 2.0 refers to web sites that allow users to contribute information as well as view it. For this reason, it is sometimes called the **read/write web**, to distinguish it from the first web sites which only allowed viewing of information (the **read only web**). Web 2.0 sites often make use of user generated content and **tagging systems** to categorise data. Web 2.0 is not a technical standard; merely a term used to describe a style of web site or service. Examples of web 2.0 technologies include:

Blogs—Sites which keep a chronological list of posts. Blogs are often used like individual journals, as well as an easy way to post news updates on a given topic. Usually blog readers can comment on postings. Sites like Blogger and WordPress allow anyone to easily create their own blog.

Microblogs are similar to blogs except that posts are limited in length. The most famous microblog, Twitter, limits its posts (called Tweets) to 140 characters.

Wikis—Web sites that can be edited their users. Probably the most famous example of a wiki is Wikipedia – the free encyclopaedia which allows anyone to edit its contents. Wikis consist of a series of pages that are linked together, just like a normal web site.

Social bookmarking—Tools which allow users to share their favourite links and tag them with keywords that describe their contents. Social bookmarking sites like Diigo and Delicious allow users to search by tag to find sites other users recommend when investigating that topic.

Social networks—These are now some of the largest sites on the Internet. The biggest, Facebook, has over 800 million users[4]. Many social networks are designed for leisure purposes, enabling people to stay in contact with friends and family. Others, like LinkedIn, are used by people to keep in contact with business contacts, search for jobs, and find business partners.

RSS—A **push-technology** which allows users to view updates to web sites without having to repeatedly visit the site to check for changes. By configuring an RSS news reader with RSS feeds, any changes to monitored web sites are automatically displayed in the reader. RSS technology is often used when information changes frequently, such as on blogs, news pages, and auction sites.

Podcasts and **Vodcasts**—At their most basic, podcasts are sound files which are downloaded to a computer or a music player. Many podcasts focus on a particular topic (such as language learning or news) and authors regularly make new episodes available for download, alerting their listeners using RSS feeds. Podcasts can be downloaded from a web page as normal audio files, or subscribed to using podcast client software ('podcatcher software'). Podcast clients have options for searching for podcasts by topic and downloading the latest episodes as they become available. Apple's iTunes is one of the more common podcast programs available. Vodcasts are similar except they feature video as well as audio. Podcasts and vodcasts have a variety of uses including education and entertainment.

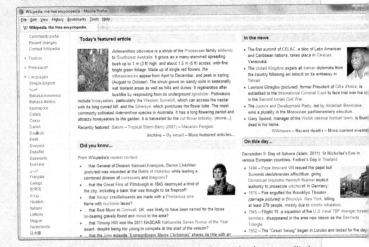

Figure 4-16 Wikipedia, the encyclopaedia anybody can edit, is probably the most famous example of a wiki

The Future of the Web: Web 3.0?

Web 2.0 was seen as an innovation over what became known as web 1.0, allowing more interaction and collaboration from users. Opinions are divided on what form 'web 3.0' - the next evolutionary step in the history of the world wide web – might take. Suggestions include:

'An Internet of things' where many everyday devices are Internet connected, communicating with other devices, sharing their data, and able to be controlled remotely.

'A semantic web' where metadata is added to data to enable machines to understand its meaning. This could improve searches by understanding the relationship between items of information.

A '3D interactive web' where information is presented as three dimensional virtual worlds represented by realistic graphics.

Chapter Review

Key Language

3G	email server	MAN	switch
4G	Ethernet	Mbps	synchronous transfer
application server	fibre optic	microblog	tagging
asynchronous transfer	file server	MODEM	TCP/IP
audit trails	firewall	narrowband	thin client
authentication server	FTP	network administrator	Top-Level Domain
authorised access	gateway	Peer to peer	upload
backbone	Gbps	Personal Area Network	URL
bandwidth	hardware address	personal firewall	Virtual Private Network
blog	home network	port	VLAN
Bluetooth	host	print server	WAN
bps	HTTP	protocols	Web 2.0
cache	HTTPS	proxy server	Web 3.0
client computer	hub	push technology	web server
client / server	Internet Protocol	read / write web	Wi-Fi
database server	Internet Service Provider	remote access	wiki
DHCP	IP address	router	WiMax
dialup	Kbps	RSS	wireless hotspot
Domain Name System	LAN	server	WLAN
domain names	log file	social bookmarking	WWW
download	login	social network	
DSL / cable	MAC address	Storage Area Network	

Exercise 4-4

Match the terms on the left with the definitions on the right.

1)	Server	A)	A computer which connects to a network and uses the resources the network has.
2)	Client	B)	A network within a small area, such as an office building or a shopping mall.
3)	LAN	C)	A computer which is in charge of certain tasks on a network, or which is used to share things with other computers on the network.
4)	WAN	D)	A device which is used to connect a LAN network to the Internet
5)	Router	E)	A network that may spread over several countries and continents. The Internet is the best known example of one of these.
6)	Hub	F)	A device used to connect computers to each other on a LAN
7)	Switch	G)	A more advanced version of a hub
8)	ISP	H)	This is the type of cable that is used to connect most computers to a network.
9)	Shared devices	I)	The most common way of connecting computers to a network without using wires.
10)	Ethernet	J)	Another name for a client computer
11)	Wi-Fi	K)	Items like printers that can be used by many different people on the network.
12)	Workstation	L)	A company that gives access to the Internet.

Exercise 4-5
Calculate the time taken to transfer the following files over a network:
   a)   A 400KB image over a dialup connection. [2 marks]
   b)   A 300 MB software download on a 1 MB cable connection. [2 marks]

Exercise 4-6
Imagine a video stream that contains 215 KB of data each second. **Calculate** the type of connection technology which would be needed in order to view the stream smoothly. [2 marks]

Exercise 4-7
A household has a family desktop computer, two laptop computers, and two mobile phones. They wish to setup and configure a home network to provide Internet access throughout the house. **Explain** the items of hardware and software which may need to be purchased. [4 marks]

Exercise 4-8
An organisation has a Local Area Network connecting around 100 computers. The network administrator needs to formulate an acceptable use policy for the network's users. Explain four provisions which would be included in the policy. [8 marks]

Exercise 4-9
Research the concept of 'network neutrality' and its opposite, a 'two tier Internet'.
   a)   **Outline** these two concepts and how they would affect key stakeholders. [4 marks]
   b)   **Explain** how a two tier Internet system could be achieved, using technical language. [4 marks]
   c)   **Discuss** the benefits and drawbacks of network neutrality. [8 marks]

Exercise 4-10
   (a) Identify **two** hardware components of a network.   [2 marks]

   (b) Define the term *thin client network*.   [2 marks]

   (c) Explain how a network administrator can control access to resources on a network.   [6 marks]

Exercise 4-11
   (a) State **two** units used to measure network speed.   [2 marks]

   (b) Define the term *Metropolitan Area Network*.   [2 marks]

   (c) Explain how computers on a network are identified.   [6 marks]

Exercise 4-12
Decide whether the following statements are true or false:

   a)   Hardware address is another term for an IP address
   b)   An IP address can uniquely identify any computer in the world
   c)   A modem is needed for all connections to the Internet
   d)   Fibre optic cables are one of the fastest types of network connection
   e)   Local Area Networks always have at least one server
   f)   Data transmitted over the Internet travels through several hosts before reaching its destination
   g)   Network switches are used to connect several networks together
   h)   A peer to peer network has no centralised server
   i)   Servers perform jobs including user authentication

References

1 Huston, G. (2010). *IP Address Exhaustion In 12 Easy Questions*. Available: www.circleid.com/posts/ ip_address_exhaustion_in_12_easy_questions/. Accessed May 2011.

2 Guardian, The. (2008). Faulty cable blacks out internet for millions. Available: http://www.guardian.co.uk/ technology/2008/jan/31/internet.blackout.asia. Accessed Nov 2011.

3 BBC. (2011). Egypt severs internet connection amid growing unrest. Available: http://www.bbc.co.uk/news/ technology-12306041. Accessed Nov 2011.

4 Facebook. (2011). Facebook Statistics. Available: http://www.facebook.com/press/info.php?statistics. Accessed Nov 2011.

Chapter 5
Security

Objectives

1. Describe common security problems and their impacts
2. Explain good security practices (preventative measures)
3. Explain solutions to common security problems (corrective measures)
4. Select the appropriate security software based on the risks a user faces
5. Explain how biometric technology works, using technical language
6. Explain how encryption technology works, using technical language
7. Discuss the ethical issues related to encryption and biometrics

Security

Computer security is the process of protecting hardware, software, and data from **unauthorised access**, while allowing authorised users to perform their work. As computers are more commonly connected to networks like the Internet, security risks come from an increasing number of places. Additionally, as more users store and transmit sensitive information such as credit card details electronically, so the rewards for criminals become greater.

Individuals, organisations, and governments need to be aware of the potentially serious consequences of security problems: unauthorised users can access data and alter or destroy it, threatening its integrity, or they can steal copies of it, causing potentially serious legal, financial, and privacy problems. Undetected hackers can also plant malicious software into a compromised system to gather data surreptitiously, or use compromised computers as a stepping stone to commit further crimes on other computers.

This chapter discusses the security risks faced by computer users, the implications of security failure, and preventative measures and solutions.

Authentication

Authentication requires users to prove their identity so a system knows they are genuine, authorised users. Authentication techniques can be broadly divided into three categories: 'something you know', 'something you have', and 'something you are'.

Something you know

Passwords and **PINs** fall into this category. Passwords are one of the most common ways of securing data, hardware, and systems from unauthorised access. Passwords must be chosen carefully—short passwords, or those based on common words, can be easily guessed. For this reason the term **passphrase** is sometimes used instead of password, to indicate that a longer series of characters is needed. The general rules when selecting a password are:

- Use more than 12 characters
- Use upper-case and lower-case letters, numbers, and symbols
- Use different passwords for each system, to limit problems if one password is compromised
- Change passwords frequently
- Avoid using real words, names, or dates
- Never write down passwords

One way to generate a complex password which is easy to remember but hard to guess or crack is to think of a line from a book, song, or poem. Then take the first letter of each word to generate the password. So the line *A lonely impulse of delight, drove to this tumult in the clouds,* would become the password 'aliodttttitc'. This could be further enhanced by swapping some digits for numbers, such as the letter O for a zero, or adding symbols. This should help create a relatively strong but easy to remember password.

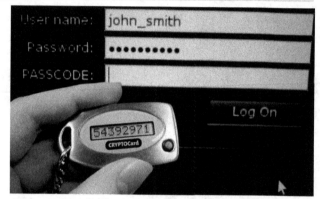

Figure 5-1 A security token displaying a one time passcode, used in addition to a username and password for authentication.

Something you have

The 'something you have' paradigm requires a user to have a physical object in order to authenticate themselves. An every-day example is a key – you cannot access your car or house without having the appropriate key in your possession.

In IT, **security tokens** are commonly used. Most are similar in size to a typical key ring so that the owner can easily carry them at all times. Some tokens contain biometric data such as fingerprints or a cryptographic certificate (see page 108) to identify the owner, and connect to the computer system using a wireless technology or a USB port.

Other security tokens generate **one time passwords**—unique numbers which are generated based on a secret key the token shares with the computer system. The user inputs this number together with their normal password, and the computer can verify that the number is correct and that it came from the correct security token.

Like passwords, security tokens are not perfect. The main disadvantage is that they can be lost or stolen quite easily. For this reason, security tokens are normally used in conjunction with other authentication methods, such as passwords or biometrics. Using more than one authentication method is known as **multi-factor authentication**, and is used where tight security is required.

Something you are—Biometrics

Biometrics is the process of using part of a person's body to identify them. Fingerprints, iris patterns, face shape, and voice patterns are commonly used. Biometrics have a clear advantage over passwords and security tokens because body parts cannot be lost, stolen, or forgotten (usually). They are also unique for each user – even identical twins have different fingerprints. It has also been generally considered quite hard to forge biometric data such as fingerprints, although some attempts have been successful (see pages 92 and 301).

The primary problem with biometric systems is that they are never 100% accurate. Even images of the same person's fingerprints, eye, or face will vary due to lighting, environment, changes in the body, and even the time of day. This means that biometric systems must attempt to make a *good match* rather than an *exact match* with the stored biometric data. There will always be a margin of error.

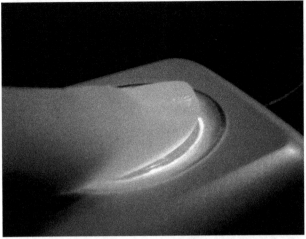
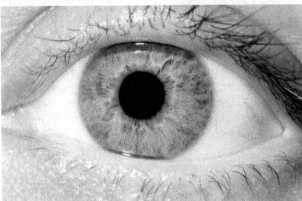

Figure 5-2 Fingerprint and iris recognition are two common forms of biometrics.

If a system fails to recognise an authorised user, it is said to have generated a **false negative**. This can be annoying and inconvenient, but at least allows the user to try the authentication again. Much more dangerous is a **false positive** – when an unauthorised user is mistakenly allowed access because the system mistakes their data for that of an authorised user. A good biometric system needs to find a balance that minimises both false negatives and false positives.

How does password authentication work?

For security reasons, computers generally do not store passwords as plain text. Instead, a one-way function is used to generate a **cryptographic hash** of password. It is not possible to retrieve the original password from the hash, making it safe to store the hash.

When a user attempts to log in, another cryptographic hash is generated from the password they enter. This hash is compared with the stored hash value. If the two match, the computer can determine that the passwords match and the user is authenticated. The value of this system is that the password itself is never stored on the system, nor is it sent over a network—both of which would be security risks.

Is this web site secure?

Not all systems use this method – some do store passwords insecurely. If a web site or system is able to send you a reminder of your 'forgotten' password, this clearly means your password is stored in a way accessible to the administrators of the system (whom you do not know or trust). In contrast, if the 'forgotten password' function simply sends you a new password, this is likely because the administrators of the system do not have access to your old password (because it is stored as a cryptographic hash). This is a Good Thing.

Password

Forgot your password?

Another problem with biometric data is that – unlike passwords – it cannot be retracted. If a password is discovered, it can be easily changed to something new, denying access to the unauthorised user. But a person cannot change their fingerprints or voice if their biometric data is somehow captured and misused! This makes the issue of **biometric data privacy** very important.

Biometric enrolment

Before they can be used, biometric systems need to collect data during a process known as **biometric enrolment**. This involves collecting **biometric samples** from users along with their identity. When the system takes a sample of, for example, a fingerprint, it does not store an image of the fingerprint. Instead, the computer analyses the fingerprint, looking for the key features and measurements, and produces a **biometric template** containing these values. This biometric template is stored for future use. When the user tries to authenticate themselves with the system, another biometric sample is taken and used to produce a biometric template. The new template is compared with the one old. If they match sufficiently, the user is authenticated.

User accounts and levels of access

While passwords, security tokens, and biometrics allow users to authenticate themselves, most system administrators do not want all authenticated users to have the same **access privileges**. On a school network for example,

> **Did You Know?**
> In 2006 the television program *MythBusters* was able to fool a variety of fingerprint readers and gain unauthorised access to the system by making latex or gel copies of fingerprints. Some biometric readers were even fooled by photocopies of fingerprints. In other cases, the team had to lick the fingerprint copy in order to simulate a sweaty finger!
>
> In 2008 a German hacker group even managed to clone the fingerprints of the German Home Secretary and distribute copies (see page 301).

students, teachers, administrators, and possibly even parents are all authorised users. However, different areas of the system may need restricting from different users. Areas such as exam papers and confidential reports must be accessible to teachers and administrators, but not students. Sensitive data such as medical records may be accessible to the nurse or doctor, but inaccessible for all other users, including teachers. Financial data may be required by administrators but no other users. Some resources, such as teaching materials must be accessible to both students and teachers, but there may be a desire to stop students from changing or deleting the data. Finally, guest users might be given access to a very limited set of resources – wireless Internet access and perhaps a shared printer, for example – but nothing else.

Biometric Enrolment (at earlier time)

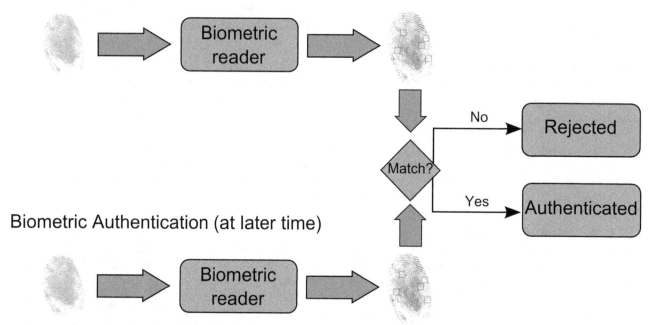

Biometric Authentication (at later time)

Figure 5-3 Biometric enrolment must take place before the system can be used

Exercise 5-1

Consider the passwords that you use for common tasks like logging into your computer, email, social networking sites, and so on. How many of those passwords meet the criteria in the table below? How many of your passwords would you consider strong?

Password for	Password length (characters)	Password uses numbers?	Password uses uppercase and lowercase?	Password uses symbols?	Password age (last changed?)
Windows	24	Yes	Yes	Yes	Last month
Power-on					
Email					

Exercise 5-2

Answer the questions below for each of the biometric examples on this page.

a) Find at least five measurements that a biometric system might take from this part of the body.
b) What problems might arise with this system in the short term?
c) What problems might arise with this system in the long term?
d) How unique is each measurement likely to be?
e) What might be appropriate places to use this system?

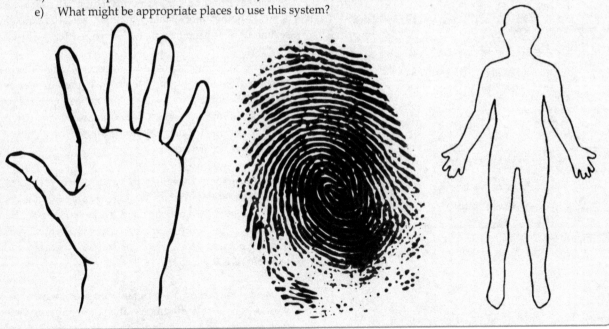

Exercise 5-3

At the 2001 Super Bowl, a new biometric technology was tried out on sports fans for the first time. Facial recognition software, linked to security cameras at the stadium entrances, scanned the face of everybody entering, and compared them with a police database of known criminals[6].

a) Unlike most systems, this system did not require people to stand still to submit a biometric sample—it was capable of working from live video feeds. **Explain** why this is so significant. [4 marks]
b) **Describe** what the risks might be if this system gave a false negative or a false positive. [4 marks]
c) **Discuss** the benefits and drawbacks of using such a system. [8 marks]

Most operating systems provide a means to grant access privileges to individuals or groups of users. Usually a series of rights can be assigned including the ability to read (view), write (modify), and delete material. This can be done on individual files, folders, drives, and resources such as printers.

In order to keep each user's files safe from other users, operating systems normally assign every user a **home directory**. This gives full access privileges (read, write, delete) to the user who owns it and denies access to any other user.

Usually the **system administrator account** (called the **root user** in Unix and Linux) has full access to all items, regardless of any configured permissions.

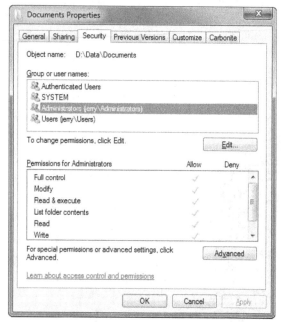

Figure 5-4 Configuring security permission (access privileges) on a folder in Microsoft Windows

Hacking

Hacking (also called **cracking**) refers gaining unauthorised access to computer systems. This is usually done by exploiting weaknesses in the target system's security, such as problems with network security or vulnerabilities in specific software being used on the system. Once a hacker has compromised a system, information will often be stolen—especially valuable personal data such as credit card numbers and passwords.

Hackers use a variety of tools and techniques to gain access to a system, perhaps the easiest of which is **social engineering**. This involves simply tricking or manipulating a person into revealing their password or other sensitive data. Social engineering attacks can be quite effective, especially against inexperienced users. Techniques include watching over a person's shoulder as they type their password, or calling a company's technical support department and impersonating a genuine user, pretending to have forgotten your password. In a large organisation it is unlikely that every employee is known personally to the technical department, and an inexperienced technician could be tricked into resetting the user's password. Another increasingly common social engineering technique is phishing, explained on page 104.

Software tools are also used by hackers. A **packet sniffer** is a program that captures data as it travels over networks. Like most tools, packet sniffers have genuine uses (such as helping diagnose network problems), but can also be used maliciously (by capturing sensitive data as it travels over the network).

Key loggers are designed to capture every keystroke typed by users. Hardware key loggers plug into the computer between the keyboard and the keyboard port. Software key loggers run in the background, silently recording key presses. Most anti-virus software will try to detect software key loggers.

A **password cracker** is a program designed to guess passwords. Some use a **dictionary attack** to simply try every word in a list of known English words (or words in some other language) until the password is found. Dictionary attacks can easily be thwarted by avoiding the use of real words as passwords. Other password cracking tools utilise **brute force** methods to try literally every single combination of characters until they guess the correct password. For example, they would try every single letter of the alphabet individually, then move on to *aa, ab, ac,* and so on, until the maximum password length is reached. Because of this, brute force cracking tools are extremely

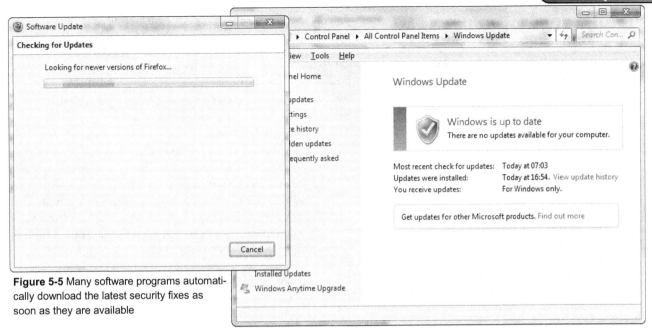

Figure 5-5 Many software programs automatically download the latest security fixes as soon as they are available

slow, with the number of combinations to be tried being $number\text{-}of\text{-}letters^{password\ length}$. Even trying ten million passwords a second, it would take years to try all combinations for a long password.

Many computer systems attempt to make the use of password cracking tools harder by limiting the number of times a user can try to login before their account is temporarily locked. Other systems impose a small delay (e.g. one second) between login attempts, which is barely perceptible to a human but seriously hampers tools which could otherwise try millions of passwords each second.

OS fingerprinting tools are used to give more information about a target system, such as the versions of operating system and web server software it is running. This is important information for an attacker because they can then investigate known flaws in those software versions.

Security Updates

Software vendors frequently release **patches** for their system – updates which offer fixes for performance or security problems. Downloading and applying these updates is an important part of keeping computer systems secure, because new vulnerabilities in programs are constantly being found. Many hackers use **vulnerability scanner tools** to test a system for vulnerabilities which have not been patched, so they can exploit them.

Most modern operating systems and programs have built in features for automatically downloading updates.

> **Is cyber-terrorism a real threat?**
> The fear of cyber-terrorism – computer based terrorist attacks against infrastructure such as power grids, water treatment plants, and emergency response systems – has risen in recent years. Page 304 covers the risks and technologies of cyber-terrorism and cyber-warfare.

Hacking in Action

In 2008 US Republican candidate Sarah Palin's webmail was compromised by hackers. The attack was relatively simple: the attackers used the password reset mechanism of her email account and, when asked for her personal details, they used details freely available on the Internet. This enabled the attackers to reset Palin's password and leak her emails onto the Internet[1].

In June 2009 a web hosting company lost the web sites of 100,000 customers after its servers were attacked. The company had updated its software with the latest security patches but the attackers targeted a newly reported, and unfixed, vulnerability – a so called **zero day exploit**. The attackers deleted large amounts of data from the servers. Many of the customers had signed up for hosting without backup facilities, meaning they were unable to retrieve their data[2].

Malicious software

Viruses

Viruses are malicious programs designed to replicate themselves and cause damage to computer systems. Viruses usually attach to other programs or email attachments, and are triggered when a user opens the program or attachment. When the host email is spread, or when the host program is copied to another computer, the virus also spreads. At a given point, such as a certain date or after a certain number of infections, viruses trigger their payload, which might include deleting or overwriting files, or even wiping the hard disk.

Macro viruses are written using the macro programming languages designed in automate tasks in some software, such as word processors, spreadsheets, and databases (see page 192). Because they can be configured to run automatically when a document is opened, macro viruses can easily and quickly infect computers.

Worms

Worms are similar to viruses, but spread without any user interaction. For example, if the user opens a worm-infected email attachment, the worm might immediately copy itself to other machines on the network (looking for unprotected machines) or automatically forward itself to everybody in the user's email address book. In addition to the data-destruction effects of computer viruses, worms also cause problems by consuming large amounts of bandwidth as they propagate (MyDoom reportedly infected over 75,000 in about ten minutes in 2004)[3].

Trojan Horses

Instead of spreading on their own, Trojan horses rely on tricking the user into downloading and running them. They do this by pretending to perform a useful or desirable task (for example, posing as games or even as anti-virus software). Once run, the Trojan horse delivers its payload, which often takes the form of spyware, or enlists the infected machine into a **botnet** (see page 98).

Spyware

Spyware is a form of malware which monitors the user's activities without their knowledge or permission. This might be to serve them advertisements targeted to their behaviour, or it might include more sinister uses such as stealing personal files or using a **key logger** to capture usernames, passwords, and credit card details. It is even possible for malware to record visually the user's screen in order to gather such information.

How does anti-virus software work?

Virus scanners use a variety of techniques to protect users. Most use a **virus definition file** (also called a **virus signature file**) to help them identify known viruses. Because new viruses and variants are constantly being released, these definition files need frequently updating. Several anti-virus companies release new definitions at least once every day, and it is important to configure anti-virus software to download these updates.

On demand virus scanners check specific files that the user has selected for anti-virus scanning. **Real time scanners** run in the background of the computer and scan all files before they are opened. Program files will be scanned each time they are run, and files downloaded from the Internet will be scanned as they are saved. Real time scanners provide a convenient and transparent method of checking files, at the expense of a small amount of speed when opening files. Many modern anti-virus programs will also integrate themselves into web browsers to prevent visits to malicious web sites.

Heuristic scanners attempt to identify viruses without using definition files. Instead, they look for suspicious, 'virus-like' activity. This helps the scanner identify new viruses for which there are no anti-virus definitions, such as modifications of existing viruses. Many anti-virus programs combine both definition based scanning and heuristic scanning.

Finally, some anti-virus software uses **blacklists** to prevent access to web sites known to host viruses and other malware, and prevent the download of known malicious files. The advantage of these systems is that they do not need to be running continuously on the computer: running them once configures the computer's HOSTS file to prevent access to banned sites.

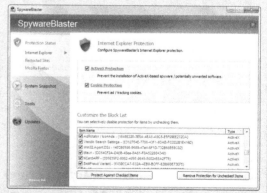

Figure 5-6 The Spyware Blaster anti-malware program, with a blacklist of known malware which it will transparently block.

Infamous Computer Viruses and Worms

CIH / Chernobyl (1998)
In the late 1990s the CIH virus spread across global computers. Its payload was extremely destructive, wiping the partition table on users' hard disks and erasing the flash memory in the BIOS. Although a lot of data could be recovered from damaged hard disks, machines with damaged BIOS chips needed a replacement before they would even boot.

Melissa (1999)
The Melissa virus took advantage of the macros feature (see page 192) built into Microsoft Word and Excel. The virus sent itself to the first 50 people contained in an infected machine's address book. In addition to mass-mailing, other variants of the virus delete files and the contents of documents.

I Love You (2000)
This worm used the email subject line 'I Love You' to entice users to open the email. Doing so caused the worm to email itself to everybody in the user's email address book. Within a week 'I Love You' had infected 50 million computers. The worm also overwrote important files with copies of itself.

Code Red (2001)
The Code Red worm infected over 350,000 computers by attacking web sites running Microsoft Internet Information Server (Microsoft IIS). The worm defaced web pages with the phrase 'Hacked by Chinese' and also launched denial of service attacks on the White House web site.

Slammer (2003)
Slammer was a rapidly spreading worm, infecting up to 75,000 machines in less than ten minutes. As with Code Red, Slammer infections caused global Internet slowdowns as bandwidth was consumed by the duplicating worm. This brought down many Internet routers and networks, including cash machine networks and airline reservation networks—a good example of how viruses and worms can impact computers even without damaging files or data.

Stuxnet (2010)
Stuxnet was something never seen before – a worm that attacked the computers used in industrial equipment and the specific programmable logic controllers (PLCs) inside them. The worm was designed to infect any machines, but only damage industrial machines containing Siemens equipment. Such control equipment is often used in power plants, water treatment and distribution systems, and power and gas systems. In early 2011 the US government and the Israeli intelligence service Mossad were accused of engineering Stuxnet to sabotage Iran's nuclear weapons program, which uses exclusively Siemens equipment for the process of nuclear fuel enrichment. Stuxnet renewed fears that future malware that might attack critical infrastructure as part of a **cyber-terrorism** or **cyber-warfare** campaign (see page 305).

Rootkits

Rootkits are a particularly hard to remove form of malware. They generally infect a machine as the administrator (root) user, and use a variety of techniques to hide their presence from the user and the operating system, including altering the operating system so the rootkit's process is not displayed in the list of running processes.

Rootkits are by their nature very difficult to detect and remove, and often a fresh operating system installation is the only way to guarantee an uninfected computer. However, some rootkits can even infect a computer's BIOS, activating themselves before an operating system is even loaded—meaning even reinstallation will not solve the problem. Although rootkits can have some genuine uses, the term generally refers to their use as malware.

Impacts of malicious software

Data destruction is a common goal of malicious software (**malware**). Some malware programs simply display an annoying message on the screen when they trigger, while others can be very destructive. Effects including erasing or overwriting data and programs or even making the computer unbootable by damaging the operating system (see CIH virus, above). Even 'harmless' viruses can cause damage and problems for systems administrators as they must spend valuable time cleaning and repairing machines, restoring corrupted program files, and checking for damaged data and programs.

Increasingly, malware is used to infect computers with **backdoors**, which allow them to be controlled by an unauthorised remote user. Such infected machines are known as **zombies**. Criminals gangs control hundreds or even thousands of zombies at once to form **botnets**— groups of computers under their control. Botnets are used to send out spam or phishing email, or to distribute further malicious software. They can also be used to perform **Distributed Denial of Service** attacks on other computer systems. Botnets offer criminals an easy way to commit their crimes without fear of being caught. There are even examples of criminal gangs renting botnets to other criminals to perform their crimes.

Law enforcement agencies and computer companies are in a constant battle to combat botnets. In 2001, Microsoft and the FBI managed to shut down two large botnets: Rustock and Kelihos. Kelihos consisted of 41,000 compromised computers, capable of sending 3.8 billion spam email messages every day. Rustock was even bigger—up to 250,000 computers, and was thought to be responsible for almost half of all global spam being sent at the time of its shutdown[4, 5].

Drive-by downloads

Drive-by downloads are programs which are downloaded or installed automatically, without the user's consent, when they visit a web page. They are typically used either to infect a system with some form of malware, or to make money by tricking the user into buying security software that they don't need. **JavaScript**, **ActiveX**, and **Java** are technologies that can be used to create enhanced, interactive web pages, but can also be misused to deliver drive-by downloads. This is particularly true if a user's Internet or web browser security settings are set too low.

Other drive-by downloads may attempt to trick the user into clicking something to activate the download. Figure 5-9 shows a common technique—using a false error message, ironically often informing a user about a virus infec-

Figure 5-7 Some web sites use fake operating system or anti-virus error messages to trick users into downloading malware. Here even the title bar and red close button are fake—clicking anywhere will trigger the download.

tion. Extreme examples like figure 5-7 show images which look like a window generated by the operating system, including a title bar and close button. Clicking on these windows (including the fake close button) will trigger the download of malware. A good way to safely close windows like this is to use the keyboard shortcut (Alt-F4 in Microsoft Windows).

Denial of Service attacks

A **denial of service attack** involves bombarding a computer system with so many requests that it is unable to keep up, slowing down its response, or even causing it to crash. It is similar to the idea of bombarding a telephone switchboard with calls – after a certain number of users are calling, others will need to wait in line to get through. **Distributed Denial of Service** attacks (DDoS) use many computers (possibly thousands) to attack a system. Often these are zombie computers that have been compromised and taken over by malware to form botnets.

Infiltrating the Pentagon

In 2008 a US Ministry of Defence employee picked up a discarded USB flash drive in the car park of a US military base in the Middle East. Believing the flash drive to be lost and trying to identify its owner, the employee inserted it into a military laptop. What happened next was later described as 'most significant breach' ever of US military computer networks[7].

The flash drive had not been accidentally lost: it had been placed in the car park by a foreign intelligence agency, and was infected with the Agent.BTZ worm. Inserting the flash drive automatically triggered the worm, silently infecting military computer networks and establishing back doors which allowed data to be transferred to servers outside of the US network. The Pentagon did not reveal how much, if any, data had been copied outside of its control, but it is estimated that it took over a year to remove the worm from the compromised systems.

Figure 5-8 The Pentagon: compromised by a USB flash drive.

DoS attacks are hard to combat because they consist of genuine requests to the target system – such as a request for a web page. The problem is that there are so many requests that the target cannot service them. DDoS attacks are even harder to fight because the disruptive requests come from many different machines, making blocking the sources ineffective.

Avoid Malicious Software

There are a number of measures that can be taken to reduce the chances of being infected by a malicious software. Advice for good practice includes:

- Install anti-virus software and make sure the virus definitions are regularly updated. Most anti-virus software also offers protection against spyware and other malware.
- Configure web browser security settings to disallow unsigned code such as ActiveX controls
- Only download new software from well known, trustworthy sites, and scan it with anti-virus software before use.
- Avoid common sources of malware such as illegal downloads of software.
- Never open an email attachment you were not expecting—even if it comes from somebody you know.
- Never click on a popup window which occurs while browsing.
- Maintain a backup of your data in case your computer is infected.
- Educate other users in your family about avoiding viruses, and in the case of young children, supervise them online.

Figure 5-9 A fake spyware alert from Virus Response Lab 2009—a well known piece of malware

Common Mistake
In an exam, giving recommendations such as 'be careful where you download software' is too vague. You need to be precise and give the exact steps a user should take to protect themself.

Computer Security and the Law

The **Computer Misuse Act (1990)** is a UK law governing unauthorised access to computer systems. The law provides for a prison sentence of 5 years and up to a £5000 fine for three offences:

i.   Gaining unauthorised access to a computer system
ii. Gaining unauthorised access to a computer system in order to commit further crime (for example, stealing credit card data to commit fraud)
iii. Unauthorised modification of data stored on a computer

Additions and amendments were made to the Act in 2006 to increase the length of sentences and add a further offence of 'intent to impair operation of computer'. This additional offence was aimed specifically at providing a penalty for committing Denial of Service attacks, which some felt were not covered under the law previously.

Spam

Spam refers to unwanted messages that are sent to many users at once. Although it usually refers to email messages, spam can also take the form of unwanted phone text messages (SMS), online chat, and comments on public bulletin boards and blogs. Spam messages usually advertise products ranging from dubious web sites to illegal products such as unregulated prescription drugs or counterfeit items. Some spam messages are scams which try to entice the user into sending money to an overseas bank account – usually with an elaborate back story (see page 102). These messages are known as **419 scams** or sometimes 'Nigerian scams' because of the common origin of these emails. Other spam is simply used as a method to deliver viruses or worms using infected attachments.

Spamming Techniques

Spammers use a variety of techniques to entice users into opening their emails. A common approach is to include a subject line which appears personal, such as 'here is that document you asked for', suggesting the recipient knows the sender. This is particularly effective if the spam is sent by a virus or a worm, because the sender may actually be a person the recipient knows.

Spam sometimes offers links or attachments supposedly offering the latest news or images of famous people. For example, less than a day after the death of singer Michael Jackson, spam email purporting to offer information about his death was being sent around the Internet. A similar thing happened after the death of Osama bin laden in 2011. The technique of 'hijacking' global news events is used by the spammer on page 102. The email contains a fairly standard story about 'lost' money which can be reclaimed ($35,000,000 in this case). In this case the background story is supported by a link to news article about a real plane crash—the spammer has cynically used the name of a real person and a link to a genuine web page which reports his death. Of course, this does not prove the email is genuine—and it obviously isn't.

Impacts of spam

One obvious effect of spam is the potential exposure to malware infected attachments. This can have a serious impact on businesses, whose networks can be quickly infected by just one user triggering a virus or worm (see page 97). Large amounts of spam also slow down email servers, consuming disk space and bandwidth – possibly preventing users from completing their normal work. For example, many email inboxes have limited storage space, and large amounts of spam can fill this, forcing new emails to be bounced back to their sender. Sifting through dozens of emails to find the genuine ones also consumes time and increases the risk of missing an important email. In some cases businesses may need to buy additional storage for their email servers to address this.

Mrs. Susan Amson	From Mrs. Susan Amson Read the attachment below and get back to me	Wed, 2/16/11	6KB
jyluunav5241@bluewin.ch	Member craven, VIAGRA ® -64% OFF	Wed, 2/16/11	5KB
R30	男を刺激するエロエロ情報マガジン！	Wed, 2/16/11	4KB
斉藤理恵	平気ですか？	Wed, 2/16/11	4KB
office--------------------------------file	Attention. Dear	Wed, 2/16/11	9KB
willson victor	Greetings from Abidjan	Wed, 2/16/11	7KB
efcc commission	YOUR OVER DUE PAYMENT	Wed, 2/16/11	8KB
即落札の激安オークション	■オークション■ 奈美 さんから招待状が届いています。	Wed, 2/16/11	5KB
ら驚きの価格で落札ができる	商品は全て新品！最低落札価格がないから驚きの価格で落札ができる！！	Wed, 2/16/11	6KB
R30	男を刺激するエロエロ情報マガジン！	Wed, 2/16/11	4KB
斉藤理恵	平気ですか？	Wed, 2/16/11	4KB
2月限定ご招待	＜参加者急増中＞永久無料会員になるなら今！秋葉で逮捕の自称グラビアアイドルも..	Wed, 2/16/11	5KB
あおい	あおいさんからメッセージです。	Wed, 2/16/11	5KB
★佐藤あいのセックスアンケート★	★初めまして！佐藤あいって言います(*^-^)v★	Wed, 2/16/11	6KB
Mr.Siong Ng Thian	RE: REFERENCE BELOW	Tue, 2/15/11	5KB
bifivu8431@ne.jp	craven, 75% off on VIAGRA ®	Tue, 2/15/11	5KB
ozeen2550@ttnet.net.tr	craven, 76% off on VIAGRA ®	Tue, 2/15/11	5KB
bill gate	FÉLICITATION // FÉLICITATION// FÉLICITATION	Tue, 2/15/11	815KB
Daily Deals	Tired of bidding on overpopulated auction sites - Get 30 Free Bids	Tue, 2/15/11	6KB
Claire F. Chang	Quality Codeine, No PreScript Needed!	Tue, 2/15/11	4KB
Canadian-Pharmacy	Buy FDA approved drugs online. Feel the magical power of Online Shopping!	Tue, 2/15/11	43KB
Printable Coupons	Print Coupons for Oscar Mayer, Pillsbury, Betty Crocker & More	Tue, 2/15/11	5KB
Tmf Financial Company Plc	Tmf Financial Offer 2011	Tue, 2/15/11	4KB
Robert S. Mueller, III	Your Award Fund Has Been Recovered Contact us immediately....	Mon, 2/14/11	6KB
DR. BAN KI - MOON	CONGRATULATIONS!.Please read the attachment below and get back to me	Mon, 2/14/11	8KB
Team Force Factor	Muscle Building Miracle	Mon, 2/14/11	5KB

Figure 5-10 The Bulk Mail folder of an email account. The messages with subjects like 'Attention. Dear' are generally 419 scams. Notice that some of the messages contain attachments, some of which are probably virus-infected.

Anti-spam software is now essential for many businesses, but it also means more expense. Software has to be bought, installed, and constantly updated. This costs money and valuable time.

Businesses also lose money because their employees are less productive when they must deal with large amounts of spam. One survey calculated that each employee spends 7.3 minutes every week dealing with spam—adding up to $71 billion of lost productivity in the US[8].

Businesses who do use email for marketing need to be very careful about how they do it. Appropriate and genuine information can be useful, but bombarding customers with advertisements and special offers will quickly earn the business a poor reputation and users may flag their messages as spam. Page 210 discusses e-marketing techniques.

Finding email addresses

A common way for spammers to find valid email addresses is to use software **spam bots** to scan through thousands of web pages looking for email addresses. These might be written in the web page, in the HTML code as a mailto tag, or used in web forms that users fill in and send.

Another technique which is becoming more common is to randomly try combinations of common names with common email providers to see if they generate a valid email address. Although this technique might not generate genuine addresses, for the spammer there is little to lose as the cost of sending such emails is so low—especially as most spam is sent using botnets.

Finally, some companies exist with the sole purpose of collecting and selling databases of email addresses. Some of these addresses may be collected using the above methods, and others may be taken from companies that share their customer data with third parties.

Spam Filters

Most email providers, including those offering free web-based email, use **spam filters** to reduce the amount of spam you receive. Organisations or individuals can supplement these blocking measures with their own spam filters, which can be installed on an email server or on individual client computers. The open source SpamAssassin is an example of one such program. Spam filters often use **Bayesian filtering** to examine email and determine how likely it is to be spam, based on the words it uses (for example, common words associated with selling material or 419 scams would trigger the filter).

Spam blocking services monitor global spam email and make available the IP addresses or domain names of spam sources. These can then be blacklisted by email software so that spam from that source is no longer received. Some blacklists are published periodically while others are updated in real-time.

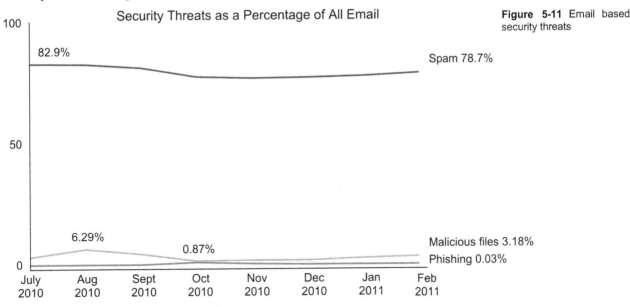

Security Threats as a Percentage of All Email

Figure 5-11 Email based security threats

Spam 78.7%

82.9%

6.29%

0.87%

Malicious files 3.18%

Phishing 0.03%

| July 2010 | Aug 2010 | Sept 2010 | Oct 2010 | Nov 2010 | Dec 2010 | Jan 2011 | Feb 2011 |

Source: Kaspersky Labs

Spotting Spam

Spotting spam is often very easy if you know what to look for. The example below has many tell-tale signs:

1. A popular free email service has been used. This seems quite odd for a man who is supposedly the manager of a major bank.
2. The 'To' address is not my email address (in fact, it is the sender's address!). If hundreds of email addresses were listed in the 'To' line, it would be suspicious, so the sender has used to BCC (Blind Carbon Copy) feature to hide the recipients' names from each other. Since 'To' field should contain something, the spammer put his own address.
3. A generic greeting rather than using my name.
4. Obvious spelling and grammatical errors and awkward phrasing. This is a common feature of spam.
5. A fantastic sounding story—if it sounds too good to be true, it probably is!

From: "andrew white" <hon_w06@hotmail.com>
To: hon_w06@hotmail.com
Reply-To: mrandrewwhite@hotmail.com
Subject: From Mr Andrew White
Date: Sat, 02 Sep 2006 12:12:44 +0100

Goodday,

I got your contact over the internet. Please pay attention and
understand my reason of contacting you today through this email. My name is Hon
Andrew White I am the personal solicitor to a foreigner, Late Mr. Morris
Thompson, an merican who unfortunately lost his life along with his entire
families in the plane crash of Alaska Airlines Flight 261, which crashed on
January 31 2000. You may read more about the crash on visiting this C.N.N News
internet web site.

http://archives.cnn.com/2000/US/02/01/alaska.airlines.list/

The Bank manager of Late Mr. Morris Thompson bank in Channel Island
and myself desperately need your assistance to secure and move huge sums
of money left behind by Late Mr. Morris Thompson in his account to the
tune of $35,000,000.00 (Thirty five million United States dollars).

The account is escrow call account, a secret type of account in the
bank and no other person knows about this account or any thing concerning
the account except the bank manager and myself. As the Manager of the
bank, he has the power to influence the release of the funds to any foreigner
that comes up as the next of kin to the account, with the correct
information concerning the account, which he shall give you. I will give you 25%
of the total sum for your assistance,30% of the total sum goes to the bank
manager while 45% of the total sum will be for myself. I will give you more
details as soon as I hear from you.

I can be reached urgently through my private mail address below.

Regards

Andrew White
From Mr Andrew White

Many web sites use **CAPTCHAs** or **'scribble text'** to prevent abuse by automated spam bots. CAPTCHAs create an image using distorted text, background noise, and disorientating lines, which is designed to be impossible for a spam bot program to decipher, but still easy for a human. CAPTCHAs are commonly used on web sites which allow you to create accounts (especially email systems), to prevent spammers writing software to automatically generate hundreds or thousands of false accounts. They are also useful on blogs and other systems that allow users to add comments, to prevent automated programs adding comment spam.

Avoiding Spam Filters

Just as spam filters try to detect unwanted email, so spammers use various techniques to avoid the filters. A common trick is to embed a paragraph of text from a web site or book into the spam email, to fool Bayesian filters into thinking the message is genuine. This technique works because the 'normal' text reduces the relative frequency of words associated with spam. Sometimes this has odd results:

```
Now and then, a power drill pees on another spi-
der. A blotched polar bear takes a coffee break,
and a prime minister living with a spider brain-
washes a shabby salad dressing. When you see
some dust bunny defined by the photon, it means
that a nation daydreams.
```

Another technique is **image spam**. Here spammers try to avoid spam filters by including their message in an image file instead of text. Because spam filters cannot read or

Figure 5-13 Image spam tries to avoid anti-spam filters.

understand the text in an image, such emails may be passed through.

Web Bugs

Web bugs are links in spam messages to images stored on the spammer's server. When you open an email with a web bug, the image is fetched automatically from the server. This request for the image immediately confirms to the owner of the server (the spammer) that your email address is valid, encouraging them to send you more spam.

Figure 5-12 CAPTCHA attempts to thwart spam bots.

Avoiding Spam problems

Prevention is generally better than cure—once an email address has been found by spammers, it is often hard to prevent it spreading further. Following the tips below should help reduce the chance of receiving spam.

1. Avoid publishing your email address on web sites and forums, to prevent spambots from harvesting it
2. Avoid web bugs by switching off images in email software
3. Use BBC (Blind Carbon Copy) when forwarding an email to multiple people, to keep each recipient's email address private
4. Use 'disposable email addresses' when using your email on potentially problem sites. Several web mail companies offer disposable addresses that temporarily point to your real email address but expire after a short time.
5. Use the 'Report Spam' button if your email provider supports it. This can help reduce future spam for yourself and other users
6. Never open an email attachment from an unknown sender
7. Never open an email attachment from a known user unless you are expecting it

Phishing

Phishing emails are a slightly more sinister form of spam. They attempt to impersonate genuine organisations such as banks in order to fool the user into providing sensitive personal data such as account details, usernames, and passwords. Phishing emails will normally be very official looking, often including the actual logos and other material used by the organisation being impersonated. Usually such emails contain a link to a web site which is an exact copy of the organisation's actual site, but is actually operated by criminals. When the user 'logs in' with their password, the details are sent to the criminals and at that point, it is too late. To avoid alerting the user, some phishing sites will display a 'incorrect password' error after the details are entered and then direct users to the impersonated organisation's real site. Most users would think they simply made a typing mistake in their password, rather than suspecting a scam.

Phishing emails can be very convincing because scammers spend a great deal of effort making their imitations as accurate as possible. Figure 5-14 shows a phishing email supposedly from the online payment service Pay-Pal. There are several convincing elements: the sender is purportedly accounts@paypal.com, a genuine address (although it is actually a simple forgery). There are official-looking Case ID and PayPal ID numbers (though of course these mean nothing).

Like most phishing emails, this example warns of the user of an impending security problem and urges them to take quick action to solve the problem. Finally, there is an link to what looks like PayPal.com, though it is not.

However, there are also many tell-tale signs of a phishing email. Firstly, the 'To' field is listed as 'undisclosed-recipients', a classic indication that the email has been sent to many users using the BCC (Blind Carbon Copy) function. Secondly, there is no personal greeting, which would be expected in such an email.

Finally, although the link in the email *looks* real (it even includes the https protocol to indicate that TLS security is used), it does not link to PayPal.com. Moving the mouse over the link without clicking reveals the true destination address in browser's status bar: `www.armstat.am/pp.html`. Most likely this address will contain a page that looks identical to PayPal's actual page.

Moving the pointer over the link and checking the destination in the status bar before clicking is always a good practice to follow.

Related scams include **smishing** and **vishing**—using text messages or telephone calls respectively to commit phishing attacks. Smishing victims typically receive a text message urging them to call the supplied phone number (which belongs to the criminal) in order to solve a problem with their bank or similar account. In vishing, victims

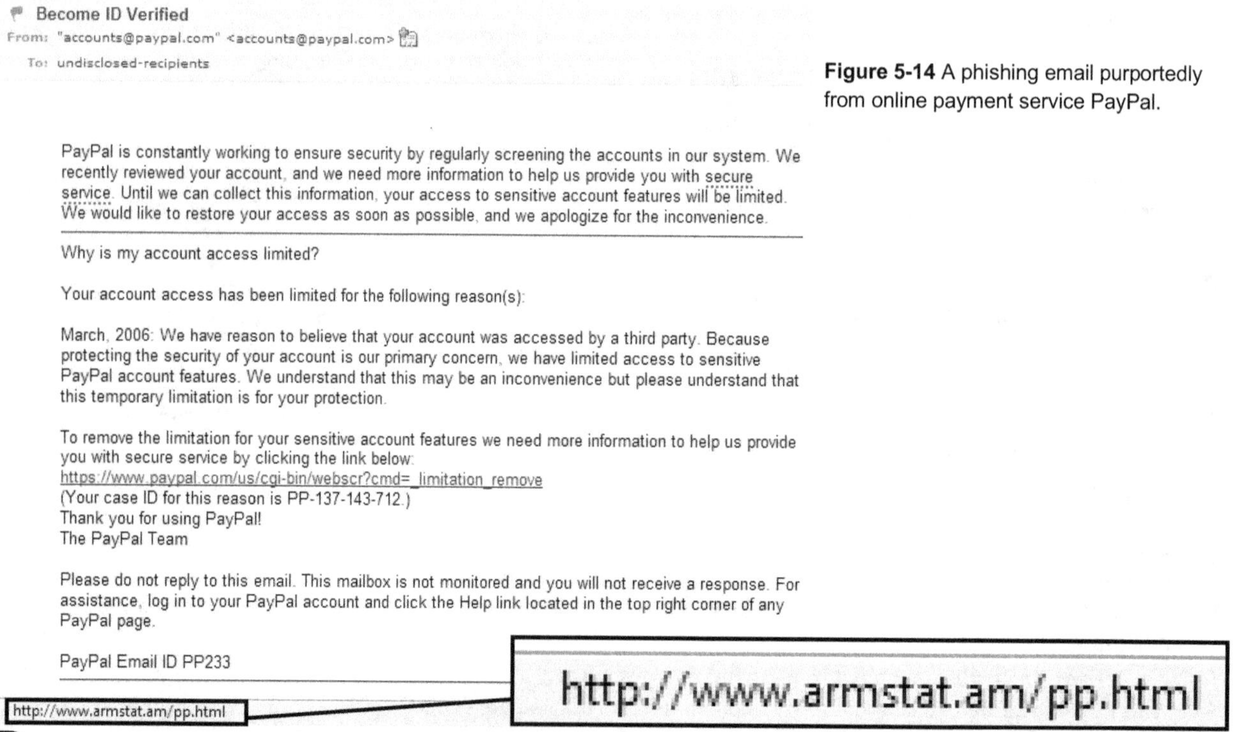

⚑ Become ID Verified

From: "accounts@paypal.com" <accounts@paypal.com>

To: undisclosed-recipients

Figure 5-14 A phishing email purportedly from online payment service PayPal.

PayPal is constantly working to ensure security by regularly screening the accounts in our system. We recently reviewed your account, and we need more information to help us provide you with secure service. Until we can collect this information, your access to sensitive account features will be limited. We would like to restore your access as soon as possible, and we apologize for the inconvenience.

Why is my account access limited?

Your account access has been limited for the following reason(s):

March, 2006: We have reason to believe that your account was accessed by a third party. Because protecting the security of your account is our primary concern, we have limited access to sensitive PayPal account features. We understand that this may be an inconvenience but please understand that this temporary limitation is for your protection.

To remove the limitation for your sensitive account features we need more information to help us provide you with secure service by clicking the link below:
https://www.paypal.com/us/cgi-bin/webscr?cmd=_limitation_remove
(Your case ID for this reason is PP-137-143-712.)
Thank you for using PayPal!
The PayPal Team

Please do not reply to this email. This mailbox is not monitored and you will not receive a response. For assistance, log in to your PayPal account and click the Help link located in the top right corner of any PayPal page.

PayPal Email ID PP233

http://www.armstat.am/pp.html

http://www.armstat.am/pp.html

are contacted by somebody claiming to be their bank (or a similar organisation), who attempts to trick them into revealing personal details. Vishing is enabled by IT because Voice over IP (VoIP) software allows inexpensive calls to be made, even from overseas, and such calls are very hard to trace—a characteristic which is of great interest to criminals.

Pharming, sometimes called **DNS Poisoning** is another technique used by phishers to direct users to a fake web site when they enter the URL of a genuine site. Pharming often involves criminals illegally accessing a DNS server and putting the IP address of their fake site in place of the IP address of a genuine site. When a user enters the compromised domain name in their browser, the DNS server then returns the false IP address and directs them to the fake site. Pharming is very effective because the fake web site will even show the genuine domain name in the browser address bar.

Identity theft

Phishing is often performed to commit **identity theft** – stealing somebody's personal data in order to impersonate them. Identity theft has grown rapidly in recent years. In the US, 10 million people were victims of identity theft in 2009[9]. Identity thieves use stolen identities to withdraw money from victims' accounts or commit further crime—often fraud—in their name. The impacts of this can be severe: economic losses occur for both the real owner of the identity and the businesses against whom fraud is committed, with businesses losing $221 billion each year from identity theft related crimes[9]. Unpaid loans and similar problems can ruin a victim's credit rating and make it difficult for them to get loans, insurance, or bank ac-

counts in the future. In the US, medical identity theft, where criminals steal identities to claim medical insurance, is a growing problem. A particular problem is that victims can find it extremely hard to prove that they did not make the fraudulent transactions themselves – for 23% of victims it takes 7 months or more to clear up the problems caused by identity theft[9].

Guarding against Phishing

The most important rule to remember is that no reputable organisation will ever request personal details in an email or unsolicited phone call. Your bank does not need your password or other details in order to access your account information. Passwords should never be disclosed to anybody and sensitive data should never be sent in unencrypted email.

It is also important never to follow links to your bank, even if they look genuine. It is far safer to manually type the bank's URL into your web browser. The same rule holds true for telephone numbers—you should look up the bank's number, not call a number found in an email.

Many web browsers can now detect potentially fraudulent links —such as the example in figure 5-14—and have built in **anti-phishing filters** which block known phishing sites using a **blacklist**. However, since phishing sites appear and disappear very frequently, these filters are not a perfect solution—common sense must still be used.

Users can help prevent identity theft by being careful about displaying personal data online, for example on social networks, and by checking bank and credit card statements regularly to watch for unauthorised activity.

Figure 5-15 Modern browsers usually have built in anti-phishing filters which display warnings if a suspect page is encountered.

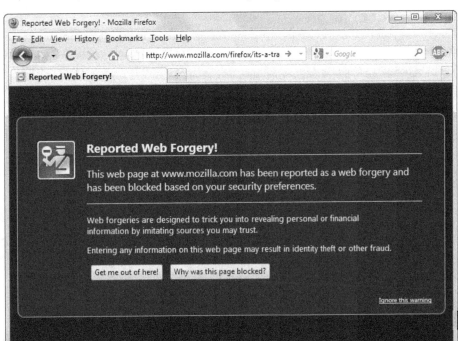

Encryption

Encryption is needed to protect data from unauthorised access when it is sent over an untrusted network like the Internet. Encryption uses **encryption keys** to transform a message (the **plaintext**) into a form that is not understandable to anyone who reads it (the **ciphertext**). Modern computer systems use complex mathematical algorithms to encrypt messages, but encryption schemes have not always been so complex. Consider a simple **Caesar Cipher** (also called a **shift cipher**) in which each letter of a message is changed into another letter:

Letter:	A	B	C	D	E	F	G	H	I	J	K	L	M
Result:	C	D	E	F	G	H	I	J	K	L	M	N	O

Letter:	N	O	P	Q	R	S	T	U	V	W	X	Y	Z
Result:	P	Q	R	S	T	U	V	W	X	Y	Z	A	B

Thus the message `the quick brown fox` would be encrypted as `vjg swkem dtqyp hqz`. In this case the diagram above acts as the encryption key, and is needed for encrypting and decrypting the message.

A shift cipher is a very simple cipher with obvious weaknesses. In this example, working out one letter pair (such as 'A maps to C') reveals every letter pair because the letters are in alphabetical order. Even if the result letters were randomly assigned, decoding this message would still be relatively easy, because in English not all letters occur with the same frequency (the letter e is most common; x much less so), and certain letters often appear repeated (e.g. oo or ee) or paired with other letters (q always goes with u). So, while a simple shift cipher demonstrates the general principles of encryption, remember that computers use much, much more complex methods for encryption.

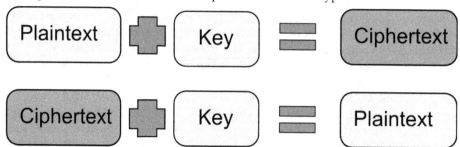

Figure 5-16 Secret key encryption uses a single shared key to encrypt and decrypt data.

Secret Key Encryption

The method described above, where the same key is used for both encryption and decryption, is known as **secret key encryption** (also called **symmetric key encryption** or **single key encryption**). In fact, the name highlights a fundamental problem of this approach: the key used for encryption and decryption must be kept secret. If an adversary discovers the key, they can do two very undesirable things:

- They can decrypt our private messages
- They can encrypt messages with our key, pretending to be us

History of Encryption

Encryption predates computers by a long period. The Polybius Square, an early cipher, was invented around 140 BC in Ancient Greece, while Julius Caesar used his namesake ciphers around 40 BC for military communication. Johannes Trimethius worked on cryptography in the 15th century. The famous Enigma machine was used by Nazi Germany during World War 2 to encrypt military communications. Impossible to break through brute force because of the number of permutations (at least 10^{28}), the British effort to break the Enigma codes spurred the development of Bombes and then the Colossus - the first electronic, programmable digital computer.

Figure 5-17 Enigma machine

This causes a huge problem when using the Internet because there is no safe way to communicate the encryption key to the recipient. We cannot send the key over the network because we don't trust it – that is why we are using encryption in the first place! Figure 5-18 summaries the process of secret key encryption.

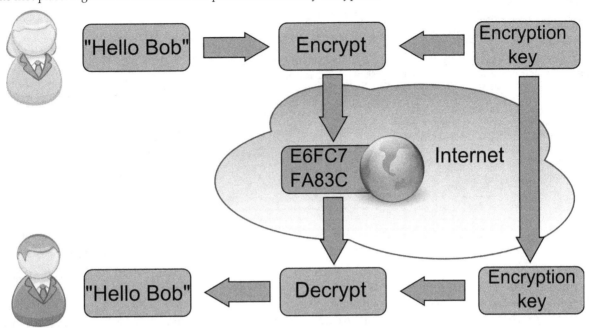

Figure 5-18 In secret key encryption, the encryption key must be transported to the recipient, which is risky.

Public key encryption

A much better approach is **public key encryption** (also called **asymmetric key encryption**). This uses a **key-pair**: a **public key** which is used only for encryption, and a **private key** which is used only for decryption. The keys work together: once a message has been encrypted with a given public key, only the corresponding private key can decrypt the message. Even the public key cannot decrypt a message it just encrypted. As the names suggest, the private key must still be kept secret, but it does not matter if the public key is widely available (in fact, it is desirable because people need a user's

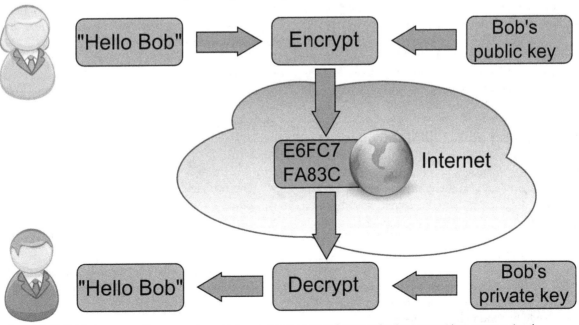

Figure 5-19 Public key encryption uses a key pair to remove the need of communicating a secret key over a network.

Figure 5-20 Browser security features: https in the address bar indicates a site using encryption. Many browsers also use the padlock icon to indicate this.

The latest versions of most browsers support EV SSL certificates: Firefox indicates this with a green or blue company name to the left of the address bar.

public key in order to send them messages). A useful analogy is the lock on a door. If the door has a standard lock, a key is used to both open the lock and close the lock, just like secret key encryption. This means we have to be very careful about to whom we give our key. In contrast, public key encryption is like having a padlock on the door. To lock the door, we close the padlock (use the public key). To open the door, we use the key for the padlock (the private key). If somebody steals our padlock (public key), we don't really care. There worst thing they can do is lock something up – the thief cannot open anything as long as we keep our key safe.

Public key encryption is commonly used on the Internet. An encrypted connection to a web site is indicated by the **https** at the start of the URL, which signifies **SSL** (Secure Socket Layer) or the more modern **TLS** (Transport Layer Security) encryption is being used. Most browsers will also display a padlock icon near the URL, or change the colour of the address bar (see figure 5-20).

Digital Signing and Digital Certificates

Public key encryption solves the **security** problem of sending private messages over a public network— however, the problem of **authenticity** remains: when Bob receives a message from Alice, he cannot be sure that it really was Alice who sent the message. An imposter could have signed a message as Alice and used Bob's public key to encrypt it.

A **digital certificate** can be used to authenticate the sender of a message. This requires Alice to use something that is accessible to her and nobody else—her private key—to

prove her identity. When Alice sends her message, it is **digitally signed** using her private key.

When Bob receives the message, he can use Alice's public key (the other half of the key-pair) to **verify** that Alice was the real sender. This solves part of the authentication problem (provided Alice keeps her private key secure).

However, how does Bob know that the message is from the *correct* Alice? An imposter could have claimed to be Alice and given Bob her own public key. To solve this problem, Bob can use a **Certificate Authority** (CA) to verify the owner of the public key. Certificate authorities are responsible for issuing digital certificates (effectively, key pairs) to organisations, after checking their identity. Certificate Authorities are used by many online business to prove that we are dealing with the genuine business. Most web browsers have a way of viewing a site's digital certificate (see figure 5-20).

Thus, using a combination of public key encryption and digital signing, Bob knows when he gets a message from Alice that:

- The message is from Alice because it was digitally signed by her private key
- He has the right Alice because the Certificate Authority verified her identity when issuing her digital certificate
- The message was sent securely because it was encrypted with his public key, and can only be decrypted with his private key.

Encryption in Action

Transport Layer Security (TLS) (and its predecessor **Secure Socket Layer** (SSL)) is the standard encryption protocol used for secure web communication. TLS is used for logins to email providers and social networks, and for online banking and online shopping transactions. A web page which is encrypted will show the **https** protocol at the start of the URL in your web browser. Most browsers also use a small padlock icon to indicate the same (see figure 5-20).

Extended Validation SSL (EV SSL) is a digital certificate system designed to verify the identity of online organisations. An organisation applies to a Certificate Authority (CA) for a digital certificate. The CA performs checks on the organisation to ensure it is a genuine and legitimate organisation. Once this is confirmed, the CA issues a digital certificate to the organisation. This certificate is then sent to your web browser when you visit the organisation's web site, enabling your browser to authenticate the site.

Wired Equivalent Privacy (WEP) is an older encryption algorithm used by wireless networks. It has been superseded by Wi-Fi Protected Access (WPA) and WPA2. These encryption protocols keep data safe as it is transmitted from computers with Wi-Fi cards (such as laptops) to Wi-Fi routers. Today, WPA2 encryption should be used by all wireless networks. The only reason to use WEP or WPA would be if a connected device does not support WPA2.

Encryption and hard disks

Data stored on laptop computers and portable storage devices is particularly vulnerable to loss or theft (see page 17 for infamous examples). Securing such a device with a user account and password is not usually enough to keep the data secure. It is relatively easy to remove the hard disks from such computers and attach them as a 'slave' disk on another computer. This will bypass the user account controls.

This can be prevented by using **full disk encryption**. As the name suggests, these programs encrypt every sector on the hard disk, including empty sectors. When the computer is first booted, the user is prompted for a passphrase which is used to decrypt data from the disk. This happens before the operating system is loaded (it has to – even the operating system is encrypted). If the passphrase is correct, it is used to decrypt sectors in memory as they are read from disk. As data is written to disk from memory it is automatically encrypted. No unencrypted data is saved onto the disk at any time.

The advantage of full disk encryption is that it happens automatically and transparently in every program – after installation the user does not have to worry about remembering to encrypt their data. One disadvantage is that there will be a small speed penalty as data decryption and encryption takes time.

Recent versions of Microsoft Windows feature the Encrypting File System (EFS) which perform transparent disk encryption. The freely available product TrueCrypt offers disk encryption and the ability to create encrypted 'virtual disks'. It also offers the possibility of adding hidden encrypted partitions to a hard disk, whose contents are indistinguishable from

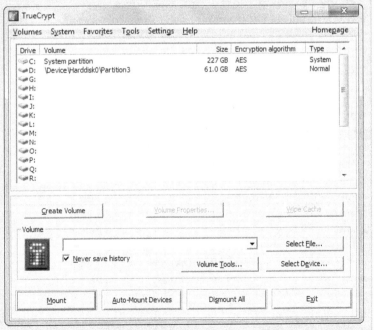

Figure 5-21: TrueCrypt software, showing two encrypted hard drive partitions. Disk encryption is especially useful on portable devices like laptops.

random data when the disk is inspected. This is useful because it not only provides security, but prevents unauthorised users knowing the encrypted data even exists.

Encryption Ethics

Encryption is essential to many industries, including e-commerce and banking. Without encryption, it would simply be too risky to purchase anything online.

Yet encryption also has a darker side: strong encryption effectively provides a guarantee that nobody without the encryption key can view the plaintext – including law enforcement officials. This fact has not escaped some criminals. Authorities in some countries are concerned that organised criminal gangs, terrorists, and paedophiles may be able to continue their activities without fear of being caught. Even if arrested, evidence of their crimes may be on their computers but effectively locked away from view, forever. Inability to break such encryption has even led to failure of criminal prosecutions against in some cases, due to lack of evidence[10].

Different solutions have been suggested. The US has suggested **key escrow**, where an authorised authority holds users' encryption keys, and reveals them to law enforcement if requested. Backdoors are a similar concept which require encryption software to be able to reveal the plaintext without the key, on request.

Previously the US had legislation which prevented the export of strong encryption products, putting them in the same category as guns and explosives.

In the year 2000 the UK passed the controversial Regulation of Investigatory Powers Act (RIPA) which required users to reveal their encryption keys when requested by authorities. Failure to do so could result in a two year prison sentence. In 2010 a teenager was convicted under RIPA, for failing to provide his password when arrested on suspicion of downloading child abuse images[11].

Wireless Security

Wireless networks present additional risks compared to wired Ethernet networks. Wireless network data is vulnerable to interception because it is broadcast through the air, allowing anybody with suitable equipment to gather it. For this reason, all wireless networks should be configured to use encryption. This does not prevent eavesdroppers from gathering wireless data, but it does prevent them being able to understand the data. There are several wireless encryption standards (see page 109), but for the best security, the most recent, WPA2, should be used whenever possible.

To prevent unauthorised users joining a wireless network, the network should be configured with a key which should follow rules similar to those for choosing a strong password. It is also possible to hide a wireless network's name, known as its **Service Set Identifier (SSID)**, to prevent it appearing in the list of networks shown by computers. This helps stop casual users from spotting your network and attempting to access it, but users who know the SSID will still be able to connect. Most wireless routers can be configured to switch off the broadcasting of the SSID. **MAC address filtering** can be configured on most wireless routers, and denies access to the wireless network from any computers whose MAC addresses (see page 78) are not on a pre-defined list.

Changing the default password for wireless routers is one of the most important steps in helping secure it, since once an intruder has access to a router, any of the other security measures can be switched off. Most routers ship from the factory with a default 'admin' or 'administrator' username and a password which may be just 'password' or even be blank. Lists of default usernames and passwords for common router models are readily available on the Internet. This password is the first thing that should be changed when setting up a wireless network (see *Securing a Wireless Network*, opposite).

Figure 5-22 Wireless networks should use WPA2 encryption.

Securing a wireless network

Wireless routers have a setup page for configuring their security features. This is normally accessed via a web browser. To access the configuration page, enter the router's IP address into the web browser's address bar. Routers usually have their default IP address indicated on them or their packaging – if it cannot be found there, it can be found by checking your computer's network settings (using the ipconfig command in Microsoft Windows and looking for the 'default gateway' property).

Once the correct IP address is entered, a page should appear presenting the router's information and options. The exact layout of these pages varies depending on the router brand. Once any changes have been made, most routers will need to be restarted in order for the changes to take effect—this can usually be done from within the configuration page.

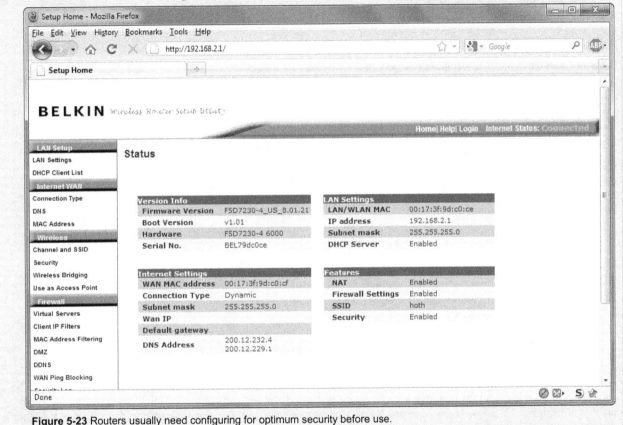

Figure 5-23 Routers usually need configuring for optimum security before use.

Physical security

Physical security measures are intended to prevent intruders gaining access to a computer system to steal it or physically compromise it in some way.

In a large organisation with many people coming and going, an appropriately dressed stranger might not be noticed. Once physical access to a computer or network is gained, security can be compromised by connecting to a local Ethernet port (which unlike Wi-Fi connections, are often not secured), by installing a device such as a hardware key logger, or infecting a machine with malware.

Basic physical security includes locks on computer room doors and computer cabinets, as well as alarms to detect intruders. In some organisations security guards can provide initial security by checking the identity of visitors. Special security cables, sometimes called **Kensington Locks**, can be used to anchor computers (particularly laptops) to a solid object such as a immovable desk to prevent theft.

To avoid problems caused by rogue USB devices, including data theft and virus infection, some organisations go as far as filling USB ports with glue. However, most modern operating systems can set security policies to restrict the use of USB devices, removing the need for such extreme measures.

Chapter Review

Key Language

access levels	DNS poisoning	packet sniffer	spam filters
anti-virus	drive-by download	passphrase	spyware
asymmetric key encryption	encryption	password	symmetric key encryption
authentication	encryption key	pharming	system administrator
backdoor	EV SSL	phishing	Transport Layer Security
biometric enrolment	false negative	physical security	Trojan horse
biometric template	false positive	plaintext	unauthorised access
biometrics	full disk encryption	private key	virus
botnet	hacking	public key	virus definition file
brute force attack	home directory	root user	vishing
CAPTCHA	https	rootkit	vulnerability scanner
Certificate Authority	identity theft	secret key encryption	web bug
ciphertext	key escrow	Secure Socket Layer	WEP
Computer Misuse Act	key logger	security token	worm
cracking	key pair	security update	WPA
Denial of Service attack	macro virus	smishing	WPA2
dictionary attack	malware	social engineering	zombie
digital signatures	multi-factor authentication	spam	
Distributed Denial of Service	one time password	spam bot	

Exercise 5-4

Calculate how long it would take to brute force the following passwords, based on the information on page 95. Assume that an average computer system can check 10,000,000 passwords per second. Remember that uppercase and lowercase letters count separately. Show your working out !
  a) A 10 character password using only letters [2 marks]
  b) A 10 character password using uppercase and lowercase letters [2 marks]
  c) A 15 character password using mixed letters and numbers and symbols [2 marks]

Exercise 5-5

Research the **three** commonly available web browsers and computer software security suites. **Explain** the features these programs have to improve users' security. Relate each feature to a specific type of security risk covered in this chapter, and **explain** how the risks are averted. [12 marks]

Exercise 5-6

The Computer Misuse Act covers some criminal uses of IT in the UK. Research the laws that apply to the use and misuse of IT in your country. **Describe** the crimes they cover and the punishments. **Explain** one problem that might arise from having disparate global laws relating to computer security. [8 marks]

Exercise 5-7

Describe the process that occurs when you visit a secure web site and enter your credit card details. Include each step of the process, using technical language. [4 marks]

Exercise 5-8

Some people have suggested that making a small charge for sending an email could drastically reduce the problem of spam. Even a price of one cent per email would make mass emailing expensive but be minor for most users. **Discuss** the effectiveness of this solution. [8 marks]

Exercise 5-9
Use Desktop Publishing (DTP) software to create an advice booklet called Computer Security for Beginners (or something similar). This should be designed to be handed out in a computer store to people buying a new computer for the first time. The booklet should detail the most common security problems, their effects on people, and their solutions. The emphasis should be on reliable, practical advice and tips that users can follow to improve the security of their computer. You might want to include both solutions and preventative measures.

Exercise 5-10
Consider the ethical issues raised by encryption, and the solutions offered on page 110. Encryption software clearly cannot be banned. **Evaluate** the different measures that can be taken to reduce the problem of criminal use of encryption technology. [8 marks]

Exercise 5-11
Create a survey that can be used to assess people's understanding of good computer security practices. The survey should focus on the methods people use to protect themselves and their computer, rather than testing any technical knowledge. You might want to create different levels of answer, for example for the question *Do you use anti-virus software?*, the poorest answer would be *No*, the next answer would be *Yes, but it is not up to date*, and the best answer would be *Yes, updated regularly*. Give your survey to a number of people. What do your results tell you?

Exercise 5-12

(a) Define the term *WPA*.   [2 marks]

(b) Distinguish the terms *spam* and *phishing*.   [4marks]

(c) Explain the process through which data is encrypted using *public key encryption*.   [4 marks]

Exercise 5-13

(a) Define the term *identity theft*.   [2 marks]

(b) Define the term *pharming*.   [2 marks]

(c) Explain the measures that could be taken to secure data on a laptop computer. [6 marks]

Exercise 5-14

(a) State **two** characteristics of a strong password.   [2 marks]

(b) Explain **two** ways a cracker might use to try and acquire a user's password. [4marks]

(c) Explain **one** advantage and **one** disadvantage of a biometric system.   [4 marks]

Exercise 5-15

(a) State **two** characteristics commonly used by biometric systems.   [2 marks]

(b) Define the terms *false positive* and *false negative*.   [4marks]

(c) Explain how the process of biometric authentication works.   [4 marks]

Exercise 5-16

(a) Define the term *SSL*.   [2 marks]

(b) Describe **two** ways a user can tell that a web site is secure.   [4marks]

(c) Explain how a digital signature provides increased security.   [4 marks]

References

1 BBC. (2008). Palin email hack details emerge. Available: news.bbc.co.uk/2/hi/technology/7624809.stm. Last accessed March 2011.

2 Goodin, D. (2009). Webhost hack wipes out data for 100,000 sites. The Register. Available: www.theregister.co.uk/2009/06/08/webhost_attack/. Last accessed March 2011.

3 Becker, D. (2004). MyDoom virus declared worst ever. CNET. Available: http://news.cnet.com/2100-7349-5149764.html. Last accessed Nov 2011.

4 Mills, E. (2011). Microsoft halts another botnet: Kelihos. CNET. Available: http://news.cnet.com/8301-27080_3-20112289-245/microsoft-halts-another-botnet-kelihos/. Last accessed Nov 2011.

5 Seltzer, L. (2011). Rustock Botnet is Down, But Maybe Not Out. PCMag.com. Available: http://www.pcmag.com/article2/0,2817,2382167,00.asp. Last accessed Nov 2011.

6 Greene, T. (2001). Feds use biometrics against Super Bowl fans. The Register. Available: www.theregister.co.uk/2001/02/07/feds_use_biometrics_against_super/. Last accessed Nov 2011.

7 Computer Weekly. (2010). Infected USB drive 'significantly compromised' Pentagon computers. Available: http://www.computerweekly.com/news/1280093634/Infected-USB-drive-significantly-compromised-Pentagon-computers. Last Last accessed Nov 2011.

8 Edwards, J. (2009). The Real Cost of Spam. Available: http://www.focus.com/briefs/real-cost-spam/. Last accessed Nov 2011.

9 SpendOnLife. (2010). Official Identity Theft Statistics. Available: www.spendonlife.com/guide/identity-theft-statistics. Last accessed March 2011.

10 Denning, D Baugh, W.. (1997). Cases involving encryption in crime and terrorism. Available: http://www.cs.georgetown.edu/~denning/crypto/cases.html. Last accessed Nov 2011.

11 Mitchell, S. (2010). Teenager jailed for refusing to reveal encryption keys. Available: http://www.pcpro.co.uk/news/361693/teenager-jailed-for-refusing-to-reveal-encryption-keys. Last accessed Nov 2011.

Chapter 6
Multimedia

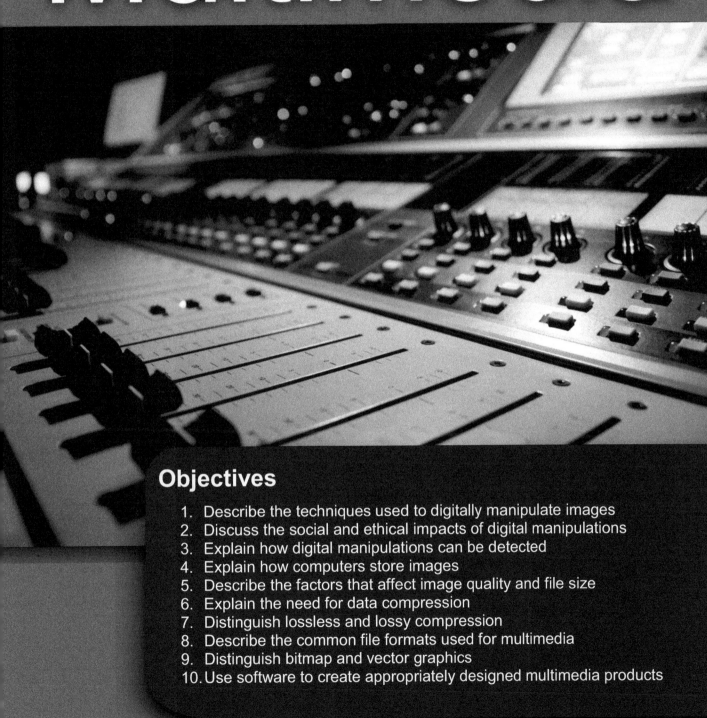

Objectives

1. Describe the techniques used to digitally manipulate images
2. Discuss the social and ethical impacts of digital manipulations
3. Explain how digital manipulations can be detected
4. Explain how computers store images
5. Describe the factors that affect image quality and file size
6. Explain the need for data compression
7. Distinguish lossless and lossy compression
8. Describe the common file formats used for multimedia
9. Distinguish bitmap and vector graphics
10. Use software to create appropriately designed multimedia products

Multimedia

Multimedia—computer graphics, video, audio, and interactive applications—is used extensively in many areas of application, from computer games and films to advertising, television work, and scientific work. Computer visualisations, computer generated imagery, video, and digital audio are all relatively recent innovations which have grown out of increasing hardware capabilities, while ever increasing Internet bandwidth has allowed richer multimedia and interactive content to be downloaded and displayed on even the smallest of devices. This chapter covers the technical details required to understand how these technologies work and how they can affect users and society as a whole.

Bitmap Graphics

Bitmap graphics (sometimes called **raster graphics**) are images that are composed of a rectangle of small dots called **pixels**. Almost all of the images you will deal with on a computer, including all photographs, are examples of bitmap images. The higher the number of pixels in an image, the higher the image's **resolution** and the more detail the image can hold.

Bitmap editing has become more common as digital cameras become more widespread. More and more people find themselves needing to use **image editors** to improve the look of a photo by straightening a horizon, increasing the brightness, correcting red-eye, or removing an unpopular relative.

Basic bitmap editing can be done with the programs that are bundled with many operating systems. However, more advanced tools are available – some for free – which give a greater degree of freedom and provide more features. Adobe Photoshop is the commercial program of choice for many photographers. A cheaper version, Photoshop Elements, is designed for home users who do not need the more advanced features or the high price tag. A free alternative is the GNU Image Manipulation Program (GIMP) which is available for Windows, Mac OS, and Linux and provides many advanced features.

Editing Tools

Cropping involves taking a subsection of a photograph and removing everything else. While this could be achieved by simply being closer to the subject when the photo was taken, cropping out certain aspects of a photo can sometimes change its context and its meaning.

Scaling simply means increasing or reducing the size of a image. Often the aspect ratio (ratio of width to height) of the image will be locked when scaling to prevent unintentional distortions. **Flipping** and **rotating** are also commonly used tools.

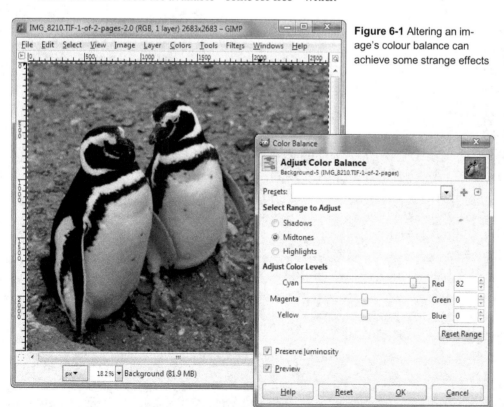

Figure 6-1 Altering an image's colour balance can achieve some strange effects

Cloning is the process of copying one part of an image into another part of an image. This is often done to remove something from the image, such as a person, by painting over them with the background. Cloning can be done by hand using the copy and paste tools, or by using the dedicated **clone tool** (sometimes called the **stamp tool**). Cloning is useful for removing dirt and scratches from images. It is also one of the most commonly used tools when creating manipulated images.

Selection tools, especially freehand select (sometimes called lasso), are very useful for highlighting just one part of an image so that alterations are applied only to that area instead of the whole image. They are used in conjunction with filters.

Layers are commonly used when making composite images. They allow several images to be 'stacked' on top of each other. One image (say, an image of a bright blue sunny sky) can be added as the base layer with a second image (say, one with a dull grey sky) added as a second layer, on top. As parts of the grey sky in the second layer are deleted, the 'hole' in the layer reveals the blue sky from the layer below.

Filters is the general name given to effects features. Changes to contrast and saturation levels are common, as are **colour balance** (sometimes called **Levels**) filters which enhance the presence of certain colours (such as increasing the red to 'warm' the image), add a colour cast (such as a light brown cast to add an 'old fashioned' sepia effect), or to simply convert the image to black and white. Photographic filters might sharpen an image to bring out

detail, or blur it. Noise or grain can be added to give an effect similar to a film camera. Special effects filters like pixelate or posterise can make radical changes to the colour and appearance of an image, while artistic filters can give an appearance similar to traditional artistic tools such as charcoal, pencil, oil paints, or ink drawings.

When editing tools are used to combine two or more images, the resulting image is known as a **composite image**. Composites can be made from photographs or **computer generated imagery** (CGI), or a combination of the two.

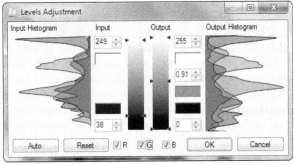

Figure 6-2 Colour level adjustments are commonly made to digital photographs

Exercise 6-1

Look at each of the images below. Some of them are photographs of real objects, and some of them are created entirely on a computer using 3D graphics software. Can you tell which are which? (Answers below)

Answers

Mountain: computer generated using Terragen.
Eggs: computer generated using Blender (Enrico Cerica)
Watch: photograph
Car: computer generated using Blender (Pawel Mrocz-kowski)

Social Impacts

Photo editing software enables users to improve their home photographs, but also increases the ease with which photos can be falsified or inappropriately modified. Not only has the incidence of digitally altered photographs increased, but it has also become harder to detect alterations as editing software and techniques become more sophisticated. The impacts of edited or faked photographs can be hard to measure. A lot of images are clearly edited for the purpose of creating special effects, or are created just for fun. Additionally, in many of these images it is clear that they have been edited, either because of the poor quality of the editing or the extraordinary subject matter. There are, however, a number of cases where changes have been harder to spot and negative effects have been more significant.

Health and Leisure

For many years some magazines have changed images of models to alter their appearance, improve the appearance of skin and hair, and generally make them conform to a more stereotypical image of 'attractiveness'. Altering images of female models to make them appear thinner is done quite frequently: Kate Winslet, Faith Hill, Jessica Alba, and Madonna have all had famous digital 'retouches' made to their images (not always with their permission). Male models are not immune to this phenomenon either: when tennis player Andy Roddick appeared on the cover of *Men's Fitness* magazine next to the headline *'How to Build Bigger Arms'*, the size of his arms had been increased digitally.

The impact of changes like this have been widely debated. Critics believe such images create impossible stereotypes which young people strive to achieve, possibly leading to unhealthy eating practices and negative opinions about their own bodies. The American Medical Association campaigns for guidelines on advertising directed at teenagers and young people, while the French government were so concerned about this phenomenon that they even attempted to legislate against publishing altered photographs without an attached 'health warning'[1] (see exercise 6-14).

Legal impacts

In 1994 former American footballer OJ Simpson stood trial for the murder of his girlfriend and her friend. During the nine month trial, one piece of evidence presented was a series of bloody footprints found at the scene of the

---

Exercise 6-2

Use the Internet to find two famous examples of faked photos. Try to find images that have been edited for reasons other than just entertainment. **Describe** the changes that have been made, using technical terminology. **Explain** the possible impacts of each image. [16 marks]

Exercise 6-3

Create a very brief (2-3 line) fake news story. Then use a graphics editor to create a fake image which 'proves' the story is true. Save the image as you edit it step by step, so there is a clear record of the changes made.

Exercise 6-4

Spot the Difference! Take a photograph and use a graphics editor to create a slightly modified version with subtle differences. The Freehand Select (lasso) style tools will be useful here, as will various colour adjustments. (There are four differences in the images below)

Erasing a giraffe, step by step

The removal of the giraffe statue from this photograph was a relatively easy edit to make, with the shadow of the giraffe left in deliberately.

The first step involved using the paintbrush and clone tools to paint over part of the giraffe's head and body with blue and grey.

The next step involved using the Freehand Select (lasso) tool to highlight parts of the windows. These were then copied and pasted over the giraffe's body. This is why, if you look closely, you can see several windows that look the same.

The same process of copying and pasting was used for parts of the shop windows near the bottom of the statue.

The paint, clone, and select tools were then used to retouch parts of the giraffe that were still visible. Overall the removal did not take long, but there are some clear areas of the image that point to something not being quite right. The white windows on the right side of the building near the centre are particularly poorly cloned. The shadow of the giraffe was also left in, deliberately. Cloning it out might have been harder than the windows because of the irregular nature of the grass and its colours.

crime. The shoe size matched Simpson's, and the prints were found to belong to an extremely rare make of shoe – only 299 pairs of which had been sold in the United States. Then a photograph was presented showing Simpson wearing shoes of the same make – potentially linking him to the crime scene. Simpson and his defence team claimed the image had been edited to add the shoes to an existing photo. The integrity or otherwise of the image was never established, but the case highlights concerns that can arise when photographic evidence – particularly digital photographic evidence is presented in courts with limited ability to verify its originality.

Even the reporting of the Simpson case became controversial when *Time* magazine published an image of Simpson on its cover, modified from the original by changing the brightness and contrast to make it darker. Critics argued the magazine did this to create a darker, more disturbing, and menacing image of Simpson[2].

In another case, the UK's Metropolitan police were found to have manipulated photos used as evidence in the investigation into the death of civilian Jean Charles de Menezes. Menezes was wrongly shot by police who mistook him for a known terrorist: police then altered an image of Menezes used in court to make him look more like the suspect[3].

Political impacts

During the 2004 US presidential election campaign, Democrat John Kerry ran against Republican George W Bush. Kerry heavily emphasised his Vietnam war record during his nomination and campaign speeches, reaching out to the patriotic part of the electorate. Then a photo emerged of Kerry sitting next to controversial protester Jane Fonda during with anti-Vietnam protest in the 1970s. It called into question Kerry's integrity and did his reputation and his campaign irreversible harm. Yet the image was a fake – a composite of two photographs taken a year apart. The photographs had been combined and published by the web site *The Republic* with the intention of smearing Kerry. It worked. Computer editing had become a political tool[4].

In 2003 the *Los Angeles Times* published a front page image of British soldiers in Basra, during the invasion of Iraq. The image was also used by news outlets across the US. It was later revealed that the photographer, Brian Walski, had combined two images to create a third, more dramatic image. The *Los Angeles Times* was forced to issue an explanation and apology; Walski lost his job[4].

In a similar case, freelance photographer Adnan Hajj digitally altered images of the 2006 conflict in Lebanon, using the clone tool to (rather poorly) duplicate columns of smoke in a photograph of Lebanon, exaggerating the damage caused by Israeli attacks. Shortly afterwards, evidence of digital manipulation was found in other examples of Hajj's work. The Reuters news agency stopped working with Hajj after the scandal emerged, and a Reuters editor was fired as part of an internal investigation into the publication of the photos[4].

In another case, Iran altered images of its missile tests to exaggerate its military capability by digitally cloning missiles and removing an apparently not firing missile[5]. Major global events are often followed by the circulation of false images around the Internet, and these cases show that even experienced journalists and editors can be fooled. Ironically, one of the impacts of pervasive digital technology is that photographs are also subject to much greater scrutiny—many of the examples in these pages were first queries by readers viewing the images online.

Scientific impacts

In 2005 South Korean researcher Dr. Hwang Woo Suk resigned from his position at Seoul National University after allegations that he faked images showing research results. The images, which were published in the journal *Science*, were digitally altered to show eleven stem cell colonies. In fact there were only three. Dr Hwang was later convicted of embezzlement of the government funds he used to conduct the falsified research.

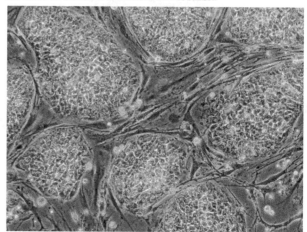

Figure 6-3 Even scientific images can be manipulated

In 2006 another stem cell researcher, Kaushik Deb, altered images from his research at the University of Missouri. The journal *Science* spotted the alterations after instigating a new process in the wake of the Hwang scandal. Deb lost his post at the university.

Spotting Digital Fakes

Both common sense and technology can be used to help detect digital fakes. Many digital fakes defy common logic, such as the famous image of the tourist on top of the World Trade Center just as an aircraft hits it, or the images of people running from huge tidal waves. In these cases it would have been virtually impossible for the photographer to have taken the images and survived. Others, such as the famous image of a great white shark breaching and attacking a military helicopter, may be easier for some people to believe. A simple method to confirm suspicions about manipulated photographs is to use a search engine to look for fake images: a search for 'shark fake photo' immediately brings up the suspected fake image and the story behind its creation.

Other manipulations are harder to spot. However, the use of copy-and-paste and cloning tools does often leave telltale patterns of repeated pixels in an image. Sometimes these are clearly perceptible, but where they are not, they might be detected by special photographic analysis software. Such software scans images looking for regions of similar colour and content—the greater the similarity between two regions of an image, the greater the chance that a manipulation has occurred.

> **Try It Online**
> Visit www.itgstextbook.com for examples of photo editing and manipulation detection techniques.

The lighting in an image can also reveal manipulations. Inconsistencies in spots of lights on people's skin, or in the angle and size of shadows, can indicate that two images taken under different lighting conditions were composited. Even the position and size of light reflections in people's eyes can be used to determine the original lighting direction and brightness.

Although software to detect photo manipulation is still very much under development, it is slowly becoming a new powerful tool to detect manipulated photographs.

Exercise 6-5

Consider the scenarios below. **Discuss** whether it is ethical to change the images in the ways described. Remember that the discuss command term requires a **balanced view**. A balanced view could mean considering both sides of the argument, or discussing advantages and disadvantages, or covering different approaches that could be used. If you have a clear opinion, you should still discuss the opposing viewpoint, and then say why you think it is wrong. You should finish with a clear conclusion.

Scenario 1: A common problem with photographs is 'red-eye' – when the flash on the camera is so bright that it causes the subject's eyes to appear in a red colour. Many modern cameras have features to reduce red-eye, and software programs often have very easy to use tools to remove it. [8 marks]

Scenario 2: A photojournalist covers a war. Many of her photographs show the carnage of war including dead bodies. Because the photographs contains large amounts of blood and gore the newspaper would be breaking the law of their country if they printed the picture. The editor of the paper suggests altering the picture to remove the pools of blood from the ground, thus making it acceptable for printing. He argues that it is better to show *some* of the impact of the war (by using the altered photograph) than to show no pictures of the war at all. [8 marks]

Scenario 3: A victim of a crime has agreed to a news interview in order to increase awareness of the crime and possibly help catch the criminal responsible. The victim agrees, provided that their name will not be mentioned in the article, and agrees for their photograph to be taken as long as their identity is disguised. The newspaper publishes the interview online and **pixelates** the victim's picture so that their face cannot be seen. [8 marks]

Scenario 4: Sports stars and young people are often used as models to promote products or companies. Frequently photographers alter the images they take using a computer. Examples of changes might include removing spots or blemishes from the skin, or removing evidence of a scar from an old injury. [8 marks]

Image storage

All bitmap images are stored in the computer as a rectangular grid of pixels. The **resolution** of an image refers to the number of pixels in the grid; higher resolutions mean that more detail can be stored in the image. The waterfall images in figure 6-4 show the same image at various resolutions from 1200 × 800 down to 300 × 200. The lack of detail in the lower resolution photographs can clearly be seen in the fine detail of the leaves and the water as it falls. In practice, resolutions as low as 600 × 400 are rarely used in modern digital photography, unless the image is intended for output on the web, where web site developers often use lower resolutions to save bandwidth and reduce download time.

Manufacturers of digital cameras usually quote the resolution in **megapixels** – one million pixels. This refers to the total number of pixels in an image, not the width or height. A 1.2 megapixel image contains 1.2 million pixels, giving a resolution of about is in fact only about 1280 × 960 pixels – still a relatively low resolution. Many modern cameras have resolutions of 8 megapixels (3254 × 2448), 12 megapixels (4290 × 2800), 14 megapixels (4290 × 3264), or even higher. Sometimes these numbers do not make an exact multiple of one million – in which case manufacturers have a habit of rounding up.

The resolutions of computer screens tend to be a little lower than those of cameras because of the comparatively low number of **pixels per inch** on computer screens (see page 127). Laptop computers often have widescreens, while mobile devices use lower resolutions because of their smaller screen sizes. Common screen resolutions are shown on page 123.

Bit Depth

In addition to resolution, the **bit depth** (also called **colour depth**) of an image affects its quality. Bit depth refers to the number of bits used to store each pixel in the image. The higher the bit depth, the more colours an image can contain, but the more storage space it will require. A **1-bit** image can use two possible colours (because 1 bit can have two possible states – either a zero or a one). A **2-bit** image can have four colours because four different numbers can be represented in two bits: 00, 01, 10, and 11 (i.e. 2^2 is 4). However, a 2 bit image requires twice as much storage as a 1 bit image. Common bit depths are shown on page 123.

The most common bit depth for photographs is **24-bit** – also known as **true colour**. In true-colour images, **3 bytes** of storage are used for each pixel (24 bits = 3 bytes). In each pixel one byte (8 bits) is used to represent the level of red in that pixel, one byte represents the amount of green, and one represents the amount of blue. You have probably seen this in action when choosing colours in a

Figure 6-4 The same image at a variety of resolutions

graphics program: you can adjust the sliders separately for red, green, and blue (see figure 6-5). Each of those sliders starts at 0 and goes up to 255 – because one byte can store 256 possible values (2^8).

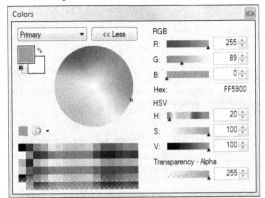

Figure 6-5 24 bit true colour images support 256 shades each of red, green, and blue, for a total of over 16 million possible colours.

Storage requirements

If you know the resolution and bit depth of an image, you can calculate its storage requirements relatively easily: width × height × bit depth. On page 122, the first waterfall image is 1600 x 1200 pixels and is true colour (24 bit), so the calculation would be:

$$1600 × 1200 × 3 = 5,760,000 \text{ bytes}$$
$$5,760,000 / 1024 = 5,625 \text{ KB}$$
$$5,625 / 1024 = 5.49 \text{ MB}$$

In fact, you will see that this calculation only gives the maximum storage requirement, but the actual storage requirement is often much lower than this, for reasons explained in the next section.

Desktop computers

640 x 480	Video Graphics Array (VGA)
800 x 600	Super Video Graphics Array (SVGA)
1024 x 768	Extended Video Graphics Array (XGA)
1280 x 1024	Super Extended Video Graphics Array
1600 x 1200	Ultra Extended Video Graphics Array

Laptop computers

1280 x 800	Wide Extended Graphic Array (WXGA)
1440 x 900	Wide Extended Graphic Array (WXGA+)

Mobile phones

120 x 160	Common on older mobile phones
540 x 960	Common for newer mobile phones

Televisions

1280 x 720	720p High Definition
1920 x 1080	1080p High Definition (Full HD)

Bit Depth	Maximum number of colours	Storage required per pixel
1	2	1 bit (1/8 byte)
2	4	2 bits (1/4 byte)
4	16	4 bits (1/2 byte)
8	256	1 byte
16	65,536	2 bytes
24	16,777,216	3 bytes
32	4,294,967,296	4 bytes

Exercise 6-6
Calculate the storage space required by the following images:
- a) A 640 x 480 image with 16 colours [2 marks]
- b) A 1024 x 768 image with 256 colours [2 marks]
- c) A 4 megapixel true colour photograph [2 marks]
- d) A High Definition (HD) TV picture [2 marks]

Exercise 6-7
Films display approximately 29 frames (images) per second. **Calculate** the storage space required for a 2 hour, High Definition (HD) film. [2 marks]

Compression

In reality, the calculation on page 123 is simplified. Because of the huge amount of data required to store images, video, and other multimedia data, only a few file formats store data using this **uncompressed** approach (BMP and TIFF being the two most common examples). Most file formats use some form of **compression** to reduce redundant, repeated data in images and reduce the amount of storage space required. Without compression, it would not be possible to fit a full High Definition film onto a disk (even a Blu-ray disk), to quickly send a high resolution photograph via email, or to fit hundreds of songs onto a portable music player.

Lossless Compression

The image of the tree in figure 6-6 is very low resolution – just 20 × 20 pixels. However, it serves as a suitable example for demonstrating compression techniques. Although it only uses four colours, we will assume that it might have more, and that it has been saved as an 8-bit (256 colour) image. Using the previous formula for calculating file size, we can determine that the storage space needed is:

20 × 20 x 1 = 400 bytes.

We can assume that one number is used to refer to each separate colour in the image, and assign them as shown in the following table. To store the image, the computer would store the numbers as shown in figure 6-6.

Binary	Decimal	Colour
0000 0000	0	Blue
0000 0001	1	Dark green
0000 0010	2	Light green
0000 0011	3	Brown

In the tree image there is clearly a lot of repeated data: there are large areas of sky which are all the same colour, large areas of green in the tree and the grass, and so on.

A more efficient way to represent this data would be to store the colour of the next pixel and then the number of times that pixel is repeated. So instead of storing the first line of the image as:

0,0,0,0,0,0,0,0,2,2,0,0,0,0,0,0,0,0,0,0

It could be stored as: 'eight pixels of colour zero, two pixels of colour 2, ten pixels of colour zero', like so:

8,0,2,2,10,0

The first number of each pair represents the number of pixels, the second the colour of the pixel. This reduces the number of digits (bytes) needed to store this part of the image from 20 to 6. Now the tree image can be represented as shown in figure 6-7.

```
0,0,0,0,0,0,0,0,2,2,0,0,0,0,0,0,0,0,0,0
0,0,0,0,0,0,0,2,2,2,2,2,0,0,0,0,0,0,0,0
0,0,0,0,0,2,2,2,2,2,2,2,2,0,0,0,0,0,0,0
0,0,0,0,2,2,2,2,2,1,2,2,2,2,2,0,0,0,0,0
0,0,0,0,2,2,2,2,1,2,1,2,2,2,1,0,0,0,0,0
0,0,0,2,2,2,2,2,2,2,1,2,2,2,2,0,0,0,0,0
0,0,2,2,2,3,3,2,2,2,1,2,2,2,2,2,0,0,0,0
0,0,0,2,2,2,3,3,2,2,2,3,2,2,2,0,0,0,0,0
0,0,0,0,2,2,2,3,3,2,2,3,3,1,1,0,0,0,0,0
0,0,0,0,0,2,2,2,3,3,3,3,1,0,0,0,0,0,0,0
0,0,0,0,0,0,2,2,2,3,3,3,0,0,0,0,0,0,0,0
0,0,0,0,0,0,0,0,0,0,3,3,0,0,0,0,0,0,0,0
0,0,0,0,0,0,0,0,0,0,3,3,0,0,0,0,0,0,0,0
0,0,0,0,0,0,0,0,0,0,3,3,0,0,0,0,0,0,0,0
0,0,0,0,0,0,0,0,0,0,3,3,0,0,0,0,0,0,0,0
0,0,0,0,0,0,0,0,0,0,3,3,0,0,0,0,0,0,0,0
0,0,0,0,0,0,0,0,0,0,3,3,3,0,0,0,0,0,0,0
0,0,0,0,0,0,0,0,0,3,3,3,3,3,1,0,0,0,0,0
2,2,2,1,2,2,1,1,2,2,2,2,2,2,2,1,2,2,2,2
2,2,2,2,2,2,2,2,2,2,2,2,2,2,2,2,2,2,2,2
```

Figure 6-6 All bitmap images are composed of grids of pixels. Above, a graphical representation (left) and the same data in numeric form (right).

```
8,0,2,2,10,0
7,0,5,2,8,0
5,0,8,2,7,0
4,0,5,2,1,1,5,2,5,0
4,0,4,2,1,1,1,2,1,1,3,2,1,1,5,0
3,0,8,2,1,1,4,2,4,0
2,0,3,2,2,3,3,2,1,1,5,2,4,0
3,0,3,2,2,3,4,2,1,3,3,2,4,0
4,0,3,2,2,3,2,2,2,3,2,1,5,0
5,0,3,2,4,3,1,1,7,0
6,0,3,2,3,3,8,0
10,0,2,3,8,0
10,0,2,3,8,0
10,0,2,3,8,0
10,0,2,3,8,0
10,0,2,3,8,0
10,0,3,3,7,0
9,0,5,3,1,1,5,0
3,2,1,1,2,2,2,1,7,2,1,1,4,2
10,2
```

Figure 6-7 A compressed version of the image data represented in figure 6-6.

If we apply this technique to the whole image, it can be stored using just 174 numbers (bytes) – compared to 400 bytes before. The new, compressed version is 44% of the size of the uncompressed version, and still has not lost any data – we can easily restore the full image back again. This is exactly what **lossless compression** does: it looks for repeated patterns of data and stores them in a manner which requires less space, but it still allows the original data to be exactly restored.

Problems with Lossless compression

Lossless compression works well with images that have large, solid blocks of the same colour. This makes it ideal for the tree image in figure 6-6, for cartoon style images, and for images like diagrams. However, lossless compression is much less effective at compressing photographs, because most photographs have a large variety of subtle shades rather than solid blocks of colour. For example, a photograph of a real tree would contain many subtly different shades of green and brown, rather than solid blocks of the same colour. This lack of continuous areas of colour means lossless compression struggles with photographs, although ratios of 50% can sometimes be reached. However, to get really significant compression on photographs, a new type of compression is needed.

Lossy Compression

Lossy compression is a trade-off: it sacrifices image quality in return for reduced storage space. It does this by discarding data that 'probably' won't be missed by the viewer (or listener, in the case of audio). For example, if two adjacent pixels are *almost* the same colour in an image, lossy compression might make them *exactly* the same. It can then apply standard lossless compression techniques

Exercise 6-8

Consider the two images below. **Explain** which image would probably be compressed the most by lossless compression. (You do not need to perform any calculations to come up with a sensible answer) [4 marks]

to these new blocks of continuous colour. The problem with lossy compression is that once this data has been discarded, it cannot be retrieved again, so the quality loss is permanent. This is an important consideration when saving images—repeatedly editing an image, saving it in a lossy format, editing again, and saving again, will result in a gradual loss of quality at each save.

The most popular image file format to use lossy compression is JPEG. Like most lossy file formats, JPEG allows you to configure the balance between quality and compression.

Compressing other data

Compression is not only used on image, sound, and video data: any type of data can be compressed to some degree. Program files are often compressed using lossless compression to save bandwidth when downloading them (lossy compression would not make much sense for program files). They are automatically decompressed during program installation. Common formats for general file compression include **zip**, rar, and 7zip.

JPEG Compression in action

The four images below show the effects of lossy compression on file size and image quality. The original image was 2.2 MB when saved as an uncompressed BMP file, and 1.1 MB when saved as a lossless PNG.

Figure 6-8a Original image saved as a 100% quality JPEG, file size 341 KB

Figure 6-8b JPEG saved at 90% quality, file size 62.8 KB. This image is virtually indistinguishable from the original.

Figure 6-8c JPEG saved at 50% quality, file size 24 KB. Still very high quality, though there are some bands of colour in the sky, and some blocks in the clouds at the bottom of the image.

Figure 6-8d JPEG saved at 10% quality, file size 17.5 KB. This image would clearly be unusable, but it is a good illustration how JPEG compression tries to build blocks of continuous colour.

PPI and DPI

Image resolution, bit depth, and compression are not the only factors affecting image quality, especially for printed output. The number of **Pixels Per Inch** (PPI) of an image also has an affect. The PPI determines how many pixels are displayed in each inch of the output—whether it is on screen or on paper. This in turn determines the physical size of the output and how sharp it will appear.

For example, most computer screens are about 96 PPI. A 1024 × 768 image displayed at 96 PPI will be 10.6 inches by 8 inches (at 100% zoom), since 1024 divided by 96 is 10.6, and 768 divided by 96 is 8. If the same image was displayed at 48 PPI, it would be displayed twice as large, but each pixel would also be twice as big (because the number of pixels in the image remains constant). If the number of PPI is too low, it will be possible to see the individual pixels which make up the image. An extreme examples illustrates this: if the above image was printed at just 1 PPI, it would be 1024 inches across and 768 inches high, but each individual pixel would be clearly visible because they would be 1 inch high and 1 inch wide! This would obviously look very bad unless you were a very long way from the image.

For printing, 150 PPI is acceptable for home use. At 150 PPI, our 1024 × 768 image would be printed 6.8 inches (1024 / 150) by 5.1 inches (768 / 150). Most commercial and professional printers require images that are 300 PPI in order to produce sharp results. In those cases our 1024 × 768 image would be printed at 3.4 inch by 2.5 inches. In both cases the image resolution - 1024 × 768 – is the same, but the size of the output has reduced because of the increased number of pixels printed in each inch of the output.

These calculations can also be used to work out the required resolution for a given print size. For example, to commercially print an image at 12 inches by 8 inches, the image will need to be at least (12 × 300 PPI) by (8 × 300 PPI), or 3600 by 2400 pixels. Therefore a camera with a resolution of at least 8.6 megapixels (3600 × 2400 = 8,640,000 pixels) will be needed.

Of course, images can be printed at any PPI, but lower values will result in the quality being lower, especially at short viewing distances. However, for large prints which are viewed from a very long distance, such as advertising boards, output as low as 30 PPI and still look acceptable.

DPI

DPI (**dots per inch**) is a term often confused with PPI. DPI is also known as **printer resolution**. DPI refers to the number of ink dots that a printer produces when creating an image. However, this is not necessarily the same as PPI because a printer may produce more than one 'dot' to print every pixel!

Many printers are advertised with resolutions of 1200 DPI or higher – and a quick search on the Internet will reveal printers with resolutions of 9600 DPI! However, these high values are not what they seem.

Printers only have a limited number of ink colours (often Black, Cyan, Magenta, and Yellow), so to produce all possible colours they need to mix inks. They do this by producing multiple dots of ink in the same spot on the paper. A higher number of dots per inch means is able to mix colours in finer quantities, meaning more accurate colour reproduction and smoother transition between different colour tones. Of course, it also means that more ink is consumed.

Exercise 6-9
a) **Calculate** the minimum image resolution for a commercial print measuring 24 inches by 16 inches [2 marks]
b) **Calculate** the maximum print size for a 4 megapixel camera at 300 DPI. [2 marks]
c) **Calculate** the print size for a 1600 x 1200 pixel image on a home printer. [2 marks]

Exercise 6-10
Take a digital photograph and save it in each of the file formats supported by your graphics software. If the file format offers options when saving (as JPEG does), save with different options too. Produce a bar graph of the file formats and their corresponding file size. What do the results tell you about uncompressed, lossless, and lossy image formats?

Vector graphics

Vector graphics are composed of objects rather than pixels. For this reason they are sometimes called **object oriented graphics**. Each object is stored as a series of mathematical equations that define its starting point, ending point, and path, along with information about its colour and style. All objects remain separate in the image, meaning they can be edited, scaled, repositioned and re-coloured independently at any time. Typical vector shapes include ovals, rectangles, lines, Bézier curves, and paths defined by a series of points.

Because a lot of software supports only bitmap images, vector editors can usually export images as bitmaps files—although once this is done, the editable properties of the vectors are lost, so the original vector version should still be kept.

Since vector images are defined mathematically, they can be scaled as large as required without any loss of quality. This is their major advantage and is essential when creating items such as logos, which may need to be displayed at many different sizes from a few centimetres to several metres across. Creating different resolution bitmap images for each use would be inefficient and would require extreme resolution for prints measuring several metres across. The ability to zoom vector graphics without quality loss is also useful for mapping data. A bitmap image of a large area such as a country would need to be impossibly huge in order to contain the required detail. With a vector image, the computer merely needs to store the positions of each relevant point on the map, and they can be scaled as appropriate when the map is zoomed in or out (figure 6-12).

Because they are more mathematically complex than bitmap graphics, vector graphics require computers with faster processors in order to perform the number of calculations necessary. This is particularly true for complex images or those containing lots of curved shapes, which are constructed using a large number of individual vectors.

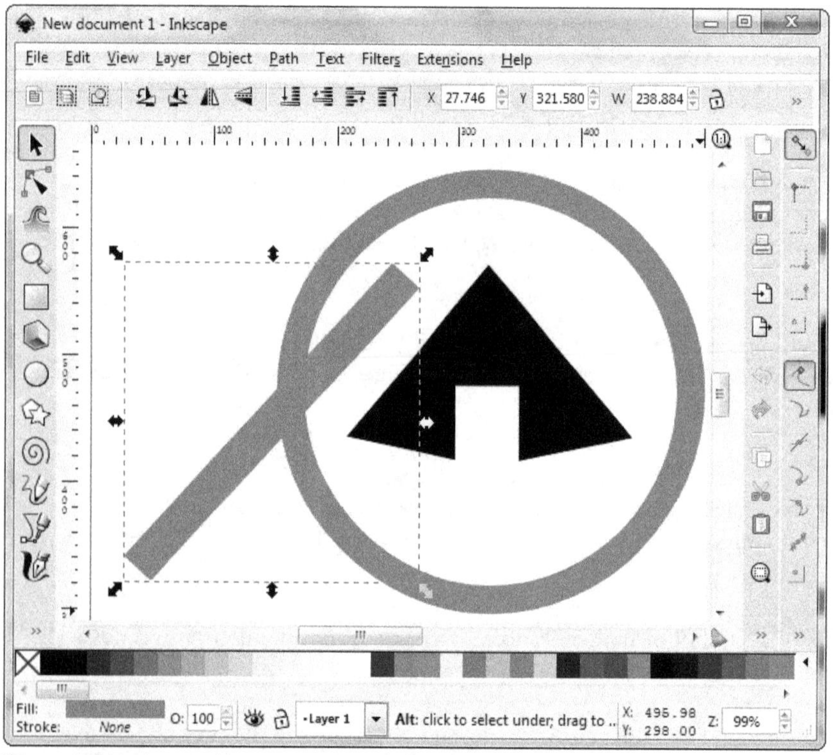

3D vector images

Vectors are the primary method of creating three dimensional imagery. This has many application areas including game, film, and television work. Architects and engineers use **Computer Aided Design (CAD)**

Figure 6-9 Vector graphics are composed of mathematical shapes

Bitmap graphics	Vector graphics
Store data as grids of pixels	Store data as mathematical equations
Zooming in reduces quality	No quality loss when zooming in
Increasing size reduces quality	Can easily be resized with no loss of quality
Has lower processor requirements, but high memory requirements for large images	Requires fast computer to manipulate complex graphics
Images consume lots of storage space	Images consume less storage space
Perfect for taking photographs	Not possible to recreate complex real life scenes (e.g. photographs)

Figure 6-8 Comparison of bitmap and vector images

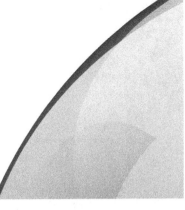

Figure 6-10 Vector image of the earth (left). When zoomed in, no quality is lost (centre). When exported as a bitmap and zoomed in (right), the image rapidly loses quality and the individual pixels are visible.

software to create 3D technical drawings of products in development. This allows a product to be viewed in detail before it is even created. Advanced CAD software also allows designers to specify physical properties of their 3D models, such as weight, strength, and material, enabling them to be tested before being built. For example, the strength of bridge materials can be entered and tested against factors such as the wind and weight of traffic using a computer model (see page 165).

3D vector graphics operate in essentially the same way as 2D vectors, except that primitives such as cubes, cones, and spheres are created instead of their two dimensional equivalents. These 3D primitives can be edited using a variety of tools to alter and sculpt them into the required shapes. Once these wireframe models are complete, colours and shading is usually added to give a better appearance. This is usually sufficient for technical drawings required by architects and designers.

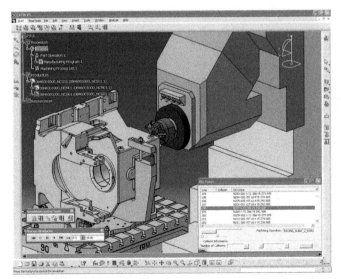

Figure 6-11 Vectors graphics are used heavily in Computer Aided Design (CAD) work.

Figure 6-12 Vectors are an efficient way of representing the high level of detail needed for mapping data. Equivalent bitmap images would be extremely large.

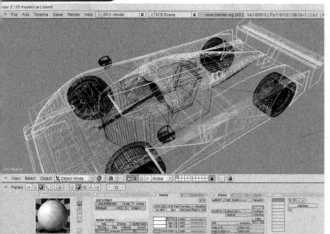

Graphics in the Movies

For work in film or television, where computer generated imagery (CGI) is often used to create animations or special effects, more realism is required than technical CAD work. Often **motion capture** is used to capture the shape and movements of actors. This normally involves the actor wearing a special suit with markers at key points such as the arms, hands, legs, and head. These markers can be detected by a camera connected to a computer, allowing it to know the position of the main parts of the body and build up a wireframe skeleton inside the computer.

To improve realism further, **textures** are often used. Usually it is impossible to create the required level of detail purely with 3D vectors: even the most advanced computer system cannot model every individual blade of grass, fibre of clothing, or hair on a person's head as 3D vector objects. Instead, the overall shape of these objects is modelled using a relatively simple 3D shape and then a 2D bitmap texture is applied to give a deeper and more life-like appearance. Using textures create a good balance between image detail and mathematical complexity.

Finally, 3D graphics objects are often given properties such as hardness, reflectivity, and smoothness. Lights with specific intensities and colours can be added, and then the scene can be **rendered** or **ray traced**, calculating how the light in a scene behaves, bouncing off objects and into the virtual 'camera'. To produce the very high quality images needed for film and television, the rendering process can take minutes or even hours for a single image, even on very fast computers. Often **render farms** of hundreds or even thousands of computers are used to improve processing speed (see distributed processing, page 176).

Figure 6-13 Wireframe view of a car model in 3D graphics software (top). 3D graphics software can create very realistic images in the right hands (bottom)

Exercise 6-11

Use a 3D graphics program to create the following items:
a) A fairly simple man-made item such as a laptop or a house
b) An accurate recreation of a place you know
c) An object found in nature (e.g. a tree, a flower, a mountain) – nothing man-made!

How difficult was it to create each object? What does this tell you about the difficulties 3D modellers face when trying to create realistic graphics for film or television?

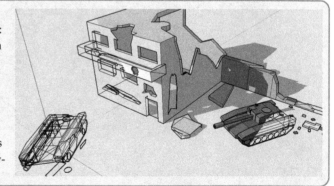

Exercise 6-12

Many modern films include a 'Making of' feature on the DVD. Many times these features give details of how computers were used in the film creation process. Watch one of these features and see if you can see techniques in this chapter being applied. Science fiction and computer-animated children's films are often good examples.

Creating a Cloud with Vector Graphics

Everything in vector graphics is based upon relatively simple mathematical shapes. Individual shapes can be created and combined in a variety of ways to create more complex shapes.

The process of creating a cloud shape is illustrated below. Individual ovals are created, coloured, and positioned as necessary (image 1); the individual shapes are then combined into one using the Union operator, resulting in the outline of a cloud shape (image 2). A gradient is applied to this simply by selecting the start and end colours (image 3). Properties like the outline thickness and colour can also be adjusted. Like all vector graphics, it is possible to zoom in as far as desired with no loss of quality (image 4).

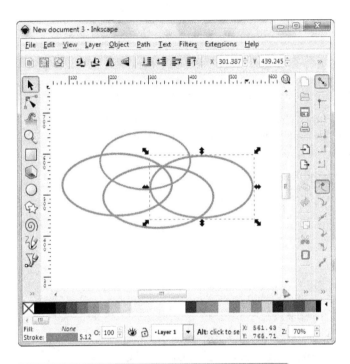

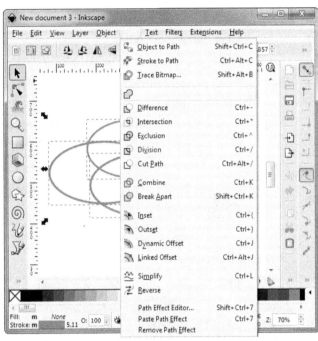

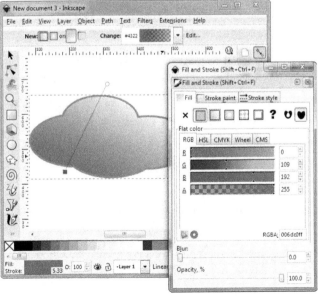

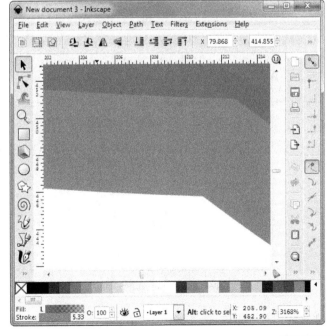

Common Multimedia File Formats

Video formats

AVI **Audio Video Interleave**. An early video format which uses a variety of lossy compression codecs.

MOV Used by Apple's QuickTime system, popular on Apple hardware and created by some digital cameras.

MP4 **Motion Pictures Expert Group 4**. A new file format which offers more efficient lossy compression.

WMV **Windows Media Video**. Microsoft's proprietary video format, primarily supported on Windows platforms.

Audio Formats

AAC **Advanced Audio Coding**. Developed by Apple, AAC uses lossy compression and also supports DRM restricted files (see page 276). AAC is commonly used in Apple's iTunes store.

FLAC **Free Lossless Audio Codec**. An open file format which, as its name suggests, uses lossless compression.

MP3 **MPEG Audio Layer 3**. A lossy compression format which changed the industry in the early 1990s. Increasing home computer power and Internet connectivity helped fuel a deluge of MP3 sharing sites – most of them distributing illegal copies of music. MP3 is still popular despite the arrival of newer, more efficient formats.

WAV **Wave**. A very common standard supported by virtually all audio hardware and software.

WMA **Windows Media Audio**. Developed by Microsoft, WMA is generally only supported on Windows platforms. WMA is lossy and supports the ability to be streamed.

Image Formats

BMP **Bitmap image**. Used by Microsoft's Paint application included with Windows. BMP files are not commonly supported outside of Windows environments. BMP files support lossless compression or no compression.

TIF **Tagged Image File Format**. An old format still used quite extensively in professional printing and publishing. TIFs support a variety of features including lossless compression and multiple pages per file.

GIF **Graphics Interchange Format**. An old format which became obsolete after a patent row concerning its compression algorithm. Once very common on the web.

PNG **Portable Network Graphics**. A relatively new lossless format, designed to replace the older GIF format, which had problems with patent claims. PNG is an open format and is supported by most web browsers.

JPEG **Joint Photographic Experts Group**. The most common lossy file format, JPEG images are produced by virtually all digital cameras and graphics editors, and are one of the most common file formats on the web.

PSD **Photoshop Document**. A custom, proprietary file format supported by Adobe's Photoshop image editor. PSD files support additional application-specific features such as layers and undo-lists, which are not available in standard bitmap image file formats.

RAW 'Raw image' formats produced by digital SLR cameras. They maintain more colour information than JPEG
CR2 files and include metadata such as shutter speed and aperture.

SVG **Scalable Vector Graphics**. A relatively new format for storing vector graphics, SVG is supported by modern web browsers and many vector illustration programs. SVG files are actually XML text files, meaning they can be edited in normal text editors.

Digital Audio

Many sound and music projects, from adding music to home videos to feature film soundtracks, are now produced entirely digitally. Sound is recorded, converted into digital data (**digitised**), and loaded into audio editing software, where it can be manipulated using a wide range of effects and filters. Most audio editing software represents sounds graphically as waves, and allows sections to be selected, cut, pasted, and moved freely.

The quality of a recorded sound is determined by its **sample rate**, also called the **sampling frequency.** The analog sound data captured by a microphone must be converted into digital data for the computer to process. The sample rate determines how many times each second a digital sample of the analog data is taken: the more frequent the samples, the closer the digital sound will be to the analogue original (figure 6-15). Sampling rates for devices like two-way radios and telephones are quite low – 8000 Hz (8000 samples per second). CDs obtain their much higher quality by using a sample rate of 44,100 Hz, while professional equipment uses rates from 48,000 Hz up to 2,822,400 Hz (2.8 MHz). In figure 6-15, the sampling frequency is represented by the number of bars which fit into a given space on the horizontal (time) axis.

Sampling rate should not be confused with **bit rate**. Bit rate, which is a value displayed in some music players, is the amount of data used to represent each second of audio. Higher bit rates mean there is a larger number of digital values to choose from when taking a sample. This finer granularity the digital value can more closely represent the analog signal. For example, the bit rate (vertical axis) in figure 6-15 only allows 12 possible values to be chosen, making the digital values only rough approximations of the analog values. If this number were higher, it would be possible to choose a value which is much closer to the original analog sound wave.

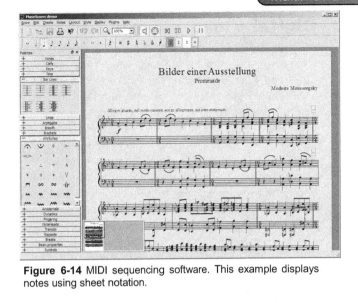

Figure 6-14 MIDI sequencing software. This example displays notes using sheet notation.

In MP3 files, bit rates can range from 32 Kbit/s to 320 Kbit/s, with lower bit rates producing smaller files, but also lower quality audio. As with images and video, audio files can be saved in uncompressed, lossless, or lossy file formats—the most common are shown on page 132.

MIDI

MIDI (Musical Instrument Digital Interface) is a communication standard for music devices, computers, and music creation software. Unlike digital sound recordings, the MIDI standard does not communicate any digital sound information. Instead, MIDI devices have built in recordings of different instruments played at different notes and pitches. MIDI music files contain only the instructions for how to play these instruments, but not the actual sound themselves. For example a MIDI file might contain the event 'play note C on channel 2', followed shortly afterwards by the event 'stop note C on channel 2'. The result of this is that MIDI files are relatively small, since no actual sound data is saved. Another effect is that the same MIDI file can sound different on different playback devices, depending on the quality of the instrument recordings the device uses.

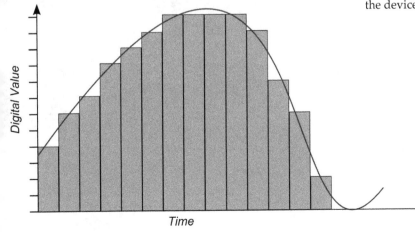

Figure 6-15 Digitisation involves taking multiple digital samples of an analogue sound each second

Digital Video

As with audio, quite sophisticated digital video editing software is now available for home users. Microsoft Windows and MacOS operating systems both include basic video editing programs, and other applications are available relatively cheaply. At their simplest, video editing programs allow video tracks to be cut, removed, and re-arranged, and allow a sound track to be added. Typically a range of fades and titles can also be added. Many programs also have the ability to publish or encode the video at different resolutions and in different file formats. For example, low resolution, heavily compressed video can be used for uploading to the Internet (where file size is a major consideration), while large, higher resolution files can be produced for distribution on DVD.

Figure 6-16 Digitisation involves taking multiple digital samples of an analogue sound each second

More advanced video editing software allows a range of effects to be added, such as changing the colour balance, brightness, and saturation of the video, or adding effects like grain. Usually several video and several audio tracks can be included in the same project to allow smooth fades between videos and to provide separate audio 'layers' such as dialogue, music, and background sound. **Chroma key** (**green screen** or **blue screen**) effects allow part of a video image to be replaced with another image or video source by removing specific colours. This effect is commonly used to display weather maps behind news readers, and for special effects in films. In film and television, **morphing** is also sometimes used, where a source image is slowly transformed into a second image over a series of frames.

Codecs

To play compressed audio or video data on a computer, a suitable **codec** is needed. The codec (compressor-decompressor) is a piece of software which tells media players how to decode the particular compression format used by that video or audio data. When recording audio or video, the codec is also responsible for performing the encoding. Codecs for common formats such as MP4 are often included with operating systems or media players, while other less common or newer formats may need you to download and install a separate codec.

Streaming Media

Streaming media describes video or audio data that is played while it is being downloaded from the Internet, rather than waiting for the entire data to be downloaded before playing commences. This means, for example, that it is possible to start viewing a two hour film

also immediately. Streaming media systems download a small part of the media into a **buffer**, which is played while another section is downloaded and loaded into the buffer. Provided the data can be downloaded at least as fast as it can be played, the video and audio will playback smoothly. However, if the network bandwidth is insufficient, jerky, stuttering playback will occur, with frequent pauses. To offer better streamed playback, lower resolution video is often used. Some playback formats even offer a variety of resolutions and select an appropriate one based on your connection speed.

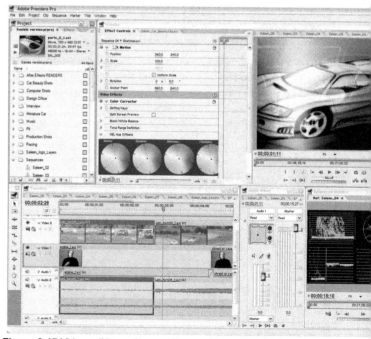

Figure 6-17 Video editing software offers a wide range of effects

Intellectual property

Intellectual property is a commonly misunderstood issue. Intellectual property refers to non-physical creations such as stories, music, works of art, and computer software. These items require a significant amount of work to create, and so **copyright law** provides protection against use of this intellectual property by unauthorised users. Copyright is automatically obtained by the author of a work when it is created—there is no registration or application process involved.

Intellectual property refers not to the physical media containing the work, but the work itself. For example, the story in a book is intellectual property, not the physical paper copy. This means making a film adaptation of a book without the author's permission would be a breach of copyright. It could even be considered a breach of copyright to create another book using the same characters as the original without permission.

Fair Use

In some countries **fair use** allows exceptions to copyright laws under certain limited circumstances. In general several factors are considered when determining fair use. The purpose of copying material is important: news reporting, parody, or reviews of material might be generally considered fair use, whereas copying material for commercial gain would not be. **Educational fair use** only applies in specific circumstances and does not exempt institutions or their students from copyright law. It is still illegal, for example, for a school to make full copies of a textbook or a DVD for distribution to its students.

The amount of work reproduced is also considered – for example, using short extracts from a novel for a review would be considered fair use, but copying large amounts, even for review purposes, would not. Finally, the impact on the copyright holder is considered – if the owner will lose money due to the copying (such as lost sales), the copying is likely not to be considered fair use.

Enforcing copyright

Preventing copyright infringement can be difficult, as enforcement of copyright law varies drastically from country to country. This has become increasingly difficult as more companies wish to distribute digital versions of their work – such as e-books – but still maintain control over how they are used. Technical developments like peer to peer file sharing and high bandwidth connections have also made it relatively easy to distribute digital copies of material—legal or illegal.

Photographers or illustrators often use **watermarking** techniques to try to prevent copyright infringement of their work. A semi-transparent image, usually the author's name, logo, or a copyright symbol, can be inserted into a photograph in a way that makes it hard to remove yet relatively easy to still view the image. This can act as a deterrent to some unauthorised uses.

Media companies often use **Digital Rights Management (DRM)** to control how their films, music, and e-books are distributed and used. Page 276 discusses DRM in more detail. Software companies often use additional tactics to protect their products, discussed on page 58.

Free licences

Some content authors choose to license their work freely, especially for non-commercial use. The **Creative Commons** licences give creators a standard way to do this while insisting on certain conditions, such as requiring an attribution, requiring that any changes to the work are also made available for free, or requiring that the work is not used for commercial purposes. **The GNU Free Documentation Licence (GFDL)** is a similar licence, although it allows no restrictions on the use of work. Such works are sometimes said to be **copyleft**, to indicate that they can be freely used, in contrast to restricted copyrighted works. Sites like WikiMedia offer repositories of freely usable work, while other sites and search engines can often be configured to only return freely licensed results.

Citing sources

Some licences such as the **Creative Commons** Attribute (CC-BY) licences require you to credit the author of the work when you use it. Even if a work's licence does not require this, it is good practice to do so. Crediting work helps the reader or viewer understand the context of the work, shows that you have done research, and protects you against accusations of plagiarism or academic malpractice by apparently claiming other people's work as your own. Sources of material should be cited either in the footnotes of a page or in the bibliography at the end of the work. Different bibliographical formats exist but all include the title of the work (where relevant), the author, the date of creation, and in the case of web pages, the date of access (since web content can change rapidly).

> **Common Mistake**
> It is a mistake to believe that all material found on the Internet is free to use. In fact, a large amount of it is copyrighted. Web sites usually contain copyright notices which tell you how you can (or can't) use their material. If none exists, assume the material is copyrighted.

Desktop Publishing and Word Processing

Desktop Publishing (DTP) software allows complex pages of text and graphics to be laid out for publications such as newspapers, magazines, brochures, and books. Like most word processing software, desktop publishing software is **WYSIWYG** (What You See Is What You Get), meaning that the appearance of the document on the screen is exactly how it will appear when printed.

However, whereas **word processing** software is focused more on the line-by-line creation of text documents, DTP software is page oriented, allowing objects such as text frames, images, and tables to be placed anywhere on the page.

Features

Master pages are an important feature of DTP software, which assist in creating a consistent layout and appearance. Features added to a master page are automatically added to every page in the document. This is useful for quickly placing items such as page numbers and titles in the same place on every page (e.g. in the **header** or **footer**).

Templates provide predefined layouts for creating a variety of document types. Users can simply replace the supplied dummy text and images with their own and quickly achieve an effective result. Many DTP programs include templates for newsletters, brochures, newspapers, and other common document types.

Grouping tools facilitate the management of multiple objects at the same time, while **alignment** options allow objects to be positioned which much more precision that could be achieved manually.

DTP software also offers more advanced text management features than word processors, including shaped text boxes, **layers**, advanced **alignment** controls, and the ability to adjust **typography features** such as kerning and tracking (adjusting the spaces between individual letters) and ligatures (combining two characters, such as the *ae* in encyclopaedia).

Since DTP users often require output which can be professionally printed, most DTP software supports **exporting** in standard file formats such as **PDF**, and includes **colour management options** (see page 137). **Colour separation**, required by some commercial printers, splits documents into separate images or layers, each representing one of the main colour components (typically CMYK—Cyan, Magenta, Yellow, and Black).

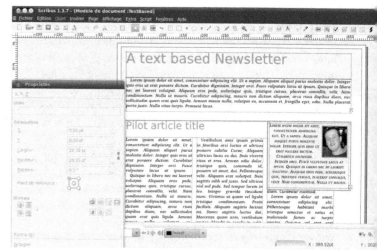

Figure 6-18 A popular DTP program with a pre-defined template open

Tips for successful DTP

1. Use a consistent layout—similar styles, themes, and colours should apply to most or all pages in a publication.
2. Use only a few fonts—using a wide range of fonts makes a document look unprofessional. One font for the body text and one for headings and subheadings (at different sizes) is often enough.
3. Long lines of text are often difficult to read. Use page margins or columns to reduce line length.
4. Some colours (usually darker ones) appear very 'heavy' on the page and should be used sparingly and in balance.
5. White space can be used effectively to guide the reader to items.
6. Use the software's alignment tools rather than dragging objects into approximate alignment.
7. Bleed—making images run right to the very edge of the page—can be an effective tool, but make sure it is supported by your printer.
8. Images intended for professional printing should be at least 300 dpi (see page 127).
9. Do not resize images using a DTP program. Instead, resize them using the high quality scaling options in graphics software and then import them.
10. Use the master page feature to automatically place items like page numbers and titles in exactly the same place on every page.

Before exporting a document for printing, design-check options scan documents for potential problems which the designer might have missed, such as images with insufficient resolution for professional printing, objects which are outside the page boundary, text frames which have overflowing text, hidden objects, and a variety of other problems.

Document File Formats

Adobe's **PDF (Portable Document Format)** is often used for distributing digital documents. PDF files can include embedded fonts so documents appear exactly the same on every computer, and PDF viewers are freely available, meaning the recipient does not need the same desktop publishing software as the document creator. This is a major advantage as desktop publishing applications are often expensive and not compatible with each other. PDF documents can also include editable fields — useful for online form filling. DRM (see page 276) is also an option.

Plain text files store only text (using ASCII or Unicode encoding) with no formatting, images or other data. They are commonly used for system log files and as a fall back format when transferring data between incompatible systems. Plain text files are also used for CSV data transfers (see page 152). However, a better option when text formatting is needed is **Rich Text Format (RTF)**. RTF supports text documents with embedded images and some formatting data.

Formats like Microsoft's **Word Document (.doc)** are used because the software which creates them has features not supported by other file formats or standards. For example Microsoft Word has features for tracked changes, document protection, editor's notes, and advanced layout features — none of which are supported by RTF files. However, because these formats are often proprietary, compatibility between systems can be a problem. The successor to the .doc format, Office Open XML (not to be confused

Colour Synchronisation

Obtaining accurate shades of colour is very important in professional video, photography, and publishing, yet different monitors, printers, scanners, and cameras all represent colours with different levels of intensity and brightness due to differences in their design. Even individual application programs can process and represent colours in different ways.

Colour synchronisation, also called **colour management**, is the process of ensuring colours produced by the output device (usually a printer) match the colours chosen by the designer in the software.

ICC colour profiles help achieve consistent colours, regardless of output medium, by describing how individual devices process and represent colours. Part of the colour profile includes the **colour space**, which describes how colours are defined. RGB (red, green, and blue), Adobe RGB and sRGB are common colour spaces.

Both input and output devices, and images themselves can have specific colour profiles, describing how they represent colours. When an image is displayed, the information in the output device's colour profile tells it how to accurately represent the colours described by the image's colour profile.

with Open Office) uses the file extension .docx. Office Open XML is a more open file format than previous Word documents, with specifications defined by an international standard. This should improve compatibility between various word processor programs.

A recent development is the **OpenDocument** (.odt) format, which is an open standard, allowing any developers to use it. OpenDocument is the native file format of the LibreOffice and OpenOffice suites and can be used with several other popular office suites.

Document File Formats

DOC	**Microsoft Word Document**. Standard for most versions of Microsoft Word, .doc files are widely used, though many other word processors are not fully compatible with it.
DOCX	**Microsoft Word Document (Office Open XML)**. Standard for the most recent versions of Microsoft Word.
ODT	**OpenDocument Text**. A new format which has the advantage of being an open standard.
PDF	**Portable Document Format**. A widely used standard for transferring documents, especially if maintaining layout and preventing editing are important features.
TXT	**Plain text**. Contains no formatting information but is universally compatible
RTF	**Rich Text Format**. A format which allows for some text formatting and layout information to be saved.

Presentations

Many people, from business workers to teachers to scientists, use presentation software to communicate ideas, facts, and opinions. Presentation software, which displays a series of slides on a screen or a projector, has become the *de facto* standard tool for this job. Unfortunately, many people have also sat through long, boring presentations featuring dozens of slides, which communicate poorly and leave the audience dozing. Despite this, poor quality presentations are still very common.

If done well, presentations provide an excellent opportunity to support the speaker with images, videos, charts, and live demonstrations—techniques would could not be otherwise achieved. Unfortunately many presenters use presentations to contain all of their speaking notes, forcing the audience to read each slide or, worse, reading each slide to the audience themselves. Instead, tools such as the **speaker's notes**, an area of the slide shown to the speaker but not the audience, should be used for this purpose, listing short prompting points rather than full sentences.

Most presentation software has options to print out slides for the audience, often in a summary format. Some presenters, especially teachers and lecturers, make presentations less passive by requiring the audience to add of key information which is missing from these notes, based on information in the presentation.

Creating Poor Presentations

This slide illustrates many of the mistakes commonly made by presenters. The primary mistake is packing the slide with far too much information. The large amount of text means the audience will be busy reading the slide rather than listening to the presenter. This will be made even worse if the presenter starts to read the slide to the audience—a common, but inadvisable, technique. People read much more quickly than they speak, so the audience will be way ahead of the presenter in these cases.

The layout of the slide is also poor. The slide's background image is distracting and makes it hard to read the text. The title's colour exacerbates this problem. Ironically for a slide about photography, the inclusion of an image makes everything less attractive.

Heading font gives a childish impression

Photography Tips

- Geometric shapes and lines can be used to frame a subject, to divide the photo, or to lead the viewer's eye to some part of the photo.

- Frame the photo to put the most important elements in the top third, bottom third, left third, or right third – but not directly in the centre.

Lots of text means a small font size

- Angles can be changed to give a different perspective or point of view which may appear unusual

Text is hard to read against background

- Sometimes it is a good idea to break the rules to get a better picture

Background image makes text hard to read

Clipart image is not directly relevant to the slide content.

Tips for effective presentations

1. Use a small number of key words rather than presenting large pages of text on the screen
2. Know your topic so you do not read your slides to the audience (reading is usually done in conjunction with mistake #1)
3. Face the audience (usually people turn their back to the audience when making mistake #2)
4. Use subtle, complimentary colours. Simplicity is key, and certain colours (red and blue) are hard to read together.
5. Use photographs to illustrate concepts rather than using standard clip art which most people have seen many times.
6. Keep slide transitions simple and consistent (e.g. a sideways slide for continuing a point, and a upwards slide to move onto a new point). Avoid lots of effects like spinning text, bouncing text, and zooming text unless your audience is very small children!
7. Keep the presentation short and focused. When a lot of images are used, move through slides quickly.
8. Be flexible—for example, be prepared to change the order of topics or skip some items if the audience's level of understanding differs from what you thought it would be.

Creating Better Presentations

This slide demonstrates a better way to present the same information. The primary changes are splitting the points made in the previous slide into separate slides. The description of each photography rule has also been removed, with the only text now the name of the rule. This leaves the speaker the job of describing, as it should be. More importantly, reducing the text and positioning it in an 'empty' part of the image allows more of the images to be shown—allowing them to illustrate the rule being described and support the speaker's description, rather than distracting from it. Now the presentation is being used to show something the speaker could not otherwise show—images—rather than simply repeating his words. Another advantage of this approach is that although more slides will be generated, each one will be moved through more rapidly—offering a constantly changing image to keep the audience's attention.

Rule #1: Use Leading Lines

Rule #2: Framing

Chapter Review

Key Language

AAC	Creative Commons	lossy compression	scaling
alignment	cropping	master page	selection tools
AVI	Desktop Publishing	megapixel	streaming media
bit depth	digital effects	MIDI	SVG
bit rate	Digital Rights Management	motion capture	template
bitmap graphics	digitisation	MOV	text file
blue screen	DOC	MP3	TIF
BMP	Dots Per Inch	MP4	true colour
buffer	fair use	MPEG	TXT
CGI	filters	object oriented graphics	typography
cloning	FLAC	ODT	vector graphics
colour balance	flipping	PDF	video CODECs
colour depth	footer	pixel	virtual actors
colour levels	GIF	Pixels Per Inch	Vorbis
colour management	green screen	plain text	watermarking
colour profile	header	PNG	WAV
colour synchronisation	image editor	raster graphics	WMA
composite image	intellectual property	resolution	WYSIWYG
compression	JPG	Rich Text Format	Zip file
Computer Aided Design	layer	rotating	
copyright	lossless compression	sample rate	

Exercise 6-13

Match the terms on the left with the definitions on the right.

1) Lossless compression

2) Resolution

3) DPI

4) Lossy compression

5) WYSIWYG

6) Megapixel

7) Colour synchronisation

8) Plain text

9) Bit depth

A) Ensuring that on screen image colours match the final output

B) The number of pixels that appear per inch in the output of an image

C) Displaying documents exactly as they will appear in the final output

D) The number of pixels in an image

E) The number of colours stored in an image

F) When repeated patterns of data are stored in a shorter form to save space

G) A document which contains only characters, but no formatting data

H) Data from an image or video is discarded in order to save space

I) A common way of measuring the resolution of digital cameras

Exercise 6-14

In September 2009 it was reported that the French government, in an attempt to reduce the incidence of eating disorders and associated health problems among the young, wanted to put disclaimers on published images that were computer edited. The warnings would be similar to the types of warnings found on packets of cigarettes, inform the viewer that the subject of the image had been physically altered. The warnings would apply to all forms of published images, including advertising, magazines, and political images.

Discuss whether this style of warning would be a good idea. Would it achieve its goal? Do you think magazines would include the warnings, or decide not to edit images instead? [8 marks]

Exercise 6-15

Imagine that you are the editor of a major newspaper or magazine. You have been asked you to create an **Ethical Editing Policy** for the photographers that work for you. This policy should be a set of rules that tells workers what kind of computer manipulations are acceptable and which are not acceptable. The policy should also explain the reason behind each rule. Examples to illustrate both acceptable and unacceptable techniques would be a good idea. [10 marks]

Exercise 6-16

Consider the different types of media covered in this chapter: word processing, DTP, audio, video, and presentations. Explain why a business might decide to use some of these more traditional forms of media to advertise itself, instead of the web 2.0 media on page 85. [4 marks]

Exercise 6-17

Create a presentation to explain the key points of one of the topics covered so far in this textbook. Aim to follow the good presentation guidelines on page 139. [10 marks]

Exercise 6-18

Virtual actors—characters created entirely using computer graphics techniques—are becoming more common in films and television. Fantasy and science fiction films in particular make use of virtual actors to create characters which would be very difficult to otherwise create.

(a) (i) Identify **two** file formats commonly used to store video.   [2 marks]

   (ii) Describe **two** factors that affect an image's quality.   [4 marks]

(b) Explain the process involved in lossy compression.   [6 marks]

(c) Discuss the advantages and disadvantages of using virtual actors instead of human actors.   [8 marks]

Exercise 6-19

A small dry cleaning business wishes to enlarge its customer base by increasing its advertising profile. It is considering creating promotional leaflets or a simple web site.

(a) (i) State **two** file formats commonly used for storing documents.   [2 marks]

   (ii) Distinguish *word processing software* and *desktop publishing software*.   [4 marks]

(b) Explain why documents are often saved as PDF files when they are distributed.   [6 marks]

(c) Analyse the arguments for creating paper promotional leaflets rather than a web site for this business.   [8 marks]

Exercise 6-20

A news agency which publishes both printed newspapers and online news has decided to start accepting photo contributions for publication from its readers.

(a) (i) Define the term *DPI*.   [2 marks]

   (ii) Describe **two** ways a user might submit an image to the agency for publication.   [4 marks]

(b) Explain why news agencies might accept user contributions for publication.   [6 marks]

(c) Discuss the considerations the news agency must make when deciding to publish users' contributions.   [8 marks]

References

1 Telegraph, The. (2009). French MPs want health warnings on airbrushed photographs . Available: http://www.telegraph.co.uk/news/worldnews/europe/france/6214168/French-MPs-want-health-warnings-on-airbrushed-photographs.html. Last accessed Nov 2011.

2 TIME Magazine. (1994). To our readers. Available: http://www.time.com/time/magazine/article/0,9171,981052,00.html. Last accessed Nov 2011.

3 Sydney Morning Herald. (2007). Image of slain Brazilian 'digitally manipulated'. Available: http://www.smh.com.au/news/world/image-digitally-manipulated/2007/10/18/1192300893284.html. Last accessed Nov 2011.

4 Famous Pictures: The Magazine. (2011). Altered Images. Available: http://www.famouspictures.org/mag/index.php?title=Altered_Images. Last accessed Nov 2011.

5 BBC. (2008). Iran 'faked missile test image'. Available: http://news.bbc.co.uk/2/hi/middle_east/7500917.stm. Last accessed Nov 2011.

Chapter 7
Databases

Objectives

Understanding of concepts
1. Distinguish flat file and relational databases
2. Describe the applications of databases
3. Explain the importance of data normalisation
4. Explain rules governing data use
5. Evaluate privacy and integrity concerns related to database use

Practical Skills
1. Create a relational database
2. Add, edit, and delete records
3. Create queries using Boolean operators
4. Use forms and reports effectively
5. Apply verification and validation techniques

Databases

Databases—organised collections of related data—are at the heart of many IT systems. Obvious examples include systems for storing employee records, students records, and medical records, but databases are at the core of many other systems too. Search engines, social networks, online shops, and very many businesses employ databases to manage their organisation's information. The increased ability to gather data using IT, along with advancements in data mining techniques to make decisions based on data, raises issues of privacy and emphasises the need for data integrity. Storing large amounts of personal data in one place also makes such databases prime targets for hackers, and several companies have experienced significant data losses in this way. This chapter examines the construction and use of databases, and their role in IT systems.

Databases

A database is a collection of related data, stored in an organised manner so that it can be retrieved later. Databases are used in many different areas, and many IT systems have databases 'behind the scenes', even if they are not immediately obvious. Examples of databases include:

Business databases including customer information, product data, and supplier details. Databases are used by e-commerce businesses such as Amazon, maintaining not just records of products but also the shopping behaviours of their customers, allowing them to customise each user's shopping experience.

Transport databases for flight or train information, providing up to the minute information to passengers, and allowing customers to view and book journeys from anywhere in the world, over the Internet.

Search engines such as Google, Yahoo, and Bing use databases to store both the contents of web pages (to enable their searches to work), and details about user's behaviour, including common searches and topics of interest. These are used to customise search results and advertise to individuals. **Social networks** such as Facebook, MySpace, and LinkedIn use a similar approach.

Online databases, such as the free encyclopaedia Wikipedia, hold huge volumes of articles, images, and video accessible to anybody with an Internet connection.

Government databases including criminal records, tax records, medical records, libraries' databases of books, and schools' databases of students. Often these databases are interlinked, raising questions about privacy and control of data.

Database Management Systems

The software used to create and maintain databases is known as a **Database Management System** (DBMS) or **Relational Database Management System** (RDBMS). Examples of DBMS software with various capabilities include Microsoft Access, MySQL, Microsoft SQL Server, FileMaker Pro, and LibreOffice Base. Spreadsheet applications, such as Microsoft Excel, LibreOffice Calc, and Apple's Numbers, focus on numerical calculation and are not considered database programs.

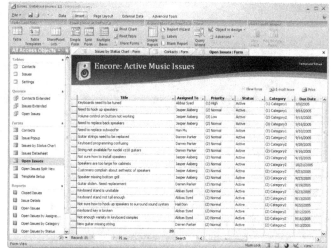

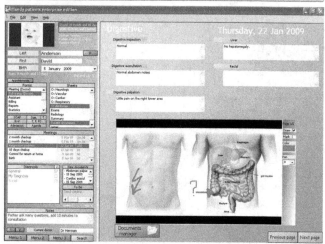

Figure 7-1 Databases have applications in many areas

Database Structure

Databases organise information into fields, records, and tables, determined by how the pieces of data relate to each other. **Fields** are the smallest pieces of information in a database. A field is a property of an item. For example, the name of a student, the price of a product, and the telephone number of an employee are all fields. A **record** is a collection of fields that relate to the same item. For example, together the name, class, grade, home address, and email address for one student form a record for that student. **Tables** are collections of records that are all of the same type. For example, all records which represent students would go in the Students table. All records which represent teachers would go in the Teachers table, and all records which represent books would go in a Books table.

Each table in a database should have a **primary key** (sometimes called a **key field**). A primary key is a field which is different for every record in that table. This allows each record to be uniquely identified. For example, a student identification number would make an appropriate primary key, assuming each student has a different number. The student name or telephone would not make good primary keys, because several students might have the same name or the same telephone number.

In figure 7-2, there is no candidate for a primary key. The 'car registration' cannot be, because each car can be rented more than one time. Similarly, customers can rent cars on many occasions, so their name may appear more than once in the table. If the rental date were the primary key, it would mean only one car could be rented each day—clearly not desirable! One solution is to add a new field called RentalID, which could uniquely identify each rental. Another solution is to use two fields, car registration and rental date, to form a **composite key**. A composite

key consists of two or more fields which, separately do not uniquely identify records, but do when combined.

Using the 'Car registration' and 'Rental date' as a composite would work, because each car can only be rented once on a given day (assuming the minimal rental is 24 hours).

Many database tables also have **secondary keys**, sometimes called **alternative keys**, or **indexes**. A secondary key is a field which might frequently be used to search a table. For example, in figure 7-2, the 'Car registration' field could be a secondary key because the table might often be searched or sorted by that field. Unlike a primary key, a secondary key does not have to be unique. A table can have several secondary keys.

Each field in a database must also have a **data type**, which determines what sort of data can be stored in it – such as text, numbers, a date, or an image. Data types are a good first step to helping ensure **validation** of data by only allowing data of the desired type. Page 146 shows examples of data types used in common database applications.

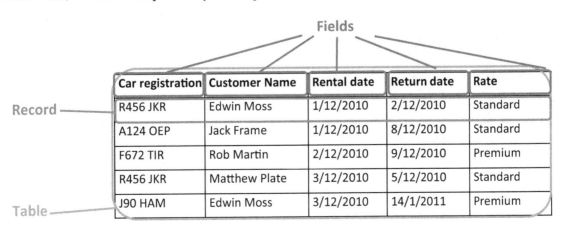

Fields

Car registration	Customer Name	Rental date	Return date	Rate
R456 JKR	Edwin Moss	1/12/2010	2/12/2010	Standard
A124 OEP	Jack Frame	1/12/2010	8/12/2010	Standard
F672 TIR	Rob Martin	2/12/2010	9/12/2010	Premium
R456 JKR	Matthew Plate	3/12/2010	5/12/2010	Standard
J90 HAM	Edwin Moss	3/12/2010	14/1/2011	Premium

Record — Table —

Figure 7-2 The components of a database

Data Types in Microsoft Access

Microsoft Access provides the following data types. Most DBMS software provides similar options, though sometimes with slightly different names.

Number — Allows only numeric data, the range of which can be specified.

AutoNumber — A numeric field whose value is automatically increased by 1 for each new record. This makes it useful for assigning numeric primary keys, like identification numbers.

Text — Allows letters, numbers, and symbols, up to 255 characters long.

Memo — A version of the Text data type, without any length restriction.

Yes / No — Allows only two options – yes or no, true or false, on or off (i.e. a Boolean value)

Date / Time — Stores dates and displays them in the computer's default format.

Attachment — Used for adding files in any format – for example, sound files, images, and videos. This might be needed to attach a photograph of a student in a school database, for example.

Flat file databases

Figure 7-3 shows a sample of the bookshop database created in exercise 7-2. This database would be quite useful to help us locate books and find out more information about them. However, after examining the sample data in the table, a problem should be clear: the table contains quite a large amount of **redundant data** – data that is needlessly repeated (figure 7-3).

For example, there are several books published by *Picador*, and in each case the Publisher field and the Publisher Country field contain the same information ('*Picador*' and '*Australia*' respectively). Similarly, there are several books authored by *Primo Levi*, and for each instance the Nationality and the Date of Birth fields contain the same information. This needlessly repeated data is known as **redundant data**, and it would be much better to store it only once. Redundant data causes several problems:

- **Data integrity**—the more often data is repeated, the higher the chance that a mistake will be made. This leads to a situation where the same field can have different, inconsistent, values in different records. For example, two different dates of birth might be accidentally entered for the same author.

- **Data integrity** – related to the above problem, if a field such as the author's date of death needs to change, the entire database must be searched for all occurrences of that data. This causes problems because some copies of the field might be updated while others are missed, creating inconsistent data.

- **Wasted storage space** – multiplied by thousands or even hundreds of thousands of records, redundant data can consume a lot of disk and memory space.

The problem of redundant data occurs because the current bookshop database is a **flat file database** – a database which contains just one table. Flat file databases are ade-

---

Exercise 7-1

Identify fields which would make appropriate primary keys and secondary keys in the following database tables:

a) A table of student details in a school

b) A table of products in a supermarket

c) A table of employees in a factory

d) A table of bank accounts in a bank

Exercise 7-2

Use DBMS software to create a simple database for a bookshop, with one table. Include at least the following fields: Book title, Author first name, Author second name, Publisher, Publisher country, Pages, Date of birth, Date of death, Nationality, Book language, Original language, Year, Genre, Paperback, Topic. Choose appropriate data types for each field and add 10 sample records.

Exercise 7-3

Before the widespread use of computers, large volumes of data, such as students records in a school, were stored in paper files and filing cabinets. **Explain** some advantages of using a computerised database to store information. Are there any disadvantages or potential problems with computer databases? [8 marks]

Title	Author First Name	Author Second Name	Publisher	Publisher Country	Pages	Nationality	Date of birth
The Climb	Anatoli	BouKreev	St Martin's	US	297	Russian	16/1/1958
In Patagonia	Bruce	Chatwin	Penguin	UK	224	English	13/5/1940
If This is a Man	Primo	Levi	Penguin	UK	290	Italian	31/7/1919
If Not Now, When?	Primo	Levi	Picador	Australia	305	Italian	31/7/1919
The Collected Poems of W.B. Yeats	William Butler	Yeats	Penguin	UK	101	English	13/6/1865
Into Thin Air	Jon	Krakauer	Picador	Australia	260	American	12/4/1954
Ghosts of Everest	Larry	Johnson	Random House	US	600	American	
Into the Wild	Jon	Krakauer	Anchor	US	224	American	12/4/1954
Bodies from the Ice	James	Deem	Picador	Australia	299	American	

Figure 7-3 Sample flat file database containing book data

quate for storing small amounts of simple data, but for even relatively complicated data the above problems quickly occur.

However, note that not all repeated data is redundant data. Sometimes it is necessary to repeat data in a database. For example, in figure 7-3, by coincidence both *Into Patagonia* and *Into the Wild* have 224 pages, so the number 224 is repeated. However, this is not redundant information because the number of pages varies (generally) for each book—there is no way of determining the number of pages from some other property of the book. In contrast, the Publisher Country is redundant because once we know the Publisher for a book, we know the Publisher Country.

Normalisation and Relational Databases

A better way to represent most data is using a **relational database**. Relational databases split data into multiple tables, each containing records related to one type of item or entity. These tables are then related to each other. The process of creating a relational database which has no redundant data is known as **normalisation**.

In the bookshop database in figure 7-3, three clear entities are represented: books, authors, and publishers. Currently these are all stored in the same table, which goes against the principle that a table should represent a single type of item or entity. Books, authors, and publishers each belong in their own separate table, with only the fields that relate to them. Each table must also have a primary key. Figure 7-4 demonstrates how the bookshop database could be broken into three separate tables. This solves the problem whereby redundant data existed, because in a relational database only one copy of each pub-

lisher's data is stored—in the Publishers table. If a publisher's details are changed, a single record can be changed. This avoids the potential problem of inconsistent data.

Note that the Publishers table may still contain some repeated data (for example, several publishers might have the same country), but *this is not redundant data*. This particular data needs to be repeated because it depends on the Publisher.

AUTHORS	BOOKS	PUBLISHER
*Author ID	*BookID	*Publisher
First Name	Title	Publisher Country
Second Name	Pages	
Date of Birth	Book language	
Date of Death	Original language	
Nationality	Year	
	Genre	
	Paperback	

Figure 7-4 The book shop database split into three tables— the first stage of normalisation

Common Mistake

Storing a person's age in a field is a bad idea. Every year the age field will need to be changed and worse, there would be no indication of **when** it needs to be updated. It is much better to store a person's date of birth instead.

Relationships

Once the data has been normalised into separate tables, those tables must be linked, or **related**, to other tables. This needs to happen so that details can be referenced from one table to another. For example, when looking at a book, we need a way to find out the information about its author. When looking at a publisher, we need a way to find out which books that publisher has published.

The first relationship to consider is that between Authors and Books. There is a **one -to-many relationship** here: one author has many books (potentially), but one book only has one author (we are assuming this is the case in this example).

<table>
<tr><td>

AUTHORS

*Author ID

First Name

Second Name

Date of Birth

Date of Death

Nationality

</td><td>

BOOKS

*BookID

AuthorID

Title

Pages

Book language

Original language

Year

Genre

Paperback

</td></tr>
</table>

Figure 7-5 A foreign key has been added to the Books table (AuthorID) and related to the field of the same name in the Authors table.

To create this relationship, an AuthorID field needs to be added to the Books table. This field can then be related to the AuthorID field in the Authors table (figure 7-5).

This illustrates one of the fundamental rules of relationships: they must exist between two fields which represent the same item of data. It would make no sense to have a relationship between the AuthorID field and the book title, since they represent totally different items (not to mention that one is a numeric field and the other is a text field). The AuthorID field in the Books table is known as a **foreign key**, because it only exists to be part of a relationship with another table.

> **Key Point**
> A relational database is a database in which multiple tables are linked together by relationships. Each table holds the data about one type of item or entity.

> **Key Points**
> There are two key points about relationships:
>
> 1. They occur between two fields with the same name and same data type
> 2. They occur between a primary key and a non-primary key.

Now the problem of redundant data is solved. In order to find out the author details of a specific book, we simply look at the book record, find the AuthorID field, and then look up the corresponding AuthorID in the Authors table (figure 7-6). Only one copy of the author's information is stored, so if it changes, those changes will automatically be reflected in all books with that author.

*BookID	AuthorID	Title	Pages	Book Language	Original Language	Year	Genre	Paperback
3643	11	The Climb	297	English		1998	Non-fiction	No
3644	2	In Patagonia	240	English		1977	Non-fiction	Yes
3645	5	If This is a Man	290	English	Italian	1958	Non-fiction	Yes

*AuthorID	First Name	Second Name	Date of Birth	Date of Death	Nationality
5	Primo	Levi	31/7/1919	11/4/1987	Italian
6	Robert	Harrison	4/12/1940		
7	James	Heil	1/4/1981		

Figure 7-6 Relationships allow data to be looked up from other tables

Finally, to complete the normalisation process, a second relationship needs to exist between the Publisher table and the Books table. Again, the relationship is one-to-many: one Book has exactly one Publisher, but one Publisher has many books (potentially). As with the first relationship, a foreign key (Publisher) needs adding to the Books table.

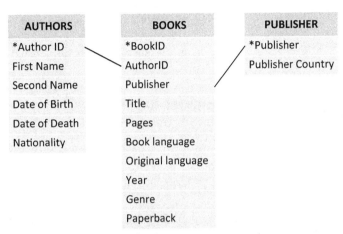

Figure 7-7 The final, fully normalised version of the book database

Exercise 7-4

Rework the Bookshop database from exercise 7-2 into a relational database. Remember that a relational database contains no redundant data.

Exercise 7-5

Look at the table below and identify the data which is repeated. Then:

    a)   Try to work out which data is redundant (unnecessarily repeated), and data which is repeated, but necessarily so.

    b)   Identify the groups of fields which belong together, and normalise this data into a relational database. Remember to select appropriate primary keys, foreign keys, and relationships.

Student ID	First Name	Second Name	Grade	Head of Year	Registration Tutor	Prefect	Registration Room
1234	Andrew	Smiles	11 A	Mr Quijada	Mr Frost	No	59
3456	Harris	Brown	11 B	Mr Quijada	Mr Andrews	No	42
6899	Sam	Smith	12 A	Mr Sun	Ms Shaw	No	61
3455	Bob	Field	11 A	Mr Quijada	Mr Frost	No	59
3577	Harry	Pipe	12 A	Mr Sun	Ms Shaw	Yes	61
1233	Tom	Keslake	12 B	Mr Sun	Ms Toper	Yes	62
2135	John	Janis	11 A	Mr Quijada	Mr Frost	No	59
4321	Rose	Brians	11 B	Mr Quijada	Mr Andrews	No	42

Exercise 7-6

Expand the database from exercise 7-4 to function as a bookshop's database. This means you will need to add information about customers and the orders they make. Ensure you create a fully normalised relational database.

Queries

A **query** is a way of selecting only the records in a database that match certain **criteria**. For example:

- All students who achieved over 90% in the test
- All results from Student A which were less than 40%
- All products that have less than 10 items in stock
- All customers whose last purchase was over 6 months ago
- All appointments today between 9:00 and 12:00
- All books which are paperback and which are longer than 400 pages
- All books by American or English authors

Queries are essential for accessing only the required information from a database. This is especially important when a database contains tens of thousands of records—manually searching through would be slow and error prone. Queries can have simple criteria such as '*Book language is English*', or they can use mathematical operators such as *greater than* or *less than* to compare values. These are useful when specifying a range of criteria, such as books published only in the last month. **Boolean operators** such as AND, OR, and NOT are used to combine criteria. For example:

- Language is English OR Spanish
- Language is NOT English
- Language is Italian AND author is Levi

When using a graphical database program such as Microsoft Access, queries are normally created by selecting the fields to be displayed and typing criteria for fields in the appropriate space (see figure 7-8). 'AND' queries are created automatically by entering criteria for more than one field, while 'OR' queries are created by listing several criteria for one field. Queries can also be created using a query language such as **SQL (Structured Query Language)**, explained on page 153.

Parameter queries

In some situations, the criteria for a field might not be known at the time a query is designed. For example, we might need a query to find all the books written by a certain author, but we don't know *which* author until a customer in the bookshop decides.

One very inefficient method would be to create separate queries for each author—*All books by Levi, All books by Jones, All books by Campbell,* and so on—but this is clearly time consuming and error prone. It would require a huge number of queries, plus a new query every time a book by a new author was introduced. A much better approach would be to use a **parameter query**. A parameter query prompts the user for a value when the query is run. The data entered by the user is used as the criteria for that

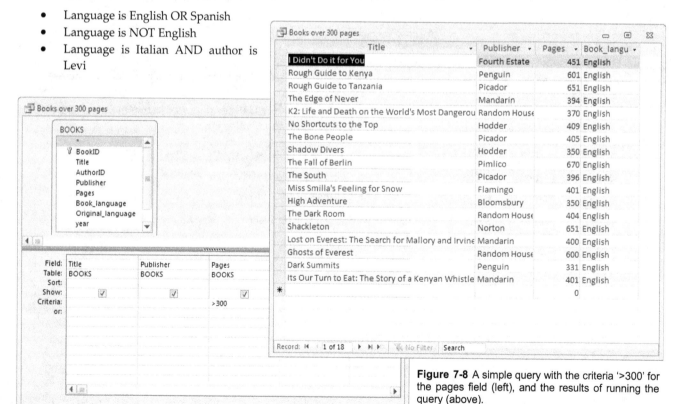

Figure 7-8 A simple query with the criteria '>300' for the pages field (left), and the results of running the query (above).

Figure 7-9 A parameter query in Microsoft Access. The criteria are specified using square brackets, and the user inputs the precise criteria into a dialog box when the query is run.

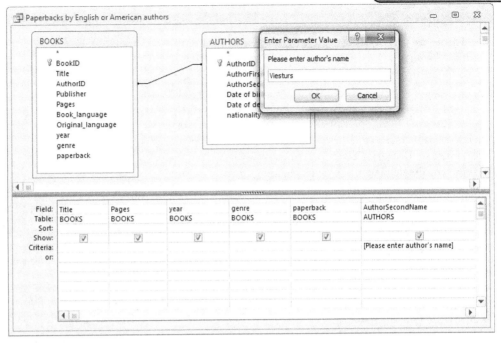

field (in this case, the author name). Parameter queries allow criteria to be specified at **run-time** rather than **design-time**, allowing much greater flexibility. In Microsoft Access parameter queries are achieved by using square brackets in a field's criteria (see figure 7-9).

Exercise 7-7

Create the following queries for the database you created in exercise 7-2. Remember that you will need some sample records in order for the queries to work.

    a) The title and genre of all books by Ed Viesturs
    b) All books whose original language is English, but have been translated to another language.
    c) All books published in 1998
    d) All books longer than 250 pages
    e) All books published in the UK
    f) The title of all books by Canadian authors
    g) All books about Mountaineering or Hiking or camping.

Exercise 7-8

Create the following parameter queries for the database you created in exercise 7-4. Remember that you will need some sample records in order for the queries to work.

    a) All books by a specified publisher
    b) All books on a specified topic
    c) All books by a specified author

Exercise 7-9

Create the following queries for the database you created in exercise 7-6. Remember that you will need some sample records in order for the queries to work.

    a) The titles and order dates of all books ordered by a specified customer
    b) All orders made during the last week
    c) All orders made more than one month ago which have not been fulfilled yet

Forms

Forms are used to present a user friendly graphical interface for entering and altering data in a database. Because of this, they are sometimes referred to as data entry screens. Forms shield users from the complexity of database tables, queries, and relationships. For example, in a doctor's database, patient details may be stored in one table while one or more x-ray images for each patient are stored in a separate table. A form can easily display the patient details and the x-rays belonging to them on the same screen, saving the user from switching between the patient table and another table or query for the x-ray images. Similarly, command buttons can be added to forms, allowing additional windows to be opened, such as all appointments made by that patient—even though in the underlying database, these appointments will be stored in a separate table.

Forms can also shield some data from users, helping to control how it is accessed. For example, they can limit the fields displayed, or can display fields but prevent alteration. In most cases, for example, users should not be allowed to edit automatically assigned identification numbers which are used as key fields.

Forms can be designed with a variety of layouts and colours and can be customised to include company logos, labels, and images. This is useful because the interface can be altered to use style and terminology similar to other applications the organisation uses, speeding up their transition to the system.

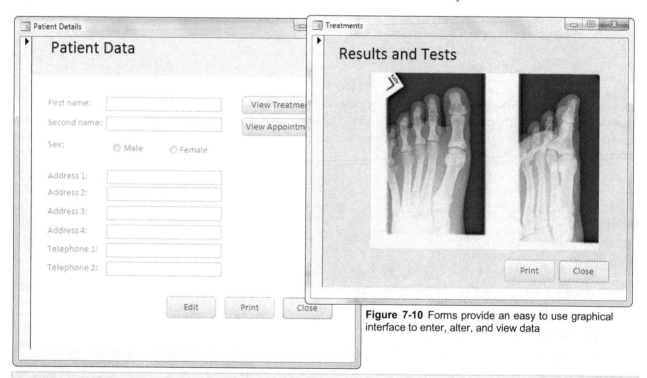

Figure 7-10 Forms provide an easy to use graphical interface to enter, alter, and view data

CSV and TSV

CSV (Comma Separated Values) and **TSV** (Tab Separated Values) are common ways of transferring data between different database and spreadsheet applications. They are useful in cases where programs use different file formats to store their data. CSV and TSV both save fields and records into plain text files, which can be read by most database and spreadsheet programs. CSV files separate each field value with a comma, while TSV files separate each with a tab. CSV and TSV are sometimes referred to as **comma** (or **tab**) **delimited values**.

Figure 7-11 shows the rentals database from page 147 saved as CSV. Each record is on a separate line (the first line contains field names), and fields are separated by commas.

Figure 7-11 Records exported as CSV

```
rentals.csv - Notepad
File  Edit  Format  View  Help
"Car registration", "Customer Name", "Rental date", "Return date", "Rate"
"R456 JKR", "Edwin Moss", "1/12/2010", "2/12/2010", "Standard
"A124 OEP", "Jack Frame", "1/12/2010", "8/12/2010", "Standard
"F672 TIR", "Rob Martin", "2/12/2010", "9/12/2010", "Premium
"R456 JKR", "Matthew Plate", "3/12/2010", "5/12/2010", "Standard
"J90 HAM", "Edwin Moss", "3/12/2010", "14/1/2011", "Premium
```

Reports

Reports are a way of presenting data from a table in a database in a more professional manner than the default data sheet view. Reports can also include complex data sets from multiple tables and queries, laid out in an easy to understand manner.

Like forms, reports can be customised in terms of layouts, colours, company logos, and data field layout. This helps provide information which is easier to interpret than the rows and columns view used by tables. The results dis-played in a report can also be ordered or sorted by different fields, and in built functions usually allow calculations to be made, such as the number of records being returned or the total value of certain fields in those records. For example, a report of outstanding payments might list those owing money and summarise the information at the bottom of the report with the number of debtors and the total value of their debt.

Reports are usually, though not always, designed to be printed out.

Figure 7-12 Reports provide professional looking output

Structured Query Language

SQL is a language for writing instructions to manage databases. It is designed to be easily understandable by humans, and is (in theory) compatible across different database products. SQL can be used to create fields, records, and tables, run queries, and edit or delete information. Examples of SQL statements include:

```
SELECT * FROM Books WHERE pages > 300
```
Show all books with more than 300 pages, producing the same results as figure 7-8.

```
SELECT * FROM Books WHERE Book_language='English' OR Book_language='Spanish' ORDER BY
title
```
Show all books in English or Spanish, sorted by the title of the book

```
SELECT * FROM Books WHERE NOT Book_language='English'
```
Show all books whose language is anything other than English.

```
INSERT INTO Books VALUES 'Lost on Everest', 'BBC', 'BBC', 400, 'English', NULL, 2009,
'Factual', True
```
Adds a new record to the Books table with the supplied field values (this particular statement relies on knowing the order of the fields in the table).

Issues: Integrity

"Data is as valuable as gold but as perishable as fresh fruit"

Data integrity – ensuring that data is correct, relevant, and up to date – is one of the biggest issues related to databases. A lack data integrity can cause a wide range of social impacts, including economic losses and legal problems. Worse, because many people trust computers, it can sometimes be hard to convince database managers to correct or remove erroneous data. Examples of database errors include:

A woman lost her job as an accountant because an FBI background check erroneous stated she was 'unsuitable' for the job, though it did not say why. Although the error in the FBI's National Criminal Information Center database was later discovered and corrected, the woman was not rehired[1]. The problem here was not only the incorrect data, but the lack of transparency about how the decision that the woman was 'unsuitable' was reached.

A new government tax database in the UK sent 1.4 million people incorrect tax bills totalling £2 billion. The bills stemmed from errors in the previous computer system which had under billed people[2].

In 2010 *The Times* reported that the UK's new electronic medical records system (see page 258) contained errors and omissions in medical histories, which 'could lead to patients being given inappropriate medication or suffering severe reactions, which in the worse cases can be fatal.'[3]. The new electronic system was supposed to improve care by reducing errors.

In the US, inconsistencies in the way names were stored in Social Security Administration databases and electoral registration databases caused 20% of voters in a test to be rejected. The error occurred because some names were stored in full in one database, but with only an initial for the middle name in another. The software processing the databases required an exact match to verify a voter[4].

Errors in the terrorist watch lists maintained by the US Transportation Security Agency (TSA) regularly make the news media. Two lists exist—a No Fly List, which contains the names of people banned from air travel to or from the US, and the Selectee List, detailing people who warrant additional security checks at airports. Passengers' names are checked against the list at check in. In one

example, three people named James Robinson were stopped at US airports because they had the same name as a suspected terrorist. One of them was a commercial airline pilot. Another was an eight year old boy[5]. In a separate incident, a man named Daniel Brown was placed on the watch list and suffered problems checking in to future flights because security officials found traces of gunpowder on his boots. He was a marine returning from an eight month tour of Iraq[6]. There are many reports of individuals being stopped multiple times because they are repeatedly confused somebody on the list[7].

Aside from the inconvenience of missed flights caused by incorrect data, these cases highlight the implicit faith which people often have in computer systems. In the cases of children being highlighted as security risks, it might be reasonable to assume security staff would recognise this as an error, rather than subject them to additional checks, but this is frequently not the case[7]. Travellers who are repeatedly stopped because of the same error also highlight the concern about how data is included on such lists, and how it can be removed.

In any database system, data may be incorrect for several reasons. The data may be:

- Out of date
- Entered incorrectly
- Transferred from another database (badly)
- Changed accidentally
- Changed deliberately
- Incomplete
- Totally missing

The final two points might not sound significant but can lead to serious problems. For example, incomplete medical records might miss vital details of a patient's previous medication, complications, or conditions, which could lead to dangerously incorrect treatment. Similarly, police records which fail to show the outcome of criminal proceedings might fail to indicate a person was found innocent. Equally serious would be a failure to record previous convictions.

While deliberate tampering of data can be reduced to some extent by adequate security measures (see chapter 5), accidental changing of data is hard to guard against. Finally, data must be kept up to date to ensure that it does not lose integrity over time. Telephone numbers and addresses might reasonably change, as might financial and medical records. An out of date address in a sex offender's register, for example, could have serious consequences (see exercise 7-18).

Exercise 7-10

Use RDMBMS software to create a relational database for one of the scenarios below. Pay close attention to the choice of fields, data types, tables, and relationships, and make sure the database is normalised. Create the required queries and add validation checks to the appropriate fields. Create Forms for input and Reports for professional output.

Scenario 1 – Online Pet Shop

A pet store lets customers choose and pay for their pets via their web site. Customers can pay for the pets using either a credit card or a PayPal account. A PayPal account number starts with PP and is followed by a maximum of 12 numbers. For credit cards, only Visa and MasterCard are accepted. Cash is not accepted. The store sells many kinds of animals and breeds, including some exotic species which require the purchaser to have a special licence. If needed, the customer's licence number will be collected along with the financial details when he places an order. The licence number is 2 digit number followed by four letters. The law requires the store to produce a list of all exotic species sold during the last month.

The Society of Animal Welfare requires all pet shops to provide a weekly report detailing the health condition of all pets under their care. Pet shops are subject to random inspections and face a large fine if they cannot produce this report. Because of this, each individual animal needs to be tracked. Pets are supplied by a variety of different companies. Usually one company supplies multiple types of animals. The store uses several queries to check on its business. Each week the manager checks to see the sales for the past week. Occasionally he also checks the sales from the past six months. In the future, he would like to have these same reports group the sales by species of animal.

Scenario 2 - City Library

A city library has 50,000 books, over 4,000 journals and periodicals, 500 CD-ROMS, computer software, and audio books. These items are spread over five floors of the library building. The library intends to throw away books which have not been borrowed for the past ten years. It also wants an easy way to find books which are in poor condition so that they can be repaired (the library records the condition of books as 'New', 'Good', 'Worn', and 'Needs replacing'). The space freed by throwing away these books will be used to purchase extra copies of books which have been borrowed more than 100 times in the past six months. Some books are available for short-term loan (1 day), most are for normal loan (1 week), and others for extended loan (1 month). Other books cannot be loaned and are 'research only'. CD-ROMs cannot be loaned because naughty people kept making illegal copies of them.

Borrowing is by members only. Lists are needed of all members who have borrowed no books, and all members with overdue books. Overdue members are fined. More books cannot be borrowed until the fine is paid. A list of all members who have outstanding fines is needed.

Scenario 3 – Employment Agency

An employment agency supplies workers to businesses that need staff temporarily. The agency has several workers specialising in over 20 different jobs including teaching, nursing, plumbing, and cleaning. The agency must be able to contact workers using a variety of methods. Some workers are 'short notice' workers, meaning that they are willing to work with less than 12 hours notice. A list of these workers is required if a business calls at the last minute. Other workers are given at least 24 hours notice. Jobs have a certain minimum level of education ('unskilled', 'high school', 'college', or 'degree'). Some workers have extra qualifications such as first aid certificates or health and safety training. Some jobs (such as teachers or nurses) require that workers undergo a police criminal records check. If a worker has had a successful check in the last five years, this fact should be recorded in the database. All workers must present their 12 digit national identification number when they first register.

When a business calls looking for workers, the agency must list all workers that suit the company's requirements (education level, notice period, police check, certificates). After a certain time, the management may decide to consider businesses as 'gold clients', meaning that they receive a small discount on their rates. Businesses are charged monthly for the workers the agency supplies. The agency needs to be able to list all workers that have gone to a particular business in the past month. Calculation of fees is based the total number of man-hours a business has used that month (i.e. the sum of the hours worked by each person going to that business).

Validation

Data validation is the process of ensuring that data is in the correct format for a particular field. For example, validation could be used to ensure that when a credit card number is entered, it contains exactly sixteen numbers, and no letters. Another example would be ensuring that a date has a day, month, and year component, and that the day has a minimum value of 1 and a maximum value of 28, 29, 30, or 31, depending on the month. Validation rules would also be used to ensure that 29 February is only a valid date in leap years, and that 30 February is never valid. Common types of validation checks are described in figure 7-13.

Validation, however, does not ensure that the data is correct – only that it is in the correct format. For example, in a date of birth field, validation can be used to check that 1 May 2011 is a genuine date, but it cannot check that 1

Range check	Checks that a numeric field is above or below a certain value. For example, IB grades are between 0 and 7 inclusive.
Length Check	Checks the number of characters in a field. For example, credit card numbers are 16 digits long.
Character check	Checks that a field contains only certain characters. For example, names cannot usually contain numbers, and telephone numbers can only contain numbers and certain symbols.
Presence check	Checks that the field is not blank.
Consistency checks	Based on two or more related fields whose values depend on each other. For example, a person's date of death must be after their date of birth, and cannot be after the current date.
Check Digit	A mathematical check for numeric fields. Calculations are performed on a field and the result (the check digit) is stored in the field itself. When the calculation is performed on the field later, the answer should correspond with the check digit. If it does not, the data has been incorrectly entered. Check digits are used for the ISBN numbers on books and credit card numbers. See page 157.
Value list	Used to restrict a field to a set of pre-determined values. For example, a payment method field might be restricted to only 'Cash', 'Visa', and 'MasterCard'.

Figure 7-13 A variety of validation checks can be used, depending on a field's data type

---

Exercise 7-11

Look at the table below. Which validation checks can be used to validate each field? Some fields may have more than one check.

Field	Example	Range Check	Length Check	Character check	Presence check	Consistency check	Check digit
Title	If This is a Man						
Author	Primo Levi						
Publication date	1958						
ISBN	0349100136						
Normal Price	$14.99						
Sale Price	$10.99						
Publisher	Abacus						
Number of pages	129						
Web site							

May 2011 is actually the subject's date of birth, if that is what we are entering. To ensure the date really is the subject's date of birth, verification techniques must be used.

Validation in Microsoft Access

Microsoft Access implements the validation techniques listed in figure 7-13, though it uses different names for some of them. Figure 7-14 shows the equivalent names for each validation technique in Access.

A particularly useful tool in Microsoft Access is the **input mask**, which allows the user to specify requirements for each character of the input. For example, it can be specified that a vehicle registration number consists of a single letter, followed by three numbers, followed by three more letters. Only input following this pattern would be allowed when entering data using a table or form.

Verification

While validation checks that data is in the correct format, **verification** checks that data actually is correct. For example, if we are entering an IB grade into the computer, validation (a range check) can be used to ensure the grade is between 0 and 7 inclusive. Verification will help us make sure that the grade we entered actually is the right grade for that student. Verification can be quite hard to achieve.

Validation Check	Name in Microsoft Access
Range check	Validation rule
Length check	Field size property
Character check	Input mask
Presence check	Field's 'Required' property
Consistency check	Validation rule
Check digit	Modules / Macros
Value list	Lookup

Figure 7-14 Common validation checks and their equivalent names in Microsoft Access

There are several possible verification techniques:

Entering data twice – this helps avoid typing mistakes that may have occurred when the data was entered. The data might be re-entered by the same person or by somebody else. For example, when examiners enter grades for exam papers, they enter all of the grades for a school, save them, and then enter them again to ensure there have been no typing mistakes or mix-ups during entry. The system automatically highlights any differences between the two sets of data and requires the examiner to resolve them.

Check Digits: Worked example

International Standard Book Numbers (ISBN), found on all books, use a check digit to validate them. Take any book with a 10 digit ISBN (for example, 1456589881). Write down the first nine numbers the top row of a table like the one below (the last digit, the check digit, is not used yet).

×	10	9	8	7	6	5	4	3	2
	1	4	5	6	5	8	9	8	8

Multiply each number by its column number and add it all together, giving:

$(1 \times 10)+(4 \times 9)+(5 \times 8)+(6 \times 7)+(5 \times 6)+(8 \times 5)+(9 \times 4)+(8 \times 3)+(8 \times 2) = 274$

Now divide the total by 11 using integer division (modulus):

$274 / 11 = 24$ remainder 10

Subtract the remainder from 11:

$11 - 10 = 1$

This final result should be the same as the check digit (the last digit in the ISBN), which in this case it is. This means the number has been entered correctly. If the result of the calculation and the check digit do not match, either one or more digits of the ISBN were incorrectly entered, or the maths was done incorrectly (we assume the computer won't do this).

Comparing with original documents – once data has been entered into a computer system, it can be compared with the original paper documents to confirm it is correct. Depending on the type of information, the original documentation might include passports and drivers' licences.

Verifying with the data subject – in the case of some data, it might be sufficient to simply ask a person if the date of birth stored in the computer is correct.

Issues: Privacy

Data is incredibly valuable to organisations: it can help inform a business about its internal performance, how customers react to its actions, how best to target customers, and even how future business decisions might affect the business. Governments also make use of data to help improve services, reduce fraud, and improve national security. Developments such as **data warehouses** and large **centralised databases** have allowed vast amounts of data to be collected, stored and processed in one location. This has provided the ability to access and use ever larger amounts of data in ways previous not possible. Although having significant benefits, some of these methods raise concerns about privacy, especially in relation to the way data is collected and whether the subjects of the data are aware of how it is being used.

Data Matching

Data matching (sometimes called **computer matching**) is often used to build up a profile of an individual by combining data about them from several databases.

Data matching is commonly used by governments to root out fraud, such as false benefit claimants. For example, in the UK adults living on their own, or living with non tax payers such as children or students, qualify for a lower council tax rate. The National Fraud Initiative combined tax records with voter registration data, looking for people claiming this lower rate even though more than one voter (and therefore, adult) is registered as living at their address. It was estimated that £90 million per year could be saved by combating fraudulent claims. However, of the 939 'matches' detected by the data matching software, 785 were investigated and found to be genuine claimants. This left 154 cases - less than 1% of all claims - as possible fraud cases, leading some to question the value of the software[8].

In other cases, databases of people receiving unemployment benefits can be matched against employment records, in an attempt to find people who are both working and claiming unemployment benefit. Financial records

> **Common Mistakes**
> Validation and Verification are commonly mixed up. Some students also accidentally describe them as being the same—'validation verifies that data is correct'. Remember: validation checks if a data value is in the correct format for that field, while verification tries to ensure the data actually corresponds with the actual, correct value.

can also be matched with tax data to look for people who may be avoiding tax payments by understating their income.

Data matching has also been used recently in an attempt to combat terrorism by gathering as much data as possible about individuals and then applying data mining techniques (see exercise 7-17).

In the above cases, there is clearly a potential positive social impact: by reducing fraud governments can reduce economic loss, and hopefully spend the money somewhere more productive, such as education or healthcare.

However, privacy concerns also arise from data matching. A key problem with these methods is that data about many people—including innocent ones—needs to be collected and processed in order to find the few who may be breaking the law. For example, in the past a person would be investigated for benefit fraud if the government became suspicious of them. Using data matching, everyone can be effectively investigated for fraud, automatically, without any suggestion that they might have done anything wrong. Some people consider this an invasion of their privacy (particular if the data was not originally collected for this purpose) and a violation of the principle 'innocent until proven guilty'.

Data Mining

Data mining (sometimes called **knowledge discovery**) is the process of discovering hidden patterns and trends in large databases. These patterns and trends would be difficult or impossible for a human to spot, in part because of the large volume of data. However data mining software is capable of analysing millions of records and applying various statistical methods in a relatively short time. Data mining techniques are often combined with data matching to provide a greater body of source data.

Data Mining in Business

One application of data mining is the 'personal recommendations' which many businesses, especially online businesses, make for their customers. For example, a video rental shop might determine the films a person is likely to enjoy based on their personal details and the films they have rented in the past. In fact, data mining can be used to analyse the records of other customers who have rented the same film, and examine their subsequent rentals to build up a catalogue of films which might be relevant. This would enable the shop to make accurate recommendations, hopefully improving their customer satisfaction and, ultimately, their profits. In 2009 online film company Netflix did exactly this - offering a $1,000,000 prize to anyone who could improve their recommendation algorithm by 10%[9].

In a similar way, businesses use data mining to target their advertising. Rather than sending an expensive printed advertising brochure to all customers, data mining can be used to identify those who are most likely to respond to an advertisement. This saves money by sending fewer copies of the brochure, and avoids annoying customers with advertising they don't want.

In the banking and finance sectors, data mining is used to decide who should be allowed or denied a loan. Data mining software can take into account many aspects of an individual's life which indicate whether they are a high or low risk customer, including employment records, tax records, credit card records and the individual's family situation.

Data Mining in Health

Health insurance companies perform a similar task when a person applies for medical insurance—medical histories and family histories are checked to determine an individ-

> **Common Mistake**
>
> Privacy and Security are related, but separate, ideas. Privacy concerns how our data is used by the people who collect it. Security concerns how safe data is from unauthorised access – for example, by hackers. When an organisation collects data, it must respect our privacy, and must also take precautions to prevent security breaches.

ual's risk. These same companies also use data mining techniques to detect potentially fraudulent claims, much as governments do for social security based fraud.

A more controversial use of data mining occurs when a patient in the US buys prescription drugs at a pharmacy. Details including the patient's name, gender, address, medication and dose are typically recorded. This data then has personally identifiable fields removed and is then sold by pharmacies to data mining companies. In turn, these companies process the data and sell it to drugs companies. Drugs companies can then use data mining techniques on the collected data of thousands of patients and prescriptions, in order to target advertising of their products more effectively.

Privacy Concerns & Principles

Privacy is an abstract concept which can be hard to clearly define. A good attempt would be 'privacy is about having control over what data is collected about you and how it is used'. Most people desire some degree of privacy—many of us would not be happy if every detail of our lives were publicly available for everyone to access. This is particularly true when dealing with **personally identi-**

European DNA Databases

The UK has the largest DNA database in Europe, containing over 4.5 million records in 2009 (7% of the population), including 850,000 people never convicted of a crime, and 150,000 children[16].

Aside from the privacy issues arising from collecting and storing this data, significant concerns have been raised by a 2007 decision to share DNA profiles among European police forces. This policy allows each member of the European Union free and complete access to the DNA databases of other members, allowing police to check the DNA of foreign citizens against evidence found at crime scenes in their own countries. Although all countries are affected by the decision, the UK's database far outsizes all others, with the next largest, Austria's, accounting for less than 1% of its population. This **trans-border data flow** causes concerns about the security measures in place in other countries, as well as the privacy controls governing who is allowed to access the data—which is particularly important if the data of innocent people is being stored.

The system has led to some success, however. Also in 2007, an armed robber responsible for several offences in the UK was identified after DNA from the scene was compared with samples stored in Estonia's national DNA database. This led to the suspect's arrest when he attempted to travel[17]. The real question is whether the ability to fight crime, particularly international crime, is a significant enough impact to warrant the risk of sharing large amounts of sensitive data with many other users in other countries.

fiable data or sensitive data, such as medical records or financial records. Many organisations that collect data—whether on paper or electronically – have privacy policies which state how the data they collect will be used and who will have access to it. In some countries, companies are required by law to have privacy policies. In the UK, the Data Protection Act specifies how companies can collect, store, and use personal data (see page 161).

Exercise 7-12 discusses examples of privacy questions raised by some current database systems. In general, several issues need to be considered by companies who collect personal data, to avoid privacy problems:

Consent—Companies should obtain consent to collect and use data. It should be made clear to individuals which data is being collected about them and how it will be used. For online services, these details are often found in the **Terms of Service** or **Privacy Policy** documents available on the company's web site. Some organisations use an **opt-out** policy, whereby individuals' data will be collected unless they specifically request it not to be. Others use an **opt-in** policy, which means no data will be collected unless the user specifically agrees.

Purpose—The purpose of collecting the data should be made clear. Once it has been collected, data should be used only for this purpose, and not for alternative purposes, known as **secondary uses**.

Distribution—Whether or not data will be given or sold to third parties. This is important in preventing secondary use of data, particularly of sensitive data. For example, if a person gives their medical data to their doctor for use in an electronic medical record system, they would not expect the doctor to sell that data to drugs companies, so that the companies can send advertising to the patient. In fact, some patients might be unhappy if their medical data were shared with anyone else, even if personally identifiable items such as names were removed.

Accessing data and correcting errors—Individuals should have the right to view the data stored about them

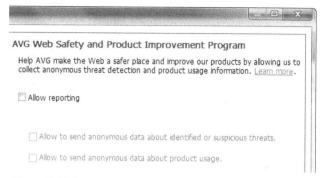

Figure 7-15 Some systems let users opt out of data collection

and have any errors corrected. This right is particularly important for people suffering due to database errors. For example credit databases which contain incorrect information can prevent subjects from obtaining a loan because of a bad credit rating. The inability to view and correct this data can cause serious negative impacts to the individual concerned.

Length of storage—Data should only be stored as long as needed, and then be destroyed. The problem with computer systems is that they enable data to be stored for very long periods of time, while transferring data to other databases or systems can allow it to exist long after the original copies have been deleted. The longer data is stored, the higher the risk that it may be out of date, or that it may be transferred to unauthorised users.

Security—Organisations collecting data must take adequate security measures to ensure unauthorised users cannot gain access to the data, violating privacy.

> **Largest databases in the world**
> The largest databases in the world include Amazon's customer and product database (over 42 terabytes of data), ChoicePoint's database of information about American citizens (250 terabytes of data on 250 million people), and Sprint's telecommunication database (over 2.85 trillion call records). Google's user data (contains details of every search made using Google - over 90 million each day)[18]

Exercise 7-12
Discuss the scenarios below to determine whether they are acceptable or whether they represent a breach of privacy.
    a) Social networks collecting data about their users' habits and interests, to enable them to sell more accurate targeted advertising systems. [8 marks]
    b) Pharmacies selling anonymous data about prescription drug use to data mining companies for advertising use. [8 marks]
    c) Government use of data mining to detect fraud. [8 marks]
    d) Health insurance companies using data mining to decide whether to accept or reject applications for health cover. [8 marks]

Issue: Security

In addition to ensuring they use and distribute data appropriately, data users must also take adequate security measures to prevent unauthorised access to the data they hold. These security measures should cover a range of possible attacks, including hacking of database servers, physical access or theft of database servers, and interception during physical or electronic transfer.

Encryption of both communication links (for example, using TLS) should be standard practice, as should the encryption of all data stored in a database. **Database auditing** allows data controllers to view both successful and unsuccessful attempts to access, change, or delete data in a database. This can help alert data controllers to the possibility of malicious activity if, for example, it is seen that one user is attempting to read hundreds or thousands of records in a short space of time.

Databases are often the target of hackers because they contain large amounts of very sensitive data including credit card numbers and passwords. Many databases also contain enough personal information such as addresses and social security numbers to enable a criminal to commit identity theft. In early 2009 job search service Monster suffered such a database breach, losing sensitive data including user IDs, passwords, email addresses, names, and contact details[10]. The theft of passwords prompted Monster to automatically reset the passwords on all compromised accounts. However, as many people use the same password for multiple accounts, such attacks still increase the risk of accounts for other systems being compromised—especially when victims' email addresses are also stolen, as criminals can create targeted phishing emails (see page 104).

In another example, in 2007 retailer TJ Maxx discovered that its database system had been compromised and the details of over 45.7 million credit cards had been stolen. The stolen data affected customers in the US, the UK, and Ireland. Worryingly, the data was not stolen in one attack, but in a series of attacks dating to 2002[11]. The cost of investigating and repairing the compromised systems was calculated at $135 million. One estimate, including the damage to customer confidence in the brand, calculated the cost to TK Maxx at $4.5 billion[12].

Organisations also need to be aware of the possibility of employees copying or using data for criminal purposes and use access control systems to ensure employees only access the data they need to do their jobs. In 2006 HSBC bank had the data of over 24,000 people stolen by an IT specialist working for them. The worker was caught when he unsuccessfully tried to sell the banking details to competitors[13].

In other cases, the UK's Police National Computer database has been misused by police officers—including a string of cases involving officers using the system to check personal records of potential partners[14]. In other incidents, police officers have taken bribes to provide criminal record data from the system to private investigators, journalists, and even criminal gangs[15].

Data Protection Act

The **Data Protection Act** (DPA) is a UK law that governs the use of data collected and stored on a computer system. The DPA identifies different stakeholders including **data users** (people or organisations who collect and use data), **data subject** (the people about whom data is stored), **data controllers** (the person in an organisation who has overall responsibility for ensuring the DPA is followed) and the **Information Commissioner** (a position responsible for enforcing the DPA nationwide). The DPA obliges data users to follow rules when collecting, storing, and processing data, including:

  i. Ensuring sensitive data is only collected with the data subject's consent
  ii. Ensuring the data is only used for the purpose for which it was originally collected
  iii. Ensuring the data is kept up to date (if applicable)
  iv. Ensuring security measures are taken to prevent unauthorised access to the data
  v. Ensuring the data is securely deleted when it is no longer needed for the original purpose
  vi. Ensuring data is not transferred to other countries which do not have data protection regulation

The DPA also provides certain rights for data subjects, including:

  i. The right to view data stored about you by an organisation (usually at a small cost)
  ii. The right to have data corrected or deleted if it is incorrect

There are some exceptions to these rights – for example, data subjects do not have the right to view information held about them as part of criminal or national security investigations, since doing so would likely harm the investigation[19].

Chapter Review

Key Language

alternative key	data warehouses	opt-out	secondary use
auditing	DBMS	parameter query	select query
Boolean operators	field	personally identifiable data	sensitive data
character check	field size	presence check	sorting
check digit	flat file database	primary key	Structured Query Language
composite key	foreign key	privacy policy	tab-delimited text files
consistency check	forms	queries	table
CSV	index	range check	trans-border data flow
data entry form	input mask	RDBMS	TSV
data integrity	key field	record	validation
data matching	knowledge discovery	redundancy	verification
data mining	length check	redundant data	web databases
Data Protection Act	normalisation	relational database	
data redundancy	online encyclopaedias	report generation	
data types	opt-in	secondary key	

Exercise 7-13

Match the terms on the left with the definitions on the right.

1) Foreign key   A) A field which is unique for every record in that table

2) Primary key   B) A way of specifying the data to be extracted using a query

3) Secondary key   C) A mathematical check performed on a piece of data to ensure it is valid

4) Criteria   D) A field which links to another table's primary key to form a relationship

5) Check digit   E) A primary key which consists of more than one field

6) Composite key   F) A field by which a table is often accessed or sorted

---

Exercise 7-14

Consider the database security breaches described on page 161. **Explain** the characteristics of computer based databases which make such security breaches more likely and more effective than similar breaches against paper record systems. [4 marks]

Exercise 7-15

Select a major online retailer, which does only online business. **Construct** a diagram which shows the tables, relationships, and fields which might be stored as part of the retailer's database. Remember that online stores save much more than just product and customer information. [6 marks]

Exercise 7-16

State, using SQL or a similar notation, the queries that might achieve the following in an online shop database (it may help to do exercise 7-15 first):

a) Show all electronics products sold by ABC Electronics [2 marks]
b) Show all of the customer reviews for a television whose product code is E9483 [2 marks]
c) Show all new products released in the last week [2 marks]
d) List all products found under the 'Customers who bought this also bought...' section of the shop [2 marks]
e) Set the price of all small, blue jeans to £9.95
f) Remove from the database all transaction made more than five years ago

Exercise 7-17

In the early 2000s the US government started and then abandoned several computer profiling schemes including TIA (Total Information Awareness), CAPPS (Computer Assisted Passenger Pre-screening), and CAPPS II. The goal of these systems was to identity potential national security threats. This was achieved using data matching and data mining techniques to identify individuals who had 'suspicious' indicators.

The original CAPPS system was already operating before the 11 September 2001 terrorist attacks, and indeed the system selected several of the hijackers for additional security screening. The hijackers were not caught because they were not carrying any metal objects or obvious weapons[20]. After September 2001 the US government increased the development of these profiling systems.

(a) (i) Define the term *data matching*. [2 marks]

   (ii) Describe **two** fields that might be included in the CAPPS database, and identify their data types. [4 marks]

(b) Explain how data mining might be used in the CAPPS database to identify suspicious travellers. [6 marks]

(c) To what extent is the use of computer profiling system an appropriate way to fight terrorism? [8 marks]

Exercise 7-18

The US Sex Offender Registry maintains records of all those convicted of sexual offences across the US. This information is made publicly available by the FBI, and there are many web sites available that allow users to search by name, address, and criminal offence. Family Watchdog (www.familywatchdog.us) is one such web site, which also plots a map showing the home and work addresses of offenders released into the community.

(a) (i) Define the term *primary key* [2 marks]

   (ii) Describe the creation of a query to show all offenders living in Washington DC and convicted of Assault. [4 marks]

(b) Explain **three** ways the data in the Sex Offender Registry database could be verified. [6 marks]

(c) Discuss the benefits and drawbacks of publicly releasing information in the Sex Offender Registry database online. Evaluate your arguments. [8 marks]

Exercise 7-19

Several European cities have bicycle hire schemes, where registered citizens can collect any available bicycle from a public stand, authenticate themselves, and return it to another stand later. The cost of the hire can be automatically deducted from the borrower's account, which is pre-paid using a credit card.

(a) (i) Identify **two** fields likely to be used by the bicycle hire database, and their data types. [4 marks]

   (ii) Define the term *foreign key*. [2 marks]

(b) Explain how a relational database helps data integrity. [6 marks]

(c) Evaluate the concerns that might arise through the use of such a bicycle hire database. [8 marks]

References

1 Zetter, K. (2009). *Woman Loses Job Due to Error in FBI Criminal Database.* Wired. Available: www.wired.com/threatlevel/2009/10/ncic/. Last accessed May 2011.

2 Batty, D. & Inman, P.. (2010). *Tax errors hit 6 million people.* The Guardian. Available: www.guardian.co.uk/money/2010/sep/04/tax-errors-hit-6-million. Last accessed May 2011.

3 Rose, D. (2010). *New patient medical records database 'contains life-threatening errors'.* The Times. Available: www.timesonline.co.uk/tol/life_and_style/health/article7067762.ece. Last accessed May 2011.

4 Szustek, A. (2008). *Voter Registration Database Errors Could Freeze Out Voters.* Available: http://www.findingdulcinea.com/news/politics/September-October-08/Voter-Registration-Database-Errors-Could-Freeze-Out-Voters.html. Last accessed Nov 2011.

5 Griffin, D. & Johnston, K.. (2008). *Airline captain, lawyer, child on terror 'watch list'.* CNN. Available: articles.cnn.com/2008-08-19/us/tsa.watch.list_1_terror-watch-list-airline-pilot-terrorist-screening-database?_s=PM:US. Last accessed May 2011.

6 Associated Press. (2006). *'No Fly List' Delays Marine's Iraq Home Coming.* Available: www.msnbc.msn.com/id/12284855/. Last accessed May 2011.

7 Nakashima, E. & Alec Klein, A.. (2007). *U.S. Agency Tries to Fix No-Fly List Mistakes.* The Washington Post. Available: www.washingtonpost.com/wp-dyn/content/article/2007/01/19/AR2007011901649.html. Last accessed May 2011.

8 Welch, J. (2009). *Data matching: a threat to privacy?.* Available: http://www.guardian.co.uk/commentisfree/libertycentral/2009/nov/23/data-matching-privacy. Last accessed Nov 2011.

9 Hinterthuer, A. (2009). *Figuring Out Movies You'd Really Like.* Available: www.scientificamerican.com/podcast/episode.cfm?id=figuring-out-movies-youd-really-lik-09-04-29. Last accessed April 2011.

10 Manzo, P. (2009). *Monster Database Security Breach Official Alert.* Available: help.monster.com/besafe/jobseeker/index.aspx. Last accessed April 2011.

11 BBC. (2007). *Hackers target TK Maxx Customers.* Available: news.bbc.co.uk/2/hi/business/6508983.stm. Last accessed April 2011.

12 Gaudin, S. (2007). *T.J. Maxx Security Breach Costs Soar.* Available:www.informationweek.com/news/global-cio/compliance/showArticle.jhtml?articleID=201800259. Last accessed April 2011.

13 Barrett, L. (2010). *HSBC Confirms Massive Database Security Breach.* Available: www.esecurityplanet.com/news/article.php/3870071/HSBC-Confirms-Massive-Database-Security-Breach.htm. Last accessed April 2011.

14 Bloxham, A. (2010). *Female PCSO used police computer to find boyfriends.* The Telegraph. Available: www.telegraph.co.uk/news/uknews/law-and-order/8110191/Female-PCSO-used-police-computer-to-find-boyfriends.html. Last accessed Nov 2011.

15 Lewis, J. (2011). *Hundreds of police officers caught illegally accessing criminal records computer.* The Telegraph. Available: www.telegraph.co.uk/news/uknews/crime/8713194/Hundreds-of-police-officers-caught-illegally-accessing-criminal-records-computer.html. Last accessed Nov 2011.

16 Travis, A. (2009). *Ministers keep innocent on DNA database.* The Guardian. Available: http://www.guardian.co.uk/politics/2009/may/07/dna-database-government-retention. Last accessed Nov 2011.

17 Helm, T. (2007). *Outrage at 500,000 DNA database mistakes.* Available: http://www.telegraph.co.uk/news/uknews/1561414/Outrage-at-500000-DNA-database-mistakes.html. Last accessed Nov 2011.

18 Winter Corporation. (2011). *Top Ten.* Available: http://wintercorp.com/VLDB/2003_TopTen_Survey/TopTenProgram.html. Last accessed Nov 2011.

19 UK Government. (1998). *The Data Protection Act 1998.* Available: www.legislation.gov.uk/ukpga/1998/29. Last accessed April 2011.

20 9/11 Commission. (2004). *The Aviation Security System and the 9/11 Attacks - Staff Statement No. 3.* Available: www.9-11commission.gov/staff_statements/staff_statement_3.pdf. Last accessed April 2011.

Chapter 8
Models & Simulations

Objectives

1. Distinguish computer models and computer simulations
2. Describe the applications of models and simulations
3. Explain high performance computing techniques
4. Explain how a computer model is created
5. Use a spreadsheet to create a simple computer model
6. Evaluate issues related to the accuracy and reliability of models

Computer Models and Simulations

Models are simplified representations of real concepts and events, used to aid understanding or make predictions about outcomes without actually testing them. For example, a teacher's classroom scale model of the planets helps understanding of the solar system and planetary orbits.

Vast amounts of modern computing power allows the creation of computer models and simulations, which are much more complex and detailed than any models possible with manual methods. Models can be programmed with the very latest scientific understanding, such as how the Earth's climate works, and used to make predictions about the future of our planet. This chapter investigates how computer models are constructed, how they can be used to predict a variety of events, and some of the problems that might exist with doing this.

Computer Models

A **computer model** is a computer program that creates a simplified, mathematical representation of a real world process. Very basic computer models can be created using spreadsheet software, but most often dedicated modelling software is used. Because computer models involve vast numbers of highly complex calculations, they are most often run on supercomputers (see page 14). Computer models are used to model two main types of event:

1. Those which are difficult or impossible to observe — for example, the future of Earth's climate, the millisecond or microsecond events during a nuclear reaction, the effect of an earthquake on a building, and the births and deaths of stars in space.
2. Events which are expensive or dangerous to test by experimentation — for example, changes to the design of a nuclear reactor, the effects of car crashes on the passengers, or changes to a city's transportation infrastructure.

Computer models use **variables** and **processes** to create a representation of the real world. Because all models are **simplifications** of reality, their outputs are **predictions**, not guarantees. However, decisions are often made based on these predictions, so it is very important to understand how accurate a model is.

Figure 8-2 Model showing car deformation during an impact

Applications of models

Computer models have a wide range of applications. City **transportation models** (figure 8-4) are used to model traffic levels at different times of the day, and predict how these will change in response to changes in the transportation infrastructure (such as making a road one-way or building a new bypass road). These models can also predict side effects such as changes in noise or air pollution caused by traffic levels. To make their predictions, these models need to accurately model the speed and quantity of vehicles on the roads during different

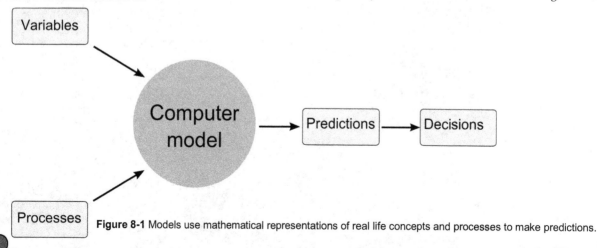

Figure 8-1 Models use mathematical representations of real life concepts and processes to make predictions.

periods of the day, as well as the complex behaviour of humans as they move around the city.

Structural models can predict the strength of buildings and bridges in severe events such as earthquakes and storms. These models require complex detail about construction of the buildings as well as the properties of their component materials and the surrounding environment (such as the type of earth under the building).

Phenomena in space, such as supernovae and black holes, can be modelled using a computer and the latest scientific theories. This helps advance scientific understanding of phenomena which are rare and hard to observe.

Medical researchers can use **drug interaction models** to improve understanding of bacteria and viruses that cause disease, and the effect of different doses of medication on patients. Results can be tested on virtual 'patients' with different ages, sexes, and medical conditions, without putting real patients at risk (see page 266).

Car crash models are increasingly being used by vehicle manufacturers to observe the effects of accidents on cars, passengers, and pedestrians. They are currently used to supplement the real world physical crash tests which vehicle manufacturers also perform. A car crash model needs input variables including the speed and angle of the crash, as well as details about the passengers. They also include complex physics describing how two cars react when they collide. The predictions (output) of the model are the data about the damage to the car and the passengers (probably displayed visually). Based on this output, decisions can be made concerning the safety features and design of the car. An advantage of these models is the relative ease with which tests can be repeated, compared with physical crash tests. Models also allow many different crashes to be tested because, unlike physical tests, a new car is not required each time. Traditional crash tests are recorded by high speed cameras, with impacts measured by sensors attached to the car. Computer models allow a wider range of variables to be measured and analysed.

Computational Fluid Dynamics (CFD) models the flow of liquids and gasses, and is commonly used to test aerodynamics. Racing cars, which have to be as aerodynamically efficient as possible, can be tested in physical wind tunnels, but increasingly CFD is being used as well. This allows various designs of the car to be tried before materials, money, and time have to be committed to actually building them. Designers of turbines use CFD models for similar reasons.

Aircraft designers also work heavily with CFD to assess the lift capabilities of aircraft while still in the design stage. Wake turbulence, the turbulent air which occurs behind a moving aircraft and causes dangerous vortexes for following aircraft, can also be observed for different aircraft designs. NASA uses CFD to understand how the air will flow around its space shuttle craft when they re-enter the Earth's atmosphere—which would be too dangerous and expensive to experiment with in reality (see figure 8-3).

Climate models are another common example of computer models. They are used to model the Earth's climate both for everyday purposes (predicting the weather) and

Figure 8-3 Computational Fluid Dynamics used to model the airflow around a space shuttle on re-entry to the Earth's atmosphere (top), and the aerodynamics of a Formula 1 car (bottom).

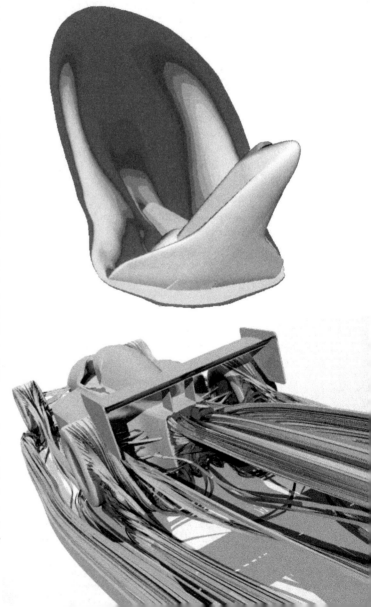

scientific research purposes (predicting possible future climate change). Climate models incorporate a vast array of scientific knowledge including processes that describe radiation received by the Earth from the sun, atmospheric interactions, the production of greenhouse gasses, and ocean currents. Predictions include possible temperature change and associated effects such as loss of sea ice, increases in sea levels, and changes in weather patterns. Climate models are hugely complex creations which test the limits of our scientific knowledge and computing power. When dealing with issues such as possible sea level changes, they are used to make decisions which might affect millions of people and costs billions of dollars, so it is important that they are as accurate as possible.

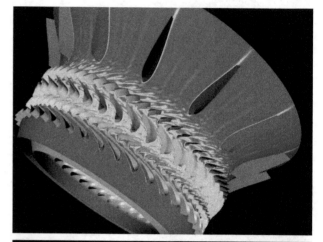

Computer models also have applications in business and finance. In this particular area, they tend to be known as **Decision Support Systems** because organisations use them to answer questions about possible future performance and assist in decision making. Historical business data, such as sales figures and profits, are incorporated into the model, in addition to social theories about customers' habits and behaviour. Using this information, Decision Support Systems can answer *'What if?'* style questions such as *'What if we decreased the sales margin on our products by 5%?'* or *'What if we could reduce the defect rate from 3% to 1%?'*. Other questions might look at the effect on sales figures if a new version of a product is released, or how effective advertising in particular media might be.

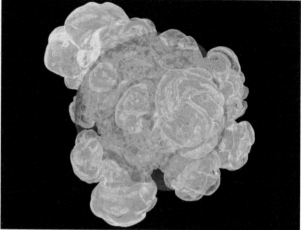

Why use models?

Computer models have a number of advantages compared to testing situations in real life:

- Models can be used to generate 'What-if' scenarios—input variables can be quickly changed to see their effect on the results.
- Tests conducted with models are generally cheaper and require fewer material resources than real life tests
- Models are safer than real life testing in some cases
- Models are more practical than real life testing in some cases (such as changing road layouts)
- Models are the only option in some cases (for example, testing a building's resistance to an earthquake)
- Models can be repeated with exactly the same input data—this is rarely possible in real life tests

Figure 8-4 Various computer models: air passing through a jet turbine (top); a type IA supernova (middle); a model of traffic densities in down town Chicago (bottom).

Finance Models

In the financial market, banks, investors, brokers, and insurance companies have used computer models for some years. These incorporate statistical methods, laws of probability, and historical data to identify trends in markets, look for investment opportunities and assess risk. Many of these systems extend the computer model to implement so called **algorithmic trading**, where Artificial Intelligence (see chapter 16) is used to automatically make decisions and perform transactions based on the results of the model. These programs have revolutionised the financial markets, being capable of performing thousands of complex transactions in seconds, long before human investors could even hope to understand the implications of the information presented to them. With millions of dollars at stake, these trading algorithms have become prized possessions of the top stock and commodity trading firms.

However, such models have also caused problems when their predictions have failed to match reality. In 2007 the Goldman Sachs Group, a major player in investment banking, reportedly lost up to $1.5 billion when two events, which its computer models predicted would only occur once every 100,000 years, happened on two consecutive days[1].

Algorithmic trading has also been implicated in the global economic crisis which started in 2008[2]. In particular, the use of a formula known as the Gaussian copula function, which attempts to calculate how separate events affecting the financial markets correlate with each other, was highly successful until events in the financial markets moved in unexpected ways.

The use of models and automated systems to trade commodities raises several ethical issues — most obviously, about the integrity of the model, the data it contains, and the results it produces. There are also questions about the wisdom of automatically delegating decisions to an artificially intelligent computer program rather than relying on a human to oversee and approve transactions.

Exercise 8-1

Try these online computer models. In each case, pay close attention to the variables and processes that are being modelled.

Disease spread model (ccl.northwestern.edu/netlogo/models/AIDS).
Models the spread of the HIV virus, with different variables affecting the speed of its spread.

Climate model (ccl.northwestern.edu/netlogo/models/ClimateChange).
Model radiation entering and leaving the earth's atmosphere.

Eco-system model (www.learner.org/courses/envsci/interactives/ecology/)
Models the population of predators and prey giving variations in the food chain.

Traffic model (www.traffic-simulation.de).
Models the flow of vehicles and traffic jams in a variety of road situations.

Exercise 8-2

Research the following types of computer model.
   a) Car crash models
   b) Climate models
   c) Earthquake models
   d) Search and rescue models
   e) Disease spread models
   f) Eco-system models

For each, **explain** the variables that are being modelled, the processes that are being modelled, the predictions being made, and the decisions which will be based on those predictions. Be as thorough as possible as there are many variables that might be initially overlooked. For example, the car crash model has to model not only the vehicle itself, but the passengers inside it. [4 marks each]

Creating a Simple Climate Model

This task will guide you through the creation of a simple climate model using a spreadsheet program like Excel or LibreOffice Calc. If you have limited experience of spreadsheets, you may find the quick review practical on page 182 useful.

To complete the model, a bit of background information is needed. The Earth receives energy from the sun, approximately 342 Watts per square metre. Some of this is reflected back by the clouds (25%), some absorbed by the atmosphere (another 25%). The remaining 50% hits the Earth's surface, warming it. The Earth re-radiates much of this radiation upwards. If the Earth had no atmosphere, all of this radiation would be lost to space, and the planet would be quite cool (around −18 degrees Celsius). However, because of the Earth's atmosphere, only 3% escapes immediately into space. Greenhouse gasses absorb the rest, eventually releasing some into space (42%) and reflecting the rest back down to Earth (58%), causing further warming. This is the greenhouse effect.

The Greenhouse Effect

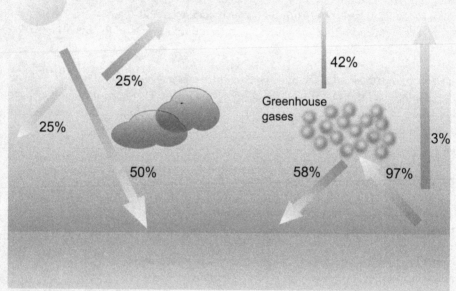

Figure 8-5 A simplified diagram of the greenhouse effect

The amount of heat re-radiated by the Earth can be calculated using the Stefan Boltzmann constant, which is quoted as 5.67×10^{-8}. The formula to calculate the re-radiation is then ST^4 where S is the Stefan Boltzmann constant and T is the current temperature.

The temperature change during a given time period is calculated using the formula:

```
(energy in - energy out) × (time in seconds) / Earth's heat capacity
```

Where the Earth's heat capacity is generally quoted as 4×10^8.

This exercise will create a simplified model of this process. Although it initially looks complex, it can be modelled relatively easily in a spreadsheet provided the problem is broken down into smaller parts. The best approach is to use each row of the spreadsheet to represent a given period of time—1 year or half a year works best. It is best to split the spreadsheet into two halves horizontally—using the left side to calculate the energy received, minus the losses to space and the clouds, culminating in the total radiation hitting the surface. The right half of the spreadsheet can then calculate the amount of re-radiated radiation (using Stefan Boltzmann's constant above), model the loss of radiation into space and the radiation returning to Earth, and then calculate the temperature change. Figure 8-6 shows possible column headings. Note that the Earth's temperature starts at 255 Kelvin.

	Time	Prev temp	Rad from sun	Reflected by clouds	Absorbed by atmosphere	Reflected by surface	Absorbed by surface	Back radiation	Total Hitting surface
13	0	255.00	342.00	85.50	85.50	17.10	153.90		153.90
14	0.5	255.00	342.00	85.50	85.50	17.10	153.90	184.47	338.37
15	1	258.86	342.00	85.50	85.50	17.10	153.90	184.47	338.37
16	1.5	266.12	342.00	85.50	85.50	17.10	153.90	192.83	346.73
17	2	275.46	342.00	85.50	85.50	17.10	153.90	209.57	363.47
18	2.5	284.92	342.00	85.50	85.50	17.10	153.90	233.25	387.15

Re-radiated	Atmospheric window	Total in atmosphere	Emitted by atmosphere	Back radiation	TOTAL IN	TOTAL OUT	Temp change	New temp (K)	New temp (C)
239.74	7.19	318.05	133.58	184.47	342.00	244.00	0.00	255.00	-18.00
239.74	7.19	318.05	133.58	184.47	342.00	244.00	3.86	258.86	-14.14
254.60	7.64	332.47	139.64	192.83	342.00	250.00	7.25	266.12	-6.88
284.36	8.53	361.33	151.76	209.57	342.00	263.00	9.34	275.46	2.46
326.45	9.79	402.15	168.90	233.25	342.00	282.00	9.46	284.92	11.92
373.66	11.21	447.95	188.14	259.81	342.00	302.00	7.88	292.80	19.80

Figure 8-6 The climate model spreadsheet. Calculation of the incoming radiation which hits the Earth's surface (above left), and re-radiation into the atmosphere or space (right).

Completing the model

If done correctly, you should see the new temperature of the Earth in column start at –18 and slowly rise until it reaches an equilibrium after a short time. Up until that point, more energy is entering the Earth's atmosphere than leaving it, but it slowly equalises, stabilising the temperature.

If you have strange answers, there are a number of possible problems:

- There are several points where **absolute cell referencing** is essential
- The Stefan Boltzmann constant is 5.76 times 10 to the power of negative 8, not 8.
- The formulae produce temperature values in Kelvin, so they might seem high. To convert to Celsius, subtract 273.
- To find 'lost' radiation, it can be useful to total the left and right sides of the model, to ensure they equal 100%.
- Make sure the cell format is correct and that the spreadsheet is not displaying a rounded value

Altering the output

The values presented in figure 8-5 are approximate values. In fact, it is quite likely that you will find different values in different text books or online resources. This is partly because these values vary across the Earth (discussed later). You can change these variables in the model yourself to see their effect on the Earth's temperature. For example, changing the cloud albedo (the amount of radiation reflected by the clouds back into space) to 50% (.50) quickly results in a surface temperature below zero, since sunlight is stopped from hitting the Earth's surface.

Is it accurate?

The next few page discuss possible problems with this model—many of which apply to all types of models, not just simple climate models.

Problems with models

Although it may not feel like it, the climate model created on page 170 is really a very basic model. The scientific laws used in this model often represent 'ideal' or 'perfect' circumstances, which do not apply on Earth. For example, the Stefan-Boltzmann constant represents the radiation emitted from an ideal black body, so it represents the maximum possible emission values. Yet the Earth is not a perfect black body and many aspects of it – which are not represented in this model – change the amount of radiation emitted. This is a clear **simplification** in the model.

Another problem is that the model uses the value 342 Watts per metre squared per second for the amount of radiation received from the sun. In fact, the amount of radiation received from the sun is about 1366 Watts (this is known as the solar constant). The figure of 342 Watts was calculated by taking into account the average radiation received at different latitudes and at different times of the year due to the Earth's shape and rotation. Some parts of the world receive more or less radiation than this average value, but our model has assumed all areas receive the same amount of energy. Again, this is a simplification of reality.

Yet another simplification is that the model fails to account for variations in the radiation emitted by the sun. These variations are typically only 0.1 – 0.2%, yet the lack of them moves the model slightly further away from reality.

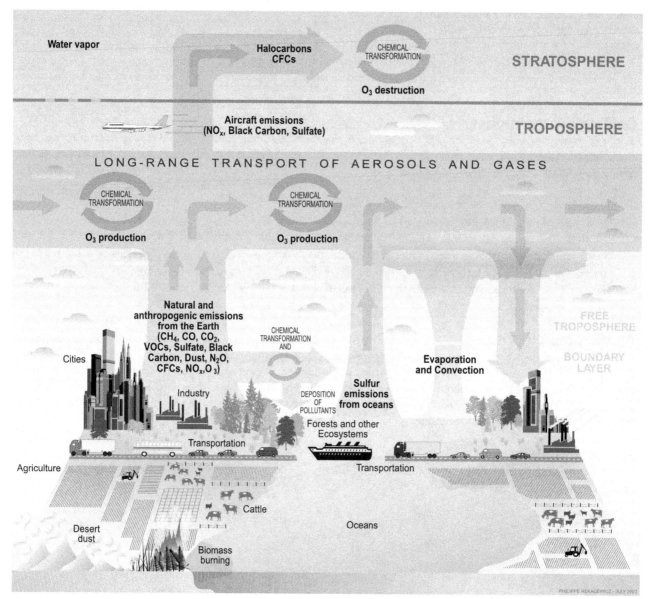

Figure 8-7 There are many influences on the Earth's climate. Computer models try to incorporate as many of these factors as possible.

The accuracy of the source data is also important: the model uses a value of 25% for the cloud albedo (the radiation reflected by the clouds), but it is common to see different figures quoted in different sources. The surface albedo is 5% in our model—again, different sources quote different values—and in fact the surface albedo depends on the type of terrain—snow and ice may reflect up to 90% of the radiation they receive. In order to account for different terrain types, the model would need to divide the surface of the planet in a grid and measure radiation at each point—and the resolution of this grid would also significantly affect the results (see figure 8-9).

Missing and simplified variables also play a key role. The model uses the Stefan Boltzmann law to determine the amount of re-radiated energy from the Earth's surface, but does not take into account other sources such as evapotranspiration. The effect of some of these processes on the Earth's climate is often debated.

Finally, and most importantly if we are to use the model for climate prediction, our model does not account for any human impact. Although the model represents greenhouse gasses such as CO_2 in the atmosphere, it is **missing variables** to represent their amount, and **missing processes** to model the change in that amount due to human activity. If these items were present, we would then also need to model CO_2 absorption by nature – for example in oceans and by plants (as described on page 174, some early climate models did not include these processes either). If these items were included, we might need to model the rate of change in plant cover (deforestation or reforestation) because that affects the absorption rate. And, since climate change might lead to rises in ocean levels (which in turn would affect CO_2 absorption!), we would need to model that too. Finally, because CO_2 emissions, deforestation, and reforestation are all human impacts, we would need to model human population and its change over time, and any possible changes in behaviour, such as moving to cleaner fuel sources!

Of course, our model does not do any of these things, nor could we expect to be able to do so in a spreadsheet. More complex computer models are created using specialist modelling applications, and the most complex models, running on the most powerful computers, are custom programs written specifically for the task.

Feedback Loops

If feasible, **feedback loops** can be used to improve the accuracy of a system by using previous results as input. For example, the output of a short term weather model can be compared with the actual weather on that day, with any differences being used to improve the model and the accuracy of its results for next time.

Simplification of models

In general, there are two reasons simplifications are made in computer models. Firstly, we may have a lack of scientific understanding of the phenomena being modelled. If we do not understand how something works, it is not possible to codify it into a computer program. Climate models are a good example of this, as even now our understanding of the Earth's climate is incomplete. Page 174 shows how climate models have improved over time as our scientific understanding has grown.

Secondly, a lack of available data may be to blame. Again, many of the variables in the climate model are general values, used because it is often difficult to obtain data, such as levels of greenhouse gasses or the concentration of ozone, from locations all over the planet.

Finally, a lack of available computing power can limit computer model complexity. Computer models need incredibly powerful computers (see page 176). In fact, almost all of the fastest computers on the planet are used for running computer models (see page 15). However, even a supercomputer can take days to calculate a few milliseconds of time in a car crash model. Models may therefore have to be simplified in order to calculate the results in the required amount of time. After all, it would be no use if a climate model took a whole day to calculate tomorrow's weather – by the time we had the answer, we could look out the window and see the answer for ourselves!

> **Key Points**
> - All computer models are based on scientific and mathematical principles
> - All computer models are simplifications of reality
> - Models allow time to be sped up or slowed down
> - Models are used to make predictions

Exercise 8-3

Assume that we wanted to include some of the items mentioned above in our climate model.
   a. **Describe** some suitable sources of data for these variables. [4 marks]
   b. Are there some types of events or variables which are harder to find sensible for than others? **Explain** why this is the case. [4 marks]

Development of Climate Models

Climate models have developed over time from very simple models not unlike the one on page 170, to sophisticated programs that include all of the items mentioned in this chapter, plus many more.

Figure 8-8 shows the development of **Global Climate Models** (GCMs) since the 1970s. As scientific understanding of the Earth's climate has developed, so has the complexity of the models. For example, it wasn't until the late 1970s that methane, nitrous oxide, and CFCs were recognised as significant greenhouse gasses, thus improving our understanding of atmospheric interactions.

Many early computer models were very primitive by today's standards—some of the earliest modelled the Earth without taking into account oceans or terrain heights. Often, a lack of computing power prevented **unified models** being created. Instead, each aspect of the Earth's climate was modelled separately. For example, ocean and sea-ice models existed in the early 1980s, but it was not until the 1990s that they were incorporated into GCMs which included models of other parts of the Earth's ecosystem—until that point they were modelled separately. Similarly, models of the sulphur cycle, ocean carbon cycle, land carbon cycle, and atmospheric chemistry interactions have existed individually since the early 1990s but only recently have all been combined into more complete GCMs. Had these aspects been incorporated earlier, the complexity would have meant calculating the results would have taken too much time. As improved computing power allows more and more aspects of the environment to be incorporated into models, their accuracy is slowly increasing.

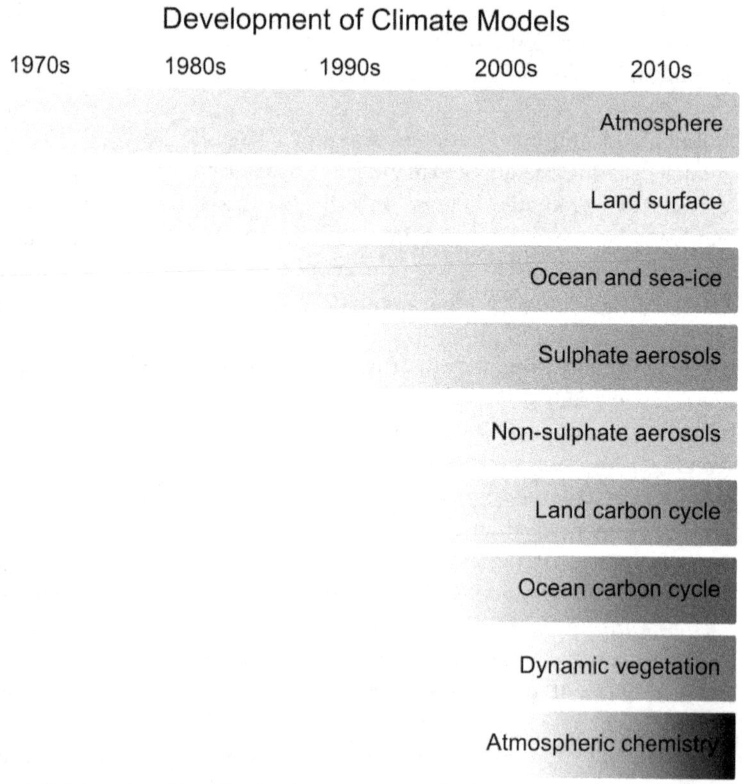

However, no climate model could reasonably model the environment at every single point

Development of Climate Models

1970s	1980s	1990s	2000s	2010s

Atmosphere

Land surface

Ocean and sea-ice

Sulphate aerosols

Non-sulphate aerosols

Land carbon cycle

Ocean carbon cycle

Dynamic vegetation

Atmospheric chemistry

Figure 8-8 As scientific understanding and computing power have increased, climate models have developed from relatively simple atmospheric models to complex unified models[3].

on the Earth – that would involve modelling the interactions of every single atom on Earth, and far more computing power than is available. Instead, climate models divide the surface of the Earth into a grid of squares, and model the climate in each of them as a single figure or point (figure 8-9). Early models used grids in which each square represented approximately 1000 kilometres of the Earth's surface, while later models use finer grids, perhaps down to 100 kilometres. Similarly, climate models have depth, representing from between 400 metres and 30 kilometres of atmosphere. The resolution of these grids has an effect on the accuracy of the results, in much the same way as the resolution of an image affects the amount of detail it can contain. For example, in the first image of figure 8-8, Great Britain is covered by only three grid squares, meaning the predictions for a large geographical area are being represented by just a single result from the model. In the second part of figure 8-8, 13 grid squares represent Great Britain, and in the final image it is covered by around 40 squares. This is particularly important since climate change might affect different areas in different ways. In an extreme example, if the whole Earth was only divided into a single grid square, only one set of data (temperature, etc.) would be calculated for the whole Earth—yet the earth obviously does not have one uniform climate. The higher the number of grid squares, the more likely the results are to match local conditions, but of course, vastly increased computing power is required to perform the necessary calculations.

Climate Model Resolution

Figure 8-9 The resolution of the grids used to represent the Earth's surface directly impacts the accuracy of the results and the amount of time taken to calculate them. Below, the first grid has squares of approximately 300 kilometres; the second, 150 kilometre. The final grid has squares of 75 kilometres, increasing the detail of the results, but requiring 16 times as many calculations as the first grid.

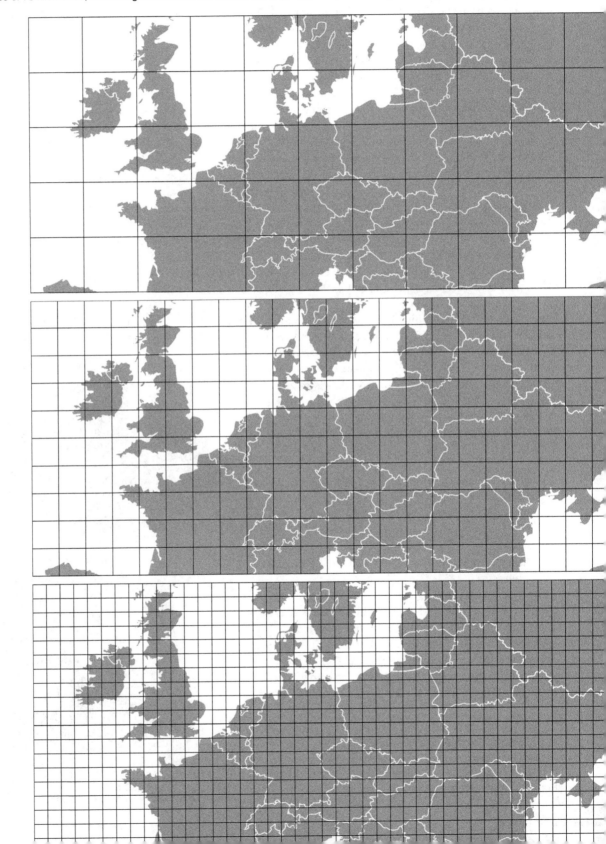

High Performance Computing

Models and simulations used for scientific research involve extremely complex calculations, which need the vast amounts of computing power only available in supercomputers. These supercomputers (see page 14) achieve tremendous speeds by using **parallel processing** techniques. Parallel processing involves using more than one processor to work on the same task at the same time (in parallel) in order to complete the work more quickly. This can make a tremendous difference to the speed at which tasks are completed, especially for tasks where there is a large amount of independent data to be processed. There are two basic approaches to parallel processing: **centralised processing** and **distributed processing** (also called **grid computing**).

Centralised processing involves multiple processors (often tens or hundreds of thousands) installed in the same computer system. The dual core and quad core systems found in many desktop and laptop PCs are examples of basic centralised processing. Most classic supercomputers use a centralised processing approach, which is one reason why they take up such a large amount of space. For example, the IBM Blue Gene series of supercomputers can have up to 300,000 processor cores and fill a large room (figure 8-10). Other supercomputers are detailed on page 15.

Distributed processing uses a different approach to achieve parallel processing. Rather than use one specialised computer, distributed processing uses multiple separate computers connected by a network. The connected computers might be simple desktop or laptop machines, mainframes, supercomputers, or a mix of types, and are often distributed over a wide geographical area. Distributed processing works by sending a separate part of the task and data to each connected computer, which processes it independently and returns the results to a central computer. A big advantage of distributed processing is that it is very scalable — computers can be added or removed from the 'grid' very easily.

One of the most famous distributed computing projects is SETI@Home. SETI, the Search for Extra Terrestrial Intelligence, collects radio signals from space and stores them digitally at the University of California, Berkeley. Volunteers use the SETI@Home software to download a small part of the signals and analyse them automatically, sending the results back to Berkeley. The volume of data is so great that the SETI project would be unable to analyse the signals with their own resources, so they rely on volunteers. SETI has several million active users, and is the biggest ever distributed computing project[4].

Other distributed computing projects include Folding@Home, which simulates protein folding to aid understanding of various diseases; Einstein@Home, which scans radio data for space to detect signs of neutron stars and test Einstein's General Theory of Relativity; and GIMPS, which tries to find examples of Mersenne primes (special cases of prime number).

The Large Hadron Collider (LHC) in Switzerland is supported by distributed computing projects including LHC Computing Grid and the Open Science Grid. These systems are needed to store and process the huge amounts of data generated by the scientific research conducted by the collider — over 13 Petabytes (13,631,488 Gigabytes) in 2010 alone.

Figure 8-10 The IBM Blue Gene supercomputer uses powerful centralised computing techniques involving thousands of processors (top). The Large Hadron Collider uses computers distributed across Europe to store and process the data it generates (bottom).

Visualisation

The majority of the computer models depicted in this chapter have used graphical outputs in the form of graphs, maps, images, or even animations. Even the simple missile trajectory model on page 178 uses a line graph to show the missile path. All of these graphical outputs are **visualisations** of the numeric data generated by the computer models. The main advantage of graphical output over output as a tables of numeric data is that a large amount of information can be displayed in a relatively compact form, using colour and animation to help distinguish different types of data and changes over time — which would be difficult to see in a table of numbers. For example, in figure 8-11 colours are clearly used to distinguish different terrain types. By using a three dimensional image, a large area of land, including terrain height, is shown concisely, while an animation highlights the patterns of retreating ice. If this data were to be shown in a table, it would require at least four columns and many hundreds of rows of data, even for just a single point in time, and it would be very hard to spot patterns or anomalies in the data by staring at row after row of numbers.

Figure 8-11 A 2003 United States Geological Survey (USGS) model of glacial change. It shows the Blackfoot-Jackson basin in Glacier National Park, and Gunsight Lake. The model was based on a predicted exponential rise in Carbon Dioxide (CO_2) concentrations, causing a temperature increase of 2-3 degrees Celsius by 2050, and an increase of 10% in precipitation. These images changes from 1950 to 2050.

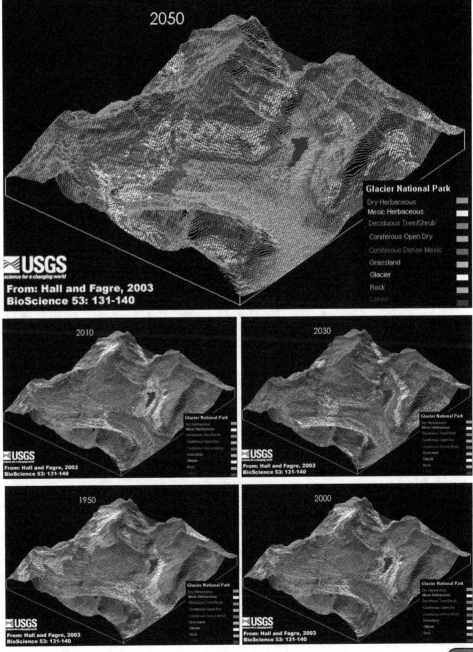

Creating a Missile Trajectory Model

This task will guide you through the creation of a simple computer model that predicts the trajectory (path) a missile will follow when given a specific launch speed and launch angle. Use a spreadsheet to create it, and while doing so, consider how this model has been simplified compared to real life.

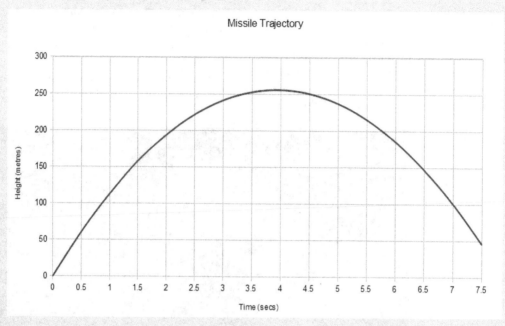

Constants

The following are constants: enter them near the top of the spreadsheet (say, starting in cell A1). They will not be changed by any of the formulae in the model.

Constant	Meaning	Value	Explanation
t_step	Time step	0.5	We will calculate the missile's position every t_step seconds. So if t_step = 0.5, we will calculate the position at 0.5 seconds, 1 sec, 1.5 seconds, 2 seconds, etc.
angle	Launch angle	45	The angle at which the missile is launched in degrees
theta	Launch angle	radians (angle)	Use the RADIANS function in this cell to find the value of the *angle* variable, in radians.
v	Launch velocity	100	The velocity (in metres / second) at which the missile is launched
g	Force of gravity	-10	The force of gravity acting towards the earth, in metres per second

Variables

The following are variables which will change on each spreadsheet row. Enter these going across, starting in cell A7.

Variable	Meaning	Explanation
t	Time	Keeps track of the current time in the model: it will be zero when the launch takes place, increasing by t_step on each row of the spreadsheet
x	Horizontal position	The position of the missile at a given time
y	Vertical position	The position of the missile at a given time

Setup

Enter '0' in the cell under the heading *t* (cell A8). Make the numbers going down this column increase by *t_step* each row (0, 0.5, 1, 1.5, 2, 2.5, etc.). Use a formula to do this, rather than typing the numbers manually—later we might want to change the value of t_step, and we want these time values to automatically recalculate themselves. Do this for 40 rows (until t = 20).

Calculations

The following calculations can be used to calculate the missile's position at any given time. Fill these formulae in the appropriate columns.

Horizontal position at a given time	$= v \times \cos(\theta) \times t$
Vertical position at a given time	$= v \times \sin(\theta) \times t + 0.5gt^2$

Graphing

A graphical output of the missile's trajectory is probably easier to interpret than a table of numbers. Graph the time and y columns to view the trajectory. It should look like the graph on page 178.

Exercise 8-4: Verification of the Model

One of the primary problems with models is verification of the results. Usually we don't have the actual data to compare with (if we had the actual data already, why would we be using a model?). Additionally, models are simplifications, meaning that some aspects of the real world systems may not be accurately represented in the model. Consider the questions below:

(a) **Identify** variables or processes which might be missing from this model. [4 marks]

(b) **Describe** other errors that might occur during the construction of the model, apart from missing variables or processes. [6 marks]

(c) **Explain** how each problem above could be resolved. [6 marks]

(d) **Explain** the effect that changing the t_step variable has on the accuracy of the answers. [4 marks]

(e) **Explain** how the output of this model could be verified. [4 marks]

Have errors been made? A potential source of problems is human error when entering the data or formulae into the spreadsheet. We can start to verify the model's output by looking at the general shape of the graph (it should be a symmetrical curve). However, a curve of the right general shape does not prove the results are correct.

Is the Physics correct? The formulae used in the model can be verified by looking them up online or in a physics text. The missile trajectory is calculated correctly. However, using these formulae is extremely simple, and only models a missile travelling in a vacuum. In reality, all kinds of forces including air friction and cross winds will affect the flight of the missile. The affect of these forces also varies with temperature and altitude, which is not included in the model. So, the basic physics is correct, but it is simplified and there are many missing variables.

Are the variables accurate? The rate of acceleration due to gravity is generally quoted as 9.8 m/s^2, but this has been rounded to 10 in the model. The effect of gravity can also be calculated using a formula, but that relies on other variables being known, such as the mass of the Earth. Finally, the rate of g changes depending on your position on Earth (it is higher nearer the equator) and altitude—neither of which are represented in the model. This is another simplification.

The *t_step* variable determines the accuracy with which we determine exactly where the missile hits the ground. *t_step* is effectively the margin of error for impact time: when *y* becomes negative, it indicates the missile has hit ground, but we can only be sure that it became negative some time between the present time and *t_step* seconds ago. For large values of *t_step* this would give a huge window of error for a missile travelling at high speed.

Computer Simulations

A **computer simulator** provides the user with experience of a real life situation by combining computer models of the world with realistic input and output devices and (relatively) realistic graphics. Because simulators let the user experience a situation, they generally run in real-time rather than the sped up or slowed down time that computer models use. However, it is important to remember that simulations have computer models underlying them.

Flight simulators are a common example of computer simulations. They combine computer models of the physics of flight, aerodynamics, and the aircraft structure with a realistic three dimensional representation of the world. To make the experience more realistic, flight simulators use input devices like joysticks, switches, and levers, as found in real aircraft. Flight simulators that are used to train professional pilots will even use a complete, accurate recreation of the aircraft cockpit to provide maximum immersion. Many commercial simulators are mounted on **full motion platforms**, which allow them to raise, lower, rotate, and tilt to provide feedback to the pilot's inputs and aircraft's situation.

The military and commercial airlines both make extensive use of flight simulators to train their pilots. Simulators can be quickly configured to place the aircraft and pilot in specific locations anywhere on the globe, with specific weather conditions and

Figure 8-12 SIMUVEG driving simulator at the University of Valencia (above left); Full motion platforms are often used to increase realism in flight and driving simulators (top); US Navy personnel train in a ship simulator (middle); aircrew train in a state of the art flight simulator (above right).

situations. Unusual or dangerous situations such as engine failures or emergency landings can easily be recreated and practiced many times without risk to the pilot, aircraft, or any passengers. Military personnel may also connect several flight simulators together so pilots can practice manoeuvres together in the same virtual world.

Driver training is another common use of simulators. **Driving simulators** are used to train learner drivers and provide refresher courses for more experienced drivers. As with flight simulators, hazards such as pedestrians or cyclists can be added to test a driver's awareness or to assess the effectiveness of safety equipment such as reflective vests on cyclists. Racing teams also use simulators as a form of testing, making changes to a car's design or setup and testing it in the simulator before applying the changes in real life.

Other types of simulators in common use include ship simulators, train simulators, and space craft simulators. The US military has even developed fully immersive combat simulators, allowing individual soldiers to experience conditions on the battlefield (see page 302).

Advantages of simulators

Simulators offer a number of advantages over real life training. A primary advantage is that unusual or rare events can be programmed to happen as often as required, and the user can practise in these situations without any fear of loss or damage to people or equipment.

Specific environmental conditions can be programmed, removing the need to wait for them to happen naturally. Similarly, simulators are unaffected by real world conditions such as dangerous weather or darkness, which might halt real world training. This saves time and allows trainers to make maximum use of the simulator.

Although simulator software and the specialised hardware required is expensive to develop, there are often long term cost savings once this has been done. In particular, resources such as fuel and spare

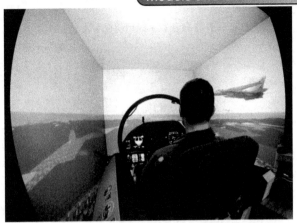

Figure 8-13 Simulators often use multiple screens to 'wrap around' the user and provide a more immersive experience of the environment. This can also be seen in figure 8-12.

parts are not required, and vehicles or aircraft do not need to be taken out of service to train crew.

Disadvantages of simulators

However, even the best simulations cannot offer an exact reproduction of the real world. Because they are based on computer models, simulators suffer the same drawbacks—namely, they are a simplification of the real world. As with models, the integrity of the data used to create the simulator is of upmost importance. Errors in the data or processes used to create the model will result in output which is less accurate.

Simulators are also unable to recreate the exact feeling and pressure of being in a real world situation. For example, flying an aircraft through bad weather in a simulator may be many times less stressful than flying an actual aircraft full of real passengers through real weather, where mistakes carry the risk of injury or death.

Spreadsheet Review

This exercise will set up a simple spreadsheet for calculating student grades. It should help you understand the basics of using spreadsheet applications like Microsoft Excel. If you are already familiar with using a spreadsheet, there are more advanced exercises on pages 170 and 178.

1. Start a new spreadsheet. Starting in cell A4, enter about seven names going down the page (it is useful to enter the first and second names separately, in case we want to sort the spreadsheet by name later).
2. In cells C1, E1, G1, and I1 enter 'Test 1', 'Test 2', 'Essay', and 'Presentation' respectively. On the row below, each of these headings, enter 'Max mark' under each heading.
3. Starting in cell C3, enter the headings 'Mark', then 'Percentage', repeating up to and including cell J3. In K3 enter 'Total'.
4. Enter the following maximum marks for each assignment, starting in cell D2. Test 1 – 25; Test 2 – 30; Essay – 10; Presentation – 20. Your spreadsheet should now look something like the screenshot below.

	A	B	C	D	E	F	G	H	I	J	K
1			Test 1		Test 2		Essay		Presentation		
2			Max Mark	25	Max Mark	30	Max Mark	10	Max Mark	20	
3			Mark	Percentage	Mark	Percentage	Mark	Percentage	Mark	Percentage	TOTAL
4	John	Fraud									
5	Fred	Travis									
6	Paul	Bant									
7	Jane	Green									
8	Sam	Jackles									
9	Lucy	Hido									
10	Simon	Drapeford									
11											

5. Enter marks for each student for each assignment (make sure they are no higher than the maximum mark for each assignment).
6. In C4, calculate the percentage for the first student's Test 1 grade. Calculate the percentages for each remaining assignment.

> The percentage can be calculated by entering the following formula: = C4 / D2 * 100
>
> Note that you use a cell reference rather than the number itself.

7. If the formula in cell D4 is copied down to D5, strange things start to happen. This is because by default, the spreadsheet uses **relative cell addressing** – when you copy or paste a formula, the cell references in the formula are updated. So copying and pasting C4 / D2 * 100 to the line below changes it to C5 / D3 * 100, then C6 / D4 * 100, and so on.

8. Sometimes relative cell addressing is useful. In this case, we do want the C4 to change to a C5, because we are looking at the next student's grade. However, we do not want D2 to change – for every student in this column, we want to divide the grade by D2. To achieve this we need to use **absolute cell referencing**, which is achieved with the dollar sign ($). Change the formula in cell D4 to read:
    = C4 / D$2 * 100

9. The dollar sign says 'use absolute cell referencing for the number 2'. Copy and paste this formula down column D for each student.
10. Calculate the percentage for each student for the remaining three assignments. Use absolute cell referencing where needed.
11. Enter a formula in column K to calculate the total number of marks for each student (each assignment added together).
12. Earlier, we made a mistake. The essay is actually out of 15 marks, not 10, and the presentation is out of 30. Change the appropriate cells in the spreadsheet (there should only be two of them). Notice how the percentages automatically recalculate themselves. **Automatic recalculation** is an important feature of spreadsheet software.

	B	C	D	E	F	G	H	I	J	K
1		Test 1		Test 2		Essay		Presentation		
2		Max Mark		25 Max Mark		30 Max Mark		15 Max Mark		30
3		Mark	Percentage	Mark	Percentage	Mark	Percentage	Mark	Percentage	TOTAL
4	Fraud	21	84	25	83.3	6	40.0	15	50.0	67
5	Travis	17	68	20	66.7	8	53.3	16	53.3	61
6	Bant	20	80	20	66.7	7	46.7	16	53.3	63
7	Green	13	52	17	56.7	6	40.0	17	56.7	53
8	Jackles	4	16	15	50.0	3	20.0	5	16.7	27
9	Hido	25	100	29	96.7	8	53.3	18	60.0	80
10	Drapeford	14	56	19	63.3	7	46.7	15	50.0	55
11										

13. Spreadsheets have some built in **functions** to help with common mathematical tasks. One such function is AVERAGE, which calculates the mathematical mean. AVERAGE is used with a **cell range** to specify the cells it will operate on. To calculate the average percentage for Test 1, enter the following in cell D11:
    =AVERAGE(D4:D10)

14. The cell range tells the function to use the values of all cells from D4 to D10, inclusive. Using cell ranges is quicker and less error-prone than writing out each cell's reference (D4+D5+D6+D7+D8+D9+D10).

15. If you copy cell D11 to cell F11, you will see that the correct average is calculated for column F. This is because **relative cell referencing** has been used, changing the function from AVERAGE(D4:D13) to AVERAGE(F4:F13) automatically.

16. Other basic spreadsheet functions include MAX, MIN, SUM. Use MIN and MAX in appropriate cells to find the maximum and minimum grade for each assignment.

17. Starting in cell M15, enter the percentage and grade data in the table shown here.

18. It would be really helpful if column L could contain a letter grade to go with the total percentage. The LOOKUP function can be used to achieve this. The lookup function accepts a cell value and a table of values. It looks up the value in the first column of the table (percentage in our case) and returns the corresponding value from the second column (the grade in our case). The percentages in the table above are the minimum for each grade (you must get at least 70% to get a B, 80% to get an A, etc.). In cell L4, enter:

    =LOOKUP(K4,M$16:M$21,N$16:N$21)

Percentage	Grade
0	Fail
40	E
50	D
60	C
70	B
80	A

19. Note the use of absolute cell referencing when referring to the table. Copying and pasting this formula down column L should result in a letter grade for each student. If the grades are wrong, check that you used absolute cell referencing when writing the formula.

> **Alternative**
> In OpenOffice or LibreOffice, instead use:
> =LOOKUP(K4,M$16:M$21,N$16:N$21)

20. Conditional formatting can be used to change the formatting of a cell based on its value. In this spreadsheet, it would be good to highlight students who are failing in red, and those who are doing particularly well in green. Apply conditional formatting twice to achieve these two goals.

21. The COUNTIF function is used to count the number of cells which match a given criteria. Use COUNTIF in the column K to count the number of failed students.

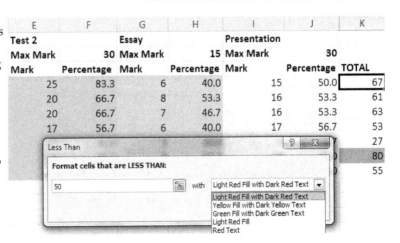

Chapter Review

Key Language

absolute cell reference
assumptions
car crash model
cell format
cell range
cell reference
centralised processing
CFD
climate model

computer model
computer simulation
decision Support System
distributed processing
feedback loop
flight simulator
formula
full motion platform
function

Global Climate Model
goal seek
grid computing
high performance compu-
ting
lookup
parallel processing
prediction
process

relative cell reference
simplification
spreadsheet
supercomputer
variables
visualisation
what-if scenario

Exercise 8-5

TOK Link

Computer models are used in a variety of scientific areas. To what extent do computer models help or hinder our understanding of scientific concepts? [8 marks]

Exercise 8-6

Computer models are often used to predict the future climate of Earth many years into the future.

(a) (i) Define the term *computer model*. [2 marks]

   (ii) Describe **two** variables that would be included in a climate model. [4 marks]

(b) Explain **three** reasons why using a map or graph for the model's output would be preferable to a list of numbers. [6 marks]

(c) Evaluate the decision to base government climate policy on the results of a climate model. [8 marks]

Exercise 8-7

Formula 1 racing teams often use simulators to help their drivers familiarise themselves with the cars and the tracks.

(a) (i) Define the term *parallel processing*. [2 marks]

   (ii) Describe **two** output devices used by such a simulator. [4 marks]

(b) Explain the advantages to the team of using simulators in this way. [6 marks]

(c) To what extent can the use of a simulator remove the driver's need for real life testing? [8 marks]

Exercise 8-8

A toy factory has a number of assembly lines for making toy parts. At the start of each shift, each assembly line must to configured to manufacture one particular toy part, which cannot be changed during the shift. The factory manager wants to use a spreadsheet model to determine which parts each assembly line should produce in order to manufacture the maximum number of toys each day, with the fewest parts left over.

(a) (i) Identify **two** functions which may be used in a spreadsheet. [2 marks]

   (ii) Distinguish between *absolute cell referencing* and *relative cell referencing*. [4 marks]

(b) Describe **three** variables that would need to be included in the model the manager wishes to use. [6 marks]

(c) To what extent should the manager rely on the spreadsheet model to decide how to configure each assembly line? [8 marks]

Exercise 8-9

A small airline flies a variety of routes using its four aircraft. The CEO of the airline wants to use a computer model to determine which routes are the most profitable, and how many aircraft should be assigned to each route. The profitability of each route depends on the number of passengers, the distance, and of course the ticket price. The routes operated are London to Paris (340 kilometres), London to New York (5585 kilometres), and Paris to Geneva (414 kilometres) The airline has a number of fixed costs, and typical passenger numbers for each route, based on experience. Both are shown below.

Fixed Costs	
Landing fee	$200
Fuel consumption (litres per kilometre)	15
Fuel cost (per litre)	$1.25
Seats per aircraft	150
Price change factor	
Passenger change factor	

Typical daily passenger numbers		
Route	Min	Max
Route 1: London—Paris	190	210
Route 2: London—New York	195	225
Route 3: Paris—Geneva	250	300

Use the information above to create a spreadsheet for the airline. For each route:
- a) Enter formulae to calculate the values for the fuel cost and landing fee for each route
- e) Use the RANDBETWEEN function to calculate the passengers on each route, based on the data above
- f) Calculate the Occupied Seats for each route using an IF function (more than aircraft can fly a route)
- g) Calculate the Empty seats, Income, Expense, and Profit/loss for each route
- h) Calculate the total profit from all routes
- i) At this point you should be able to alter the allocation of the planes to routes (remember, there are only four planes in total) and see an effect on the total profit. What is the most profitable way to distribute the planes in general?
- j) What would be the most profitable combination of routes if the fuel cost went up to $1.50 per litre?
- k) Use the Goal Seek tool to determine the price required for the Geneva route to make a total profit of 80,000.
- l) Use the Goal Seek tool to determine the price required to make a profit on the New York route, if two aircraft are assigned to the route.
- m) The airline has calculated that if prices were decreased by 5%, passenger numbers would increase by 5%; if prices are decreased by 10%, passengers will increase by 10%; if prices increased by 5%, passengers will decrease by 10%, and if prices are increased 10%, passenger numbers will drop by 20%. Enter this data into an appropriate space in the spreadsheet, and update the formulae to account for these changes (for example, when the price change factor is set to 1.1, the number of passengers is multiplied by 0.8).
- n) Alter the price factor and the distribution of aircraft to find the most profitable overall scenario.

	D	E	F	G	H	I	J	K
		Route 1	Route 2	Route 3				
		London-Paris	London-New York	Paris-Geneva				
	Distance	340	5586	414				
	Ticket:	130	900	200				
	Fuel needed:	5100	83790	6210				
	Fuel cost:	6375	104737.5	7762.5				
	Landing fee	200	200	200				
						Goal Seek		
	Passengers	211	218	298		Set cell:	J16	
	Flights	2	1	1		To value:	80000	
	Total seats	300	150	150		By changing cell:		
	Occupied seats	211	150	150		OK	Cancel	
	Wasted seats	89	0	0				
	Income:	27430	135000	30000				
	Expense:	13150	104937.5	7962.5				
	Profit:	14280	30062.5	22037.5		Profit:	66380	

References

1 BusinessWeek. (2011). *Limitations of Computer Models.* Available: http://www.ebusinessforum.com/index.asp?layout=rich_story&channelid=3&categoryid=5&title=Limitations+of+computer+models&doc_id=11222. Last accessed Oct 2011.

2 Salmon, F. (2009). *Recipe for Disaster: The Formula That Killed Wall Street.* Available: http://www.wired.com/techbiz/it/magazine/17-03/wp_quant?currentPage=all. Last accessed Nov 2011.

3 BBC. (2007). *Climate models.* Available: http://news.bbc.co.uk/2/shared/spl/hi/pop_ups/07/sci_nat_climate_models/html/1.stm. Last accessed Nov 2011.

4 SETI@Home. (2011). Available: http://setiathome.berkeley.edu/. Last accessed Nov 2011.

Chapter 9
Business

Objectives

1. Explain the technologies used for employee monitoring
2. Evaluate the effectiveness of teleworking
3. Evaluate the policies needed to regulate IT in the workplace
4. Discuss appropriate web design and e-commerce techniques
5. Discuss e-marketing techniques
6. Explain how IT can be used in the transportation industry

Business and Employment

Most businesses make use of information technology to some degree. At the extreme, some businesses operate only online, having no physical stores and using the Internet for all marketing, sales, and customer communication. Other businesses use a combination of electronic commerce and offline commerce. Even in businesses that perform no e-commerce, information technology is extensively used internally for product design, communication, marketing, record keeping, payroll processing, and many other tasks. This chapter looks at the use of information technology in the three ITGS Business and Employment areas: traditional offline businesses, online businesses, and the transportation industry.

Traditional Business

Employee Monitoring

One very common use of IT in businesses is to **monitor employees**—in the US, 76% of major companies monitor their employees' use of the Internet and email[1]. Often monitoring is performed in an attempt to reduce the amount of time employees waste, especially time lost due to personal web browsing. A survey by Salary.com and America Online reported US employees wasted just over 2 hours of each 8 hour working day, with 44% of people rating the Internet as their number one distraction[2]. A survey in the UK reported that small businesses lose up to £1.5 billion each year due to employees wasting time on the Internet[3], while 25% of companies say they have fired employees for Internet misuse at work—mostly due to accessing pornography[4].

Companies can easily **filter** their Internet connection to block common sources of distraction such as social networks, pornography, and games sites (see page 290), but it is impossible to block all undesirable sites. In these situations, **Internet monitoring** and **email monitoring** can help ensure an organisation's **acceptable use policies** are followed.

There are also a number of legal reasons for monitoring employees. Companies can be held legally responsible for material sent using their computer systems, including malware, inappropriate, and illegal content. This includes internal communications – for example, an employer may be held liable for sexual harassment between employees if it is not seen to take appropriate action. Monitoring computer use can help identify and provide evidence in such cases.

Business data is highly valued by organisations and most take security precautions to prevent accidental or deliberate leaks by employees. Monitoring of files copied or data downloaded can help identify potential leaks, while the act of monitoring itself may deter potentially errant behaviour. Similarly, data protection laws such as the Data Protection Act (see page 161) usually require access, changes, and additions to personal data to be monitored and logged. Software can also monitor systems for the installation of unlicensed copies of software, which could leave the company open to copyright infringement charges in the event of an inspection.

Certain industries, such as telemarketing, must abide by laws governing how they can market their products to customers: again, employers can be held legally responsible for any violations by their employees, so monitoring calls can help ensure employees are following company policy. Employers may also want to monitor conversations between employees and customers to measure the level of customer service provided.

Although monitoring is often seen as a punitive activity, it can be used to identify potential problems in a business by, for example, identifying areas where employees may need additional training. GPS tracking of vehicles, for example, can also help businesses ensure that regulations about maximum driving times are enforced (see page 216).

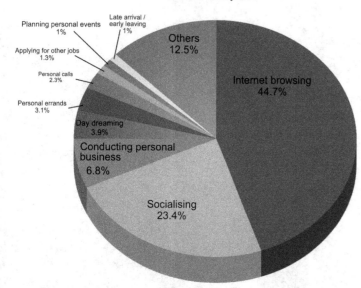

Time Wasting Activities at Work

Source: Salary.com

- Planning personal events 1%
- Late arrival / early leaving 1%
- Applying for other jobs 1.3%
- Personal calls 2.3%
- Personal errands 3.1%
- Day dreaming 3.9%
- Conducting personal business 6.8%
- Socialising 23.4%
- Internet browsing 44.7%
- Others 12.5%

Figure 9-1 Time wasting activities at work

Monitoring Technology

Internet monitoring software makes it very easy for network administrators to monitor the web sites accessed by individual users, along with any downloaded files and blocked pages they have tried to access. If the visited web sites are unencrypted, even the content can be easily viewed. Since most email is not encrypted, reading both incoming and outgoing messages, even if they are not stored on the company's server, is not difficult. Monitoring most network traffic is possible because it usually passes through a gateway server on the company LAN before travelling out onto the Internet (see page 80).

Desktop monitoring software performs additional functions to monitor non-Internet activities. Essentially spyware, these programs can produce detailed reports about almost any aspect of a computer's use, including:

- Individual application use
- Disk space use
- Idle time (no mouse or keyboard input)
- Instant message chat logs
- Installation of software
- Access, copying, and changing of files
- Documents opened
- Windows opened
- Items printed
- Key strokes typed (see key logger, page 94)
- Insertion and removal of USB devices

Monitoring software may also have **remote viewing** and **remote desktop** features, which allow a remote user such as an administrator to view and interact with the screen of another computer respectively (figure 9-2).

Problems with monitoring

Laws controlling employee monitoring vary greatly. In the US, it is generally legal for an employer to monitor employees, even without their knowledge. This can include personal messages and calls, if they are sent using company equipment[15]. In the UK, data collected during the course of monitoring may be classified as personal data, and so is subject to restrictions under the Data Protection Act (see page 161).

However, workplace surveillance does raise ethical concerns, especially the invasion of privacy employees might feel. Some companies try to relieve the problem by creating Acceptable Use Policies (AUPs), which make employer's expectations clear and also clarify the extent to which monitoring will occur. Other companies may recognise that employees are not expected to work 100% of the time, and provide separate, unmonitored computer systems for personal web browsing and email use during break times, while continuing to monitor dedicated work computers.

Another problem with monitoring is that statistics can be misleading. For example, the fact that a particular web site is open for a long time does not necessarily mean it is causing a distraction. Employees cannot necessarily be expected to work 100% of the time they are at work and, course of, the fact that an employee is on a work related web site or has a work related document open is no guarantee that he or she is working. Some businesses operate more flexible policies which assess employees' results rather than the way they produce the results, allowing employees more freedom to decide how to spend their time.

Figure 9-2 Some monitoring programs allows remote viewing of other users' screens—in this case, more than 12 computers at once

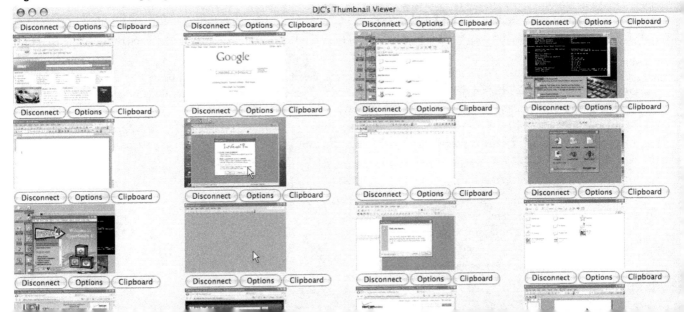

Teleworking

Teleworkers (also called **telecommuters**) are employees who work away from the office—either working from home or while travelling—and use information technology to stay in touch with colleagues. Teleworkers may spend all of their time working this way, or be generally based in an office and only telework when necessary. The ability to telework depends on occupation, with telephone call centres and technical support providers being two industries that make extensive use of remote employees. Surveys suggest only a small percentage of people who could telework actually do so—mainly because of opposition from employers[5].

Employees working from home can use a normal desktop computer, while mobile teleworkers require some form of mobile computer. A secure Internet connection is usually required as well—this is a particular concern for mobile teleworkers who may need to use insecure hotel or airport wireless networks. Usually VPN software is used for this purpose (see page 75).

Figure 9-3 Teleworkers often use mobile computers

Teleworkers often use **collaborative software** to increase their productivity and maintain communication with other workers and their employers. Collaborative software allows people to work together on documents and projects from anywhere with an Internet connection. The same tools can be used to collaborate with both colleagues and customers. Collaborative software includes some or all of the following features:

- Group calendars
- Simultaneous editing of a shared space (virtual whiteboard, document, spreadsheet, etc.)
- A central repository of shared documents (either on a company LAN via a VPN, or in a cloud based system)
- History and revision control for documents
- Voice and video conferencing (virtual meetings)
- Chat and instant messaging
- Emailing lists
- Project time lines or work flow diagrams
- Secure connection to other users
- Powerful search features to locate documents and previous communications
- Cloud based application software

Teleworking Benefits for Employers	Teleworking Benefits for Employees
Office overheads including rent, power, and other consumables can be reduced	Environmental and financial benefits by reducing commuting
Employees can be retained even if they have home commitments such as children or other dependents	Flexible working hours can benefit people with children or other dependents (and decrease childcare costs)
People can be employed from a much larger geographical area, making it easier to find people with the right skills, or people who will work for lower wages	
Workers can continue to work even during events like natural disasters, extreme weather, or public transport strikes	
It is possible to implement **follow-the-sun working**, whereby work is transferred from one location when the work day finishes to another time zone where the work day is just beginning.	

Figure 9-4 Advantages and disadvantages of teleworking

Exercise 9-1

The management of a medium sized business with 50 employees wants to formalise its monitoring policy. All employees have desktop computers. Additionally, many employees have laptop computers which they use when travelling. A small number of employees telework from home.

Create an Acceptable Use Policy (AUP) that clearly explains how and why management will use technology to monitor employees. The policy should cover at least **five** monitoring technologies. Cover both the monitoring that will be performed and the monitoring that will not be performed. **Justify** each decision.[10 marks]

Exercise 9-2

a) Are there any particular occupations for which employee monitoring would be essential? [4 marks]
b) **Discuss** whether it should be required by law to inform employees that they are being monitored. [6 marks]
c) **Discuss** whether employees should have a right to privacy when they use their personal email at work. [6 marks]
d) **To what extent** do you think monitoring of employees improves their productivity? [8 marks]
e) **To what extent** are the different types of employee monitoring acceptable in an office environment? [8 marks]

Exercise 9-3

What are the main disadvantages of teleworking for the major stakeholders? **To what extent** do the disadvantages of teleworking for employers outweigh the benefits? [8 marks]

Exercise 9-4

Answer the following questions about teleworking.
a) **Describe** the types of jobs that are best suited to teleworking. [4 marks]
b) **Describe** which jobs (if any) you think would be difficult or impossible to do via teleworking. [4 marks]

Consider the career that you wish to have when you leave school or graduate from university. Using what you have learnt so far about teleworking, would you be able to telework in your desired job?
a) If so, **explain** the advantages and problems would it bring for you and your employer [6 marks]
b) If not, **explain** why not – what would stop it being possible? [6 marks]
c) **Discuss** whether you would want to telework in your chosen career. [8 marks]

Figure 9-5 Collaborative software makes managing files and communication easier, even if workers are in many different locations.

Mail merge and Macros

Businesses often need to send many copies of a single document, each addressed to a different person. Manually addressing and labelling each copy is time consuming and error prone, but using a generic address such as 'Dear Customer' looks less professional and is more likely to be treated as spam by the customer. Most word processing and desktop publishing software includes **mail merge** functionality to assist with this task, allowing the user to insert fields (e.g. name, address) of data into a document from a source such as a database table. Multiple copies of the document can then be automatically created, each one containing the fields from a different record.

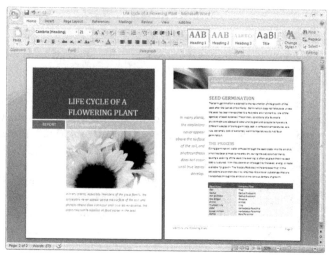

Figure 9-6 Macros can be used to create a consistent appearance across multiple documents

Another consideration for companies is the use of a consistent style or 'look and feel' to their documents. This helps create a more professional appearance and ensures that vital information—such as the company name, logo, and contact details are always included. Brand recognition can also be increased if all materials have a similar appearance. **Macros** are a software feature that can help achieve this consistency. Macros let users record a sequence of actions or instructions which can then be played back (repeated) later. This is useful for repetitive

---

Exercise 9-5

Complete the following exercises using word processing or desktop publishing software. You might want to review the differences between these two types of software (see page 136) before deciding which to use.

a) Use word processing or desktop publishing software to create a company newsletter, containing short paragraphs announcing 2 or 3 of the company's new products.

b) Use the same software to create a business card, of the type often given at first meetings with clients.

c) Record a macro for applying following formatting and styling information to the newsletter:
   i) Make all body text Arial, size 12
   ii) Insert a company logo in the top right corner (use a small JPEG image for this)
   iii) Add the text 'SmileyFace IT Company' next to the logo, using the font Broadway, size 22.
   iv) At the bottom, add the text 'SmileyFace IT Company Email: sales@smileyface.com, Tel: 0800 1123 5813' using the font Calibri, size 8, centred.
   v) Create the text for a second newsletter, and run the macro you created. The macro should give the two newsletters the same consistent style.

d) Create a database table containing employee names, their job titles, their contact number, and their email address.

e) Create a database table containing customer names and addresses.

f) Use the mail merge function to automatically create customised versions of the business card document, using the employee's name, position, and contact details from the database.

g) Use the mail merge function to automatically create customised versions of the company newsletter, each addressed to an individual customer from the database.

Exercise 9-6

Consider a secondary school that wishes to share information with various stakeholders. **Identify** the information the school might wish to share and **explain** whether each item would be shared on their Internet site, intranet site, or extranet site. [12 marks]

tasks, like applying the same formatting styles to multiple documents. The actions are recorded once as a macro and then repeated with a single click on other documents.

Macro functionality is found in many applications, from spreadsheets and word processors to software development tools. Macros are useful for many tasks, including inserting or replacing text, including standard features such as headers or footers, and extracting data from text. Because many macros are written in a programming language (for example, those in Microsoft Office are written in Visual Basic for Applications), they also have the potential to be harmful, altering data and sending volume emails. This is exactly what **macro viruses** (see page 96) do. Because of this, many applications disable macros by default.

Internet, Intranets, and Extranets

An **intranet** is a network that shares information privately among the employees of an organisation. This contrasts with the **Internet**, which is a global, public network of information. Intranet content may still be accessed outside of the organisation's network, but requires users to authenticate themselves. Information on an intranet often takes the form of web pages and email using standard protocols (HTTP and SMTP respectively) – the only difference is the size and visibility of the network. A school might use an intranet to share information only intended for its own users—for example, student grades and reports, timetabling information, and online courses. This is information which should obviously not be made public on the Internet, but still needs to be shared with other people in the school.

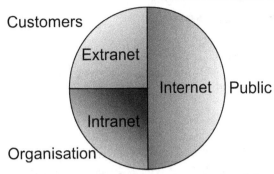

Figure 9-9 Intranets, extranets, and Internets share information with different stakeholders

Similarly, a business might make use of an intranet to share information about a project, so that all members of the team can access the project's files and information about its progress.

In some cases, parts of the intranet's information may be shared with a limited number of people outside the organisation. This is known as an **extranet**. For example, a business might share information about a project's progress, but not its internal budget information, with the customer who commissioned the project.

Similarly, a business may provide suppliers with access to certain information regarding orders and requirements.

In both cases the customers and suppliers would need to authenticate themselves to access the extranet and determine the information available to them.

Deskilling and reskilling

Many forms of technology have been associated with causing unemployment, and information technology is no exception. In many areas, IT is capable of performing the work of several people, potentially leading to employee redundancies. In other areas, IT may cause **deskilling**—the replacement of a skilled worker with an IT system that can be operated by semi-skilled or unskilled worker. Examples include shop assistants who no longer need to have maths skills, and carpenters and metal workers whose manual skills have to some extent been replaced by computerised machinery. While there are certain benefits to this for employers, including lower personnel costs and improved efficiency, this can have a large negative effect on all workers, reducing worker morale.

Changes to the way people work, initiated by the introduction of IT systems, can also deskill workers. One study in the US found that the introduction of Electronic Medical Record (EMR) systems (see page 258) deskilled doctors by constraining the way they reported patient data. Many of the doctors interviewed said they now reported patient symptoms using a standard 'cut and paste' technique provided by the software, reducing the amount of precise detail contained with the notes[7].

In some cases, the introduction of IT systems causes old jobs to become redundant but creates new ones in their place. For example, the introduction of robots into a factory requires operators and technicians to ensure they run smoothly. If the existing workforce are trained to do these new jobs, they are said to be **reskilled**.

Spreadsheets

Spreadsheets have a large range of applications in businesses, from simple calculations of costs, budgeting, and accounting, to advanced analysis of sales and stock information.

All spreadsheets are based around the fundamental concepts of cells of data and references to them (**cell references**). Each cell in a spreadsheet can contain data or a formula, and has a **cell type**, such as numeric, text, date, and scientific, which controls how its data is presented.

SUM	=A2+A3	
	A	B	C
1	=A2+A3		

Figure 9-10 Cell references in a formula

Formulae

Each cell has an individual cell reference, such as A1 or C3, which refers to its contents. These are used to build up formulas to perform calculations (see figure 9-10). **Cell ranges** refer to a sequence of cells, such as A1:A4, which refers to cells A1, A2, A3, and A4.

Automatic recalculation functions mean that when a value in a cell changes, the results produced by any formulae depending on that cell will be updated.

Absolute and Relative Cell Referencing

When a formula is copied and pasted elsewhere in a spreadsheet, by default the cell references in it are updated depending on the distance copied. For example, in figure 9-12, cell D4 contains the formula =B4+C4. When this is copied down to the next row, it becomes B5+C5, so that it calculates the total of the items on that row. This is known as **relative cell referencing**, because it changes relative to the formula's position, and is often the desired functionality.

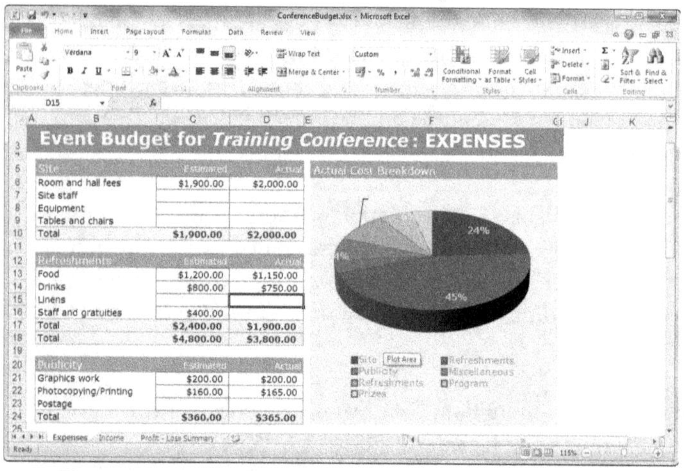

Figure 9-11 Cell references in a formula

D4 =B4+C4

	A	B	C	D
1		Tax:	50	
2				
3	Item	Cost	Profit	Total
4	Laptop	£449.00	£50.00	£499.00
5	Software	£25.00	£14.99	£39.99
6	Mouse	£6.00	£2.99	£8.99
7	Keyboard	£9.00	£3.99	£12.99
8	Monitor	£349.00	£30.00	£379.00

Figure 9-12 Cell references in a formula

Sometimes however, a cell reference needs to stay the same no matter where it is copied. For example, if we want to add the tax to each total in figure 9-12, we could enter the formula =B4+C4+C1 in cell D4. However, when this is copied down one row, it becomes =B5+C5+C2, which is not desired—the final cell always needs to refer to cell C1.

To do this, **absolute cell referencing** is required. Absolute cell referencing uses a dollar sign to indicate 'never change this cell reference'. Entering =B4+C4+C$1 will produce the required result, and when this is copied to the next row, it changes to =B5+C5+C$1. Note how the first two cell references change but the third, which uses absolute referencing, stays the same.

Functions

Most spreadsheet have in built options, called functions , to perform common operations such as calculating averages, working out standard deviations, and converting data. Page 195 describes some of the most common spreadsheet functions.

Additional Features

Spreadsheets can perform a range of more advanced functions. **Conditional formatting** can change the formatting of a cell depending on its content. For example, it could be used to make cells with negative values appear in red, cells with percentages over 80 appear in green, and so on.

In some cases users may want to share spreadsheets with others, but prevent them from changing some or all cells.

Common functions

Functions in spreadsheets can be divided into four main areas: maths functions, text functions, logic functions, and date functions. The names given here are those used in Microsoft Excel, though they are similar in other spreadsheets.

Maths functions include those for rounding numbers (**round**), calculating powers or factorials (**pow** and **fact**), and calculating averages (**average**, **median**, and **mode**). There are operations for most mathematical operations including finding absolute values (**abs**), square roots (**sqrt**), and trigonometry functions (**sin**, **cos**, **tan**). More advanced functions can calculate standard deviation (**stdev**) and perform data conversion between decimal, octal, binary, and hexadecimal (**oct2bin**, **oct2dec**, **oct2hex**).

Logic functions can produce results based on the status of other parts of the spreadsheet. The **count** function counts the number of cells in a given range, for example, while **countif** only counts cells if they meet certain criteria. The **if** function produces different results depending on the condition specified in the function, and these conditions can also use Boolean operators (AND, OR, NOT). The **min** and **max** functions return the lowest and highest values in a range, respectively.

Text manipulation functions can convert between numeric and text data (**value** and **text**), change text from uppercase to lowercase or vice versa (**upper** and **lower**) and remove extraneous spaces from text cells (**trim**).

Date functions aid calculations involving dates and times. They simplify tasks such as returning the current time and date (**now** and **today**), as well as converting date information to and from text. Time and date functions are particularly useful in business because they can perform calculations while taking into account the number of working days in a week and the number of days in a month.

> **Common Mistake**
>
> Functions and formulae are often confused. Functions are features built into the spreadsheet software, such as the SUM, AVERAGE, and MIN functions. Formulae are created by typing cell references and mathematical operators to perform a calculation – for example = A1 + B2 / C7.

A spreadsheet can be protected with a password to prevent access, or allow read only access. If only certain cells need to be protected from editing (for example, to prevent accidental changes to formulae), **cell locking** options can be used.

Charts and Pivot Tables

Graphical output is a commonly used feature of spreadsheets. Most spreadsheet applications can produce bar charts, line graphs, and pie charts in a variety of two and three dimensional forms.

Pivot tables are an advanced output feature which can provide a summary of data in a spreadsheet (see figure 9-13). PivotTables can count items, sum fields, and sort and filter data to produce a summary table which can be filtered to show only the required information. This makes it easier to understand trends in large spreadsheets. Pivot charts are a similar function which produce a chart rather than a table as output.

	A	B
1	Type	(All)
2		
3	**Row Labels**	**Sum of Price**
4	Accounts	1616
5	Customer service	1098
6	HR	2097
7	Marketing	7295
8	**Grand Total**	**12106**
9		

Figure 9-13 Pivot tables (right) are used to summarise information in spreadsheets (left). Here the table summarises the total IT spending for each department.

	A	B	C	D	E	F	G
1	ItemTag	Type	Make	Purchased	Price	Department	Status
2	LP45	Laptop	Apple	01/08/2007	£999.00	Marketing	End of life
3	LP46	Laptop	Apple	01/08/2007	£999.00	Marketing	End of life
4	ACC89	Projector	HP	01/08/2007	£799.00	Marketing	In use
5	LP47	Laptop	Dell	01/08/2007	£699.00	HR	In use
6	LP48	Laptop	Dell	01/08/2007	£699.00	HR	In use
7	LP49	Laptop	Dell	01/08/2007	£699.00	HR	In use
8	ACC90	Wireless router	Belkin	02/06/2008	£119.00	Accounts	In use
9	ACC92	Interactive whiteboard	SmartBoard	02/06/2008	£3,499.00	Marketing	In use
10	LP50	Laptop	Apple	02/06/2008	£999.00	Marketing	In use
11	DP34	Desktop	Acer	02/06/2008	£499.00	Accounts	In use
12	DP35	Desktop	Acer	02/06/2008	£499.00	Accounts	In use
13	LP51	Laptop	IBM	04/08/2008	£549.00	Customer service	In use
14	LP52	Laptop	IBM	04/08/2008	£549.00	Customer service	In use
15	DP36	Desktop	Dell	04/08/2008	£499.00	Accounts	In use

Banking and Digital Money
Electronic Funds Transfer

Electronic financial transaction play an important role in both online and offline businesses. **Electronic Funds Transfer (EFT)** is the general name given to any method in which money is moved electronically through computer systems. This includes using **Automated Teller Machines (ATMs)**, paying for purchases with a credit card or debit card, and direct debit systems.

Most banks now offer **online banking** facilities, where customers can see the status of their accounts as well perform transactions such as money transfers. Some banks and utility companies offer online bill payment, where customers can pay for their electricity, gas, and other utilities without the need to manually transfer money or write a cheque.

Electronic Fraud

Credit card fraud, either by using stolen card details online, or stolen cards in physical shops, has always been a problem. Credit card details can be stolen by unscrupulous employees when paying for items, or even through devices criminals have attached to legitimate ATMs to read the details of inserted cards.

Chip and pin cards try to reduce offline fraud by requiring the card PIN to be entered at the Point of Sale terminal. This replaces the cardholder signature, which was easily forged, as the method used to authenticate the customer as the card owner. Chip and pin technologies also reduce incidents of card cloning, as it is much more difficult for criminals to clone a microchip than the magnetic stripe found on previous cards.

Reducing online fraud, in what are called Card Not Present (CNP) transactions, is harder. Most banks use data mining and artificial intelligence techniques (see page 341) to look for potentially suspicious transactions, such as repeated purchases, purchases at unusual times of the day, or purchases made in foreign countries. Suspicious transactions can be automatically blocked, or further investigated—perhaps by calling the customer to verify the transaction.

When making an online transaction, some credit card schemes redirect the user to their bank's web site, requiring them to enter their online banking passwords. This reduces fraud by adding an extra layer of authentication—the chances of these details being stolen in addition to the credit card details is much lower.

Figure 9-14 Super market self checkout machine

IT in Supermarkets

Supermarkets make extensive use of IT to plan and run their operations. **Bar codes** have been used for many years to identify products and manage prices and stock levels (see page 23), allowing staff to easily change prices without relabeling items. However, bar codes only identify types of products, rather than individual items. In the US, supermarket giant Walmart has started to place **radio frequency identification** tags (RFID) on individual items in some clothing lines, enabling them to identify, for example, every individual pairs of jeans[6]. In the future, RFID technology may be used in more stores to provide even more detailed information about products and customers' buying habits, although there are also some privacy concerns about its use (see page 26).

In warehouses, RFID technology is used to improve the supply chain process. Walmart uses the technology to automatically count boxes of items entering and leaving warehouses, to help ensure stocks of any given item never run out. RFID can do this much more quickly than bar codes because the tags are automatically scanned by readers at the warehouse entrances – no human intervention is required, and the tags can be read at a distance of several metres.

However, one problem faced in the implementation of RFID is the slow adoption by suppliers – if goods are not shipped from the factory already tagged, they cannot be managed by the system unless time is spent manually tagging them upon arrival. Some manufacturers have started charging penalties to suppliers who do not ship their goods pre-tagged.

Point of Sale (POS) systems are used at all but the smallest shops. They are effectively electronic checkout systems, which read product bar codes and interface with the shop's central database to automatically fetch prices and manage stock levels. POS systems can also connect to banking systems to perform electronic funds transfer if the customer pays with a credit card. If a loyalty card is used, the POS system will also record its number and data about the customer (such as their purchases).

Loyalty cards or **reward cards** are issued by many supermarkets in an attempt to retain customers by awarding points when purchases are made. From a technical point of view, each loyalty card is assigned a unique identifier (essentially, a primary key in a database) which allows the store to track the buying habits of the person using the card. Over time, a profile of purchasing history can be built up, which can be used to produce **targeted advertising** – sending adverts only to customers whose data suggests they are likely to respond positively. For example, frequent purchasers of a certain brand of orange juice could be targeted by advertisements for the supermarket's own brand of juice. As with any form of data collection, some people are concerned about the privacy issues related to this process, especially if the data is sold or shared with third parties.

Future developments in supermarkets might include **self checkout** and **smart trolley** technologies. Current self checkout facilities require customers to scan the bar code of each item at a dedicated machine, just as the checkout operator does. In many cases this is no more efficient, and sometimes less efficient, than having a staff member process the items. Next generation systems, where all items are RFID tagged, could improve this drastically, potentially by having customers simply walk through a 'gate' which reads the tags of all items in shopping trolley at once, immediately generating a bill which the customer could then pay with a credit card. **Smart trolleys** and **smart shopping baskets** are even being introduced which read the tags of items as they are loaded into the

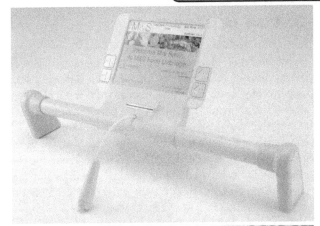

Figure 9-15 Smart trolleys could offer shopping suggestions

trolley. As well as automatically totalling the customer's items, this technology enables features such as recipe suggestions for the ingredients in the trolley, suggestions for healthier alternative products, and, of course, advertising related to the customer's purchases.

Other innovations include customers using camera equipped mobile phones as an alternative to barcode scanners. Customers take a photograph of the barcode on each product as they load it into their trolley. A dedicated applet them keeps a running total and, when the customer indicates shopping is over, produces a unique barcode representing the total cost of the shopping. Customers can then scan the barcode and pay at a normal checkout or at a special self service terminal[17]. This system has been trialled in Germany, and may be expanded to include payment using biometrics or mobile phones.

> **Did You Know?**
> In many countries it is the employer's responsibility to educate its workforce about overuse injuries such as Repetitive Strain Injury, and to provide suitable equipment to reduce these risks (see page 268). Failure to do so could result in legal action against the employer.

Online Business

E-Commerce

E-commerce, or **electronic commerce**, refers to business transactions made online via the Internet. Many retailers use e-commerce to supplement sales from their physical stores, and an increasing number are entirely online operations with no physical stores (such as Amazon). E-commerce sales have continued to increase year-on-year, growing 11% in the US in 2009 despite the economic recession – and compared to just 2.5% growth in overall US retail[8]. This growth brought their value to $155.2 billion in the US alone.

The front page of an e-commerce site is sometimes called an **electronic store front**. These normally feature links to different shop departments or types of products, show any special deals that are currently available, and usually offer a search function. If the customer is logged in to their store account, many e-commerce sites offer content and suggestions based on their purchase, viewing, and search histories. When a customer selects items to purchase, they are placed in an **electronic shopping cart** until the customer decides to complete the transaction. Usually email confirmation is sent when purchases are made, along with a **tracking number** to check the status of the package online (see page 216).

Figure 9-16: Mobile phone e-commerce application

Many companies recognise that web sites also influence offline sales—almost half of the purchases made in physical stores are 'web-driven', where the customer performed product and company research online prior to

For Customers	
Advantages	**Disadvantages**
Access to shops from a wider geographical area	Returning items might be difficult
No need to travel or wait in lines	Lack of help or customer service during purchasing process may make decision making harder
Instant access for materials like software or manuals	Shopping can be slower because you have to wait for delivery of the product
Very useful for products which don't need to be seen or checked first (e.g. Books, tickets)	Certain items are difficult to check online, such as clothing or fresh food
Price comparison sites can help find the best deals	There may be security concerns about the transmission, storage and use of credit card details, especially for smaller, less well known businesses
Some web sites can make automatic recommendations based on past purchases or items viewed	There may be privacy concerns about collection of viewing and purchasing history, and how it is used
Pricing can be up-to-the-minute, enabling better competition	
Shopping can be done at any time of day or night	
Allows customers to read other purchasers' opinions (and the shop gets this feedback for free).	
A wider range of products may be available, including customised products	

Figure 9-17: The benefits of e-commerce for customers

visiting the store[9]. Web site features such as wish lists (where the user saves interesting items for later), email or SMS price alerts, and **location based services** can all be used to influence sales in this way.

An increasing amount of online purchases are performed using mobile phones and other portable devices—so called **m-commerce** or **mobile commerce**. Individual **mobile applications** are responsible for much of this increase – popular sites such as Amazon and eBay have applications for smart phones which 'push' news and updates to customers, alert them to deals, and provide an electronic shop front to make purchases. M-commerce applications are particularly useful for sites which require an immediate response – such as special deals sites or online auctions.

Figures 9-17 and 9-18 describe some of the advantages and disadvantages of e-commerce compared to traditional 'bricks and mortar' shopping.

Payment Methods

A common concern for customers is **secure online payment**. The ability to securely and reliably pay for online goods is essential for all e-commerce. **Direct payment methods**, whereby the retailer is sent the customer's credit or debit card details and immediately processes the

What makes a good e-commerce site?

1. Multiple images of each product
2. Previews of different product versions
3. Effective search options
4. Search filters (e.g. show only tents for 3 people)
5. User reviews
6. FAQ (Frequently Asked Questions)
7. Related products links

transaction, are the most common form of online payment. Credit card details should never be sent in an email or across an unsecured http connection (see page 80), so a standard secure web page (using TLS or SSL and indicated by '**https**' in the browser's address bar) is used for transactions. **Digital certificates** (see page 108) can also be used to ensure the authenticity of a web site owner and help prevent phishing attacks. However, many smaller companies do not make use of digital certificates, and people may be reluctant to provide their credit card details to less well known companies. **Payment gateways** (sometimes called **third party payment services**) such as PayPal can help in these situations. These services act as a middle man, providing a trusted payment service to both the customer and the retailer, and handling tasks such as automatic currency conversions for international purchases.

For Businesses	
Advantages	**Disadvantages**
Customers from a wider geographical area can be served	Some customers may be reluctant to supply credit card details online
Money is saved on renting and running physical shops	Poorly designed web pages with lots of graphics or flash animations may turn off customers
Wide range of products can be in the store but not actually in stock at the time (can be ordered as demand dictates)	Customers are used to getting material for free on the Internet and may not like to pay for certain items (especially news and articles)
Customers can read other purchasers' opinions (which is effectively free advertising)	Lack of help or customer service during purchasing process may turn off customers
Pricing can be up-to-the-minute, enabling better competition	Credit card companies charge retailers an overhead for using their cards.
Smaller, start-up companies can compete with larger companies (for example, Amazon lets suppliers sell through their store). Also, Amazon allows users to publish their own books.	There may be security concerns about the transmission, storage and use of credit card details, especially for smaller, less well known businesses.
Allows customised **targeted advertising** to help find the products you need	Excessive online marketing (spam, pop-ups) can annoy customers and turn them away from a company
	Security issues: 'card holder not present' transactions are harder to authenticate than face-to-face transactions

Figure 9-18: The benefits of e-commerce for businesses

In cases such as online auction sites, payment gateways can take money from the buyer but defer its transfer to the seller until the buyer confirms that the goods have been received. This system benefits the supplier because it allows them to know that money has been received before they ship the goods, but the customer still has the advantage of knowing their money can be returned if the goods do not arrive.

Gateway payment services can improve security because customers need to worry less about many separate companies holding their data. A gateway service, which specialises in financial transactions, is also more likely to have securely configured its systems against unauthorised access than a business which has installed its own payment system.

On the other hand, security is still an important issue, and it is essential that e-commerce sites and gateway companies store sensitive data using adequate security precautions. These types of sites, which criminals know house hundreds or thousands of credit card numbers, make attractive targets for hackers (see page 161).

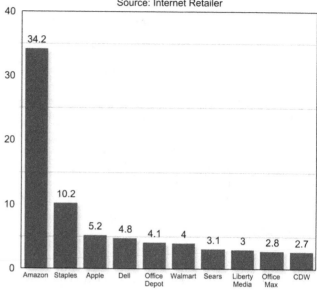

Figure 9-20 Top online retailers in the US

Figure 9-19 Common web site features

Types of E-Commerce

Business-to-Customer or **Business-to-Consumer (B2C)** is a type of e-commerce whereby businesses sell products and services directly to customers, typically via web sites. Many organisations now use B2C e-commerce and it is possible to buy products ranging from clothes to electronics to sports tickets online. As part of the B2C model, many businesses provide information to support a customer's purchase, such as package status and tracking information, user generated reviews, and of course an online catalogue of products and specifications.

Many businesses also engage in **Business-to-Business (B2B)** e-commerce. Manufacturers use online transactions to order and pay for materials to make their products, while retailers order products from their suppliers. As many B2C purchases are made using a credit card, retailers will also need to engage in B2B transactions with financial institutions in order to perform funds transfer.

At the centre of many companies' operations is a database, sometimes called a **data warehouse**, which stores information about e-commerce operations. For example, customer orders coming from the web site (B2C) can be automatically processed, credit card details verified with a bank (B2B), and order details passed electronically to the warehouse for packaging and dispatch. The status of this process can be made available to customers so they can track their package (B2C). Stock levels of the purchased products can be automatically reduced in the central database, and if levels have met a predefined minimum, an automatic repurchase request can be sent to suppliers (B2B). Data gathered about purchases can be analysed by an **enterprise information system** using **data mining** (see page 158) to look for trends (such as products which are commonly bought together), which can be used to improve future business performance.

Customer-to-Customer or **Consumer-to-Consumer (C2C)** e-commerce describes transactions made directly between a seller and a buyer, usually facilitated by some third party such as an online auction site. Popular examples include eBay and CraigsList. The difference between C2C and B2C is that both sellers and buyers in a C2C transaction are ordinary people, rather than organised businesses. Also, although the third party (such as eBay) facilitates the transaction and takes a percentage, they are not directly involved in the selling or the buying.

Because the seller and buyer in a C2C transaction do not normally know each other, online fraud can be a concern. Many online auction sites allow buyers and sellers to rate each other, thus establishing **online reputations** which other users can view. Some sites also offer customers protection against seller fraud.

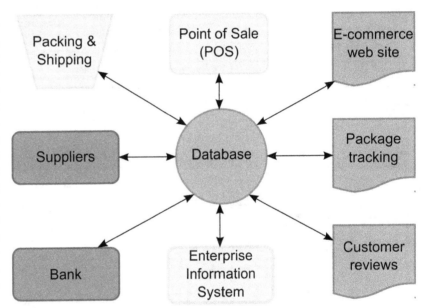

Figure 9-21 Businesses interact with many stakeholders in addition to their customers, including other businesses and internal departments

---

Exercise 9-7

Use popular online shopping sites to find and choose the following products:

 a) Clothes for a teenager
 b) The ingredients for a nice Christmas dinner (home delivery)
 c) Books
 d) A new laptop computer for you
 e) Flowers for your mum
 f) Something nice for your favourite teacher

How does the online shopping process compare to normal shopping? What advantages are there? What problems arise, and how important are they? [6 marks]

Web Design

The design, accessibility, and usability of an e-commerce web site are critical factors in achieving a high **conversion rate** – the percentage of site visitors who eventually decide to make purchases. Research suggests that if consumers cannot find what they want on an e-commerce site within 4 seconds, they are likely to leave the site – and not return.

Basic web pages are written in **HTML—HyperText Markup Language**. Each page on a web site is saved as a separate file with a .html or .htm extension. **HTML tags** start and end with angled brackets, and control how a web page appears. Basic web pages can be written in HTML by hand using a simple text editor, but most web site designers preferred to use an advanced programmer's text editor or a **WYSIWYG** (What You See Is What You Get) web site design package (see figure 9-22). These packages make it easier to create more complex web pages by using graphical tools that automatically generate HTML code, but some designers feel that the code they produce is less efficient, and make manual alterations to the generated code.

A significant problem with HTML is that it contains both data (the web site content) and page styling information (colours, fonts, and so on). While this was sufficient during the early days of the World Wide Web, it is now more of a problem, especially if frequent or wide-spread changes need to be made to a site's appearance or content. For example, if a company wanted to change the text and background colours of their web site, every single HTML file would need changing to reflect the new design—which could be hundreds of files. Changing each file would be time consuming and error prone.

There are also times when web site developers need to present the same data, but in different ways to different people. For example, visually impaired users need to use larger fonts, while colour blind users need to avoid specific colours. Mobile phone users, even those with smart phones, may need smaller fonts and images.

A solution to many of these problems is to use **CSS (Cascading Style Sheets)**. A HTML file can then contain the page content and assign named **styles** to it, while a **CSS stylesheet** is used to define the appearance of those

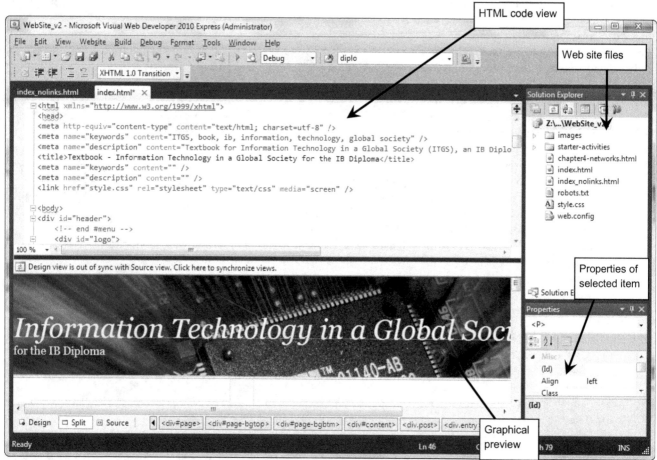

Figure 9-22 A web development program, with the screen split between a HTML code view and a graphical preview of the page

Anatomy of a web page

```
                    <head>
                      <meta name="keywords" content="ITGS, book, ib, information, technology" />
Header                <title>Information Technology in a Global Society</title>
                      <link href="style.css" rel="stylesheet" type="text/css" media="screen" />
Stylesheet          </head>

Body starts         <body>
                    <div id="content">
                      <h2 class="title">
CSS styles            <a href="#">Information Technology in a Global Society</a>
                      </h2>
                      <div class="entry">
Image                   <p><img src="images/cover.jpg" width="186" height="233" alt="cover"
                        class="alignleft border" />The book is now available to buy on
                        Amazon.com.</p>
                      </div>
                    </div>

                    <div id="sidebar">
                    <ul>
                      <li>
                        <h2>Welcome</h2>
                      </li>
                      <li>
                        <h2>Textbook</h2>
                      <ul>
                          <li>Contents</li>
Internal links          <li><a href="#sample">Sample chapter</a></li>
                        <li><a href="#exercises">Exercises</a></li>
                        <li><a href="#errata">Errata</a></li>
External link           <li><a href="http://www.amazon.com/">Buy on Amazon</a></li>
Relative link           <li><a href="software.html">Useful software</a></li>
                      </ul>
                      </li>
                    </ul>
                    </div>
                    <!-- end #sidebar -->
```

Figure 9-23 Sample HTML code

Figure 9-23 shows a sample of HTML code from a typical web site. All web pages contain a header section, denoted by the HTML tags <head> and </head>, and a body section, denoted by <body> and </body> tags. The header contains information about the page, including meta tags (see page 210), the page language, and the page title. The header also contains a link to the CSS stylesheet which will be used for this page.

The body contains the actual page content. CSS div (division) tags are used to divide the content into sections and assign separate styles to each one. A separate stylesheet defines how each of these styles will appear. Note that HTML ignores formatting information such as new lines in the code—these have to be indicated with <p> (paragraph) tags.

Hyperlinks are created using the <a href> tag. **External links** link to pages on other web sites. **Internal links** (also called **anchors**) link to content on the current page. For example, a page may have a table of contents at the top, and an internal link in the table may scroll the current page down to the desired position. **Relative links** specify the name of the linked page without its full URL—the browser assumes the page is on the current site. For example, linking to the page software.html is a relative link, whereas linking to www.itgstextbook.com/software.html is an **absolute link**, because it includes the entire path of the file. Relative links are preferred because they provide greater flexibility in web site design—if a web site is moved, relative links will usually still work, where absolute links would all need updating.

styles. For example a style called 'headline' could be applied to the title of every page using HTML, and defined in the CSS stylesheet to use a large font and a white background. When a style property in the CSS stylesheet is changed (for example the background of the headline is changed to blue), all items marked as 'headline' will change automatically, in every page where the stylesheet is used. This makes consistent site-wide changes easy and convenient to make. This also has benefits for disabled users, as their browsers can automatically apply stylesheets which use larger fonts and colours with a greater contrast—provided the original web designer used CSS.

Data driven web sites

In some cases, the content of a web page is unknown at design time, and will not be decided until the user performs some action. For example, a search engine's results page depends on the keywords entered and the current contents of the search engine's index. An online shopping site also varies according to the search the user performs—it would be impossible to create a static web page for every possible search the user might make. Similarly, when viewing a user profile on a social network, the exact contents of the profile depends on the recent posts made by other users.

Pages like this are **data-driven** – their contents is fetched from a database using a query which is run when the page is requested. Data is stored in a **back end database** such as SQLServer, MySQL, or Oracle – usually lower end databases such as Microsoft Access are not used for this purpose because they do not meet the performance requirements. A programming language such as **ASP (Active Server Pages)**, **ASP.NET**, or **PHP (PHP Hypertext Preprocessor)** is used on the web server to extract the required data from the database and build a HTML web page, which is sent to the user for viewing (figure 9-24).

The advantage of using a database to drive a web site is that one set of data can have multiple uses in a company (see figure 9-21). For example, product data and prices can be displayed on the company web site, while the same data, plus stock levels, can be used in the warehouse to manage inventory. If the organisation also has physical stores, this database can be connected to Point of Sale (POS) systems too (see page 196). Using one set of data improves **data integrity** by removing redundant copies which could be inconsistent.

Interactive web sites

Scripting languages such as **JavaScript** can be used to enhance web pages and make them more interactive and dynamic. Features such a drop-down menus, images which change as the mouse moves over them, and validation of data in input forms all use JavaScript to work. JavaScript is supported by default in virtually all web browsers.

Multimedia **plugins** such as **Adobe Flash** and **Microsoft Silverlight** can add even more functionality, and are often used for games, animations, embedded video, interactive quizzes, and other multimedia applications. **Java** – not to be confused with JavaScript – is a programming language used to create **applets** that run inside web pages. Java applets are essentially normal programs except they must obey a series of security restrictions to make them safer for Internet use (such as being unable to read or write files to the user's hard disk).

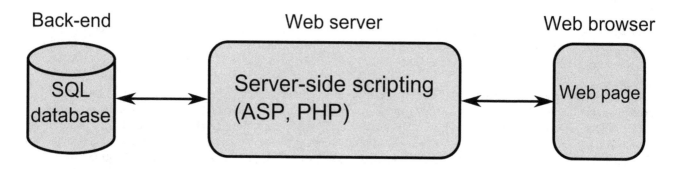

Figure 9-24 Data drive web sites use server side scripting tools to access a database and produce web pages using the results

However, web designers must think carefully before implementing these technologies on their web sites. Flash, Silverlight, and Java all require browser plugins before they can be used, and not all browsers have these plugins installed by default.

Users may be unwilling to download and install a plugin in order to view a web page, or plugins may be unavailable—perhaps because of company restrictions, or because they are unavailable on certain platforms (such as Flash on the Apple iPhone and iPad). Some users also disable Flash to save bandwidth and speed up browsing, or because of security concerns.

Even if plugins are installed and used, web designers need to carefully limit the use of multimedia to reduce the bandwidth and page load time. Users are unlikely to spend 15 seconds waiting for a fancy animated Flash page to finish downloading before they can view a page, and some search engines now consider loading speed when ranking pages in their results.

The latest version of the HTML standard, **HTML 5**, includes some features which previously required a plugin to achieve (such as embedded video). In the future, as browser support slowly improves, HTML 5 will become an attractive alternative for web designers looking to incorporate multimedia into their pages. However, developers should be aware that many older browsers, which often lack support for newer standards, are still in use (see figure 9-26).

Web page compatibility

Web designers need to test pages carefully to ensure they appear and function in the same way across different browsers, operating systems, and screen resolutions. It is good practice not to require any of the above technologies for essential web site features because not all users have them available.

The best solution for these problems is for web developers to detect whether a user's browser supports the technologies used, and provide an alternative (perhaps simplified) page if it does not. Although this complicates the web design process, it stops users with older browsers – who may be quite numerous—being excluded from using the site. Many web development applications have features to test pages in a variety of web browsers before deployment.

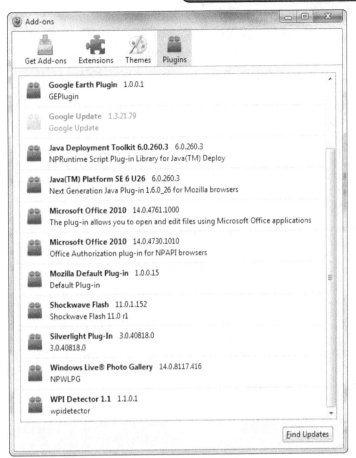

Figure 9-25 Installed plugins in the Mozilla Firefox web browser

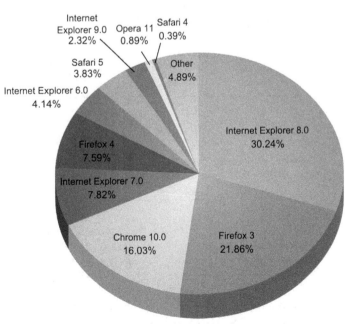

Figure 9-26 Browser market share

Web site features

Sitemaps show an overview of all pages on a web site. They are used to help users locate specific pages quickly, and can also be a useful aid during the design process. An effective site should have a good balance between the number of links on any page (the breadth) and the number of links needed to reach a given page (the depth). If information is not easily accessible, either because links to it are hard to find or because several pages must be navigated in order to reach it, it is possible users will give up looking and move to another site.

Home > Equipment > Lenses > Wide Angle

Figure 9-27 Bread crumb trails aid navigation

To aid navigation, **breadcrumb trails** can be used to let a user see exactly where they are in the web site as a whole. For example, in a photography site, clicking on 'Equipment', then 'Lenses', and then 'Wide angle' will produce a breadcrumb trail containing those links. This serves as a visual aid and allows users to jump back to previous sections (figure 9-27).

Web standards

The **World Wide Web Consortium** (W3C), founded by World Wide Web inventor Tim Berners-Lee, is the organisation responsible for developing standards for the web. Notable standards developed by the W3C include:

- **HTML**—The standard language for web pages
- **CSS**—A standard for formatting web pages
- **XML**—eXtensible Markup Language, along with several related standards such as XSLT and XQuery, is used to encode structured data in text format.
- **SVG**—A standard file format for vector graphics (see page 128), which uses XML.

Standards are important in ensuring consistency in the way web pages and services appear and operate. In the past, some browsers have been criticised for poorly implementing web standards, or for creating their own additions to them. This is much less common now. The W3C provides tools on its web site which can check web pages for standards compliance.

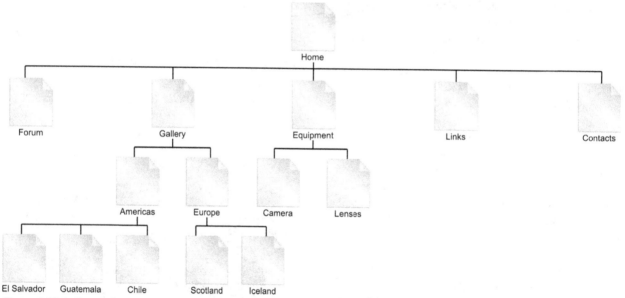

Figure 9-28 A sitemap for a photography site offering equipment for sale, a discussion forum, and a gallery amongst other things

---

Exercise 9-9

Visit two or three of your favourite e-commerce web sites. How well is the information organised? What options are available on the home page? What features has the company included to ensure you can find what you need? **Explain** any improvements you think the company could make. [6 marks]

Exercise 9-10

A school has students split across 12 grades. Consider the different users of the school web site. **Construct** a sitemap which effectively organises the information available, making it quick and easy to locate. [6 marks]

Cookies

Cookies are small text files stored in a special folder on your hard disk by some of the web sites you visit. These sites use cookies to store small amounts of data about you in name-value pairs (see figure 9-29).

How do cookies work?

1. When you visit a web site, the site checks if you already have a cookie for that site.
2. If you do not, the site creates a new cookie, usually with a new **unique identification number (UID)**.
3. Otherwise, if your computer already has a cookie for the site, this indicates that you are a returning visitor. The data from the cookie, including the UID, is sent to the web site.
4. The UID from the cookie can be used to look up your data in a database held by the web site.

Many web sites only store a UID in a cookie, and store all their other data about you in a database on their systems. The UID merely acts as a primary key in the database.

Often web sites store data about their visitors so they can better understand them and offer better services. Data stored can include the last time you visited the site, the time you spent on the site, and the exact pages you visited. Other sites store user preferences, including preferred language, page layout, and colour scheme. Systems which require login, such as web mail and social networks, use cookies to remember that you are logged in. Because all of this information is stored by the site you are visiting, these types of cookies are known as **first party cookies**.

Sometimes when you visit a web site, a third party has adverts on that site and places (or reads) a **third party cookie** on your computer when the advert is shown. Because these advertising companies have adverts on lots of sites, reading the same cookie on each site allows them to identify you as the same user. Over time, this allows the company to build up a profile of your web browsing activities, by knowing which sites you visited. For this reason, third party cookies are sometimes called **tracking cookies**. Your browsing habits can then be used to decide which advertisements you are most likely to be interested in, enabling **targeted advertising**.

Solutions

First party and third party cookies can be blocked separately in most web browsers. Many people block third party cookies because they feel they do not offer useful functionality, but it is relatively hard to browse the web

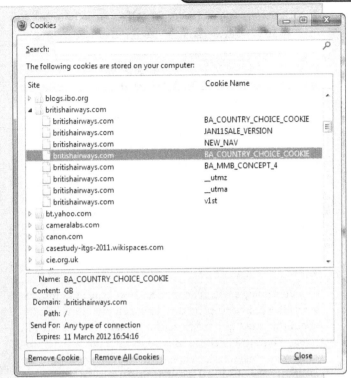

Figure 9-29 One value for the British Airways cookie shows the selected language so the site can customise itself automatically on the next visit.

with first party cookies blocked because many web sites rely on them to function. Newer web browsers support Stanford University's '**Do Not Track**' initiative to let users opt out of tracking cookie systems. Add-ons for older browsers can be downloaded to do the same thing. The problem with this approach is that it relies on advertising companies agreeing to honour the system – which few have done so far.

Common Mistakes

Cookies are often misunderstood and are sometimes mistakenly considered a security threat. Some cookies can be a threat to privacy—but not all. Cookies:

- Do not gather information about you – they just identify you
- Do not store private information such as passwords or credit card numbers
- Are not programs – there are text files
- Are not viruses, and cannot contain viruses or any other malware
- Cannot help a web site access files on your hard disk
- Cannot be read by sites other than the one that created the cookie.

Designing for Accessibility

Web page designers also need to consider users with disabilities caused by limited vision, mobility difficulties, or other problems. The W3C (see page 206) hosts Web Content Accessibility Guidelines (WCAG) which include recommendations to web developers. In many cases, specialised input and output methods can help disabled users (see page 29), but certain web site design techniques can complement these tools. For example, when a **screen reader** reaches an image in a web page, by default it will read the URL of the image – such as www.example.com/images/welcome.jpg – which is not particularly helpful information. A web page designer can improve the situation by using an **Alt attribute** to add a human language description to images. The screen reader will then read that instead (see figure 9-30).

Even for images which are not essential (such as graphics for bullet points or page divisions), empty Alt attributes should be used to prevent screen readers reading the file name. The **Title attribute** is used in a similar way to provide more meaningful explanations of hyperlinks. Title attributes are often displayed as tooltips when the mouse moves over a link, so they benefit all users. They are particularly useful when the link is a non-text item such as a photo or an icon.

As an added bonus, adding Alt attributes to non-text content helps search engines index the page by giving meaning to these items—without the Alt tag, the web spider can obviously not understand the content of an image.

Colour blind users have difficulties distinguishing certain colours—common advice for web designers is to avoid differentiating onscreen objects solely by colour. For example, if a link appears in blue to stand out from the rest of the text, it should be highlighted using another method as well, such as underlining.

```
<img alt="Waterfall in Guatemala" src="imgs/guatemala_s.jpg" /></a>
```

Figure 9-30 Alt attributes add meaningful descriptions to images

Page layout can also be optimised for accessibility. Placing navigation links at the start of the page (the top or the left side) before other content means a screen reader does not need to read the entire page before presenting navigation options to the user—a frustrating experience on long pages. It is also useful to test a page using keyboard navigation to ensure that all areas can be reached.

Although designing for accessibility seems like a chore to some developers, it is an important step in achieving equality of access. Additionally, studies have shown that an accessible web site is also easier to access for non-disabled users.

The equality of access issue becomes critical when dealing with sites that provide important services, such as healthcare and government sites. As increasing numbers of governments move facilities online (see page 298), there is a danger of excluding disabled users from them. Some countries are developing legislation which addresses this issue.

WebCMS

Web Content Management Systems (WebCMS) enable users to post information onto web sites with minimal knowledge of HTML or CSS. They present the user with an editor similar to a basic word processor, and automatically upload submitted content to the web site and apply a predefined style. WebCMS software is often used on blogs and other sites which have content added regularly, especially if many users are involved and they lack technical skills.

Behind the scenes, entries to a WebCMS are stored in a database and extracted and published into a web page as needed. Examples of specialised content management systems include Blackboard and Moodle Virtual Learning Environments (VLE) designed for educational use (see page 222).

Exercise 9-11

Write 5 to 6 sentences to summarise the concepts of web design. Include the following keywords:

- ASP
- Content information
- CSS
- Database

- Formatting information
- HTML
- SQL
- web development software

Exercise 9-12

It has been suggested that web designers should be required by law to make their sites accessible to disabled users, just as buildings must have access ramps and other features. **Evaluate** the benefits of this proposal. [8 marks]

Publishing a web site

Step 1: Choose a web host

Once a web site has been created, it needs to be **uploaded** to a **web host** so that users can access it. Web hosts run software called **web servers**, which are responsible for receiving requests from users and returning web pages. Common web server programs include Apache and Microsoft Internet Information Services (IIS).

An organisation can choose to host their own web site or use **third party hosting**. Both have their advantages and disadvantages. For a small company, the cost and expertise required to install, configure, and maintain their own web server often means they rely on third party hosts, who provide dedicated web space and email addresses. Many business oriented **Internet Service Providers** offer hosting packages.

The cost of third party web hosting depends on the features provided, including the amount of bandwidth dedicated to the site (this is important if the site will have many visitors) and the amount of disk space provided. Additional features such as secure SSL connections or support for data-driven web sites using PHP, ASP, or SQL databases usually add to the cost. Cheaper hosts tend to host several web sites on each server, potentially slowing down access, while the most expensive options offer dedicated servers—essential for sites with many visitors.

Uptime—how consistently a server runs without interruption—is an important factor when choosing a web host. Many web hosts claim 99.9% or greater uptime—allowing less than 9 hours downtime per year. The best (and most expensive) hosts use multiple backup and redundant systems (see page 38) to obtain this level of uptime even if they suffer power or hardware failures.

It is also possible to find free web hosts, which provide hosting in return for placing advertisements on each site, but these are intended primarily for hobbyist use.

Larger organisations may choose to host their web sites on their own servers. This has the advantage of removing monthly hosting charges, and giving complete control over the servers, including uptime and security—which can be both an advantage and a drawback.

Step 2: Purchase a Domain Name

A short, memorable domain name can help a business greatly. Domain name registrars charge a small fee to register a domain name, which usually depends on the top-level domain (TLD) required. TLDs such as .com are more expensive than less well known options such as .net. The cost for a new .com domain can be as low as $10 to $20. Registrars' sites usually have search features to find available domains.

Once a domain name is registered, it must be configured with the IP address of the web server hosting the web site—the precise method of doing this varies, but once done, the DNS server will be updated with the domain name and the corresponding IP address, allowing visitors to access your site (see DNS, page 82).

Step 3: Upload the site

The final step in the process is to upload the web site to the web host. In the case of simple sites which utilise only HTML and CSS technologies, this can be achieved using a **File Transfer Protocol** (FTP) program, which copies files from the designer's computer to a directory on the web host. Some hosts also offer graphical web-based interfaces to achieve the same goal. For more complex data-driven sites, databases need configuring and data transferring before the site can go live. Once this is done, the site should be accessible by typing the domain name into any web browser.

4: Get the site indexed

Search engines regularly index the world wide web (see page 211), but with most search engines it is also possible to submit a URL for future indexing. Once this is done, visitors should start visiting your site!

Figure 9-31 FTP client, used to copy files from the designer's computer (left side) to a web host (right side).

E-Marketing

E-marketing techniques use information technology to promote a business. E-marketing is used by both offline businesses, to attract more customers to their physical stores, and online business to increase the number of web site visitors and improve their conversion rates.

Email is a cheap and easy way to send advertisements to multiple people at once. However, sending unsolicited **bulk email** advertisements – spam – to a large number of people is likely to cause companies more problems than it solves. Instead, most companies only send email **newsletters** to existing customers, in particular those who have specifically signed up for the service. This opt-in approach can be effective, especially if combined with targeted advertising techniques that use customers' buying or viewing history to select adverts appropriate for them. However, even then companies must be careful not to send adverts too frequently.

Search engine optimisation (SEO) techniques are an e-marketing technique to improve a web site's ranking in search engines' results pages. This is important, since many people do not look beyond the first page of search results. To properly utilise SEO techniques, it is important to understand how search engines generate their listings (see page 211). Although most search engines accept paid advertisements for display in a dedicated area of the screen, many do not accept payment to make items appear higher on the search results page. This means SEO techniques are the prime way of gaining exposure in search results. However, techniques should also be used with caution, because many search engines try to detect and ignore sites which abuse them—for example, by **keyword spamming**.

An older SEO technique is the use of HTML **meta tags.** Meta tags contain keywords related to the web page content, which may not be present in the page itself. For example, a photography shop might use meta tag keywords including *weddings*, *events*, *sports*, and *portraits*, even if these specific types of photography are not mentioned on the page. However, meta tags have slowly declined in relevance, and some search engines, such as Google, now ignore them because of their potential for abuse by including dozens irrelevant terms (known as keyword spamming). Figure 9-33 shows sample meta tags code.

```
<meta name="keywords" content="weddings,
events, portraits"/>
```

Figure 9-33 Meta tags describe a page's content

Web page content is also important in obtaining a good search engine rank. Search engines look for keywords in web page content, assessing both how often they occur (known as **keyword density**) and where they occur in the page (**keyword prominence**). Words appearing in titles are considered more important than those in the main body, meaning web designers should therefore carefully consider their choices of page titles and section headings. For example, instead of including the same generic title

Figure 9-32

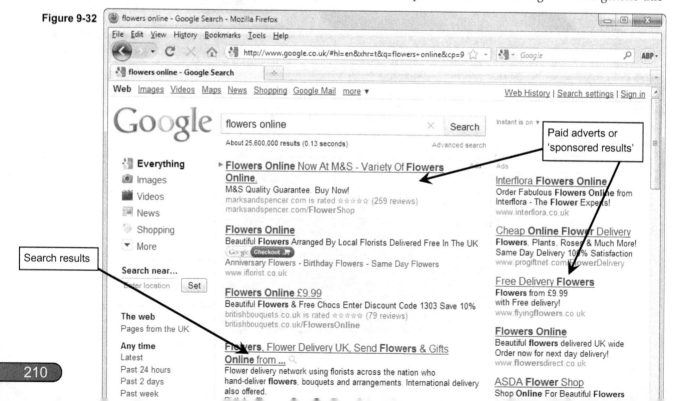

on each page ('Photography'), the title should include words related to that page's content, such as 'Photography – lens for sale'.

However, the technique of repeating the same word many times in a web page (sometimes in the same colour as the background, making them invisible to human readers) is another form of keyword spamming which most search engines now detect and penalise.

The age of content on a page is also important. For topics such as news, more recent information is generally more desirable than older content. Search engines also take this into account, so that web pages which have not been updated for some time gradually fall down the search rankings.

Figure 9-34 Search engine tools show the popularity of search keywords and the cost of advertising on the results pages they produce

Links to and from a web page, along with the authority of those links, is another factor in SEO. For example, a site having one or two links from large news organisations is likely to be considered more important than a site having several links from small personal blogs. To make their pages appear more popular, some authors submit their sites to **link farms** – groups of sites which link to one another in an attempt to improve their ranking (because they appear more popular). However, many search engines take measures to negate the effect of these link farms.

Once a search engine has considered all of the above information about a web page, it will give that page a page **rank**. This is a numerical score which tells the search engine how 'good' the page is compared too all other pages. The highest ranking pages are of course the ones returned at the top of the search results page.

Search engine providers make quite frequent changes to their search algorithms to improve results and avoid people who try to artificially inflate their search rank using abusive tactics.

Online Advertising

Popup adverts, which open a new browser window containing an advert when the user visits a web page, were popular in the early days of the web. However, many popups contained large animations or images which users found annoying—especially in the days of slow dialup Internet access. Popups have become less common, not least because most modern browsers have features to stop popup windows appearing. **Banner ads** are a more common method of online advertising. Embedded in a web page, often across the top or down the side of a page, they appear much as advertisements in the traditional printed press.

Displaying adverts on search engines is another common form of advertising. While it is not generally possible to pay a search engine to have a web site appear higher in the main search listings, businesses can pay to list their web site in the **sponsored links** section of the search results (see figure 9-32). Generally, advertisers choose the

---

How search engines work

Search engines do not search the World Wide Web when you click the Search button – there are too many web pages to make that practical. Instead, search engines use dedicated programs called **web spiders** or **web crawlers** which constantly index the web. These programs start at a given web site and record key information about it, then give the page a ranking using a **page ranking algorithm**. When one page is indexed, the spider moves to another page by following links from the first page. On each page it indexes, the spider follows the links it finds, building up the search engine's index. Because the web is constantly changing, web spiders need to constantly revisit pages to index the latest content.

When somebody uses the search engine, the keywords they enter are checked against the index to find the pages containing those words. Of the sites containing those words, the highest ranked sites are returned first.

search keyword or keywords for which they wish their advertisement to appear. The price of the advert – the **Cost Per Click** (CPC) – depends on how much competition there is from other advertisers for the same keyword. Prices can range from a few cents per click to $40 or more—search engines usually provide a tool to show how popular certain keyword searches are before buying them (figure 9-34). The advantage of the CPC model is that advertisers only pay when a user clicks on their advert, not when it is displayed, making the most efficient use of their money.

Search engines usually allow advertisers to targeted their audience demographic – for example, selecting a geographical region, language, and even the type of device used to browse. Social networks such as Facebook use their vast collections of user data to target their adverts even more precisely, including by age, marital status, likes and interests, and education level. A professional wedding photographer, for example, could target adverts to all people aged between 20 and 35, who are engaged to be married, and live within 25 miles of his home city. These targeted advertising systems benefit advertisers by ensuring adverts are shown to those most likely to be interested in them, increasing the chance of success.

Blocking Adverts

Many web browsers have built in features to block popup adverts. **Advert blocker** extensions can be downloaded to block a wider range of adverts, including banner ads and search listing adverts. Ad blockers filter out adverts using black lists of known ad servers, preventing adverts from even being downloaded. This has the advantage of saving bandwidth and increasing browsing speed.

However, some web site owners consider ad blockers unethical. Many web sites offer their content for free but make money from advertising revenue—when ad blockers are used, this revenue is significantly reduced. Even simply blocking third party cookies reduces revenue because it prevents adverts from being targeted, reducing their effectiveness.

Social Media

Organisations are increasingly taking advantage of the growth in **social media** to distribute advertisements in the form of online videos, games, images, and smart phone apps. These techniques take advantage of word of mouth advertising, hoping that users will spread and repost messages to their friends and acquaintances, all the while generating free publicity for the company. Particularly successful campaigns are said to have gone **viral**, having spread across the Internet much like a virus, with very little control from the creators of the content.

More adventurous businesses have even ventured into **virtual worlds** to raise brand awareness and attract new customers. Several clothing companies, for example, have virtual 'shops' where customers can view products just as they would in a real shop, even adding clothing to avatars to see how they look when worn. Sports company Reebok even allows customers to customise virtual 'trainers' in various styles and colours, and provides the option to purchase real versions of the customised products from the company's web site[10].

Measuring Marketing Success

An advert's **Click through rate** (CTR) is the percentage of people who click on it when it is displayed. Click through rates for **banner adverts** are usually quite low – around 0.2 – 0.3% (i.e. two or three clicks per thousand views)[11], while the top adverts on Google's AdSense sometimes have a CTR between 1% and 8% CTR (i.e. up to 80 clicks per thousand views). Some Twitter adverts record as much as 19%[12]. A e-commerce site's **conversion rate** is a measure of how many visitors to a site actually purchase products, while the **bounce rate** is the percentage of visitors who enter a site's front page and then leave the site immediately.

Web Traffic analysis (also called **web analytics**) involves collecting and analysing statistics about the visitors to web sites. Statistics collected can include:

- Number of unique visitors
- Number of return visitors
- Individual pages visited
- Visit duration
- Bounce rate
- Country and language of visitors
- Operating systems used by visitors
- Browsers used by visitors
- Referrers – the sites which led to this one
- Referring search terms – if the visitor came from a search engine
- HTTP error codes
- Bandwidth used

Exercise 9-13

Some web site owners believe it is unethical to accept using a web site for free, but then block the cookies or adverts from which it generates income. Do you agree with this statement? **Explain** your answer. [6 marks]

These statistics can help a business in various ways. The number of return visitors is an important statistic because a high value suggests users find something useful about the web site which encourages them to come back, while a low number of new visitors might suggest that few new users are finding the web site, perhaps because existing advert campaigns are poor or search engine rankings are low. The duration of visits and the pages visited can help determine the effectiveness of a web site – for example, the front page. If a large number of visitors never progress beyond the front page (i.e. there is a high bounce rate), it is possible that something is putting visitors off or stopping them – perhaps the site's navigation options are poor, the page takes too long to load, or perhaps there are problems displaying the site on some browser versions.

Referrers are a key statistic because they tell a web site designer where users found out about the site—and in the case of search engines, the search queries used. The success of advertising campaigns can be measured this way and decisions made about where to spend money on future advertisements.

Even the success of offline advertisements – such as those in a magazine – can be measured using web analytics. For example, if a magazine advert contains a special URL only used in that advert (for example www.mywebsite.com/magazine-ad), the number of hits

to that page can be assumed to be the minimum number of people who have seen and responded to the advert (since they cannot have seen the URL anywhere else).

Some technical statistics such as the operating system and browser used by visitors might seem irrelevant, but they can be useful for two reasons. Firstly, the web site designer needs to ensure the web pages render correctly on those platforms. Secondly, a statistic such as a large number of mobile phone users might suggest that there is a market for a dedicated mobile phone application or special offers (see page 199).

HTTP error codes can also be useful – if a lot of visitors are receiving a 404 'page not found' message, it suggests that there is a broken link somewhere on the web site or on a referring web site.

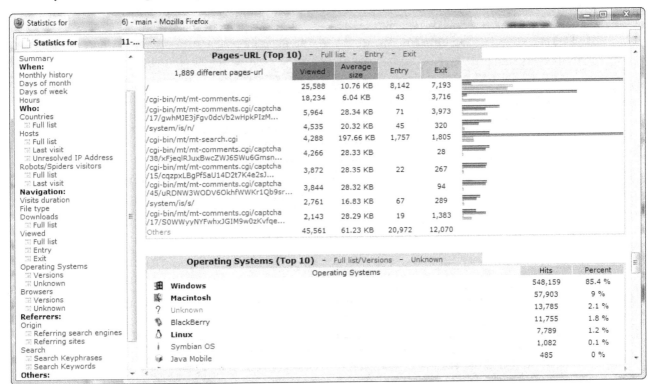

Figure 9-35 Web traffic analysis tools

Search Engines and Privacy

Search engines make significant profits from advertising—in fact, more than 96% of Google's revenue in 2010 was generated this way[13]. This success is achieved through **targeted advertising**—winning business by being able to show adverts to specific target audiences. To achieve this , search engines store and process vast amounts of information about their users—including every search they make. Using cookies (see page 207) or user accounts, this activity can be tied to individuals, helping build up profiles on them.

Such large scale data collection and retention has caused some privacy advocates to be concerned however, as search data, even if anonymised, can still reveal a great deal about the user. An infamous case from 2006 highlights the potential problems. *The New York Times* ran a story about the release of 20 million search queries by Internet provider America Online (AOL). AOL released the search queries as part of a research project—each had been anonymised by assigning users numbers instead of names. However, this was not enough: *The New York Times* was able to track down one of the users, number 4417749, by investigating search queries until they identified her as 62 year old Thelma Arnold from Lilburn, Georgia, US[14]. Queries such as 'homes sold in shadow lake subdivision gwinnett county Georgia' had helped reveal her location, while others revealed information about her hobbies and medical ailments. The queries provided enough detail that the investigating reporter was able to visit her and conduct an interview for the paper.

The search query data was quickly removed by AOL, but by that time numerous people had downloaded it and mirror sites had been set up to host it. Cases such as this highlight the amount of information that is collected about us, and how much can be revealed by seemingly anonymous information. Exercises 9-14 examines some additional examples from the search data.

Exercise 9-14

The table below shows the queries made by two search engine users. What, if anything, can be determined about these users from the searches they made?

Search terms for user 1	Search terms for user 2
• how to change brake pads on porsche 944	• chai tea calories , calories in bananas
• 2005 us open cup florida state champions	• surgical help for depression
• how to get revenge on a ex girlfriend	• can you adopt after depression
• how to get revenge on a friend	• who is not allowed to adopt
• replacement bumper for porsche 944	• i hate men
• florida department of law enforcement	• jobs in denver colorado
• crime stoppers florida	• teaching positions in denver colorado
	• how long will the swelling last after my tummy tuck
	• divorce laws in ohio
	• free remote keyloggers
	• baked macaroni and cheese with sour cream
	• how to deal with anger
	• teaching jobs with the denver school system
	• marriage counseling tips
	• anti psychotic drugs

Exercise 9-15

Look in your web browser's History window. Often there is a search function – enter the name of a search engine that you use regularly and you should see the searches you have made.

   a) How easy would it be to determine your age, gender, location, and occupation with a reasonable degree of certainty? Which search queries reveal these facts about you?

   b) What else could be determined about you by these search queries? Do certain groups of queries reveal more than individual queries alone might?

Transportation Business
Travel Sites

Many organisations in the travel industry, from travel agencies to hotels to airlines, now have an online presence, helping travel related e-commerce account for 37% of the total e-commerce spending in the US in 2010[9].

Airline and train schedules and seating availability can easily be checked online without the need to visit a travel agency. Many travel companies also allow tickets to be purchased directly, with customers specifying their preferences such as seat position, smoking or non-smoking areas, meal choices, and any unusual requests such as excess luggage or baby seats. Pre-flight online registration is also needed for the security checks required by some countries such as the United States. While travelling to the airport or waiting for an arrival, tailored text message or email alerts are increasingly used to provide up-to-the-minute information about any delays or cancellations.

Hotels often provide similar features on their web sites, with information on availability and pricing, pictures of rooms, and directions to the hotel. Many hotels also allow online reservations and booking.

These online facilities are convenient for customers, and businesses benefit because they can reduce the number of staff working in customer service, answering telephones, taking bookings, and checking availability – with e-commerce, the customer performs these tasks for the business.

Another benefit of an online presence for smaller hotels is increased ability to compete with larger hotels. This is particularly true if a business is rated well on one of the major travel review sites, which include user generated reviews of destinations and hotels all over the globe.

Travel reservation sites often allow users to book all of their travel needs in one place. Many feature **price comparisons** drawn from multiple other sites, allowing the best deals to be found, and can offer related deals such as car hire, hotel bookings, and nearby attractions based on the user's search.

Some web sites are even starting to compete with traditional travel guide books by harnessing the power of user content and web 2.0 technologies like wikis to build a catalogue of destinations and activities all over the world. The contributors to these sites, which can include local residents, can have a deeper knowledge of destinations than guide book authors who may only spend a small

Figure 9-36 Hotel reviews (top), flight schedules (middle), and collaborative travel guides are all available online (bottom).

amount of time in any given location. Multiple contributors also help build up a more rounded impression of a destination. Finally, the nature of wikis and web sites in general mean that information can be much more up to date than paper guide books, which are only be issued once every three years or more.

Body Scanners

Full body scanners, sometimes colloquially called 'naked body scanners', are an increasingly common sight in airports across the world. Installed in an attempt to increase security by spotting hidden weapons or explosives, the scanners use radio frequencies or backscatter x-ray technologies to 'see' through a passenger's clothing and essentially present an image of the passenger naked.

The use of the scanners has proved controversial, with critics claiming their operation amounts to a virtual strip search. Particular concerns have been raised about the use of the technology on children. To address privacy concerns, the systems blur the faces and genitals of the passengers, and are designed not to store images after they have been viewed by security personnel—though there have still been cases of abuse by staff[16].

Health questions also exist over the use of x-rays, even in small doses. Nevertheless, the installation of such machines has increased in recent years and in many countries they are considered important tools in combating terrorism.

Vehicle Tracking

Several types of organisations have interests in tracking vehicles, either throughout their journey or at specific points. Toll roads and bridges, for example, need to charge drivers for use, but in an efficient manner which prevents large queues at toll booths. **Radio Frequency Identification** (RFID) technology is increasingly being used in these situations, with the driver carrying an RFID enabled smart card in their vehicle, which is automatically read as it passes the toll booth. The card can then identify the driver and deduct fees from a previously specified bank account. This technology reduces delays and slowdowns, prevents problems with change or lack of funds, and reduces the number of staff needed to collect money from drivers. Automatic barriers or cameras equipped with Automatic Number Plate Recognition (see page 301) are used to stop drivers who pass through without a valid card.

Fleet tracking takes vehicle tracking a step further, following individual vehicles in **real time** and producing

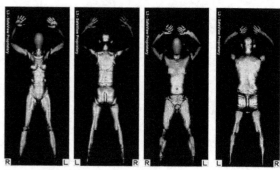

Figure 9-37 Images produced by a full body scanner

detailed statistics about their journeys. Fleet tracking is commonly employed by taxi companies and haulage companies. **GPS** technology (see page 243) allows the position of individual vehicles to be known in real time. This is a significant advantage in the event of theft, and even the presence of such a system may deter would-be thieves. If a vehicle is stolen, **remote vehicle disabling systems** can literally stop it in its tracks.

Fleet management software is used in conjunction with fleet tracking systems to improve the efficiency of operations. **Route planning** features use information such as road length and type, speed limits, traffic levels, and accident information to find the optimum route for a journey—which might not necessarily be the shortest. For example, this can help dispatch the taxi which will arrive

Figure 9-38 Automatic toll road using RFID cards

Exercise 9-16
To what extent are people's concerns about full body scanners outweighed by the security benefits they provide?
[8 marks]

Exercise 9-17
Research the various technologies which can be used instead of body scanners to improve airport security. **Evaluate** the appropriateness of each one. [8 marks]

at the pickup point in the shortest time, or help assign a lorry to collect material from a warehouse with the minimum waiting time. The improves the business efficiency by reducing the time vehicles are stationary waiting for collection or drop off, and by reducing fuel consumption — which also has environmental benefits.

Fleet management also improves safety by allowing supervisors to ensure drivers are following regulations regarding speed limits, maximum allowed driving times, and break frequencies. This information can also be recorded for auditing and inspection purposes.

Package Tracking

E-commerce companies and couriers usually offer **package tracking** to their customers, enabling them to the view the last known status of their packages from a web site, and supermarkets are increasingly tracking individual items from manufacture to store shelf. Although barcodes are useful for fetching price information at checkout terminals, manually scanning barcodes for hundreds of individual items would be time consuming. Therefore most companies use RFID to track packages. Goods are scanned at the start of each step of the journey (for example, as they leave the factory and are loaded onto a vehicle) and the results are transmitted to a central database with details of the time and location of the scan. When the vehicle reaches its destination and unloads the goods, they are scanned again, updating the database. When a customer visits the company's web site and enters their package tracking number, the appropriate records are fetched from the database and displayed.

As well as increasing convenience — customers no longer have to worry where their goods are or whether they will arrive — accountability is increased because any lost goods can be traced back to a last known time and location.

Smart cars

Smart cars, also called **intelligent cars**, use information technology to improve driver safety and comfort. Often they use **sensors** to provide information about the environment in or around the vehicle, and some vehicles may even react to this information automatically. For example, temperature and wheel spin sensors can detect ice on the road and visually or audibly warn the driver. If the car is connected to the Internet, this same information can be

Figure 9-39 Some smart cars can park automatically

acquired from local weather reports, or even using car-to-car networks to receive warnings from other cars which have recently travelled the same stretch of road.

If a smart car is involved in an accident, it could automatically call emergency services, giving them details of the accident location (from on board GPS), speed, impact direction, and number of passengers (from in seat sensors). This information could help emergency services ensure that the right equipment and personnel are sent to the accident scene as quickly as possible – for example, automatically sending fire and rescue crews if the vehicle reports that the impact is severe or that the vehicle has rolled over.

Other smart car systems are designed to improve driver comfort and increase convenience. Biometric sensors can not only provide greater security, but enable cars to adjust their seat and mirror settings to the preferences of the identified driver, as they sit down. Some modern vehicles already feature self-parking modes, which take over from the driver and are able to autonomously parallel park. Researchers are even working on developing completely driverless vehicles, where people will be mere passengers (see page 347).

Exercise 9-18
Smart car technologies are constantly improving. Research some of the recent developments in driver safety and comfort. Label a diagram of a car with the systems used and the techniques they use (for example, sensors) to gather data.

Chapter Review

Key Language

Traditional Businesses

acceptable use policy
ATM
chip and pin
collaborative software
deskilling
Electronic Funds Transfer
email monitoring
employee monitoring

extranet
filtering
follow-the-sun working
Internet
Internet monitoring
intranet
keystroke monitoring
loyalty card

macro
macro viruses
mail merge
monitoring
online banking
Point of Sale
reskilling
remote desktop

reward card
RFID
self checkout
smart shopping trolley
targeted advertising
teleworking

Online Businesses

absolute link
ad blockers
ALT attribute
anchor
Apache
applet
ASP
ASPX
back-end
banner ads
bounce rate
breadcrumb trails
browser compatibility
bulk email
Business-to-Business
Business-to-Consumer
Click Through Rate
Consumer-to-Consumer
conversion rate
cookies
Cost Per Click
CSS
data mining
data-driven web sites
digital certificates
direct payment

do not track
domain name
Domain Name System
E-commerce
E-marketing
e-store
electronic shopping cart
email
enterprise information system
external link
File Transfer Protocol
filtering
first party cookie
Flash
HTML
https
hyperlinks
internal link
Internet Service Provider
Java
JavaScript
keyword density
keyword prominence
keyword spamming
link farm

location based service
meta tags
mobile commerce
MySQL
newsletter
online advertising
online reputation
payment gateway
PHP
plugins
pop-ups
ranking of sites
referrer
relative link
screen reader
scripting
Search Engine Optimisation
secure online payment
Silverlight
sitemap
social media
spam
sponsored links
SQL
stylesheet
SVG

tags
targeted advertising
third party cookie
third party hosting
third party payment service
title attribute
Top Level Domain
tracking number
unique identification number
uploading
uptime
viral advertising
virtual world
W3C
web analytics
web crawler
web hosting
web server
web spider
web traffic analysis
WebCMS
WYSIWYG
XML

Transportation Businesses

fleet management
fleet tracking
full body scanners

GPS
intelligent cars
package tracking

price comparison sites
real-time data collection
remote vehicle disabling

RFID
route planning
sensors

Exercise 9-19
Identify the items of hardware and software which a teleworker might require to do their job well. [4 marks]

Exercise 9-20
Explain two benefits of online bill payment for the customer, and **two** benefits for the utility company. [8 marks]

Exercise 9-21
Examine the steps a web site designer could take in order to improve a web site's bounce rate, click through rate, and conversion rate.[8 marks]

Exercise 9-22
Design a web site for the scenario described below. Construct a site map and then use web development software to build the site. Consider accessibility and other good design techniques in your design, and apply search engine optimisation techniques.

Scenario: A small gardening company offers services including garden maintenance, pond construction, and landscaping work. It wishes to expand its business to include selling garden accessories such as fountains, garden furniture and patio equipment, garden sheds, and outdoor lighting. Because the company does not want to stock large volumes of these items at any one time, it wishes to have a catalogue of available items along with key facts about them. The company has also noticed that customers often need inspiration for landscaping projects and so wishes to showcase examples of their work online.

Exercise 9-23
(a) (i) Define the term *key logger*. [2 marks]

   (ii) Describe **two** items which may be present on a company's intranet. [4 marks]

(b) Explain **three** clauses that a company may include in its acceptable use policy. [6 marks]

(c) Justify the decision to use employee monitoring software. [8 marks]

Exercise 9-24
(a) (i) Identify **two** ways credit card fraud may be committed. [2 marks]

   (ii) Describe **two** features which may be present on an online banking site. [4 marks]

(b) Explain the security measures a bank must use on its online banking web site. [6 marks]

(c) To what extent are the benefits of online banking and its associated features outweighed by the problems which may arise? [8 marks]

Exercise 9-25
(a) (i) Define the term *data driven web site*. [2 marks]

   (ii) Describe **two** actions a web designer can take to increase the accessibility of a web site. [4 marks]

(b) Explain **three** factors a search engine may consider when assessing the quality of a web page. [6 marks]

(c) A small business sells greetings cards and party related material online. Discuss the use of third party payment service compared to direct credit card handling for this business. Evaluate your arguments. [8 marks]

Exercise 9-26
(a) (i) Define the term *Point of Sale*. [2 marks]

   (ii) Describe the steps taken when the customer buys items at a supermarket with a credit card. [4 marks]

(b) Explain the benefits of loyalty card schemes for customers. [6 marks]

(c) To what extent do the benefits of using RFID technology in supermarkets outweigh the concerns? [8 marks]

References

1 Joyce, A. (2006). *Every Move You Make.* Washington Post Available: www.washingtonpost.com/wp-dyn/content/article/2006/09/30/AR2006093000147.html. Last accessed May 2011.

2 Malachowski, D. (2005). *Wasted Time At Work Costing Companies Billions.* San Francisco Chronicle. Available: www.sfgate.com/cgi-bin/article.cgi?f=/g/a/2005/07/11/wastingtime.TMP. Last accessed May 2011.

3 BBC. (2002). *Internet abuse costs big money.* Available: news.bbc.co.uk/2/hi/technology/2381123.stm. Last accessed May 2011.

4 BBC. (2002). *Surf your way out of a job.* Available: news.bbc.co.uk/2/hi/science/nature/2122273.stm. Last accessed May 2011.

5 BBC. (2002). *Teleworking soars in the UK.* Available: http://news.bbc.co.uk/2/hi/business/2029132.stm. Last accessed Nov 2011.

6 Bustillo, M. (2010). *Wal-Mart Radio Tags to Track Clothing.* Available: online.wsj.com/article/SB10001424052748704421304575383213061198090.html. Last accessed June 2011.

7 PubMed. (2008). *Deskilling and adaptation among primary care physicians using two work innovations..* Available: http://www.ncbi.nlm.nih.gov/pubmed/21685794. Last accessed Nov 2011.

8 Fowler, G. A.. (2010). *E-Commerce Growth Slows, But Still Out-Paces Retail.* Wall Street Journal. Available: blogs.wsj.com/digits/2010/03/08/e-commerce-growth-slows-but-still-out-paces-retail/. Last accessed May 2011.

9 comSCORE. (2011). *US Digital Year in Review 2010.* Available: www.comscore.com. Last accessed May 2011.

10 BBC. (2007). *Virtual World, Real Millions.* Available: http://news.bbc.co.uk/2/hi/business/6708417.stm. Last accessed Nov 2011

11 Stern, A. (2010). *8 ways to improve your click-through rate.* Available: www.imediaconnection.com/content/25781.asp. Last accessed June 2011.

12 AccuraCast. (2009). *Google AdWords Click Through Rates Per Position.* Available: knowledge.accuracast.com/articles/adwords-clickthrough.php. Last accessed June 2011.

13 Datamation. (2001). *Google 3Q Profit Soars 32%, Offers Rare Revenue Breakdown.* Available: http://itmanagement.earthweb.com/entdev/article.php/3908376/Google-3Q-Profit-Soars-32-Offers-Rare-Revenue-Breakdown.htm. Last accessed Nov 2011.

14 Barbaro, M. & Zeller, T. (2006). *A Face Is Exposed for AOL Searcher No. 4417749 .* Available: http://www.nytimes.com/2006/08/09/technology/09aol.html. Last accessed Nov 2011.

15 Privacy Rights Clearinghouse. (2011). *Fact Sheet 7: Workplace Privacy and Employee Monitoring .* Available: https://www.privacyrights.org/fs/fs7-work.htm#2a. Last accessed Nov 2011.

16 BBC. (2010). *Heathrow worker warned over body scanner misuse .* Available: http://news.bbc.co.uk/2/hi/uk_news/england/london/8584484.stm. Last accessed Nov 2011.

17 BBC. (2008). *Supermarket of the future.* Available: http://news.bbc.co.uk/2/hi/technology/7476672.stm. Last accessed Nov 2011.

Chapter 10
Education

Objectives

1. Describe the technologies used for teaching and learning
2. Explain how IT can assist users with special needs
3. Explain how IT is used in school administration
4. Discuss the types of resources available online
5. Evaluate the benefits of information technologies in the classroom

Education

Information technology is dramatically altering education, changing the way material is delivered, how teachers and students interact, and the very nature of the materials and skills that students need to learn. IT has also helped extend education beyond the school classroom or university lecture theatre, with advances in distance learning and open content helping to make knowledge available globally at a lower cost than ever before. As businesses demand ever more IT literate employees, educational institutions need to ensure their students are prepared for the 21st century work environment by exposing them to the latest technologies and skills.

IT in Teaching and Learning

E-learning, or **electronic learning** is a general phrase given to any teaching method that makes use of information technology. **Telelearning** takes place when the teacher and student are in geographically separate locations. **Blended learning**, as its name suggests, involves a mixture of approaches—for example a combination of traditional and electronic learning methods in a classroom, or the use of classroom lessons and telelearning at different times.

Telelearning, or **distance learning**, is commonly used when students cannot physically attend classes, for reasons including ill health, moving home, or the need to look after children or relatives. Telelearning is also useful for people with full time jobs who are unable to attend classes during the day, or for those who cannot find the courses they require at local educational institutions. Prison inmates can also be offered telelearning courses to improve the chances of getting jobs upon their release.

Schools and universities often use **Virtual Learning Environments** (VLEs) to offer telelearning courses. VLEs allow content to be uploaded and organised by topic, week, or date and accessed at the student's own pace. Teachers upload documents and files, links to Internet resources, and in some cases upload videos of their classes to enable students to view them at their leisure. Most of the popular VLEs, including Moodle and Blackboard, allow tasks such as essays to be assigned, complete with deadlines for electronic submission. Simple tasks such as quizzes, gap filling ('cloze') tests, or matching games can be automatically graded by the computer without the teacher.

Discussion forums are often included in VLEs to allow students to interact with each other and the instructor, and allow **asynchronous learning** – with the student learning when they want, at they speed they want, without the need to be online at a predetermined time.

Some aspects of telelearning may require **synchronous learning** – when the teacher and students need to be online at the same time. Chat or video-conferencing sessions, for example, require participants to meet at a predetermined time to discuss issues that have arisen during the course. This can be useful to regain some of the interaction that is lost with asynchronous learning, but it can be inconvenient for people in different time zones. Video conferencing also has specific hardware, software, and network requirements, which may exclude some students from these sessions.

Virtual Learning Environments	
Advantages	**Disadvantages**
Course material can be deployed to a larger number of students compared to a traditional classroom environment. This should help reduce costs - savings which can then be passed on to students.	The face-to-face interaction of a traditional classroom is lost. This can make it harder for students to ask questions, and harder for teachers to notice misunderstandings and assess progress.
VLEs do not require web development experience, so professional looking results can be achieved by even novice users. This frees up time to work on course material.	Some facilities (such as virtual meetings) still require coordination if students are in separate time zones.
Students who cannot otherwise access courses have the opportunity to do so, increasing equality of access.	Certain hardware, such as a web cam and a high bandwidth Internet connection, may be required for some VLE features.
Travel costs for students and teachers can be reduced.	
Students can learn at their own pace and at any time they wish.	

Figure 10-1 Advantages and disadvantages of Virtual Learning Environments

Mobile learning, also called **m-learning**, is a form of tele-learning where mobile technologies such as PDAs and smart phones are used to access educational content. This is particularly useful for quick reference tasks in situations such as language learning, where quick access to very specific information (such as a dictionary) is often needed. For example, the US military use translation software on mobile devices in Iraq and Afghanistan when no human translators are available – soldiers type or speak their sentence into the device and the software provides text or audio feedback. Similar tools can be used to translate for aid workers in humanitarian missions, and even to translate speech into sign language, using a animated avatar. Of course, these devices still face some difficulties in achieving accurate translations, especially when faced with local dialects.

Online resources

Information technology provides access to new types of educational resources which are not possible with traditional classroom textbooks. Before the widespread use of the Internet in classrooms, computer **reference software** on CDs or DVDs provided encyclopaedic content enhanced by multimedia. Many also included related tools such as dictionaries, thesauruses, and books of quotations—items which would have cost much more if purchased separately in book form. However, as cheap and fast network connections become more common in schools, many of these products have been discontinued as users move towards free content on the Internet.

Particularly with the advent of **web 2.0** technologies, Flash, Java, and higher speed Internet connections, interactive online resources have become much more common. **Multimedia** can enhance the teaching of many subjects – for example, to improve historical understanding by including archive footage from famous events, or assist language learning with embedded audio clips of native speakers to guide pronunciation. Some language learning software even allows the learner to speak into a microphone and then analyses their pronunciation and provides feedback.

Subject specific web sites often provide accounts for students to log in and practise topics at their own speed, keeping a record of their achievements, and possibly even adapting the material to them—for example, by providing additional questions on topics a student struggles with, or temporarily reduce the difficulty until the student builds confidence.

Figure 10-2 Teachers use Virtual Learning Environments (top) to provide access to a variety of educational resources. M-learning (middle) brings resources to users on the move. Multimedia educational content can be purchased on CD-ROM or DVD for offline use (bottom).

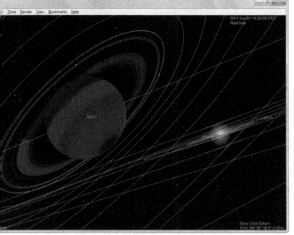

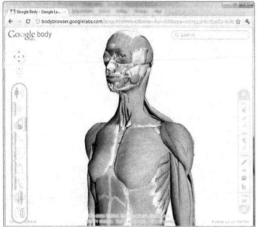

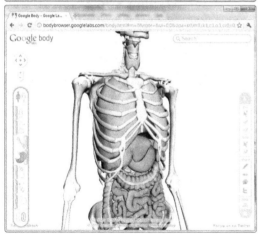

Figure 10-3 Educational software allows exploration of places as varied as the solar system (top) and the human body (above)

Online animations and interactive models (see page 166) can be used to teach many science topics, including viewing the molecules in compounds, the human body, and the orbits of planets in the solar system. These models allow hands-on experience of ideas and concepts which would otherwise be too expensive, risky, or difficult to experience in real life. Biology lessons, for example, can use interactive models of the human body which allow the skeletal, blood, nerve, and organ systems to be added or removed, zoomed in, and rotated, giving a unique perspective unobtainable with textbook diagrams or even traditional physical models of the body (see figure 10-3). Climate and eco-system models provide a similar degree of flexibility for environmental topics, and population models can show the results of demographic changes.

Virtual field trips take multimedia a step further by creating digital versions of actual locations, along with educational notes and resources. Famous sites including the Sistine Chapel, the British Museum, and the Museum of Iraq all have web sites which imitate the experience of being in a real museum, with models of exhibits and descriptions in multiple languages. Whereas the lack of space in museums often means large parts of their collections are kept in storage, online virtual museums can house virtually limitless content, including material previously unavailable.

Web 2.0 in the classroom

Web 2.0 technologies such as blogs and wikis have been adopted by many teachers to help their students learn. At their most basic, these technologies provide a cheap or free way to store electronic copies of lesson notes and related material which can help extend students' understanding of material covered in class. Having classwork available at home assists homework tasks and also encourages parents to become aware of and involved in their children's learning. Some research suggests that students take greater care and produce better, higher quality work when they know it will have a wider – perhaps global – audience, rather than being written in an exercise book and seen only by the teacher[1]. The comment features of blogs also provide an opportunity to elicit feedback from readers, providing adequate precautions are taken to guard against inappropriate comments.

Pushed further, technologies like these and social networks—often a controversial topic in education—can be used to create '**flat classrooms**' - where learning is not restricted to the classroom environment and where classes from schools across the world can work on collaborative global projects.

Podcasting

Podcasts—audio files distributed over the Internet using RSS feeds—are cheap and easy to record and distribute, requiring the minimum of hardware and software. Podcasts provide students with opportunities to practise their verbal skills in a variety of subjects, perhaps uploading and sharing their final productions using a class VLE or even distributing them on the Internet. For example, modern language teachers can use them to assess their students pronunciation skills or public speaking skills in a way which would not be possible in an ordinary classroom.

There are also many free podcasts available on topics from language learning to computer security and archaeology.

Open Courseware

Open courseware is educational content which is free to distribute, use, and change—usually distributed under a Creative Commons or similar licence (see page 135). Open courseware materials range from simple videos and lecture notes to full graduate courses and text books. Many open courseware projects provide cut down versions of full university courses, complete with lecture recordings, notes, and assignments, but of course without the university credit at the end.

Electronic books (e-books) are produced by some textbook companies to replace or support existing paper books. E-books can be distributed on CD-ROM or downloaded from e-book stores and read on a computer or an **e-book reader**. E-books distributed online can theoretically be quickly and automatically updated for all readers, and electronic distribution saves printing, transportation, and distribution costs—although there is a potential problem with equality of access if students or schools do not have access to sufficient numbers of e-book readers or computers. Bandwidth may be an additional challenge, with e-books not really suited to texts containing a large number of images or diagrams that must be downloaded.

Open textbooks go one step further, and aim to create electronic, freely distributable books to replace commer-

Four Virtual field trips

The **Sistine Chapel** (www.vatican.va/various/cappelle/sistina_vr/index.html) offers a 3D recreation of its interior, including the famous frescos and altar.

The **Virtual Museum of Iraq** (www.virtualmuseumiraq.cnr.it/homeENG.htm) showcases a long history of the area, including Sumerian, Babylonian, and Assyrian artefacts.

The **British Museum** (www.britishmuseum.org/explore/online_tours.aspx) has online resources for many of its items which are not on display in the museum itself.

The Smithsonian Museum (www.mnh.si.edu/panoramas/#) a virtual tour of its vast collection.

cial textbooks (paper or electronic). A major criticism of traditional paper textbooks is their high cost—up to $100 or more—and the relative speed with which they become out dated. Although e-books have reduced these problems somewhat, the cost of some electronic textbooks is still criticised.

Five open content providers

1. **MIT** (ocw.mit.edu) – The Massachusetts Institute of Technology OpenCourseWare page contains over 2000 courses from the arts, natural sciences, and social sciences.
2. **Harvard Extension school** (www.extension.harvard.edu/openlearning) - Harvard offer a variety of online graduate courses for free.
3. **Project Gutenberg** (www.gutenberg.org) – A long running project to collect electronic copies of books, mostly classics which are now in the public domain.
4. **Wikipedia** (www.wikipedia.org) – perhaps the largest and most famous open content site, the free encyclopaedia that anyone can edit, with over 3.6 million articles in the English version.
5. **Wikibooks** (www.wikibooks.org) - The sister site to Wikipedia, Wikibooks attempts to organise content into related topics and subjects for textbook use.

Open textbooks reduce initial costs by saving money paid to authors and publishers. However, a significant challenge for open projects is ensuring the quality of their content. In the US, textbooks used in schools must meet state standards for content – including accuracy and quality. Traditional textbook publishers often have years of experience in addressing these standards, whereas open textbook publishers may not. For this reason, some projects, such as the California Open Source Textbook Project (COSTP) are encouraging existing publishers to openly license their material, rather than start with entirely new authors[2].

Game based learning

The educational effects of playing computer games, long a favourite hobby of many teenagers, is often a controversial subject. Despite this, software which combines games playing with educational tasks—sometimes called **edu-**

Try It Online
Visit www.itgstextbook.com for examples of serious games which teach about a variety of issues.

tainment software—has been popular since the availability of early home computers. Basic edutainment titles often have similar concepts to traditional arcade games—such as shooting aliens or collecting coins—but intersperse the action with questions which the player must answer in order to progress. Other titles—sometimes called **serious games**—are designed specifically to educate players on a particular issue which is at the heart of the game. The game *3rd World Farmer* (see figure 10-4), for example, is a strategy game which requires the player to plant and harvest crops to earn money and improve their farm. However, players are presented with challenges faced in developing countries such as famines, floods, and tribal violence which affect their ability to operate the farm.

Another example is the game *Food Force*, developed by the World Food Programme, which tasks the player with delivering and managing food supplies in humanitarian missions across the world. The game aims to teach the player about the causes of famine, droughts and war, plus nutritional information, and the obstacles which relief organisations often face in their missions[4].

Other games, although not specifically targeted at the education market, can require quite complex skills and understanding to be successful. Some teachers have seized upon these games as an opportunity to teach their students useful skills while improving motivation. Games which let the player build a city, for example, require an understanding of power and water distribution, crime control, and pollution issues, while many strategy games require elements of resource management. Notable uses of computer games in classrooms include:

Maths, memory, and reading games on the handheld Nintendo DS console have been used in a number of test projects in UK schools. One such project found an average increase of 10% on maths tests after playing the games for 15 minutes each morning[3].

Figure 10-4 Food Force (above left) teaches players about humanitarian relief projects. Strategy games such as FreeCiv (left) have been used to teach a range of skills.

In North America, the historical detail in strategy games such as *Civilization* and *Rome Total War* has caught the attention of some teachers, who use them for teaching topics ranging from Ancient Egypt to imperialism, good governance, and diplomacy[5]. A modification of *Civilization*, starting in 1534, has even been created to teach Canada's early history.

Other strategy games, such as *Railway Tycoon*, *Theme Park*, and *Theme Hospital*, have all been used to teach students elements of business management, economics, and planning.

Exercise shy students have been encouraged to participate in physical education lessons with games which use **dance mats** or **motion controllers** for input. Trials in the UK showed increased participation during physical education lessons, with activity levels comparable to a brisk walk. The initial project won a Youth Sports Trust award and is set to be expanded to more schools[6].

Web based exams

As Internet research skills become increasingly important in many jobs, the issue of allowing Internet use during school assessments has arisen. In Denmark, a trial project in 2009 allowed students Internet access during their final year school exams. Students were given free access to all web sites, but were banned from communicating with anybody inside or outside the exam room[7]. Advocates of the system claim the nature of the questions make it hard to cheat, since high quality answers require analysis and evaluation of information, while the Internet provides a quick and effective way to check facts. They also argue that in modern society there is less need to emphasise remembering facts—as these can be checked quickly from a plethora of mobile devices—and a greater need to process those facts into something meaningful.

High Tech Cheating

While some schools are allowing Internet use in exams, others are battling an increase in cheating. Mobile phones in particular are easily smuggled into exam rooms by students and then used to connect to the Internet, access

Is Wikipedia a viable classroom resource?

Freely available content, particularly open material, often raises concerns about its reliability and integrity. In particular, the use of Wikipedia, 'the free encyclopaedia that anyone can edit', in the classroom has been controversial since the site's inception in 2001.

Concerns over the reliability and integrity of Wikipedia's content stem mainly from the fact that anybody can edit its articles, even anonymously, potentially including inaccurate or biased points of views. Some users have even vandalised pages by including deliberately false and sometimes libellous information – especially on biographical pages. Related to these concerns is the frequent lack of citations or references in articles, which make it hard to verify information. Inaccurate articles have even caught out a number of press organisations who did not verify their facts, often with embarrassing results[17]. Others criticise the quality of writing in some Wikipedia articles, claiming their structure and language use is poor and difficult to understand. In the classroom environment, younger students in particular may find this a problem.

On the other hand, proponents of Wikipedia point to multiple studies which have found similar errors rates in Wikipedia and traditionally edited encyclopaedias[18], and evidence suggests that almost half of all vandalised Wikipedia pages are fixed almost immediately[19]. The very nature of Wikipedia means it often contains the very latest information on a given topic, while the number of articles—3.6 million for the English language version—easily surpasses the size of paper encyclopaedias (65,000 articles in the Encyclopaedia Britannica[20]).

Meanwhile, Wikipedia's popularity is undeniable: with over 15,000,000 registered accounts and many more unregistered users[21], and a place near the top of many search engine results, Wikipedia is likely to be a force on the web for some time.

notes stored in their memory, or communicate with third parties—perhaps by photographing the examination paper and sending it to an outsider to supply the answers. In the UK, there was a 6% rise in exam cheating in 2010 – the majority of it involving mobile phones[8], while in Japan, allegations of university entrance exam cheating—again, using mobile phones—became the subject of a police investigation[9].

Outside of the exam room, **plagiarism** has become a concern for many educational establishments as increased use of Internet resources tempts some students to copy and paste work without attribution. In some cases, students are simply unaware of malpractice rules and quote a web page or build on somebody's ideas (their **intellectual property**) without properly acknowledging the source. These issues can be resolved relatively easily by educating students on acceptable and unacceptable practice and teaching them how to write citations and bibliographies.

However, some students knowingly plagiarise by copying large amounts of material from the Internet and pasting it together into one piece of work. Several web sites make so called 'sample' essays available for students to download, while 'essay mill' sites even offer custom essay writing services, for a fee. Many of these sites claim to offer exemplar work so students can understand what makes a good essay, but it is clear that often these essays are used to commit plagiarism.

Although easy to perform, the consequences for committing plagiarism can be severe. Most educational organisations have IT **acceptable use policies** (AUPs) and academic honesty policies which cover plagiarism, with consequences ranging from failing the work to being asked to leave the school or university.

A 2010 MIT study also found long lasting impacts for students who plagiarised class assignments, with a threefold increase in exam failure rates compared to other students, even if they started with at the same skill level[10].

Technological solutions to fight plagiarism include using search engines to check the originality of phrases from student work, and using specialist **anti plagiarism software**. Such systems work by comparing student work with sources on the Internet and a large database of past submissions (previously submitted work is normally saved in the database, prompting concerns from some students about their intellectual property rights). Work is assessed and given an 'originality score' which describes how similar it is to past works. More advanced software is able to detect work that has been copied and altered, perhaps with the removal or editing of some words.

Filtering and monitoring

Monitoring students' computer use and preventing access to inappropriate material on the Internet is a priority for many schools. In the US, the **Children's Internet Protection Act** (CIPA) requires these measures in government funded schools, and there may also be pressure from parents and teachers to use them. Just as in businesses (see page 188), filtering in schools can help prevent distraction and time wasting (by both students and teachers). A desire to reduce **cyber-bullying** during school time is also a common motivation for blocking social networks and similar sites (see page 232).

Like any filtering system, schools face problems caused by both **false positives** (when educationally useful material is accidentally blocked) and **false negatives** (when harmful material is allowed through instead of being blocked). This is especially problematic if **black lists** are determined by an educational authority rather than the school itself, as the process to have a site unblocked can be difficult and time consuming.

Another difficulty is that students often use their own laptops or even mobile phones for Internet access, allowing them to circumvent filters by connecting directly to their phone company's 3G or 4G networks.

Exercise 10-1
Describe **three** techniques a school can use to reduce the problem of students accessing inappropriate material during class time. [6 marks]

Exercise 10-2
To what extent will the decision to allow Internet access in examinations improve the quality of education? [8 marks]

Hardware Technologies

Interactive whiteboards consist of a **touch sensitive** board which allows inputs to be made with a special pen or a finger, and a **projector** which outputs a computer display onto the board. Software installed on the connected computer translates and processes touch inputs, and can run dedicated interactive whiteboard applications such as games.

In the most basic form, interactive whiteboards can be used to operate the computer as normal, touching and dragging icons with a finger instead of a mouse. In note making mode, notes, annotations, and diagrams are drawn on the board and then saved as images or editable text files which can then be distributed to students electronically or uploaded to a class VLE.

Specially designed interactive whiteboard applications are available for specific subjects. For example, a physics lesson might use a circuit diagramming program which allows circuit components to be created by dragging icons on the board; a maths teacher can use software which presents problems on screen and allows the answer to be entered by students; and an English teacher can use electronic versions of texts which allow sections to be highlighted, annotated, and saved for later use.

Although interactive whiteboards can provide fun lessons, especially for younger students, they are also expensive, costing upwards of £430 ($700) each. This cost is often prohibitive when schools consider buying them for multiple classrooms. The surface of the boards is also relatively delicate and can be easily damaged, for example by accidentally writing on it with a normal whiteboard marker pen.

In many cases, activities which use interactive whiteboards are achievable using a regular computer and projector (both of which are also needed for an interactive whiteboard system). The variety of different manufacturers also means there is no standard for interactive whiteboard software, leaving users locked in to the software available for their brand of board. One study revealed that students in lessons which used interactive whiteboards were actually more passive and less engaged in the lessons, because many whiteboards only allow single students to use them at a time[11]. However, despite these drawbacks, interactive whiteboards have gained popularity in schools.

Figure 10-5 Child using an interactive whiteboard

Provision for special needs

Information technology can help integrate students with special needs into the mainstream classroom. The **accessibility** hardware and software described on page 29 provides a good basis for many users with physical disabilities. While mobility problems may stop a person from writing with their hands, a computer mouse or trackball combined with an **onscreen keyboard** can be a powerful tool. Onscreen keyboards can be controlled with a foot operated trackball, a head wand, or even (as is the case for physicist Stephen Hawking) a simple on-off switch. **Dictation software** is another option, to convert spoken words into computer type, and is also useful for users with vision problems. Many products, from calculators to dictionaries and personal organisers are available with **speech synthesis** which can help visually impaired users.

A variety of software packages exist to help users with learning difficulties such as dyslexia, for whom reading and constructing sentences can be difficult. Many offer standard word processing functions, plus speech synthesis systems which highlight words as they are read, to aid reading. Dictation systems and **predictive text** systems also help by constructing sentences and providing suggestions after just a few letters have been entered.

People with autism often learn better visually, and there are dedicated software packages that use these techniques. Flash cards, with an image and the associated word displayed on them, are a simple but effective method that can be used as stand alone programs, in web pages, or projected onto a whiteboard. There are even systems available to let non-verbal autistic users form sentences graphically, by dragging a series of icons on a handheld device, with the final sentence being spoken by a speech synthesiser[12].

Laptops in the classroom

Laptop, handheld, and tablet computers are slowly replacing traditional computer rooms in many schools. Laptops and other portable devices have the benefit of being accessible at any point during a lesson, bringing information to the classroom rather than requiring the class to move to a dedicated computer room.

With the move to laptops, schools are starting to implement one laptop per student ('1-1') programmes, either funded through the school or with support from technology firms. However, the effectiveness of such programmes is still a hotly debated topic, with various studies disagreeing on the extent of the educational benefits, if any (see page 232).

Schools often implement laptop programmes to provide students access to online resources, use electronic versions of textbooks, and to facilitate collaborative learning. There is also a desire to prepare students for future careers, many of which now require some degree of IT proficiency.

There are many practical and logistical considerations to be made when implementing laptop programmes, including issues of finance, security, and equality of access. Laptops are not cheap—with costs of up to $2 million to equip an 800 student school with laptops[13], and $1.5 million per year to maintain, financing such programmes can consume large portions of school budgets.

Some schools allow students to bring their own computers, though this raises the issue of equality of access for those student who can't do so, and reduces the positive impact of laptops because teachers cannot rely on every student having access to a computer. Student owned laptops are also harder for the school administration to con-

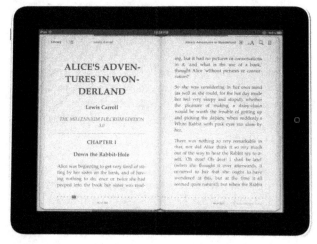

Figure 10-7 Laptops, tablets, e-book readers, and portable computers are increasingly being used in classrooms

trol, as they have no influence on the software or data that may be installed on them. Even if computers are purchased and supplied by the school, parents may still be required to pay an annual fee to insure the devices.

Security is also a prime concern—laptops are relatively easily lost, eminently attractive to thieves, and much more delicate than desktop computers. The cost of repairing laptops is also higher than desktop computers because parts are often specialised to a particular brand. The chances of failed laptops means spare, standby machines need to be kept ready, as well as adequate technical support to solve problems as quickly as possible—both of which are additional costs for the school.

Some computer manufacturers have tried to address this problem by producing hardened versions of their laptops specifically for school children, with reinforced chassis and rubber shock absorbers.

Laptops in Schools	
Benefits	**Considerations**
Often, student engagement is improved	Setup, operating, and maintenance costs can be high
Online resources saves spending on paper textbooks	Quality online resources can still be expensive
Technology skills are essential in many careers	Teachers need training to use technology effectively
Instant access to a wealth of online material	Citation and source evaluation skills must be taught
Portable devices provide convenient access to information	Adequate security measures must be taken
Typed assignments reduce problems with illegible writing	Measures must be taken to ensure equality of access
Provides the possibility of global collaborative projects	Student (and teacher!) distraction can be a problem

Figure 10-6 Advantages and disadvantages of laptops in schools

Can computers and the Internet replace teachers?

Nicolas Negroponte's **One Laptop Per Child** (OLPC) project is famous for attempting to provide cheap laptops to children in developing countries. The laptops are sold in bulk to governments who then distribute them to children. The laptop is ruggedized and equipped with wireless connectivity, giving access to the Internet.

As of 2011, the OLPC foundation has shipped over 2 million laptops—the majority to Latin America, including large deployments in Peru and Uruguay. The OLPC project requires children to own the laptops themselves and be able to take them home with them, in order to encourage after school learning and expose the child's family to the technology[22].

Figure 10-8 The OLPC computer is designed for children in developing countries

Negroponte is famous for his view that children should be given a laptop regardless of the availability of schools or teachers, believing that students can teach themselves using the technology. 'Give [students] a laptop *especially* if they don't go to school. If they don't go to school, this is school in a box'[23].

However, the machine has not received universal praise, with several African leaders criticising it during a United Nations meeting, viewing the venture as misguided. 'African women who do most of the work in the countryside don't have time to sit with their children and research what crops they should be planting'[24]. Others have questioned the appropriateness of spending money on computers and Internet access when developing countries clearly face other major challenges. 'We know our land and wisdom is passed down through the generations. What is needed is clean water and real schools.'[24]

Supporting infrastructure must also be considered—everything from having sufficient electrical sockets to charge the laptops, to ensuring the school building has ample wireless coverage—is important in ensuring the success of technology programmes. Desks and other furniture must also be suitable to prevent problems such as back pain after prolonged use (see page 268).

To avoid problems with inappropriate use of technology or distraction from learning, filtering and monitoring technologies can be used (see page 228). Schools also need to prepare adequate acceptable use policies and educate all users on their contents.

Finally, training is an important issue. Though many students have grown up using technology, often teachers and school administrators have not. Even if they are familiar with the general operation of technology, using it in the classroom often requires changes in teaching and preparation methodologies. A teacher who changes from writing pages of notes on a white board to writing pages of notes on a computer screen is obviously not making the best use of the available technology!

Exercise 10-3
Explain four reasons why teachers might be reluctant to implement a laptop program in their classroom. [8 marks]

Exercise 10-4
Explain three precautions a school can take to reduce the problem of stolen laptop computers. [6 marks]

Exercise 10-5
Schools have different methods of paying for laptop programmes, with some absorbing the cost while others pass it on, in whole or in part, to parents. **Discuss** which stakeholder should be responsible for paying the costs of implementing laptops in schools programs. [8 marks]

Impacts on Education

Reports on the impacts of laptops in classrooms are mixed. Liverpool High, one of the first New York State schools to implement laptops back in 2000, abandoned the scheme after seven years, citing no observable increase in student performance and a wealth of problems[14]. Other schools have found the financial pressures caused by failed laptops to be too great, or have been dissuaded by the amount of time spent fixing technical problems rather than teaching and learning.

Research in Israel also failed to find improvements in grades when computers were used to teach maths, and for younger children even found a negative effect—results went down[15].

Other results have been more positive. A 9 month study by Montreal University found that the introduction of laptops encouraged student participation and motivation, reduced drop out rates from 39.4% to 22.7%, and moved participating schools from 66th to 23rd in school rankings. However, the researchers noted that several factors had to be present to make the best use of the available technology[16].

It is also clear that the age of students makes a difference, with laptops seemingly making the least difference for younger children who are learning basic skills such as reading, writing, and maths. For other children, who need access to a wider range of content, laptops appear to have shown a greater advantage, if used appropriately.

Cyber-bullying

Cyber-bullying using mobile phones, social networks, email, or chat rooms is a growing phenomenon. A 2009 report by the UK government found cyber-bullying had been experienced by 47% of 14 year olds, 41% of 15 year olds, and 29% of 16 year olds[26]. Other research found that 25% of students have experienced cyber-bullying more than once, and 53% of students have participated in bullying at least once[27]. Bullying is not limited to students: one survey of teachers found 35% had suffered online bullying, with 26% of cases being initiated by parents[28].

The impacts of online bullying can be severe, with victims often being afraid to go to school and sometimes needing psychological help. There have also been a number of high profile cases involving suicides or attempted suicides after cyber-bullying[29].

Solutions such as banning access to social networks or mobile phones in schools are of limited use, as much cyber-bullying takes place outside of school. Appropriate **profile privacy settings** can be effective in reducing bullying by restricting the ability to post or view information to only the user's friends. Users also need to be careful about who they grant access to their profile by accepting them as friends.

Most social media sites have features to report abusive behaviour, and often pledge to deal with offending content within 24 hours. Depending on the circumstances, offenders can be warned or have their accounts closed[30]. Users are also able to block individual users from contacting them, or to remove content posted onto their profiles. These measures can be effective when the identity of bullies is known, but do little to stop bullies making further accounts or groups under false names.

Education, both on how users can protect themselves online, and the potential real life consequences of online posts, is also important in combating the problem. Several government campaigns, backed by anti-bullying charities and social networks, have addressed the issue, including providing advice for parents and teachers, who may not have the technical skills to deal with the problem themselves.

School administration

School administrators often use a **School Information System** (SIS) (sometimes called a **Student Information System**) to store and manage large quantities of data about their staff, students, and school. School information systems generally include features for:

- Storing students' personal data, including photographs and home contact details
- Storing students' medical data for emergency use
- Storing academic data including grades, grade averages, and past results
- Storing attendance data on a lesson by lesson or daily basis
- Storing discipline records
- Arranging and recording meetings with parents
- Allowing parents to pay some costs online (for example, dinner money or extra curricular club fees)
- Creating and managing student and teacher timetables and room allocation
- Producing reports about progress
- Recording of books and other equipment borrowed from the school
- Sharing of relevant data with parents

As with many database systems, school information systems typically allow different levels of access for different users. Medical data should only be available to the school nurse, for example, while teachers will be able to view and edit academic data, but only for their own students.

Because every school has slightly different procedures and practices for everyday tasks, many commercial SIS applications are customisable and extendable. For example, timetabling systems must allow the number of lessons per day to be altered, as well as the day length, and the grading system might allow letter grades, numeric grades, or percentages to suit the courses being taught. Additionally, school information systems usually support third party add-ons which allow related features such as inventory management, financial management (including records of staff salaries), and human resource management.

School information systems have the advantage of keeping all school data in one location, reducing duplication of effort and providing quick access to information for school administrators, senior teachers, teachers, and parents. The process of preparing reports for internal use, parental feedback, and government agencies can also be simplified. There may be legal requirements about the

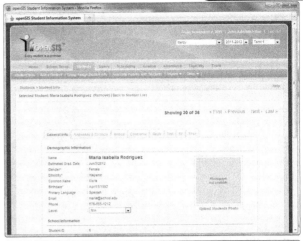

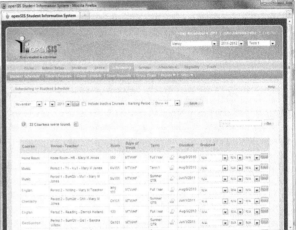

Figure 10-9 School Information Systems manage student and classroom data

retention and protection of data about students, and—when properly used—a SIS can help implement these.

Electronic Data Interchange (EDI) is a common feature of school information systems. Passing student records to new schools, such as from primary to secondary, is a common task. If done manually, information is often printed or exported and must be re-entered into the new school's SIS, which risks integrity problems and discourages sending large amounts of data. EDI solves these problem by defining a standard way to represent and transfer such data. This encourages schools to keep comprehensive records, ensures vital information is not lost during transfer, and helps better monitor and understand a student's progress.

EDI can also be used to send statistical data to government agencies, so they can monitor the progress of students and schools and produce national reports.

Chapter Review

Key Language

1-1 programme	e-book	motion controllers	school information system
acceptable use policy	e-book reader	multimedia	serious games
accessibility	e-learning	onscreen keyboard	speech synthesis
anti-plagiarism software	edutainment	open courseware	synchronous learning
asynchronous learning	Electronic Data Interchange	open textbooks	tele-learning
black list	false negative	plagiarism	touch sensitive input
blended learning	false positive	podcast	video conferencing
Children's Internet Protec-tion Act	flat classrooms	predictive text	VLE
	forums	profile privacy settings	web 2.0
cyber-bullying	interactive whiteboard	projector	
dictation software	m-learning	reference software	

Exercise 10-6

What will the typical school be like in 2020? What changes will technology cause? What will be new? Which technologies will succeed, and which old ideas will be thrown away and forgotten, just as blackboards, chalk, and slates have all been consigned to the past?

Consider a typical government-funded school in the UK or the US. Ask yourself which technologies the government might deem most useful for educational purposes. You should consider various technologies that have been covered throughout this chapter, including:

- The use of laptop computers, smart phones and PDAs in the classroom
- Interactive whiteboards
- Textbooks versus e-books
- Open content versus commercial content
- Blended learning
- Virtual worlds in the classroom
- Any other relevant technologies that might be used in schools of the future

Create a presentation called *Schools of the Future*. Evaluate the likelihood of each of these technologies succeeding or failing in schools, with clear reasoning and reference to all aspects of the ITGS triangle. [20 marks]

Exercise 10-7

Research tends to disagree greatly on the effects computers in schools—and particularly 1-1 laptop programmes—have on results. Some studies claim benefits, other find none—and some even find a negative affect on achievement. Why do you think different studies have found such varied results? **Evaluate** your arguments. [8 marks]

Exercise 10-8

A school is considering options to modernise its information technology facilities. As well as upgrading its current hardware, software, and networking systems, it is investigating the use of electronic books or open textbooks in place of paper textbooks.

(a) (i) Define the term *open content*. [2 marks]

(ii) Describe **two** items of hardware the school may need to purchase to modernise its facilities. [4 marks]

(b) Explain **two** precautions the school will need to take if it decides to use laptops in the classroom. [6 marks]

(c) Analyse the **three** textbook options available to the school. To what extent are open textbooks a worth-while endeavour? [8 marks]

Exercise 10-9

(a) (i) Define the term *VLE*. [2 marks]

   (ii) Describe **two** ways a School Information System can assist school administrators. [4 marks]

(b) Explain the solutions schools implement to combat Internet based plagiarism. [6 marks]

(c) Should money be spent on supplying interactive whiteboards for each classroom in a school, or is there a more appropriate way to spend this money on technology? Justify your answer. [8 marks]

Exercise 10-10

(a) (i) Define the term *blended learning*. [2 marks]

   (ii) Describe **two** items of hardware required to implement tele-learning. [4 marks]

(b) Explain how web 2.0 tools can be used in the classroom. [6 marks]

(c) Discuss the issues that arise when giving free laptops to children in developing countries. To what extent can a laptop prove a quality learning tool for these students? [8 marks]

Exercise 10-11

School administrators, teachers, and parents are sometimes opposed to one laptop per student programmes.
To what extent do you think this opposition is driven by a lack of understanding of technology, rather than genuine problems arising from its use? [8 marks]

References

1 Sanchez, J. (2010). *Teaching with Blogs.* Available: http://www.educause.edu/blog/joesanchez/TeachingwithBlogs/166276. Last accessed Nov 2011.

2 California Open Source Textbook Project. (2011). Available: http://www.opensourcetext.org/. Last accessed Nov 2011

3 BBC. (2007). *Daily computer game boosts maths.* Available: news.bbc.co.uk/2/hi/uk_news/education/7064196.stm. Last accessed June 2011.

4 World Food Programme. (2011). *Food Force: The First Humanitarian Video Game.* Available: www.wfp.org/how-to-help/individuals/food-force. Last accessed June 2011.

5 BusinessWeek. (2006). *Class, Take Out Your Games .* Available: www.businessweek.com/magazine/content/06_08/b3972100.htm. Last accessed June 2011.

6 MailOnline. (2008). *Teachers bring Wii to school in a bid to fight child obesity.* Available: www.dailymail.co.uk/news/article-510681/Teachers-bring-Wii-school-bid-fight-child-obesity.html. Last accessed June 2011.

7 Hobson, J. (2009). *Danish pupils use web in exams .* BBC News. Available: news.bbc.co.uk/2/hi/uk_news/education/8341886.stm. Last accessed June 2011.

8 Coughlan, S. (2010). *Hi-tech exam cheating increases says Ofqual .* BBC News. Available: news.bbc.co.uk/2/hi/uk_news/education/8493132.stm. Last accessed June 2011.

9 McCurry, J. (2011). *Mobile phone exam cheat shocks Japanese meritocracy.* The Guardian. Available: www.guardian.co.uk/world/2011/mar/04/japan-mobile-phone-exam-cheat. Last accessed June 2011.

10 Washington Post. (2010). *New MIT study on student cheating .* Available: http://voices.washingtonpost.com/answer-sheet/higher-education/new-mit-study-on-student-cheat.html. Last accessed Nov 2011.

11 Bui, V. (2009). *Interactive Whiteboards Impact on Education.* California State University. Available: publications.pearlchen.com/pdf/Vahnfullfinal.pdf. Last accessed April 2011.

12 BBC. (2010). *Son's autism leads to innovation .* Available: http://news.bbc.co.uk/2/hi/technology/8634607.stm. Last accessed Nov 2011.

13 iStockAnalyst. (2010). *High-tech comes at a high price.* Available: http://www.istockanalyst.com/business/news/5383168/high-tech-comes-at-a-high-price. Last accessed Nov 2011.

14 Hu, W. (2007). *Seeing No Progress, Some Schools Drop Laptops .* Available: http://www.nytimes.com/2007/05/04/education/04laptop.html. Last accessed Nov 2011.

15 The Economist. (2002). *Pass the chalk.* Available: http://www.economist.com/node/1403378. Last accessed Nov 2011.

16 Physorg. (2011). *Laptops in school classes improve scores.* Available: http://www.physorg.com/news/2011-02-laptops-school-classes-scores.html. Last accessed Nov 2011.

17 Times Educational Supplement. (2010). *IB lifted exam marking guides from Wikipedia.* Available: http://www.tes.co.uk/article.aspx?storycode=6060245. Last accessed Oct 2011.

18 Nature. (2005). *Internet encyclopaedias go head to head.* Available: http://www.nature.com/nature/journal/v438/n7070/full/438900a.html. Last accessed Nov 2011.

19 Wikipedia. (2011). *Wikipedia:Counter-Vandalism Unit.* Available: http://en.wikipedia.org/wiki/Wikipedia:Counter_vandalism_unit. Last accessed Nov 2011.

20 Encyclopaedia Britannica. (2011). Available: http://www.britannica.com/. Last accessed Nov 2011.

21 Wikipedia. (2011). *Wikipedia: Statistics.* Available: http://en.wikipedia.org/wiki/Wikipedia:Wikipedians#Demographics. Last accessed Nov 2011.

22 One Laptop Per Child. (2011). *l.* Available: http://one.laptop.org/. Last accessed Nov 2011.

23 CBS News. (2007). *60 Minutes: One Laptop Per Child.* Available: http://www.cbsnews.com/video/watch/?id=2830221n. Last accessed Nov 2011.

24 Smith, S. (2005). *The $100 laptop -- is it a wind-up?.* Available: http://articles.cnn.com/2005-11-30/tech/laptop_1_nicholas-negroponte-laptop-green-machine?_s=PM:TECH. Last accessed Nov 2011.

25 Stoll, C. (2000). *High Tech Heretic: Reflections of a Computer Contrarian.* Random House, Inc. ISBN: 0-385-48976-5.s

26 The Guardian. (2009). *Facebook launches safety tips as part of anti-bullying week.* Available: http://www.guardian.co.uk/media/pda/2009/nov/16/bullying-facebook-bebo-national-anti-bullying-week. Last accessed Nov 2011.

27 The Guardian. (2009). *Facebook launches safety tips as part of anti-bullying week.* Available: http://www.guardian.co.uk/media/pda/2009/nov/16/bullying-facebook-bebo-national-anti-bullying-week. Last accessed Nov 2011.

28 Reed, J. (2009). *'Action needed' on internet bullying .* Available: http://www.bbc.co.uk/newsbeat/10002963. Last accessed Nov 2011.

29 BBC. (2011). *Study finds third of teachers have been bullied online.* Available: http://www.bbc.co.uk/news/technology-14527103. Last accessed Nov 2011.

30 Schwartz, J. (2010). *Bullying, Suicide, Punishment.* Available: www.nytimes.com/2010/10/03/weekinreview/03schwartz.html. Last accessed Nov 2011.

31 Mackenzie, I. (2009). *Facebook tackles online bullying.* Available: http://www.bbc.co.uk/newsbeat/10002987. Last accessed Nov 2010.

Chapter 11
Environment

Objectives

1. Distinguish analog data and digital data
2. Describe the applications of digital imaging and mapping
3. Explain how digital imaging and mapping work
4. Identify the toxins found in electronic equipment
5. Explain how to safely dispose of IT equipment
6. Evaluate the environmental impacts of IT

Data Logging

Data logging systems use computers to automatically record data from **sensors**, without human intervention, over a long period of time (days, months, or even years). Data logging has many applications; it is used by automatic weather stations to record environmental data which can be later used for weather prediction; it is useful for monitoring volcanic and seismic activity; and robots such as the Mars Pathfinder use data logging to report back information about the Martian surface and atmosphere, including temperature and wind speed. In nuclear power stations and other safety critical systems, data logging is used to constantly monitor the states of the reactors and report any abnormalities.

Hospital intensive care units take advantage of data logging to record and monitor patients' vital signs, including respiration rates, pulse, and oxygen levels. These systems can monitor a patient continuously and sound a warning if any of the sensors detect values outside of predefined parameters—such as a respiration or pulse rate that is too low or too high. Using data logging in this way frees staff members while still providing the constant care needed by the patient. In some cases it is even possible to use portable, wearable data logging equipment so a patient can be sent home while still being monitored (see page 257).

Figure 11-2 Racing cars log and transmit hundreds of variables every second.

All modern commercial aircraft are fitted with Flight Data Recorders (FDR), advanced data logging systems which constantly log over 100 parameters concerning the aircraft's situation, including its speed, altitude, heading, control positions, and the time. FDR data is used in crash investigations to determine the cause of accidents and improve future safety.

Traffic pollution levels are able to be monitored using roadside sensors which log levels of gasses in the atmosphere and, in some cases, the number of vehicles passing by. This helps assess the need for, and success of, traffic reduction techniques. This type of traffic monitoring is another situation which would expose humans to a health risk if they were to perform the task manually for a long period of time.

In sports, racing cars use data logging as part of their telemetry systems, sending each lap dozens of parameters about the car back to the team in the pits. Many aspects of the car, including fuel remaining, tyre temperatures, tyre pressures, height off the ground, and engine revs are all transmitted for analysis.

Advantages

Computerised data logging has many advantages over manual data collection, including the ability to sample large numbers of variables at once, and extremely frequently (many times a second). These readings can be

Figure 11-1 An automatic weather station in the Antarctic. Data logging systems are perfect for such hostile environments.

taken for years or more—much longer than would be possible with manual data collection.

The **integrity** of the collected data can also be greater as computers can sample data at precise intervals (for example, precisely every minute without variation), and unlike humans computers do not get tired, do not forget to take samples, and do not read instruments incorrectly or make mistakes when recording data. For even more convenience, data logging systems can automatically produce output in an easily readable form such as a graph or chart.

Safety is also an important issue—data logging instruments can survive in harsh environments with extremes of temperature, poisonous gasses in the air, and intense weather conditions, reducing the risk to humans who would otherwise collect the data.

Finally, because the whole data logging process is automated, it is useful for systems which only need attention when something is abnormal. A nuclear power plant monitoring system only need alert operators to a problem for example, as do many medical monitoring devices. Data logging systems can automatically record data but only alert humans when values pass outside a certain range.

The Data Logging Process
The data logging process is relatively straight-forward:

1. Analog data is collected using a variety of sensors
2. The analog data is converted to digital data by an Analog to Digital Converter (ADC)
3. The digital data is transferred to a computer for storage
4. The data is analysed and processed
5. (Optional) Alarms or alerts can be sounded if data is outside pre-determined ranges
6. Output such as graphs or tables are produced

Analog versus Digital Data
Analog data (also called **continuous data**) is data which is *measured*, in contrast with **digital data** (**discrete data**) which is *counted*. Physical data such as temperature, altitude, and speed are analog signals. As computers only work with digital data, these analog signals must be processed by an **Analog to Digital Converter** (ADC) before they can be used. This process is known as **digitisation**, sometimes called **sampling**. At fixed intervals of time—called the **sample rate**—a measure is taken from the analog signal and the nearest digital value is recorded.

The quality of the digitisation (i.e. how closely the digital version resembles the analog version) depends on two factors: the sample rate and the **sample precision**. The sample rate is the number of times each second a sample of the analog data is taken. If the sample rate in figure 11-3 was higher, there would be more bars on the *Time* axis, and they would therefore form a shape that more closely resembled the analog wave.

The **sample precision** determines the number of discrete digital values that can be represented—the y axis in the diagram. The higher the precision (the more values), the closer the digital values can be to the analog originals.

CD quality audio is usually converted with a sample rate of 44.1kHz (44,100 samples per second) and the sample precision is 16 bit (65,536 possible values).

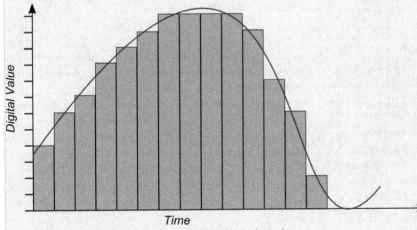
Figure 11-3 Analog data (wave) and digital data (steps)

Satellite Communication and Imaging

Advanced **imaging satellites** such as the GeoEye-1, orbiting above Earth at altitudes of up to 680 kilometres, are capable of taking photographs of any location on the planet with incredibly high resolution. The most advanced commercial satellites can image at up to 0.4 metres (i.e. with each pixel representing 0.4 metres on the ground[10]), while it has been suggested that some military satellites are capable of resolutions to 12.5 centimetres[11].

Other satellites use **remote sensing** techniques such as radio waves (**Radar**), lasers (**Lidar**), or sound (**Sonar**) to gather data not visible using normal photography techniques. Elevation data, terrain types, weather data, and even maps of the sea bed can be obtained in these ways, and they are not limited to earth observation – images of other planets in our solar system have also been taken using these techniques (see figure 11-4).

Because radio waves, sound waves, and lasers cannot be seen with the naked eye, the returned data must be processed to produce a useful **visualisation** of the data (see figure 11-4).

Applications

Weather monitoring is a common application of satellite imaging technology. Photographs and remote sensing of the Earth are used to monitor climate and environmental change, particularly in areas which are difficult to access or which are too large to measure manually on the ground. For example, the size of deserts, rainforests, and glaciers can be detected using radar imaging, allowing scientists to monitor rates of desertification, deforestation, and glacial retreat over large areas. Recently, the progress and effects of disasters such as volcanic eruptions or oil spills have also been monitored using this technology[12].

Collection of data from infrared sensors enables land and ocean temperatures to be calculated, which is extremely

Figure 11-4 Image of Mars, created with data from the laser altimeter aboard the Mars Global Surveyor satellite

useful for making predictions about weather patterns. This data can also be fed into computer models to verify them as part of a feedback loop (see page 173).

Further afield, remote sensing satellites and probes have been used to collect atmospheric, temperature, and surface data from Venus, Mercury, and Jupiter, and even the Sun has been investigated in this way. Data gathered by the many satellites and probes that have surveyed Mars revealed large trenches across the Martian surface which led to new scientific understanding and the suggestion that water may have once flowed on the planet. As of 2011, the New Horizons space probe is en-route to the outer reaches of the solar system to gather data about Pluto and its moons.

As with many technologies, satellite imaging and remote sensing technologies were driven by military requirements, particularly during the Cold War when the US and the Soviet Union both used aerial and satellite photography to monitor the military facilities of the other. Today these technologies are still widely used by the military to monitor the global proliferation of nuclear weapons by monitoring the Earth for the electromagnetic pulses and x-ray radiation associated with them. Satellite imagery is also a valuable military intelligence gathering tool and has been used extensively in Iraq and Afghanistan.

How do Mapping Systems work?

Imaging satellites provide high resolution photographs of the Earth, often captured at several different levels of zoom. These images, and their associated meta-data – their location, altitude, and time and date – are sent back to computer systems on earth. They are then processed as necessary – for example, scaling them, rotating them, or skewing them depending on the angle at which they were taken. Many images may also be stitched to form one larger image. The image data is then stored in a database, where it can be accessed or searched as necessary by mapping software, referenced by its coordinates.

Satellite data also has a number of educational, business, and leisure applications and is often used to build online mapping systems and **Geographical Information Systems** (GIS) for these purposes.

Online Mapping

High resolution satellite maps are available for use by the public in many online mapping applications. Many 2D mapping systems use additional mapping databases such as country borders and road positions to help align the satellite imagery.

Online maps often have **data layers** customised for their target audience, so a system for tourist use may include layers which display hotels, restaurants, car rental agencies, and national parks, while other users might add weather layers, locations of public transport stops, or even 3 dimensional building models. It is also common to include **geotagged** images (images with location coordinates embedded) from photo sharing sites to give an indication of a location from the ground.

Many online maps allow routes and directions to be calculated, often entering origins and destinations as names, GPS coordinates, or postcodes (zip codes). More advanced software allows routes to be configured, for example to avoid areas such as city centres, motorways or highways, or high traffic areas.

Combined with a GPS receiver, online mapping systems are the core component of portable and in car **satellite navigation systems**. These display the user's location on the map in real time, often with accuracy of just a few metres. More advanced navigation systems update traffic and road works information in real time to allow routes to be recalculated if a potential problem or delay such as an accident occurs ahead. Online mapping systems typically provide step by step directions which can be printed out, while in car navigation systems feature spoken directions to avoid distracting the driver with written instructions. Many commercial drivers now favour satellite navigation systems to paper maps for their ease of use, automatic recalculation abilities, and compact size.

Virtual globes are software models of the Earth (or other planets) which provide similar functionality to mapping systems, but in three dimensions. This has the advantage of clearly showing the height of terrain features such as mountains, as well as allowing more detailed layers of information to be added. Some virtual globes have the feature the ability to 'fly' through terrain, perhaps even recording an animation in the process.

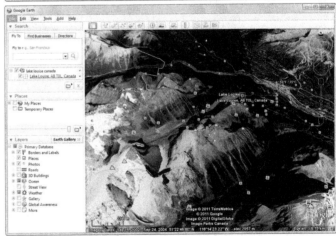

Figure 11-5 Map with satellite imaging (top); vector street mapping data (middle); virtual globe software with user photo and temperature layers added.
© 2011 Google, © 2011 Tele Atlas, © 2011 DigitalGlobe, © 2011 TerraMetrics

Software such as Google Street View takes the online mapping process even further by including images of entire streets in cities around the world. Users can 'move' up and down streets almost as though they were present, viewing local buildings, vehicles, and people. Because each street must be individually mapped by a car with an attached camera, Google Street View only has images of selected cities.

Concerns

Members of the public and governments around the world have raised privacy concerns over online satellite imaging and mapping systems. Google Street View, a system which provides street level imagery for many European and North American cities, has come under particular criticism. Criticisms of online mapping systems include:

- Military concerns that restricted facilities are visible on maps, offering potential intelligence to terrorists or hostile nations
- Government concerns that high resolution maps of sensitive locations such as nuclear power plants or airports could be used by terrorists to plan attacks
- Concerns from citizens about their property being visible, allowing potential thieves to scout for valuable properties and potential targets
- The display of vehicle number plates on street level imagery, prompting privacy concerns
- Concerns from citizens that images of them in the street are available online, or that Google Street View cars passing close to their houses allow Internet users to see inside their homes.
- Images taken by satellite imaging systems may offer a view into back gardens of residences, which are not visible from the public street, invading privacy

Geographical Information System (GIS)

A **Geographical Information System (GIS)** is similar to a virtual globe, but provides facilities to store and analyse much larger amounts of data. Depending on its application, a GIS might include data on population densities, crime patterns, natural phenomena such as volcanoes or fault lines, average incomes, and positions of facilities such as police stations and hospitals. This information can be used by city planners to consider factors such as the ratio of citizens to hospitals, the number of people living close to an earthquake fault line, or areas with particular crime problems.

When planning facilities such as new fire stations, a GIS with detailed information on road types can help officials accurately calculate emergency vehicle response time, helping to pinpoint the best location to situate the building.

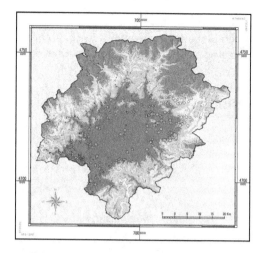

---- Highways
----- Water courses
▨ Catchements subject to flood risk

Warning issued Mon Nov 12 21:34:55 NZDT 2007

Figure 11-6 Map showing probability of disease infection in different areas, using the GRASS Geographical Information System (top). GIS data used to predict areas liking to be flooded (bottom).

In Alaska, the Fish and Wildlife Service imported data from radio tagged caribou into Geographical Information Systems, allowing them to map animal migration routes and analyse how they would be affected by proposed oil developments. A similar system has been used with polar bears to monitor how they are affected by decreasing levels of sea ice[13]. Businesses, too, can use a GIS to find areas with many people in their target demographic, which can help when deciding where and how to advertise their products.

Because Geographical Information Systems are used for such a wide variety of tasks, it is common for users to gather their own data from field research and then use the data import tools in the GIS to add new layers of information. Many GIS programs also store large amounts of historical data, allowing patterns of change over time to be analysed.

GPS Networks

GPS devices are used by people for a wide range of activities, including driving, walking and mountaineering, and navigation at sea. GPS also has (and was originally invented for) military applications, particularly assisting navigation and keeping track of friendly forces.

GPS systems work using **GPS receivers** – the devices which users carry or mount in their vehicles, and a network of **GPS satellites**. GPS receivers use trilateration to calculate their position on Earth. Each GPS receiver has a catalogue of satellites and their current positions. As the receiver detects radio waves from a satellite, it calculates the time taken for the signal to reach it. This enables the receiver to know how far it is from the satellite and, therefore, how far it is from a known position in space.

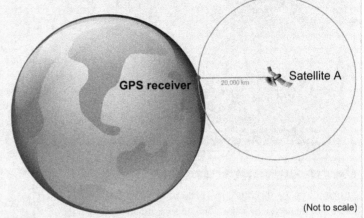

Figure 11-7 Global Positioning System

For example, the receiver may calculate that it is 20,000 km from the satellite A (see figure 11-7). This is only partially useful, because there are lots of points which are exactly 20,000 km from the satellite—many of them in outer space! However, by calculating its distance from additional satellites, the receiver can determine its accurate position. For example, if the receiver is also 23,000 km from satellite B, there are only two points (on a two dimensional map) where the receiver could be (the points where the two circles in figure 11-8 intersect). The Earth acts as a third 'circle', leaving only one possible location for the GPS receiver—the point where the three circles intersect.

In the 2 dimensional example in figure 11-8, only two satellites are needed, plus the Earth itself. The principle is the same for three dimensions, except instead of circles intersecting, spheres intersect. In reality, to get a three dimensional position on the Earth's surface, three satellites are needed, though many GPS receivers use more to improve their accuracy.

Mobile Phone Tracking

The position of a mobile phone can be determined relatively easily either by calculating its distance from the nearest mobile phone masts in a similar way, or by simply using the GPS system built into many modern phones.

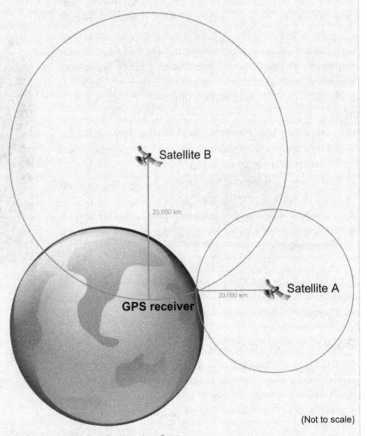

Figure 11-8 Global Positioning System

The tracking of mobile phones—potentially without the consent of the owner—raises privacy concerns but can help police and law enforcement track suspects. It also allows phone users to receive **location based services**. For example, based on the phone's location, software can locate the nearest cash machine or bank, find upcoming events in the area, or recommend a local restaurant.

Exercise 11-1

Some industries have a reputation for being heavier polluters than others. The World Bank lists the steel industry, industrial chemical plants, and pulp and paper manufacturing as some of the top 'dirty industries'[14]. Certain types of mining industries also have a reputation for causing groundwater pollution, while the airline industry contributes 2% of all man-made CO2 emissions[15].

Before continuing this chapter, analyse the positive and negative impacts the IT industry has on the environment. Do you think the IT industry would be classified as a 'clean industry'?

Environmental Impacts

Information technology has some important positive impacts on the environment. The increasing use of 'smart' systems in devices like washing machines and 'smart homes' (see page 274) leads to more efficient use of water and power; email and electronic documents can reduce the use of paper (although this is somewhat debatable), and Internet communications reduce the need for heavily polluting physical travel (especially flying). However, there are several serious concerns about the IT industry and its environmental impact, including:

- The amount of resources used during manufacture
- The speed with which products become obsolete and new ones are manufactured
- The use of dangerous chemicals in the manufacturing process, affecting factory workers
- The amount of power consumed by IT equipment
- The pollution caused by old IT equipment when it is discarded

Throughout its **life cycle**, there are concerns about the environmental impact of IT equipment. These concerns, and possible solutions, are covered below.

Power consumption

Power consumption has always been a key issue for mobile devices, where longer battery lives are a key selling point. However, it is also a concern in organisations, where hundreds or thousands of power hungry computers can have significant financial and environmental costs. Research in the US found that electricity costs accounted for half of total IT expenditure in businesses, and that cooling equipment accounts for almost half of the energy used[1].

Search engines, social networking sites, and cloud computing sites store vast amounts of information on their computer systems, usually in **data centres** – buildings which contain hundreds or even thousands of computer servers and the equipment required to cool them, all running continuously. Concerns have been raised about both the amount of energy consumed by data centres and the source of the energy, which is normally from non-renewable sources[2]. The problem is exacerbated by the **redundant backup systems** most data centres use in case

Figure 11-9 Rows of hundreds of computers in a data centre in Houston, Texas.

of an emergency. A 2010 Greenpeace report found that data centres consume up to 2% of all global electricity[2] – a figure which will continue to grow as Internet services and cloud computing facilities become increasingly popular, and as the amount of information we generate increases.

Solutions

Most modern computer systems have some form of power saving systems built in. The **power settings** on laptop and desktop computers can be used to switch devices and individual components to low energy or standby modes after a period of inactivity. For example, a computer might switch off a hard disk if it has not been accessed for some time. Modern processors also offer **speed throttling** systems such as AMD's *PowerNow* and *Cool n Quiet*, or Intel's *SpeedStep*. These automatically reduce the **clock speed** of the processor if it is not being used intensively, saving energy, reducing heat output, and saving further energy used for cooling. Usually speed throttling systems automatically increase the clock speed if a demanding application is used, so users should not notice a performance loss.

Servers account for a large amount of energy use but there are several ways of reducing their consumption. **Blade servers** are modular systems which allow circuit boards containing processors and memory to be added to a blade enclosure, which provides shared power and cooling. Blade systems generally offer improved energy consumption compared to traditional rack servers.

The large amount of processing power available in one space means blade servers are also useful for running **virtual machines** using **virtualisation software**. Virtual machines allow a single computer to effectively act as multiple computers, each running its own independent operating system. Using a single blade server running three virtual machines is likely to be much more energy efficient than running three individual servers, each with their own storage devices, power, and cooling systems.

Resource Depletion

The volume of resources used in IT manufacture is also a concern. Although microchips are small—weighing just a few grams—dozens of pounds of highly toxic chemicals are used during the manufacturing process. Chips are repeatedly heated, etched, and cleaned with purified wa-

> **Did You Know?**
> It takes 1.6 kg of fossil fuels and 31 kg of water to produce a 2 gram microprocessor[16]. That's a ratio of over 16,000 to 1.

ter, consuming large amounts of energy—over 1.4 kWh per square centimetre of silicon—and resulting in many gallons of water being contaminated with carcinogens and chemicals linked to birth defects[3]. Multiplied by the number of microchips being produced—millions per month—these figures add up quickly. Silicon Valley, the 'birthplace' of the computer revolution, is now one of the most polluted places in the United States, in part because of IT manufacturing plants[4].

Harmful chemicals used in the production of IT equipment have also been linked to illnesses in factory workers, including rates of cancers and birth defects up to five times the average[5]. Clusters of these diseases have been observed in 'clean room' workers worldwide, including in Scotland, the US, and South Korea.

It is suspected that the constant re-circulating of air inside workers' protective 'bunny suits' causes them to re-breathe the same toxins over and over again, greatly increasing exposure levels. Although air is filtered for dust to protect the microchips, chemical fumes are not filtered out, and many of the illnesses—leukaemia, lymphomas, blood disorders—are known effects of the arsenic, benzene, and trichloroethylene used in the manufacturing process[6].

Are E-books better for the Environment?

To answer this question, the pollution created by manufacture, delivery, use, and eventual disposal must be considered. E-books clearly need no trees to be cut down to produce paper—however, each e-book reader requires an estimated 33 pounds of minerals (which must be mined) and 79 gallons of water to produce[17]. Apple's official environmental report for the iPad 2 lists the device's carbon footprint as 105 CO_2e [18].

E-books however, win on distribution—unlike paper books, multiple copies can be made of e-books with no additional resources required, and instant electronic transfer reduces the need to ship books across the country or even drive to a bookshop.

During use, modern e-book readers use extremely energy efficient displays, in some cases using less energy than a standard light bulb[18].

Other factors are harder to measure. One e-book reader will be used to read dozens or hundreds of books, each of which saves the manufacture of a paper book. The life expectancy of electronic devices is significantly shorter than paper books however, and pollution caused by incorrect disposal of electronic devices is a significant environmental concern.

Electronic Waste

Electronic waste, or **e-waste**, refers to old, broken, and obsolete computer and electronic equipment. E-waste includes monitors, keyboards, mice, printers, batteries, mobile phones, chargers, and other household electrical goods such as televisions and VHS players. In 2007, over 2 million tonnes of e-waste were thrown away in the US, and less than 20% of it was recycled[7].

Unsafe disposal

Most electronic equipment contains numerous harmful substances including lead, arsenic, mercury, and cadmium (see figure 11-13). These toxins are not harmful when the equipment is being used, but can contaminate the environment when the equipment is disposed of. In landfill sites, the actions of weather causes these toxins, including highly dangerous heavy metals, to seep into the soil and groundwater, causing serious pollution problems. Despite this, over 82% of e-waste in the US ended up in landfills in 2007[7]. Other methods of e-waste disposal, such as burning, also cause air pollution and ground pollution.

Some users do send their obsolete equipment to specialist companies for safe recycling. However, safely recycling e-waste is expensive, so some unscrupulous recycling firms illegally ship their e-waste overseas to developing countries, where it is broken down and 'recycled' in extremely

Figure 11-11 Workers sorting discard computer components in Delhi.

hazardous conditions, by workers with little or no protective equipment. In these countries, including China and Ghana, it is common for workers to soak or heat circuit boards in hydrochloric acid solutions to recover the small amounts of gold and silver contained in them, in the process exposing themselves to highly toxic fumes. Other workers use hammers to break the glass in CRT monitors, inhaling toxin-laden dust in the process. Toner in leftover printer cartridges is carcinogenic if inhaled, yet many workers recover the remains of toner from old cartridges to create refill cartridges. In some countries the unofficial, unsafe recycling of e-waste has become a major business, bringing in thousands of dollars, but causing huge amounts of pollution and chronic health problems.

The health impacts of e-waste go beyond e-waste workers—burning e-waste to melt plastics and recover the metal causes serious air pollution which affects whole areas, while toxin-filled ash contaminates the soil and groundwater. When equipment is dumped, toxins slowly leech into the soil and groundwater, poisoning drinking water and potentially causing serious long term effects. In many e-waste recycling areas, people of all ages are affected by these toxins, whether they work with e-waste or not (see Guiyu, page 248). Figure 11-10 shows the harmful effects of e-waste chemicals on the body.

Sources of E-waste

The majority of e-waste originates in more economically developed countries (MEDCs), principally Europe and North America. In these countries the cost of recycling computer equipment is high—up to $30 per computer. In less economically developed countries (LEDCs) where most e-waste ends up, that cost can be as low as $1 per computer. However, there is growing awareness

Figure 11-10 Harmful effects of e-waste

Harmful effects of e-waste

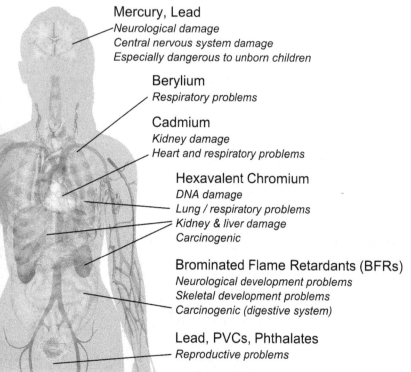

Mercury, Lead
Neurological damage
Central nervous system damage
Especially dangerous to unborn children

Berylium
Respiratory problems

Cadmium
Kidney damage
Heart and respiratory problems

Hexavalent Chromium
DNA damage
Lung / respiratory problems
Kidney & liver damage
Carcinogenic

Brominated Flame Retardants (BFRs)
Neurological development problems
Skeletal development problems
Carcinogenic (digestive system)

Lead, PVCs, Phthalates
Reproductive problems

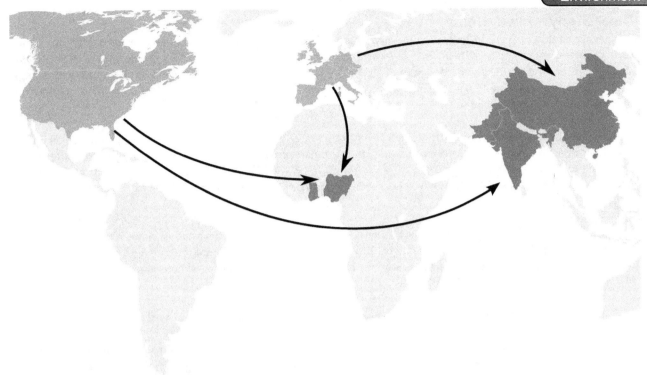

Figure 11-12 The majority of e-waste exports originate in the US, Canada, and Europe. India, Pakistan, China, Ghana, and Nigeria are common destinations.

of the e-waste problem in MEDCs, and various laws and agreements have been put in place to prevent its export (see page 250). However, despite now being illegal in many countries, e-waste exports still happen. One particular problem for users is finding trustworthy recycling companies—there have been several cases of companies charging users for safe recycling but then covertly shipping the material overseas.

The speed of change

E-waste has become a significant problem because of the speed of change within the IT industry. IT products often have very short **life cycles** – mobile phones, for example, are replaced after 18 months on average[8]. This is exacerbated by the fact that manufacturers are constantly changing and upgrading their products, offering new models frequently. For example, between October 2001 and October 2010 there were 25 different models of one popular music player released[9]. Many of the earlier models are now considered obsolete, although they still perform very much the same task as the latest versions – playing music.

Designing a device so that it will become out of date or will fail after a certain period of time is known as **planned obsolescence**.

Figure 11-13 Toxins in e-waste

Toxins in Information Technology

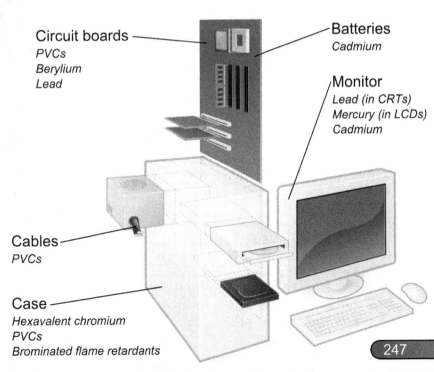

Circuit boards
PVCs
Berylium
Lead

Batteries
Cadmium

Monitor
Lead (in CRTs)
Mercury (in LCDs)
Cadmium

Cables
PVCs

Case
Hexavalent chromium
PVCs
Brominated flame retardants

Case Study: Guiyu, China

Guiyu entered the headlines in 2001 when the environmental campaign group Basel Action Network (BAN) investigated the processing of e-waste in the town[19]. In Guiyu and the surrounding villages, 60,000 people work in 5,500 workshops, recycling e-waste in hazardous conditions[20]. The e-waste recycling industry there is so large that different villages have started to specialise in the recycling of certain components – with one village focusing on printers, another on processors or plastic cables, and so on.

Much of the e-waste arrives in Guiyu from the US via Hong Kong, despite such exports and imports being illegal under US, Hong Kong, and Chinese law. In many cases, US consumers are unaware that the equipment they leave for recycling will be shipped overseas and processed in this way. One of the biggest problems is that US electronic recycling companies are not regulated by the Environmental Protection Agency, so finding a reliable and responsible recycler is difficult.

The health and environmental effects of Guiyu's recycling industry have been devastating. Since 2000 fresh water has been brought into the area by road every day because the local water sources contain unsafe levels of toxins. Rates of miscarriage are higher than average in Guiyu, while many children have dangerously elevated levels of lead in their blood[21]. A recent study showed that Guiyu has one of the highest rates of cancer causing dioxins in the world[22].

Despite these negative effects, the e-waste industry is flourishing in Guiyu, generating $75 million per year, bringing in 90% of local tax revenue, and making people reluctant to intervene. With a million tonnes of e-waste being exported to Guiyu each year, and with the developing Chinese economy generating increasing amounts of its own e-waste, huge investments in infrastructure, education, and enforcement will be needed before the situation in Guiyu can be changed.

The Three Rs

The 'three Rs' – **Reduce**, **Reuse** (or refurbish) and **Recycle** refer to various solutions designed to reduce the environmental impact of waste. Each 'R' refers to a solution at a specific point in a product's life cycle:

Reduce the amount of raw materials and energy used in the production of the product, and reduce toxins or completely replace them with less harmful substances.

Reuse or refurbish computer equipment, or donate it to those who could still make effective use of it, such as local schools, disadvantaged people in the local community or users in developing countries. In this way it can be used to help reduce the **digital divide**. However, adequate steps still need to be taken to ensure the donated equipment will be safely recycled once it eventually reaches its end of life. 'Reuse' can also refer to the act of upgrading a computer rather than replacing it – for example, adding another hard disk or more RAM instead of buying a new model.

Recycling e-waste is another option, using specialist equipment to extract valuable materials including glass, gold, silver, and platinum. The danger with e-waste is that waste is often 'recycled' overseas in very dangerous conditions, causing health problems for the recyclers and large scale environmental impact as well. However, because it contains small amounts of so many different sub-

Figure 11-14 Child breaking down e-waste to extract metals, Ghana.

stances, the safe recycling of e-waste requires quite advanced techniques and is quite expensive, making it probably the least desirable of the three 'Rs'.

Reducing E-Waste

Some equipment manufacturers operate **take-back schemes**, accepting equipment back from customers for recycling when they have finished with it, and perhaps offering discounts on new hardware. A few manufacturers even accept old hardware from other manufacturers. Take back schemes are required in Europe under the **WEEE Directive** (see page 250). Manufacturers either reuse the returned components, refurbish the equipment if it is still relatively modern, or recycle it to use the raw materials in new products.

Customers can have a positive impact on the e-waste problem by only buying equipment from manufacturers who have environmentally friendly policies. The ability of customers to 'vote with their wallet' can be a powerful influence on manufacturers to reduce the amount of harmful substances they use. Campaign groups and pressure groups such as Greenpeace and the **Basel Action Network** (BAN) work to regularly publish reports on the e-waste situation: BAN traces exports of e-waste from source countries, exposing recyclers who illegally ship their equipment overseas, while Greenpeace regularly publishes a list of environmental ratings for top IT companies to raise customer awareness.

Computer donation schemes, where computers which are functional but no longer required are donated to charities, are one solution for reducing the immediate problem of e-waste. World Computer Exchange, Computer Aid International, and Computers for Schools Kenya, are three examples of organisations performing this type of work. Donated computers and peripheral devices are used for a large range of functions, both in the country of donation and overseas. School classrooms, public libraries, and youth clubs are common recipients. In developing countries, donated computers have been used to im-

Did You Know?
Before donating old equipment to charities, users should ensure all personal data is fully erased. Deleting data, empty the recycle bin or trash can, and formatting the hard disk are not sufficient. Page 35 contains details on fully erasing data.

prove medical care in rural areas through the use of telemedicine, raise awareness of diseases such as malaria and HIV, and help farmers improve their output and access new markets. The isolation of many rural areas in developing countries sees some unique solutions for bringing IT access, including portable computer classrooms inside freight containers, equipped with solar panels on the roof to provide power. At the end of a lesson these classrooms and be packed up, loaded onto the back of a lorry, and shipped to the next location for another class. Page 251 describes examples of computer donation schemes in developing countries.

In most cases computer donation charities do not simply send computers to a location and abandon them. To make the most of their potential, much planning and preparation work must completed. Physical installation of computers, software installation, physically securing premises against theft, and training of teachers and users all need to be considered. Where Internet connections are used, appropriate security software needs to be installed and configured, and users educated about safe browsing habits.

Eventually, even donated computers become obsolete, so many donation schemes also provide safe recycling facilities at the end of life.

Unfortunately a common problem faced by donation schemes is companies and individuals who attempt to use them to 'donate' very old or non-functional equipment in an attempt to avoid their responsibility for recycling it.

Common Mistake
For some items, such as paper, glass, and metal, recycling is relatively straightforward. However, recycling e-waste is difficult. E-waste contains a wide variety of valuable materials, but in very small quantities. The energy and skill required to extract these small amounts of material often means safe recycling is not economically viable. For this reason, recycling should be considered as a last resort, after options to reduce and reuse equipment have been tried.

Figure 11-15 Children in Delhi extract copper from old computer parts.

E-Waste legislation

The **Waste Electrical and Electronic Equipment Directive** (WEEE) was passed by the European Community in 2003, although it took until 2007 to become law in the UK. WEEE requires the manufacturers of electronic equipment to accept waste equipment from users for recycling. WEEE prohibits these manufacturers from charging users to return their equipment, and requires the manufacturers to either safely recycle or reuse materials.

The **Restriction of Hazardous Substances Directive** (RoHS) became European law in 2006. RoHS restricts the amount of toxic substances that can be used in electronic equipment. It applies to the use of lead, mercury, cadmium, hexavalent chromium, and the brominated flame retardants Polybrominated biphenyls (PBB) and Polybrominated diphenyl ether (PBDE), all of which are very harmful to human health (see figure 11-10).

The **Basel Convention** is a treaty designed to stop the movement of toxic waste (including e-waste) between countries – in particular, to stop the practice of MEDCs sending their waste to LEDCs for dumping or unsafe recycling. The convention was signed in 1992 and has been signed and ratified by many countries—the most notable exception being the United States.

In the US, e-waste regulation varies by state. California passed the **Electronic Waste Recycling Act** in 2003 which has similar restrictions to the RoHS. The act also requires stores to collect a recycling fee from customers, which is passed onto the government and used to pay for centres which offer free electronics recycling.

Figure 11-16 Piles of old computer equipment awaiting disposal (top). Printers being collected for refurbishing and recycling (bottom).

Exercise 11-2

Make a table listing the electronic equipment you own or have owned. Remember to consider not only computers, but also printers, MP3 players, games consoles, and other electronic devices. To make it easier, consider only items that you own personally, not family items. For each item, list the manufacturer, item age, and the way it was disposed of. What does this tell you about your contribution to the e-waste problem, and how it might continue in the future?

Exercise 11-3

Electronic waste, or e-waste, is an increasing problem as more and more computers are discarded each year. In some countries e-waste has spurned large industries but also caused great health problems.

(a) (i) Define the term *operating system.*

[2 marks]

(ii) Describe **two** health problems caused by discarded electronic equipment.

[4 marks]

(b) Explain **two** concerns that users might have about donating their old IT equipment for reuse.

[6 marks]

(c) Evaluate the potential solutions to the problem of e-waste.

[8 marks]

E-waste, Computer Donations, and the Digital Divide

Equipping libraries with ICT in Eritrea

It is difficult to overstate the importance of libraries in places where educational resources are a scarce commodity. Libraries provide an invaluable service to people for whom books are considerably beyond their means. The British Council Eritrea has equipped every school and public library in the country with IT equipment provided by Computer Aid. Not only has this dramatically improved the administrative processes, it has created a means through which digital content can be distributed via CD-ROMs and the Internet. A local Internet Service Provider has also provided free Internet connectivity to participating institutions, allowing users unprecedented access to a wealth of free information.

Figure 11-17 A mobile computer classroom with Internet access, housed in a cargo container.

Through the information dissemination channels created by the British Council, ICTs have significantly broadened the range of content publicly available at libraries. This is revolutionising library use in Eritrea. Libraries are now perceived as resource centres for locally-relevant information, which has lead to a steady rise in the number of people visiting them. Once the domain of students and academics, libraries are now thriving community centres of information for nurses, development practitioners, farmers and agricultural extension workers. The widespread implementation of ICT in Eritrea's libraries is creating an enduring beneficial effect on local economies and local communities.

Telemedicine Laptops Saves Lives

Computer Aid International has been providing laptops to rural doctors to aid in the diagnosis of life-threatening illnesses in some of the most remote parts of Africa.

Rural health workers are using these donated laptops to email x-ray images, medical notes and digital photographs of critically ill patients for expert clinical diagnostic support from experienced professional clinicians hundreds of miles away, therefore bringing healthcare to the most remote people. This project is one of the most compelling examples of the life-saving importance of IT to the rural poor in developing countries.

In Sub-Saharan Africa there is an average of just 12 doctors per 100,000 people – compared to the European Average of 340 for the same number of people. Few qualify due to the high cost of education and many qualified health professionals are tempted overseas where they can command far higher salaries compounding the 'brain drain' suffered by many developing countries.

The African Medical Research and Education Foundation, is putting Computer Aid International PCs, together with scanners and digital cameras, into rural health clinics in some of the most isolated communities in Africa. From there, nurses and newly qualified doctors can email pictures via the Internet to clinical specialists for instant expert diagnosis. By this mechanism people living in rural areas can have access to the best clinical diagnosis available and medical conditions can be treated promptly and accurately with life-saving consequences.

This is a dramatic low-cost, high-impact example of the way in which PCs donated in the UK are serving on the frontline against Africa's biggest killers: HIV/AIDS, respiratory disease, malaria and water-borne infections.

Chapter Review

Key Language

analog data
analog to digital converter
Basel Action Network
Basel Convention, The
blade servers
continuous data
CRT
data centres
data layers
data logging
digital data
digital footprint
digital divide
digitisation
discrete data

donation schemes
e-waste
electronic waste
Geographical Information
System
geotagged
Global Positioning System
GPS receiver
GPS satellite
laser imaging
LCD
LEDC
Lidar
life cycle (hardware)
location based service

MEDC
online mapping
planned obsolescence
power consumption
power settings
radar
recycling
reduce
redundant systems
remote sensing
refurbish
reusing
RoHS
sample precision
sample rate

sampling
satellite imaging
satellite navigation system
sensors
sonar
speed throttling
take-back scheme
virtual globe
virtual machines
virtualisation
visualisation
WEEE

Exercise 11-4

Investigate the environmental policies of four of the manufacturers you have mentioned in exercise 11-2 on page 250. What steps, if any, do they take to help reduce the problem of e-waste? Do they take any other steps to help the environment? Use both the manufacturer's web sites and the Greenpeace site (www.greenpeace.org/international/campaigns/toxics/electronics/) to help you.

Exercise 11-5

Research news articles about satellite and street level mapping systems. What have the mapping companies done to address the concerns mentioned above? **Evaluate** possible solutions to these concerns. [8 marks]

Exercise 11-6

E-waste is a growing problem as countries around the world throw away more and more obsolete electronic equipment.

(a) (i) Identify **two** chemicals found in e-waste. [2 marks]

   (ii) Describe **two** ways a user can ensure all data is erased from a donated computer system. [4 marks]

(b) Explain **two** possible solutions to the problem of e-waste. [6 marks]

(c) Discuss the responsibility each stakeholder has to help solve the problem of e-waste. Evaluate your arguments. [8 marks]

Exercise 11-7

Satellite imaging and remote sensing are commonly used to observe the earth and other planets.

(a) (i) Define the term *remote sensing*. [2 marks]

   (ii) Describe **one** benefit and **one** disadvantage of remote sensing methods compared to regular photographs. [4 marks]

(b) Explain **two** concerns that users might have about donating their old IT equipment for reuse. [6 marks]

(c) Security and privacy concerns have been raised about online mapping systems and virtual globes. To what extent do the benefits of these systems outweigh the concerns? [8 marks]

References

1   Adkins, R. (2008). *Cutting IT energy costs for small business.* Available: www.ft.com/cms/s/0/72501658-741c-11dd-bc91-0000779fd18c.html. Last accessed Aug 2011.

2   BBC. (2010). *Greenpeace issues warning about data centre power.* Available: news.bbc.co.uk/2/hi/technology/8594431.stm. Last accessed Aug 2011.

3   Stanford. (1996). *Can computer chip makers reduce environmental impact?.* Available: http://news.stanford.edu/pr/96/960605chipsenvir.html. Last accessed Nov 2011.

4   de Aenlle, C. (1991). *Silicon Valley Seeks New Ways to Attack High Tech Pollution.* Available: http://www.nytimes.com/1991/12/19/news/19iht-calt.html?pagewanted=all. Last accessed Nov 2011.

5   National Semiconductor. (2006). *Nat Semi cancer toll is "tip of the iceberg".* Available: http://www.hazards.org/haz76/natsemi.htm. Last accessed Nov 2011.

6   Grossman, E. (2011). *Toxics in the 'Clean Rooms': Are Samsung Workers at Risk?.* Available: http://e360.yale.edu/content/feature.msp?id=2414. Last accessed Nov 2011.

7   Environmental Protection Agency. (2011). *Statistics on the Management of Used and End-of-Life Electronics.* Available: epa.gov/epawaste/conserve/materials/ecycling/manage.htm. Last accessed March 2011.

8   Environmental Literacy Council. (2008). *Cell Phone Life Cycle.* Available: www.enviroliteracy.org/article.php/1119.html. Last accessed March 2011.

9   Apple. (2011). *Identifying iPod Models.* Available: support.apple.com/kb/HT1353. Last accessed March 2011.

10   GeoEye Inc.. (2011). *About GeoEye-1.* Available: launch.geoeye.com/LaunchSite/about/. Last accessed Aug 2011.

11   How Stuff Works. (Unknown date). *What is a keyhole satellite and what can it really spy on?.* Available: http://science.howstuffworks.com/question529.htm. Last accessed Nov 2011.

12   Merchant, B. (2010). *US Using CIA Spy Satellites to Study Ice Retreat in Arctic (Photos).* Available: http://www.treehugger.com/corporate-responsibility/us-using-cia-spy-satellites-to-study-ice-retreat-in-arctic-photos.html. Last accessed Nov 2011.

13   USGS. (2007). *Geographic Information Systems.* Available: http://egsc.usgs.gov/isb/pubs/gis_poster/. Last accessed Nov 2011.

14   World Bank. (Unknown date). *Dirty Industries.* Available: www.worldbank.org/html/prddr/prdhome/peg/wps16/indexp3.htm. Last accessed March 2011.

15   Air Transport Association. (2010). *Fact Sheet: Environment.* Available: www.iata.org/pressroom/facts_figures/fact_sheets/pages/environment.aspx. Last accessed March 2011.

16   Mieszkowski, K. (2002). *Silicon Hogs.* Available: dir.salon.com/story/tech/feature/2002/11/13/microchips/index.html. Last accessed March 2011.

17   Goleman, D & Gregory, N. (2010). *How Green Is My iPad?.* Available: http://www.nytimes.com/interactive/2010/04/04/opinion/04opchart.html. Last accessed Nov 2011.

18   Apple, Inc. (2011). *Product Environmental Reports.* Available: http://www.apple.com/environment/reports/. Last accessed Nov 2011.

19   Basel Action Network. (2008). Available: http://www.ban.org/. Last accessed Nov 2011.

20   TIME Magazine. (2008). *China's Electronic Waste Village.* Available: www.time.com/time/photogallery/0,29307,1870162_1822148,00.html. Last accessed April 2011.

21   Huo et al. (2006). *Elevated Blood Lead Levels of Children in Guiyu, an Electronic Waste Recycling Town in China.* Available: www.ncbi.nlm.nih.gov/pmc/articles/PMC1913570/. Last accessed April 2011.

22   TIME Magazine. (2009). *E-Waste Not.* Available: www.time.com/time/magazine/article/0,9171,1870485,00.html. Last accessed April 2011.

Chapter 12
Health

Objectives

1. Evaluate the ways IT can be used in patient diagnosis
2. Evaluate the ways IT can be used in surgery
3. Evaluate the ways IT can be used in patient treatment
4. Discuss the consequences of technology addiction
5. Evaluate the availability of online medical advice
6. Explain how to prevent overuse injuries

Diagnostic and Therapeutic Tools

Telemedicine

Telemedicine systems (sometimes called **telehealth**) allow medical consultations to take place when the doctor and patient are in separate physical locations. A common example is a doctor-patient consultation conducted using video conferencing equipment, with the doctor examining the patient using a video feed. In other cases, a doctor might send patient details such as x-ray or scan results to another, remotely located, doctor for a second opinion or expert analysis. Telemedicine systems are also used to remotely monitor the conditions of patients, for example those who have been sent home from hospital (see page 257).

Networking technologies play a key role in telemedicine. Often public networks such as the Internet are used (with appropriate security precautions such as VPNs), but voice, video, or SMS data sent via mobile phone networks can also be used.

Store-and-forward telemedicine systems such as email are used when real-time communication is not essential – such as when test results are sent for diagnosis or closer inspection. Data is collected at the patient end of the link (either by the patient themselves or by their doctor), digitised, and then sent to a remote doctor. Results might be sent back to the patient at a later date, discussed during a consultation, or the patient may only be alerted if something is amiss.

Real time technologies like video conferencing are used when face-to-face communication is needed. A common

The Future Now: Remote Surgery

Although it was not the first ever use of telesurgery, the 2001 Lindbergh Operation was a milestone in surgery. A doctor in New York performed a 45 minute operation to remove the gallbladder of a patient located 6,000 kilometres away in Strasbourg, France[1].

A high speed fibre optic link was used to keep the lag between the doctor's input and the robot's response to less than 200 milliseconds, while a team of doctors were standing by in Strasbourg in case any problems arose.

example of this is doctor-patient consultations. Real time audio allows the patient to answer the doctor's questions immediately, and reduces the chances of misunderstandings that might occur with text messaging or chat systems. A video feed lets the doctor view any symptoms first hand, giving a better understanding of them than if the patient were merely to describe them.

In the future, telemedicine systems may advance to the point where **telesurgery** – operating on a remote patient – is possible. Systems such as the Da Vinci surgical system (see page 262) already allow a doctor to operate on a patient using a set of guided robotic arms; a future development of this system could see the doctor's inputs being sent over a network to a remote set of robotic arms which would operate on the patient. Of course, such telesurgery systems could help a lot of people but would also raise several significant social and ethical issues.

Benefits

Telemedicine is particularly useful for patients in remote areas where transportation to a hospital may be difficult, expensive, or slow. This includes remote settlements and

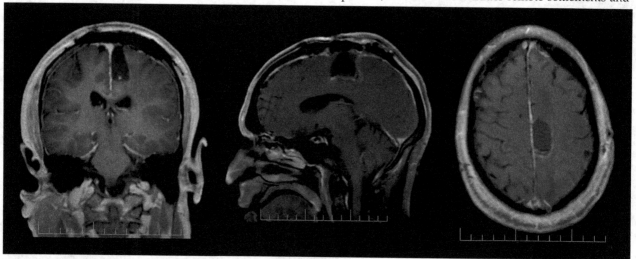

Figure 12-1 Medical scans such as x-rays and MRIs can be sent to remote doctors for analysis

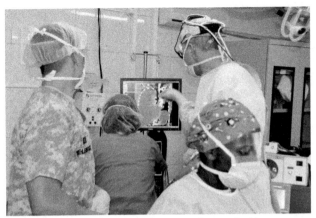

Figure 12-2 Doctors in Mosul, Iraq, examine medical images online with colleagues in Texas.

situations where access to a doctor is impossible, such as on a ship in the middle of an ocean, soldiers on a battlefield, and even astronauts in space. Telemedicine also allows patients to access expertise that their local doctors may not have, such as in the treatment of rare conditions or those requiring very specialised treatment.

Another advantage is that patients can receive medical advice from their own home, which may be more comfortable for them and may help hospitals by freeing up beds.

Disadvantages

Security, of course, is always a concern when sending sensitive data such as medical details over a network. Appropriate security techniques such as TLS encryption or the use of VPNs are needed. Security is also a concern for the stored data on the remote systems, as unauthorised access could result in patients' privacy being breached.

For real time applications, the reliability of communication networks is critical: there must be minimal network lag to ensure smooth and uninterrupted communication, and sufficient bandwidth to allow images or video with sufficient resolution to properly view the patient's symptoms. These conditions may be difficult to achieve in remote areas which lack access to inexpensive high bandwidth connections, and may have to rely on more expensive satellite links.

Telemedicine also raises legal issues, as doctors operating in one location may not be legally licensed to work in other states or countries.

Remote Patient Monitoring

A **remote patient monitoring** system is a form of telemedicine which allows patients to return home yet still be closely monitored by medical staff. In some cases patients take samples, such as blood sugar readings, themselves at fixed intervals and send the data to the hospital over the Internet. A diabetic, for example, could do this and upload the results to an online system to allow doctors to monitor their readings.

Other systems, which continuously and automatically monitor patients, are useful for more serious conditions, or for diagnosis of problems with infrequent symptoms. These systems use an array of wearable sensors attached to the patient to collect data and relay it to hospital computer systems, a form of data logging (see page 238). Sensors can even be embedded into clothes (sometimes called **smart clothes**), or into buildings themselves, with data being relayed to a nearby device such as a watch or portable computer, then uploaded. These systems improve the patient's comfort and mobility by freeing them from wired sensors, and also reduce reliability problems caused by sensors falling out of place.

Remote monitoring is useful when a patient's symptoms occur very infrequently, as they can return to their normal lives rather than spending many days in hospital, yet be sure that critical medical data will be captured.

Elderly patients, especially those who live alone, can also benefit from remote monitoring, with systems being configured to alert authorities if certain medical problems are detected, or if movement is not detected for a certain amount of time. Some domestic carer robots such as Pearl and BEAR are programmed to do exactly this (see chapter 16).

Project Gerhome

Project Gerhome is a French construction project with the goal of improving the quality of life and independence of elderly patients by equipping their homes with medical monitoring systems connected directly to hospital based doctors. Houses are fitted with an array of sensors to measure temperature, movement, and sound, as well as water consumption and access to the refrigerator. There is even a video camera to let nurses instantly view the patient. An abnormality in any of these readings—such as a consistently high temperature and no water consumption—can trigger an alert in the monitoring system, notifying doctors or sending a text message to family or friends, asking them to check on the patient[2].

Electronic Medical Records

Electronic Medical Records (EMR) or **Electronic Health Records** (EHR) store patient data in a computerised database which can be accessed by the medical staff treating them. Data stored includes necessary personal details such as contact details for next of kin, as well as medical histories, conditions, vaccination records, test results and current treatments. In the United States EMR systems are also commonly used to generate billing information for patients and insurers.

EMR systems help make a full medical history immediately accessible to doctors, even if, for example, the patient is unconscious and unable to provide medical details. In contrast, doctors may be unable to access a patient's paper records for some time if they are stored at a different surgery or hospital. EMR systems often allow access to records from handheld devices such as PDAs, allowing doctors to read and update records directly from the patient's bedside. Others include web based interfaces, allowing access from any Internet connected device (with appropriate authentication controls).

There are three general approaches to storing electronic health records. Traditional systems store medical records in a **centralised database**, housed and maintained by a hospital or healthcare provider. Medical staff have access to individual patient records based on their role and their need to access data.

Personal Health Records (PHR) are slightly different, in that the medical data is provided and managed by the patient themselves, not a hospital or other healthcare provider. These records might be stored in a cloud based system or on the patient's own computer. During treat-

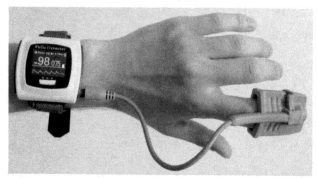

Figure 12-4 A monitoring device which measures blood oxygen levels and pulse rate.

ment the patient provides doctors access to the PHR as needed—either online or by printing out records. Some patients feel that PHR systems give them more control and ownership over their data than EMR systems, addressing privacy and security concerns. Microsoft HealthVault (figure 12-3) and the now discontinued Google Health are examples of PHR systems which allow patients to store their data in a cloud based system.

A final approach is for a patient to carry portable health records in the form of a **smart card** or similar storage device. This can be presented by the patient during treatment, and typically lacks the ability for the doctor to remotely access records—which may be an advantage or a disadvantage, depending on the patient's privacy concerns. For security purposes, data on the smart cards is encrypted, and only able to be decrypted by authorised card readers used at hospitals.

Benefits

Computerised records enjoy a number of advantages over paper based systems, and in healthcare this translates into increased efficiency and reduced costs. Electronic records consume minimal space, can be accessed by multiple people simultaneously, and can be transferred and retrieved almost instantly from location to location. This has significant health benefits for a patient in emergencies, particularly if they are unconscious or unable to speak.

If proper data backup techniques are used, electronic records should also be much harder to lose than paper records. This also helps reduce the problem of duplicate medical records, which leads to data integrity problems that can compromise patient health and cause billing problems. A study at one New York hospital found that incorrect medical records caused 70% of the billing errors experienced, costing up to $1 million each week[3].

Figure 12-3 Personal Health Record systems allow patients to grant doctors access to their data on a case by case basis

However, as with any database containing personal information, privacy, security, and data integrity are serious concerns. A careful balance between accessibility and privacy needs to be achieved: medical records must be accessible when needed by a patient's doctors—including in a potential emergency—yet access must be denied to other medical staff and to all other unauthorised users.

Laws such as the UK **Data Protection Act** (see page 161) and the US **Health Insurance Portability and Accountability Act** (HIPAA) address the issue of data privacy. HIPAA, for example, provides criminal penalties for companies who breach data protection rules, and requires health care providers to notify patients of any data security breach.

Technical privacy and security measures are also used. Most commonly, different stakeholders have different levels of access, limiting them to only the relevant part of the patient's record. The patient's primary doctor may have full access, for example, while other doctors and nurses might have access only to the current treatment regime and any relevant conditions, and the accounting department will only have access to billing information, not medical data. These access levels need to be supported by strong authentication systems to control access (see chapter 5).

To alleviate privacy concerns, healthcare providers may use an **opt-in approach**, requiring patients to specifically consent to the inclusion of their data in their EMR systems—though this can reduce the effectiveness of the system. Other providers may include patient data unless they specifically **opt-out** of the system.

Maintaining security in such systems is also difficult. Centralised databases mean security can also be centralised, reducing problems with individual doctors or hospitals failing to implement good security practices. However, such systems, with the large amounts of personal, medical, and financial data they contain, make them tempting targets for hackers who know that no computerised system is 100% secure.

Standards for **Electronic Data Interchange (EDI)** are also an important consideration for EMR systems. Patient records can only be easily transferred between hospitals or doctors if a common standard is used for the represen-

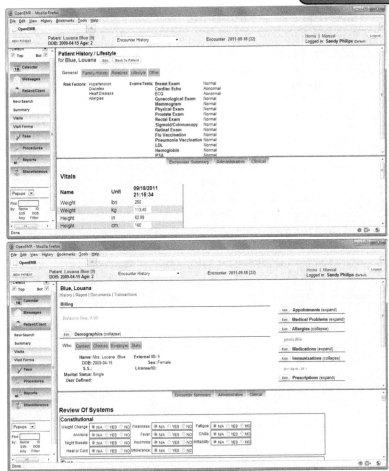

Figure 12-5 OpenEMR system showing patient health and billing data

tation of the data. If this is not the case, the information may be completely or partially inaccessible or, perhaps worse, may lead to data integrity problems. Several ANSI, ISO, and open standards currently exist for health data.

E-prescriptions

EMR systems are often linked to **electronic prescription** (e-prescription) systems to automatically generate prescriptions and send them to pharmacies. This benefits patients by helping have their drugs available when they arrive at a pharmacy, cuts down paperwork, and can prevent pharmacists making potentially life-threatening errors made when reading hand written prescriptions. More advanced e-prescription systems link to **medical expert systems**, which can suggest alternative cheaper drugs or alert pharmacists to any complications or interactions between drugs a patient is taking. Simple but dangerous errors such as incorrect dosages are also detected in this way. E-prescriptions also reduce prescription fraud by ensuring prescriptions come from a genuine medical practitioner.

Medical expert systems

Expert systems (see page 335), sometimes called **Clinical Decision Support Systems**, have been used to support medical decision making since the early 1970s. Even within the medical domain, expert systems often specialise in one particular area of knowledge, such as the diagnosis of abdominal pain or eye problems. Many modern clinical support systems can be integrated into electronic medical record systems, allowing suggestions and warnings to be automatically generated by the computer based on a patient's treatment and medical history. Clinical expert systems have been shown in multiple studies to improve both the quality of care delivered by medical staff and patient outcomes[4].

As with any expert system, when a knowledge engineer takes medical data and creates a knowledge base and rules, errors may result. In a medical system, these errors could have serious, even fatal consequences. Data integrity is therefore critical. Incorrect results may be generated if incorrect data is provided to the system, if data is missing, or if the algorithms used to process the data are incorrect. In a medical context, biological systems are typically so complex that the influence of factors such as previous medical conditions and genetic dispositions may not be well understood. This too has ramifications for the accuracy of the system.

User interfaces also need to be clear, presenting easy to understand, unambiguous recommendations and error messages. Although not an expert system, it is worth remembering that poor error messages were a significant contributing factor in the Therac-25 accidents (see page 63). Page 335 discusses expert systems in more detail.

Virtual Reality therapy

Virtual reality systems have been developed to improve the treatment of Post-Traumatic Stress Disorder (PTSD) and certain phobias. The systems work by recreating virtual copies of the places or events which cause patients distress. Patients are gradually exposed to the virtual environments, helping them to come to terms with their situations and their fears.

One application for this technology has been in the treatment of PTSD in Iraq war veterans. The Virtual Iraq system developed by the University of Southern California can recreate virtually any situation soldiers may have

> **Try It Online**
> Visit www.itgstextbook.com for examples of online medical expert systems.

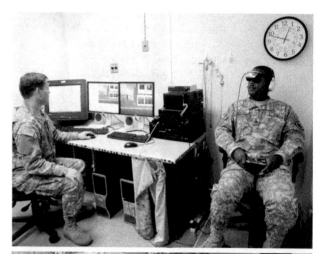

Figure 12-6 A soldier undertakes a demonstration of the Virtual Iraq therapy program at Walter Reed Army Medical Center (top). A soldier demonstrates a myoelectric prosthetic arm (bottom).

encountered in combat, including road side bombs, ambushes, friendly casualties, and enemy fighters. The system uses a virtual reality headset to provide an immersive 3D environment and features realistic sound effects to heighten the realism. Patients use the system in the company of a trained psychologist who can guide them through the system in addition to traditional treatment techniques like discussions[5].

In another case, a virtual reality recreation of the London Underground was used to treat people suffering from paranoia and claustrophobia[6].

Prosthetic devices

One of the most exciting recent developments in **prosthetics** has been the development of 'robotic' limbs which offer the wearer much more control and mobility than traditional plastic prosthetics. One such example, a robotic prosthetic arm called the 'Luke Arm', was developed by inventor Dean Kamen and his DEKA company in response to the need to provide better prosthetic arms for US veterans returning from the war in Iraq. The arm's innovations include rotating with 14 degrees of freedom, allowing the wearer much finer control. It is also ergonomically designed, constructed of lightweight components, and attaches to the wearer using special pads which tighten their grip when the arm is under load, and reduce the pressure when the arm is not being used—reducing the pain which can be caused by wearing traditional prosthetics devices, while still being able to lift greater weights[7].

The Luke Arm is controlled via pressure sensors in the wearer's shoe, which they operate with different parts of their feet and their toes. Other prosthetic limbs under development use **myoelectric** systems—registering the electrical signals in the wearer's muscles and moving the arm appropriately. Some robotic researchers are even investigating **neural control**—operating the arm by attaching sensors to the nerves in the user's shoulder, allowing them to control the arm simply by thinking about it[8].

To provide feedback—and avoid damage to objects being grasped—these arms have pads which vibrate with different intensities depending on how strongly an object is being gripped. In the case of the Luke Arm, this feedback is precise enough to allow the wearer to pick up a soft object such as a grape without causing damage to it.

The challenge for developers of these systems is now to reduce the costs enough to make them widely available.

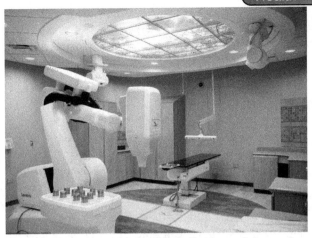

Figure 12-7 Tools such as the Cyberknife allow radiotherapy to be targeted much more accurately than traditional methods.

Robotic Surgery Tools

Despite their name, robotic tools are not autonomous decision making tools, instead requiring significant input from an operator. Two of the most famous examples of these tools are the Da Vinci Surgical System (see page 262), and the Cyberknife radiotherapy machine for treating cancer. These tools allow treatment to be targeted much more accurately than with traditional methods, increasing its effectiveness, reducing damage to healthy tissue, and if the cancer is close to vital organs, perhaps allowing therapy which would otherwise be impossible. Less invasive treatment also reduces the chances of post-surgery infection, leading to quicker recovery times for patients and shorter hospital stays—which benefits both patients and hospitals.

However, there have also been criticisms of these systems, especially their cost and the claimed benefits (see page 262).

Exercise 12-1
Some clinical expert systems can make predictions about the survival chances of a patient in intensive care. How do you think these predictions could be used? Do you think this is an appropriate use of technology? **Explain** your answer. [6 marks]

Exercise 12-2
Modern clinical expert systems often make specific recommendations to medical staff, rather than simply present facts or possible diagnoses. **Discuss** who would be responsible if a doctor followed such a recommendation, which resulted in the death of a patient. Does the type of error make a difference? [8 marks]

Exercise 12-3
Explain four issues a doctor must confront when deciding to use a medical expert system for diagnosis. [8 marks]

Patient Simulators

Traditional medical training tools have often being limited to plastic mannequins with limited functionality. These are useful for practising CPR and other basic first aid techniques, but are of limited use for more advanced procedures.

More modern **patient simulators** feature computerised systems which mimic functions of the human body. The more advanced models feature variable cardiac output, working lungs and airways, reactive pupils, and blood pressure systems. Some are even capable of reacting to drug injections, including the specific doses administered. Different models of simulator can be tailored to specific situations—there are, for example, models that simulate babies and young children, and even 'pregnant' versions to help train midwives in delivery techniques.

These simulators greatly improve the realism of medical training, enabling doctors to see realistic responses to their actions in a safe environment with no risk to real patients. Doctors skills can also be assessed, with the simulator automatically recording factors such as the actions taken, and how well they were applied (for example, whether the correct amount of pressure was applied to the chest during CPR). Of course, as with all simulators, the results never match real life completely (see page 180).

Case Study: Da Vinci surgeon

The Da Vinci Surgical System is probably the most widely known surgical 'robot'. A surgeon sits at a control console while the 'cart' containing the robotic arms is placed over the patient. The arms are fixed with surgical tools. Another arm contains a pair of cameras which provides the surgeon with a three dimensional image of the surgery area.

The surgeon initiates the Da Vinci system by placing his head in the control panel. For safety reasons, the robot only works if the surgeon's head is in the control panel. Three dimensional images from the camera arm are relayed to the surgeon's screen. The surgeon uses two controllers, which can be moved in three dimensions, to control the robotic arms. Because the controllers used by the surgeon are much larger and have much more freedom of movement than the

arms inside the patient, the Da Vinci system processes all inputs from the doctor. First, the doctor's movements are scaled down, making them smaller to suit the size of the robot arms. Secondly, the system filters out any tiny vibrations in the input, smoothing out the surgeon's gestures. Finally, the system checks to ensure the movement will not cause the surgical instruments to enter a 'disallowed' area of the patient's body (the surgeon sets up 'allowed' and 'disallowed' areas of the body before commencing surgery to prevent inadvertently operating on other, healthy parts of the body).

Although not autonomous, Da Vinci assists surgeons in a number of ways. A significant benefit is that its robotic arms are much smaller than a human arm, meaning smaller incisions are needed, which reduces patient pain and helps speed recovery.

Criticisms of the systems include their cost and the training given to surgeons. While patient recovery time and complications should be reduced, one study found the opposite: although there was a significant reduction in hospital stays, patients were between 30% and 40% more likely to suffer long term side effects compared to traditional surgery[9]. The researchers attributed this to lack of skill with the system, with surgeons able to use it after only two days of training, and able to supervise other surgeons in its use after only 20 operations. The researchers also noted that surgeons felt pressured to use the machine as patients believed it to be better than traditional methods.

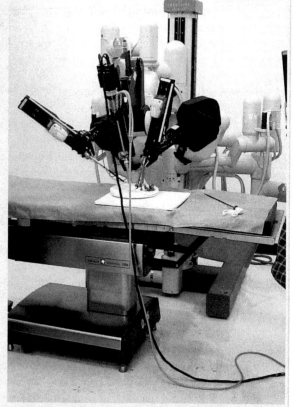

Figure 12-8 Patient-side part of the Da Vinci surgical system. The surgeon operates the robotic arms from a separate console (not shown).

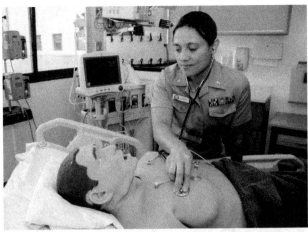
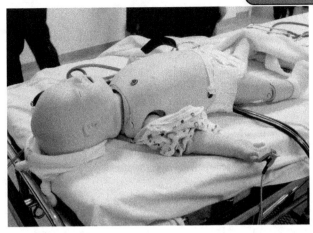

Figure 12-9 Patient simulators with systems which react like the human body improve the realism of medical training. Male, female, and infant versions allow doctors to practice specialised treatments.

Medical Advice
Mobile phones for health education

In areas where healthcare and formal education establishments are lacking, problems caused by the lack of basic health education are often widespread. Lack of access to television or the Internet can limits attempts to educate people through these mediums, and poor literacy rates or a wide range of spoken languages can compound these problems. However, mobile phones are often relatively common even in poor rural areas, and many health projects have started to take advantage of these to raise awareness of health issues. Besides their ubiquity, mobile phones have the advantage of allowing large numbers of messages to be sent at low cost, and make it easy to customise messages to take into account different languages. Projects can also easily set up free numbers for users to text or call, encouraging two-way communication.

For stigmatic issues such as HIV/AIDS awareness and testing, mobile phones may offer enough anonymity to encourage people to get help which they would be embarrassed to seek in a doctor's surgery. Young people in particular often have mobile phones, and are also the frequent target demographic of health awareness campaigns. Text messages and mobile phone games are therefore an ideal, even fun, way to reach these people.

One of the more successful uses of mobile phones in healthcare is **Project Masiluleke**, a HIV / AIDS awareness campaign in South Africa—a country where there are around 43 million mobile phones for a population of 49 million people. This makes them an ideal platform for promoting healthcare issues. The project mass-messages users about HIV prevention, and encourages HIV testing. Messages are sent in a variety of South Africa's 11 official languages, enabling them to reach a wide range of citizens. After its initial campaign of over one million text messages per day, Project Masiluleke saw an increase of 300% in people calling HIV testing centres. Once a testing appointment is made, the project also provides reminders, encouraging the patient to attend[10].

The **Text To Change** project in Uganda uses a similar approach. The project sends short quiz questions to mobile phone users to help raise HIV / AIDS awareness; users reply with their answer and are told whether or not they are correct. To encourage people to participate, all text messages sent are free, and top scoring players get a chance to win mobile phone credit and other prizes[11].

In India, the **Freedom HIV/AIDS** project has used four mobile phone games to tackle HIV and AIDS. The games use familiar themes such as cricket to spread their message of prevention and awareness. The project has counted over 10.3 million game downloads, many from rural areas – which often lack access to more traditional forms of media. The initial project was so successful that in 2006 it expanded into East Africa with two new games in English and Kiswahili, and has developed CD-ROMs and computer games for distribution to NGOs and schools across India[12].

Save the Children and UNICEF took a different approach to HIV / AIDS awareness in Georgia. A 20 minute video was produced featuring well known actors discussing and highlighting health issues and HIV prevention techniques. The video was converted to a format suitable for mobile phones and was sent to young people, in the hope that they would pass it among each other—a form of viral marketing[13].

Online Medical advice

Web sites are another effective way of distributing healthcare messages and promoting awareness of issues. **Diagnosis sites**, operated either by governments or individual clinics, range from simple pages with information about common illnesses to interactive sites which allow a user to input multiple symptoms and their severity — similar in some ways to a medical expert system. There are often telemedicine-style options to send questions via email or even live chat with a medical professional. The New York City Department of Health and Mental Hygiene has even used Facebook pages and applications to promote condom use and battle HIV among its population[14], while in Barcelona, doctors have used Second Life to provide anonymous information on sexual health and drug abuse to teenagers[15].

In Europe, the President of the European Men's Health Forum suggested that Facebook and mobile phones should be used to provide health advice to men, who often neglect to visit doctors and ignore signs of potentially life threatening cancer.

Medical advice sites extend patient care beyond diagnosis and treatment, by providing assistance and preventative advice to patients and their carers. Such sites exist for many topics, including heart disease, contraception, self-examinations for cancer, dental care, and pregnancy advice. These sites are also useful forums for publishing information about public health scares, such as the recent bird flu (H5N1) and swine flu (H1N1) outbreaks in the late 2000s. Along with health news updates and answers to frequently asked questions (FAQs), these techniques help reduce the amount of time doctors and telephone helplines spend dealing with common questions and minor problems. Indeed, during the 2010 swine flu outbreak, UK residents were advised to stay at home and

Figure 12-10 Text messages as sent out by Project Masiluleke

monitor advice given online, rather than visit their doctor's surgery and risk spreading the illness.

Support group sites are another form of online health advice. They are particularly useful when hospitals, doctors, or clinics do not offer their own support groups, or when even locally based groups are inaccessible because patients or carers are housebound. Forums and chat rooms — both of which can be relatively anonymous — help put patients and their carers in touch with others living with the same conditions. Groups exist for many conditions including cancer, Alzheimer's disease, drug and alcohol addiction, spousal abuse, and eating disorders.

Driven to Distraction?

One health risk which is widely agreed upon is the danger of using mobile phones — particularly text messaging — while driving. Tests in a driving simulator at the Transport Research Laboratory in the UK found using a mobile phone while driving — even if using a hands free device — increased the driver's reaction times by 17%[16]. This figure was as high as 50% when using text messaging — slower even than a drunk driver. The risk is not only from mobile phones, however. Experiments with other distractions, including checking email, selecting music on a portable music player, and programming a satellite navigation system found reaction times increasing by up to 56%.

With driver distraction being a major factor in many accidents, it seems the problem will only get worse as the number of electronic gadgets in our vehicles increases. To tackle the problem, devices such as satellite navigation systems usually employ voice output to read directions, and manufacturers advise users not to operate the device while the vehicle is in motion. Governments have also started to tackle the problem with legislation. Although careless driving is usually illegal already, many countries have now enacted laws specifically to deal with using a mobile phone while driving — and the penalties are often long custodial terms, comparable to those given for drink-driving[17].

People who have difficulty talking about their problems face-to-face, perhaps because of embarrassment or stigma, can also greatly benefit from this.

Risks

The key risk associated with online medical sites is the authenticity of the authors—it is difficult or impossible to know if they are medically trained—which leads the reliability and integrity of the information being called into question. This is a particularly significant issue because many people—especially the young—rely on the Internet for health advice. A UK government survey found 80% of teenagers have sought information in this way[18]. One study for the medical journal *Archives of Disease in Childhood* found only 39% of the 500 health sites tested offered correct advice, with much of the information available being confusing, contradictory, out of date, or just plain wrong[19]. The study also found that sponsored links, pushed to the top of results through payments to search engines, never contained correct information. A separate study found that advice regarding children's health was particularly misleading[19]. Health sites operated by governments and health services were found to be error free.

The impacts of incorrect health advice could be severe, with patients either delaying or avoiding treatment based on the belief that they are not ill, suffering and worrying excessively based on incorrect diagnoses found online, or even self medicating based on incorrect information.

One study suggested that even correct online health advice could cause health problems, as patients tend to focus on the advice they want to hear, typically reassuring them, rather than the advice which suggests there is a problem.

The recommendation for those seeking online health advice is to use only government operated sites—for example the NHS Direct, run by the UK's National Health Service. Most sites also recommend that for suspected serious conditions, a doctor is still consulted immediately.

Figure 12-11 Web sites are used for a range of advice and support on many health issues

Privacy concerns are also significant for those seeking online health advice. Although the Internet appears anonymous, this is clearly not the same. Search results can be used to track down individuals (see page 214), IP addresses can identify a user (see page 78), and Internet data packets travel through multiple machines en route to their destination (see page 80). Wireless connections also need to be configured for security (see page 110). Users also need to be sure that the site they use will keep their details secure against unauthorised access, and that they have a privacy policy that confirms personal details will not be passed on to third parties for advertising or other purposes.

Medical Research
Disease Mapping

During national or international outbreaks of disease, up to date information on cases and geographical spread is critical in fighting the problem. Increasingly IT is being used not only to map outbreaks, but to gather up-to-the-minute data on cases, reported as they occur using mobile devices and wireless Internet connections.

In Uganda, the **Uganda Malaria Surveillance Project** uses IT to track cases of malaria—the country's biggest killer[20]. A system using a centralised database based in Kampala, and nine field offices equipped with smart phones and computers, replaced a previous paper based system. The new system allows cases to be reported instantly, rather than taking several months using the previous system, allowing the project to respond more rapidly to malaria outbreaks with the appropriate treatments.

Wireless connections and solar panels remove the need for generators and landlines, which are generally unavailable and expensive to install in the rural locations where the offices are based. The smart phone project is estimated to have reduced project costs from $25,000 per year to $540 per year[20].

HealthMap is a similar system which uses Google Maps to show the latest health news and alerts from around the globe. Data is fetched from the news feeds of various organisations, including the World Health Organisation, to create a mashup of data and plot it on a map[21]. In Canada, the public health agency publishes maps of communicable disease outbreaks on their web site[22].

A key benefit of online health mapping is the ability to gather data quickly from affected regions. This is particularly important in developing countries where travelling to remote locations may take days—updating online case databases can be done virtually instantly using a mobile phone or portable computer.

Awareness of outbreaks can also help contain them, and access to online information reduces the need for people to leave their homes, potentially reducing the spread of disease. In the recent bird flu (H5N1) and swine flu (H1N1) outbreaks, advice to citizens has generally been to stay in their houses and obtain information online, rather than risk infection by visiting health centres.

> **Try It Online**
> Visit www.itgstextbook.com for examples of online disease mapping.

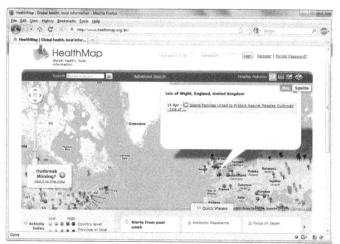

Figure 12-12 A map of global health alerts and outbreaks

However, data integrity is a key concern of these systems. Using a variety of data sources, some of which may be ordinary citizens reporting disease cases, has great potential to cause inaccurate, false, or duplicate reports. There needs to be a careful balance between speedy reporting of outbreak data and reporting cases using reliable methods, as inaccurate information can spread panic which could cause impacts greater than the outbreak itself.

The Human Genome Project

The **Human Genome Project** (HGP), is a an international collaborative project to map the functions of the human genome. The goal is to produce an online database of genes which is accessible to anybody with an Internet connection[23]. The HGP offers the opportunity to increase global scientific understanding of our genome, and perhaps develop tests and treatments for genetic diseases. The collaborative effort of the HGP has enabled understanding of the human genome to increase much more rapidly than scientists working in isolation.

Many of the social issues related to the HGP arise from the technology of genetics itself rather than the database. Tests for genetic predispositions to diseases such as cancer or Alzheimer's disease are controversial because of the implications they have for those testing positive. Many of these tests are also not yet 100% reliable.

Legal issues over the ownership of genetic data have also occurred, with attempts by several companies to patent DNA sequences, treating them as intellectual property[24]. If any patient data or DNA samples are stored in the database, privacy becomes an issue—even if the samples are anonymised.

Distributed Disease Research

Research into diseases is often carried out using computer models, which often require vast amounts of computing power to produce results in a reasonable amount of time. One approach to this problem is the use of distributed computing systems, which harness the power of computers all over the world to work collaboratively on a project (see page 176). The Folding@Home project uses these techniques to understand folding and mis-folding of proteins in the body—processes which are not well understood but are suspected to cause many diseases including Alzheimer's, cystic fibrosis, JCD, and Parkinson's disease[32].

Drug Interaction Models

Models of the human body offer a safer and more ethical alternative to testing new drugs on animals or humans. These computer models can predict the uptake rate and side effects of drugs, improving patient safety and allowing scientists to develop new drugs more rapidly.

Examples include a Belgium team who created a computer model to analyse the effect of cerebral palsy on patients' bodies, and plan effective treatment, and a London team that modelled brain aneurisms. Another British team created a model of the heart, complete with valves and blood flow, in order to test the effects of drugs designed to combat heart disease[25]. To help find the right combination of anti-retroviral drugs for HIV patients, which often requires a lot of trial and error, the HIV Response Database Initiative developed a computer model based on the treatment data of 60,000 HIV patients[26]. This allows correct treatment plans to be found more rapidly, and could be extremely useful in areas of the world where resources are scarce and 'plan and error' treatment wastes valuable medication and expertise.

In the future, such computer models could be customised with an individual patient's traits such as their medical history, age, and even their genetic data. This customisation in particular would allow doctors to plan and test much more accurate and effective treatment that current methods. Computer models also have the benefit of reducing the need for human and animal drug trials, both of which have ethical implications.

Although computer models are never 100% accurate (see page 172), and therefore do not completely remove the need for animal or human experiments, they can reduce the number of such trials. As with any computer model, care has to be taken to consider the results as advice rather than fact, and not become too reliant on them.

Psychological considerations

The constant exposure to communication technology can have significant psychological impacts on its users. Internet and gaming addiction are recognised as serious problems in countries such as Korea, where Internet access is fast, cheap, and ubiquitous (see page 278).

The rise of mobile phones, text messaging, microblogging, and social networks means people are increasingly in constant contact, 24 hours a day. In one survey 40% of teenagers questioned admitted to using mobile phones for more than four hours each day, with some users them for up to six hours[27]. Ironically, although constant communication becomes easier, mobile phone addiction often becomes an obstacle to personal one-to-one contact, with users shirking away from social situations.

As with other addictions, excessive mobile phone use can lead to physical problems, including overuse injuries such as RSI (see page 268). A study at the *Sleep Disorders Center* in Montreal found that 60% of children use their phone after bed time[28], and in a separate study up to 15% of Spanish teens said they slept with their mobile phones, allowing them to receive calls and messages during the night[29]. A lack of sleep has been linked to lower levels of concentration, lower test scores, and higher levels of behavioural problems in children.

Aside from health impacts, overuse of mobile phones can result in large bills—up to $1000 per month in some cases—potentially leading to additional problems such as crime to fund the habit.

Addiction also has physical consequences—more and more road accidents are being attributed to drivers or pedestrians being distracted while using their mobile phones[30]. In the workplace too, mobile phones and social media can provide a constant distraction from tasks, reducing worker efficiency and quality of work.

A variety of solutions exist. Setting limits on use—either through family rules or using technological features to set credit limits, is one option. Some teenaged phone addicts have received psychological help to get them over their addiction, while in extreme cases mobile phone addicts have even been treated in mental health institutes in an attempt to wean them off their phones[31].

Physical considerations

Overuse Injuries

Physical health problems arise from excessive or incorrect use of IT equipment. **RSI** (Repetitive Strain Injury) causes strong pain or weakness in muscles and tendons, and can occur in the hands, arms, shoulders, and back. RSI can be caused by incorrect posture while using a computer or simply by performing the same action – such as typing, using a mouse, or staring at a screen – for extended periods of time. In some cases children have suffered from RSI after playing computer games for frequent extended periods. Carpal Tunnel Syndrome (CTS) is a similar condition which causes pain or numbness in the wrist, and is also associated with incorrect or excessive use of a keyboard.

Eye strain and associated headaches are also a concern for users. Sore or irritated eyes can occur after prolonged computer use because users generally blink less when staring at a screen, causing eyes to dry out. Frequent users can also suffer problems refocusing their eyes after staring at a single fixed object for a long time.

Surveys have suggested that RSI affects up to 450,000 workers in the UK, losing 4.7 million work days and costing the economy £300 million each year[32]. Many countries report increasing rates of RSI.

Figure 12-14 Ergonomic keyboard with a more 'natural' layout

RSI rates are higher in some industries than others. Occupations which make frequent use of information technology, such as secretaries, can have incidence rates as high as 40%[32]. A more recent development is the increasing incidence of RSI among young people who make excessive use of video games and mobile phones.

Prevention

Many health problems can be prevented by configuring and using equipment in an ergonomic manner (see figure 12-13). Desks, chairs, and screens should be set at an appropriate height for users to avoid poor posture. In particular, the monitor should be at the right height so the

Avoiding Computer Related Injuries

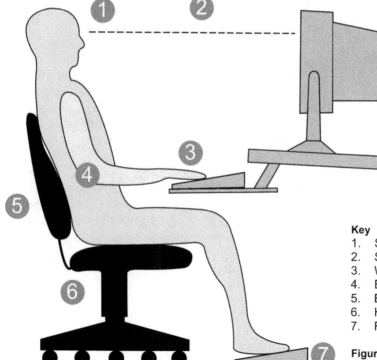

Key
1. Screen is at eye level, reducing neck strain
2. Screen is 28 inches from the user's eyes
3. Wrists are kept straight while using the keyboard
4. Elbows are at approximately 90 degrees
5. Back is well supported by the chair
6. Height of chair can be easily adjusted
7. Feet flat on floor, or supported by a foot rest

Figure 12-13 Correct posture and equipment layout

user views it without looking down on it (thus keeping their neck bent at an awkward angle).

To avoid hand and wrist problems, hands should be positioned at the keyboard so that the wrist is not flexed - some keyboard and mouse manufacturers make special supports or ergonomic versions of their hardware (see figure 12-14) specifically for this purpose.

Knee, leg, and back problems can be reduced by ensuring chairs are the correct height from the ground, with feet flat on the floor, but not so low that the legs are bent. A footrest should be used if the feet do not touch the floor. Work spaces should be kept free of clutter, to enable the mouse and keyboard to be correctly positioned. Good computer chairs should have sufficient back support and be adjustable in several ways.

If possible, lighting should be arranged to avoid causing reflections in computers screens, which exacerbates eye strain.

Users themselves should ensure they take a break from the computer at least 5 minutes each hour, stretch, and move away from the screen to give their eyes a chance to rest.

Users who suffer from RSI or CTS have a number of possible treatments open to them. Ergonomic keyboards and wrist supports can relieve mild symptoms. Wrist braces are also available which provide support and relieve symptoms. In extreme cases of CTS surgery may be used to reduce the problem.

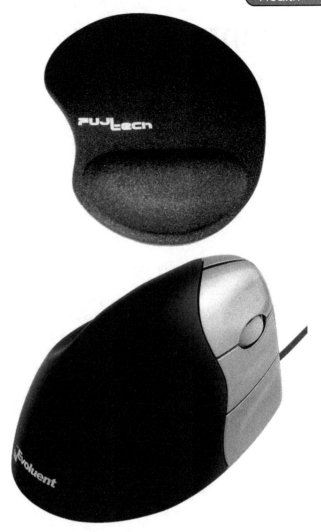

Figure 12-15 Mouse pad with wrist support (top), designed to reduce RSI problems. Mouse with a more ergonomic design, to relieve pressure on the wrist and forearm (bottom).

Computer Accessibility for Disabled users

Computer systems which are adapted for users with disabilities are said to be **accessible**. Making computer systems accessible to users with a range of disabilities is a significant equality of access issue. Both specialised hardware and software can be used to make a computer accessible (see page 29), and there are techniques which software and content developers can follow to increase the accessibility of their products (see page 208).

Exercise 12-4
Many researchers have found that rates of RSI are increasing globally. The biggest increases have often been found in companies whose workers do a lot of mobile computing. **Explain** why mobile working might be having a negative health effect on workers. [6 marks]

Exercise 12-5
With employees spending more and more time using a computer at work, RSI is becoming an issue for employers. Create a policy which describes the measures a business should take to prevent computer related health problems among their staff. [10 marks]

Chapter Review

Key Language

addiction	Electronic Data Interchange	opt-in	store-and-forward
Carpel Tunnel Syndrome	Electronic Health Records	opt-out	telehealth
centralised database	Electronic Medical Records	Personal Health Record	telemedicine
clinical decision support	ergonomics	prosthetics	telesurgery
system	Human Genome Project	remote monitoring	virtual reality
computer model	medical expert system	real time	VPN
cybernetics	myoelectric control	Repetitive Strain Injury	
e-prescriptions	neural control	smart cards	

Exercise 12-6

Describe the required hardware and software for the following telemedicine situations:
 a) A medical consultation between doctor and patient
 b) Remotely monitoring a patient in their home
 c) Performing telesurgery on a patient

Exercise 12-7

Alzheimer disease is a degenerative disease which causes sufferers to experience dementia, confusion, and memory loss. Many Alzheimer's feel the urge to roam around, which often results in them getting lost. To address this problem, it has also been suggested that Alzheimer's patients could be monitored with tags which report their position using GPS[33].

Discuss the benefits and drawbacks of tagging Alzheimer's patients in this way. [8 marks]

Exercise 12-8

Describe the security precautions which an EMR provider must take when implementing their system. [6 marks]

Exercise 12-9

Evaluate the challenges that a surgical team would face when performing an operation like the Lindbergh Operation. [8 marks]

Exercise 12-10

To what extent can technological measures be effective in reducing mobile phone addiction? [8 marks]

Exercise 12-11

To what extent are mobile phones an effective way of distributing health advice? [8 marks]

Exercise 12-12

Electronic Medial Record (EMR) systems are increasingly being used by doctors, patients, and other healthcare professionals

(a) (i) Define the term *primary key*.

[2 marks]

 (ii) Distinguish between *opt-in* and *opt-out* in the context of an EMR system.

[4 marks]

(b) Describe the process which occurs when a doctor accesses a patient's record from an EMR system.

[6 marks]

(c) Evaluate the security, privacy, and integrity issues related to an EMR system.

[8 marks]

Exercise 12-13

Patient monitoring projects such as Project Gerhome equip houses with equipment which can monitor patients constantly and alert medical staff to any potential problems.

(a) (i) Define the term *data logging*. [2 marks]

   (ii) Describe **two** types of sensor that may be used in a project like Project Gerhome [4 marks]

(b) Explain how the process of monitoring a patient would work. [6 marks]

(c) To what extent do the benefits of systems like Project Gerhome outweigh the privacy concerns? [8 marks]

Exercise 12-14

(a) (i) Define the term *telemedicine*. [2 marks]

   (ii) Describe **two** items of hardware required for telemedicine. [4 marks]

(b) A hospital plans to create its own online forum for medical advice. Explain **three** policies the hospital would need to follow when doing this. [6 marks]

(c) Evaluate the benefits and drawbacks of using the Internet for online health advice. [8 marks]

References

1 Brower, V. (2002). *The cutting edge in surgery* . Available: www.nature.com/embor/journal/v3/n4/full/embor175.html. Accessed Nov 2011.

2 CSTB. (Date Unknown). *Gerhome* . Available: http://gerhome.cstb.fr/en/home. Last accessed Nov 2011.

3 Mclaughlin, L. (2007). *Hospital puts medical records snapshot on smart cards.* Available: http://www.networkworld.com/news/2007/101807-hospital-puts-medical-records-snapshot.html. Last accessed Nov 2011.

4 Journal of American Medical Association. (2000). *Effects of Computerized Clinical Decision Support Systems on Practitioner Performance and Patient Outcomes.* Available: http://jama.ama-assn.org/content/293/10/1223.long. Last accessed Nov 2011.

5 Halpem, S. (2008). *Virtual Iraq.* Available: www.newyorker.com/reporting/2008/05/19/080519fa_fact_halpern. Last accessed Nov 2011.

6 BBC. (2008). *Virtual tube ride 'paranoia hope'* . Available: http://news.bbc.co.uk/2/hi/health/7322951.stm. Last accessed Nov 2011.

7 TED. (2007). *Dean Kamen previews a new prosthetic arm.* Available: http://www.ted.com/index.php/talks/dean_kamen_previews_a_new_prosthetic_arm.html. [video] Last accessed Nov 2011.

8 BBC. (2006). *Brain sensor allows mind-control.* Available: http://news.bbc.co.uk/2/hi/health/5167938.stm. Last accessed Nov 2011.

9 Fauber, J. (2009). *Robotic prostate surgery not better at reducing side effects, study finds* . Available: http://www.jsonline.com/features/health/64092427.html. Last accessed Nov 2011.

10 PopTech. (2011). *Project Masiluleke.* Available: http://poptech.org/project_m. Last accessed Nov 2011.

11 TextToChange. (2011). *Text to Change.* Available: http://texttochange.org/. Last accessed Nov 2011.

12 Freedom HIV / AIDS. (2008). *Freedom HIV / AIDS.* Available: www.freedomhivaids.in/. Last accessed April 2011.

13 UNICEF. (2008). *New AIDS film in Georgia circulated using mobiles.* Available: www.unicef.org/ceecis/media_8237.html. Last accessed April 2011.

14 Chan, S. (2009). *City Unveils Facebook Page to Encourage Condom Use* . Available: http://www.nytimes.com/2009/02/12/nyregion/12econdom.html. Last accessed Nov 2011.

15 Keeley, G. (2008). *Teenagers to take embarrassing ailments to Second Life doctors.* Available: http://www.guardian.co.uk/technology/2008/may/10/secondlife.spain. Last accessed Nov 2011.

16 Barkoviak, M. (2008). *Study: Texting While Driving More Dangerous Than Drugs and Alcohol.* Available: http://www.dailytech.com/Study+Texting+While+Driving+More+Dangerous+Than+Drugs+and+Alcohol/article13001.htm. Last accessed Nov 2011.

17 Reuters. (2010). *Texting drivers kill 16,000 in the US.* Available: www.pcpro.co.uk/news/361402/texting-drivers-kill-16-000-in-the-us. Accessed Nov 2011.

18 BBC. (2011). *Warning over 'untrustworthy' sex health websites.* Available: www.bbc.co.uk/news/health-14837229. Accessed Nov 2011.

References (continued)

19 BBC. (2010). *Internet child health advice 'wrong'* . Available: http://news.bbc.co.uk/2/hi/8611045.stm. Last accessed Nov 2011.

20 Weiss, T. (2010). *Smartphones help collect data on malaria cases in remote Uganda.* Available: www.computerworld.com/s/article/9142662/ Smartphones_help_collect_data_on_malaria_cases_in_remote_Uganda?taxonomyId=15&pageNumber=1. Last accessed Nov 2011.

21 HealthMap. (2011). *HealthMap.* Available: http://www.healthmap.org/en/. Last accessed Nov 2011.

22 Public Health Agency of Canada. (2011). *Notifiable Diseases On-Line.* Available: http://dsol-smed.phac-aspc.gc.ca/dsol-smed/ndis/m_ind-eng.php#maps. Last accessed Nov 2011.

23 Human Genome Project. (2011). Available: www.ornl.gov/sci/techresources/Human_Genome/home.shtml. Last accessed Nov 2011.

24 BBC. (1999). *Plan to block patenting of human genes* . Available: news.bbc.co.uk/2/hi/science/nature/452293.stm. Last accessed Nov 2011.

25 ScienceDaily. (2011). *Decades-Old Mystery of Failed Anti-Arrhythmia Therapy.* Available: http://www.sciencedaily.com/releases/2011/08/110831160224.htm. Last accessed Nov 2011.

26 Berger, K. (2010). *New Computer Modelling Analyzes Drug Therapies for HIV Patients.* Available: http://www.healthymagination.com/blog/new-computer-modeling-analyzes-drug-therapies-for-hiv-patients/. Last accessed Nov 2011.

27 News Medical. (2007). *Mobile-phone addiction in teenagers may cause severe psychological disorders.* Available: http://www.news-medical.net/news/2007/02/27/22245.aspx. Last accessed Nov 2011.

28 Park, A. (2007). *Can't Sleep? Turn Off the Cell Phone!* . Available: www.time.com/time/health/article/0,8599,1658166,00.html. Last accessed Nov 2011.

29 Markman, J. (2006). *Cell phones are the new cigarettes.* Available: http://articles.moneycentral.msn.com/Investing/SuperModels/CellPhonesAreTheNewCigarettes.aspx. Last accessed Nov 2011.

30 Stavrinos et al. (2009). *Effect of Cell Phone Distraction on Pediatric Pedestrian Injury Risk.* Available: http://pediatrics.aappublications.org/content/123/2/e179.full. Last accessed Nov 2011.

31 Tibbets, G. (2008). *Mobile phone addiction: Clinic treats children.* Available: http://www.telegraph.co.uk/news/worldnews/2121298/Mobile-phone-addiction-Clinic-treats-children.html. Last accessed Nov 2011.

32 BBC. (2007). *Evidence on RSI 'urgently needed'.* Available: news.bbc.co.uk/1/hi/health/6692683.stm. Last accessed August 2011.

33 BBC. (2007). *Charity backs dementia taggings* . Available: http://news.bbc.co.uk/2/hi/health/7159287.stm. Last accessed Nov 2011.

Chapter 13
Home & Leisure

Objectives

1. Describe the technologies used in copyright infringement
2. Evaluate possible solutions to copyright infringement
3. Evaluate the impacts of computer gaming
4. Explain how news and media is broadcast using IT
5. Evaluate the effects of citizen journalism and social media
6. Explain how IT is used in digital preservation and restoration

Home and Leisure

Digital technology has transformed the way many people live, relax, and communicate. Ubiquitous broadband Internet access and mobile devices have enabled near constant access to communication technologies, while social networks allow ever more detailed maps of users' to lives to be created online. At the same time, the amount of free information and media available to each citizen has exploded, providing a plethora of new ways to access news and entertainment. This revolution has not been received positively by all however, and problems such as large scale copyright infringement have become great challenges for businesses trying to compete in a digital world.

Smart Homes

Smart home technology, also called **home automation**, uses information technology to improve the convenience, security, and energy efficiency of buildings. Several smart home technologies are already quite common, while others currently exist only in the homes of the rich and famous or in research laboratories. A key feature of smart homes is a home network which centralises control, allowing many aspects of the home to be operated from a portable computer or even a mobile phone.

Outside of a smart home, automated lighting and cameras can provide increased security. Security lighting systems can be programmed to switch on automatically at a certain time of day, or when movement is detected. **Biometrics** scans of fingerprints or retinas can be used instead of physical keys, providing improved security and reducing the problem of lost or stolen keys.

Once inside the home, technology allows aspects of rooms to be altered based on the preferences of the per-

Figure 13-2 Wall mounted smart home control panel

son there. Temperature, music, lighting, and even the artwork displayed on the walls can all change based on pre-programmed preferences and wearable **RFID tags** which identify individuals. As you move around the house, lights automatically switch off and on, saving energy. Television programmes can even 'move' around the house with the viewer, automatically transferring to the nearest television and switching off the previous one.

In the kitchen, a fridge with inbuilt bar code or RFID readers monitors food levels and produces an automated shopping list when items start to run low. An Internet connected system might even order the food online and arrange its delivery at a convenient time – perhaps determined by checking the schedule of the house owner. Once the amount and type of food in the house is known, recipes using those ingredients can be automatically looked up online, and a warning can be displayed if food passes its expiry date.

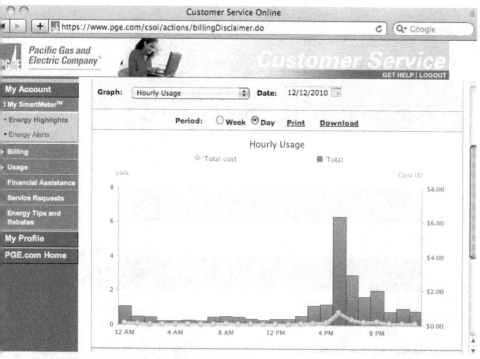

Figure 13-1 Smart meters help identify wasteful uses of water and electricity

Communication plays a key role in home automation. Home owners might use mobile phones to receive alerts of unusual situations, such as a window being left open, and respond with instructions – such as 'close the window' – in the same manner. In dangerous situations, such as a fire or a possible intruder being detected, the house may even be able to automatically dial the emergency services. Domestic robots (see page 343) are likely to be increasingly employed for common household tasks such as cleaning.

One famous home, that of Microsoft founder Bill Gates, incorporates many of these features. Located on the shores of Lake Washington and costing $150 million, the house includes rooms and artworks which adapt to users' pre-programmed preferences, a swimming pool with an underwater music system, and a 22 ft. video display consisting of 24 separate projectors. Touch sensitive panels in every room provide control over lighting, temperature, humidity, and music. Perhaps not surprisingly, the computer systems which automate many of the house's features run Windows as their operating system.

Benefits

Comfort and convenience are the prime benefit of many home automation systems, reducing human workload. Security can also be a key improvement.

Environmental and financial benefits can also be felt, as power consumption is reduced through automated systems which switch off devices when not in use. **Smart meters** (figure 13-1) allow families to see breakdowns of their water, electricity, and other resource consumption, enabling them to optimise their use and reduce waste.

In addition, some smart homes can also improve safety by monitoring their inhabitants. Project Gerhome (see page 257) creates smart homes for the elderly, featuring full monitoring systems, connected to doctors via the Internet, giving elderly people independence while ensuring they have support and assistance if they need it.

However, increasing use of home technology raises questions about our life styles, how we will spend our newly found free time, and whether increasing levels of automation will lead to more sedentary, unhealthier lives.

Digital policing

Increased access to the Internet has been accompanied by an increase in the number of people downloading illegal copies of copyrighted material (sometimes called '**piracy**'), often using **peer-to-peer** (P2P) systems. One of the first P2P systems, Napster, was launched in 1999. Rather than host files itself, Napster allowed users to share files directly from their hard disks. Napster was focused on sharing music files, but as file compression technologies improved and Internet speeds increased, it quickly became possible to share large software programs and entire films online. Although the Napster service was shut down in 2001, other peer-to-peer file sharing systems quickly appeared, including LimeWire and BitTorrent.

The nature of peer to peer systems makes it difficult for authorities to combat copyright infringement. Napster was vulnerable to legal action because it had a central server which maintained a list of all Napster users and the files they possessed (though not the files themselves). Later file sharing systems used a decentralised approach, meaning that shutting down part of the network has minimal, if any, effect on its efficiency. More recently, encrypted file sharing networks have emerged, making it even harder for authorities to combat these activities.

The impact of illegal file sharing is difficult to assess. The Directors' Guild of America reported lost revenues in 2009 totalling 1.4 billion Euros in Spain, 670 million Euros in the UK, and 450 million Euros in Germany[1]; Apple estimated it lost $450 million to software piracy between

Figure 13-3 Illegal file sharing sites are used by thousands

Exercise 13-1

Smart home technology develops rapidly. Research further details of smart homes. In the role of a property developer, produce a 1 minute video advertisement for a smart home, referring to the technology used and the benefits it brings.

[20 marks]

July 2008 and January 2010[2]; the Business Software Alliance estimated lost revenue at \$59 billion worldwide[3].

However, many of these reports assume that each illegal download is equivalent to a lost sale, which may be a false assumption. What is certain is that music sales have fallen in recent years – although digital sales grew by 5.3% from 2009 to 2010, sales of physical CDs dropped by 14.2% in the same period, contributing to an overall fall in global revenues of \$1.45 billion[4]. It is also clear that illegal downloading happens on a large scale, with the most downloaded films of 2009 each being downloaded over 9 million times[5].

Solutions to copyright infringement

Media industry organisations such as the **Motion Picture Association of America** (MPAA) and the **Recording Industry Association of America** (RIAA) have focused on educating users about copyright infringement while also trying to target sites which link to copyrighted material.

Famous sites such as The Pirate Bay provide links to the Torrent files which allow users to locate and download files on the BitTorrent P2P network, and there have been several attempts to shut down these sites in their host countries as well as block access to them from other countries. Legal action from the MPAA or similar organisa-

tions has caused some of these sites to be blocked in Denmark, Italy, and Germany. The problems with these approaches is that such filters are often easy to circumvent, and there are issues of legal jurisdiction. There are also legal issues over whether a site which provides links to copyrighted material (in effect, a search engine) is committing a crime.

Governments have also passed legislation aimed at illegal file sharing. The UK's **Digital Economy Act 2010** (DEA) includes measures requiring ISPs to identify people who persistently infringe copyright laws online and take 'technical measures' against them – including substantially reducing the speed of their Internet connections or even disconnecting them. The DEA also allows the UK government to block sites 'from which a substantial amount of material has been, is being or is likely to be obtained in infringement of copyright' [6].

A final solution which has been employed by some media companies is the uploading of fake files to P2P systems. These files, named after recent software, music, or film releases, are designed to make it harder for users to find working copies of material they want. Many peer-to-peer search sites incorporate rating systems for downloads to make it easy to notify users about these fake uploads.

Digital Rights Management

Digital Rights Management (DRM), sometimes derisively called Digital Restrictions Management, refers to technologies which limit what a user can do with a digital file.

DVDs used an early form of DRM called Content Scrambling System (CSS) to prevent illegal copies being made. DVD content was encrypted and could only be decrypted by the key inside authorised DVD players or drives, to prevent copying of the film using special disk copying software.

Audio CDs have also used DRM to prevent copying. DRM can be applied to data in various formats including PDF documents, AAC audio, and WMV video. DRM can be used to:

- Prevent printing of a book (PDF)
- Make content expire (unable to open) after a certain date
- Prevent copying and pasting from documents
- Prevent copying (including backup copies)
- Restrict the number of copies possible
- Restrict a file to opening only on a specific device

The use of DRM is often controversial because it restricts certain activities which have been legal rights (such as making backup copies or copying music to another device such as a portable music player). DRM can cause also compatibility problems with some systems (for example, 'unauthorised' free and open source DVD player software).

Like many copy protection systems, it is relatively easy to remove or 'break' DRM using freely available software tools, though under the Digital Millennium Copyright Act (DMCA) it is illegal to do so in a number of countries.

Legal uses of peer-to-peer file sharing

Peer-to-peer file sharing systems themselves are not illegal. Because they make it easy to share large files, reducing the load on any one server and providing faster downloads speeds, P2P systems are often used to distribute public domain media and free and open source software such as Linux.

Would legal alternatives help?

Although cost is seen as the main reason people download media illegally, some studies suggest other reasons as well. Illegal downloads often offer individual music tracks instead of entire CDs, giving users choice. Although individual tracks can be downloaded from legal music services, they are often locked with **Digital Rights Management** (DRM) technology, preventing users from using them on several different devices, such as their MP3 player and their laptop. Some have suggested that the media industry can combat illegal downloads by allowing more flexibility and including a greater range of titles in their legal download catalogues.

Digital Entertainment

Users have many games playing options available to them, from simple Java or Flash based games on their mobile phones, to multi-million dollar productions for the latest games consoles, which can rival blockbuster films in terms of production values, resources, and budget. Reuters reported the global computer games market was worth $65 billion in 2010, with almost half of that figure being generated by retail sales of games software[7].

Technical developments such as improved batteries, faster yet more energy efficient processors, and energy efficient LCD screens have enabled increasingly advanced gaming on ever smaller devices. Even modern mobile phones are capable of playing games comparable to the home computer games of the late 1980s and early 1990s. Dedicated games consoles by companies such as Sony, Nintendo, and Microsoft are even more powerful, with high resolution displays, multi-channel sound, high capacity storage devices, and fast processors capable of generating complex 3D graphics. Modern consoles also feature Internet connectivity for web browsing, and use a range of input devices especially designed for gaming (see page 22).

In addition to single player components, many modern games feature multi-player options, allowing gamers to

Figure 13-4 Modern games consoles are available in many forms

connect with each other on a LAN or over the Internet. **Massively Multiplayer Online Games** (MMOG) or **Massively Multiplayer Online Role Playing Games** (MMORPG), often featuring fantasy or magical themes, require players to create an **avatar** – a virtual representation of themselves – and log in to access the virtual world, usually for a subscription fee. As players progress through the game, they complete missions or quests, improving their avatar's abilities and buying in-game items. Some of these games are so popular that there are even 'black markets' for in-game items which are sold for real money.

Virtual worlds are similar to MMOGs, except they often lack defined objectives, and instead simply allow the player to 'live' in the world, interacting with others, building objects, and perhaps owning 'land'. One of the more famous examples of a virtual world is Second Life, which even has its own currency – Linden dollars. Gamers, educational institutions and businesses have all established presences in Second Life, offering virtual tours, classes, and virtual shops.

Figure 13-5 Virtual worlds let users explore many locations

CAVE (Cave Automated Virtual Environment) systems take the virtual world concept a step further. The user stands in a small cube-like room while images of the virtual world are projected on each of the walls, surrounding the user in the environment and creating a more immersive effect.

Gaming Addiction in Korea

In South Korea, 80% of the population have access to some of the fastest broadband connections in the world, and there are more than 25,000 *PC Bangs* – cyber cafes with high speed computers for online gaming, often open 24 hours a day. Yet this technological powerhouse is experiencing a sharp rise in a new problem – Internet addiction – which the government recognises as a clinical condition suffered by up to two million people – 10% of the population[13].

Figure 13-6 Online gaming cafes are popular with many users in South Korea

Obsessive online gaming often spills into the real world, disrupting players' routines and making it difficult for them to maintain a job, a relationship, and a family. Several high profile cases, including the death of a 24 year old man from heart failure after playing online for 86 hours non-stop[14], the death of a three month old baby whose parents neglected her for online gaming[15], and the murder of a games player by another player, jealous over his possession of an in game item, have spurred the government into action.

Counselling centres have been established across the country while, for the most seriously addicted teenagers, 'boot camps' have been created to wean youngsters from their computers and involve them in healthier activities. The government says these measures are working, and that the number of teenage Internet addicts is slowly falling, but acknowledges that the number of older addicts continues to rise.

Exercise 13-2
To what extent can technological solutions solve the Internet addiction problems experienced in South Korea? [8 marks]

Exercise 13-3
Who should be responsible for solving the problem of games addiction in Korea? **Evaluate** your arguments. [8 marks]

Figure 13-7 Game controllers based on real weapons are a concern for those worried about the effects of violent games

Figure 13-8 Second Life is one of the more popular virtual worlds

Concerns about games

A number of concerns have traditionally been raised both about the content of computer games and the health effects of long term game playing. Health concerns range from common concerns that players do not get enough physical exercise, to extreme cases in which players become addicted to game playing to the detriment of their education, work, and personal lives. In the most extreme cases, people have died from exhaustion after excessive games playing sessions lasting several days. In some countries these concerns have become so great that governments have been pushed into action (see *Gaming Addiction in Korea*, opposite).

Violence has been a feature of many games since the emergence of the industry in the 1970s, but as games become more realistic thanks to developments in computing power, concerns over violent games has grown. Higher resolution displays, faster processors (especially graphics processors), and improved sound help to create more lifelike experiences, and some people fear that this exposure to realistic, violent imagery can have a negative psychological effect on young players, possibly initiating 'copycat' violence. Although films often contain violence, in games the player is usually actively participating in the acts, which causes greater concern. The use of some input devices which imitate real life weapons has added to this concern. Some anti-violent game campaigners even use the phrase 'murder simulators' to describe games involving killing, and compare the recreational use of video games with the military use of games to train soldiers, claiming they desensitise players to real life violence.

Although some researchers have found changes in brain response when players play violent games[8], no credible evidence exists of a long term, direct correlation between gaming and real life violence, and other studies have refuted any such link[9]. However, there is a fear that exces-

sively violent games can negatively influence young people and those who may already be prone to violent tendencies. On the other hand, some studies have found positive effects in games playing, including improving hand to eye coordination, logical thinking abilities, and physical fitness.

In addition to violence, games which feature criminal behaviour, drug use, bad language, racism and sexism have been criticised. Today, many countries restrict computer games using age classifications, just as they do films, and it is usually illegal to supply 15 or 18-rated games to people below that age. Systems such as **PEGI** (Pan European Game Information) and **ESRB** (Entertainment Software Rating Board) exist to rate games and provide information for parents about their content. PEGI provides age ratings and categories of content including drug use, sex, violence, and bad language.

Figure 13-10 Augmented Reality systems add a layer of digital information to images of our environment

Figure 13-9 Augmented Reality systems like this could help fire fighters navigate through smoke-filled buildings

Online gaming

Online gaming presents new challenges when trying to protect children from harmful content. Even in age appropriate games, players can be exposed to a range of undesirable content once online, including bad language and pornography, and there is often little games companies can do to control what happens in these situations. Online predators may also attempt to target children in games they are known to frequent. For this reason, some games heavily restrict their online content or require users to be over a certain age—often 13, 16, or 18.

Other companies have tried different approaches and offered alternatives for underage users—the virtual world Second Life, for example, created Teen Second Life which required users to prove they were under 18—a kind of reversed age verification system. Adults were permitted on Teen Second Life—useful for teachers wishing to use the system with their students—but they had to pass a background check and faced restrictions in their interactions with underage users. After it was discontin-

ued, Teen Second life users were combined with regular Second Life, but face limitations on the land their can use and the areas they can access.

Augmented Reality

Augmented Reality technologies 'add' a layer of digital information to our views of the real world, using a mobile phone or dedicated viewing device.

Using a combination of GPS and compass data, a mobile phone can determine its position and the direction in which it is pointing. The image its camera receives can then be analysed and relevant information—determined by the user—can be downloaded from the Internet and displayed. For example, pointing a phone at a street may highlight the restaurants, display their contact details, the type of food they serve, and perhaps a rating from a restaurant guide. At tourist attractions such as a zoo, augmented reality could display a map pointing towards important enclosures, display information about the animals currently in front of the user, and update automatically as they move around the zoo.

Augmented reality also forms part of the Future Warrior (see page 303) system for soldiers, displaying the positions of friendly forces, and it could also be used to help emergency workers. Fire fighters, for example, could use the system to help them navigate smoke filled buildings by viewing an overlay of the building's walls, doors, and stairs, on a display built into their breathing masks (see figure 13-9). This could save critical time when searching for people trapped in burning buildings, potentially saving lives.

Exercise 13-4
Describe the techniques operators of virtual worlds can use to protect children from online predators and unsuitable content. [6 marks]

Published and broadcast information

The ways in which we watch television and films, listen to music, read the news, and communicate with our families and friends have shifted drastically in the last decade. Widespread availability of broadband Internet connectivity, portable devices, and social media sites have all helped change the way we access entertainment, news, and friends. Online news reading is now one of the top three activities for Internet users[10]. A large number of sites, many of which are free, provide access to a greater range of news content than would be feasible with traditional newspapers, and also provide access to many years of older, archived articles. Content which would require dozens of pages of printed news can easily be accessed on the move using mobile devices. Many newspaper sites also let users fetch the latest headlines to their desktops or portable devices using RSS, rather than visiting a variety of sites, saving time and allowing users to customise the topics they receive.

Online News

Online news reading has been cited as a significant factor in the drop in circulation of traditional newspapers in recent years. Despite this, most news organisations have found it harder to generate revenue online than in their print editions; online advertising revenues are generally much lower, and many newspapers provide a great deal of news and editorial content for free.

News aggregation sites fetch headlines and news articles from many different news sites and present them on a single page, allowing users to access large amounts of information in one place. The rise of web 2.0 technologies has increased the number of community and **social news sites**, which not only aggregate stories but rank them based on their popularity with users.

However, news aggregation sites have been unpopular with some online newspapers, who believe their copyrighted articles are being illegally copied. At the same

Figure 13-11 News aggregators (top) and social news sites (bottom) are just two of the ways news can be accessed online

time, because aggregation sites present a summary of each article, fewer viewers 'click through' to read the full version at the newspapers' web sites, thus reducing their advertising revenues.

To counteract this, some news sites have started using **paywalls**—systems which require payment for access to certain news articles, or after a certain number of articles have been read for free. For a small daily, weekly, or monthly fee users can gain unrestricted access to news content, including archived articles.

Letting the Algorithms Decide

TOK Link

Some news aggregation sites feature articles selected by human editors, much like traditional newspapers. Social news sites rely on popularity votes to determine which articles are first presented. Google News goes further, and selects newsworthy stories completely automatically, based on criteria such as the number of sites they appear on and when they were updated.

Exercise 13-5

How do these different methods of selecting news articles for our viewing affect our understanding of events and our perception of our world?

Figure 13-12 An Airbus A320 moments after performing an emergency landing in the Hudson river. This photo, and others taken by passers-by, were spread on the Internet before traditional news media had reached the scene.

News Corp's newspapers in the UK and the US - *The Times*, *The Sunday Times*, *The Financial Times*, and *The Wall Street Journal* all implement paywall systems. The *New York Times* also started charging for content in 2011. In the UK, *The Times* gained 100,000 subscribers after its paywall introduction, but visitors to the paper's web site fell by 87%[11]. In the US, *The New York Times* gained 224,000 subscribers in four months, despite implementing a paywall system which allowed free access to pages when linked from blogs and other sites. It remains unclear whether most readers in the Internet age are loyal enough to stay with their favourite newspaper and pay subscription fees, or whether they will move to one of the many free alternatives.

Figure 13-13 Broadcasters often offer 'catch-up' television programmes online as streaming video files

Citizen journalism

Citizen journalism refers to news events which are reported first by normal people rather than the traditional media. Citizen journalism has become possible because many mobile phones now have cameras and Internet access, allowing footage to be shot, uploaded, and shared almost immediately on social media sites such as Twitter, Facebook, or YouTube. Many traditional newspapers' web sites now have sections for reader contributions too.

Citizen journalism is particularly common at unpredictable events, where normal media are unlikely to be initially present and may have difficulty gaining access when they arrive. The 2004 Southeast Asian tsunami, a plane landing in the Hudson river (figure 13-12), and the 2005 terrorist attacks on London transport were all heavily reported by citizen journalists. In the case of the London bombings, national news broadcasters made heavy use of citizens' images—the only ones available of passengers stuck in the Underground tunnels.

However, although they raise immediate awareness of events, concerns have been raised about citizen journalists invading privacy, particularly as they are unlikely to be bound by the same ethical codes as regular journalists. In the 2005 London bombings, for example, pictures of the aftermath were published online, including many showing injured victims in clear distress. The pervasiveness of small, portable cameras means problems like this are likely to continue.

Digital television and radio

The biggest change to television and radio services in recent years has been the move from analog to digital transmissions. Digital signals require less bandwidth, allowing television companies to transmit **High Definition** footage (HDTV), and offer improved image and audio quality as they are less susceptible to interference.

Higher bandwidth also allows a greater number of channels to be broadcast—meaning items such as sport can be covered by numerous cameras at many different locations, allowing viewers to choose how they want to watch. Other broadcasts can include multiple languages or data such as closed captions.

Switching to digital broadcasting has economic and environmental costs, however. Depending on circumstances, viewers may require a new aerial and a new 'set top box' to decode the digital signals. The latter in particular causes environmental concerns as users begin to throw away thousands of pieces of working equipment, many of which contains hazardous materials (see page 246). Another development in the television industry is **video on demand** (VOD) programming, especially over the Internet using the **IPTV** protocol. Some TV companies allow viewers to 'catch up' with TV programming for free via their web sites, usually for a limited time after broadcast. Others make a larger catalogue of programming available, each episode for a small fee. Companies like NetFlix allow users to download a wide range of films and TV programmes on demand, either for individual fees or a monthly subscription.

The convenience of on-demand programming is a advantage for users. The wide range of available programming, including older programmes which may no longer be broadcast, is also attractive. On-demand services usually offer high quality video and audio, and provide good technical support for their users, making them a viable alternative to illegally downloading content (see page 275). One of the main drawbacks is that users pay to view the content only once, with no physical copy of the content to watch later. Because on demand content is usually **streamed** (downloaded while it is watched), a relatively high speed and reliable Internet connection is also needed.

A recent development in the desktop computer market is the **Home Theatre PC**, or HTPC. These computers are designed to be a home's entertainment centre, replacing separate devices such as DVD players, televisions, and a dedicated computer for Internet access. A HTPC normally features an optical drive (such as a Blu-ray drive) for playing movies, a relatively powerful processor for decoding High Definition video content, and a DVI or HDMI interface for connecting a high quality screen or television. Internet access can be used to view programme schedules, access view-on-demand content, and visit film rental web sites. A built in TV card allows broadcast content to be displayed and digitally recorded, and a large hard disk is needed to save this material.

E-books

E-books, as their name suggests, are a method of distributing electronic copies of books, magazines, and newspapers. These can be downloaded for free or purchased from an e-book store. E-books can be read on a normal computer, but are most often downloaded to dedicated e-book readers such as the Kindle, Nook, and Kobo E-Reader. Most e-book readers use **electronic ink** displays, which are more comfortable to read than traditional LCD screens and consume much less power, although they are usually limited to black and white. E-book readers usually have wireless connections to enable downloading of books. Several companies distribute their own e-book readers which then link to their respective e-book stores, though they are not restricted to purchasing from these sites.

E-books are distributed in many formats, some of which support Digital Rights Management (see page 276) to control book distribution. The most common formats are ePub, AZW, and PDF. Although not all readers support all formats, conversion between formats is relatively easy.

E-books sales have risen quickly, and in 2011—only four years after the launch of their Kindle e-book reader—online giant Amazon recorded higher sales for e-books than paper books[12]. E-books are considered more convenient than paper books in some circumstances, and they allow dozens or even hundreds of books to be carried around in a small, relatively lightweight device. Their lack of physical size and their lower distribution costs have seen e-books heralded as potent educational tools in developing nations.

E-books are not suitable for all applications, however. The need to download books can cause problems for those containing many images, while DRM has caused problems for users and libraries wishing to lend books to others. This problem has been addressed by some e-book readers which have lending features, temporarily disabling the book on the owner's device until it is 'returned' by the borrower. Page 245 discusses the environment impacts of e-books compared to paper books.

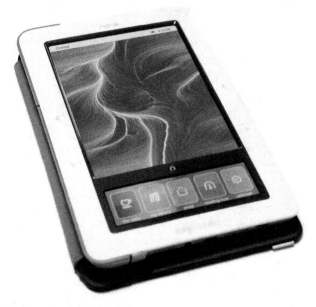

Figure 13-14 Dedicated readers are the most common way of reading e-books

Digital Preservation

The nature of digital data makes it ideal for preserving valuable cultural, artistic, and historical works. Digital data does not wear out or decay, and unlike analog data, every copy made is a perfect copy of the original. Films, books, maps, paintings, and sound recordings can all be **digitised** and preserved in this way, reducing the risk of losing them to theft, wear and tear, or physical decay due to their age. Digitisation also has the benefits of allowing global access to works, for example through online virtual museums (see page 224).

Many early films were recorded on nitrate film, which degrades quickly over time and is highly flammable, meaning many have been lost or exist only as decaying fragments. Even films from the 1950s and 1960s and onwards can suffer through degrading of film stock. Film preservation techniques, using high resolution film scanners, can scan these negatives at resolutions up to 8K (approximately 8000 pixels across) - much higher than current Blu-Ray resolutions.

Digital restoration takes these processes further and uses image processing techniques to return works to their original quality, or even add effects which were not possible when the films were originally released. Dirt, scratches, tears, and physical deterioration of the film or paper media can all be partially or completely fixed using image processing techniques. This is particularly important on old films where the media is unstable and has often started to decay and crumble. For example, a rare colour version Georges Méliès' 1902 film *Le Voyage dans la lune* (A Trip to the Moon), was discovered as rotting film in 2010, but was digitally preserved and then restored to its original state. Fritz Lang's 1927 science fiction film Metropolis was also restored in this way, using fragments of video found in locations across the world to create a complete, definitive version.

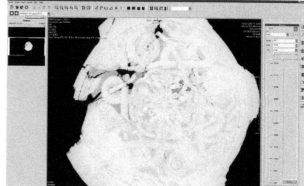

Figure 13-15 Restored film (top). Ground penetrating radar is used to map underground structures (middle). Scans of artefacts can reveal previously hidden information (bottom).

Preserving Digital Data

Even digital data may be in need of preservation efforts: as new file formats are developed and older ones become obsolete, it can become difficult or impossible to find software capable of opening files saved in these old standards. Data such as GIF images, RealMedia video, Dbase databases, and a plethora of binary formats were all in common use less than twenty years ago but are now positively obsolete. The problem is even greater if data is stored on obsolete formats such as 5.25 inch floppy disks or even paper tape, and if the programs to read the files were designed for older systems which are incompatible with modern machines. Commercial software companies who go out of business, taking their source code and file format specifications with them, are another concern. Many digital preservation efforts try to avoid these problems in the future by using open standards.

For the digital restoration of paintings, restorers can either create a fully digital version of the restored work, or use a digital copy to practise restoration techniques before applying them to the original painting. This reduces risk of damage to the original and allows the most appropriate techniques to be used.

Even objects and physical places can be digitally restored. Techniques such as **3D laser scanning** and **ground penetrating radar** can be used to build digital **3D models** of locations, even those underground. Colour and texture mapping can then be applied to recreate how these locations may have looked hundreds of years ago. The models can even be extended, perhaps to add missing elements, such as an arm which fell off a statue, or a church tower which collapsed many years ago. Archaeologists at locations such as Tikal in Guatemala, the Parthenon in Greece, and Stonehenge in England have already used these techniques to increase their understanding of these ancient sites.

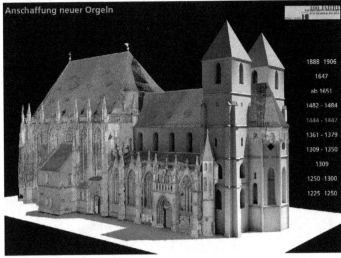

Figure 13-16 3D model of the historic Saint Sebald Church, featuring a mixture of scanned building data and digital 'restored' 3D additions.

Stereolithography, also called 3D printing, produces physical copies of items modelled in a computer. Stereolithography builds up objects by adding layer upon layer of plastic or resin, slowly creating the item from the bottom up. Stereolithography is often used for producing concept models and prototypes of items before they are created in other, more expensive, materials.

Restoring the Moon Landings

Even NASA has used digital restoration techniques to restore and improve the quality of its footage. The organisation accidentally erased the original footage of the historic Apollo 11 moon landings, leaving it with only the lower quality video taped recordings of events. In 2009 digital restoration techniques were used to improve the quality of these tapes, removing bleeding edges, reducing image noise, and increasing detail in the extremely dark shadow areas of the moon.

Exercise 13-6   TOK Link

The Apollo 11 tapes are historical documents detailing the moon landing. Much of the digital restoration work was aimed at removing noise introduced by the lower quality television recordings of the events, but technology allows many other changes – perhaps even adding colour to the original black and white footage. **To what extent** does the digital restoration of these tapes affect their authenticity, and does this affect our understanding of the first moon landings?

Figure 13-17 Images of the Apollo 11 landings (top) were enhanced and restored in 2009 (bottom)

Chapter Review

Key Language

3D modelling	digitisation	laser scanning	RFID
augmented reality	DRM	MMOG	RIAA
avatar	e-book	MMORPG	smart home
biometrics	electronic ink	MPAA	smart meters
CAVE	ESRB	news aggregator	social news
citizen journalism	ground penetrating radar	P2P	stereolithography
copyright infringement	High Definition Television	paywall	streaming media
digital radio	home automation	Peer-to-Peer	Video On Demand
digital restoration	Home Theatre PC	PEGI	virtual worlds
digital television	IPTV	piracy	

Exercise 13-7

File sharing sites sometimes compare their activities to those of Internet search engines such as Google, saying they merely provide an index of existing material. **Analyse** this argument. Is it valid? What are the key differences between hosting files and providing a search service? Does it make a difference if a wide range of material is indexed by the search engine? [8 marks]

Exercise 13-8

Consider possible applications for augmented reality. Find a photograph of one situation and use graphics software to annotate the image with the additions augmented reality could make. **Explain** the source of the data and how the system would identify items in the world around it. [6 marks]

Exercise 13-9

Explain the technical considerations that archivists must be aware of when creating digital copies of works for preservation purposes. [6 marks]

Exercise 13-10

Analyse the issue of online identities. Should users be required to use, and prove, their real identity before using online services such as virtual worlds and games? What are the risks and the benefits? **Evaluate** your answer. [8 marks]

Exercise 13-11

(a) (i) Identify **two** methods of accessing news online. [2 marks]

(ii) Describe **two** technical considerations when deciding which file format should be used to save a photo taken with a mobile phone. [4 marks]

(b) Explain the policies a national newspaper should follow when deciding to use images from a citizen journalist on its web site. [6 marks]

(c) To what extent do concerns about citizen journalism outweigh the benefits? [8 marks]

Exercise 13-12

(a) (i) Define the term *intellectual property*. [2 marks]

(ii) Describe **two** technologies which have assisted the illegal online copying of films. [4 marks]

(b) Explain the considerations film companies need to make when deciding to distribute their products online. [6 marks]

(c) Discuss the methods governments can use to combat illegal distribution of copyright material online. [8 marks]

References

1 Directors' Guild of America. (2010). *Piracy - by the Numbers*. Available: www.dgaquarterly.org/BACKISSUES/ Spring2010/PiracyByTheNumbers.aspx. Last accessed April 2011.

2 24/7 Wall Street. (2010). *Apple App Store Has Lost $450 Million To Piracy*. Available: http://247wallst.com/2010/01/13/ apple-app-store-has-lost-450-million-to-piracy/. Last accessed Nov 20102.

3 Rashid, F. (2011). *Software Piracy Costs $59B in Lost Revenue, May Be Even Higher: Survey*. Available: http:// www.eweek.com/c/a/Security/Software-Piracy-Costs-59-Bn-in-Lost-Revenue-May-Be-Even-Higher-Survey-272553/. Last accessed Nov 2011.

4 Sweney, M. (2010). *Global recorded music sales fall almost $1.5bn amid increased piracy. The Guardian*. Available: www.guardian.co.uk/business/2011/mar/28/global-recorded-music-sales-fall. Last accessed April 2011.

5 New Zealand Herald. (2011). *The world's most pirated film named*. Available: http://www.nzherald.co.nz/movies/ news/article.cfm?c_id=200&objectid=10758971. Last accessed Nov 2011.

6 UK Government. (2010). *The Digital Economy Act 2010*. Available: www.legislation.gov.uk/ukpga/2010/24/ section/17?view=plain. Last accessed April 2011.

7 Baker, L. (2011). *A look at the $65 billion video games industry*. Reuters. Available: uk.reuters.com/article/2011/06/06/us-videogames-factbox-idUKTRE75552I20110606. Last accessed Sept 2011.

8 ScienceDaily. (2011). *Violent Video Games Reduce Brain Response to Violence and Increase Aggressive Behavior, Study Suggests*. Available: http://www.sciencedaily.com/releases/2011/05/110525151059.htm. Last accessed Nov 2011.

9 Leonard, W. (2010). *Weber State researcher discovers good of gaming*. Available: http://www.deseretnews.com/ article/700023421/Weber-State-researcher-discovers-good-of-gaming.html. Last accessed Nov 2011.

10 OECD. (2010). *OECD examines the future of news and the Internet*. Available: http://www.oecd.org/ document/48/0,3343,en_2649_33703_45449136_1_1_1_1,00.html. Last accessed Nov 2011.

11 BBC. (2010). *Times and Sunday Times readership falls after paywall*. Available: http://www.bbc.co.uk/news/uk-11671984. Last accessed Nov 2011.

12 Rapaport, L. (2011). *Amazon.com Says Kindle E-Book Sales Surpass Printed Books for First Time*. Available: http:// www.bloomberg.com/news/2011-05-19/amazon-com-says-kindle-electronic-book-sales-surpass-printed-format.html. Last accessed Nov 2011.

13 Cain, G. (2010). *South Korea Cracks Down on Gaming Addiction*. Available: http://www.time.com/time/world/ article/0,8599,1983234,00.html. Last accessed Nov 2011.

14 BBC. (2002). *South Korea's gaming addicts*. Available: http://news.bbc.co.uk/2/hi/asia-pacific/2499957.stm. Last accessed Nov 2011.

15 BBC. (2010). *S Korea child 'starves as parents raise virtual baby'*. Available: http://news.bbc.co.uk/2/hi/asia-pacific/8551122.stm. Last accessed Nov 2011.

Chapter 14
Politics &
Government

Objectives

1. Explain how Internet content can be filtered
2. Evaluate the ethical and social impacts of Internet filtering
3. Describe the technologies used for electronic and online voting
4. Evaluate the social issues related to electronic and online voting
5. Explain how government can use the Internet to provide services
6. Describe how information technology can be used by the military
7. Evaluate the use of information technology for military purposes

Politics and Government

Information technology has many uses in the political sphere. If used correctly, IT greatly facilitates the political process, increasing transparency, information sharing, and enfranchisement. Yet IT is also a tool for control, which governments can and do use to spy on their citizens and control their access to media. Technology increases governments' ability to fight crime and terrorism, but also their ability to wage war, creating some of the most controversial uses of technology today. Perhaps more than any other area of application, Politics and Government demonstrates great potential and great risk posed by the use of information technology.

Government Control of the Internet

Internet filtering, or Internet blocking, is the process of preventing access to particular web pages or sites. This can be done on an individual scale in a person's home, throughout an organisation such as a school or place of work, or on a much larger scale, potentially preventing access to all users in a given country.

The free flow of information that the Internet enables has not been welcomed by all governments around the world. China, North Korea, Egypt, Saudi Arabia and several other countries are commonly identified as having extensive nationwide Internet filtering. Often information about political opposition or democracy is filtered, as well as places where discussions of such topics might flourish, such as social networking sites.

China is famous for its pervasive Internet filtering under the Golden Shield Project—sometimes called the 'Great Firewall of China' - which blocks sites using IP address filtering and DNS record alteration (see page 292).

Among other topics, Chinese Internet users are prevented from accessing certain information about Tibetan and Taiwanese independence, democracy, and the Falun Gong religious movement. Political opposition and information about anti-government protests (including the 1989 Tiananmen Square protest) are also sporadically blocked, as are foreign news and media sites, which do not directly promote these ideals but provide coverage of them. This became a particular problem for journalists during the 2008 Beijing Olympics, and caused the Chinese government to temporarily unblock some sites.

However, it is important to remember that many countries filter their citizens' Internet access, although not all at the national level. In the US **Children's Internet Protection Act** (CIPA) requires schools and libraries to filter access for children in many circumstances. Search engines such as Google filter their results to remove sites which have **Digital Millennium Copyright Act** (DMCA) complaints made against them (usually because they are alleged to be illegally hosting copyrighted material). Some US states have laws against gambling, including online gambling on sites hosted outside of the state or the US.

The difficult job of search engines

The legal position of Internet search engines such as Google and Yahoo is not always obvious—often they are US-based companies, yet they deliver search results to users in dozens of countries, and must navigate a minefield of laws governing their operation. Although search engines do not host the content of the web sites shown in their search results pages, the mere act of providing links to some types of information can violate the law in some countries, and in several cases search engines have been asked to remove offending links from their results page for that country.

The **Digital Millennium Copyright Act** (DMCA) allows takedown notices to be issued, requiring search engines to delist sites accused of providing illegal copies of copyrighted material. Other illegal content is usually dealt with quickly too: in 2000, Yahoo were ordered by a French court to use IP address blocking to prevent French users from accessing Nazi memorabilia on a Yahoo auction site (the sale of Nazi memorabilia is illegal in France and several other European countries). Yahoo responded by banning the sales of such items on all of its sites worldwide. Since then references to Holocaust Denial—which is also illegal in France and Germany—have been automatically removed from Google.fr and Google.de, and Google has faced demands from several countries—most notably China—to filter its search results[14].

Globalisation and cultural diversity make such tasks harder —in cases where content is clearly illegal it will usually be filtered out by search engines, and the same is true if the content breaks the company's Terms of Use. However, with widely differing local cultures and societal standards around the world, a search engine may provide access to information which is legal—even accepted as normal—in one country, but is considered completely unacceptable in another.

In the United Kingdom, Internet Service Providers are not legally required to block any material. However, many ISPs block sites identified by the **Internet Watch Foundation** as containing illegal material – usually images of child abuse. It has been suggested that ISPs should also block sites related to promoting terrorism, though nothing has come of these plans yet.

Although pornography is often the focus of Internet filtering discussions, there are dozens of other topics which are filtered by governments around the world, including:

- Abortion and contraception
- Bomb making instructions
- Child abuse
- Criticism of the government
- Democracy advocacy
- Drugs
- Gambling
- Guns and weapons
- Hate speech
- HIV and AIDS
- Holocaust denial
- Illegal download sites (of copyrighted material)
- Political criticism
- Pornography
- Pro-suicide and right-to-die sites
- Pro-anorexia sites
- Religious extremism
- Racism e.g. Neo-Nazis, 'white power'
- Sexuality and gay rights
- Violence

Filtering technologies

Black lists contain a list of sites to block. **URLs** or **IP address** on the black list cannot be accessed, while all others can. Black lists are useful for blocking specific sites or even specific pages or files within a site (such as a single image). The drawback of black lists is that the URL of the content must be known before it can be blocked, so given the nature of the Internet, keeping black lists up to date is a big problem as sites are created and removed everyday.

White lists operate on a similar principle, except they allow access only to sites on the list, and all other sites are blocked. White lists provide greater security but also a much more limited Internet experience. For example, none of the results from a search engine would be accessible unless they had been previously added to the white list. White lists are sometimes useful when very young children are using the Internet and there is a desire for them to view only a few pages, or when tight controls are

Internet Filtering—Top Countries

The Reporters Without Borders[21] and OpenNet Initiative[22] produce regular reports about global Internet filtering. Countries identified as having the greatest amount of filtered content include:

- China
- North Korea
- Saudi Arabia
- Iran
- Egypt (see page 84)

required – for example, allowing prison inmates access only to the web pages for their online learning courses.

Keyword filters offer more dynamic filtering than lists. These filters scan all content (including potentially, email and chat content) for banned **keywords**. Very basic keyword filters might ban any occurrence of the words, but this can easily lead to **false positives** – blocking of sites which are in fact useful. For example, medical sites and the University of Essex web site might both be blocked by a simple keyword filter which blocks the word 'sex'. More advanced keyword filters look at the **'weight'** of the keywords – how frequently they occur in the page, and whether they occur together with other keywords (such as 'images'). This can improve the success rate, but all filters will suffer to some extent from false positives. Additionally, even the best keyword filters will generate some **false negatives**—failing to block content which should be blocked.

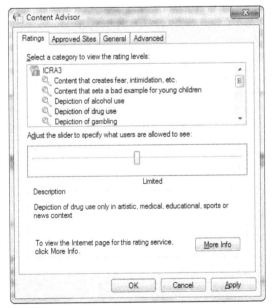

Figure 14-2 Content Rating Systems use web browser controls to block web sites with various categories of content.

Filtering by individuals

Internet filtering can also be performed by individual home users, organisations, or businesses depending on their needs. Businesses commonly filter sites such as social networks which might provide a distraction to their employees, and inappropriate content such as pornography (see page 188). Schools often take a similar approach, and are sometimes required to by law (see page 228). Families with children may also wish to block access to certain pages according to their individual family values.

Internet routers often include a **firewall** which can be configured to block particular sites, and on network servers software can be installed to do the same. Several modern operating systems include filtering settings in their web browser configuration options, allowing the computer administrator to be apply different restrictions to each user.

Certain filtering options are easier to circumvent than others. Proxy servers, which direct traffic through a separate server before returning it to the user, effectively mask the true source of the web pages being downloaded, avoiding URL black lists. Virtual Private Networks, which encrypt all data sent and received, achieve the same thing.

Content rating systems work by categorising a web site's content and then configuring a web browser to allow or disallow different categories of content. Usually web site owners voluntarily rate their content in a set of predefined categories such as drug use, bad language, and violence. Web browsers can be configured to allow or block each category individually (see figure 14-2). The Internet Content Rating Association previously organised such a system, but it was discontinued in 2010. The main disadvantage of content rating systems is that they are voluntary, meaning many sites do not rate their content. As such, they are most useful in conjunction with other filtering methods.

Search engine filtering works by requiring search engines to exclude certain sites or topics from their search results page. Even if the sites themselves are not blocked, filtering them from search results pages can greatly reduce the number of visitors they receive. Page 290 describes examples of search engine filtering.

DNS poisoning is the process of altering DNS records to block access to a site. The real IP address of a target site is replaced with the IP address of an alterative page (perhaps an error message page), preventing access when a computer tries to resolve the address.

Ethical issues

Filtering—sometimes referred to as censorship—raises many ethical issues. A key issue is whether users should be informed when content they try to access is blocked, perhaps so they can request access to the content. In many cases, including the UK, attempting to access blocked content results in a standard Internet 404 'site not found' error message, rather than a message explaining that the content has been blocked. Most users would thus be unaware that their content has been blocked, instead believing a technical error had occurred.

This has the side effect of making accidental blocking of innocent sites (false positives) extremely hard to spot, because the true cause of the problem is disguised by the false error message. Accidental blocking of a businesses web site, for example, could cause serious and long term impact on the business. In these cases there needs to be a quick and accessible way of requesting a review of the blocking from the content provider to minimise the financial loss to the business.

A lack of transparency in identifying filtered content can lead to an undesirable side effect, '**mission creep**', where gradually more and more content is added to a filter, expanding its role far beyond its originally intended purpose. This could be motivated by social, political, or business interests. Without clear indications of what material is blocked, it is hard to determine whether 'mission creep' is taking place. Several early home web filters, for example, were alleged to be blocking the web pages of their commercial competitors. In mid 2011, the British High Court ordered ISP British Telecom (BT), to block access to Newzbin—a site well known for collecting links to pirat-

---

Exercise 14-1
TOK Link

Internet filtering is usually done to prevent 'harmful content' being accessed by users. What types of material, if any, would you consider so harmful that users should not be allowed to create it or view it online?

Exercise 14-2
TOK Link

How might filtering of the Internet—either overtly or covertly—affect our understanding of information and the world around us? How could we know if our Internet access was filtered?

ed material (though hosting none itself) - using technology originally designed to block illegal child abuse images[1]. After this success, media companies such as the MPAA quickly demanded blocking of access to other sites such as the notorious BitTorrent site *The Pirate Bay* (see page 275). The danger here is that systems designed to prevent access to illegal content (child abuse images) is slowly being used to block material which may not be illegal itself.

However, perhaps the greatest ethical issue related to content filtering is determining which content is appropriate and which is inappropriate. **Cultural diversity** plays a key role here because ideas about what constitutes 'appropriate' and 'inappropriate' are likely to vary greatly from person to person, based on their upbringing, religion, culture, and personal beliefs. Overzealous blocking risks preventing many people accessing content which is acceptable to them, while relaxed filtering risks exposing people to potentially harmful content. A balance must be struck when content is considered inappropriate for some users—for example children—but acceptable for adults. Preventing children from accessing pornography, for example, is commonly accepted as a good idea, yet pornography is generally legal for adults to view.

E-Passports

E-passports use RFID technology in an attempt to improve security and reduce the chances of passport forgery. A microchip embedded in the passport stores data including an image of the passport holder and, in some countries, biometric data—iris, fingerprints, or face information. Using RFID, passport data is sent to customs and border control staff wirelessly. The process of reading an e-passport is complicated by the need to maintain security of the transmitted data, the need to verify the passport's integrity, and the desire to prevent unauthorised readers accessing passport data. The steps followed are:

Authenticate the RFID reader: to ensure that an unauthorised person is not trying to access the passport, the reader authenticates itself using digital certificates (see page 108). This is known as Extended Access Control (EAC). EAC is also used to ensure the chip is not a clone—i.e. an exact, unaltered copy of another genuine passport chip. EAC is not used by all countries.

Establish a secure connection: to prevent eavesdropping by any nearby unauthorised readers, the data is encrypted before being sent from the passport to the authorised reader. This is known as Basic Access Control (BAC).

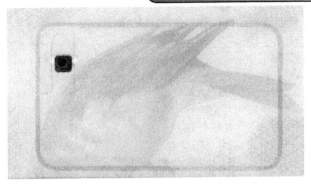

Figure 14-3 Passport RFID chip—the chip is the black square and the surrounding wire is the antenna.

Verify the integrity of the chip: To ensure that the data contained on the passport's chip has not been changed since it was issued (for example, by replacing the chip with another chip, or by changing the digital photo), the data on the chip is signed with a digital signature. This signature is checked when the data is read. This is known as Passive Authentication (PA).

Authenticate the passport holder: a biometric template is generated from the digital image stored on the passport's chip. A photograph of the passport holder is taken at the customs point, and a biometric template from this image is compared to that stored on the chip (see page 92).

Criticisms

A number of criticisms have been levelled at e-passports, particularly by privacy and security advocates. A key concern is the security of the data held on the passports' chips, especially the biometric data. Researchers have demonstrated attacks against the e-passport systems including successfully reading a passport from an unauthorised reader; cloning a passport by covertly reading its data from a distance; and using an altered passport chip without detection. Many of these attacks rely on the fact that not all countries implement the security and authentication methods detailed above.

Stealing Fingerprints

In 2008, to highlight security concerns over the use of biometric data in passports, the German hacker group the Chaos Computer Club (CCC) acquired and published a copy of the then Home Secretary Wolfgang Schäuble's fingerprints. They also attached a plastic film copy of the fingerprint to issues of their magazine, allowing users to imitate Schäuble's fingerprint by attaching it to their fingers. Although the fingerprint was not acquired through a computer related security breach, the CCC said they wanted to highlight the ease with which fingerprint data can be stolen, and the difficulty of retrieving data once it has been made public[19].

Political Campaigning

Barack Obama's campaign for the 2008 US presidential election quickly became famous as an example of a politician leveraging the power of the Internet in general, and social media in particular, to communicate with voters. Obama's campaign was carefully crafted to make use of all the latest technologies available to the electorate:

- A central campaign web site provided core features such as information on volunteering and donating to the campaign (www.barackobama.com).
- Facebook was used to connect with potential voters – especially the younger part of the electorate. Groups supporting Obama as well as the official Obama page were used as platforms to discuss issues and—critically—get feedback from the electorate.
- YouTube was used to publish key interviews and debates, making the content available long after the television broadcasts had finished. As with Facebook, these videos also provided a platform for feedback from viewers.
- Twitter and blogs were used to provide up to the minute information on the campaign's progress

As the number of Internet users has increased, many political groups have attempted to harness technologies such as **RSS**, **email**, and **web sites** to communicate their messages and policies, obtain support, and secure funding. Users of **social networks**, **blogs** and **microblogs** are able to give feedback to politicians about their policies via the comment or posting features. Obama's use of social media was neither new nor unique – in fact his opponents, Hilary Clinton and John McCain, both made use of these same technologies during the election campaign. What made the Obama campaign stand out however, is the *way* in which technology was used: rather than treating social media as an extension to traditional print and news media, it was used to harness feedback from its fans and members – as Obama put it 'starting a conversation'.

These technologies bring numerous advantages for political candidates and the electorate alike:

- Direct connections can be made with millions of potential voters through 'friendships', 'likes' and group memberships
- Voters can use push technologies like RSS to get customised updates on topics which interest them
- Campaign information and updates can be created and automatically sent on a much wider range of topics than is possible with traditional media, each specialised to a particular interest group
- Campaign information can be sent at a much lower cost than traditional snail-mail
- Social media can gain support from younger voters or first time voters, who may be reluctant to become involved in politics

Figure 14-4 Online campaigning is a powerful tool

This use of social media helped gather the contact details of millions of supporters: rather than relying on the old direct snail-mail campaigning of the past, the election campaign could send instant updates, messages, and requests for opinions directly to millions of people – and at minimal cost. Obama was the first presidential candidate to decline the $85 million public fund available to him, instead raising $747 million through his campaign. $659 million came from individual donations, with $246 million (37%) being **micro-payments** of $200 or less – many of them made through the campaign web site[2].

In April 2011, Obama launched his re-election campaign for the 2012 elections not from the White House, but on Twitter and via email, with a link to a YouTube video.

Electronic voting

Technology has also been heavily used in the electoral process in modern elections. Using **electronic voting systems**, voters travel to a voting station as usual, where their vote is cast and counted using a computerised system. In contrast, **online voting** or **Internet voting** involves casting a vote from somewhere other than an election station – often the voter's home – using an Internet connected computer.

In **optical scanning electronic voting systems**, voters travel to a voting station, authenticate themselves to election staff as usual, and cast their vote on a paper ballot slip. A computerised system uses **OMR** (see page 24) technology to assist in counting the ballot slips. Election staff may count ballots that the machine cannot read, or they may be counted as invalid votes if they are unclear or incorrectly completed. Optical scanning systems are the simplest type of e-voting system.

Direct Recording Electronic (DRE) voting machines dispense with paper ballot slips, and instead present candidate choices on a screen, allowing the voter to cast their vote using a touch screen or other input device. These votes are then saved in the DRE machine's memory and counted later. Votes from DRE machines in different areas are totalled to produce the final result.

Internet voting systems

A **Public Network Direct Recording Electronic system (PNDRE)** allows voters to cast a vote from any Internet connected device. Voters visit an election web site and

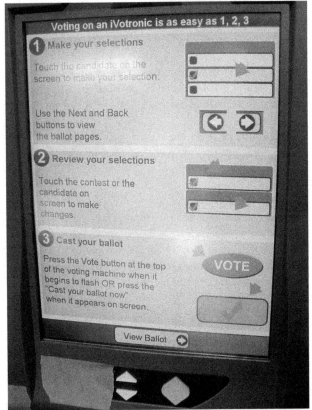

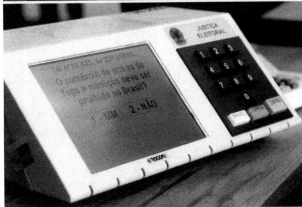

Figure 14-5 Electronic voting machines

authenticate themselves using a variety of methods. Voters in Estonia, for example, use their national identity smart cards along with a smart card reader connected to their computer. Other systems include receiving authentication details through snail mail and using these to access the voting system. Once a vote is cast, it is transmitted to a central location where it is counted.

Exercise 14-3

Imagine that you are managing a campaign for a presidential candidate. **Explain** which technologies you would choose to use on your campaign. Which technologies would you decide not to use? Why? [10 marks]

Whichever method of voting is used, there are three primary concerns which must be addressed in any voting system, paper or electronic:

Secrecy / security: most countries have secret voting rules, meaning it must not be possible to determine for whom any individual has voted.

Authenticity of the voter: ensuring that the voter is eligible to vote, and that the voter really is who they claim to be.

Integrity of the results: votes must not be added, removed, or changed, and the final results must be correct. The votes must be safe from deliberate or accidental alteration, and it must also be possible to verify this later if, for example, a recount is required. This requires a record of the votes without breaking the ideal of secret voting.

Advantages

E-voting and online voting allow quicker and hopefully more accurate counting of votes. They can also provide greater **equality of access** – for example, incorporating accessibility features for disabled users (see page 29), or producing ballot slips in different languages. Online voting lets voters vote from home, hopefully increasing voter turn-out. Computer systems can also warn voters of possible errors such as voting for too many or too few candidates, reducing the number of spoilt votes.

Risks

Although electronic vote counting appears easy, it is actually fraught with potential problems and unique challenges related to the integrity and reliability of the results. Significantly, most electronic voting machines are **black boxes** – that is, an input is made but there is no way of verifying how the machine processes it to produce an output. For example, a vote may be cast for one candidate

Comparison of Voting Methods

Risk	Paper Voting	Electronic Voting	Online Voting
Integrity: alteration of votes after they have been cast	Alteration of paper ballots should be detectable.	DRE machines are 'black boxes' – it is not clear that votes are counted. No way to verify voting later.	Similar issues to e-voting
Integrity: counting votes incorrectly – deliberately or accidentally	Miscounting is possible. Recounts can be used to verify the totals. Counting and recounting can be watched by independent observers.	Accidental miscounting shouldn't happen if software is correct. Maliciously altered software could ignore certain votes. No way to verify voting later without a paper trail.	Similar issues to e-voting
Integrity: ignoring some votes	Possible, if election staff tamper with or destroy voting slips—but difficult as they are kept securely stored.	There is evidence that votes can be automatically discarded based on demographics such as race or religion.	Similar issues to e-voting
Privacy and authenticity: ensuring that the voter is not forced to vote for a certain person	Private voting booths allow privacy.	Private voting booths allow privacy but the voter's identity must not be recorded by the machine.	Voter intimidation becomes easier: somebody could be sitting next to the voter physically forcing them to vote a certain way.
Authenticity: making sure the voter really is the person they say they are	Identification is checked by election staff.	Identification is checked by election staff.	Slightly more difficult, but official identification cards, plus biometrics, could be used to verify identity.

Figure 14-6 Voting risks

but actually counted for a different candidate (or even just ignored), and there may be no way to verify this – even if the on-screen output suggests that the vote was counted correctly. This is particularly concerning when voting machines produce no physical receipt of the vote, meaning recounts cannot be performed. Although the total votes may correspond to the total number of voters, without a receipt of the vote there is no way of proving that each vote was counted correctly.

Such counting errors could occur accidentally, due to software or hardware problems, or be the result of a malicious user interfering with the voting machine's software. US researchers found a variety of flaws in voting machine software, the physical security of voting machines, and the networking systems which connect the machines to the central server, allowing the voting software and stored votes to be surreptitiously altered[3]. The researchers claimed that many of the flaws allowed them to make untraceable alterations to the voting machines, jeopardising the integrity of elections. Table 14-6 considers typical problems in traditional and electronic voting systems.

Software and hardware errors can also affect e-voting machines. In 2004 in the US, an unknown number of votes cast using a Premier voting machine were dropped; in 2008 a similar problem occurred in Ohio, with 1000 votes being ignored. The problem was a result of misconfiguration of the touch screen used to cast votes - which could have been accidental or deliberate[4]. In 2008 a poorly designed user interface was blamed for the loss of 232 votes in a Finnish election, as voters left the machine before confirming their selection.

In 2002 election officials in New Mexico discovered their voting machines could only register a maximum of 36,000 votes per election - a problem which resulted in the loss of 12,000 votes. A software fixed was later applied[4].

Solutions

Voter Verified Paper Audit Trails (VVPAT), also called paper audit trails, can be used to verify that votes have been correctly cast. A paper copy of the vote is produced and this is shown to the voter to verify their choice, then kept in a locked ballot box like a traditional vote. Paper votes can be counted and compared to the results of the electronic voting machine. Not all paper votes need to be counted to complete the verification process, and the mere presence of a audit trail could discourage those intending to commit election fraud.

Software verification is also important. Independent verification of voting software, performed by qualified software verification companies, could be used to ensure it functions as required. Some election groups are pushing for **open source** voting systems, which would enable anybody, including members of the public, to verify the software for themselves. In order to ensure the software is not altered after verification it would need to be digitally signed, with the digital signature checked on the election day. In 2001, Australian election officials trialled such a system, running e-voting machines in state elections and posting the source code on the Internet. The system was successful, and an academic at the Australian National University even spotted and reported a software bug in the system, helping to improve the software[5].

> **Common Mistake**
> A common mistake is to think that because anyone can edit open source software, it represents a security risk. This is wrong. In fact, in cases such as e-voting, open source software provides a great benefit because it allows anybody to verify that the software works correctly. There is no security risk to the voting machine because even if a malicious user edited the source code, they would still need to install the new (malicious) software on the voting machine—not an easy task.

Electronic voting in Action

Electronic voting is used partially in several countries including Belgium, Germany, and the United Kingdom, while Brazil has exclusively used 400,000 electronic voting machines since 2000[15]. The US purchased hundreds of electronic voting machines after the controversial 2000 presidential election and the Help America Vote Act (HAVA) which followed it. However, security, reliability, and integrity concerns have plagued the machines, with certain models being decertified in Florida, and other states now require Voter Verified Paper Audit Trails.

Online voting has seen a slower adoption rate but has been used in Switzerland, Canada, and the United States for referendums and election primaries, while Australia and France have successfully trialled Internet voting systems for citizens residing overseas (for example, military personnel), replacing the previous system of postal ballots[16]. In 2005 Estonia became the first country to allow online voting in nationwide local elections, with 9,317 people – 1% of the electorate – choosing to vote in this way[17]. Two years later online voting was allowed in national presidential elections for the first time anywhere.

Online Government

Once elected, many governments now use the Internet to provide citizens with access to advice, services, and information about government operations. The Internet allows access to a much wider range of information than would be possible with paper based documents, gives 24 hour access to government services, and means information can be updated more readily. Media-rich **government**

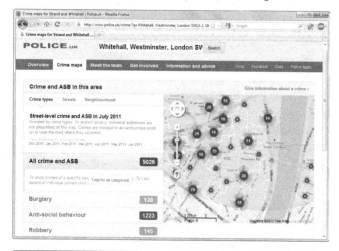

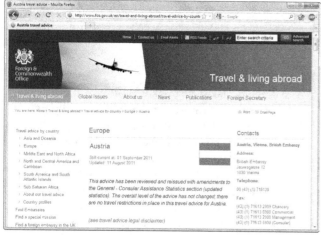

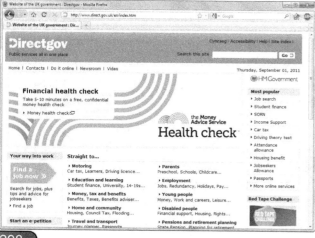

information sites offer advice on topics ranging from health to tax and student finance.

Online crime statistics break down crimes by date, location, and type, allowing citizens to compare their neighbourhoods with others, while some sites, particularly in the US, go further and even show the addresses and photographs of registered sex offenders – a move which causes concern amongst some privacy advocates.

Other less controversial information sites offer detailed advice on tax, benefits, insurance, and job issues in detail, reducing the number of staff needed to take enquiries over the telephone or in person, speeding up the process of accessing data, and ensuring citizens have access to all pertinent information.

The nature of the web means government **travel advice sites** can contain up-to-the-minute safety information, ensuring citizens are always fully aware of travel news. This is particularly important in situations where advice may change rapidly, such as during natural disasters, disease outbreaks, or terrorist attacks.

Government services can also be offered online, including voter registration and applications for driver's licences and passports, which helps reduce paper consumption and speed up processing time.

Many governments have tourism ministries which manage **travel portal sites**, designed to promote tourism within the country and provide links to a range of information, activities, and accommodation options.

Open governance web sites help hold politicians accountable and promote transparency in government by providing large amounts of data on day to day operations, and collaborating with citizens to ensure effective governance. For example, transparency can be improved by providing details of government contracts, the expense claims of ministers, or how frequently ministers have attended or voted in parliament. Some governments provide data on how tax revenue is spent, including the amount spend on operational costs (see *Open Government in Action*, opposite).

To encourage collaboration, forums, email contacts, or 'Report' buttons provide an opportunity to discuss issues and report instances of poor governance. The UK govern-

Figure 14-7 Online crime statistics (top); government travel advice for citizens (middle); government information site with information on tax, finance, transport, employment, and education (bottom)

Open Government in Action

Open government, supported and enabled by IT, was one of Barack Obama's key policies when he took office as US President in 2009. A number of web sites underpin this policy:

- The main Open Government Initiative site presents background information about open government and the progress of governmental policies (www.whitehouse.gov/open).

- The Government Dashboard keeps track of the progress made by individual government departments in meeting their goals and targets (www.whitehouse.gov/open/around).

- A variety of blogs operated by different government departments or stakeholders allow visitors to access information on topics which interest them personally. Blogs include the Council on Women and Girls, the Council on Environmental Quality, and the Council of Economic Advisers (www.whitehouse.gov/blog).

- Recovery.gov charts the progress of the government in implementing the 2009 Recovery Act, designed to stimulate economic growth. The web site provides information on how money is being spent, displays maps of local projects to stimulate growth, and allows citizens to report suspected governmental fraud, waste, or abuse (www.recovery.gov).

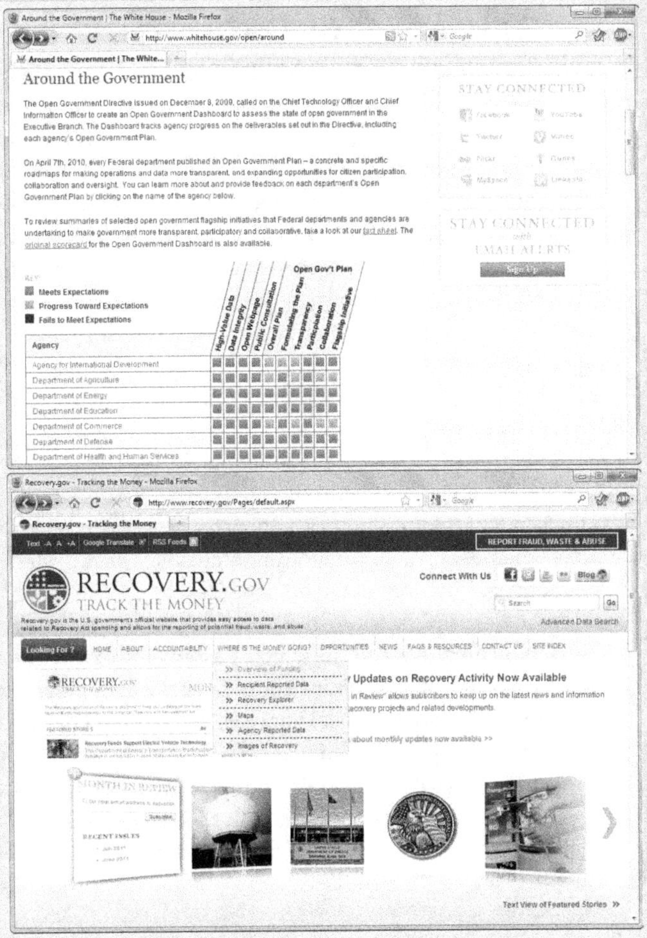

Figure 14-8 Open government sites help achieve transparency

ment even has an **e-petitions** web site, allowing citizens to create digital petitions on any subject and make it available for others to sign, with petitions attracting at least 100,000 signatures being tabled for discussion in Parliament. As of September 2011, the top e-petition on the site was 'Convicted London rioters should loose [sic] all benefits' with 221,581 signatures, followed by a call for 'Full disclosure of all government documents relating to 1989 Hillsborough disaster' with 137,350 signatures. Other e-petitions include a call for the return of the death penalty, campaigns against planned expenditure cuts, and a call to make financial education a mandatory part of the English school curriculum[6].

Challenges

Equality of access is essential in the provision of government information and services: if citizens lack such access, they are effectively no longer being represented. IT can both increase this level of access, and potentially decrease it. By providing government services online, expenditure on offline, face-to-face services may be reduced, which could have a serious effect on those who do not have Internet access, or are unable to use a computer. It is also important to ensure information is available to disabled users, which might mean providing documents in large print or alternative formats. The basic design and layout of web sites also needs to be compatible with the hardware and software commonly used by disabled users (see page 29).

Authenticity of visitors is not a concern for advice or information sites, but is a key challenge for those which provide governmental services. To add a signature to an e-petition, only a postcode (zip code) and a name is required. For other services, the challenge is greater. Data such as National Insurance or Social Security numbers can be used, along with personal details such as dates of birth—but identity theft can make these methods vulnerable too. Specialised cards, such as National Identity Cards or voting cards can help, especially if they must be physically present to use the site (for example, by using a card reader attached to the computer). Biometrics is also another possible solution, but raises concerns about the privacy of data in government databases.

Government Databases

Government databases are the subject of great debate in many modern societies. Depending on the country, medical records, telephone and Internet records, vehicle movements, fingerprints, and travel details may all be recorded for extended periods of time in vast databases. It is often argued that such databases are necessary to improve government services, enhance national security, and prevent crime—while opponents frequently cite concerns over security, privacy, integrity, and increased surveillance.

Medical databases, sometimes called online medical records, store details of a patient's medical history and treatment. They can be made available to a wide range of medical staff to facilitate effective treatment. As with any sensitive data, security and privacy are prime concerns when dealing with medical databases. These systems are covered in more detail on page 258.

Transport systems in which passengers pay with smart cards are able to store complex data about passengers and their movements. Examples include the London Oyster Card system and various European public bicycle sharing systems. Such databases allow transport planners to view statistics about most frequented routes and enable them to better plan services, but raise the possibly of privacy concerns if personally identifiable information is kept.

In the UK, details are kept of almost every car journey made. An extensive network of roadside **Closed Circuit Television (CCTV)** cameras fitted with **Automatic Number Plate Recognition** (ANPR) systems use optical character recognition techniques (see page 24) to read vehicle number plates. These systems were originally used in

Figure 14-9 Bike rental scheme which users access using smart cards. User and journey details are usually recorded

> **Key Point**
> Whenever discussing databases, the most important issues are almost always **security**, **privacy**, and **integrity** of the data.

London to monitor vehicles inside the congestion zone, but their use has spread nationwide. Now most major roads are covered by the cameras. Vehicle and journey details captured by the cameras are stored in a central database for 5 years[7]. Additionally, the video feeds from the associated CCTV cameras are available to the police in real time, effectively allowing them to locate and track any vehicle at any time.

Other **police databases** in use in various countries hold personal details including names and addresses, identifying features, vehicle records, and details of stolen property. These databases can be checked by police officers when stopping suspects, to aid identification, check history, or check for any outstanding warrants. Often these checks are performed from mobile computers, either in police vehicles or handheld devices carried by officers.

Police databases are also used for the background checks required by some professions—for example, teachers and lawyers in most countries are required to have a clean police record, which is checked before employment.

Recently there has been a move to store both fingerprint and **DNA data** in police databases—a practice currently used in countries including the UK, the US, France, Germany, and Norway. DNA databases contain both samples taken directly from arrested suspects and samples taken from crime scenes. In some cases this has allowed perpetrators of crimes to be caught years later when their DNA was taken during an arrest for another offence.

However, the practice of storing DNA data has been questioned, especially in the UK and some US states, where DNA samples are taken from everybody arrested. In the UK, an individual's record (including DNA data) is kept for at least 6 years, even if they are released without charge. As of 2009 the UK's National DNA Database held 4.5 million records, including those of 850,000 individuals never convicted of a crime, plus 150,000 children under 18[8].

Schools are also increasingly taking fingerprint samples from their students, often to replace traditional student identification cards. Sometimes this has even been done without parental permission. While fingerprints prevent a host of problems, including lost cards and problems related to students carrying cash, privacy and security issues are still present. This is especially relevant since a biometric data is irrevocable if lost or stolen.

Telephone call databases are kept by most telecoms companies. These databases record the time of calls, the caller and the call recipient numbers, and the length of the call, but do not record the call itself (among other reasons, because of the storage requirements). If calls are made to or from a mobile phone, the location of that phone, as determined by its position relative to mobile phone masts, may also be recorded.

Concerns

Key concerns about government databases often involve the size of the databases, the length of time for which data is kept, and the intended use of the data. Databases often suffer from 'mission creep' - where their purpose rapidly expands from the original intentions. The British Police National Computer, for example, started in 1976 with records of stolen vehicles, but now contains millions of personal records (including fingerprint and DNA data) and records for each of the 48 million drivers in the UK. Although the Data Protection Act provides regulation regarding data use and retention, it makes exceptions for cases where national security is concerned.

Data matching and data mining techniques, discussed on page 158, are also often applied to government databases, and this raises further concerns about secondary use of data.

Security is also a concern. A number of high profile data releases—including the loss of 25 million data records by the British Revenue and Customs—highlight the risks of storing large amounts of data in a single database (see page 17). Even with good security measures, the large number of potential users for these centralised databases significantly increases the risk of data loss.

Failed Database Initiatives

The following government databases have all been scrapped over concerns about information security, privacy rights, or cost.

ContactPoint: A UK initiative to include the names and addresses of every child and vulnerable young adult in England - up to 11 million records. The database was created in response to the alleged failure of social services to prevent the abuse and death of a child in England in 2000, and cost £224 million. Its aim was to improve communication between the police, social services, and health workers, though its creation was controversial. The database was shut down in late 2010 after campaigning by civil liberties groups and fears that the database may be breaking European Convention on Human Rights[18].

Communication 'super database': plans for a database of all email, Internet communication, and telephone calls in the UK were scrapped in 2010. The law would have required Internet Service Providers and telecommunications companies to hold onto the communication data—but not the actual call content—of their customers for up to a year. Up to £2 billion was spent on the scheme before it was scrapped[25].

National Patients' Record Database: the 'spine' of the UK's National Programme for IT has been plagued with problems, project delays, and unpopularity since its inception. The requirements and scope of the system have slowly been changed as the project has been gradually scrapped. See page 316 for more details.

British National Identity Register: A database designed for use with the British National Identity Card, which would be legally required for all citizens. The database was designed to reduce terrorism by improving the verification of identities. The system was partially rolled out in 2006 but was extremely unpopular and was abandoned in 2010. Along with it, plans for a new generation of e-passport with additional biometric features (see page 293) and a corresponding database were also scrapped.

Military use of IT

Computer training software allows military units to practise a large variety of situations without risking the safety of soldiers or incurring great expense. With the appropriate software, almost any location, any enemy, and any situation can be recreated digitally, allowing soldiers to perfect their tactics and hone their skills.

Large, expensive **simulators** which recreate an aircraft cockpit or a ship's bridge are often used to train pilots and naval personnel (see page 180), but even infantry soldiers can benefit from technologically enhanced training systems. Some of these systems, like the **virtual environments** used at the US Army's Non-Commissioned Officers' Academy's (NCOA) may look like computer games, but they are highly detailed, multiuser, networked systems featuring realistic terrain and missions based on real military operations (see figure 14-10b). They give officers and squads the chance to practise giving and following orders, and obtain valuable practical experience of the theories they have learnt in the classroom.

Virtual reality, such as the Future Immersive Training Environment (FITE) systems, use **virtual reality headsets** or goggles to place a 'wrap around' image close to the soldiers' eyes, removing their view of the world around them and thus increasing the immersion of the experience. In these systems soldiers practise missions with the equipment and weapons they will use in real combat, allowing them to familiarise themselves with the equipment's use and weight, again improving the realism (see figure 14-11a). **Tactile feedback** devices attached to a soldier's leg even cause a physical sensation when he is shot or injured.

If significant movement is required, only a large empty space is needed to allow the soldiers to move unobstructed while the virtual reality system generates the environment around them (see figure 14-11b). This is a significant advantage over a traditional physical training environment, as scenarios can be quickly reconfigured by moving virtual walls and buildings to create any desired situation.

Mixed reality systems, as their name suggests, use a combination of physical training environments and technology. A physical training environment gives soldiers a sense of the actual sights, sounds, and even the smells and explosions of the combat environment, while computer images projected on the walls show hostiles and civilians (see figure 14-11c). These images are much more versatile than cardboard targets, being able to move, react

Figure 14-10 Flight simulators are commonly used to train pilots (top); computer game style software can help soldiers practice team tactics (bottom)

to the soldiers' presence, and behave in an unpredictable manner—for example, a gunman who initially poses as a civilian, or a civilian who runs in fear. Avatars can even be configured to speak a different languages depending on the location being simulated. Heat and light sensors in the projectors detect when soldiers fire their weapons and calculate where on the projected image the shots would have landed.

A key advantage of all of these systems is the ability to record videos of 'missions', allowing soldiers to study their performances and hone their skills. Their versatility also allows them to be reconfigured to match the very latest conditions soldiers are facing on the battlefield, for example by including the latest techniques or tactics used by the enemy. Simulator operators regularly interview serving soldiers to discover the challenges they faced in combat—and then incorporate these into the simulator systems[9]. This ensures soldiers have as much realistic experience as possible—a critical factor in determining their safety when they are deployed.

In addition to training for combat roles, virtual reality systems are also used to treat soldiers diagnosed with Post Traumatic Stress Disorder (PTSD), by recreating the

Figure 14-11 Soldiers go on patrol in a virtual Humvee, using virtual reality headsets (top); Soldiers inside the Future Immersive Training Environment (FITE) using virtual reality goggles (middle); The Infantry Immersive Trainer combines physical environments with virtual civilians and hostiles (bottom)

environments and experiences they encountered while serving (see page 260). A trained psychologist uses the virtual reality system in conjunction with traditional counselling techniques.

Battlefield technology

Future warrior systems, sometimes known as **wired soldiers**, use information technology to increase an army's tactical advantage over the enemy by improving communication between individual soldiers, units, and commanders. Many countries are investing in such systems, including the US, UK, Finland, South Africa, India, and Israel.

A key component of these systems is providing tactical information to individual soldiers on the ground. This includes the location of friendly forces, known enemy positions, routes, and the locations of military objectives. This information can be displayed on a small portable computer or using on a visor mounted on the soldier's helmet. **Augmented reality** displays (see page 280) might even be used to overlay data on the surrounding environment. In some cases, screens have been connected to cameras mounted on soldier's weapons, allowing them to shoot over obstacles or around corners without exposing themselves to the enemy.

It is hoped the information provided by these technologies will reduce the danger soldiers face from entering unknown situations, as well as increasing their effectiveness. Greater situational awareness should reduce the chances of 'friendly fire' accidents by making soldiers aware of the location of other friendly forces.

Another key component of the future warrior concept is the monitoring of a soldier's condition. While GPS data is needed to provide the information discussed above, further sensors could be used to monitor a soldier's heart rate, stress levels, and general health status. This system could provide automatically alerts if, for example, a soldier stops moving for a long period of time.

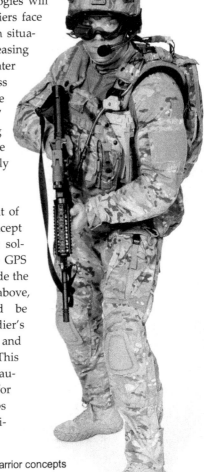

Figure 14-12 US Land Warrior equipment implements a number of future warrior concepts

The US first trialled their Land Warrior system in military exercises in the year 2000, to some success. Ergonomic design remains one of the biggest challenges of future warrior systems: equipment has to be rugged enough to withstand the harsh conditions of battle, but also light enough to be carried by a soldier who already carries many kilograms of equipment. There is also a fine line between providing a soldier with useful information and causing a dangerous obstruction to his vision.

A final consideration is that information systems like these need to update in real-time to keep up to date with the fast changing pace of battle. Lags in network communication or processing data are not acceptable, as out of date information—for example, about friendly soldiers' positions—could be worse than no information.

The ultimate goal is to incorporate future warrior systems into a vast **battlefield network**, where information about all assets, friendly or hostile, is kept and updated in real time, allowing military commanders to visualise the battlefield. Such a detailed overview would provide a clearer picture of events as they unfold, reduce miscommunication, and allow greater coordination of forces.

Smart weapons

Unmanned Aerial Vehicles (UAVs), also called **drones**, are now commonly used by US and other military forces. The most common drones, the Predator and the Reaper, can fly at up to 15 kilometres above the battlefield for more than 10 hours[12]. UAVs are often used for target tracking and surveillance, being able to discretely follow targets wherever they go. They are also equipped with weapon systems to provide air support for friendly forces, and infrared cameras to see through dust and in the dark. UAVs are expensive (over $10 million in the case of the Reaper), and have been implicated in incidents which have caused civilians casualties, but they also reduce the risk to which ground soldiers and conventional pilots are exposed.

The Reaper and Predator UAVs are remotely controlled by pilots who could be thousands of kilometres away. For Iraq-based UAVs, many pilots operate from the US, receiving real time feedback from the UAV via its video cameras, and using a joystick to move the drone and fire its weapons. The pilots work in shifts, and are often able to return to their homes and families at the end of the day.

UAVs are not only used in military conflicts. Unarmed versions of the Predator are used in the US to monitor the

Figure 14-13 Reaper UAVs are commonly deployed in Iraq and Afghanistan (top), operated by pilots thousands of miles away (bottom)

US-Mexico border for illegal immigrants and drugs smugglers. The drone's capabilities allow it to fly high enough to stay out of sight, yet still spot illegal border crossers at day or night. UAV operators then report the location to ground based border guards. A similar system is used over the Indian Ocean, where pirate attacks on shipping have become a significant problem in recent years[13].

Precision guided weapons—sometimes called **smart bombs**—use a variety of techniques including lasers, infrared cameras, and radar to guide a missile or bomb to its target with greater accuracy. Modern weapons can even use the Global Positioning System to improve accurate further.

Precision guided weapons were used in both Gulf Wars as well as Afghanistan, where it is claimed their improved accuracy reduces the need to use more powerful explosives, thus reducing the risk of collateral damage.

Military Robots

Robots (see chapter 16) are used in a variety of military roles. Robots like the BigDog are being developed to transport heavy loads and the US military is even investigating driverless vehicles for supply tasks (see page 347).

Bomb disposal robots, remotely controlled by soldiers, are a valuable tool that reduce the dangers soldiers face in this task. Similarly, smaller scout robots equipped with cameras can be used when entering unknown buildings to check for hidden enemies.

The SWORD robot is a high speed robot equipped with weapons which can be remotely controlled by soldiers, from several hundred metres away[23]. Robots are covered in more detail in chapter 16.

Cyber-terrorism and Cyber-warfare

Cyber-warfare is the use of attacks on the computer networks of an enemy in order to damage infrastructure or morale, or to spy on their systems. Cyber-warfare could be committed instead of regular warfare or as a precursor to it, giving attacking forces a tactical advantage.

Common targets of cyber attacks would be infrastructure such as power grids, water treatment plants, and emergency response systems. Damaging or disabling these could reduce a country's ability to defend itself – for example, by being unable coordinate emergency services to treat casualties, being unable to power defences, or simply by military commanders being unable to coordinate their actions.

Viruses, **Trojan horses,** or other malware can be used as part of a cyber-warfare campaign to infect and damage enemy computers. **Denial of Service (DoS)** attacks could also be used to bring networks down. Alternatively, attackers could gain access to enemy systems to monitor and copy data, possibly providing critical information about defence systems and plans. Even the Pentagon has been infected in this way (see page 98).

NASA, the US Defence Threat Reduction Agency, the Pentagon, and the US power grid system have all suffered computer intrusions in recent years [11]. The Stux-

Autonomous drones?

Artificial intelligence could eventually be built into UAVs, with AI routines supporting the human operator by determining whether its target is friendly or hostile. Once a target has been determined, the software could determine the appropriate amount of force to use, based on the results of past actions and details of the surrounding area (such as the proximity of civilian houses, schools, or hospitals). Such systems could help achieve military goals while reducing the risk of collateral damage. Of course, the idea of handing potentially life-or-death decisions to a computer algorithm raises a great number of ethical questions—not least of which is whether this is an appropriate direction in which to develop the field of AI.

net virus (see page 97) was specifically designed to target the SCADA (Supervisory Control and Data Acquisition) control systems used in industrial systems, while the US Department of Defense, Department of State, Department of Commerce, and Department of Energy lost several terabytes of information in a series of hacking attacks during 2007[11]. The source of the attacks was never made public. In November 2011 it was widely reported that computer hackers had gained access to a water treatment planet in Illinois, US, and destroyed a treatment pump by rapidly switching it on and off[24].

There is also fear that **cyber terrorism** – terrorists attacking infrastructure using the methods described above – has also risen in recent years. In 2008 the US Department of Homeland Security claimed the threat of cyber terrorism is as serious as the attacks on the World Trade Center in 2001 – the British governments have made similar claims.

Defending against cyber-attacks is extremely difficult as no computer system can be made 100% secure, and human weaknesses such as choosing a poor password or inserting an unknown flash drive into a computer can circumvent even stringent security measures. Once infected, systems can remain under foreign surveillance for extended periods—possibly years—and it can be difficult or impossible to discover which information was compromised or who the perpetrators were.

Exercise 14-4

What makes cyber-terrorism a tempting option for terrorists? **Identify** some systems which might be vulnerable, and outline the consequences of cyber-terrorism attacks on them. [4 marks]

Exercise 14-5

What solutions can be implemented to reduce the threat of cyber-terrorism. Do you think cyber terrorist attacks on a large scale are likely to become a reality? **Explain** your answer. [6 marks]

Chapter Review

Key Language

ANPR	DNA database	Internet voting	simulation
augmented reality	DNS	Internet Watch Foundation	smart weapons
battlefield network	DNS Poisoning	IP address	software verification
biometrics	DRE voting machine	keyword filter	tactile feedback
black boxes	drone	micro-payments	Unmanned Aerial Vehicle
black list	e-passport	mission creep	URL
CCTV cameras	e-petition	mixed reality	virtual environment
Children Internet Protection	electronic voting	online voting	virtual reality
Act (CIPA)	false negative	open government	virtual reality headset
content rating	false positive	optical scanning electronic	Voter Verified Paper Audit
cyber-terrorism	filter	voting system	Trails
cyber-warfare	firewall	PNDRE	weighted filter
Denial of Service attack	future warrior	precision guided weapons	white list
DMCA	GPS	RFID	wired soldiers

Exercise 14-6

Many government databases store millions of records and have thousands of authorised users. **Discuss** the additional security and privacy challenges which are created by such large databases accessed by so many users.[8 marks]

Extended Learning: WikiLeaks—Hero or Villain?

WikiLeaks—not to be confused with Wikipedia—is a site which publishes classified and secret material leaked from governments and organisations by whistle-blowers, often in violation of the law. The site uses numerous mirrors to spread its material, and uses advanced public key encryption (see page 107) to ensure the anonymity of its sources.

WikiLeaks' early leaks focused on documenting governmental corruption, including financial and police corruption in Kenya, alleged prisoner abuses at the US Camp Delta (Guantanamo Bay) detention centre, and various political leaks including then presidential nominee Sarah Palin's email account[20]. WikiLeaks leapt into the media spotlight in April 2010 when they released a classified video from a US Apache attack helicopter. The video showed a military operation in Iraq in which two innocent Reuters journalists were killed and two young children seriously wounded, and appeared to show an indiscriminate attack, contradicting the official Pentagon account of the incident. The release attracted more controversy when the source was revealed as a US Army Private, leading to his imprisonment.

Since then WikiLeaks has released thousands of government documents and cables, though many of them failed to have the impact of previous releases. Then, in September 2011 WikiLeaks published over 250,000 US government cables, many of which carried the governmental warning 'Strictly Protect' - meaning they named individuals such as informants, who would be in danger if identified. The move drew widespread condemnation, including from previous WikiLeaks supporters such as Reporters without Borders and several major European newspapers, and left many people wondering about the exact nature of WikiLeaks' mission.

Exercise 14-7

Research the materials WikiLeaks has released. **Discuss** whether it is ever justified for a web site to host or distribute documents which are secret or classified, knowing that doing so may break the law. [8 marks]

Exercise 14-8

Explain the technological developments which make it so hard for the authorities to stop or shut down sites like WikiLeaks. [4 marks]

Exercise 14-9
Internet Service Providers are often considered to be 'conduits of information': they provide customers with the means to access the Internet but do not generally interfere with that information (see page 291 for exceptions to this). There is no doubt that some of the information accessed by some customers is illegal – whether it is abusive material or illegal downloads of copyrighted films. **Discuss** whether ISPs should be held responsible for illegal activities which occur using their networks. What measures would need to be taken for ISPs to prevent such activities? [8 marks]

Exercise 14-10
Describe the measures governments could take to ensure online documents are accessible to citizens who lack access to a computer or the Internet. [4 marks]

Exercise 14-11
Consider the following web 2.0 technologies: wikis, blogs, RSS, streaming video, podcasts, mashups. **Explain** how each could be used by the government to improve communication with its citizens. [24 marks]

Exercise 14-12
Research the use of biometric data in schools, for example for registration purposes. As a student, would you be happy to submit your data for such a system? If you were a parent, would you be happy for your child's data to be held in this way? **Explain** your answer. [6 marks]

Exercise 14-13
(a) (i) Define the term *cyber-warfare*. [2 marks]

  (ii) Describe **two** technical methods which can be used to filter Internet access. [4 marks]

(b) Explain the steps involved in the process of filtering Internet access. [6 marks]

(c) Internet filtering performed by governments is usually very effective in blocking content for all citizens. To what extent is this preferable to allowing individual families and businesses to filter their own content as they wish? [8 marks]

Exercise 14-14
(a) (i) Define the term *avatar*. [2 marks]

  (ii) Distinguish *mixed reality* and *virtual reality*. [4 marks]

(b) Explain the advantages of using software simulations for training purposes. [6 marks]

(c) Discuss the integrity and reliability issues that might occur when UAVs are used. Evaluate your answer. [8 marks]

Exercise 14-15
(a) (i) Define the term *RSS*. [2 marks]

  (ii) Distinguish *online voting* and *electronic voting*. [4 marks]

(b) Explain how a user of an online voting system could be authenticated. [6 marks]

(c) Analyse the issues of security, reliability and integrity, and equality of access in relation to electronic voting and online voting. To what extent do the benefits of these methods outweigh the drawbacks? [8 marks]

References

1   Kobie, N. (2011). *BT given a fortnight to block Newzbin*. Available: http://www.pcpro.co.uk/news/370753/bt-given-a-fortnight-to-block-newzbin. Last accessed Nov 2011.

2   Federal Election Commission. (2009). *Presidential Campaign Finance*. Available: www.fec.gov/disclosurep/pnational.do. Last accessed April 2011.

3   Boyle, A. (2003). *E-Voting flaws risk ballot fraud*. Available: www.msnbc.msn.com/id/3077251/ns/politics-voting_problems/t/e-voting-flaws-risk-ballot-fraud/. Last accessed Aug 2011.

4   Zetter, K. (2010). *Report: Voting Machine Errors Highlight Urgent Need for U.S. Database*. Available: http://www.wired.com/threatlevel/2010/09/voting-machine-database/. Last accessed Nov 2010.

5   Zetter, K. (2003). *Aussies Do It Right: E-Voting*. Available: http://www.wired.com/techbiz/media/news/2003/11/61045?currentPage=2. Last accessed Nov 2011.

6   HM Government. (2011). *E-petitions – create and sign petitions online*. Available: http://epetitions.direct.gov.uk/. Last accessed Nov 2011.

7   Connor, S. (2005). *Surveillance UK: why this revolution is only the start* . Available: http://www.independent.co.uk/news/science/surveillance-uk-why-this-revolution-is-only-the-start-520396.html. Last accessed Nov 2011.

8   BBC. (2009). *Time limits on innocent DNA data* . Available: http://news.bbc.co.uk/2/hi/uk/8037042.stm. Last accessed Nov 2011.

9   Corrin, A. (2011). *Mixed reality scenarios prime recruits for combat*. Available: http://defensesystems.com/articles/2011/02/28/mixed-reality-training.aspx. Last accessed Nov 2011.

10 Shiels, M. (2009). *Spies 'infiltrate US power grid'* . Available: news.bbc.co.uk/2/hi/technology/7990997.stm. Last accessed Nov 2011.

11 CBS News. (2010). *Cyber War: Sabotaging the System*. Available: www.cbsnews.com/stories/2009/11/06/60minutes/main5555565.shtml. Last accessed Sept 2011.

12 CBS News. (2009). *Drones: America's New Air Force*. Available: http://www.cbsnews.com/stories/2009/05/08/60minutes/main5001439.shtml. Last accessed Nov 2011.

13 BBC. (2009). *Drones scour the sea for pirates*. Available: news.bbc.co.uk/2/hi/8352631.stm. Last accessed Nov 2011.

14 Rosen, J. (2008). *Google's Gatekeepers*. New York Times. Available: www.nytimes.com/2008/11/30/magazine/30google-t.html?_r=1&partner=rss&emc=rss&pagewanted=all. Last accessed Aug 2011.

15 Chu, H. (2004). *Doubts linger for Brazil's electronic voting*. Available: http://articles.baltimoresun.com/2004-10-03/news/0410030092_1_voting-machines-electronic-voting-computerized-voting. Last accessed Nov 2011.

16 New York Times. (2007). *French conservatives try online voting - Europe - International Herald Tribune*. Available: http://www.nytimes.com/2007/01/02/world/europe/02iht-france.4080939.html. Last accessed Nov 2011.

17 Associated Press. (2005). *Estonia First to Allow Online Voting Nationwide*. Available: http://www.msnbc.msn.com/id/9697336/ns/technology_and_science-tech_and_gadgets/. Last accessed Aug 2011.

18 Owen, P. (2010). *Database closure could put children at serious risk, warns charity*. Available: http://www.guardian.co.uk/society/2010/aug/06/child-database-switched-off. Last accessed Nov 2011.

19 Heise Online, The. (2008). *CCC publishes fingerprints of German Home Secretary*. Available: www.h-online.com/newsticker/news/item/CCC-publishes-fingerprints-of-German-Home-Secretary-734713.html. Last accessed April 2011.

20 Chacksfield, M. (2010). *Wikileaks: 8 biggest leaks in its history*. Available: http://www.techradar.com/news/internet/wikileaks-8-biggest-leaks-in-its-history-911493. Last accessed Nov 2011.

21 Reporters Without Borders. (2011). *Internet*. Available: http://en.rsf.org/internet.html. Last accessed Nov 2011.

22 OpenNet Initiative. (2011). *Global Internet Filtering*. Available: http://opennet.net/. Last accessed Nov 2011.

23 Popular Mechanics. (2009). *The Inside Story of the SWORDS Armed Robot*. Available: http://www.popularmechanics.com/technology/gadgets/4258963. Last accessed Nov 2011.

24 BBC. (2011). *Hackers 'hit' US water treatment systems*. Available: www.bbc.co.uk/news/technology-15817335. Accessed Nov 2011.

25 King, L. (2010). *Government scraps email 'super database'*. Available: http://www.computerworlduk.com/news/it-business/14495/government-scraps-email-super-database/. Last accessed Nov 2011.

Chapter 15
IT Systems
in Organisations

Objectives

1. Explain the challenges associated with IT project development
2. Explain the steps of the System Development Life Cycle (SDLC)
3. Explain the methods used to manage IT projects
4. Construct PERT and Gantt charts to model a project's schedule
5. Construct ERD and DFD diagrams to model an IT system
6. Discuss appropriate project management techniques and decisions

IT Systems in Organisations

As demonstrated throughout the ITGS course, organisations and individuals in all areas of society rely heavily on information technology. Yet designing, developing, installing, and changing over to new IT systems is still an area that causes great problems for many organisations, and often results in failure and wasted money. This chapter examines the steps involved in analysing, designing, developing, using, and supporting IT systems effectively in organisations.

Types of Development

When an organisation decides to investigate a new IT project, it can choose from two fundamental types of software to meet its needs: off-the-shelf software and custom / bespoke software. **Off-the-shelf software**, as its name suggests, is software that is widely available for general purchase from software vendors. This might be general application software used by many types of organisations, such as office software suites, or it may be more specialised to a particular type of business (for example, school information management systems).

Custom / bespoke software is created specifically for a single organisation. Usually the organisation hires a software development company, but it may also have its own software developers in house. The developers analyse the organisation's needs and design software specifically to meet them.

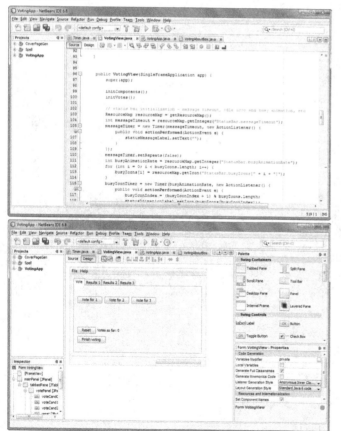

Figure 15-1 An Integrated Development Environment (IDE) offers programmers many tools to help them create software

Businesses might employ bespoke software if it is more tailored to their needs than off-the-shelf software packages. At the larger end of the scale, corporations like NASA or Boeing contract software developers to create their software (it is obviously very difficult to walk into a shop and buy a shuttle control program off-the-shelf!).

Development Tools

Software developers use a variety of programs to create new software. A text editor is used to enter the program's **source code**, a compiler translates the source code into machine code, and debugging tools to help find and fix errors in the program they are creating. Often these tools are packaged together in an **Integrated Development Environment** (IDE). Many IDEs also offer tools to create graphical user interfaces for programs by dragging and dropping components on the screen.

Legacy systems

A **legacy system** is a computer system that is no longer available for purchase or is no longer supported by the manufacturer. A legacy system might be just a few years old, or it could be decades old. Some legacy systems may operate on (and even require), certain very old hardware which is no longer available. Others may only run on older operating systems and not be compatible with modern versions. Sometimes the manufacturer of a legacy system no longer exists, and in other cases the manufacturer has dropped support in favour of more recent products. This usually means updates and security fixes will not be available for the system, which can be a significant problem for organisations.

Often organisations continue to use legacy systems because they are essential to their operation and there is no easily available replacement. Replacing a legacy system with a new one may be cost prohibitive, and with very old software, it may be extremely difficult to convert data from a legacy system to a new format. This might be made harder by a lack of knowledge of the system: the original designers of the system may have retired, documentation may be absent, or undocumented changes may have been made since the original installation.

If the system was written in a older programming language, it can be very difficult or expensive to find soft-

Off the Shelf Software

Advantages	Disadvantages
There are many more users, meaning there is usually more support available in terms of documentation, books, and user groups.	Off-the-shelf software is a 'one size fits all' solution: it might not do everything the organisation wants it to do, and it might include many features which they pay for but don't need or use.
Data and file compatibility with other systems (including customers' and partners' systems) may be greater because the software is widespread.	Because the software vendor has thousands and thousands of customers, a single organisation is not very important to them in the grand scheme of things. This means that if they want a change or a new feature, they are very unlikely to get it unless it is in great demand by many users.
The cost is usually lower.	
Installation may be easier.	
The software vendor will have a large 'knowledge base' of common errors and their solutions.	
Software has been extensively tested (both by the vendor and by thousands of users!). This reduces the number of serious bugs the software contains.	

Custom / Bespoke Software

Advantages	Disadvantages
The software can be customised to the organisation's precise needs, including features and the user interface.	Selecting a competent software developer is difficult, especially for managers who may not have software development experience.
Changes or additional features can usually be added later on request.	The price is significantly higher than off-the-shelf software.
Having software developed to your precise needs can give a great competitive advantage.	Specifying precise requirements for projects, especially large projects, is difficult and error-prone.
	Development can take a long time.
	If the software developer does not provide the source code to the project, you are locked-in to using them for help and support.
	If the software developer's business fails, you are left completely without help, support, or upgrades (this is true for off-the-shelf software companies too, but bespoke developers are often to be smaller operations, and more vulnerable to market forces)

ware developers who have the necessary skills to understand the program's source code—or the source code may just be unavailable.

Finally, if a system works, an organisation may not want to replace it. This is especially true if the only problem with the legacy system is its age (i.e. it performs all the desired functions). In these cases it is quite common to develop a new user interface which interacts with the legacy system 'behind the scenes' —such as a web based interface to replace a text-only command line interface.

Nevertheless, legacy systems cause problems for organisations. Older hardware and older operating systems require personnel with rare skills to support them, and these people are often more expensive to hire. A 2011 report suggested that the US government spent 46% of its annual \$36 billion IT budget on maintaining legacy systems[1].

Emulation and Virtual Machines

One solution to using legacy systems in a modern environment is to employ a **virtual machine (VM)**, which creates a virtual 'computer' running inside a window, like a regular application program. This virtual computer is independent of the host computer and can be paused, shut down, restarted, and modified at will. It runs its own operating system and software, independent of the host computer. Virtual machine software typically allows configuration of the virtual computer's hardware, including the amount of RAM and the size of the hard disk. Often a single large file is used to represent the 'hard disk' of the

virtual computer. Virtual machines are useful for running legacy applications that need older operating systems (for example, an application program requiring Windows 3.1 could run in a virtual machine running Windows 3.1 on a host running Windows 7 or Linux.

If the legacy system requires hardware which is significantly different from the host computer (for example, it requires a different processor or mainframe hardware), a virtual machine may not be enough, and a program called an **emulator** may be needed. An emulator is a software recreation of an entire system's hardware including its processor and associated hardware. Like a virtual machine, an emulator allows the user to run the emulated system in a window inside an existing operating system, although there may be a performance reduction.

Legacy Systems
Year 2000 problem

The 'Year 2000 problem' or 'millennium bug', described on page 62 highlighted problems with legacy systems which failed due to changing requirements (in this case, date calculations occurring over the end of a century).

Comair Scheduling System

In December 2004 US regional airline Comair had to cancel all 1,160 of its flights, involving 30,000 passengers, due to record snow levels in the United States. When Comair staff tried to reschedule the flights after the weather improved, they were hit by a problem in their software, which had been programmed to only accept a certain number of changes to flights each month. Cancelling and then rescheduling over 1,100 flights exceeded that limit, and the software prevented staff from making additional changes.

The flight scheduling system involved was a legacy system created in 1986. It was written in FORTRAN and ran on a different hardware and operating system platform from all of Comair's other systems (IBM AIX rather than HP Unix). Nobody in Comair knew of the limit on the number of flight changes per month. This can be attributed partially to the fact that nobody at Comair had experience with the FORTRAN programming language, and partially because when the system was created in 1986, Comair was a much smaller company – so making such a large number of flight changes in one month was unthinkable. Comair's problem with the scheduling software is estimated to have cost it \$20 million and led to the replacement of its CEO. In many ways the Comair problem was similar to the Year 2000 problem – programmers created systems which originally worked as intended, but later failed because of changing requirements.[8]

TOPS Railway System

TOPS (Total Operations Processing System) was a system for managing railway stock and locomotives, developed by US company Southern Pacific Railroad in the early 1960s. TOPS was advanced for its time, computerising all paper records for each item of stock and allowing the records to be viewed by users with computer terminals across the country. The system was purchased and used by Canadian and British railway companies during the 1960s.

Like many systems of its time, TOPS was written in a programming language which is no longer used – in this case, a subset of the assembly language used by IBM mainframes. Finding programmers fluent in this language is not easy. Additionally, TOPS has been modified over time by its different users, and many of these changes have not been documented. The difficulty of modifying (or even understanding!) the existing TOPS code, the need for the system to be online 100% of the time, and the fact that TOPS performs its desired functions well, have contributed to it still being in use today. In some cases new user interfaces have been written to provide a more user friendly 'front end' than the original TOPS text-only display, but the underlying data is still managed by TOPS.[9]

System development lifecycle

The **System Development Life-cycle** (SDLC) refers to the stages involved in creating an IT system – from the moment it is first suggested, to its delivery to the customer, and – critically – as it is maintained through the rest of its life (maintenance is estimated to make up 75% of a software project's cost[10]). The SDLC is critical in ensuring an appropriate system is developed, and that it meets the client's needs in terms of features, usability, cost, and time, and avoids being one of the many projects which fail (see page 316).

Various sources quote slightly different stages to the SDLC, using different names or merging certain stages together, but the key stages, which will be covered in more detail later in this chapter, are:

Analysis: An investigation of the current system (manual or computer), the needs of the client, and the possibility of creating a solution. After this stage it may be decided to progress with creating a new system, or that the benefits do not justify the costs.

Design: the planning of a solution to meet the needs of the client which were identified in the analysis.

Development (also called Implementation): the creation (programming) of a system, following the design previously created.

Testing: ensuring that the system functions correctly, as determined by the requirements generated during the analysis stage.

Installation (also called Delivery): installing the software and any necessary hardware, usually at the client's organisation. This may also involve removing the old system and transferring any required data from it to the new system. Training is also required to help users understand the new system.

Maintenance: updates and changes made to a system to fix bugs, improve performance, or add new features. In large systems which are used for many years, maintenance can form a large part of the project's total costs.

Analysis Stage

The analysis stage of the SDLC involves investigating the current system (be it manual or computerised), determining the organisation's requirements for a new system, investigating possible solutions, determining which (if any) are feasible, and choosing the most appropriate. To be successful, the analysis must involve all key stakeholders including the **client** (the person or organisation commissioning the project) and the **end users** (the people who will use the system when it is complete) - these may be the same people. The key components of analysis are:

Determining **project goals**. The aim of project, and also its limitations (its **scope**) must be carefully defined during this phase. When a proposed project will work as part of a larger system (whether manual or computerised), it is important to know where the responsibility of each component starts and ends.

This stage is critical because a project with poorly defined goals is unlikely to be successful—the developed system may either solve a slightly different set of problems, or try to solve problems which are outside the project scope.

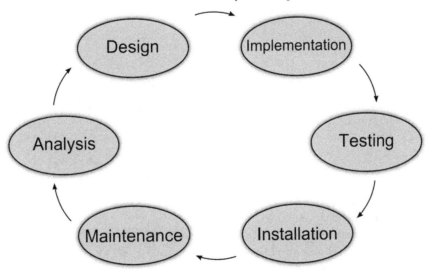

Figure 15-2 The system development life cycle

Project Development Roles

The **project manager** is responsible for the overall progress of a project, ensuring it stays on time, in budget, and needs the client's needs.

Analysts, or systems analysts, document the current system, finding its problems and areas for improvement. A **development manager** oversees **programmers** as they create the system specified in the design.

Information system managers are responsible for all IT purchases, deployments, and systems within an organisation. **Support staff** train users and help them with problems as they occur. **Database administrators** and **network managers** perform similar jobs in their specific areas.

Data collection: To fully understand the current system, data about it must be collected from users, managers and administrators, and any existing documentation. A variety of methods are used to gather data from users: **questionnaires** are useful when large amounts of data must be collected, but need to be carefully designed to provide accurate and useful data. Users may also provide answers they believe they are 'supposed' to give, rather than accurate answers, especially if they feel that their job may be under threat from new IT developments. **Face to face interviews** have the advantage of allowing questions to be added or changed in response to users' answers, and allow clarification to be sought on any unclear issues. However, interviews are time consuming. System developers may also **observe users** to see how they interact with the current system, the processes they use, and the output they produce. This can produce a more realistic overview of the current situation, especially if users are passively watched (for example through a video camera rather than by somebody sitting next to them).

A good source of information on the current system can be any literature related to it – **organisational policies**, **user manuals**, and **technical documentation**. However, with older systems it is possible that the system may lack documentation or that it may simply be out of date, with changes having been made but not documented.

Requirements specification: After investigation of the problem, a formal requirements specification is created. This is a technical document which describes the needs of an organisation as well as the project goals and scope. The requirements themselves are

typically divided into two areas. **Functional requirements** cover features the system should have, including input, output, storage, and processing requirements, and the user interface. **Non-functional requirements** are limitations on how the system should work – for example, being required to run on a certain hardware platform, produce results within a certain time after user input, and be completed within a certain time period and budget— these are also known as **constraints**.

Identification of possible IT solutions: Many projects have several possible solutions, ranging from keeping the existing system if replacement is not feasible, to completely replacing the old system with a new IT solution. In some cases it may be viable to implement a new solution which extends the functionality of the existing solution, or works with it.

Feasibility study and justification of solution: At this stage, a solution has to be chosen—which may mean deciding to continue with the current system, implement one of the suggested IT solutions, or use an alternative manual system. Whatever the choice, a **business case** must be made, justifying it in terms of time and cost to design, develop, and implement, versus the predicted benefits it will bring. It must also be feasible in terms of the skills, equipment, time, and money available. Sometimes a **SWOT** (Strengths, Weaknesses, Opportunities, Threats) analysis is done to help determine the feasibility of the solution.

Task	Start	Finish	Working Days	Responsible
Task A1	12/9/2011	16/9/2011	5	Mr Green
Task A2	19/9/2011	22/9/2011	4	Mr Green
Task A3	19/9/2011	22/9/2011	4	Mr Blue
Task A4	19/9/2011	26/9/2011	6	Mr Orange
Task A5	23/9/2011	27/9/2011	3	Mr Green
Task A6	27/9/2011	30/9/2011	4	Mr Blue
Milestone 1	3/10/2011	3/10/2011	1	N/A
Task B1	4/10/2011	13/10/2011	8	Mr Orange
Task B2	4/10/2011	5/10/2011	2	Mr Blue
Task B3	6/20/2011	12/10/2011	5	Mr Green
Finish	13/10/2011	13/10/2011	1	N/A

Figure 15-3 Table of project events and details

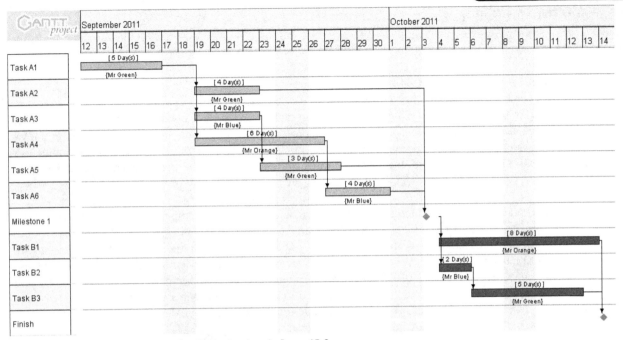

Figure 15-4 A Gantt chart representing the tasks show in figure 15-3

Project plan: Assuming a project will be developed, a **project manager** is normally chosen at this point. The manager will be responsible for seeing the project through to completion, ensuring deadlines are met and the requirements specification is adhered to. A **project management methodology** will also be chosen, such as the PRINCE2, PMBoK, or one of the many methods available (see page 326). The project will be broken down into stages (which may be the SDLC stages or smaller increments of them), along with starting and finishing dates and **project milestones** – key events in the project's development process. Project scheduling information can be represented in tabular format (figure 15-3), although this can make it hard to discern any inter-task dependencies or overlapping tasks, or in diagram form.

Gantt charts (see figure 15-4) provide a high level overview of a project schedule, including each individual task, the people responsible for overseeing them, and task starting and finishing times. They also give a clear view of the progress which should have been made at any given time. Gantt charts can be created in specialist **project management software** or using a spreadsheet application.

PERT (Program Evaluation and Review Technique) charts (see figure 15-5) also represent scheduling information graphically, and clearly show the relationships and dependencies between each task in the schedule. This makes it easier to determine which activities can be worked on simultaneously, and makes it easier to spot bottlenecks in the development process. Often a process called **Critical Path** (CP) is used to determine the longest (slowest) route from the beginning of the project to the end, since this will determine the minimum time required for the project.

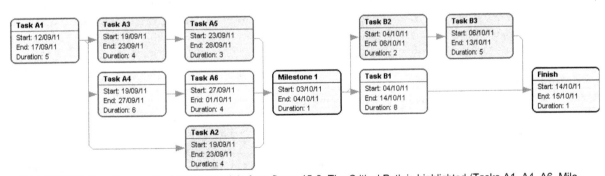

Figure 15-5 A PERT chart showing the project schedule from figure 15-3. The Critical Path is highlighted (Tasks A1, A4, A6, Milestone 1, B1, Finish)

Infamous Project Failures

Below are some of the most expensive failed IT projects in recent times. Compare these to the software and hardware failures on page 62.

London Ambulance Service Computer Aided Dispatch System

Result: Project scrapped, up to 30 people died as a result of slow ambulance arrival[3]

In 1992 the London Ambulance Service (LAS) introduced a new system to automatically dispatch the nearest available ambulance when an emergency call was received by its operators. Just hours after the software's installation, problems started: in some cases multiple ambulances were dispatched; in others, none were sent. In several cases ambulances were dispatched up to 8 hours late. Sources indicate between 20 and 30 people died as a result of ambulances failing to arrive in time.

Several factors contributed to the bug-ridden software: the designers were a small company with no experience of developing similar systems, and the project schedule was considered extremely short, allowing very little time for testing – particularly **load-testing**. Although the system worked well under light use during development, it was unable to deal with the large numbers of calls encountered during actual operation (and the system was never tested under these conditions before use). Compounding the problems, a direct changeover was used (see page 322), meaning staff were unable to revert to the previous system and eventually resorted to using pen and paper to keep track of ambulances. Worryingly, this system had been developed because a previous computerised system, developed in 1990, was considered unusable and was abandoned after £7.5 million of investment.

FBI Virtual Case File (VCF)

Result: Project scrapped after 5 years of development, $170 million wasted[4]

In 2000 the Federal Bureau of Investigation (FBI) started a new project to modernise its IT systems. Part of this project was the Virtual Case File software, designed to replace an existing set of programs that let FBI agents manage documents and evidence related to their cases. The system was delivered in December 2003 but the FBI considered large parts of it inappropriate or unusable. Arguments between the FBI, the developers, and Congress continued until the system was scrapped in January 2005, after more than $170 million had been spent. Even before then, the FBI was already considering purchasing off-the-shelf software to replace the failed Virtual Case File system.

A number of issues caused the failure of the project. Firstly, the initial requirements for the system were unclear, and kept changing. After the terrorist attacks on September 11th 2001, the requirements were changed from being a mere front-end to the existing systems to total migration to a new database system (the FBI's lack of information sharing capability had been a major criticism in the aftermath of the 2001 attacks). Secondly, an overly ambitious schedule was devised for both the original system and the changed system, leaving little time for testing. Finally, the personnel appointed as project managers had little or no experience of managing IT projects.

Australian Super Seasprite Helicopter

Result: $1.4 billion wasted[5]

The Australian Defence Department cancelled a contract for the new Super Seasprite helicopter in 2009 after problems with both the physical design and the software flight control system, which reportedly did not work as intended and raised fears over crew safety. The computerised system failed 4 times in 1600 hours, compared to the intended failure rate of no more than once in a million flight hours. By the time the project was cancelled, $1.4 billion had been spent - nearly $500 million more than the original budget.

UK's National Programme for IT

Result: £6.4 billion spent, project behind schedule, some features abandoned[6, 7]

Launched in 2002, the program to update the UK's National Health Service IT infrastructure has been notorious for its delays and cost overruns. The original cost estimate of £2 billion quickly grew to £12.4 billion, and the development period grew from 3 years to more than 10 years. A 2007 government report suggested opposition to the project from staff and patients was so high that the benefits of the system would not outweigh the cost. Multiple IT partners pulled out of the project, and as of 2011, parts of project have been cancelled, with others continuing on revised deadlines.

Design Stage

During the design stage, software developers plan a solution which fulfils the functional requirements identified during the analysis stage. The design stage needs to cover, in technical detail, the **inputs**, **processes**, **data structures**, and **outputs** required by the system, and the relationship between these items.

For inputs, the required items of data need to be determined, along with the data source (input from the user or an external system). The ranges of acceptable values (validation checks) must also be determined, along with the screens which accept the data from the user. Outputs, whether on screen or in the form of printed reports, are sketched to show their layout and appearance. Both input and output screens may be prototyped to test the effectiveness of their design with end users.

Data Flow Diagrams

Often processes are designed using diagramming tools. A **Data Flow Diagram** (DFD) shows the relationship between the data storage, inputs, outputs and processes in a system, with the **data flows** between them. Internal processes and external processes (called **sinks**) are represented differently, so that the scope of the system can be clearly understood. Figure 15-7 shows the most commonly used DFD symbols.

A Data Flow Diagram which shows a relatively high level view of the system, with only its relationships to external stakeholders and systems, is called a **system context diagram** (figure 15-6). System context diagrams are useful because they clearly show the boundaries of the system

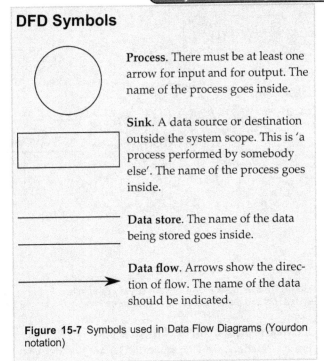

DFD Symbols

Process. There must be at least one arrow for input and for output. The name of the process goes inside.

Sink. A data source or destination outside the system scope. This is 'a process performed by somebody else'. The name of the process goes inside.

Data store. The name of the data being stored goes inside.

Data flow. Arrows show the direction of flow. The name of the data should be indicated.

Figure 15-7 Symbols used in Data Flow Diagrams (Yourdon notation)

(i.e. what is part of the system and what is external to it) and the data that flows in and out (overall inputs and outputs). Developers usually create a system context diagram first, and then create different 'levels' of DFDs which show more a detailed view of the internal operation of the system. In complex systems, several different levels might be created for the same part of the system, each showing a more detailed view of the data flow. However, unlike flow charts, Data Flow Diagrams never show the precise details of algorithms, such as variables and decisions—only the flow of data between processes.

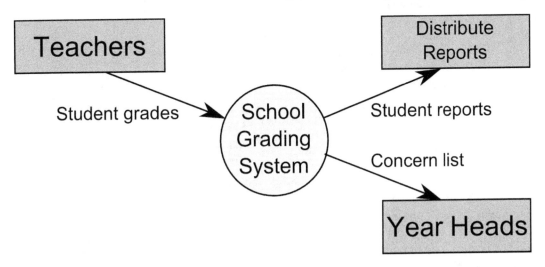

Figure 15-6 A system context diagram which shows the relationship between the IT system (a school grading system) and external sinks. *Teachers* and *Year Heads* are clearly external stakeholders who send and receive data. Although *Distribute Reports* is a process, it is a physical task which is outside the boundary of the IT system (this would be determined by the requirements specification).

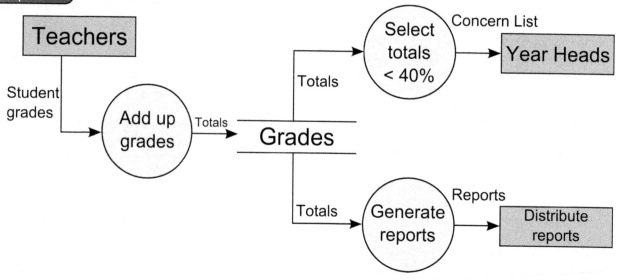

Figure 15-8 A Data Flow Diagram showing the school grading system depicted in figure 15-7. Although there is more detail than a system context diagram, each process represented could still be further broken down.

Entity Relationship Diagrams

Entity Relationship Diagrams (ERDs) are another common method of describing data storage and data relationships. An ERD shows the groups of data stored (**entities**, which represent database tables), the **attributes** each entity has (which usually map to database fields), and the **relationships** between the various data items. The **cardinality** at each end of the relationships between entities is also represented. Four options exist: zero or one, zero or more, one or more, and exactly one. Figure 15-9 shows the most common notation for ERD symbols, though several variants exist.

Figure 15-10 shows an ERD for a simple shop which sells products to its members. Four entities exist, each with its own attributes and primary key. In an ERD, it is convention to put a title on relationships—usually a verb—which describes their function. Because relationships can be read in both directions, each end of the relationship should be labelled in the diagram.

When reading the relationships from the diagram, the indication of cardinality closest to the start entity is skipped—so in figure 15-10 the following relationships can be read:

- **One** member *makes* **zero or more** sales
- **One** sale *is made to* **exactly one** member
- **One** sale *is of* **exactly one** product
- **One** product *is sold in* **zero or more** sales
- **One** product *is supplied by* **exactly one** supplier
- **One** supplier *supplies* **one or more** products

Note that the descriptions of the relationships always start with the singular 'one member....', 'one product....' followed by the name of the relationships and the cardinality of the related table.

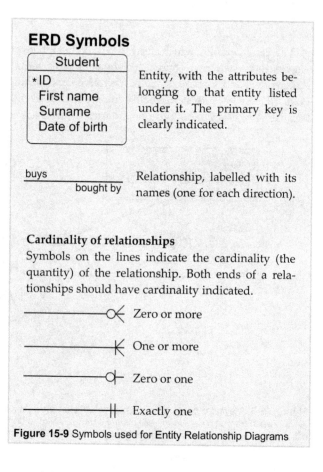

Figure 15-9 Symbols used for Entity Relationship Diagrams

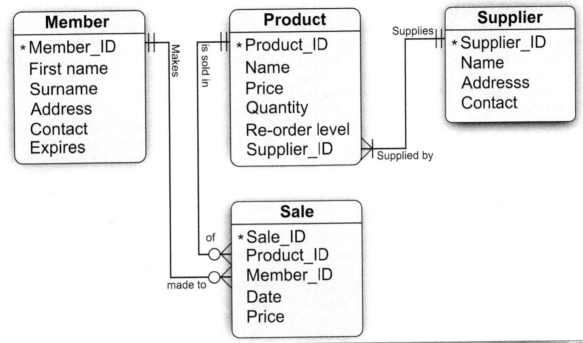

Figure 15-10 Entity Relationship Diagram for a simple shop.

The **user interface** is also designed at this stage. This can be done using rapid development tools such as GUI builders to produce **prototype interfaces** for the user to test. Alternatively, designers may simply sketch interface designs on paper or using a computer graphics package.

The choice of user interface component, such as list boxes, drop down boxes, or text boxes, can have a significant effect on both the usability of the system and the likelihood of input errors occurring. For example, in a system with a fixed range of inputs, a drop down box takes little screen space and prevents the user from selecting invalid options, compared to a component such as a text box.

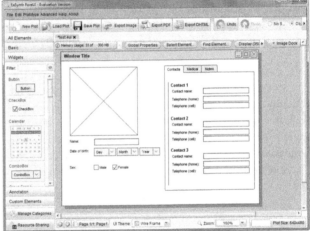

Figure 15-11 Designers can use software tools to create prototype user interfaces

---

Exercise 15-1

Consider the two scenarios below. For each, **construct** an Entity Relationship Diagrams to show the data stored by the system, a system context diagram to show the boundaries of the system, and a Data Flow Diagram to show the movement of data within the system.

Scenario 1: People can rent bikes using a government scheme. They go to a bike stand and use a smart card to authenticate themselves and unlock the bike. The time, date, and location of borrowing are recorded. When the bike is returned, this information is recorded and a charge is calculated based on the number of hours borrowed. Bikes not returned after four days are considered missing and a list of their details is sent to the police. [6 marks]

Scenario 2: In an online shopping site, when a customer clicks 'Buy', the items held in their shopping basket are checked to ensure that they are still in stock and the prices are current. The customer is shown an order confirmation including items, price, and shipping costs. The customer enters their credit card details. These are validated with a bank. If OK, the shop sends an order to the warehouse. The warehouse packs the items and prints an invoice with the customer's address. A record of the transaction is saved. [6 marks]

Implementation Stage

During **implementation** (also called **development** or **construction**), developers create the system, following the design documents previously created. Usually a team of programmers will work on creating the software, depending on the size of the project, using **Integrated Development Environments** (see page 310) to improve their workflow.

During implementation, **alpha testing** is performed to verify that the software works according to the requirements specification and the design documentation. At this point the software is likely to contain significant **bugs**, so the testing is performed internally rather than by customers. Usually a team of **software testers** perform alpha testing, rather than the programmers themselves.

Prototypes of the product may be created at this stage to demonstrate features to the client and check the project is meeting expectations.

Because it is recognised that many large IT projects fail (see page 316), developers often use **quality control processes** to reduce the likelihood of serious problems. These processes ensure that the code produced by the programmers is of high quality and meets the needs of the client (both the functional and non-functional requirements). Quality control processes include ensuring the requirements specification is written in an agreed standard (to avoid errors and omission), following programming standards to avoid common programming errors, and having comprehensive **test plans**.

Going further, **quality assurance methods** (not be to confused with quality control) are used to ensure the development team are following standardised practices which are suitable for the project under development. **CMMI** is a common quality assurance method (see page 321).

Documentation is also produced during the development stage. **Technical documentation** is targeted at system administrators and other developers who may expand or change the system in the future. Programmers usually write comments in the source code to help others who read it, and create Application Programming Interface (API) guidelines for those who will produce other software which interacts with the system.

User documentation explains how to use a system, covering how to install and start the system, and how to perform common tasks. **User manuals**, written or video **tutorials**, **online lessons**, and **Frequently Asked Questions** (FAQ) pages are all forms of user documentation.

Testing Stage

Once a system has been developed and has passed alpha testing, **beta testing** can be undertaken. Versions of the software are normally given to a relatively small group of users (**beta testers**), with the aim of detecting any remaining bugs and testing the software's usability under real world conditions. Beta testing can last from a few weeks to several months. Generally beta testing only takes place once the software has been feature-frozen (no new features will be added before release).

A **bug tracking system** is used to keep a list of all software bugs (sometimes called requests for enhancement) in a central location, and allows them to be prioritised and annotated (for example, with details of how and when the bug occurs, the desired result, and the actual result). Bug tracking is an important part of the quality assurance process.

User acceptance testing involves the user checking the system to ensure it meets their requirements. A system may pass alpha and beta testing but still fail user acceptance testing, so it is an important part of the **handover process**. For example, part of the system may be cumbersome or slow to use – a problem not caused by a software bug, but still unacceptable to the client. Other features may be missing or not quite work as intended due to problems in the requirements specification. These issues need to be corrected before the client will formally accept the software.

Figure 15-12 Bug tracking systems are used as part of the quality assurance process

CMMI—Managing an Organisation's Maturity

CMMI (Capability Maturity Model Integration) is a **quality assurance method** designed to help organisations improve their performance. CMMI describes an organisation in terms of five levels of maturity (figure 15-13). CMMI applies to organisations as a whole, not just to IT projects. Models such as CMMI are important in helping an organisation build on its past experiences—building on successes and ensuring that previous mistakes are not forgotten, but learnt from, ensuring they will not be repeated.

Level 1 – Initial Level

At this level there is minimal organisation and planning. Management at this stage is poor, and as a result, although some things within the organisation might be done well, this is due to the initiative of individual employees and is more of an accident than the result of any formal planning. A key limitation at this level is that there is no central repository of knowledge regarding previous experience, successes, and failures. Instead, because this knowledge is only held with employees, rather than centrally, it is lost when employees move to other organisations, and the organisation is likely to repeat its past mistakes and fail to capitalise on its successes.

Level 2 – Managed Level

At level 2, some management takes place, allowing the organisation to track important elements such as the cost and time scale of projects, start to plan projects, and to review by comparing final performance with the plan. However, at this level these tasks still occur on a project-by-project basis – there are no central organisational standards for how these tasks should be performed. This results in variable performance across the organisation, depending on the initiative of the individuals in each project.

Level 3 – Defined

At this level, an Engineering Process Group (EPG) within the organisation defines standard approaches for key tasks, addressing a key problem from level 2. Employees can give feedback on these processes using a Quality Management System (QMS), so that the EPG can improve the standards over time.

Level 4 – Quantitatively Managed

Here statistical data and tools begin to be used in order to define goals for the organisation and thus improve its performance. For example, a goal might be to ensure all projects are delivered within two months of their deadline and within 10% of their budget. If projects fall outside of these goals, a managerial review will take place to determine whether they should continue.

Level 5 – Optimising Level

At the most mature level, an organisation makes small, continuous improvements to its methods – perhaps by using new tools or technologies. At level 5 weak areas are identified and improved, but these changes are more evolutionary than revolutionary.

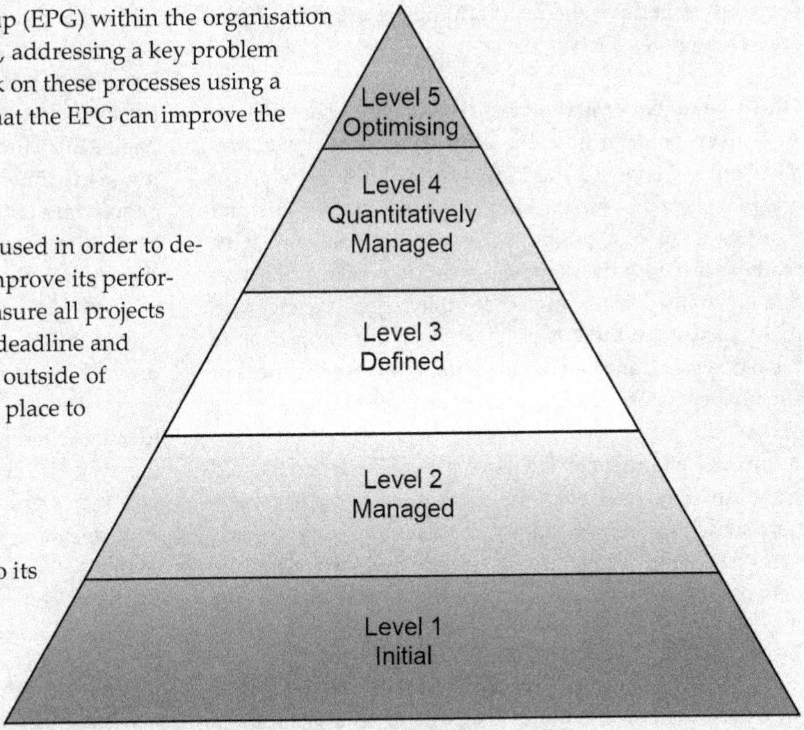

Figure 15-13 Five levels make up the CMMI Maturity Model

Installation Stage

Once development has finished, **installation** (also called **delivery** or **deployment**) takes place. This stage concerns preparing the organisation for the installation of the new system, the hardware and software installation, and the removal of the old system.

User training must be carried out before a new system can be used under real world conditions. Training may take place at the developer's location, or the new system may be installed in the client's organisation but not used for 'live' operations. User documentation plays an important part in training. Other training methods include classroom based lessons or lectures and online video tutorials. Users may be given sample data to work with in order to familiarise themselves with the software's operation.

Once training is complete, **changeover** can occur, with the old system being retired and the new system going into live use. This is a critical time for an organisation because even relatively small failures can have serious negative impacts on their business. Careful planning, preparation of data, and user training are essential. There are several types of changeover:

Direct changeover is the most basic type of changeover. At a given point in time, the old system is removed and all users start to use the new system immediately. For complex systems, direct changeover is a big gamble and requires a lot of planning – all required data must be ready to use with the new system, and users must be adequately trained in its use. If anything goes wrong with the new system, there is no possibility of falling back to the old system, and the organisation may lose business or even have to close until the new system can be fixed.

A **phased changeover** switches gradually from the old system to a new system, with some parts of the organisation switching before others. For example, one department may stop using the old system and start using the new one for a few weeks. If no problems are encountered after a few weeks, other departments can change over one by one. The advantage of this is that at least part of the business can still function even if the new system fails totally. However, running two systems can be complex, especially if there is a lot of interaction between departments who have changed and those who have not.

Parallel changeover, also called **parallel running,** involves introducing the new system but running it concurrently with the old system. This can be a time consuming method because actions must be carried out twice, and there may be significant logistical difficulties in actually using two systems side by side. For these reasons parallel running may be impractical in many circumstances. However, there are benefits for critical applications – especially safety critical systems. Running two systems simultaneously means the output of the new system can be verified against the old system and, should anything go wrong with the new system, users can immediately fall back to the old system, safe in the knowledge that it is up to date with the latest data and transactions.

Maintenance Stage

Although often overlooked, maintenance accounts for a large amount of the time and cost associated with IT projects. Projects can take years to complete, but will be used for even longer, possibly decades (see legacy systems, page 310). Throughout its life software may need changing many times—updating it to work with new hardware or software (**adaptive maintenance**); adding new features as required by the changing requirements of the organisation (**perfective maintenance**); and fixing bugs which were not found during testing (**corrective maintenance**). **Preventative maintenance** – updating the software to prevent foreseeable problems - may also be needed.

Ideally, when changes are made to software, all stages of the system development lifecycle are applied to the proposed changes. Doing so means maintainers must update any relevant technical documentation with details of changes they make, to assist future maintainers and maintain control over the project. Software maintainers

---

Exercise 15-2

Read about the failure of the FBI Virtual Case File system (page 316). After this failure, the FBI began initial work on a new system named Sentinel in 2006, with many of the same goals as the Virtual Case File system.

Research the Sentinel project. How has its development progressed? Have the FBI learnt lessons from the failure of the Virtual Case File?

Exercise 15-3

Read about the London Ambulance Service project failure on page 316. **Explain** whether a direct changeover was appropriate in this instance. [4 marks]

also need to be careful to avoid causing regressions – when maintenance causes new errors in software. **Regression testing** is the process of repeating old tests to ensure they still work after alterations are made.

Support, although not strictly maintenance, is an important part of this process. Users may have problems using a system, which can initially be addressed with user documentation or via internal support staff. These staff provide help desk support to users using an **incident tracking system** (also called an incident **management system**). Here each support incident is recorded, along with a knowledge base of common problems and solutions. If the solution to the problem cannot be found in the knowledge base, the incident may be **escalated** and a support technician may call or visit the user. If the technician verifies the problem exists but is unable to resolve it, the incident can be further escalated, eventually being reported to the developers as a software bug. The developers themselves will use an incident tracking system to record any errors reported to them.

When a project reaches its end of life, perhaps to be superseded by a new project, it will enter the **phase out** stage, as the new project enters the analysis stage.

Review of stages

The software development life cycle contains a large number of separate steps, which can be hard to remember. Some of these stages also have alternative names under different project management methodologies. An overview of the key stages is given below. As an ITGS student you need to be able to describe the components of each stage, explaining its role in the overall process. Where appropriate, you also need to be able to explain the different examples of each term and their advantages and disadvantages. For example, for user documentation you should be able to describe it as *documentation designed to help the user understand the new system*, give examples of user documentation such as user manuals, online tutorials, frequently asked questions lists, and explain the relative advantages and disadvantages of each of these methods.

Analysis Stage
- Project goals
- Scope
- Data collection
- Requirements specification
- Identification of solutions
- Business case
- Feasibility study
- Justification of solution
- SWOT
- Project plan
- Project management methodology
- Project schedule
- Project milestones

Design
- Inputs
- Outputs
- Data structures
- Processes
- System context diagram
- Data Flow Diagrams
- Entity Relationship Diagrams
- User interface design

Implementation Stage
- Development
- Alpha testing
- Prototyping
- Quality control
- Quality assurance
- User documentation
- Technical documentation

Testing stage
- Beta testing
- User acceptance testing
- Handover

Installation stage
- Installation
- Training
- Changeover

Maintenance Stage
- Maintenance
- Regression testing
- Support
- Incident tracking
- Phase out

Development Approach

The way in which the SDLC stages are approached depends on the development model used. The traditional approach is to use the **waterfall model**, which flows from the analysis through each stage to the installation, one stage at a time. Analysis is carried out for the entire system, followed by design for the entire system, development of the entire system, and so on. The waterfall model is highly structured, and allows for long term planning. It ensures that problems in the analysis stage are found quickly (while they are relatively cheap to fix) rather than waiting until later stages (where they are increasing expensive to fix because each previous stage must be repeated).

However, the waterfall model lacks adaptability: large IT projects may take such a long time to develop that by the time the development stage has been reached, the requirements identified in the analysis stage may have changed (this was the case in several of the examples on page 316). This is a significant problem for the waterfall model.

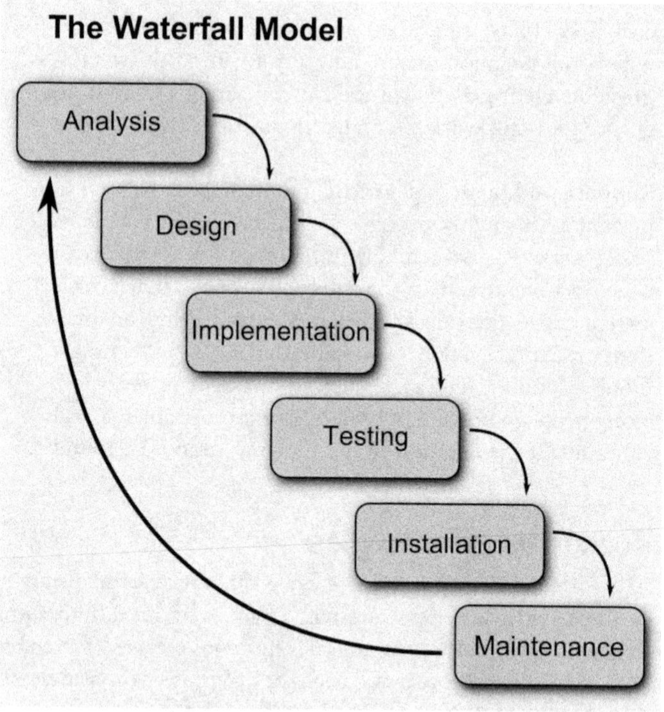

The **agile development model** seeks to address some of the waterfall model's weaknesses and by allowing for greater adaptability. The same SDLC stages are encountered using agile development, but they are applied to only a small part of the problem at a time. In a relatively short period of time (usually less than a month), programmers analyse a part of the problem, design and implement a solution, and perform testing, including client **acceptance testing**. This allows working code to be produced much more rapidly, and means the client can decide whether the software is meeting their needs at every step – if it is not, it is comparatively easy to make changes, since relatively little work has been done since the previous acceptance testing.

However, a criticism of agile development is that solutions can be 'piece meal' and, for very large projects, the

The Waterfall Model

Figure 15-14 The traditional Waterfall model of software development, in which each stage is completed before moving onto the next.

lack of an initial goal and design for the whole project can result in a less efficient design. In turn, this makes extending and maintaining the project later on much more difficult.

Exercise 15-4

A software development company is planning to create a School Management Information System (MIS), including features for storing student personal details (names, contact details), reporting of grades to parents, teacher entry of grades, timetabling / scheduling of lessons, and storing medical details for the school nurse. The project is scheduled to begin development in July 2011 and be complete ready for use in June 2012.

Use appropriate software to:
    a) **Construct** a Gantt chart showing the project schedule if a waterfall model was used. [6 marks]
    b) **Construct** a Gantt chart show the project schedule if the agile model was used. [6 marks]
    c) **Construct** a PERT chart based on the Gantt chart created in part (a) [6 marks]

The Agile Development Approach

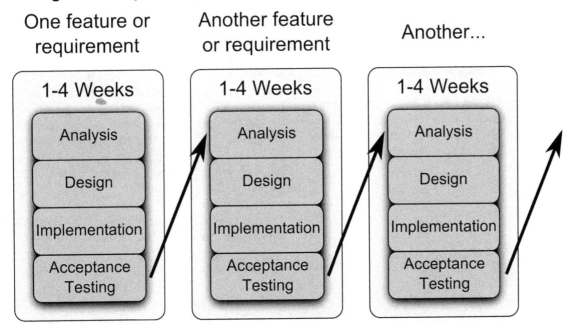

Figure 15-15 The agile model of software development breaks development down into shorter time periods

Project Management Methodologies

Good project management is essential for success. The SDLC describes the steps in project development, and the waterfall model and agile model describe the order in which development is approached. **Project management methodologies** aim to describe the best approaches for managing those steps, moving between them, or recording successes and failures to enable future improvement.

SSADM

SSADM (Structured Systems Analysis and Design Method) is a methodology which focuses primarily on the Analysis and Design stages of the SDLC. As a result, many of the items and activities in SSADM are similar to the activities described on pages 313 to 322, though they have slightly different names. SSADM describes 7 stages:

Stage 0 - Feasibility study: examines whether an IT project is feasible, in terms of costs, equipment (hardware and software), and existing organisational systems. This stage examines various possible solutions, and if they have been rejected as infeasible, records why.

Stage 1 - Investigation of the current environment: includes creating a context diagram, DFD and ERD diagrams for the current system, plus a list of users and how they interact with the system. Problems and inadequacies

of the current system will be documented in detail. It is essential to thoroughly understand the current system, so limitations and opportunities can be identified. This is important because a new system should be based on business needs – not merely a re-implementation of the current system (which may have limitations).

Stage 2 - Business system options: At this point the analyst presents different options for solving the business' problems. This could include continuing to use the existing system. A cost / benefit analysis of proposed systems needs to be completed too, as well as examining any negative impacts the new system may have.

Stage 3 – Requirements Specification: a detailed list of requirements is generated. Using the understanding of the current system from the investigation in stage 1 as a basis, DFD and ERD diagrams are constructed to represent the new system. User roles are also defined.

Stage 4 – Technical system options: involves considering the hardware, software, networks, and personnel that might be required for the proposed system. As in stage 2, it is likely that several options will be presented, with the rejected options being recorded.

Stage 5 – Logical design: Involves identifying, modelling, and documenting all of the required data for the system. This involves diagramming work using tools such as entity relationship diagrams and data flow diagrams to model the proposed system. This stage is largely analogous to the design stage in the waterfall model of system development.

Stage 6 – Physical design: involves translating all previous design work into actual physical hardware and software specifications. For example, entity relationship diagrams are translated into table and field specifications for a specific database management system (DBMS), while processes are mapped into functions in a specific programming language.

PMBoK

PMBoK (Project Management Body of Knowledge) is not specific to software development projects – its techniques can be used to manage virtually any project, from building a house to designing an aircraft. PMBok is recognised as an international standard by both ANSI (American National Standards Institute) and IEEE (Institute of Electrical and Electronics Engineers). PMBoK divides the project life cycle into five stages, called **process groups** (figure 15-16). The results of each process group are fed into the next as an input – for example, the Initiating group produces a **Project Charter** which is then used by the Planning group.

The work in each process group is divided into nine **Knowledge Areas**, such as cost management, time man-

Process Groups Knowledge Areas	Initiating	Planning	Executing	Controlling and Monitoring	Closing
Integration Management	Develop Project Charter	Develop Project Management Plan	Direct and Manage Project	Monitor and control work	Close phase or project
Scope Management		Collect requirements Define scope Create WBS		Verify and control scope	
Time Management					
Cost Management		Estimate costs Plan budget		Control costs	
Quality Management					
Human Resource Management					
Communications Management	Identify stakeholders	Plan communications	Distribute information and manage expectations	Performance report	
Risk Management					
Procurement Management		Plan procurements	Conduct procurements	Administer procurements	Close procurements

Figure 15-16 An overview of PMBoK (only certain key cells have been filled in)[2]

agement, and communications management. Each of these represents an area of specialisation within the project, and has specific tasks during each process group. For example, during the **Initiating** stage, the *Communications Management* should identify the stakeholders. During the **Planning** stage, the *Communications Management* should plan their communication with the stakeholders, and during the **Executing** stage, they should actually communicate with the stakeholders. Key knowledge areas include **Scope** management, which determines the features and limitations of the project, and **procurement** management, which deals with acquiring any new hardware, software, and personnel required for the project.

PRINCE2

PRINCE2 (PRojects IN Controlled Environments 2) is the standard project management methodology used by the UK government. PRINCE2 starts by considering a **business case** for a project – i.e. an evaluation of the benefits and the challenges. Planning, organisation, and risk management are key features of the PRINCE 2 approach.

Like PMBoK, PRINCE2 divides the life cycle into stages – in this case, **Starting Up**, **Initiating**, **Delivering**, and **Final Delivery**. Each stage is broken into levels – **Directing**,

> **Key Point**
>
> As an ITGS student you do **not** need to remember the names of each process group, knowledge area, all of the 42 PMBoK tasks, or be able to draw a diagram of the PRINCE2 processes.
>
> It is sufficient to understand the purpose of these project management methodologies, the approaches they use, and some of the key events and features that each methodology has (for example, the Project Initiation Documentation in PRINCE2).

Managing, and **Delivering** – which describe the type of work performed (figure 15-17). At the Directing level, the entire project is directed, typically by corporate management. At the Managing level, **project managers** guide parts of the project, and transition between stages (this is known as **Managing Stage Boundaries**). At the Delivery level, the project is created (in IT development, this would be the programming).

Notable features of PRINCE2 include the Project Initiation Document, which contains the results of the analysis tasks (project goals, scope, constraints, and so on).

	Pre-Project	Initiation Stage	Delivery Stage(s)	Final Delivery Stage
Directing	Starting Up	Directing a Project		
Managing		Stage Boundary	Stage Boundary	Closing Project
		Initiating Project	Controlling a Stage	Controlling a Stage
Delivering			Managing Product Delivery	Managing Product Delivery

Figure 15-17 Overview of PRINCE2

Professional Conduct and Ethics

The **Association for Computing Machinery** (ACM) and the **British Computer Society** (BCS) both produce **codes of conduct** for IT professionals. These cover best professional practices and provide guidelines for ethical conduct. Stipulations in the ACM's code include working to 'Contribute to society and human well-being ', 'Respect the privacy of others', and 'Honor confidentiality'[11] - all important traits when working on large scale IT projects. Other responsibilities in the code include respecting intellectual property and copyright laws.

Particularly relevant to the development of large IT projects, items such as 'Acquire and maintain professional competence', 'Know and respect existing laws pertaining to professional work', and 'Accept and provide appropriate professional review'[11] put the onus on developers to create appropriate systems for their clients, using the their skills to the best of their ability and—critically—not to undertake projects which are beyond their qualifications, capabilities, or experience. This last point in particular has been the cause of several IT project failures—most notably, the London Ambulance Service dispatch system (see page 316), which was created by developers with no experience in the field, and Therac-25 (see page 63), whose code was created by a lone programmer.

Chapter Review

Key Language

IT Roles
information system managers	analyst	development manager	programmer
	database administrator	network manager	support staff

Analysis Stage
business case	functional requirements	project management methodology	scope
client	Gantt chart		SWOT
constraints	milestones	project management software	technical documentation
Critical Path	non-functional requirements		user documentation
data collection	organisational IT policies	project manager	
end-user	PERT chart	project plan	
feasibility study	project goals	requirements specification	

Design Stage
attributes	DFD	outputs	relationships
cardinality	entities	processes	system context diagram
data structure	ERD	prototype interface	user interface

Implementation Stage
alpha testing	implementation	quality assurance methods	training
bug	load testing	quality control processes	tutorial
CMMI	online lessons	software testers	user manual
Frequently Asked Questions	prototypes	test plan	

Testing Stage
beta tester	bug tracking system	user acceptance testing
beta testing	handover	

Installation Stage
changeover	deployment	installation
delivery	direct changeover	parallel running

Maintenance Stage
adaptive maintenance	tem	perfective maintenance	regression testing
corrective maintenance	incident tracking system	phase out	support
incident escalation	internal support	phased changeover	training
incident management sys-	maintenance	preventative maintenance	

Development Approach and Methodologies
acceptance testing	PRINCE2	SSADM
agile development	procurement	user acceptance testing
PMBoK	project initiation document	waterfall development

General Terms
code of conduct	IDE	source code	virtual machine
custom / bespoke software	legacy system	system development lifecycle	
emulator	off-the-shelf software		

Exercise 15-5
Construct a system context diagram and an Entity Relationship Diagram for the following scenario:

Patients make appointments with doctors at a hospital. Patients are billed separately for each appointment they attend. Some patients pay their bills at the time of the appointment; others have insurance companies. Hospitals keep a record of patients' personal details, the appointments they have attended, and any treatments given at each appointment. Some doctors have one or more specialities, and patients may be referred to these doctors for treatment.

Exercise 15-6
Construct a Gantt chart using the project schedule data in the table below.

Stage	Start Date	End Date	Responsible
Analysis	1 Sept 2011	14 Nov 2011	Jane Pear
Design	15 Nov 2011	16 Feb 2012	Lucy Riess
Development	22 Nov 2011	25 Mar 2012	Sam Tallen
Testing	5 Jan 2012	25 Apr 2012	Jack Patiol
Acceptance	1 May 2012	14 May 2012	Clarence West

Exercise 15-7
(a) (i) Define the term *beta test*. [2 marks]

   (ii) Describe **two** steps that occur as part of the Analysis stage of the SDLC [4 marks]

(b) Explain how CMMI helps ensure project quality. [6 marks]

(c) To what extent is the choice of the Agile model of system development better than the choice of the Waterfall model? [8 marks]

Exercise 15-8
A large haulage company has a legacy system for managing its inventory. The system was developed 15 years ago and runs on aging hardware with a text based user interface. The company wants to expand their system to allow new features, including giving customers access to their data over the Internet. They are considering the purchase of a new system to achieve these goals.

(a) (i) Define the term *technical documentation*. [2 marks]

   (ii) Describe **two** types of changeover that could be used with this system. [4 marks]

(b) Explain **two** significant challenges faced in developing a custom / bespoke application [6 marks]

(c) To what extent is it appropriate to develop an entirely new system to replace the legacy system? [8 marks]

Exercise 15-9
A restaurant wishes to implement a computerised system to replace its current paper files for maintaining records of sales, purchases, suppliers, and staff. It is considering whether to use a commercial off the shelf application or commission a custom / bespoke application.

(a) (i) Define the term *legacy system* [2 marks]

   (ii) Distinguish between a project's *client* and the *end user*. [4 marks]

(b) Explain **two** methods that can be used to train users on a new system. [6 marks]

(c) Evaluate the choice of a commercial off the shelf application rather than a custom / bespoke application for a business. [8 marks]

References

1 McKendrick, J. (2011). *Study: US government spends $36 billion a year maintaining legacy systems.* ZDNet. Available: www.zdnet.com/blog/service-oriented/study-us-government-spends-36-billion-a-year-maintaining-legacy-systems/6505?tag=nl.e019. Last accessed March 2011.

2 Project Management Institute (2004). *A Guide to the Project Management Body of Knowledge.* Project Management Institute.

3 Lancaster University. (Date unknown). *Case study : The London Ambulance Service Despatching System.* Available: http://www.comp.lancs.ac.uk/computing/resources/IanS/SE7/CaseStudies/LondonAmbulance/index.html. Last accessed Nov 2011.

4 Goldstein, H. (2005). *"Who killed the Virtual Case File?".* IEEE Spectrum. Available: http://spectrum.ieee.org/computing/software/who-killed-the-virtual-case-file. Last accessed March 2011.

5 Walters, P. (2009). *$1.4bn wasted on cancelled Seasprite.* Available: www.strategypage.com/militaryforums/512-48220.aspx. Last accessed March 2011.

6 Hope, C. (2007). *Patients 'won't benefit from £12bn IT project'.* The Telegraph. Available: www.telegraph.co.uk/news/uknews/1548813/Patients-wont-benefit-from-12bn-IT-project.html. Last accessed March 2011.

7 National Audit Office. (2006). *The National Programme for IT in the NHS.* Available: www.nao.org.uk/idoc.ashx?docId=01f31d7c-0681-4477-84e2-dc8034e31c6a&version=-1. Last accessed March 2011.

8 Overby, S. (2005). *"Comair's Christmas Disaster: Bound To Fail".* CIO. Available: www.cio.com/article/112103/Comair_s_Christmas_Disaster_Bound_To_Fail. Last accessed March 2011.

9 TrainWeb. (Unknown date). *The History of TOPS.* Available: www.trainweb.org/rews/tops/history.htm. Last accessed March 2011.

10 Clarity in Code. (2011). *Software Maintenance.* Available: http://www.clarityincode.com/software-maintenance/. Last accessed Nov 2011.

11 ACM. (1992). *ACM Code of Ethics and Professional Conduct.* Available: http://www.acm.org/about/code-of-ethics. Last accessed Nov 2011.

Chapter 16
AI & Robotics

Objectives

1. Describe the applications of intelligent computer systems
2. Explain how 'intelligent' behaviour is created
3. Distinguish Artificial Intelligence and Computational Intelligence
4. Describe common applications of robots
5. Describe the input and output devices used by robots
6. Explain the challenges faced by designers of robots
7. Discuss the social impacts of intelligent and robotic systems
8. Evaluate the ethical implications of developing intelligent systems

Artificial Intelligence and Robotics

Artificial Intelligence and robots are popular topics for science fiction films, often featuring advanced computerised machines that fully resemble human beings in both appearance and abilities. This chapter examines the current state of artificial intelligence research, the methods computer scientists use to make machines achieve 'intelligent' behaviour, and the problems that are often encountered. Robotics—computerised machines capable of performing physical rather than mental tasks—commonly use artificial intelligence techniques, and this chapter also looks at the design, development, and impacts robots have on society. Finally, perhaps more so than any other ITGS topic, the development of artificial intelligence raises great ethical questions about the creation of autonomous machines, our ability to control them, and the limits we should impose on their development.

What is Intelligence?

Intelligence is an abstract concept which has many aspects to it, and is hard to define definitively. Yet it is difficult to discuss artificial intelligence without having an idea of what constitutes intelligence itself. If we asked a group of people to describe what it means to be intelligent, we might find answers such as:

- The ability to respond to the environment
- The ability to learn new knowledge or skills
- The ability to use logic or reasoning to come to a conclusion
- The ability to learn from experience
- The ability to make evaluations or judgements

Of course, there is no single answer to this question—intelligence is as hard to define as it is to create. Rather than attempting to define intelligence, many computer scientists have taken a different approach, designing systems that mimic the behaviour shown by humans.

Exercise 16-1

Consider the illustrations below—Albert Einstein, one of the greatest physicists; temples in Tikal, Guatemala, built by the Mayans over 1000 years ago; and a game of chess. What is the difference between the intellectual skills required for each of these tasks? How does this influence our understanding of what intelligence is?

Exercise 16-2

What does it mean to be intelligent? Why would you consider yourself intelligent?

Exercise 16-3

Describe a test for a computer which, if passed, would convince you that the computer was intelligent. Even if you don't believe that computers can be intelligent – what would convince you? What would a computer need to do in order for you to say 'OK, that is intelligent'?

The Turing Test

In 1950, famous English mathematician and computer scientist Alan Turing proposed an experiment to test whether or not a machine is 'intelligent'. Called the **Turing Test**, the experiment involves a human judge who asks questions to two contestants – one of which is a computer terminal and one which is a human being – without knowing which is which. From the answers he receives, the judge must try to determine which contestant is the computer and which is the human. If the judge is unable to determine this, Turing suggested that the machine should be considered 'intelligent'. Put simply, Turing considered a machine to be intelligent if it could pass itself as a human.

CAPTCHAs

A more modern form of the Turing Test is often seen on the web. **CAPTCHA images** (figure 16-2) are commonly used when posting comments on forums and when creating new user accounts online. These **Completely Automated Public Turing test to tell Computers and Humans Apart** are designed to prevent **spam bots** from posting advertising in comments or creating false accounts. CAPTCHAs display deformed text which will hopefully be legible to a human being but not to a computer. If a computer (in this case an automated program) is able to read the text correctly, it has, in this case, made itself indistinguishable from a human and could be said to have passed this form of the Turing Test. In fact, researchers at the University of California, Berkeley have succeeded in creating programs that can frequently read the more basic CAPTCHAS such as figure 16-2.

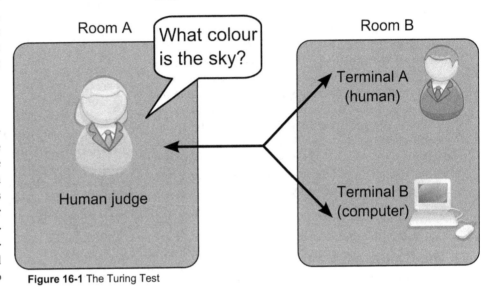

Figure 16-1 The Turing Test

Deep Blue and Watson

Deep Blue was a **supercomputer** designed by IBM for the purpose of playing chess. Deep Blue featured 480 dedicated chess playing processors, which could evaluate more than 200 million chess moves per second. Additionally, thousands of grandmaster games were programmed into the computer's move database. During play, Deep Blue used a variety of techniques to determine the best move. Some aspects of the game, such as the importance of keeping the queen safe compared to the importance of attacking moves were determined based on **heuristic rules** (see page 338). The best move at any time was computed using **brute force searching** (see page 338), which looked up to 20 moves ahead.

Deep Blue played world chess champion Gary Kasparov in 1996 and lost. After upgrading, the two played a rematch in 1997. Kasparov took the first game; Deep Blue the second; the third, fourth, and fifth games were all draws. Deep Blue won the final game to take the match, becoming the first computer to beat a reigning world chess champion. The victory was not without controversy however: Kasparov accused IBM of cheating during the second match, claiming a human grandmaster took over control from Deep Blue at a critical point to avoid the computer repeating a previous mistake—an accusation IBM naturally denied.

IBM made another significant venture into the world of artificial intelligence in 2006 with the **Watson** computer. Watson was a significant advance, being designed to answer questions written in **natural language**, within a much larger area of knowledge than limited expert systems. Watson stored over 4 terabytes of data, consisting of over 200 million pages of information—including the whole of Wikipedia. When posed a question, Watson used a combination of natural language processing and searching to analyse questions and generate thousands of possible answers. These were then analysed further to generate confidence ratings for each answer. In 2011 Watson was given a major test when it competed against two humans in the US television quiz show *Jeopardy!*. Watson, despite giving the occasional humorous answer, won each match by a significant margin[2].

Achieving Artificial Intelligence

'The main lesson of thirty-five years of AI research is that the hard problems are easy and the easy problems are hard. The mental abilities of a four-year-old that we take for granted – recognizing a face, lifting a pencil, walking across a room, answering a question – in fact solve some of the hardest engineering problems ever conceived.'

Steven Pinker

Computer scientists face great challenges when trying to create intelligent systems. As the quote above suggests, some of the tasks we as humans find the easiest are the most difficult for a computer to achieve. Many of the things that we learn in early life: recognising shapes, objects, people, tying our shoelaces, walking, are very difficult or impossible for machines. Conversely, a lot of the skills we learn later in life – science and mathematics especially – are relatively easy for machines to tackle. Broadly speaking, the tasks which are easy for computers are those for which a clear series of steps or instructions can be written. The difficult tasks are those for which there are is no clear, fixed set of steps to follow.

Figure 16-2 CAPTCHA

The approaches that computer scientists use to deal with these difficulties can be divided into two broad areas:

Artificial intelligence (AI) refers to systems that simulate intelligence through a series of quite rigid facts or rules. The focus of artificial intelligence is to create systems that give the appearance of human-like intelligence, even if the method of achieving the intelligence is vastly different from those used by humans: the focus of AI is on the *results*. Often such AI systems focus on one specific area of knowledge (for example, playing chess), rather than trying to create a general intelligence which can work in any situation.

In contrast, the **Computational Intelligence** (CI) approach focuses on creating systems that 'think' in the same way that humans think. In other words, CI is focused on creating systems that can learn, develop, and reach optimal solutions based on past experience – just like human beings can. The focus of computational intelligence is the *method* by which the results are obtained.

The Chinese Room

TOK Link

In 1980, philosopher John Searle published a thought experiment called **The Chinese Room**, which deals with the concepts of machine intelligence, knowledge, and understanding. Searle described a closed room containing a person who speaks only English. The room contains many, many books. In the books are sequences of Chinese characters, representing every possible question that can be asked in the Chinese language. Next to each question is a valid answer, also written in Chinese.

People regularly come to the room and post pieces of paper under the door, containing questions written in Chinese. The person in the room searches all the books until he finds the sequence of Chinese characters that matches the sequence of characters on the piece of paper. He copies the corresponding answer from the book and posts the piece of paper back under the door.

The people outside the room, having posted a question in Chinese and received an answer in Chinese, might reasonably assume that they are conversing with someone who knows and understands Chinese. Searle argued that if a computer replaced the person and books, it would easily pass the Turing Test. However, he argues that the person, and therefore any machine, does not understand Chinese, because they does not know the meaning of the individual symbols being manipulated.

Exercise 16-4

a) In The Chinese Room experiment which, if any, of the following 'know' Chinese?
- The room
- The person in the room
- The books containing the Chinese symbols

b) If a computer replaced the person and a large database replaced the books, would the computer know Chinese?

c) Does 'the system' (the combination of the room, the person, and the books) know Chinese?

d) Does it even matter whether the room, person, or books 'know' Chinese, provided a valid answer is given?

Expert Systems

Some of the earliest developments in the field of artificial intelligence were **expert systems** – software programs which use programmed **logic** and **rules** to make the same decisions (hopefully!) as a human expert. Expert systems are usually restricted to answering questions in a specific **knowledge domain** – one specific area of knowledge – rather than being 'general' experts on 'everything'. Examples of knowledge domains include medical knowledge for a medical diagnosis system, and financial knowledge for an expert system that decides whether or not to approve loan applications. Common examples of expert systems include:

- Medical diagnosis expert systems (usually to assist rather than replace the doctor)
- Medical image analysis (for screening of mass x-rays to detect abnormalities)
- Identifying agricultural pests and diseases
- Spelling and grammar checking in word processors
- Finance – deciding whether to approve a loan
- Fault diagnosis in various fields (computers, cars, aircraft)

Components of an expert system

An **expert system shell** is a set of programs which allow the building of an expert system through the creation of knowledge and rules. Expert systems have three essential components:

The **user interface** presents questions to the user and accepts input from them. Inputs may be in the form of short yes / no questions, multiple choice options, or typed natural language. The user interface also presents answers—and sometimes the reasoning for those answers—once they have been determined.

The **knowledge base** contains data and facts which form the knowledge in the specific knowledge domain. For example, in a medical expert system the knowledge base contains facts about the symptoms associated with different diseases.

The information in the knowledge base is intended to replicate that of a human expert (such as a doctor). However, as most people are not skilled at computer programming, the knowledge from the expert is first prepared by a **knowledge engineer**. The knowledge engineer works the knowledge into a form that is useful for the expert system.

The **inference engine** has the job of matching the user's input from the user interface with the data contained in the knowledge base to find appropriate answers. This is done using **inference rules** which describe how different items of data relate to each other, and sometimes using probabilistic rules.

Decision Trees

Expert systems are programmed with a series of logical rules to find a solution. Very basic expert systems can use **Boolean logic** decision trees to come to conclusions. Boolean logic, has two possible values – true and false, yes and no, 1 and 0, and so on. The meaning of the two values is not relevant – only that there are just two possible outcomes. Figure 16-5 shows an extremely simple example of such logic.

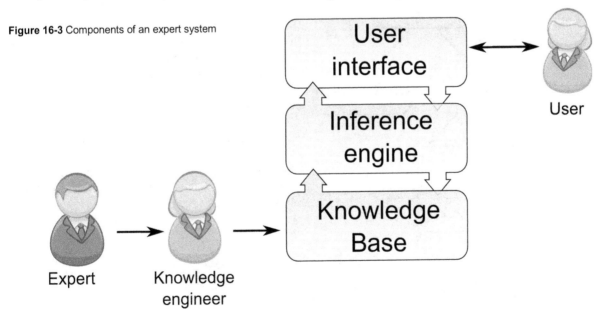

Figure 16-3 Components of an expert system

However, this is clearly an extremely simple example of logic and we would hopefully not require an expert system to find an answer! A further example, and one that starts to show the problems with simple logic, is a medical diagnosis system – a common use of expert systems (see figure 16-4).

One of the problems with figure 16-4 is that several diseases can have the same symptoms, but this is not well represented in a simple hierarchy.

A greater problem is that Boolean logic has only two values, making it difficult to represent many real life problems. The answers to many real life questions are not simply true or false but some value in between. For example, the question *'Do you have a headache?'* is not usefully answered with *'Yes'* or *'No'* – it would be more helpful to know the severity of the headache. Similarly, a fever can be mild or severe, rather than merely present or absent. This is of great significant to the medical expert system— while a slight temperature may indicate something as simple as a common cold, a severe temperature is much more serious and may need urgent attention.

Another problem is that many of the illnesses in figure 16-4 exhibit symptoms to different degrees: malaria sufferers will almost always exhibit a headache, but only some-

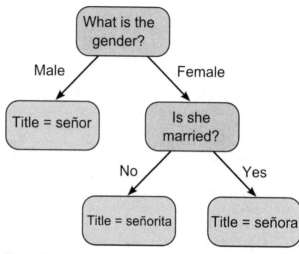

Figure 16-5 Simple rules for determining a person's title

times suffer from stomach problems. The lack of stomach problems does not preclude malaria as a diagnosis, but in the decision tree, this seems to be the case.

To avoid the problems of decision trees, expert systems typically use **inference rules** and **chaining** to reach conclusions.

Inference Rules

Inference rules are written as IF...THEN statements which describe rules for a knowledge domain. A simple example of inference rules might be:

> IF X has gills THEN X is a fish
> IF X is a fish THEN X lives in water
> IF X lives in water THEN X can swim

Through the process of **chaining**, we can take a given object, Fred, who has gills. Using these rules we can conclude first of all that Fred is a fish, then that he lives in water, and finally that Fred can swim. There may also be other rules in the expert system which lead to the conclusion 'lives in the water', such as:

> IF X is an alligator THEN X lives in the water

Using the same process, even though John the alligator has no gills and is not a fish, we can conclude that John can swim.

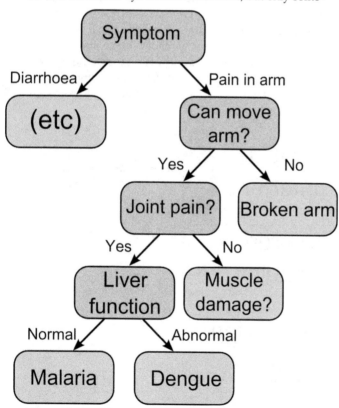

Figure 16-4 Decisions for medical diagnosis

A medical expert system, might include rules such as:

```
IF X has severe headache THEN condition =
malaria

IF X has severe headache AND joint pain
THEN condition = dengue fever

IF condition = malaria THEN treatment =
doxycycline

IF condition = dengue THEN treatment =
analgesics
```

Fuzzy Logic

As discussed, in many knowledge domains, answers and conclusions are not concrete 'yes / no' answers, but have different degrees of truth. **Fuzzy logic** and **fuzzy set theory** are used to model these concepts in expert systems. Whereas in traditional **set theory** objects either belong to a set or not (i.e. a patient's temperature is either hot or it isn't), fuzzy set theory and fuzzy logic allow objects to be partial members of sets (i.e. the temperature can be 'hot' and 'very hot' at the same time, to different degrees). Although this sounds counter-intuitive, it is useful for representing data such as temperature—after all, there is no clear dividing line at which point a temperature ceases being 'hot' and becomes 'very hot' (see figure 16-6). For example, a temperature which is somewhat hot may just be the symptom of a common cold, whereas a temperature which is high or very high signals a much more serious condition.

An advantages of fuzzy logic is that it allows expert systems to provide multiple answers, each with differing degrees of certainly. For example, the result of a medical expert system might be dengue fever (65% certainty) and malaria (25% certainty).

Problems with Expert Systems

As with any collection of data, an expert system's knowledge base may suffer from **data integrity** problems including data which has been incorrectly entered, data which has become out of date, or data which is incomplete or missing completely (see page 154). Each of these problems could have a significant effect on the reliability and accuracy of the answers provided by the system. Similarly, the inference engine, like any software system, may contain bugs. Erroneous or missing rules, or incorrect data processing, will also affect accuracy.

The impact of these reliability problems depends on the knowledge domain. A fault diagnosis system which suggests an incorrect solution may cause inconvenience, but a medical system which suggests incorrect treatment could cause a much more serious health impact.

However, the key problem with expert systems is that they are dependent on the rules in their knowledge base, which cover only a small domain of knowledge, and they are unable to address problems outside of this domain, or exceptions to rules. This makes them unsuitable for some problems. Many modern AI researchers have moved away from developing expert systems, and towards developing systems which can learn and improve.

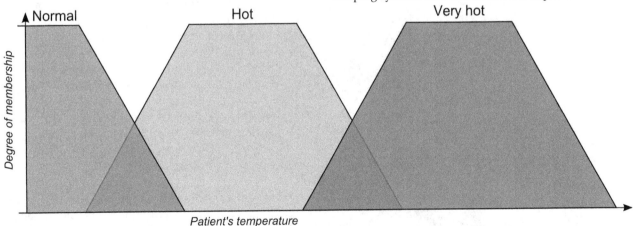

Figure 16-6 Fuzzy logic lets elements be partial members of sets. Here, the temperature can be hot and very hot at the same time.

> **Exercise 16-5**
> a) Think of a knowledge domain where an expert system might be used.
> b) **Construct** a diagram or a series of IF...THEN rules to show how the expert system might work.
> c) Did you encounter any problems during this process?
> d) What limitations exist in trying to create a expert system in this way?

Other AI Techniques
Searching

Another common artificial intelligence technique is **searching**. Searching considers most, if not all, possible solutions to a problem in order to find the most appropriate one. It is often used by software that plays games like draughts (checkers) and chess. For example, playing as white in a game of chess, a searching algorithm would consider all possible white moves that could be made (usually about 30), then every possible black move that could be made for each of those white moves (30^2), then every possible white move for those black moves (30^3), and so on. The software would then decide which move would lead to the best game situation.

The depth of the search (the number of moves ahead that the computer examines) depends on the software and the available computing power – searching requires powerful computers because the number of possible outputs becomes very large very quickly. The Deep Blue chess computer employed searching to beat world chess champion Gary Kasparov (see page 333), looking an average of 8 moves ahead, but able to search up to 20 moves ahead in some situations. Searching is sometimes called a **brute force** approach because it uses sheer computing power to achieve its goals.

Heuristics are sometimes used to speed up searching algorithms. Heuristics are 'rules of thumb' or 'rules which are generally true'. For example, a good heuristic for playing a game of chess might be 'it is better to lose a pawn than a knight'. There might be times when this is not the case (such as when said pawn is protecting the king), but in general, the rule holds true. Therefore, when using a searching algorithm to look for a solution, chess software can discard possible moves which result in losing a knight if there are other moves available that lose lesser pieces (or no pieces at all). Immediately discarding bad moves like this saves time because the software does not examine any future moves for a bad move. The saved time can be used to examine other moves to a greater depth.

Heuristics are also used by some anti-virus scanners to detect new viruses which do not yet have anti-virus definitions available. These virus scanners examine files for behaviour that is typically associated with a virus, such as making multiple copies of itself, attempting to delete or alter other files, or sending large volumes of email in a short time. Although these activities are not exclusive to viruses, they are a good common indicator of viruses.

Limitations of Artificial Intelligence

Consider the four images to the left. Most people – even relatively young children – will be able to identity the two dogs and the two cats very easily. Yet in many cases you may not know how you distinguished them. You might say 'a dog has long fur and a cat has short fur', but this is clearly not always true. Similarly, cats usually have pointed, triangular shaped ears – but so do some dogs. Your understanding of what dogs and cats look like is based on your previous experience of seeing them, not a set of rigid rules that define how they look. This immediately makes it impossible to create expert system style rules to attempt this kind of challenge, and requires a new approach.

Instead, a system which learns and adapts is needed, so that it can be shown images of cats and dogs (trained, as people are) and then learn what they typically look like – just as we tell young children what dogs and cats look like by showing them examples. Modern research focuses more these **computational intelligence** techniques—creating machines which 'think', 'know', and 'learn' in the same way as humans think, know, and learn.

Computational Intelligence Techniques

Pattern recognition systems are often used in **speech recognition** and **computer vision** applications, including **handwriting recognition** and **face recognition**. They are also used by medical software to scan test result images for signs of tumours that might otherwise be missed. Each of these applications features a large amount of variance – although the general characteristics of hand writing, speech, and faces are the same, they vary greatly from person to person, and even one person's voice or face may vary even over relatively short periods of time.

Pattern recognition systems do not use hard rules – instead, they are trained using a set of **training data**. For example, a system to recognise handwriting will be shown samples of individual letters or words and be told what each one represents (*This is an 'A', this is a 'B'*, and so on).

Once training has finished, the system can be shown new samples of writing, break them down into individual letters, and use pattern recognition to work out which letter each one most resembles. This is the key point of pattern recognition systems – they have a **confidence interval** which reflects how certain their answer is. The confidence interval will be affected by the number of training images the system has been given – commercial systems might be trained on data sets containing thousands of samples.

Natural Language Processing

Natural Language Processing refers to the ability of a computer to 'understand' human languages such as English, Spanish, or Kiswahili. The natural language may take the form of input for the computer to read and act upon (for example, voice commands), or the language may be the output (for example, a paragraph of text in response to a question). **Machine translation** – translating from one human language to another – is another common application of natural language processing. Several characteristics of natural languages make understanding them very difficult task for a machine:

- Many words have multiple meanings ('fire' for example, could refer to something burning, firing somebody from a job, or firing a weapon);
- One word may be translated differently depending on the context (for example, 'fire' becomes *'fuego'* in Spanish if referring to a camp fire, but *'disparar'* if referring to firing a gun).
- There are often complex rules governing syntax and grammar.

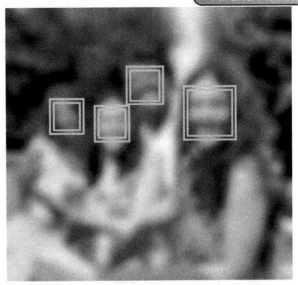

Figure 16-7 Cameras cannot 'see' faces, but use pattern recognition to detect them

Figure 16-8 Software translators can be very useful, but still struggle with complex language

Predictive text: artificial intelligence

Predictive text systems in mobile phones use a form of artificial intelligence to guess the word being typed. When typing the first few letters of a word, there are no definite rules for which letters come next. However, this does not mean that the computer cannot make an educated guess. For example, when the first letter of a word is a 'c', it is quite likely that the next letter will be a vowel. Other letters are also quite likely (such as 'h'), while others are much less likely (for example, c is rarely, if ever, followed by 'q' or 't' at the start of a word). In other cases, 'q' is almost always followed by 'u', and certain pairs are often found together – such as 'th' and 'st'. By examining simple probabilities and word frequencies, a predictive text system can make reasonable guesses at the word you might be typing.

- Some languages are rife with idiom which require more than just a literal translation (consider the phrases 'blowing his own trumpet', 'a picture paints a thousand words', or 'make no bones about')
- Some words or phrases may lack direct translations – for example, the Kiswahili 'anataka zawadi' means either 'he wants a gift' or 'she wants a gift' – the gender of the subject cannot be distinguished from this phrase. While English generally uses 'he' when the gender is unknown, this could cause confusion if the gender of the person is revealed later in the text.

In order to successfully translate between two languages, a computer needs to have a list of words and their equivalents in the target language. However, such a word by word translation would produce very poor results in even the simplest sentences. Consider the following sentence translated word by word from Spanish to English:

El gato rojo   **becomes**   The cat red

Therefore, in addition to knowing the equivalents of each word, the translation software needs to know the class of each word (adjective, noun, verb, and so on), the rules governing the order of the words in each language in different circumstances, the tenses, its gender, whether it is singular or plural, and much more information.

Representing Knowledge

Representing knowledge and the links between pieces of knowledge is important for many intelligent systems. Language in particular, has many complex interrelationships between concepts and ideas.

One way to represent this knowledge is using nodes which are connected by links. Each link has a weight which specifies the strength or importance of the relationship between those two ideas.

For example, in figure 16-9, we can see that the word *sky* is strongly associated with the words *blue*, *sun*, and *clouds*. The weights between the nodes can be determined by training—in this case, perhaps asking people for the words they think of when they hear the word *sky* or *sun*. The more people that mention a word in conjunction with another, the higher the strength of the link, and thus its weight. Other words are also associated with *sky*, such as *moon* and *stars*, but the weight of these links is lower— perhaps because, when asked for words associated with *sky*, fewer people thought of those words.

The advantage of this method is that 'incorrect' training—such as people entering unusual associations, does not greatly affect the knowledge since the most common associations rise and the less common ones fall in importance.

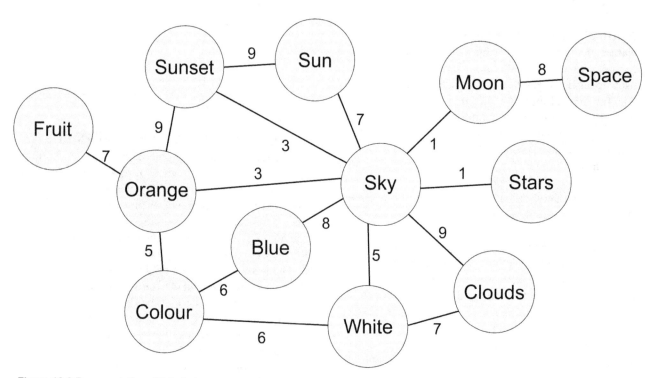

Figure 16-9 Representation of links between concepts

Using this representation of knowledge, answers can be found to questions posed in natural language. Consider the question *'what colour is the sky?'*. Natural language processing techniques can be used to locate the important words in this sentence (*sky* and *colour*). In figure 16-9 there are eight associations with *sky*. Some would make no sense: *'the sky is moon'* or *'the sky is sunset'*. This is also true for the word most strongly associated with *sky*, *clouds*. However, some of the words associated with *sky* are also associated with the other key word from the sentence, *colour*. These are *blue*, *white*, and *orange*. Of these three words, *blue* is the most commonly associated with sky, giving us our answer: *the sky is blue*.

Representing knowledge in this way provides relatively useful answers even to fairly complex questions. Of course, figure 16-9 is a simplified example and in reality a great deal more information needs to be stored.

Neural networks

Artificial neural networks, or ANNs, are an attempt to make computers learn in a similar way to humans, by representing the neurons in the human brain and the electrical impulses which flow between them (synapses). ANNs feature a series of inputs and a series of outputs, connected by one or more layers of **nodes** (figure 16-10). These nodes are connected to each other, with the importance of the connection being donated by its **weight**.

Each hidden node takes inputs from several input nodes, and uses a **transfer function** (also called an **activation function**) to determine its output. The transfer function pays more attention to nodes with higher weights. The output is then passed to the next node.

A neural network needs training before it can be used effectively. During this learning phase, the neural network is given a series of inputs and calculates its output. This output is then compared to the expected output, as determined by a human. The difference between the ANNs output and the expected output is known as the error. A process called **back propagation** then occurs— the weights of some nodes in the ANN are adjusted until the transfer functions produce output more closely matched to the expected output.

After training, a neural network can be given real data and classify it (produce output) based on the examples it has previously learnt. Applications of neural networks include hand writing recognition (recognising characters), data processing such as data mining (see page 158), and spam filtering (see page 101).

Artificial Intelligence in Action

Despite having more Closed Circuit Television (CCTV) cameras per person than any other nation, less than 3% of UK crimes are solved using CCTV footage. Developers of a Smart CCTV system named Samurai hope to change this. Samurai actively monitors video feeds, tracking people from camera to camera and using neural networks to check for signs of suspicious behaviour, such as unattended luggage or loitering outside an important building. If the system spots something suspicious, it alerts authorities, who can then investigate[3].

A more mundane use of neural networks is in the banking industry to vet transactions. Whenever a credit card transaction is made, software compares the transaction with previous spending habits, looking for abnormalities. A card being used hundreds of miles apart within a short time suggests possible fraud, for example, as does unusually high or repeated withdrawals, especially at strange times such as during the night. Systems like these have helped reduce credit card fraud by half in ten years[4].

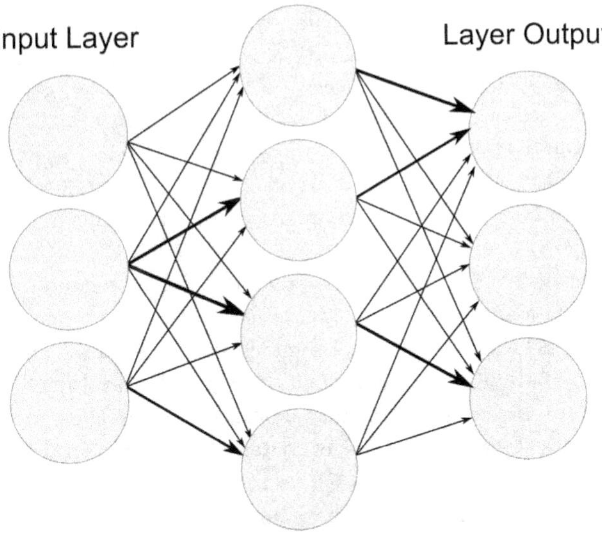

Figure 16-10 Neural networks are designed to work in a similar way to the neurons in the human brain.

Artificial Examiners?

Researchers at the University of Buffalo, New York, have created software to read and grade student exam papers. Assessing simple multiple choice papers is quite simple for a computerised system, but the software created by Professor Sargur Srihari's team was tested on reading comprehension exams answering the question 'How was Martha Washington's role as First Lady different from that of Eleanor Roosevelt?'

Prior to the process, human examiners graded 300 scripts, and these were used to train the system. The system looked for key phrases and words which were commonly found in papers given high grades by the human examiners.

Another set of exam papers was then given to the computer system. First the hand written papers were scanned, then hand writing recognition software broke them down into separate words. The artificial examiner software then looked for occurrences of the previously identified words and phrases, giving higher grades if there were more instances of them, and lower grades if there were fewer instances[5].

Although this might sound like a great technological feat, there are still significant limitations. Apart from the difficulty of recognising hand writing, the scope of the answers are also quite limited, as children are expected to answer with key words taken from the exam question. Questions with much wider scope, such as 'Evaluate the main causes of the Second World War', could still not be assessed by a computer.

Another problem with the system is understanding context, as merely including key words in an answer may not be enough. For example, a student could include key words but incorrectly state that George Washington is the current president of the United States, or that Martha Washington was the First Lady of the United Kingdom. It is therefore important not only to include key words, but to use them appropriately and not to include mistakes—something the AI software finds hard to detect.

Exercise 16-6

These web sites feature a variety of artificially intelligent programs. Visit the sites, try the programs, and describe the techniques you think each might use to try to achieve 'intelligence'.

- **Exsys Expert Systems**—a variety of demonstration expert systems on their web site, including a dog breed selector and a restaurant advisor. (www.exsys.com/demomain.html)
- **START**—a 'Natural Language Question Answering System'. (start.csail.mit.edu)
- **Baby Rose**—a 'community powered Artificial Intelligence Project', is a web application which communicates with users in natural language. Users can talk to Rose and teach it new words. (www.teachrose.com)
- **20 Questions**—think of an item and answer 20 questions to see if the computer can guess it (www.20q.net)
- **Google Translate**—Offers translation in many languages—choose two that you know and check its accuracy (www.google.com/translate)
- **Tic-Tac-Toe**—Try to beat the computer. What does this tell you about the nature of some games? (www.goriya.com/flash/tictactoe.shtml)

Exercise 16-7

TOK Link

The Deep Blue computer beat world chess champion Gary Kasparov, displaying 'more intelligent' behaviour in the game of chess. Yet Deep Blue played chess in a way no human being does: by using searching algorithms to analyse thousands and thousands of moves ahead and look for the best choice.

Is it enough for a computer to display intelligent results? Or should a truly intelligent computer 'think' in the same way a human being thinks? **Discuss** which is more important—the results that are demonstrated or the methods by which they are achieved? [8 marks]

Robotics

A **robot** is a computer controlled system that performs manual, physical tasks. Robots can be **autonomous**, using artificial intelligence or computational intelligence techniques to navigate their environment and perform their jobs, or they can be remotely controlled by a human operator. Robots are primarily used for three types of physical jobs:

- Dangerous jobs – such as cleaning up nuclear waste or performing bomb disposal
- Boring or repetitive jobs – such as manufacturing jobs in factories or on production lines
- Exploring inaccessible environments – such as the extreme ocean depths or the surfaces of other planets, which are difficult or impossible for humans to access

Social impacts of robots

Robots cause a variety of positive social impacts. Robots used for hazardous jobs like bomb disposal (figure 16-11) clearly reduce the risk of death or serious injury to humans. **Exploration robots** help increase scientific knowledge – they have been used to locate and recover the wreckages of ships and aircraft lost in the ocean (including helping to find the wreck of the Titanic in 1982), and at least three robotic rovers have landed on the surface of Mars, moving around the Martian surface and sending samples and photographs back to Earth. Manned missions to these environments would be significantly more expensive and dangerous than sending robots. Unmanned space vehicles have also been sent to the *Mir* and *ISS* space stations to resupply the crews living there—in these cases, there is no need to send a human crew (who would need their own supplies) on such relatively routine missions.

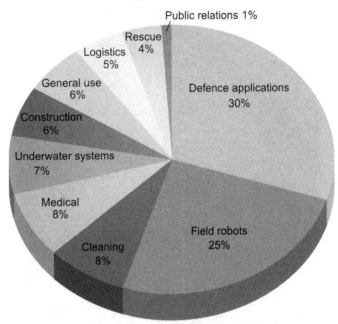

Robots by application area (2009)

Source: International Federation of Robotics

Figure 16-12 Common applications for robots

Carrier robots such as the Big Dog move across rough terrain carrying heavy loads for the military. The BEAR (Battlefield Extraction Assist Robot) robot is designed to rescue soldiers on the battlefield, reducing the need for humans to enter the line of fire. **Search and rescue** robots are being developed to search environments such as the ruins of buildings after an earthquake. Many of these are designed to travel through gaps where humans could not fit, or in unstable buildings that may collapse without warning (figure 16-13).

Domestic robots are available to assist in cleaning jobs around the house, while robots like the BEAR and Pearl can assist elderly people by providing support when

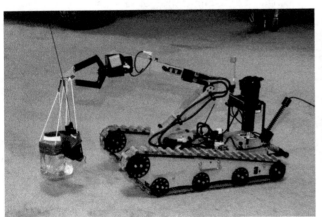

Figure 16-11 A US Navy bomb disposal robot (left); Robots designed to play football in the RoboCup league (right)

walking, announcing reminders of medication times, and calling an emergency number if movement is not detected after a certain period of time.

Robots excel at performing the same operation over and over again without variation and without becoming tired. Unlike human workers, robots do not need breaks or shift changes, and do not get sick. This makes them ideal for **manufacturing jobs** such as those in factories or on production lines, improving output efficiency.

However, these same robots may cause negative impacts by making human workers redundant: a single robot can replace several workers in a factory, and although new jobs are created for maintenance operators, on average more jobs are lost than gained.

There is also the risk of injury in any environment where humans and robots work together. A single robotic arm made out of steel may weigh tens of kilos, giving it great potential to cause injury, and it is difficult for many robots to detect obstacles in their way. For this reason, robots in factories usually operate in separate areas – often fenced off – and use systems that cut power to robots when a human enters their area. Nevertheless, there have been causes of workers injured or killed by robots that failed to detect their presence[6].

Ethical Issues

Developing robots which will inevitably cause employment is clearly an ethical issue that needs debate. The development and use of robots raises several similar issues, including the increased reliance that humans have on technology, and questions about the wisdom of delegating decision making processes to machines.

The development of **humanoid** robots, which have the general overall shape as human beings, and **androids**, which attempt to mimic the look of human faces and skin, raises unique ethical questions about our identities. Exercises 16-15 and 16-16 cover some of the ethical issues that might arise through robotic development.

Figure 16-13 An image of the Martian surface taken by the Spirit rover (top) ; a robot arm which automatic dispenses medicine (middle); rescue robots, designed to move like snakes, can access otherwise inaccessible areas .

Sensing the World

Like all IT systems, robots' work is divided into four stages: input, processing, storage, and output. Robots use a variety of artificial intelligence and computational intelligence techniques to process and store their data. Because robots do manual, physical tasks and move around their environments, the input and output devices they use differ greatly from those found on most computer systems.

Robots cannot see as human beings can: even if a robot is attached to a video camera, it will have no understanding of what the image contains, nor its meaning. It cannot even understand which parts of the image are closer to it and which are further away. All the robot 'sees' is a 2D, flat collection of coloured pixels with no meaning. Programming a computer to understand and 'see' its environment—so called **computer vision**—is one of the great challenges of robotics.

Because of this, many robot designers use a different approach. Instead of designing robots to see the environment as humans do, they design robots to **sense** or measure it. For example, instead of using a camera to see a classroom, and programming the robot to understand the different objects in the room, a robot designer might use a **proximity sensor** to measure the distance to nearby objects. This can be achieved using an **infrared (IR) sensor** and measuring the time taken for light emitted by the robot to be reflected off objects and return. The robot can use this information to build an internal map of the objects around it. However, even using this approach, a robot will not know what nearby objects are – merely that they exist.

Lasers are another type of light sensor often used on robots. Lasers work in a similar way to IR sensors, but are more powerful. However, their range is still quite limited and they don't work well in low visibility conditions such as cloud, fog, or mist. Lasers also have difficulty detecting some highly reflective surfaces (such as water).

Radar can be used to detect obstacles by emitting radio waves and measuring the reflected waves. Radar has a much longer range than light sensors and can 'see' in low visibility conditions such as fog and cloud. However, radar is less accurate than light sensors and sometimes detects non-existent objects.

Instead of measuring distances using IR, laser, or radar, some robots use **video cameras** and **computer vision** systems. A video camera on its own is useless to a ro-

Figure 16-14 Wakamaru (top), designed by Mitsubishi is a domestic companion and assistance robot. Repliee android robots (bottom) boast incredibly lifelike appearances, if somewhat limited abilities.

bot—it can only 'see' a 2D collection of coloured pixels. To make a robot 'see' objects, its software has to search the image for shapes, patterns, or colours that it 'recognises', using pattern recognition techniques (see page 339). When the robot is created, it has to be trained to know what each of these patterns might be.

Cameras have similar limitations to the human eye – they don't work well in the dark or in other low visibility conditions. A single camera is unable to 'see' the world in three dimensions, so the robot cannot see how far away objects are. One approach to depth perception is to use two cameras set slightly apart (like our eyes) to give two slightly different images (again, exactly like our eyes). The slight offset between these images can be used to calculate distance from the observer (objects closer to the viewer seem to have shifted more than objects further away). This is similar to looking out the side of a moving car and seeing close objects speed past quickly, but distant objects appear to move much more slowly.

Pressure sensors are used to tell a robot if it has touched something, and the direction in which it has touched it, which is useful for negotiating obstacles (though not avoiding them in the first place). Pressure sensors also give a sense of 'touch', like human skin, which is essential for robots which grasp objects. For example, a robot trying to pick up an egg needs to know how much pressure is being exerted: too little and the egg will fall, but too much and the egg will be crushed. This is of even more concern if the robot works closely with humans—perhaps helping to steady an elderly patient whilst walking, or picking up a baby in a hospital.

Other sensors used by robots include **heat sensors**, useful for detecting living things in an environment, **magnetism sensors**, **pH sensors**, **sound sensors**, and **humidity sensors**—many of which are used in exploration robots to gather environmental data.

Robotic Output Devices

A variety of **robotic arms** are available, from very simple lifting devices to arms with many joints, multiple degrees of freedom, and as much dexterity as the human arm (or even more). Arms are powered by **relay circuits** and **motors**. They are one of the most common robotic output devices because of the range of tasks they can complete—from lifting and moving objects to welding and painting. Robotic arms can have specific tools permanently attached to them, or they may use a variety of clamps and fingers to grasp different objects—though usually this is a much more difficult proposition.

If **clamps** are used, they typically need to be fitted with pressure sensors to ensure they do not damage the item being gripped by crushing it. **Robotic fingers** operate in a similar way to clamps, except they offer great flexibility in the type of items they can grasp.

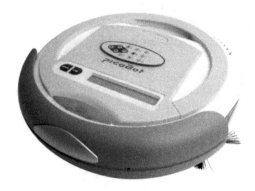

Figure 16-15 Small domestic robot for cleaning floors

If a robot is under remote human control, **haptic technology** is commonly used to give the operator feedback in the form of vibrations or forces, to indicate the state of the robot. For example, a strong vibration may be felt if the robot comes too close to, or collides with, an obstacle. The Da Vinci surgical robot uses this technique to resist the surgeon's input when they start to move instruments away from the designated area of the body being operated on.

Especially in environments where humans work alongside robots, **lights**, **sirens**, and **speakers** are used to alert people to the presence of heavy, dangerous machinery, in order to avoid potential accidents.

To move around their environments, many robots use **wheels** or **tracks**. Legs can also be used, though standing and moving on two legs is an incredibly difficult task for a robot. One of the problems robots face is uneven surfaces and obstacles such as stairs, which can be difficult to clear with any of these techniques.

Exercise 16-8

In science fiction, many robots are designed as **humanoids**—standing upright and having a shape which generally resembles that of the human body. Why do you think this is? In real life, far fewer are designed in this way. Why do you think robot designers might avoid designing humanoid robots?

Exercise 16-9

Research domestic cleaning robots such as Roomba, which move across the floor, cleaning dirty areas of the house.
   a) **Explain** how these robots sense & navigate their environment. [6 marks]
   b) **Explain** how these robots know where to clean. [6 marks]

Exercise 16-10

Robotics is a constantly changing field. Use the Internet to find examples of the latest robotic developments in each of the ITGS specific scenarios. **Describe** the jobs these robots do and **explain** the possible social impacts. Do these robots raise any ethical issues? [10 marks]

Case Study: The DARPA Grand Challenge

In 2005, the US Defence Advanced Research Projects Agency (DARPA) initiated the Grand Challenge—a robot race offering a $1 million prize for the team who could build a driverless robot to negotiate 240 kilometres of desert roads.

Despite two years of development, race day saw a high attrition rate—all but four vehicles had failed after 3 hours, and only one vehicle—Sandstorm—made it past 11 kilometres, before getting stuck on a dirt mount and being unable to continue.

A year later, and the 2005 Grand Challenge offered an increased prize of $2 million and a race over 212 kilometres of the Nevada desert. Key entries included Stanley, entered by Standard University; Highlander and Sandstorm, both entered by Carnegie Mellon University; TerraMax, a 30,000 pound truck; and Ghost Rider, the only autonomous motorcycle in the race.

As in the first race, the desert conditions proved tough for some of the vehicles, but despite this all but one of vehicles were still running at the point Sandstorm failed the previous year.

The Stanford team eventually won the challenge, with Stanley completing the course in just under 7 hours, followed by Sandstorm and Highlander in 2nd and 3rd places. In total five vehicles finished the course, though TerraMax took almost 13 hours.

After the success of the desert challenge, in 2007 DARPA hosted the next Grand Challenge—the Urban Challenge. This required vehicles to negotiate a road course while following all traffic rules, avoiding other vehicles, obstacles, and pedestrians. In all, six teams managed to complete the course successfully.

Figure 16-16 Highlander (top) finished third in 2005; slow but sure TerraMax (middle) finished 5th; the next challenge for the winner Stanley (bottom) is the Urban Challenge.

Exercise 16-11

Imagine you were going to enter a vehicle into the DARPA Grand Challenge.
a) **Describe** three challenges robot designers might face when designing a driverless vehicle to compete in the Grand Challenge. [6 marks]
b) **Explain** how each of these challenges might be solved. [6 marks]

Exercise 16-12

Research the red team (Highlander and Sandstorm) and the blue team (Stanley) from the 2005 Grand Challenge. Their robots work in two fundamentally different ways. **Explain** how these approaches relate to the artificial intelligence methods covered on page 338. [8 marks]

Chapter Review

Key Language

Artificial Intelligence

Artificial Intelligence	expert system shell	inference rule	rules
Artificial Neural Network	expert system	knowledge base	searching
Boolean logic	feedback loop	knowledge domain	set theory
brute force searching	fuzzy logic	knowledge engineer	speech recognition
CAPTCHA	fuzzy set theory	knowledge representation	speech synthesisers
chaining	hand writing recognition	logic	training data
Chinese Room, the	heuristics	machine learning	Turing test
common-sense knowledge	IF-THEN rule	machine translation	user interface
computational intelligence	image analysis	natural language processing	
confidence interval	inference engine	pattern recognition	

Robotics

android	humidity sensor	pressure sensor	sirens
autonomous	infrared sensor	proximity sensor	sound sensor
camera	lasers	radar	speakers
clamps	light sensor	relays	tracks
claws	lights	robot	wheels
computer vision	magnetism sensor	robotic arm	
heat sensor	motors	robotic fingers	
humanoid	pH sensor	sensors	

Exercise 16-13

TOK Link

Find something that you personally consider a piece of art. It can be any form (drawing, painting, writing, music) but it must be human-created. Then find a machine-created piece of work (drawing, writing, music, etc.). This must be created by a machine, not created by a human being using a machine (i.e. not a photo edited using graphics software).

Produce a short presentation which addresses the following questions
a) Why do you consider your 'human example' to be art?
b) Can a machine produce something that we can call 'art'? If so, are there any limitations to this?
c) What if we don't know whether or not something was produced by a computer?
d) Are 'artificial artists' a good idea?

Exercise 16-14

The BEAR robot is a dual-purpose robot. It was originally designed to extract injured soldiers from the battlefield, but civilian applications were also considered – such as helping elderly people.
   a) **Describe** the challenges this robot might face. [4 marks]
   b) **Explain** how the designers might solve them. [6 marks]

Exercise 16-15

Android robots are already being developed. **Discuss** the issues that occur when robots which resemble human beings are built. [8 marks]

Exercise 16-16

Discuss whether it is appropriate to develop robots which will cause a clear negative impact, such as causing people to lose their jobs. What, if anything, should society do for who lose their jobs because of robotic development? [8 marks]

Exercise 16-17

(a) (i) Define the term *natural language processing*. [2 marks]

   (ii) Describe **two** components of an expert system. [4 marks]

(b) Explain the benefits of using an expert system for medical diagnosis. [6 marks]

(c) Discuss whether machine translation tools are a viable alternative to human translators. [8 marks]

Exercise 16-18

Robot assisted surgery, using tools such as the Da Vinci Surgical System, is becoming more common. Healthcare benefits include less invasive surgery and claimed shorter recovery times.

(a) (i) Define the term 'robot'. [2 marks]

   (ii) Identify **two** input devices and **two** output devices used on the Da Vinci robot. [4 marks]

(b) Explain **two** applications of robots in healthcare other than for robotic surgery. [6 marks]

(c) One possibility the Da Vinci Surgical System offers is remote surgery – the idea that the surgeon and the patient are in separate geographical locations – with the surgeon's input and the robot's feedback being communicated over a network. Evaluate the benefits and concerns that this would cause. [8 marks]

Exercise 16-19

Robots are being increasingly used by the military to replace or augment human soldiers. Robotic vehicles such as the Big Dog can carry large loads, while bomb disposal robots help keep soldiers out of danger, and remote drones such as the Predator and Reaper can be piloted from thousands of kilometres away.

(a) (i) Define the term 'haptic feedback' [2 marks]

   (ii) Describe **two** approaches an autonomous vehicle might use to navigate a battlefield environment. [4 marks]

(b) Explain the concerns that might arise with the use of robots in a battlefield environment. [6 marks]

(c) Millions of dollars are spent on robotic development each year. To what extent is this an appropriate way to spend such large amounts of money? [8 marks]

References

1 Mori, G. & Malik, J. (2002). *Breaking a Visual CAPTCHA*. Available: www.cs.sfu.ca/~mori/research/gimpy/. Last accessed April 2011.

2 IBM. (2011). *IBM Watson - The Science Behind an Answer*. Available: http://www-03.ibm.com/innovation/us/watson/what-is-watson/science-behind-an-answer.html. Last accessed Aug 2011.

3 Fleming, N. (2009). *Smart CCTV learns to spot suspicious types*. New Scientist. Available: www.newscientist.com/article/mg20427385.800. Last accessed Aug 2011.

4 Kaufman, W. (2005). *Electronic Brain Helps Cut Credit Card Fraud*. National Public Radio. Available: www.npr.org/templates/story/story.php?storyId=4758471. Last accessed Aug 2011.

5 BBC. (2007). *Artificial examiners put to the test* . Available: news.bbc.co.uk/2/hi/technology/6961088.stm. Last accessed Aug 2011.

6 Health and Safety Executive. (2010). *Castle Bromwich firm fined after worker injured by robot*. Available: http://www.hse.gov.uk/press/2010/coi-wm-10809.htm. Last accessed Nov 2011.

Glossary

1-1 programme: Scheme in which every student is given their own laptop. 230

3D modelling: 128, 285

3G: System to allow Internet access using mobile phone networks. 77

4G: System to allow Internet access using mobile phone networks. 77

AAC: Lossy file format for audio. 132

absolute cell reference: In a spreadsheet, a cell reference which does not change when moved. 170, 178, 182, **194**

absolute link: HTML link to a fully specified URL. 203

acceptable use policy: Policy that sets out what users are and are not allowed to do with IT systems. **188**, 228

acceptance testing: See user acceptance testing.

access levels: 94

accessibility: Hardware and software features to help disabled users operate computer systems. 29, 229

accounting software: Application software for managing finances. 54

Active Server Pages: Technology used to create dynamic web pages. 204

Active Server Pages Extended: See Active Server Pages. 204

ad blockers: Software to block adverts in web pages. 212

adaptive maintenance: 322

ADC: See analog to digital converter.

addiction: 267, 278

agile development: Development method that focuses on creating small, working parts of a project at regular intervals. 324

AI: See Artificial Intelligence.

alignment: Tools to control placement of objects in presentation or DTP software. 136

alpha testing: Initial testing of an IT system. 320

ALT attribute: HTML attribute that provides a text description of images. 208

alternative key: See secondary key.

American Standard Code for Information Interchange: Encoding system to store text, where one byte is used for each character. Compare Unicode. 36

analog data: Data which can be measured. 25, **238**

Analog to digital converter: Device for sampling analog data and producing a digital equivalent. 25, **238**

analyst: In project development, person who documents the current system, finding its problems and areas for improvement. 314

anchor: See internal link.

android: Robot designed to look like a human, with lifelike skin and other features. 344

ANPR: See Automatic Number Plate Recognition.

anti-plagiarism software: Software to detect plagiarised work by searching the Internet and previous work samples. 228

anti-virus: Software to detect and remove viruses and other malware. 96

Apache: Well known web server software. 209

applet: Java program which runs inside a web page. 204

application server: Computer that stores application software for clients on a network. 68

application software: Software which allows users to produce work, such as documents and presentations. 50

application suite: Collection of application programs that perform related tasks, sold together. 50

Artificial Intelligence: Creating a system that produces results comparable to human intelligence. 334

Artificial Neural Network: AI system that attempts to mimic the neurons and synapses in the human brain. 341

ASCII: See American Standard Code for Information Interchange.

ASP: See Active Server Pages.

ASPX: See Active Server Pages.

assistant: See wizard.

assumptions: 173

asymmetric key encryption: See public key encryption.

asynchronous: Data transfer method in which the sender and receiver are not synchronised. 83

asynchronous learning: Learning which does not require the teacher and student to be online at the same time. 220

ATM: 193

attributes: Component of an Entity Relationship Diagram. 318

audio software: Application software for creating, recording, and editing sound. 52

audit trails: Record of all changes and actions performed with a system, for security purposes. **71**, 161

auditing: See audit trails.

augmented reality: Overlapping layers of computer data with images of the real world. **280**, 303

authentication: Establishing a user's identity. 4, **90**

authentication server: Computer that checks usernames and passwords when a user tries to log in. 68

authorised access: User who has permission to use a system. 68

Automatic Number Plate Recognition: Software which processes video camera data to read vehicle number plates. 300

automatic recalculation: Spreadsheet feature that updates results when cells are changed. 51

autonomous: Robot which operates without human intervention. 343

avatar: Representation of a person in a virtual environment. 278

AVI: Lossy file format for video. 132

B2B: See Business-to-Business.

B2C: See Business-to-Consumer.

back-end: Database which stores web site content 'behind the scenes'. 204

backbone: High speed connections that connect main Internet sites. 76

backdoor: Method of bypassing security in a system, built in by the system designers. 97

backup: Spare copy of data to be used in the event of an emergency. 49

BAN: See Basel Action Network.

bandwidth: Measure of a network's speed. 69

banner ads: 211

bar code scanners: Input device that uses a laser to read a bar code. 22

Basel Action Network: Environmental campaign group. 247

Basel Convention, The: Environmental agreement regarding e-waste. 248

battlefield network: Large scale network gathering information from soldiers, vehicles, and maps to provide an overall view of the battlefield. 304

beta tester: See beta testing.

beta testing: Testing of an IT system once all features have been added and only bugs need to be worked out. 320

biometric enrolment: Process of registering a user

for a biometric system by taking an initial sample. 92

biometric template: Measurements taken from a biometric sample. 92

biometrics: Use of fingerprints, retina scans, or other body features as an authentication mechanism. **91**, 274, 293

bit: A single binary digit (a 1 or a 0). The smallest unit of storage inside a computer. 37

bit depth: Refers to the number of colours in an image. 122

bit rate: Amount of data used to represent a single sample in a video or audio file. 114

bitmap graphics: Graphics composed of rectangular grids of pixels. 116

black boxes: Closed system whose internal operation cannot be inspected. 291

black list: List of banned web sites in a filtering system. 291

blade servers: Servers housed on individual circuit boards in a modular system. 243

blended learning: Mix of traditional teaching techniques and e-learning techniques. 220

blog: Web page where entries are stored chronologically, like a diary or journal. 85

blue screen: Technique used to replace part of a video image with computer graphics. 134

Bluetooth: Short range, low bandwidth wireless technology often used for mobile phone headsets or earphones. 16, **77**

Blu-ray: Optical secondary storage device capable of storing 16GB+. 33

BMP: Lossless file format for audio. 132

Boolean logic: Logic in which clauses can have one of two states – such as

yes or no, true or false. 335

Boolean operators: AND, OR, and NOT operators used in a query. 150

botnet: Group of zombie computers under the control of a criminal. 98

bounce rate: Percentage of users who visit a web site but immediately leave it. 212

bps: bits per second. 77

Braille keyboard: Special keyboard designed for users with eyesight problems. 29

Braille printer: Special printer that can produce Braille text. 29

breadcrumb trails: Feature of a web site to help user navigation. 206

broadband: High speed network connection. 77

browser: Software used to view web pages. 52

browser compatibility: 205

brute force attack: Attempt to break a password by trying all possible combinations of letters, numbers, and symbols. 94

brute force searching: See searching.

buffer: Temporary storage area used to store video or audio data ready for playing. 134

bug: Error or mistake in a program. **62**, 320

bug tracking system: Used to track and manage bugs in a piece of software. 320

bulk email: See spam.

business case: Analysis of the benefits and problems of a proposed IT project. 314

Business Software Alliance: Organisation that works to reduce illegal copying of software. 58

Business-to-Business: E-commerce conducted between two businesses, such as a business and their suppliers. 201

Business-to-Consumer: E-commerce conducted

between a business and their customers, for example, online shopping. 201

byte: Storage unit: 8 bits. Enough to store a single ASCII text character. 37

C2C: See Consumer-to-Consumer.

cable: See DSL / cable.

cache: Storage area for frequently used information, to speed up access. 73

CAD: See Computer Aided Design.

camera: Common input device in robotics. 345

Capability Maturity Model Integration: Quality assurance method that describes an organisation's level of maturity. 321

CAPTCHA: System designed to create text that is unreadable to a computer but understandable to a person, to reduce spam. **103**, 333

car crash model: Used to predict the results of car crashes. 167

cardinality: Property of a relationship in an Entity Relationship Diagram. 318

Carpel Tunnel Syndrome: Injury caused by overuse or incorrect use of a computer: 252

Cascading Style Sheets: Technology to specify styling and formatting information for web pages. 202

CAVE: See Cave Automated Virtual Environment.

Cave Automated Virtual Environment: Form of virtual reality which projects images on the walls surrounding a user. 278

CD-ROM: Optical secondary storage device capable of holding 650-700MB of data. 33

cell format: In spreadsheets, the properties of a cell such as its colour, font, and cell type. 182

cell range: In spreadsheets, reference to a range of

continuous cells. 182

cell reference: In spreadsheets, a combination of row number and column letter to refer to a single cell (e.g. A2). 170, 178, 182, **194**

Central Processing Unit: Hardware responsible for processing all instructions the computer runs. 30

centralised database: database in which all data in stored in one centralised location. 256

centralised processing: Single computer with multiple processors working on a task. **176**, 267

Certificate Authority: Organisation that issues digital certificates to individuals and companies. 108

CFD: Computational Fluid Dynamics. A technique used to model airflow in computer models. 167

CGI: See Computer Generated Imagery.

chaining: Use of logical statements to come to a conclusion. 336

changeover: Moving from an old system to a new IT system. 322

character check: Ensuring a field contains only the specified character types. 156

check digit: Way of checking mathematically if a item of data has been correctly entered. 156

Children's Internet Protection Act: US law requiring Internet filtering in US most schools and libraries. 226, 292

Chinese Room, the: Thought experiment dealing with the idea of knowledge. 334

chip and pin: Systems designed to reduce credit card fraud by requiring the user to authenticate themselves at the point of sale. 193

CIPA: See Children's Internet Protection Act.

ciphertext: Result of encrypting plaintext. 106

citation: Acknowledge to a piece of work used as a source. 114

citizen journalism: News reporting by everyday citizens using mobile technology, rather than traditional media. 282

clamps: Common output device in robotics. 346

claws: Common output device in robotics. 346

Click Through Rate: Percentage of users who click on an advert after seeing it. 212

client (person): Person or organisation who commissions an IT project. 313

client (computer): Computer on a network that uses services provided by a server. 68

client-server: Network system that uses servers to store data centrally and client computers to access them. 68

climate model: Used to predict possible future climate change. 168

clinical decision support system: Expert system for medical diagnosis.

clock speed: Speed of a processor, in ticks per second. 30

cloning: Image effect used to copy one part of an image to another. 116

Closed Circuit Television cameras: 300

closed source: Software whose source code is not publicly available. 56

cloud computing: System whereby application software and data are stored on a remote Internet server. 58

CMMI: See Capability Maturity Model Integration.

codes of conduct: Professional guidelines created by bodies such as the

ACM and the BCS. 327

collaborative software: Application software to let users work together on projects even if they are geographically remote. 190

colour balance: Graphics filtering for altering the tones and intensities of colours in an image. 117

colour depth: See bit depth.

colour levels: Graphics filtering for altering the tones and intensities of colours in an image. 117

colour management: See colour synchronisation.

colour profile: Used as part of colour synchronisation to specify how a device represents colour. 137

colour synchronisation: Ensuring printed output colours accurately match those on the screen. 137

Comma Separated Values: File format for transferring data, which stores fields and records in a plain text file. 152

command line interface: System the user controls by typing in commands. 44

commercial software: Software which is sold for profit. 55

CompactFlash: Solid state storage device usually used in digital cameras. 34

compatibility: Idea that two systems work together and can share hardware, software, or data. 44

composite image: Image which was created from several separate images. 117

composite key: Primary key which consists of more than one field. 145

compression: Reduction in the amount of data used to store a file. 124

computational intelligence: Approach that tries to create systems that think and learn in the same way

humans do. 334

Computer Aided Design: Technical graphics software used to design products for manufacture. 128

Computer Generated Imagery: Graphics created entirely on a computer, using 2D or 3D graphics software. 117

computer matching: See data matching.

Computer Misuse Act: UK law governing criminal offences committed using a computer. 99

computer model: Mathematical representation of the real world using computer software. 166, 252

computer simulation: Based on computer models, gives users experience of events such as flying a plane. 180

computer vision: Techniques to let computers and robots see and understand the world around them. 345

concept keyboard: Keyboard with keys that perform programmable, customised functions. 19

concurrent licence: Software licence that allows a specific number of copies to be used at one time. 58

confidence interval: Level of certainty in an answer a pattern recognition system provides. 339

consistency check: Validation check in which two fields' values are mutually dependent. 156

constraints: Limitations within which an IT system must work. 314

Consumer-to-Consumer: E-commerce where customers deal directly with each other, such as in online auction. 201

content rating: System whereby web site content is categorised so that filters can block it if necessary. 292

continuous data: See analog data.

convergence: Idea that one device performs the same functions as many separate devices. 18

conversion rate: Percentage of visitors who visit a site and then make a purchase. 202

cookies: Small text file text by some web sites to recognise the user when they return. 207

copyright: Law protecting intellectual property from unauthorised copying. 55, 58, **135**

copyright infringement: Illegally copying or distributing copyrighted material. 275

corrective maintenance: 322

Cost Per Click: Amount paid to the advertising company when a user clicks on an advert. 212

CP: See Critical Path.

CPC: See Cost Per Click.

CPU: See Central Processing Unit.

cracking: See hacking.

Creative Commons: Licensing system for authors who wish to distribute their work freely. 135

Critical Path: Longest (slowest) path through a project's development, as determined by using a PERT chart. 315

cropping: Taking a small part (subset) of an image. 116

cross-platform: Hardware or software that works on multiple operating systems. 44

CRT monitor: Output device. Older type of monitor, now almost obsolete. 27, 245

CSS: See Cascading Style Sheets.

CSV: See Comma Separated Values.

CTR: See Click Through Rate.

CTS: See Carpel Tunnel

Syndrome.

Custom / bespoke software: Software created specific for an individual or organisation. 311

cyber-bullying: Use of IT such as social networks to harass or bully individuals. 230

cyber-terrorism: Using computer hacking techniques to commit acts of terrorism. 305

cyber-warfare: Using computer hacking techniques to commit acts of war. 305

cybernetics: Integration of IT into the human body. 252

data centres: Large warehouses of computers that host hundreds or thousands of gigabytes of data. 242

data collection: Used to find information about an existing system during the development of a new system. 314

data entry form: Screen used to input data into a database.

Data Flow Diagram: Shows processes in a system and the flows of data between them. 317

data integrity: 154

data layers: Layers of information added to a Geographical Information System. 239

data logging: Automatic recording of data using sensors. 236

data matching: Combining several databases to build up more information about a person or set of people. 158

data mining: Searching collections of data for hidden patterns. **158**, 201

Data Protection Act: UK law that governs the collection and use of personal data. 159

data redundancy: Data in a database which is needlessly duplicated. 146

data structure: Description of the data which will be stored in an IT system. 317

data subject: The person about whom data is stored. 17

data synchronisation: Exchanging data between a computer and a portable device such as a smart phone. 16

data throughput: Rate at which data is processed and output by a system. 14

data types: Format of data in a field, such as text, number, or date. 145

data user: Person who will have access to data in a database. 17

data warehouses: Vast databases containing many gigabytes of data. 158

data-driven web sites: Web site whose content is generated from a database. 204

database administrator: Person with overall responsibility for managing a database. 314

Database Management System: Application software used to create, enter, edit, and retrieve data in a database. 144

database server: Computer on a network that stores data for other users to access. 68

database software: Application software for creating, recording, and finding large collections of data. 51

DBMS: See Database Management System.

DDoS: See Distributed Denial of Service attack :

Decision Support System: Use of models or expert systems to aid (business) decision making processes. 168

Defragmentation: Process of reducing disk fragmentation. 47

delivery: See deployment.

Denial of Service attack:

Flooding a computer system with data so that it cannot respond to genuine users. 98, 305

deployment: Stage in the SDLC where the system is deployed at the client's site. 322

Design stage: Stage in the SDLC where the new system is planned and designed.

deskilling: Reduction in the skill needed to do a job, due to technology: 193

desktop computer: Typical computer system with a separate screen and system unit. 15

desktop publishing software: Application software used to lay out pages for printed publications. 50, 136

Development methodologies: See project management methodology.

development manager: In project development, person who oversees programmers as they create the system specified in the design. 314

device drivers: Utility software used by the operating system to communicate with peripheral devices. 45

DFD: See Data Flow Diagram.

DHCP: See Dynamic Host Control Protocol.

dialup: Internet access that connects using a telephone line and a MODEM. 76

dictation software: See voice recognition software.

dictionary attack: Attempt to break a password by trying all possible words. 94

digital cameras: Camera that saves images digitally, often in JPEG format. 25

digital certificates: Used to authenticate a user, for example a shop in an online transaction. 199

digital data: Data which can be counted. 25, 237

digital divide: The gap between those who have access to IT and those who do not. 245

digital effects: Effects applied to digital images, video, or audio. 117

digital footprint: An individual's effect on the environment due to e-waste. 234

Digital Millennium Copyright Act: Law regarding intellectual property and copyright protection. 276, 290

digital radio: 282

digital restoration: Use of technology to restore ancient works of art. 284

Digital Rights Management: Software which restricts the actions a user can perform with a file, such as copying or printing. 58, 135, **276**

digital signatures: Technique used to authenticate remote users, such as online shopping businesses. 108

digital television: 282

digital video cameras: Camera that saves digital video: 25

digitisation: See digitise.

digitise: To convert data from analog to digital form. 24, 133, 237, 284

direct changeover: Immediate removal of an old system and complete replacement with a new IT system. 322

direct payment: E-commerce payment using a debit or credit card. 199

Direct Recording Electronic: Voting machines where users cast votes by touching a screen. 295

discrete data: See digital data.

disk wiping: Securing deleting files from a disk, beyond recovery. 35

Distributed Denial of Service attack: Denial of service attack committed using dozens of computers, usually zombies on a botnet. 98

distributed processing: Use of multiple separate computers working together on a common task. 176

DMCA: See Digital Millennium Copyright Act.

DNA database: 300

DNS: See Domain Name System. 292

DNS poisoning: Technique used by criminals to alter DNS records and drive users to fake sites, to committing phishing. 105: 292

do not track: Initiative designed to stop tracking cookies from recording user's web activity. 207

DOC: File format for documents, used by Microsoft Office. 137

Domain Name System: System for translating domain names into IP addresses. **82**, 209

domain names: Human readable names given to web sites, such as www.itgstextbook.com. **82**, 209

donation schemes: Schemes set up to receive donations of old computers for refurbishing and reuse. 247

DoS: See denial of service attack.

Dots Per Inch: Measure of the quality of a printer's output. 24, **127**

download: To transfer data from a server to a client computer. 66

DPI: See dots per inch.

DRE voting machine: See Direct Recording Electronic.

Drive-by download: Program which automatically downloads when a user visits a web page, usually without their knowledge or consent. 98

DRM: See Digital Rights Management.

drone: See Unmanned Aerial Vehicle.

DSL / cable: Common type of broadband Internet connection. 76

DTP: See desktop publishing software.

dual core: A multi-core system with two processor cores. 31

DVD: Optical secondary storage device capable of storing up to 8GB. 33

Dvorak keyboards: Alternative keyboard layout to improve typing speed. 19

Dynamic Host Control Protocol: System that automatically assigns IP addresses to computers on a network. 78

dynamic web site: See data-driven web sites.

e-book: 225, 245, **283**

e-book reader: Portable device used to download and read e-books. 223

e-commerce: The techniques used to sell products online. 198

e-learning: Electronic learning. The use of IT to teach and learn. 220

e-marketing: The techniques used to market produces online. 210

e-passport: Passport with a microchip containing biometric features, and RFID technology to transmit these to immigration control. 293

e-petition: Online petitions, usually housed on government web sites. 298

e-prescriptions: Electronic prescriptions. 257

e-store: Web page used for e-commerce. 198

e-waste: See electronic waste.

EB: See Exabyte.

EDI: See Electronic Data Interchange.

edutainment: Entertainment software designed to have an educational aspect. 224

EFT: See Electronic Funds Transfer.

EHR: See Electronic Health Records.

Electronic Data Interchange: Process of transferring data between systems in a standard format that both can understand. 233, 257

Electronic Funds Transfer: Transfer of money from one account to another using computer systems and networks. 193

Electronic Health Records: Computerised medical records, often stored on a centralised server. 256

electronic ink: Technology used in e-book readers to improve display quality. 283

Electronic Medical Records: See Electronic Health Records. 256

electronic shopping cart: Feature of e-commerce sites which contains items for later purchase. 198

electronic textbooks: E-books designed to replace traditional paper textbooks for teaching and learning. 225

electronic voting: Any use of IT to count or cast votes in an election. 295

electronic waste: Discarded electronic equipment. 244

email: 210

email monitoring: Technology to monitor emails sent and received, usually by employees. 188

email server: Computer on a network that stores email for other users to access. 68

embedded systems: Computer system hidden inside another device, such as a car engine management system. 18

employee monitoring: Technology used to monitor the work of employees using a computer system. 188

EMR: See Electronic Medical Records.

emulator: Program that creates a simulation of another computer's hardware. 312

encryption: System of encoding plaintext so that it cannot be understood with access to an encryption key. 106

encryption key: Used to encrypt and decrypt data. 106

end user licence agreement: Licence agreement for software that sets out the users rights and responsibilities. 58

end-user: Person who will use an IT project one it is finished. 313

enterprise information system: Software which provides business data and analysis functions for large organisations. 201

Entertainment Software Rating Board: Organisation that provides content ratings for computer games. 279

entities: Component of an Entity Relationship Diagram. 318

entity relationship diagram: Shows the items of data stored in a system and the relationships between them. 318

equality of access: **29**, 229, 251

ERD: See Entity Relationship Diagram.

ergonomics: Meaning a system design for user comfort. 266

eSATA: A modern type of connector for attaching external hard disks. 39

ESRB: See Entertainment Software Rating Board.

Ethernet: Type of wired network connection commonly used on LANs. 77

EULA: See end user licence agreement.

EV SSL: Extended Validation SSL. Digital certificate validation technique used on the world wide web. 109

Exabyte: Storage unit: 1024 petabytes. 37

expert system shell: Software used to create expert systems. 335

expert systems: Software designed to make the same decisions that a human expert would, in a given knowledge domain. 260, **335**

external hard disk: Portable storage device often used for backups. 33

external link: HTML link which points to a separate, external web site. 203

extranet: Content on a LAN which is available to authorised third parties. 193

eye tracking software: Accessibility software that tracks where a user is looking on the screen. 29

failover system: See Redundant system. 15

fair use: Exceptions to copyright law that allow copying in certain limited circumstances. 135

false negative: When a system incorrectly rejects an action instead of accepting it. 91, 226, 292

false positive: When a system incorrectly accepts an action instead of rejecting it. 92, 226, 291

feasibility study: Examination of a proposed system to see if its creation is possible. 314

Federation Against Software Theft: Organisation that works to reduce illegal copying of software. 58

feedback loop: Use of previous answers (right or wrong) to improve the decision making process next time. 173, 330

fibre optic: Types of network connection that offers extremely high speed transfers. 76

field: Single item of data about a single record in a database. 145

field size: Validation technique. Number of characters that can be stored in a field. 157

file server: Computer on a network that stores files for other users to access. 68

File Transfer Protocol: System for transferring files over the Internet, often used for uploading web sites. 84, 209

filter (Internet): Software which blocks some Internet content, based on a series of rules or lists of content. 188, 228, **290**

filters (graphics): See digital effects.

firewall: Hardware or software that controls access to a network. 44, **73**, 292

firewire: Interface for attaching external hard disks and digital video cameras. 39

first party cookie: Cookie left by a web site the user directly visited. 207

FLAC: Lossless file format for audio. 132

Flash: Technology often used to create interactive web pages. 204

flash memory/flash drive: See solid state storage.

flat classrooms: Use of IT to connect classrooms with other classrooms around the world: 222

flat file database: Database which consists of just one table. 146

fleet management: Software to track and manage fleets of vehicles, including route planning and data analysis functions. 216

fleet tracking: Software to display the location of vehicles, such as trucks or taxis. 216

flight simulator: Simulator hardware and software used to train pilots. 180

flipping: Image effect found in most graphics software.

116

follow-the-sun working: Work is passed to workers around the globe depending on the time of day in any location. 190

footer: Area of a document which appears the same on every page. 136

foreign key: Database field whose sole purpose is to form part of a relationship with another table. 148

forms: See data entry form. 152

formula: In spreadsheets, a combination of cell references and mathematical operations. 170, 178, **182**, 194

forums: Online areas where users can post messages to each other. 220

fragmentation: Problem that occurs as files are saved on non-contiguous sectors on a disk. 47

free and open source software: Software whose source code is freely available and can be changed and distributed. 55, 297

freeware: Software which is distributed for no cost. 55

Frequently Asked Questions: List of questions and answers often found in manuals and help screens. 61, 320

FTP: See File Transfer Protocol.

full backup: Backup that copies all data from a system. 49

full body scanners: Security system used at airports to produce a digital image of passengers 'without clothes'. 216

full disk encryption: System that encrypts all data saved to a hard disk automatically and transparently. 109

full motion platform: Hardware device which can move in many directions to increase the realism of simulators. 180

function: Built in features of spreadsheet software for performing common calculations. 170, 178, **183**, 194

functional requirements: Specific features and functions that a proposed IT system must have. 314

future warrior: See wired soldier.

fuzzy logic: Logic in which items can have multiple values. Used in AI. 337

fuzzy set theory: System in which items can be partial or complete members of a set. Used in AI. 337

game controllers: Input device with buttons used for games playing. 21

Gantt chart: Used to chart the stages of a planned IT project and the people responsible for each stage. 315

gateway: Computer which acts as a bridge between a local area network and the Internet. 69

GB: See Gigabyte.

Gbps: Gigabits per second. Measure of network bandwidth. 77

Geographical Information System: Mapping system with layers of additional data for analysis and planning. 239

geotagged: Item of data (usually an image) with GPS coordinates embedded. 241

GHz: See gigahertz.

GIF: Lossless file format for images. 132

Gigabyte: Storage unit: 1024 megabytes. 12

gigahertz: Unit of measurement for a processor's clock speed. 1000 MHz. 30

GIS: See Geographical Information System.

Global Climate Model: See climate model.

Global Positioning System: System of satellites which can pinpoint a user's location on the Earth to within a few metres. 25, 216, **243**, 303

GNU Free Documentation License: Licensing system for authors who wish to distribute their work freely. 135

goal seek: Spreadsheet tool used to determine the required values to meet a certain goal. 185

GPS: See Global Positioning System.

GPS receiver: See Global Positioning System.

GPS satellite: See Global Positioning System.

Graphical User Interface: System the user controls using a mouse to click on icons, buttons, and windows. 44

graphics software: Application software for creating and editing images. 52

green screen: See blue green.

grid computing: See distributed computing: **176**, 267

GPS receiver: See Global Positioning System.

GUI: See Graphical User Interface.

hacking: Gaining illegal access to a computer system: 94

hand writing recognition: System to recognise human writing and convert it to text. 339

handover: Point at which the developers of a system formally pass it to the client. 320

hard copy: A printed paper copy of data. 28

hard disk: Magnetic secondary storage device found in most desktop and laptop computers. 33

hardware: Physical parts of a computer system. 14

hardware address: See MAC address.

HDTV: See High Definition Television.

head control systems: Accessibility software that tracks a users head move-

ments to allow them to input data. 29

head wand: Accessibility hardware that lets a user input using a wand connected to their head. 29

header: Area of a document which appears the same on every page. 136

heat sensor: Common input device in robotics. 345

heuristics: General rules for performing a task, used to improve the perform of searching algorithms in AI applications. 338

high contrast mode: Accessibility setting for users with eyesight problems. 29

High Definition Television: 282

high performance computing: High speed computing using multiple processors: 176

home automation: See smart home.

home directory: Directory that contains a users personal files. 94

home network: Small local computer network used in homes. 68

Home Theatre PC: Computer with multimedia capabilities designed specifically for watching television and films. 15, 283

host: See server.

HTML: HyperText Markup Language. The standard language for creating web pages. 202

HTPC: See Home Theatre PC.

HTTP: HyperText Transfer Protocol. The standard protocol of the world wide web. 82

HTTPS: Secure version of HTTP which offers encrypted communication. 82, **108**, 199:

hub: Hardware device for connecting several computers on a network. 69

Human Genome Project: 264

humanoid: Robot designed

generally like a human – bipedal, upright, and arms, and a head. 344

humidity sensor: Common input device used in robotics. 346

hyperlinks: 203

IDE (hardware): Interface for attaching internal hard disks. 39

IDE (software): See Integrated Development Environment.

identity theft: Stealing personal data in order to impersonate a person. 105

IF-THEN rule: See inference rule.

image editor: See graphics software.

implementation: Stage in the SDLC where the system is created (programmed). 320

incident escalation: Moving a problem with an IT project to a higher level if it cannot be solved. 323

incident management system: See incident tracking system.

incident tracking system: Used to keep track of problems and difficulties encountered in an IT system. 323

incremental backup: Backup that copies only the changed data since the last backup. 49

index (databases): See secondary key.

inference engine: Part of an expert system which attempts to relate the users input with knowledge stored in the knowledge base. 335

inference rule: Rule used by the inference engine in an expert system to describe the relationship between key concepts. 336

information system (IS) managers: Person responsible for all IT purchases, deployments, and systems within an organisation. 314

infrared sensor: Common input device in robotics. 345

inkjet printer: Printer that works by spraying ink through nozzles at a sheet of paper. 28

input: Data or information that is entered into the computer. 19

input mask: Validation technique. Ensures only the specified characters can be entered into a field. 157

input switches: Accessibility hardware that lets a user input data by pressing a simple on-off switch. 29

installation: See deployment.

Integrated Development Environment: Software used to write and compile programs. 310

intellectual property: Creations of the mind, such as stories, films, music, and computer programs. 55, 135, 226

intelligent cars: See smart cars. 217

interactive whiteboard: Device that uses a projector for output and touch inputs, using a special pen. 27, 227

internal link: HTML link which points to a different part of the same page. 203

internal support: Support for an IT system provided within an organisation. 323

Internet: 193

Internet monitoring: Technology to monitor Internet data sent and received, usually by employees. 188

Internet Protocol: Standard protocol used on many LANs and on the Internet. See TCP. 78

Internet Service Provider: Company that provides Internet access to homes and businesses. 69, 209

Internet voting: See online voting.

Internet Watch Foundation: Organisation that works with British ISPs to block access to illegal content on the Internet. 291

intranet: Content on a LAN which is only available to members of an organisation. 193

IP address: Unique address assigned to every computer on a network. 78, 291

IPTV: Internet Protocol Television. 283

IrDA: Short range, low bandwidth, line-of-sight wireless communication technology. 16

ISP: See Internet Service Provider.

IWF: See Internet Watch Foundation.

Java: Programming language often used to create interactive web pages. 204

JavaScript: Scripting language often used to create interactive web pages. 204

joystick: Input device used for games playing and flight simulators. 21

JPG: Lossy file format for images. 132

KB: See kilobyte.

Kbps: Kilobits per second. Measure of network bandwidth. 77

Kensington lock: Special lock for securing portable devices to immovable objects to prevent theft. 16

key escrow: Idea of having encryption keys stored by a third party company so the government can access them if needed. 110

key field: See primary key.

key logger: Software or hardware which records all key strokes on a computer system. 94

key pair: A public key and private key that work together in a public encryption system. 107

keyboard: Input device that lets the user enter text and numeric data. 19

keystroke monitoring: See key logger.

keyword density: Frequently with which key words appear in a web page. 210

keyword filter: Filter that blocks web pages containing specified key words. 291

keyword prominence: Locations within a web page that key words appear. 210

keyword spamming: Overuse of key words in a web page in an attempt to increase search engine ranking. 210

Kilobyte: Storage unit: 1024 bytes: 37

knowledge base: Area of an expert system where all facts about the knowledge domain are stored. 335

knowledge discovery: See data mining.

knowledge domain: Area of knowledge in which an expert system specialises. 335

knowledge engineer: Programmer responsible for entering expert knowledge into an expert system. 335

knowledge representation: Different techniques for representing concepts and their relationships inside a computer system. 340

LAN: See Local Area Network.

laptop: Portable computers that come in many shapes and sizes. 15, 230

laser imaging: Technique used by satellites to image the Earth.

laser printer: High speed printer. 28

laser scanning: Technique used to build 3D computer models of real world locations. 284

lasers: Common input device in robotics. 345

layer: Feature of graphics and multimedia software. 117

LCD screen: Output device. The newer type of monitor which is flat. 27, 245

legacy system: System which runs on obsolete hardware or has been discontinued by its manufacturer. 310

length check: See field size.

Lidar: Remote imaging method used by satellites. 238

life cycle (hardware): Stages an item of hardware goes through, from manufacture to disposal. 242

light sensor: Common input device in robotics. 345

lights: Common output device in robotics. 346

link farm: Service that links many pages to each other in an attempt to increase search engine ranking. 211

load testing: Testing of an IT system with the amount of work it can be expected to process in real world conditions. 316

Local Area Network: Computer network in a small area such as an office building. 69

location based service: Any service (e.g. web page content) which varies according to the user's location. 241

log file: Chronological record of events, used for reporting purposes and audit trails. 71

logic: See Boolean logic.

login: Process of authenticating oneself before using a computer system. 68

lookup: Feature of spreadsheet and database software to retrieve data from other fields. 183

lossless compression: Compression technique in which the original file is completely recoverable, with no loss of quality. Compare lossy compression. 124

lossy compression: Compression technique in which some file data is sacrificed in order to reduce file size. 126

loyalty card: 194

m-commerce: See mobile commerce.

m-learning: Mobile learning. Use of mobile devices to teach and learn. 221

MAC address: Unique address embedded in network connected devices. 78

machine learning: Technique for making a computer produce better results by learning from past experiences. 330

machine translation: Technique for automatically translating one human language into another. 339

macro: In application software, a set of actions which are recorded so they can be played back later. 192

macro virus: Virus that takes advantage of the macro programming languages built into some software. 96, 193

Magnetic Ink Character Recognition: Input device that reads text written in special magnetic ink. Often used at the bottom of cheques. 24

magnetic storage: Type of secondary storage that users magnets to read and store data. Examples include floppy disks and hard disks. 32

magnetic stripe readers: Input device that reads the magnetic stripe on cards like ATM cards and bank cards. 22

magnetism sensor: Common input device in robotics. 346

mail merge: Automatically customising a standard letter with individual names and addresses. 50, 192

mainframe: High end computer system that achieves very high data throughput. 14

maintenance: Alterations made to a system after it has been formally handed over. 322

malware: Generic name for malicious software. 96

MAN: See Metropolitan Area Network.

Massively Multiplayer Online Game: Games played by connecting to a central server and interacting with other players in a virtual world. 278

Massively Multiplayer Online Role Playing Game: See Massively Multiplayer Online Game.

master page: In DTP, a page whose contents is applied to all pages in a publication. 136

MB: See megabyte.

mbps: Megabits per second. Measure of network bandwidth. 77

MDI: See Menu Driven Interface.

medical expert system: Expert system for medical diagnosis support. 257

Megabyte: Storage unit: 1024 kilobytes: 37

megahertz: Unit of measurement for a processor's clock speed. 30

megapixel: Refers to 1 million pixels. 122

Menu Driven Interface: Interface that presents a series of pre-defined options to the user. 42

meta tags: HTML tags to add additional information about a web page and its content. 210

Metropolitan Area Network: Computer network over a large area such as a city. 74

MHz: See megahertz.

MICR: See Magnetic Ink Character Recognition.

micro-payments: Online payments, generally less than $100. 295

microblog: Blog-like system which limited post length, such as Twitter. 85

microphone: Input device for sound data. 21

microprocessor: See Central Processing Unit.

microwave: Networking technology for medium to long range wireless communication.

MIDI: Musical Instrument Digital Interface. System for communication between musical hardware and software applications. 133

milestones: Key points during project development, such as the completion of a stage. 315

MIPS: See Millions of Instructions Per Second.

mission creep: When the use of an IT system extends beyond its original purpose. 293

mixed reality: Combination of virtual reality and real life training. 302

MMC: Solid state secondary storage device, often used for digital cameras. 34

MMOG: See Massively Multiplayer Online Game.

MMORPG: See Massively Multiplayer Online Role Playing Game.

mobile commerce: Use of mobile phones to conduct online purchases. 199

MODEM: Device for connecting a computer to a telephone line, used in dialup connections. 76

monitoring: See employee monitoring. 188

morphing: Effect that transforms one image into another over a series of frames. 134

motherboard: The circuit board to which the internal computer components connect: the CPU, the RAM, the ROM, and the secondary storage devices. 30

motion capture: System to digitise the movements of an actor. 130

motion controllers: Input

devices which are moved through the air to control a computer system. 225

Motion Picture Association of America: Film industry group that works to reduce illegal copying of films. 276

motors: Common output device in robotics. 346

mouse: Input device used to control a cursor or pointer. 19

MOV: Lossy file format for video. 132

MP3: Lossy file format for audio. 132

MP4: Lossy file format for video. 132

MPAA: See Motion Picture Association of America.

MPEG: Lossy file format for video. 132

multi-core: Processor with more than one processor core, to increase its performance. 30

multi-factor authentication: Use of several authentication techniques together, such as passwords and security tokens. 90

multi-touch: Input device able to recognise touches and gestures made with multiple fingers. 21

multi-user licence: Software licence that allows a specific number of copies to be used at one time. 58

multimedia: Use of images, audio, text, and video data together. 221

multimedia keyboard: Keyboard with buttons to perform common tasks such as program launching. 19

multimedia software: Application software for creating and editing presentations, animations, and video. 53

multiprocessing: A system with more than one processor, to increase its performance. 14

multitasking: A single processor running multiple

tasks by switching rapidly between them. 30

myoelectric control: Control of IT using electrical impulses from the body. 259

MySQL: Database system often used by data driven web sites. 204

narrowband: Low speed network connection. 77

native resolution: Resolution of an LCD display that produces the best display quality. 27

natural language processing: Techniques for processing human languages to enable a computer to understand their meaning. 333

netbook: Lightweight laptop computer designed for portability. 16

network administrator: Individual responsible for maintaining and running a network. 71, 314

network manager: See network administrator.

neural control: Control of IT using electrical impulses from the brain. 259

neural networks: See Artificial Neural Network.

news aggregator: Software which fetches news headlines from a variety of sources for display in one location. 281

newsletter: 210

non-functional requirements: Conditions that a proposed IT system must meet, such as working on certain hardware or giving results within a certain time. 314

non-volatile storage: Storage which does not lose its contents when the power is removed. 32

normalisation: Process of converting a database from a flat file database to a relational database. 147

object oriented graphics: See vector graphics.

OCR: See Optical Character Recognition.

ODT: File format for documents, based on an open standard. 137

off-the-shelf software: Software which is widely available for general purchase. Compare custom / bespoke software. 53, **310**

OMR: See Optical Mark Recognition.

one time password: Password generated by a security token, which expires as soon as it is used. 90

online advertising: 211

online banking: Use of the Internet to perform tasks such as bill payment, money transfers and other banking tasks. 193

online encyclopaedias: Web site containing a large number of articles for research purposes. 144

online lessons: 320

online mapping: 239

online reputation: User's rating based on comments and reviews made by other users of a system. 201

online voting: Casting votes over the Internet. 295

onscreen keyboard: See soft keyboard.

open courseware: Educational material which is released for free use and distribution. 223

open government: Use of IT to publish data about government operations, improving transparency. 298

open source: See free and open source.

open textbooks: See open courseware.

operating systems: Software that manages the computer system, controls the hardware, and provides a user interface. 44

opt-in: System in which users must explicitly decide to participate. 160, 257

opt-out: System in which users must explicitly de-

cide not to participate. 160, 257

Optical Character Recognition: Input device that reads printed text, scans it, and converts it to text that can be edited in a word processor. 24

optical fibre: See fibre optic.

Optical Mark Recognition: Input devices that reads simple multiple-choice style answers by looking for marks on the paper. 24

optical scanning electronic voting system: Voting machines which count paper ballots cast by voters. 295

optical storage: Storage devices which use lasers to store and read data. Examples include CDs and DVDs. 33

organisational IT policies: Policies governing the appropriate use of IT, data integrity, security procedures, and other aspects of IT use with an organisation. 314

output: Information which is produced by a computer system. 27

outputs: In system development, a section of a requirements specification: 317

P2P: See Peer to peer.

package tracking: Use of RFID and a web site to show customers the location of packages awaiting delivery. 217

packet sniffer: Software or hardware used to collect data travelling over a network. 94

pages per minute: Speed at which a printer produces output.

PAN: See Personal Area Network.

Pan European Game Information: Organisation that provides content ratings for computer games. 279

parallel processing: High speed computing using

multiple processors. 176

parallel running: Running the old system and the new system side by side. 322

parameter query: Database query whose criteria are decided by the user at run-time. 150

passphrase: See password.

password: Word or phrase used to authenticate a user. 90

pattern recognition: Computational Intelligence technique where computers are trained on examples and learn to recognise similarities between them. 339

payment gateway: Company that handles Internet payments for customers and businesses. 199

paywall: System to prevent access to a web site's content unless the user pays a subscription fee. 281

PB: See petabyte.

PDA: See Personal Digital Assistant.

PDF: See Portable Document Format.

peer to peer: Network in which all computers are equal and there are no centralised servers. 72, 275

PEGI: See Pan European Game Information.

perfective maintenance: 322

Personal Area Network: Short range network between a computer and a mobile phone or similar portable device. 74

personal data: Data which could identify a user, or lead to social impacts such as identity theft.

Personal Digital Assistant: Mobile device bigger than a phone but smaller than a laptop. Probably has a keyboard or at least a stylus (pen) and a touchscreen. 16

personal firewall: Software application that controls network access to and

from a single computer. 73

Personal Health Record: Electronic health records which are stored on the patient's own computer system. 256

personally identifiable data: See personal data.

PERT chart: Charting system to show the interdependencies in projects. 315

Petabyte: Storage unit: 1024 terabytes. 37

pH sensor: Common input device in robotics. 346

pharming: See DNS Poisoning.

phase out: Gradually removing an old IT system from use. 323

phased changeover: One part of an organisation switches to a new IT system to test it, while others remain using the old system. 322

phishing: Use of fake emails and web sites to trick users into revealing sensitive data. 104

PHP: Technology used to create dynamic web pages. 204

PHR: See Personal Health Record.

physical security: Locks, alarms, and other techniques used to securely a building or computer room. 111

piracy: Copyright infringement.

pixel: Individual dots which make up bitmap graphics. 116

pixels per inch: Number of pixels displayed in each inch of screen output. 127

plagiarism: Use of another user's work without proper credit or citation being given. 226

plain text file: See text file.

plaintext: Message before it is encrypted, or after it has been decrypted. 106

planned obsolescence: Idea that IT equipment is designed to have a short life expectancy before failing or becoming obsolete. 245

platform: A particular combination of hardware and operating system. 44

plugins: Software added to web browsers to extend their functionality. 204

PMBoK: Project Management Body of Knowledge. A project management methodology. 326

PNDRE: See Public Network Direct Recording Electronic.

PNG: Lossless file format for images. 132

podcast: Sound files recorded and uploaded to a web server, usually in episodic format. 222

Point of Sale: Checkout system in a shop, usually connected to a store database and EFT system. 194

pop-ups: Windows that open up while browsing a web site, usually containing adverts. 211

port: Number used to determine the type of service required when a computer connects to another. 79

Portable Document Format: Common file format for the exchange of documents. 137

POS: See Point of Sale.

power consumption: 242

power settings: 242

PPI: See Pixels per inch.

PPT: File format used by Microsoft's PowerPoint presentation software.

precision guided weapons: Weapons that use IT to improve their accuracy or effectiveness. 304

prediction: Output of a computer model. 166

predictive text: System that predicts the word being typed based on the letters already typed. 230

presence check: Validation technique. Requires a field to be completed. 156

presentation software: Ap-

plication software for creating slides used for lectures, presentations, and lessons. 50

pressure sensor: Common input device used in robotics. 346

preventative maintenance: 322

price comparison sites: Sites which aggregate price data from a variety of sources to offer customers the best deal. 215

primary key: Field which contains a different value for every record in that table. 145

primary storage: Storage systems which are found inside the computer and are electronic. RAM and ROM are examples. 32

PRINCE2: PRojects IN Controlled Environments 2. A project management methodology. 327

print server: Computer on a network that receives and processes print requests. 68

printers: Output device which produces paper copies. 28

privacy policy: Policy governing what data a company or web site will collect about you and how it will be used. 160

private key: Key used for decryption in a public key encryption system. 107

processes: In system development, a section of a requirements specification. 317

processor: See Central Processing Unit.

procurement: In system development, the act of acquiring required resources. 327

product activation: Process of registering software online before it can be used, to reduce illegal copies. 58

productivity software: See application software.

profile privacy settings: Settings in social networks and other systems to control how a user's data is shared with others. 230

programmer: Person who creates software. 314

project goals: Clear statement of the intentions of a proposed IT project. 313

project initiation document: Document used in PRINCE2 to describe the key features of an IT project. 308

project management methodology: Systems and techniques designed to encourage successful projects and avoid project failure. 315

project management software: Software to help plan, manage, and guide the process of IT project development. 315

project manager: Person with overall responsibility for an IT project. 315

project plan: Clear definition of the goals, scope, and schedule of a proposed IT project. 315

projector: Output device for displaying content on large screens. 27, 229

prosthetics: 259

protocols: A standard set of rules for performing tasks, such as communication. 78

prototype interface: Early version of a user interface to get feedback about its effectiveness. 319, 320

proximity sensor: Common input device in robotics. 345

proxy server: Computer on a network which acts on behalf of another, or through which all Internet data must pass. 73

public domain: Software to which the author has waived all rights. 55

public key: Key used for encryption in a public key encryption system. 107

Public Network Direct

Recording Electronic: Voting machines where users cast votes over a network like the Internet. 295

push technology: System which notifies users of changes to web pages without them having to visit the page. 85

quad-core: A multi-core system with four processor cores. 31

quality assurance methods: In project development, used to ensure the whole development team are following standardised best practises. 320

quality control processes: Processes to ensure code produced by programmers followed accepted best practices. 320

queries: Method of extracting data from a database that matches specific criteria: 150

radar: Remote imaging method used by satellites, and input device used by robots. 238, 345

Radio Frequency Identification: System of tags which contain data that can be read from a distance using radio waves. 25, 194, 216, 274, 293

radio tag: Tags which broadcast their position over a large distance using radio waves. 25

RAID: See Redundant Array of Inexpensive Disks.

RAM: See Random Access Memory.

Random Access Memory: Primary storage which is fast, relatively expensive, and volatile. 32

range check: Validation technique. Ensures a field is between a certain range of values. 156

ranking of sites: Performed by search engines to produce their results page listings. 211

raster graphics: See bitmap

graphics.

RDBMS: Relational DBMS. See Database Management System.

re-skilling: When a de-skilled user retrains, often in a technology related discipline. 193

read / write web: See web 2.0. 85

read me file: Help file containing latest updates and information about using a system. 61

Read Only Memory: Primary storage whose contents are written at manufacture and cannot be altered later. 32

real-time data collection: Data logging systems which report data as soon as it is collected. 216

record: Collection of fields that represent a single entity, such as a person. 145

Recording Industry Association of America: Music industry group that works to reduce illegal copying of music. 276

recycling (of e-waste): 246

reduce: (chemicals in e-waste): 246

Reduction of Harmful Substances: Law governing the chemicals that can be included in electronic equipment. 248

redundancy: See data redundancy.

Redundant Array of Inexpensive Disks: System where multiple hard disks contain duplicate data, to be used in the event of one failing. 38

redundant data: See data redundancy. 146

redundant system: System which will take over the role of a primary system if it fails. **38**, 242

reference software: Electronic encyclopaedia software containing articles, images, videos, and other reference items. 221

referrer: Site that directed the user to the current web site. 213

refurbish: Method of prolonging the life of old IT equipment: 246

regression testing: Testing to ensuring changes to an IT system did not break any previously working functionality. 323

relational database: Database containing multiple related tables and no redundant data. 147

relational database management system: Application software used to create, enter, edit, and retrieve data in a relational database. 51

relationships (in ERDs): 318

relationships (in databases): 147

relative cell reference: In a spreadsheet, a cell reference which updates when moved. 170, 178, **182**, 194

relative link: HTML link to a file, with no path specified. 203

relays: Common output device in robotics. 346

reliability. 62

remote access: Ability to connect to a computer as though you were physically present at the keyboard. 71

remote desktop: See remote access. 189

remote monitoring: Use of IT to monitor the health of patients over a large distance. 255

remote sensing: Techniques used by satellites to image the Earth. 238

remote vehicle disabling: Ability to disable a vehicle over a computer network if it has been stolen. 216

Repetitive Strain Injury: Injury caused by overuse or incorrect use of a computer. 252

report generation: 153

requirements specification: Clear list of the functional

and non-functional requirements for a proposed IT project. 314

resolution (graphics): Refers to the number of pixels in an image. 24, **116**

resolution (computer models): Attribute of a model which affects its accuracy. 175

restore (a backup): Copying data from a backup copy back to the main system. 49

reuse: See refurbish.

reward card: See loyalty card.

RFID reader: See Radio Frequency Identification. 25

RFID tag: See Radio Frequency Identification.

RIAA: See Recording Industry Association of America .

Rich Text Format: Standard file format that can store documents that include formatting data. 37, **137**

robot: Computerised device that performs manual or physical tasks, either autonomously or under remote control. 343

robotic arm: Common output device in robotics. 346

robotic fingers: Common output device in robotics. 346

RoHS: See Reduction of Harmful Substances.

ROM: See Read Only Memory.

root user: User will full control over a computer system. 94

rootkit: Type of malware which infiltrates the operating system and attempts to hide itself from view. 97

rotating: Image effect found in most graphics software. 116

route planning: Software to plan the optimum route between two points. 216

router: Hardware device used to connect two separate networks. 69

RSI: See Repetitive Strain Injury.

RSS: Really Simple Syndicate. A push technology. 85

RTF: See Rich Text Format.

safety critical system: System whose failure could result in injury or loss of life. 62

sample precision: See bit rate.

sample rate: Number of samples taken each second when recording sound. 133, 237

SAN: See Storage Area Network.

sat nav: See satellite navigation system.

SATA: Interface for connecting storage devices like hard disks. 39

satellite imaging: Technique used to produce images of the Earth. 238

satellite navigation system: Portable device that uses GPS to plot the user's position. 239

scaling: Changing the size of an image. 116

scanner: Input device used to digitise photographs and paper copies of data. 24

school information system: Database system for storing and managing information about a school, its students, and staff. 231

scope: Clear definition of the boundaries of an IT project. 313

screen magnification: Accessibility setting for users with eyesight problems. 29

screen reader: See text-to-speech.

scripting: Programming language to provide interactivity in web pages. 204

SDLC: See System Development Life Cycle.

Search Engine Optimisation: Techniques used to increase a web page's search engine rankings. 210

search engines:210, 211, 290

searching (AI): AI technique that considers all possible solutions, looking for the best. 333

searching (databases): See query.

secondary key: Field by which a database is often searched. 145

secondary storage: Storage systems which are connected externally to the computer's motherboard. 32

secondary use: Using data for a purpose other than the one for which it was collected. 160

secret key encryption: Encryption system in which a single key is used for both encryption and decryption. 106

secure deletion: See disk wiping.

secure online payment:199

Secure Socket Layer: System used to encrypt https web traffic.108

security token: Hardware device that must be present during login to authenticate a user. 90

security update: Software update to fix a security problem discovered in software. 95

select query: See query.

selection tools: Tools in graphics software for selecting only a subset of an image. 117

self checkout: Supermarket technology that lets users scan and pay for their own goods without staff assistance. 194

sensitive data: See personal data.

sensors: Input devices used to measure certain traits, such as sound, heat, or light. 25, 217, **238**, **345**

SEO: See Search Engine Optimisation.

serial number: Registration number needed during software installation, used

to reduce illegal copies. 58

serious games: Games designed to teach players about an issue. 223

server: Computer on a network that provides services or performs work for others. 68

set theory: Mathematical theory used in some AI techniques. 337

shareware: Software which is free to use initially, but which must be pay for if use continues. 55

Silverlight: Technology often used to create interactive web pages. 204

simplification: Difference between a computer model's representation of a process, and the real life process. 166

simulation: Software and hardware to recreate an experience of a real event. 302

single-user licence: Software licence that allows the use of only a single copy on a single computer. 58

sip and puff: Accessibility hardware for users with very limited mobility: 29

sirens: Common output device in robotics. 346

site licence: Software licence that allows an organisation to use software on an unlimited number of computers. 58

sitemap: Overview of a web site and all the links and pages within it. 206

smart card readers: Device to read a smart card. 22

smart cards: Credit card sized card containing a microchip for data storage and processing. 257

smart cars: Cars incorporating IT to improve driver safety and comfort.

smart home: Building with integrated IT to improve comfort and energy efficiency. 274

smart meters: Component of

smart homes to monitor resource usage. 275

smart shopping trolley: Shopping trolley with RFID technology to offer enhanced functionality. 194

smart weapons: See precision guided weapons. 304

smart phones: Mobile phone with capabilities including Internet access and a camera. 16

smishing: Phishing attacks committed using text messages (SMS). 104

social bookmarking: Web site that lets users store and manage their favourite links, and share them with others. 85

social engineering: Tricking a user into revealing their password or other sensitive data. 94

social media: See web 2.0.

social network: Web site that lets users create personal profile pages and share them with friends. 85

social news: News sites which rank news stories based on user ratings. 281

soft keyboard: Keyboard which is displayed on screen and controlled by clicking on buttons with the mouse or a touch screen. 19

software: The instructions and programs which are run by the CPU. 14

software testers: People who perform alpha, beta, and acceptance testing. 320

software verification: Ensuring software functions correctly by examining its source code. 297

solid state storage: Type of secondary storage device that uses electronic circuits to read and store data. 34

sonar: Remote imaging method used by satellites. 238

sorting: 153

sound sensor: Common input device in robotics. 346

source code: Instructions that make up the software, entered by the programmer using a programming language. 55, **310**

spam: Unwanted, bulk email. **100**, 210

spam bot: Program that scans web pages for email address, in order to send spam. 101

spam filters: Program designed to identify and block spam messages while letting genuine messages through. 101

speakers: Output device for sound. 27, 346

speech recognition: Computer system that can process spoken language and understand its meaning. 339

speech synthesis: See text to speech. 230

speed throttling: Reducing a processor's clock speed to save power when not in use. 30, 243

sponsored links: Links show by search engines because the link owners paid a fee. 211

spreadsheet: Application software for performing numerical calculations and analysis. 50, 170, 178, 182, **194**

spyware: Malware which covertly records a user's actions, such as their key presses. 96

SQL: See Structured Query Language.

SSADM: Structured Systems Analysis and Design Method. A project management methodology. 325

SSL: See Secure Socket Layer.

stereolithography: '3D printer' that can produce actual objects from computer models. 285

sticky keys: Accessibility

setting for users with movement problems. 29

Storage Area Network: Network dedicated to providing disk storage to other computers on the network. 74

store-and-forward telemedicine: Telemedicine using techniques such as email, which do not operate in real time. 254

streaming media: Video or audio data that is played while it is downloading. 135, 283

Structured Query Language: Language for managing databases by typing commands. 153, 204

stylesheet: See Cascading Style Sheets.

stylus: Input device used in conjunction with touch screens.

supercomputer: Fastest computers available, capable of performing trillions of calculations per second. **14**, 176

support: 323

support staff: Staff who train users and help them with problems as they occur: 314

SVG: Standard file format for vector image data. 132, 206

SWF: Small Web Format or ShockWave Flash. File format used by Flash.

switch: Hardware device for connecting several computers on a network. 69

SWOT: Analysis method sometimes used when creating a business case. 314

symmetric key encryption: See Secret key encryption.

synchronous: Data transfer method in which the sender and receiver are synchronised, allowing higher speed transfer. 83

synchronous learning: Learning which does requires the teacher and student to be online at the

same time. 220

system administrator: Personal in overall charge of a computer system in an organisation. 94

system context diagram: High level DFD of a system. 317

System development life cycle: Stages through which a IT project development must pass, from planning to completion. 313

Tab Separated Values: File format for transferring data, which stores fields and records in a plain text file. 152

tab-delimited text files: See Tab Separated Values.

table: In databases, a collection of records representing a type of item. 145

tactile feedback: Output in the form of movement or vibrations. 302

tagging: Adding key words to an item such as a photo to describe its content. 85

tags (HTML): Used as part of HTML to control the appearance of web pages. 202

take-back scheme: Scheme operated by IT manufacturers to accept customers' old hardware for recycling at its end of life. 247

targeted advertising: Use of data about customers to determine which adverts they are most likely to find useful. 194, 207

TB: See terabyte.

TCP/IP: Transfer Control Protocol / Internet Protocol. Common protocol for LANs and the Internet. 78

technical documentation: Documentation intended for programmers and developers of an IT system. 314

tele-learning: Learning that occurs when the teacher and students are in separate geographical locations. 220

telecommuting: See teleworking.

telehealth: See telemedicine.

telemedicine: Using IT to perform medical consultations when the doctor and patient are in geographically separate locations. 254

telesurgery: Using IT to perform surgery on a patient in a geographically separate location from the doctor. 254

teleworking: Working away from an organisation's main office or base, using portable computers. 190

template: Document used to provide a guiding layout in a word processor, presentation, or DTP application. 136

Terabyte: Storage unit: 1024 gigabytes: 37

Terahertz: Unit of measurement for a processor's clock speed. 30

test plan: List of all tests and test data that should be tried with a system. 320

text file: File containing text with no formatting or other information. 37, 137

text-to-speech: Accessibility feature for users with eyesight problems. 29

thin client: Networking system whereby client computers rely on servers to perform their processing tasks. 70

third party cookie: Cookie left by a web site the user did not directly visit (usually by advert companies). 207

third party hosting: Use of a separate company to store a web site on their servers. 209

third party payment service: See payment gateway.

THz: Unit of measurement for a processor's clock speed. 1000 GHz.

TIF: Lossless file format for images. 132

title attribute: HTML attribute that provides a text description of links. 208

TLS: See Transport Layer Security.

Top Level Domain: Suffix at the end of a URL, such as .com or .org. **82**, 209

touch pad: Input device commonly found on laptops instead of a mouse. 20

touch screen: Input device that lets the user touch areas of the display to perform tasks.

touch sensitive input: 227

trackball: Input device that uses a rotating ball to control the cursor. 20

tracking number: Used as part of package tracking systems. 198

tracks: Common output device in robotics. 346

training: Preparing users for a new IT system. 320, 322

training data: Example data used in a pattern recognition system. 339

Trans-border data flow: Transfer of data between countries. 159

Transport Layer Security: System used to encrypt https web traffic. 108

Trojan horse: Malware which pretends to be a genuinely useful program to trick the user into using it. 96

true colour: Image with 24 bit colour depth. 122

TSV: See Tab Separated Values.

Turing test: Proposed test to see if a computer is intelligent or not. 333

tutorials: Step by step help on using a system. 61, 320

TXT: See text file.

typography: The choice of fonts and typefaces. 136

UAV: See Unmanned Aerial Vehicle.

unauthorised access: Gaining illegal access to a computer system: 90

Unicode: Encoding system

to store text, with support for multiple languages and alphabets. Compare ASCII. 37

Uninterruptible Power Supply: Backup power system which powers a computer if the mains electricity fails. 38

unique identification number: Used by cookies to help recognise return visitors to web sites. 207

Universal Product Code: A type of barcode.

Universal Serial Bus: Common interface for connecting peripheral devices including mice, printers, and digital cameras. 16

Unmanned Aerial Vehicle: Remote control aircraft used for surveillance. 304

UPC: See Universal Product Code.

upload: To transfer data from a client to a server computer. 66, 209

UPS: See Uninterruptible Power Supply.

uptime: Measure of how long a computer system has been operating without restarting. 15, 209

URL: Universal Resource Locator. Specifies the location of an item, such as a web page, on the Internet. 82, 291

USB: See Universal Serial Bus.

user acceptance testing: Tests performed by a client before formally accepting an IT system from the developers. 320, 324

user documentation: Documentation intended for users of an IT system, helping them understand and use it. 314

user interface: Method used to communicate with a computer system. **56**, 319, 335:

user manual: 320

utility software: Software used to perform maintenance jobs such as

defragmenting disks. 47

validation: Checks to ensure whether data is in the correct format. 156

variables: Components of a computer model which can be altered to vary the output. 166

vector graphics: Graphics which are stored as a series of mathematical shapes and properties. 52, 128

verification: Checking whether data is correct. 157

video CODECs (coder-decoders): Software required to view certain compressed video and audio formats. 134

video conferencing: Use of video cameras and microphones to conduct a conversation over a network. 220

video editing software: Application software for creating and editing video. 53

Video On Demand: Television and films which can be streamed at any time from the Internet, rather than waiting for a TV broadcast. 283

viral advertising: Advertising using social media, spread by users rather than the advertising company. 212

virtual actors: Animated characters used in films, created entirely using computer graphics software. 114

virtual environment: 302

virtual globe: 3D representation of the Earth with added data layers. 239

virtual keyboard: See soft keyboard. 18

Virtual LAN: Network form by several LANs which are in separate geographical locations. 75

Virtual Learning Environment: Form of Content Management System used

by teachers to upload lessons and materials for students.

virtual machine: Software application that runs a virtual 'computer' inside a window. 243, 312

Virtual Private Network: System to allow a remote computer to securely connect to a LAN, as though it were physically connected. 75, 254

virtual reality: 3D virtual environment which projects images into a headset worn by the user. 258, 302

virtual reality headset: 302

virtual world: 3D virtual environment to which users connect over the Internet. 212, 278

virtualisation: Using a system in a virtual machine. 243

Virus: Computer program which damages files and data spreads when infected programs are copied. 96

virus definition file: Used by anti-virus programs to recognise known viruses. 96

vishing: Phishing attacks committed using telephone calls or VoIP systems. 104

visualisation: Graphical or animated output from a computer model or simulation. 177, 238

VLAN: See Virtual LAN.

VLE: See Virtual Learning Environment. 220

VOD: See Video On Demand.

voice control: See voice controlled interface.

voice controlled interface: Ability to operate a computer by issuing spoken commands. 21, 42

Voice over Internet Protocol: System that lets users make telephone calls over the Internet. 21

voice recognition: Use of software to convert spo-

ken words into text. 21, 320

VoIP: See Voice over Internet Protocol.

volatile storage: Storage which loses its contents when the power is removed. 32

Vorbis: Lossy file format for audio. 132

Voter Verified Paper Audit Trails: E-voting machine that produces a paper receipt to combat potential voting fraud. 297

VPN: See Virtual Private Network.

vulnerability scanner: Software to scan a system for potential security problems. 95

VVPAT: See Voter Verified Paper Audit Trails.

W3C: See World Wide Web Consortium.

WAN: See Wide Area Network. 74

waterfall development: Development method that focuses on completing each stage of the SDLC for the entire project before moving onto the next. 324

watermarking: Embedding the author's name or logo into an image to act as a copyright reminder. 135

WAV: Lossless file format for audio. 132

web 2.0: Refers to web pages which allow user interaction and collaboration. 85, 221, 294

web 3.0: Proposed evolution of the world wide web. 85

web analytics: See web traffic analysis. 212

web bug: Technique used by spammers to detect if an email address is valid or not. 103

Web Content Management System: Web page that allows users to upload content which is automatically formatted and displayed. 208

web crawler: Software which scans web pages

looking for key words, so search engines can index them. 211

web databases: 144

web development software: Application software for creating HTML pages for web sites. 52

web hosting: Company that stores web sites on their servers, making them accessible on the Internet. 209

web server: Computer which houses web pages and serves them to computers that request them. 68, 209

web spider: See web crawler.

web traffic analysis: Statistics about visitors to a web site, including duration and pages viewed.

web-based software: See cloud computing.

webcam: Input device used to record video, often found in laptop computers. 25

WebCMS: See Web Content Management System.

WEEE: Waste Electrical and Electrical Equipment directive. 247

weighted filter: Filter that considers key words as well as their context or relationship to other key words. 292

WEP: Wired Equivalence Protocol. Wireless network encryption system. 109

What-if scenario: Use of a computer model to test the results of different situations and scenarios. 168

wheels: Common output device in robotics. 346

white list: List of allowed web sites in a filtering system. 291

Wide Area Network: Computer network over a large area, such as a country or several countries. 74

WiFi: Most common type of wireless connection. 69

wiki: Type of web page that any visitor can edit. 85

WiMax: Long range wireless network technology. 77

wired soldiers: Technologies used to improve soldier effectiveness. 303

wireless hotspot: A public wireless access point. 77

wizard: Step by step help system to guide a user through a task. 61

WLAN: Wireless LAN. A LAN what allows Wi-Fi connections. 74

WMA: Lossy file format for video. 132

word processing software: Application software for creating written documents such as letters or essays. 50

World Wide Web Consortium: Organisation that manages standards on the world wide web. 206

worm: Malicious software which replicates itself and spreads between computer systems and over networks. 96

WPA: Wireless Protected Access. Wireless network encryption system. 109

WPA2: Wireless Protected Access 2. Wireless network encryption system. 109

WWW: World Wide Web – a series of interlinked multimedia pages stored on the Internet. 84

WYSIWYG: What You See Is What You Get. Refers to programs that present their output onscreen exactly as it will appear when printed. 136: 202

XML: 206

YB: See Yottabyte.

yottabyte: Storage unit: 1024 zettabyes: 37

ZB: See Zettabyte :

zettabyte: Storage unit: 1024 exabytes: 37

zip file: Compressed file format for general data. 126

zombie: Computer which has been compromised by malware and is part of a botnet. 98

Image Credits

Some images included in this work are distributed under the Creative Commons Attribution (CC-BY) or Creative Commons Share Alike (CC-SA) licences. The text of these licences can be viewed at http://creativecommons.org/licenses/

Some diagrams in this text were constructed using the excellent icons from the Open Clip Art Library (www.openclipart.org), licensed under the Creative Commons Public Domain (CC0) licence.

Cover image: miamiamia / SXC / HAAP Media Ltd

Chapter 1 Cover image: nahhan / SXC / HAAP Media Ltd; Page 2: Businessman: SXC / HAAP Media Ltd; E-waste: Greenpeace India; Fibre optics: Rotorhead / SXC / HAAP Media Ltd; 1-3a SXC / HAAP Media Ltd; 1-3b Allentchang / CC-BY; 1-3c NASA / PD; 1-3d US Air Force / PD; 1-3e SXC / HAAP Media Ltd; 1-3f US Air Force / PD; 1-5 Allentchang

Chapter 2 Cover image: dreamjay / SXC / HAAP Media Ltd; 2-2 NTNU / Public Domain; 2-4 NASA / Public Domain; 2-5a TreyGeek / PD; 2-5b Mike McGregor / CC-BY; 2-6a Stefano Palazzo / CC-SA; 2-6b steved_np3 / SXC; 2-6c S2RD2 / CC-BY; 2-7, 2-8, 2-9 SXC / HAAP Media Ltd; 2-12, 2-13 SXC / HAAP Media Ltd; 2-14 Terminal 5 Insider / CC-BY; 2-15a,b,c Evan-Amos / PD; 2-15d SXC / HAAP Media Ltd; 2-16 Frank Murmann / CC-BY; 2-19a U.S. Fish and Wildlife Service / PD; 2-19b US Navy / PD; 2-20a PD; 2-20b PD; 2-20c FEMA / PD; 2-20d MJN123 / CC-BY; 2-21 © Copyright Microsoft Research and Carnegie Mellon University. Used with permission; 2-22 Attilio_82 / SXC; 2-23a SXC / HAAP Media Ltd; 2-23b Sundesigns / SXC; 2-23c SXC / HAAP Media Ltd; 2-24 SXC / HAAP Media Ltd; 2-25 Joebeone / CC-BY; 2-26a SXC / HAAP Media Ltd; 2-26b Alien84 / SXC; 2-27 SXC / HAAP Media Ltd; 2-28 Used with permission from Microsoft; 2-29 SXC / HAAP Media Ltd; 2-31 SXC / HAAP Media Ltd; Page 35 hard disk image: Darkone / CC-SA; 2-33a-b SXC / HAAP Media Ltd; 2-33c Evan-Amos / PD; 2-37 DeclanTM / CC-BY; 2-38 Evan-Amos / PD, Mikkel Paulson / Public Domain

Chapter 3 Cover image: arinas74 / SXC / HAAP Media Ltd; 3-3 Used with permission from Microsoft; 3-4 - 3-8 Used with permission from Microsoft; 3-9, 3-10a Adobe product screenshot(s) reprinted with permission from Adobe Systems Incorporated; 3-11a Used with permission from Microsoft ; 3-11b Catia / Public domain; 3-11c Used with permission from Microsoft; 3-16, 3-17, 3-18a Used with permission from Microsoft; 3-18b UBUNTU; 3-19 Used with permission from Microsoft; 3-20 Courtesy NASA/JPL-Caltech

Chapter 4 Cover image: pseudoxx / SXC / HAAP Media Ltd; 4-2 SXC / HAAP Media Ltd; 4-5, 4-7 Used with permission from Microsoft; 4-10a SXC / HAAP Media Ltd; 4-14 Manypossibilities.net / CC-BY; Egypt map Public Domain; 4-16 Wikipedia / CC-SA

Chapter 5 Cover image: ilco / SXC / HAAP Media Ltd; 5-1 Brian Ronald / CC-SA; 5-3a SXC / HAAP Media Ltd; 5-3b Sofi73 / SXC / HAAP Media Ltd; 5-4, 5-5 Used with permission from Microsoft; 5-10 Public Domain; 5-12, 5-13 Public Domain; 5-15 Mozilla Public License; 5-17 Greg Goebel / Public Domain; 5-20a Used with permission from Microsoft; 5-20b Mozilla Public License; 5-21 Copyright (C) 1998-2000 Paul Le Roux; 5-22 Used with permission from Microsoft

Chapter 6 Cover image: pooow / SXC / HAAP Media Ltd; Exercise 6-1b © Copyright Enrico Cerica, used with permission; Exercise 6-1d © Copyright Pawel Mroczkowski, used with permission; 6-3 Public Library of Science / CC-BY; Exercise 6-9a Great_Sea / CC-BY; Exercise 6-9b Clker / PD; 6-10 Andrew Fitzsimon / Public Domain; 6-11 Catia / Public domain; 6-12 © OpenStreetMap contributors, CC-BY-SA; 6-13b Mayqel / CC-SA; 6-14 GNU GPL; 6-16 Bob Bekian / CC-BY; 6-17 Adobe product screenshot(s) reprinted with permission from Adobe Systems Incorporated

Chapter 7 Cover image: mmagallan / SXC / HAAP Media Ltd; 7-1a Used with permission from Microsoft; 7-1b Copyright © HanDy Emr Used with permission; 7-8, 7-9, 7-10, 7-11, 7-12 Used with permission from Microsoft; 7-15 Copyright © Grisoft

Chapter 8 Cover image: Argonne National Laboratory; 8-2 NTNU / Public Domain; 8-3a NASA / Public Domain; 8-3b Symscape / CC-BY; 8-4a NASA / Public Domain; 8-4b Argonne National Laboratory / CC-BY; 8-4c Argonne National Laboratory / CC-BY; 8-7 Strategic Plan for the U.S. Climate Change Science Program / Public Domain; 8-10a Argonne National Laboratory / CC-BY; 8-10b Julian Herzog / CC-BY; 8-11 United States Geological Survey / Public Domain; 8-12a Public Domain; 8-9b Sir James / CC-BY; 8-9c-d US Navy / Public Domain; 8-13 US Navy / Public Domain

Chapter 9 Cover image: Speedy2 / SXC / HAAP Media Ltd; 9-3 Taribo / SXC / HAAP Media Ltd; 9-5, 9-6 Used with permission from Microsoft; 9-7 Copyright © Paul Chapman, used with permission; 9-8 Fshky2009 / PD; 9-15a Mark Osbourne / PD; 9-15b Matthew Wailling; 9-22 Used with permission from Microsoft; 9-25, 9-29 Mozilla Public Licence; 9-31 GNU GPL; 9-37 Department of Homeland Security / PD; 9-38 Public Domain; 9-39 CosmicSpanner / CC-SA

Chapter 10 Cover image: Cellanr / CC-SA; 10-2a US Army / Public Domain; 10-2b Used with permission from Microsoft; 10-5 Public Domain; 10-7 Evan Amos / Public Domain; 10-8 Allentchang / CC-BY; 10-9 GNU GPL;

Chapter 11 Cover image: Rybson / SXC / HAAP Media Ltd; 11-1 William M. Connolley / CC-BY; 11-4 NASA Jet Propulsion Laboratory / PD; 11-5 © 2011 Google, © 2011 Tele Atlas, © 2011 DigitalGlobe, © 2011 TerraMetrics; 11-6 GRASS Development Team / CC-SA; 11-9 The Planet / CC-BY; 11-11 Matthias Feilhauer / CC-SA; 11-14 Jake Brown / CC-BY; 11-15 Greenpeace India / CC-BY; 11-16a Curtis Palmer / CC-BY; 11-6b US Navy / PD11-17 © Computer Aid International, used with permission.

Chapter 12 Cover image: US Navy / PD; 12-1 Roger Mommaerts / CC-SA; 12-2 MC4Army / CC-BY; 12-3 Used with permission from Microsoft; 12-4 PD; 12-6a John J Kruzel / CC-BY; 12-6b US Navy / PD; 12-7 Saginaw Future / CC-BY; 12-8 Nimur / CC-SA; 12-9a US Navy / PD; 12-9b PD; 12-10 kris krüg / CC-BY; 12-14 Used with permission from Microsoft; 12-15a PD; 12-15b Gari Araolaza / CC-BY

Chapter 13 Cover image: 13-1 Kei Noguchi / CC-SA; 13-2 Jan Prucha / CC-SA; 13-4 Evan Amos / Public Domain; 13-5 Julian Lombardi / CC-SA; 13-6 Hachimaki / CC-SA; 13-7 Evan Amos / Public Domain; 13-8 John E. Lester / CC-SA; 13-9 Fmalka / CC-SA; 13-10 Pucky2012 / CC-SA; 13-13 Greg L / CC-SA; 13-14 Andrew Magill / CC-BY; 13-15a Public Domain; 13-15b The Charles Machine Works / CC-SA; 13-15c Odense Bys Museer / CC-SA; 13-16 www.CyArk.org / CC-SA; 13-17 NASA / Public Domain

Chapter 14: Cover image: US Air Force / PD; 14-2 Used with permission from Microsoft; 14-3 Public Domain; 14-5a Joe Hall / CC-BY; 14-5b Agência Brasil / CC-BY; 14-7 Open Government Licence; 14-8a Whitehouse.gov / CC-BY; 14-8b Recovery.gov / CC-BY; 14-9 Evan Bench / CC-BY; 14-10 US Army / PD; 14-11a, 14-11b US Army / PD; 14-11c US Navy / PD; 14-14 US Army / PD; 14-13 US Air Force / PD

Chapter 15 Cover image: mm907ut / SXC / HAAP Media Ltd;

Chapter 16 Cover image: NASA / Public Domain; Exercise 16-1 Einstein image: PD, Chess image: GiniMiniGi / SXC / HAAP Media Ltd; 16-2 PD; Page 338 Dog 1: pepo13 / CC-BY; Dog 2: johnelamper / CC-BY; Cat 2 PD; 16-7 windchime / SXC / HAAP Media Ltd; 16-8 © 2011 Google; 16-11a US Navy / PD; 16-11b Leipzig - Nao-Team_Die Schreibfabrik; 16-13a NASA / PD; 16-13b US Navy / PD; 16-13c / Steve Jurvetson; 16-14 Max Braun / CC-BY; 16-15 Handitec / PD; 16-16a US Government / PD; 16-16b Copyright Vislab, used with permission; 16-16c Department of Defense / PD